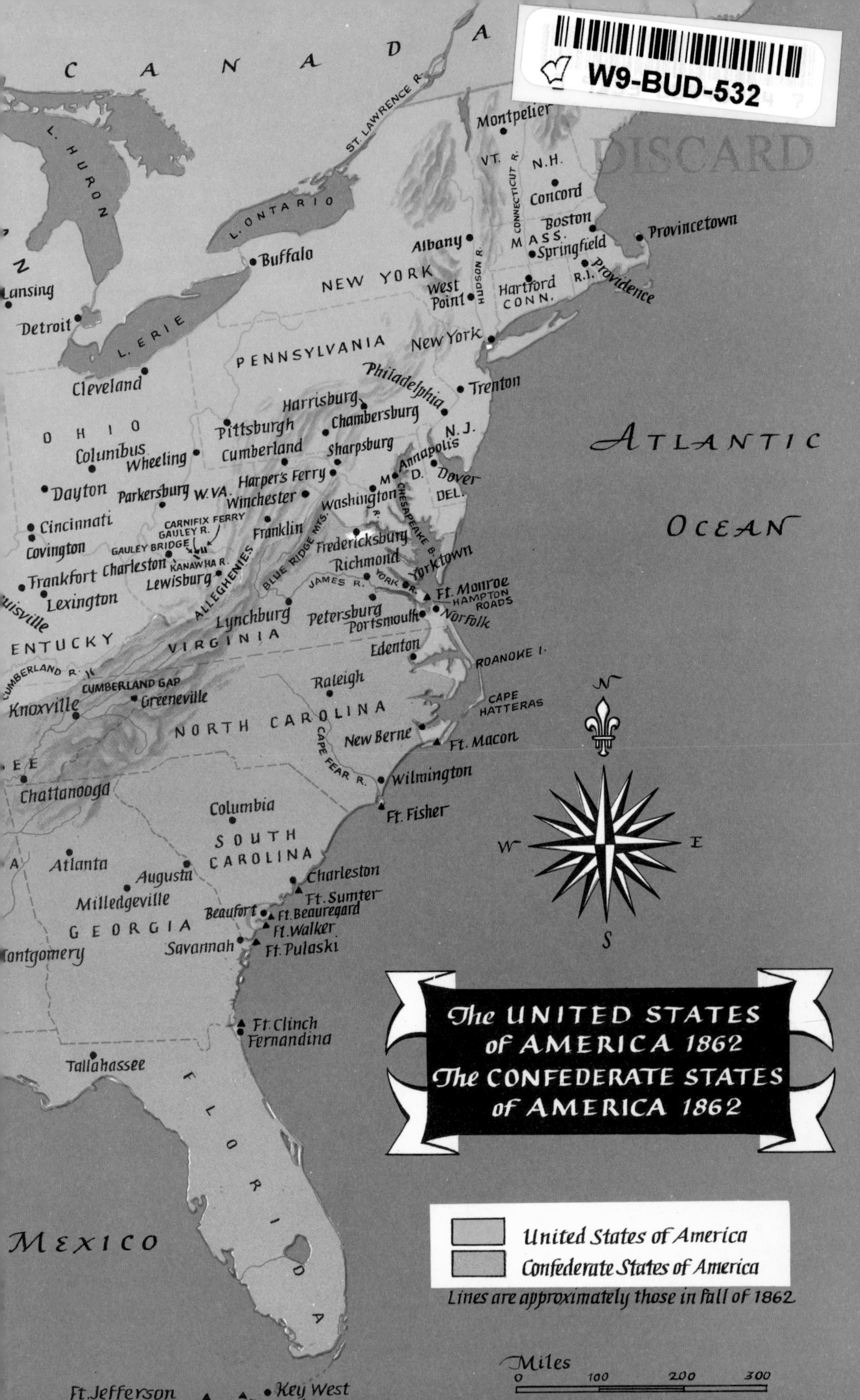

The UNITED STATES of AMERICA 1862
The CONFEDERATE STATES of AMERICA 1862
United States of America
Confederate States of America
Lines are approximately those in fall of 1862
Miles
0
100
200
300
CANADA
ATLANTIC
OCEAN
MEXICO
L. HURON
L. ONTARIO
L. ERIE
ST. LAWRENCE R.
Montpelier
VT.
N.H.
CONNECTICUT R.
Concord
Boston
MASS.
Springfield
Provincetown
Albany
HUDSON R.
NEW YORK
West Point
Hartford
CONN.
R.I.
Providence
Buffalo
Lansing
Detroit
New York
PENNSYLVANIA
Cleveland
Philadelphia
Trenton
Harrisburg
Chambersburg
Pittsburgh
OHIO
Columbus
Wheeling
Cumberland
Sharpsburg
N.J.
Annapolis
MD.
Dover
DEL.
Harper's Ferry
Dayton
Parkersburg
W.VA.
Winchester
Washington
CHESAPEAKE B.
Cincinnati
CARNIFIX FERRY
GAULEY R.
Franklin
Covington
GAULEY BRIDGE
KANAWHA R.
Charleston
BLUE RIDGE MTS.
Fredericksburg
Richmond
Yorktown
Frankfort
Lewisburg
ALLEGHENIES
JAMES R.
YORK R.
Ft. Monroe
HAMPTON ROADS
Lexington
Lynchburg
Petersburg
Portsmouth
Norfolk
VIRGINIA
ENTUCKY
Edenton
ROANOKE I.
CUMBERLAND R.
CUMBERLAND GAP
Raleigh
Knoxville
Greeneville
CAPE HATTERAS
NORTH CAROLINA
CAPE FEAR R.
New Berne
Ft. Macon
Wilmington
Chattanooga
Ft. Fisher
Columbia
SOUTH CAROLINA
Atlanta
Augusta
Charleston
Ft. Sumter
Milledgeville
Beaufort
Ft. Beauregard
Ft. Walker
GEORGIA
Savannah
Ft. Pulaski
ontgomery
Ft. Clinch
Fernandina
Tallahassee
FLORIDA
Ft. Jefferson
Key West
N
S
E
W

TERRIBLE SWIFT SWORD

VOLUME TWO

The Centennial History of the Civil War

BOOKS BY BRUCE CATTON

Terrible Swift Sword

The Coming Fury

The American Heritage Picture History of the Civil War
(*narrative*)

Grant Moves South

This Hallowed Ground
(*adult and young reader's versions*)

Banners at Shenandoah
(*a novel for young readers*)

U. S. Grant and the Military Tradition

A Stillness at Appomattox

Glory Road

Mr. Lincoln's Army

The War Lords of Washington

America Goes to War

The Centennial History of the Civil War

VOLUME TWO

TERRIBLE SWIFT SWORD

Bruce Catton

E. B. Long, Director of Research

Doubleday & Company, Inc., Garden City, New York

Library of Congress Catalog Card Number 62–15937

Printed in the United States of America

To Thurber Catton

PUBLISHER'S NOTE

Terrible Swift Sword is Volume Two of a projected three volume work, The Centennial History of the Civil War. The first volume, *The Coming Fury*, was published in 1961.

The Centennial History of the Civil War is a project begun in 1955 by Doubleday & Company, Inc., in conjunction with the New York *Times*. That newspaper is carrying articles based on the work.

Each book in the series may be read and understood separately. It is part of the original plan that the three volumes will constitute a modern history, based on the fullest as well as the most recent research. The author's note in the Foreword of Volume One with reference to Mr. and Mrs. E. B. Long is intended to be considered as a part of this book as well.

Mr. Long is preparing an "Almanac," or factual reference book, based on the research for the Centennial History. *The American Heritage Picture History of the Civil War*, already published, with a narrative by Mr. Catton, is an illustrated volume which is a graphic companion volume to this series.

CONTENTS

☆ ☆ ☆ ☆ ☆

CONTENTS

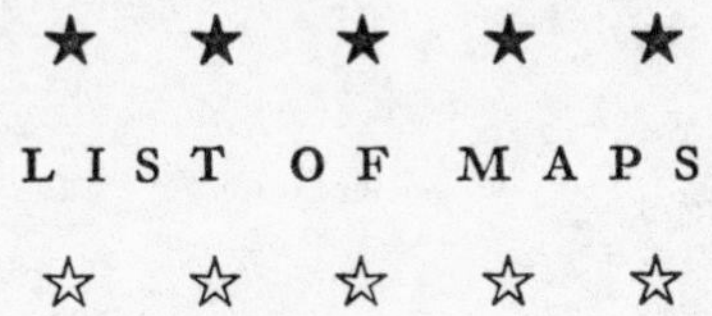

LIST OF MAPS

On the above listed maps the black arrows or bars indicate the Confederate forces, the blue bars or arrows indicate the Federal forces. In both cases, when the arrow lines are interrupted or dotted, it means either retreat or regrouping.

TERRIBLE SWIFT SWORD

VOLUME TWO

The Centennial History of the Civil War

The Leaders and the Led

1: *Tornado Weather*

On the Monday after the Battle of Bull Run the Congress of the United States went about its duties in a dignified and abstracted calm. Human fragments of the routed army drifted up and down the streets of Washington, clotting the sidewalks and alleys, eddying sluggishly about the bars, as soiled and depressing to see as fragments of the broken republic itself, but the legislators had little to say openly about the defeated soldiers or about the disaster that had taken place. In the Senate the new tariff was up for consideration, and there was also discussion of a proposal to increase the naval medical corps; and in the House the members devoted themselves to Mr. Crittenden's bill defining the cause and scope of the war.

That the war might grow and change immeasurably because of what had happened during the last twenty-four hours was neither argued nor, apparently, thought about. Mr. Crittenden's bill was static. It asserted that the war had been forced on the country by Southern malcontents, and held that the Federal government's only aim in pressing on toward an assured final victory was "to preserve the Union with all the dignity, equality and rights of the several states unimpaired." This was the definition of a small war, and the shattering defeat just experienced was a disturbing sign that the war was not going to be small. It might grow very great indeed—great enough to involve at last the dignity, equality, and rights of human beings as well as of states—and if it went in that direction there was no telling what might come of it.

But the House was in no mood to examine the future. Avoiding the hysteria which Bull Run had evoked in so many quarters, the House was still willing to see the war as something manageable, an incident rather than a cataclysm. Even Thaddeus Stevens, the Republican leader, brooding darkly on the tragedy whose ultimate dimensions he perhaps saw more clearly than anyone else, warning the legislators that the terrible laws of war were their only guide now—even Stevens was content to vote for this enactment, and in the end Mr. Crittenden's measure was adopted with just two votes cast against it.[1]

One of these dissenting votes came from Congressman Albert Gallatin Riddle, an antislavery man from Ohio's Western Reserve who confessed that he could hardly believe his ears as he heard member after member vote for an explicit statement that the war would be fought in such a way that it would not affect the institution of slavery in the slightest degree. He went to the members' lobby after he had voted, and there some of his colleagues urged him to go back and change his vote. Riddle flared up at them. Slavery, he said, was doomed to die, and every sensible man knew it, and when it died it would not simply be voted out of existence; it would be abolished "by convulsion, fire and blood," and the convulsion had already begun. The convulsion was, in short, this war which (as Mr. Riddle felt) was being so badly defined, and he wanted the war recognized as the thing that would kill slavery: "I mean to make a conquest of it; to beat it to extinction under the iron hooves of our war horses." Northerners who thought that the war could be fought without touching the slavery issue (he said) were like children who tiptoed about in the dark for fear of waking a destroying ogre. For himself, he believed that the ogre was already awake and that the thing to do now was to kill it.[2]

In the middle of that summer of 1861, the thing Mr. Riddle was talking about was actually more disturbing than the Bull Run defeat itself. The military disaster was humiliating, even infuriating, but it was not—to a people who, after all, were fairly tough-minded—really frightening. It might even help to inspire them to put down secession and to restore the shattered American past in all its beauty. But to say flatly that the war would be fought against slavery (thereby implying unmistakably that it would be fought for slavery's opposite, freedom, which is unlimited) was to bid an eternal goodbye to the cherished past, to confess that it could never be restored on earth. It was to invoke revolution, far-ranging and uncontrollable, in order to put down mere rebellion; and at this point in their development the people were not ready for any such invocation.

Still, there it was: if the war became great it would transcend the intentions of its authors. This might have momentous results at home, and it was beginning to be apparent that it could also have consequences overseas. It was apparent, at least, to the Secretary of State, William H. Seward, who had sought to make use of the fact in his conduct of the nation's foreign policy.

This policy struck Charles Francis Adams, the minister to England, as almost inconceivably bold and aggressive, so reckless that for a time he suspected that someone in the administration had gone mad. Mr. Adams reached London two months before the battle of Bull Run was fought, and soon after he got there he received a letter from Secretary Seward saying that the United States would unhesitatingly make war on any European nation or combination of nations which extended aid, comfort, or recognition to the Southern Confederacy.

It was hard to be sure about Mr. Seward. Mr. Adams's son Henry, looking at the man from his own special vantage point, saw a slouching figure with "a head like a wise macaw," a gravelly voice, disorderly clothes, and a baffling way of indulging in loose talk which might or might not reflect his inner thoughts. Mr. Seward, the younger Adams reflected, had worn a politician's mask so long that neither he nor anyone else was always sure whether the impression he made at any given moment was real or contrived. Seward had a basic integrity which impressed the older Adams (along with an uncomplicated sense of fun which appealed to President Lincoln) and Mr. Adams believed that someone else must have fathered his foreign policy. In his diary he remarked that a conflict with "a handful of slave-holding states" seemed to be giving the Lincoln administration all that it could handle, and he wondered: "What are we to do when we throw down the glove to all Europe?"[3]

If he had known all of the facts Mr. Adams would have been even more painfully baffled. The policy was not merely Mr. Seward's own, but it reached London in a form much less sharp than Mr. Seward had originally intended. As the Secretary drafted it, the letter had been downright provocative, a taunting challenge to the British government to view secession, the blockade, and all related matters precisely as Washington saw them—or to fight. Furthermore, Mr. Seward had planned that the unexpurgated text of the letter should be given to Lord John Russell, the British Secretary for Foreign Affairs, immediately upon its receipt in London. Henry Adams wrote that if his father had shown the letter to the Foreign Secretary "he would have made a war in five minutes,"[4] and it may be that this was just what Mr. Seward had in mind. In March he had suggested a war overseas as a means of reuniting America, and the idea continued to fascinate him; not until after the Bull Run disaster did he abandon the notion that most Southerners would rally around the old flag if some foreign nation could be maneuvered into firing on it.

It was Abraham Lincoln who had toned the letter down by careful editing; and it was Lincoln who had added the all-important proviso that the letter was simply a statement of policy for the minister's guidance and was not under any circumstances to be shown to anyone else.[5] The policy enunciated remained stiff enough, in all conscience; everything that Mr. Adams said and did in London must be said and done in the knowledge that his government would make war on an England openly friendly to the Confederacy. But he did not have to go around with a chip on his shoulder, or publicly tell the British government to mend its ways. Much was left to his discretion, which was unfailing. What he did not know was that this opportunity for the exercise of discretion would never have been opened to him if President Lincoln had not first exercised discretion of his own.

Charles Francis Adams was prepared to expect nothing of the kind, for his opinion of Mr. Lincoln just then was low. Mr. Adams was the son of one President and the grandson of another; he had lived in Paris and in London as a boy, he had studied law in the office of Daniel Webster, and he had served in the Massachusetts legislature and in the United States Congress; he was Boston and Harvard at full strength, undiluted and not susceptible of dilution; and he had not been impressed by President Lincoln. Mr. Seward had taken him to the White House late in April, just after his ministerial appointment had been arranged, and in the Presidential quarters which still (in this caller's mind) seemed almost to belong to old John Quincy Adams there was this long, ungainly, loose-jointed man, awkward, apparently ill at ease, with big coarse features, shabbily dressed, in shapeless pants and worn carpet slippers—Abe Lincoln of Illinois with the bark on. It was no sight for an Adams; nor was memory of the sight made more pleasant by the fact that instead of discussing foreign policy and the British the President talked to Mr. Seward about some petty matter of political patronage in far-away Chicago.[6]

Better knowledge of the President lay in the future. Meanwhile, Mr. Adams did the best he could; as modified, the letter left him a good deal of leeway. He wrote that his function seemed to be "to prevent the mutual irritation from coming to a downright quarrel," and Lord John Russell was a man he could talk to: elderly, reserved, thoughtful, with a cold blue eye—a man not altogether unlike Mr. Adams himself. His Lordship confessed that he had twice talked, unofficially, with the Confederate commissioners sent to London by Jefferson Davis, and when Mr. Adams remarked that a continuation of these unofficial conferences "could hardly fail to be viewed by us as hostile in spirit" the Foreign Minister said that he had no expectation of seeing the commissioners any more. By July, Mr. Adams felt that relations with Great Britain were in a fairly promising condition; "I have no idea that anybody wants war."[7]

Yet the British did not quite seem to understand the kind of war the American government was fighting. "They think this is a hasty quarrel, the mere result of passion, which will be arranged as soon as the cause of it shall pass off," wrote Mr. Adams. "They do not comprehend the connection which slavery has with it, because we do not at once preach emancipation. Hence they go to the other extreme and argue that it is not an element of the struggle." Bull Run, to be sure, set off a wave of pro-Confederate sentiment, but

Mr. Adams believed that it was important to remember that "Great Britain always looks to her own interest as a paramount law of her action in foreign affairs."[8]

This was the point Secretary Seward was thinking about when he drafted his defiant letter. His tart sentences had been framed to warn the British ruling class that this American war was one they just could not afford to enter. If they did get into it, Seward remarked, the result would be another war between "the European and American branches of the British race," strongly resembling the war for American independence, fought less than a century ago. "Europe atoned by forty years of suffering," he wrote, "for the error that Great Britain committed in provoking the contest. If that nation shall now repeat the same great error, the social convulsions which will follow may not be so long but they will be more general. When they shall have ceased it will, we think, be seen, whatever may have been the fortunes of other nations that it is not the United States that will have come out of them with its precious constitution altered or its honestly obtained dominion in any degree abridged." It would be well, the Secretary concluded, for the British to reflect that in such a war "our cause will involve the independence of nations and the rights of human nature."[9]

Secretary Seward thus was brandishing democracy and inviting the conservative British to contemplate it (hinting as well that the loss of privilege might be accompanied by the loss of Canada). He was saying, almost in so many words, that a revolutionary upheaval was germinating somewhere below the surface of this war between North and South, and he was suggesting that the American government could survive such an upheaval but that the governments of the established nations of Europe could not. To his wife he had written that if war did develop between America and England "it will be the strife of the younger branch of the British stock, for freedom, against the elder, for slavery"; he believed that it would be dreadful, "but the end will be sure and swift."[10]

Secretary Seward, to be sure, may have been talking through his hat. So far, revolution was only germinating. Whatever values and perils might be added if the war became an all-out struggle for human rights, that change had not yet been made and there was no sure indication that it ever would be made. Congress was all but unanimous in its declaration that the war had nothing whatever to do with slavery, and when it spoke thus Congress unquestionably spoke for a majority. The slavery issue, like a fulminate of mercury cap which could set off an immense explosion, had been carefully wrapped in protective swaddling so that it might not be jarred unduly. If the war could be fought with some restraint, limited by the sober design of its leaders and kept always under proper control, the disastrous shock could very likely be averted.

But the people who were fighting one another were most unlikely to exercise much restraint or to submit to effective discipline. They were already beginning to take the war into their own hands, and they were so muscular, tenacious, and impatient that they might easily give it dimensions large enough to develop any and all of its potentialities. The pressure for action which had compelled a reluctant general to put an unready army into the fight at Bull Run was still rising. This was a war in which anything could happen.

There was a young mining engineer who raised a company of mountaineers in northern Georgia and led them off to serve the Confederacy, only to be halted in Atlanta by the news that Georgia's quota had been filled; the governor could not take any more recruits just now. The mountaineers promptly mutinied—if that term can be applied to men who were not yet members of any accredited military organization—and refused to go home. If the governor of Georgia did not want them, they said, they would find some other governor who did. They camped on the edge of Atlanta, a wild, spirited, uncontrollable company which would do anything on earth but disband, and in the fullness of time a place was found for them in an Alabama regiment; and in the end they got, for their enthusiasm, four years of desperate fighting. After the war their former captain wrote: "The literal truth is that the people were leading the leaders."[11]

Behaving thus, the people were by no means disagreeing with those leaders who wanted to conduct the war without reference to the explosive issue of slavery. They simply wanted action, responding to a reflex that ran from the emotions through the muscles, and they showed what they wanted in various ways. From Charlottesville, Virginia, a correspondent of the Charleston *Mercury* wrote that "the cool western breeze which is rippling the tasselled corn into endless waves comes laden with the hum of war from the distant Alleghenies," and he reflected sagely: "Go where you will over this broad land, the air is instinct with strife." A spirit less pastoral, and also much less conventional, moved a citizen of Alabama who wrote to the Confederate Secretary of War proposing the formation of volunteer companies of freebooters which would make war at no cost to the Confederacy, supporting themselves by the seizure of Yankee goods and chattels: "Such companies propose going and fighting without restraint and under no orders, and convey the property captured to their own private use, thereby benefiting their own pecuniary circumstances as well as doing their country good service by crippling the enemy." This proposal got nowhere, but the editor of the Richmond *Examiner* called for harsh measures, asserting: "The enemy must be made to feel the war. They must be made to understand that there is a God that punishes the wicked, and that the Southern army is His instrument."[12]

The notion that those led might get ahead of their leaders was general. Early in May, governors of the Northern states lying west of New England met to urge vigorous prosecution of the war, and their feelings were expressed in a letter drawn up by Governor Alex Randall of Wisconsin and forwarded to President Lincoln.

"There is a spirit evoked by this rebellion among the liberty-loving people of the country," wrote Governor Randall, "that is driving them to action, and if the Government will not permit them to act for it they will act for themselves. It is better for the Government to direct this current than to let it run wild. So far as possible we have attempted to allay this excess of spirit, but there is a moral element and a reasoning element in this uprising that cannot be met in the ordinary way. There is a conviction of great wrongs to be redressed and that the Government is to be preserved by them. The Government must provide an outlet for this feeling or it will find one for itself. If the Government does not at once shoulder this difficulty and direct its current there will come something more than a war to put down rebellion—it will be a war between border States, which will lose sight, for the time, of the Government."[13]

Using different words, these Northerners and Southerners were all testifying to a common belief—that this war which was going to mean fighting, pain, destruction, and tremendous anger was destined sooner or later to go out of control. It could not be just "a war to put down rebellion." Its elements were too violent. Men who had never learned to endure wrongs with patience had become convinced that wrongs were being done to them. People eternally eager to dedicate themselves had come to feel that there were noble causes to be served. Finally, there were enemies to be hurt in a land where the only rule about a blow struck in anger was that it must be struck with all of the strength one had.

. . . Tornado weather: sultriest and most menacing, as the Wisconsin governor had said, along the border—that cross section of nineteenth-century America that ran for a thousand miles from Virginia tidewater to the plains of Kansas, reaching from the place of the nation's oldest traditions to the rude frontier where no tradition ran back farther than the day before yesterday. Here was where the fighting was beginning—along the border—and here was where the war was going to take shape.

For a long time the shape of it would be hard to make out, partly because the pattern would be slow in taking form and partly because it was so easy to look for it in the wrong place. Then as now, the eye was drawn to Virginia, to the legendary country between the Potomac and the James, the floodlit stage where rival governments would have formal trial by combat. The Bull Run frenzy had gone to its limit here, arrogant overconfidence blowing up at last in a froth of pride and shame and panic; and the governments were thought to have learned something by it. They would take their time now, organizing and equipping and drilling with much care, moving (when it was time to move) according to professional plan and not because of pressure raised by "Forward to Richmond!" headlines in an overheated press. Here, it was said, was where the final decision would be reached, and all that happened elsewhere would be secondary.

But the border ran a long way, and eastern Virginia was no more than a fraction of it. Beyond were Allegheny valleys and Cumberland plateau, western Virginia and eastern Tennessee, Kentucky with its rich Bluegrass farmland going west from the mountains all the way to the central artery, the Mississippi; and beyond them was Missouri, stretching out to the Kansas-Nebraska vastness where the war had had at least one of its beginnings. In each of the related segments of this border the war had a different guise and a different meaning. Here it was a battle in which ill-equipped armies learned their trade in blundering action; there it was a matter of shadows in the dusk, neighbor ambushing neighbor, hayrick and barn blazing up at midnight with a drum of hoofbeats on a lonely lane to tell the story, or a firing squad killing a bridge-burner for a warning to the lawless. The separate scenes were monstrous, confusing, ever-changing; put together, they might make something planned neither in Washington nor in Richmond.

2: *A Mean-Fowt Fight*

John Charles Frémont brought to Missouri a great reputation, a brand-new commission as major general, and a formidable set of abilities which did not quite meet the demands that Missouri was about to make. He entered the Civil War at the precise place where it wore its most baffling aspect, and although he presently saw with tolerable clarity what needed to be done he knew hardly anything about the way to go about doing it. He was famous as The Pathfinder, the man who had charted trails across the untracked West; he had been the first presidential candidate of the new Republican party in 1856, helping to make another sort of trail into an even more trackless wilderness; and now he was in Missouri, a bewildering jungle where a trail could be blazed only by a man gifted with a profound understanding of the American character, the talents of a canny politician, and enormous skill as an administrator. Of these gifts General Frémont had hardly a trace.

Perhaps nobody really understood what was going on in Missouri, and the fault was partly Nathaniel Lyon's. Lyon was like a sword—hard, narrow, and sharp—and he had gone slashing through the complex loyalties of this border state so vigorously that almost everyone was adrift. A captain in the Regular Army, exercising a highly irregular authority and leading troops which were almost equally irregular, he had in May surrounded, captured, and disarmed a contingent of Missouri state militia legally camped in a St. Louis suburb, with subsequent gunfire and the killing of sundry civilians. Then, elevated abruptly to the position of brigadier general, Lyon had in effect declared war on the governor of the state, secessionist-minded Claiborne Jackson, driving that functionary off toward the Ozarks and occupying Jefferson City, the state capital. Missouri had not seceded—could not really secede, now, because all of the machinery of state government was gripped by the Federal power—and a majority of its people almost certainly had been Unionists, at least to a degree, from the start. The state probably would have stayed in the Union in any case, but Lyon took no chances. He kept thinking, no doubt, of a fact which greatly worried hard-drinking Frank Blair, the brother of Lincoln's Postmaster General and son of that tough activist, Old Man Blair of Maryland: Francis P. Blair, Jr., Republican leader in Missouri and Lyon's principal sponsor. Blair complained that one big problem was the presence of a great many good men "who liked the Union very much but did not see the necessity of fighting for it"; men who thought that "the best way to put down the rebellion was to make a show of force but not to use it at all." Lyon believed in using it; did use it, with the result that Missouri was divided into factions and sub-factions, with almost everybody in the state apparently either making war or preparing to make war—on his next-door neighbor, as often as not.[1]

This was what Frémont stepped into when he reached St. Louis on July 25, and he can hardly be blamed if he found it confusing. His responsibilities were broad, his means were limited, and the crisis seemed immeasurable. He was supposed to safeguard Missouri and all the Northwest, and he was also expected to organize, equip, and lead an army down the Mississippi to New Orleans, reclaiming the great valley and reopening it to commerce and breaking off the whole western part of the Confederacy. He had about 23,000 troops, more than a third of which were three-months volunteers whose terms were about to expire. Governors of the Western states were sending recruits to him, but he had hardly any arms for them, nothing much in the way of uniforms or other military equipment, scanty rations and transportation, and no money. As far as he could learn, every county in the state contained "a Rebel faction . . . at least equal to the loyal population in numbers and excelling it in vindictiveness and energy." St. Louis struck him as "a Rebel city" whose upper classes were unanimously secessionist; bands of night riders were despoiling loyalist citizens all across the state, and the militantly anti-Union state guard was alleged to have 25,000 men under arms. Worst of all, there were said to be nearly 50,000 Confederate soldiers in Arkansas and Tennessee ready to invade Missouri, seize its railroads, reclaim its capital, capture St. Louis, and occupy Cairo, Illinois, at the point where the Ohio River joined the Mississippi. If they did all of this the war in the West would be gone beyond redemption and the independence of the Confederacy would be virtually assured.[2]

The picture actually was not quite that dark. Frémont's informants had more than doubled the size of the state guard and had nearly doubled the strength of the Confederate armies beyond the borders, and they had totally ignored the great difficulties the commanders of those forces would encounter once they began a co-ordinated offensive: and anyway St. Louis was not really as much a "Rebel city" as Frémont considered it. But the picture was dark enough. If the Federals were to make war in the West with any success at all they had to secure Missouri and the mouth of the Ohio and then move down the Mississippi in great strength, and although the authorities in Washington knew this they were not devoting much attention to it because they were concentrating on problems nearer home. They did not exactly suppose that the Missouri situation would take care of itself but they did expect that Frémont would take care of it for them, and they were not going to pay detailed attention to what he did unless he got into serious trouble. Things being as they were, it was almost inevitable that this would happen.

It began, as so many things in Missouri had begun, with Nathaniel Lyon. When Frémont reached Missouri Lyon was far off in the southwestern part of the state, near the market town of Springfield, gloomily uncertain whether he was nearing the conclusion of a triumphant offensive or the beginning of a disastrous defeat. He had done a good deal for the Union cause thus far. He had exiled the governor and forced the secessionist militia to operate without a base, a war chest or an adequate legal footing, and he had given the Unionists time to set up a state government which would co-operate with the administration in Washington. But he had done all of this by prodding a hornets' nest with a stick, and the turmoil he had raised threatened now to overwhelm him.

Lyon had taken 7000 troops to southwest Missouri. By the end of July these had dwindled to 5000, what with the loss of time-expired three-months men and the general wastage that came of poor training, sketchy supplies and no pay, and he was a long way from home. His enemies were gathering to pounce on him—30,000 of them, Lyon believed: fewer than half that many in sober fact, but still more than twice his own strength. He believed that he could neither advance, hold his ground nor retreat without heavy reinforcements, and he had been demanding help for weeks without getting any.[3]

Frémont knew that Lyon needed help but he did not think that he could do much for him. There were some 6000 Federal troops in northeastern Missouri, trying to tamp down a mean guerrilla warfare; they had their hands full and Frémont felt that he could not remove any of them. He believed that he had to hold the railroads that fanned out west and southwest from St. Louis; to guard the line of the Missouri River and hold Jefferson City, and to garrison St. Louis itself; and there was very little manpower to spare. Frémont was getting reinforcements, but for the immediate present they were of little use; he wrote that the new regiments were "literally the rawest ever got together . . . entirely unacquainted with the rudiments of military exercise," and most of them had no weapons.[4] Worst of all, Frémont's intelligence service told him that the Confederates were planning to move on Cairo—a fairly correct appraisal, although the move was not nearly as imminent as Frémont's people believed—and Cairo was the most sensitive spot of all; the one place which the Union had to hold if it was ever to wage offensive warfare in the Mississippi Valley. Cairo at the moment was all but defenseless. The Federal post there was commanded by Brigadier General Benjamin M. Prentiss, who was supposed to have eight regiments but in fact had only two and who could muster hardly more than 600 effectives for duty.

It was against this background that Lyon's calls for help had to make themselves heard, and they came through but dimly. Frémont found that he could scrape together a disposable force of 3800 men, and he concluded that they were needed at Cairo more than at any other point. At the end of July he took them to Cairo personally, making a big parade of their departure from St. Louis in order to impress the rebellious with the fact that the weak spot was weak no longer. He wrote to Lyon telling him, in substance, to use his own judgment—hang on if he could, retreat if he thought he had to—and somewhat tardily he ordered two regiments to join him.[5] The regiments had a long way to go, and Lyon never saw them. When Frémont's steamers left the wharf at St. Louis and started downstream for the mouth of the Ohio, Lyon's number was up.

Apparently Lyon knew it perfectly well. He was a score of miles beyond Springfield, his advanced base, and the Confederates were threatening to side-slip and occupy that town in his rear. If he went back to Springfield he was not strong enough to stand a siege there, he was woefully short of supplies, and the nearest point of safety was a town called Rolla, one hundred miles northeast of Springfield, at the end of a railroad to St. Louis. There seemed to be nothing for it but to retreat to Rolla, but his march would be very slow and the Confederates—who had a great deal of cavalry, an arm of which Lyon had practically none—would almost certainly surround and destroy him en route. He wrote a letter to Frémont remarking, with calm understatement, "I find my position extremely embarrassing," and he confessed that he did not know just what he ought to do; and as a matter of fact no good choice was open to him. He pulled back from his advanced position to the town of Springfield, and he wrote that he would hold this place as long as he could even though this might "endanger the safety of my entire force."[6] It was a desperate sort of letter, written by a man beset, and by the time Frémont got it Lyon was dead—victim of the decision Frémont had made, of his own impetuosity, of the unfathomable civil war that had burst into flame along the untamed border.

At the end of the first week in August, Lyon was going about Springfield smoldering with glum anger, inspecting his outposts with the air of a man who had been abandoned to the fates, breaking out now and then with profane denunciations of the distant Frémont who was sending no help. He was still full of fight. When a subordinate asked him when the army would leave Springfield he snapped: "Not until we are whipped out." He held a council of war, apparently concluded that a retreat would ruinously dishearten the Union people of all western Missouri, and at last made up his mind to take a long gamble. Unable to stand still or to fall back he would attack in spite of the odds, staking everything on one throw. He drew up his plans and got his little army in motion.[7]

It was an odd sort of army, wholly representative of its time and place. Lyon had, to begin with, a handful of regular infantry and artillery, tough and disciplined, full of contempt for volunteers, home guards, and amateur soldiers generally, whether Union or Confederate. He also had several regiments of Missouri infantry, principally German levies from St. Louis, short of equipment and training, most of them grouped in a brigade commanded by Franz Sigel. Sigel was an émigré from the German revolutionary troubles of 1848, trained as a soldier, humorless, dedicated, unhappily lacking in the capacity to lead soldiers in action; a baffling sort, devoted but incapable, who induced many Germans to enlist but who was rarely able to use them properly after they had enlisted. There were two rough-hewn regiments from Kansas and there was a ninety-day outfit from Iowa, a happy-go-lucky regiment whose time was about to expire but whose members had agreed to stick around for a few days in case the general was going to have a battle. (The Iowans did not like Lyon at all but they trusted him, considering him a tough customer and competent.)[8] There were also stray companies and detachments from here and there whose numbers were small and whose value was entirely problematic. In miniature, this was much like the Union army that had been so spectacularly routed at Bull Run except that it was even less well equipped and disciplined.

Yet if this army was odd the army which it was about to fight was ever so much odder—one of the very oddest, all things considered, that ever played a part in the Civil War. Lyon's army would have struck any precisionist as something out of a military nightmare, but it was a veritable Prussian guard compared to its foes. The Southerners were armed with everything from regulation army rifles to back-country fowling pieces, a few of them wore Confederate gray but most of them wore whatever homespun garments happened to be at hand when they left home, and for at least three fourths of them there were no commissary and quartermaster arrangements whatever. The various levies were tied together by a loose gentleman's agreement rather than by any formal military organization, and many of the men were not Confederates at all, owing no allegiance to Jefferson Davis, fighting for Missouri rather than for the Confederacy. The war was still a bit puzzling, in these parts.

The core of this army (from a professional soldier's viewpoint, at any rate) was a brigade of some 3200 Confederate troops led by Brigadier General Ben McCulloch, veteran of the Mexican War and one-time Texas Ranger, an old pal of Davy Crockett who looked the part, an officer who liked to sling a rifle over his shoulder, get on his horse, and do his scouting personally. His men were well armed, most of them wore uniforms, and they had had about as much military training as anybody got in those days—enough to get by on, but nothing special. There were also 2200 state troops from Arkansas, one cavalry and three infantry regiments led by Brigadier General N. B. Pearce. These men had good weapons but no uniforms and little equipment—they carried their ammunition in their haversacks for want of better containers—and they had brought along two batteries of artillery, guns which until quite recently had reposed in the United States arsenal at Little Rock.[9] And, in addition, there was the Missouri State Guard under Major General Sterling Price.

No one quite knew how many men Price had—between 9000 and 10,000, probably, of which number only about 7000 could be used in action; the rest had no weapons at all. There were a few regimental organizations, but for the most part the formations were nothing more than bands bearing the names of the men who led them—Wingo's infantry, Kelly's infantry, Foster's infantry, and so on. The men had no tents, no supplies, no pay, hardly any ammunition and nothing whatever in the way of uniforms; an officer could be distinguished by the fact that he would have a strip of colored flannel on his shoulders, and one of the men described General Price himself with the words: "He is a large fine looking bald fellow dressed in common citizen clothes an oald linen coat yarn pants." None of them had been given anything which West Point would have recognized as drill; one group, led by former country lawyers, was called to quarters daily by the courtroom cry of "Oyez! Oyez!" and customarily addressed its commanding officer as "Jedge." Not even in the American Revolution was there ever a more completely backwoods army; these men were not so much soldiers as rangy characters who had come down from the north fork of the creek to get into a fight. Their commissary department consisted of the nearest cornfield, and their horses got their forage on the prairie; and a veteran of the State Guard wrote after the war that any regular soldier given command of this host would have spent a solid six months drilling, equipping, organizing, and provisioning it, during which time the Yankees would have overrun every last county in Missouri once and for all. He added that although Price's men had very poor weapons—some of them actually carried ancient flintlocks—they knew very well how to use them, and they did not scare easily. They were wholly devoted to General Price, whom they always referred to as "Pap."[10]

Price was in truth worthy of devotion, and the mere fact that he was out here at all testified to the strange complexity of the war on the border. A handsome, stalwart man in his early fifties, Virginia-born and a resident of Missouri for thirty years, Price was a good lawyer and a good politician; had served in the state legislature, in Congress and as governor, and had led a regiment in the Mexican War, winning a brigadier's star for gallantry. He was no secessionist; on the contrary he had counted himself a good Union man even after the bombardment of Fort Sumter and President Lincoln's call for troops, and although he had not been prepared to help destroy the Confederacy he had not been prepared to help establish it either. He had taken to the warpath, in fact, only after Lyon compelled everyone in Missouri to choose sides; he was definitely fighting against the Federals now, but he was not so much fighting for the Confederacy as for the vain hope that the war could be kept out of the front yards of the people of Missouri. He wanted to put limits on the war, so that no one but soldiers need be hurt. Later this fall he would sign a formal agreement with Frémont providing for an end to guerrilla warfare, cessation of arrests for political opinion, and a mutual pledge that "the war now progressing shall be exclusively confined to armies in the field."[11] The Federal authorities would quickly disavow this agreement, and in the end Missouri knew all of the horrors civil war could bring, but nobody could say that Price had not done his best.

In a military sense Price was an orphan, serving a government which was adrift in no man's land, and although he was a major general and Ben McCulloch was a brigadier, McCulloch's commission came from Jefferson Davis, a full-fledged President, and Price's came from Claiborne Jackson, who was only a fugitive; if Price and McCulloch were to go to the wars together it would have to be on McCulloch's terms. Price learned this a few days before his troops, Pearce's Arkansans and McCulloch's brigade made camp together by a stream called Wilson's Creek, ten miles southwest of Springfield. Lyon had just moved back into Springfield, and it was obvious that the combined force ought to attack him immediately. But McCulloch had a poor opinion of Price and a worse one of Price's troops, and he was not entirely sure that he himself ought to be in Missouri at all: the Confederate government, he had been informed, did not want to wage aggressive warfare on foreign soil, which seemed to include Missouri, and he had visions of disaster. Price had a hot argument with him, threatening to attack Lyon unaided, telling him: "You must either fight beside us or look on at a safe distance and see us fight all alone the army you dare not attack even with our aid."[12] In the end Price won the argument by putting himself and his entire command under McCulloch's orders; and McCulloch at last ordered that on the night of August 9 the combined force take to the road and crush Lyon's army.

Defective military equipment can modify tactics. It rained that night, and McCulloch–reflecting that the men had no proper ammunition boxes but carried their paper cartridges in cloth haversacks, where they would almost certainly get soaked on a march in the rain –canceled the orders.[13] It made little difference, in the end, because at the same time Lyon issued his own orders for an attack on the Confederates, and on the morning of August 10 the two armies collided in a remarkably bloody battle at Wilson's Creek.

Lyon's plan was bold–the sort of plan that is called brilliant if it works and foolhardy if it fails. His troops plodded out of their camp in the evening drizzle. Sigel, with 1200 men, swung south on a wide flanking march, to come in on the Confederate right and rear. His men were ragged, wearing gray shirts trimmed in red, many of them shoeless, some of them lacking pants; they looked, indeed, much like the Arkansas and Missouri soldiers, which led to a good deal of confusion during the fight. While Sigel was moving, Lyon with the rest of the troops–4200 men, or thereabouts–marched straight ahead to fall on the Confederate center and left. Lyon apparently shared McCulloch's feeling: Price's Missourians were so poorly trained and armed that he could attack despite their advantage in numbers.

Just before the columns moved, Lyon rode down the lines on his dapple-gray horse, telling the men they were about to go into battle, urging them to fire low, and repeating: "Don't get scared; it's no part of a soldier's duty to get scared." As an inspirational eve-of-battle speech, it was not a success; Lyon looked exhausted and spoke in a monotone, and one of the Iowa irrepressibles was heard to mutter: "How is a man to help being skeered if he *is* skeered?"[14] Some time after midnight the men halted for a rest. At daylight they moved on and the battle was begun.

Just at first things went well for the Federals. Sigel got into position, wheeled up his artillery, and routed a camp of Confederate cavalry, then led his men forward across an open valley to press his advantage. But this move was made slowly and inexpertly; McCulloch saw that the force was not large, and put on a sharp counterattack; Sigel's men broke and fled, abandoning five guns and streaming away so incontinently that the battle saw them no more, Sigel himself going all the way back to Springfield, the private soldiers going off every which way.[15] Lyon, meanwhile, drove in the pickets in his front and got into a savage fight on a low ridge, an open meadow and a strip of timber, where he quickly learned that he had been mistaken about Pap Price's militia. The ridge became known that day as "Bloody Hill."

It was a small battle but a very hard one, devoid of tactical subtleties once Sigel's flanking move dissolved. It came down to simple head-on slugging, on a battlefield hardly more than half a mile wide—the smallest major battlefield in all the war. A Confederate officer said about all that needs to be said of it when he called it "a mighty mean-fowt fight." Now and then, inexplicably, silence would fall on the field, while the two armies caught their breath; then the fighting would flare up again, deep smoke settling on the ground, the opposing lines no more than fifty yards apart. Pap Price kept riding to the front to see what the Federals were up to, his men calling to him to get back out of danger; on the Federal side, Lyon was twice wounded and his horse was killed, and he confessed to an aide that he feared the day was lost. Strange little pictures survive: the 1st Iowa holding its fire and calling on its neighbors not to shoot while a mounted Texan galloped boldly out into an open field, in point-blank range, to retrieve a fallen flag; a Federal soldier, crouching alone, his rifle pointed straight up at the sky, feverishly firing, reloading and firing again as fast as he could, valiant as a man could be, harming no one; a Confederate colonel telling his men to shoot the Yankees in the belly because a man dying of such a wound died slowly and so had time to prepare to meet his Maker; one of Price's Missourians, carried to the rear with a broken thigh, struggling and demanding that he be put down, crying: "I want to kill more Yankees!"[16] Participants remembered many scenes like these; they do not seem to have recalled seeing very many men on either side running off in panic.

It lasted most of the morning; an amazing battle, in which raw recruits fought like veterans, disorganized Missourians and time-expired Iowans going to it as steadily as the regulars themselves, providing an odd refutation of the Bull Run lesson and its teaching about the dreadful folly of putting armies into battle before they are ready. Perhaps it was Lyon and Price personally who made the difference, or perhaps the difference lay in the men in the ranks; or, possibly, it was just that this happened in Missouri rather than in Virginia. Anyway, the battle ended in no rout. It ended, logically enough, when Nathaniel Lyon got killed; the fighting died down when the flaming fighting spirit died. Somewhere around eleven o'clock in the morning a part of the Union line seemed to be giving way, and Lyon (remounted now, carrying on in spite of his wounds) galloped over to get things in order. He waved his hat, got laggards back into action, moved the line forward, and then was shot from his horse with a bullet in his heart. The line held, and after a time the fighting came to an end. The Federals discovered that their highest-ranking officer then available on the field was Major Samuel D. Sturgis of the regulars, and so Major Sturgis took command of the army. Sensibly enough, he led it back to Springfield. The Confederates made no pursuit. As the man said, it had been a mighty tough fight.[17]

The figures show it, as far as figures can. The Federals had roughly 5400 men on the field and lost approximately 1300 in killed, wounded, and missing; just about 25 per cent of the total number present, a high figure for any battle. Probably more than 10,000 Confederates were present, but thousands of them never got into action; the casualty list–Missourians, Arkansans, and McCulloch's brigade, all together–ran to slightly more than 1200. All in all, the battle put at least 2500 men out of action.[18]

Near the place where one of the Confederate batteries had been posted there was a farmhouse, and during the battle the farmer's wife had taken refuge in the cellar. She came out after the battle ended and found a party of soldiers helping themselves to apples from her trees. An officer rode up and told the men to stop it, but the woman assured him that she did not mind; there were plenty of apples, everybody had had a pretty bad morning, let them take all they wanted. Then, looking at the boys fresh from the battle that had been raging at her own doorstep, she asked, as an afterthought, a question which might have been asked by the harassed Missouri majority, the farm people on whose homesteads the fighting and the marauding were taking place and who stood to be plundered and fought over no matter which army was present. "Are you Lincoln's folk, or Jeff Davis's folk?" she inquired. Jeff Davis's folk, the boys said.[19]

3: *The Hidden Intentions*

Lyon had done more than was immediately apparent. He had lost a battle and he had lost his life, but he had won the summer—the crucial ten weeks in which Missouri's fate rested on a knife's edge—and the Lincoln administration would in the end win the state. Late in July, while the campaign around Springfield was coming to a climax, a state convention met in Jefferson City with Unionists in full control—a thing which Lyon's offensive made possible. The convention promptly deposed secessionists by declaring all state offices vacant; then it filled those offices with solid loyalists, naming Hamilton R. Gamble as provisional governor, and the Confederate cause in Missouri thereafter was a losing cause. The machinery by which the state could impose taxes, collect money, organize troops and then arm, feed and support them had passed forever into the hands of the Confederacy's enemies; which meant that General Price and his amazing militia, along with any other Missourians who wanted to go forth and fight for the South, could never make their weight felt. They were waifs and waifs they would remain, and the handicap was too much for them.

More than three months later General Price explained the handicap in a long letter to Jefferson Davis, an epistle which sounds a little bit like the Apostle Paul tabulating his woes. Most of the people of Missouri, he said, favored the Confederacy, but they were in an almost impossible position. They were "without any military organization and but few military men; without arms and without an army; overrun by Federal armies before a blow on our side could be stricken; pursued as fugitives from the state capital at the moment when the governor called our people to arms; fleeing with a handful of men to the extreme southwestern corner of the state . . . having to fight for the arms we have and to capture nearly all the appliances of war with which we are now supplied; with a powerful foe extending his lines across the state, so as effectually to cut off our succor and recruits from the north side of the Missouri River, our metropolis all the while in the hands of the enemy, thus giving him control of the railroads and rivers as well as the banks and channels of commerce and centers of intelligence, the war being waged as well upon the people of the country and private property as upon the army." His soldiers, he went on, were no more than "half fed, half clothed, half supplied with the necessary means of subsistence and comfort." They had never been formally recruited and organized; they were simply men "caught up from the woods and the fields—from the highways and byways, by night and by day—without an hour's or a day's preparation." He believed that he could add 20,000 men to his force if he just had some backing; Missouri, he was sure, could take care of herself, "once the Confederate government renders us such assistance as to make our force available."

The pressure was on him; the war was changing, and he was changing with it. In the beginning he had opposed secession and had wanted to do no more than to keep the war out of Missouri; now he was a militant Confederate, declaring that he had "placed home and comfort and property and family and life on the altar of my country's safety," pledging his state to make war to the end if the Confederacy would give the proper help.[1]

There was a pressure on General Frémont, too. Like General Price he would in the end commit himself to a cause which had not been his when he got his commission. The news from Wilson's Creek sounded like sheer catastrophe—Lyon dead, his crippled army in full retreat, armed Rebels rampaging about unchecked, a big Confederate offensive imminent—and St. Louis itself seemed no better than an echoing cave of the winds. There were soldiers without weapons or supplies, military contracts going unfulfilled for lack of money, and a dismaying lack of the administrative firmness that could remedy these defects. Placed in a position where he was bound to make a certain number of mistakes, General Frémont had the unhappy knack of making exactly the kind of mistakes that would get into the headlines and offend the very people whose support he needed most.

It began with headquarters itself—with the look of it, the atmosphere that pervaded it, and the people who were visible there. Headquarters had been housed in a good three-story dwelling that lay behind a pleasant lawn enclosed by a stone wall, at Chouteau Avenue and Eighth Street, rented for $6000 a year. The building was not actually too big and although the price was high it perhaps was not really excessive, in view of the fact that this was one of the most important military departments in the United States; but somehow the place seemed a little too imposing. Frémont had guards all over the premises, and there were staff officers to sift his callers—the unending stream of people who simply had to see the general, most of whom had no business getting within half a mile of him—and presently people were muttering that the man lived in a vast mansion and surrounded himself with the barriers of a haughty aristocracy.

Many of these complaints reflected nothing more than the inability of a young republic to understand that an overburdened executive must shield himself if he is to get any work done. (After all, this was the era when the White House itself was open to the general public, so that any persistent citizen could get in, shake the hand of the President and consume time which that harassed official could have used in more fruitful ways.) But it is also true that Frémont brought a great many of these complaints on himself by his inability to surround himself with the right kind of assistants.

Frémont had a fatal attraction for foreigners—displaced revolutionists from the German states, from Hungary and from France, fortune hunters from practically everywhere, men who had been trained and commissioned in European armies but who knew nothing at all about this western nation whose uniform they wore and whose citizens they irritated with their heel-clickings and their outlandish mangling of the American idiom. Frémont was taking part in a peculiarly American sort of war—Price's backwoods militia was wholly representative—and Missouri had felt from the beginning that the German-born recruits from St. Louis were a little too prominent. Now headquarters had this profoundly foreign air, and when a man was told that he could not see the general—to sell a load of hay or a tugboat, to apply for a commission, to give a little information about Rebel plots, or just to pass the time of day—he was given the bad news in broken English by a dandified type who obviously belonged somewhere east of the Rhine. It was all rather hard to take.[2]

To add to his troubles, Frémont made enemies of the Blair family. These aggressive manipulators were largely responsible for his appointment in the first place; Lincoln remarked that Frémont went to Missouri as "their pet and protégé,"[3] and the Blairs expected a protégé to stay in line. Also, he had been no better than the Blairs' second choice. Nathaniel Lyon was the man they really wanted for the Missouri command, and when Lyon died at Wilson's Creek the Blairs felt bitterly that Frémont had failed to give him proper support, and they complained that he sadly lacked Lyon's flaming drive and aggressive spirit.[4] Worst of all, Frémont had sorely offended Frank Blair in the matter of army supply contracts.

The supply problem would have made trouble in any case. Frémont had to buy enormous quantities of every conceivable kind of military equipment and he had to get delivery in a thundering hurry; buying things so is both expensive and wasteful, and unless some very good watchdogs are on hand it is apt to be honeycombed with graft to boot. Frémont had little business sense and almost no administrative capacity, and he had practically no watchdogs at all. His chief quartermaster was Major Justus McKinstry, another Blair protégé who had wandered off the reservation, a man who was blamed (whether justly or unjustly) for all manner of malpractices. Also, Frémont innocently surrounded himself with various businessmen whom he had known in California before the war and who were delighted now to make money by helping their old friend get horses, mules, beef, rifles, forage, tents, and other necessities. William Tecumseh Sherman had been a San Francisco banker in Gold Rush days and he had seen something of these men on their home soil; seeing them now in St. Louis, and reflecting that tall stories about corruption and extravagance were going the rounds, Sherman was minded of the old saying: Where the vultures gather there is sure to be a carcass. Sherman knew vultures when he saw them.[5]

So the supply situation was becoming an open scandal, partly because the overtaxed Frémont was unable to keep a good grip on affairs and partly because it was impossible to spend so much money so fast without irregularities. The whole War Department, in point of fact, was getting into trouble for the same reason, and Secretary Simon Cameron himself would be forced out within six months; but Frémont's case was made immeasurably worse by the fact that Frank Blair's friends were not getting what they considered their fair share of the spoils. What good is a protégé, if he cannot steer business to one's friends? Frank Blair made complaint, with lungs of brass; Adjutant General Lorenzo Thomas prepared to look into the situation, and so did a committee of Congress, and Frémont definitely was under a cloud.[6]

All of this might have been passed over if there had been a general feeling that Frémont was getting on with the war, but after the tragedy at Wilson's Creek this feeling disappeared. The Blairs, estranged by the matter of contracts, were even more vexed because the whole war effort was lagging, in Missouri and everywhere else. Impatient Frank Blair spoke for many when he wrote angrily: "How long O Lord, how long, is the despairing cry of all who wait on the inexplicable and fatal delays of the administration."[7] General Winfield Scott himself was losing favor because he appeared to favor a leisurely sort of war. Frémont's only chance for salvation was to start winning victories. He knew this as well as anyone, and to the best of his ability he tried to get things moving.

In one respect his luck was in: the Confederates failed utterly to follow up on their victory at Wilson's Creek. What was left of the Federal Army had to make a 110-mile retreat to the town of Rolla. Lyon had considered it impossible to do this successfully even before the army had been beaten; now, defeated and having lost a fourth of its numbers, the army had to move through a country where its friends were few and where the recent battle had given vast encouragement to all Southern sympathizers. It was encumbered with a big wagon train, and a hostile army twice its size, possessed of several thousand mounted men, was in position to take it apart. The little army could have been destroyed, and Sterling Price knew it, but he never could make Ben McCulloch see it; the retreating Federals were not pursued at all, and the big chance was lost. McCulloch had not wanted to enter Missouri in the first place, and now he flatly refused to go any farther. The victorious army lay idle at Springfield; then, presently, McCulloch took his brigade and followed Pearce's Arkansans (whose time was expiring) off to the southwest, clear out of the state. Price led his militia northward to see if he could not destroy a Federal garrison which occupied Lexington, far up the Missouri River. The result of all of this was that what Lyon had won by making his campaign stayed won. The Union cause had lost a man it could have used, but it had not lost the state.[8]

Frémont's great design was to invade the deep South, but first he had to secure Missouri. The northeastern part of the state, along the line of the Hannibal and St. Joseph Railway and on up nearly to the Iowa line, was racked by guerrilla warfare, with innumerable bands of night riders swirling sporadically cross country, wrecking bridges, despoiling the farms of Unionists, and in general stirring up trouble. Federal troops were bringing this area under control, their efforts directed by a blustery, tall-talking brigadier general named John Pope, who had a skyrocket's career (fast up and fast down) not far ahead of him. It is possible that some of the regiments that were kept busy on this constabulary duty might have been spared to help Lyon, but it was too late to worry about that now; John Pope had lots of drive, and this part of the state no longer offered any great problems.

Radiating out from St. Louis toward Confederate territory were three railroads. One followed the Missouri River to Jefferson City, sending a tentacle sixty miles beyond to Sedalia; the second went southwest to Rolla, haven for the defeated army; and the third ran seventy-five miles south to Ironton, in the hills. Frémont resolved to hold these railroads by fortifying and garrisoning Rolla, Jefferson City, and Ironton. He would protect the Mississippi River by planting a force at Cape Girardeau, he would strengthen Cairo itself, and he would fortify St. Louis. With all of this done—with the effervescent guerrillas suppressed and the discontented secessionists in St. Louis brought under firm control—this end of the border would be firmly anchored. Then, with the army of maneuver which would be forming while these security measures were being taken, Frémont could go South. He was full of confidence: "My plan is New Orleans straight . . . I think it can be done gloriously."[9]

All in all, the idea was not bad, although it was an idea rather than a plan. Despite the pomp, the confusion of tongues, and the men on the make at department headquarters a fairly good foundation was laid. Looking ahead to the move down the river, Frémont bought two steamers and had them converted into gunboats, and he ordered a fleet of mortar boats for the bombardment of secessionist forts. He sent espionage agents inside the enemy's lines, to get maps and other data that would be useful later on. Also, he made one appointment that was going to have far-reaching effects. Casting about for the right man to command the important post at Cairo, he selected an unobtrusive, seemingly colorless brigadier general named Ulysses S. Grant.

Perhaps it was important, just here, that Frémont had never belonged to the club—the closely knit little corps of West Pointers in the prewar army, men who had known one another for years, whose professional standards were rigid and sometimes narrow, and who tended to follow judgments based on the eternal round of gossip, small talk, and rumor that filled the air at every post and cantonment. In this circle Grant had been typed: a drifter and a drunkard, a man who had had to leave the Army because he drank too much, who had gone from one civil-life failure to another for half a dozen years thereafter, who had had trouble getting back into the service when the Civil War began and who owned a brigadier's commission now only because Congressman Elihu B. Washburne of Illinois, who had taken a fancy to him, had a great deal of influence in Washington. Everybody in the Old Army liked Sam Grant, but nobody seemed to have much confidence in him. But Frémont was an outsider, to whom the Old Army's verdicts meant nothing, and he could look at Grant with his own eyes. He had considered sending John Pope to Cairo, but Major McKinstry took Grant in to see him, and after the war Frémont wrote that he saw in Grant the qualities of "unassuming character not given to self elation, of dogged persistence, of iron will." Grant got the appointment and at the end of August set out for Cairo to take charge.[10]

Yet if Frémont had done some things well, the summer as a whole was frustrating, to him and to his superiors. Washington was far away, the Blairs were enemies and the President was uncommunicative, and mutual misunderstandings and suspicions were sprouting. Once, just when the need for troops in Missouri was greatest, Frémont was ordered by General Scott to send 5000 infantry to Washington. The order was quickly modified, but the mere fact that it had been issued struck Frémont as ominous.[11] So did the new provisional government of Missouri, thoroughly Unionist but representative of Democrats and slaveowners, conciliatory in a spot where the general was preparing a mailed fist. Governor Gamble was reassuring the planters about the security of their animate property and at Lincoln's suggestion he had recently proclaimed amnesty and protection for all secessionists-in-arms who would lay down their weapons and go home; and Frémont, convinced that the air was electric with unseen menaces, proclaimed martial law in St. Louis and sent Major McKinstry clattering though the street with cavalry patrols by night to overawe the treasonous.[12]

From Washington the view was depressing. Lyon was dead and unavenged, the uproar about graft, favoritism, and extravagance was rising day by day, and the extensive fortifying and garrisoning of cities and railheads began to look like undue caution and a devotion to defensive warfare; and the Blairs, who had to be listened to, were muttering audibly, just off-stage. Odd rumors drifted about; it was said that when Frémont did move south he would take a leaf from Aaron Burr's book and try to set up an independent principality in the Southwest, and Missouri loyalists complained that he cared nothing about the future of the state. One credulous citizen of St. Louis assured skeptical Attorney General Edward Bates that Frémont was an opium eater—"his behaviour and manner, his staring and contortions prove it." A correspondent of the elder Blair declared angrily that Frémont "is a huge humbug," said that true Union men could not talk to him, and concluded: "The fact is Frémont is endeavouring to play the Grand Monarch—and so far has proven to be a man of no great capacity."[13]

It was the grand monarch atmosphere that hurt. Frémont had managed to surround himself with a gang that made western America fear the worst, and the posturing of his aides and guards apparently affected his own judgment. A European army officer, visiting St. Louis early in September, felt that he was seeing something common enough in Europe but extraordinary in America. The glittering display suggested "both a commander-in-chief and a proconsul," and Frémont displayed "an ardent, ambitious personality" which "obviously is inclined to dictatorship." The place hardly seemed American. Frémont was "French, but revolutionary French," he disliked not only the Democrats but "all governmental parties," and all West Pointers to boot, and the European summed him up in words that would have interested Abraham Lincoln: "He is one of those men who serve a government, not according to official instructions but rather with an understanding of its hidden intentions, men who understand in half-words what is expected of them."[14]

That was the real trouble. All of the men suddenly raised to high place in 1861 were supposed to understand hidden intentions, to know how to act on half-words, to see far below the surface and to learn what the times required of them before the requirement was actually stated. This called for both vision and balance, and Frémont had only the vision. The balance was gone, distorted by the proconsul's trappings and the immeasurable ambition, by the sense of isolation from Washington, by the unending pressures of administrative chaos, probably also by the feeling that the Missouri situation was slipping out of control. Swollen with the need to perform a drastic act that would set everything straight, Frémont moved on to an act of immense folly—an act which his government would quickly disavow, but which nevertheless had at its haunted center something that must eventually be attended to.

Very early on the morning of August 30 the general sat at his desk at one end of a broad upper hall at headquarters; alone, for the day's routine had not begun and the big building was silent, with gray dawn light coming in through the tall windows. The general had been at work, and there was a sheaf of papers in front of him. He finished his morning coffee and then sent for two people—Edward Davis of Philadelphia, a friend who was visiting him at the time, and Jessie Benton Frémont, the general's wife, personal secretary and often his guiding spirit: an excessively energetic and self-confident lady who at times seemed to be executive officer and second-in-command for the entire Western Department. These two came, and the general picked up the papers and read to them what he had written.

What they heard was a proclamation, signed by Frémont and addressed to the public at large. It began by asserting that because of the general disorganization in Missouri—"the helplessness of the civil authority, the total insecurity of life, and the devastation of property by bands of murderers and marauders" who were out to settle old scores with private foes and "who find an enemy wherever they find plunder"—it was necessary for the commanding general to "assume the administrative powers of the state." The commanding general was therefore proclaiming martial law throughout Missouri. Within the lines of the "army of occupation"—the area, that is, which was enclosed by the chain of fortified towns, running from Cape Girardeau through Ironton, Rolla, and Jefferson City all the way up to the northwestern tip of the state—it was decreed that all persons found with weapons in their hands should be court-martialed and, if convicted, shot to death. In addition: "The property, real and personal, of all persons in the state of Missouri who shall take up arms against the United States, or who shall be directly proven to have taken an active part with their enemies in the field, is declared to be confiscated to the public use, and their slaves, if any they have, are hereby declared freemen." The proclamation went on to warn everybody not to engage in treasonable correspondence, to destroy railroad tracks, bridges, or telegraphs or to circulate "false reports or incendiary documents," and closed with the assertion: "The object of this declaration is to place in the hands of the military authorities the power to give instantaneous effect to existing laws and to supply such deficiencies as the conditions of war demand."[15]

Nothing ever really daunted Jessie Frémont, but Mr. Davis was somewhat stunned, and he got to his feet to warn the general: "Mr. Seward will never allow this. He intends to wear down the South by steady pressure, not by blows, and then make himself the arbitrator." Frémont calmly replied that the thing went beyond any question of what Seward might or might not approve. It was a war measure, and he proposed to "bring the penalties of rebellion home to every man found striving against the Union." There was a printing press at headquarters, and without further ado the general had the proclamation printed and made public. He also sent a copy to Washington, for the President's guidance.

Secretary Seward might well disapprove of this document, as a matter of policy, if his opinion was asked. But Frémont's vein was much the vein of Seward himself, in that letter which had startled Charles Francis Adams. He was making explicit what Seward had elaborately hinted at . . . the slow development, deep in this war for reunion, of an uncontrollable and undesigned war for human freedom.

4: *End of Neutrality*

And so the war had changed its character, a thousand miles from Washington. If a general in the field could displace the civil government, set the bondsmen free, and bring in firing squads to settle neighborhood disturbances, the struggle might quickly be what Wisconsin's Governor Randall had feared it might become—an unlimited war, far greater than a mere fight to put down rebellion. It was a peculiarity of the situation that although this had happened because of the unvarnished energy with which the border folk made war, it was nevertheless the people of the border whom Abraham Lincoln had most in mind when he tried to keep the war limited. They would fight for the Union, he believed, but they would not fight to suppress slavery, which was where Frémont's proclamation unquestionably would take them; and on September 2 the President sent the general a firm but not unfriendly letter.

There must be (said the President) no shooting of men taken in arms, because the Confederates could play the same game, with reprisals and counter-reprisals keeping firing squads busy from the Potomac all the way to Kansas; therefore the general must order no executions without first getting specific approval from Washington. In addition, and more importantly, there was the matter of the emancipation of slaves. This, wrote the President, "will alarm our Southern Union friends, and turn them against us—perhaps ruin our rather fair prospect for Kentucky." Frémont therefore was requested to modify that part of his proclamation, putting it in line with a recent act of Congress which provided only that slaves actually used in service of the Confederate armed forces could be taken from their owners, the subsequent status of such slaves being left most indefinite.[1]

General Frémont would not retreat. He wrote that he had been in a hot spot, "between the Rebel armies, the Provisional Government, and home traitors," and his proclamation was "as much a movement in the war as a battle"; if he modified it of his own accord it would imply that he felt that he had made a mistake, and he did not feel that way. Consequently, he would modify it only if the President publicly ordered him to do so. He was satisfied that "strong and vigorous measures have now become necessary to the success of our arms," and he hoped that his views would receive the President's approval.[2] Meanwhile, General Frémont sent Jessie off to Washington to argue the case with the President in person.

By this time the general was in far over his depth. What he was saying, in effect, was that the military problem in his own bailiwick justified him in committing the entire nation—both the states of the

Federal Union, and the Confederate states which had declared their independence—to an entirely different kind of war; a remorseless revolutionary struggle which in the end could do nothing less than redefine the very nature of the American experiment, committing the American people for the rest of time to a much broader concept of the quality and meaning of freedom and democracy than anything they had yet embraced. The war might indeed come to that. Secession was at bottom a violent protest against change, and extended violence would almost certainly destroy the delicate unspoken understanding by which the rival governments fought a limited war. But this was a problem for Washington, not for a general in the field. Frémont was making a decision that lay beyond his competence, and in his message to the President there was a proconsular arrogance that American soldiers are not supposed to display.

President Lincoln acted promptly. He publicly ordered Frémont to modify the clause about emancipation, he sent Postmaster General Montgomery Blair to St. Louis to talk to the general and give the President a fill-in on the situation, and when Jessie Frémont reached the White House he gave her an exceedingly cold reception. Jessie's trip in fact did Frémont much harm. Mr. Lincoln said afterward that "she more than once intimated that if General Frémont should decide to try conclusions with me, he could set up for himself,"[3] and although she denied vehemently that she ever said anything of the kind she undoubtedly helped to confirm the President's dawning suspicion that Frémont, in a decidedly tough situation, was trying to protect his fences by winning the support of the abolitionists. At one point, Jessie explained that only an edict of emancipation would keep England and France from recognizing the Confederacy; and the President, who had devoted agonizing hours to the question of preventing European intervention in this war, cut her short with the curt remark: "You are quite a female politician." The next day the elder Blair (who had been Jessie's friend for many years) scolded her, crying out: "Who would have expected you to do such a thing as this, to come here and find fault with the President?" All in all, she had a most unhappy visit.[4]

Overruling Frémont, Mr. Lincoln was thinking of a principle

and of a point of tactics, and the explanation which he did not bother to give Jessie Frémont he gave to his old friend and political supporter, Senator Orville Browning of Illinois. Writing to Browning not long afterward, Mr. Lincoln said that the principle was simple but basic. As a general Frémont could seize all sorts of property—a Missouri farm, or even a Missouri slave—for purely military purposes, but the effect of such seizures was only temporary. "When the need is past it is not for him to fix their permanent future condition. That must be settled according to the laws made by law-makers, and not by military proclamations." What Frémont did was nothing less than an act of dictatorship. The United States no longer had a constitutional government if a general, or a President, "may make permanent rules of property by proclamation." Reflecting that the acts of a general were in the end the acts of the President himself, Mr. Lincoln went on to write a sentence that would echo powerfully a year later: "What I object to is that I as President shall expressly or impliedly seize and exercise the permanent legislative functions of the government."

So much for principle. There was also work-a-day practicality, for Frémont had packed both moral error and tactical blunder into one ill-advised pronunciamento. Tactically, the case rested largely on Kentucky; on Kentucky's geographical position and on its divided state of mind, representative of the divided minds of so many millions who lived elsewhere. Kentucky was still at peace, delicately poised between the warring sections, and Kentucky's sentiments were fearfully, tragically mixed, strong devotion to the Union going hand in hand with cheerful acceptance of slavery and outright horror of anything that smacked of racial equality. Fighting an abolitionists' war, the Federal government might well lose Kentucky entirely, and the President wrote soberly: "I think to lose Kentucky is nearly the same as to lose the whole game . . . we would as well consent to separation at once, including the surrender of this capital."[5]

So far the war was incomplete. It had two ends and no middle, which is to say that although it was being fought at full strength in Virginia and in Missouri it was not being fought at all in the 400-

mile length of Kentucky. Here was where North and South touched one another most intimately, and perhaps came closest to a mutual understanding; here was the vital center of the whole border country, which in reality was no border at all but a broad corridor straight through the heart of America. Once the war broke into Kentucky it could begin to develop its full potential, which was likely to be much greater than had been bargained for by either of the two Kentuckians, Abraham Lincoln and Jefferson Davis, who headed the opposing governments.

Kentucky had tried hard to stay out of the war, thus reflecting not only the split in popular feeling but also the fact that Governor Beriah Magoffin leaned toward secession while a majority of the state legislature opposed it. Immediately after Fort Sumter Governor Magoffin notified Lincoln that the state would furnish no troops "for the wicked purpose of subduing her sister Southern states," and a group called the State Union Committee agreed that Kentucky could not send such troops "without outraging her solemn convictions of duty, and without trampling upon that natural sympathy with the seceding states which neither their contempt for her interests nor their disloyalty to the Union has sufficed to extinguish." On May 20 the governor made formal announcement of the state's neutrality, warning "all other states, separate or united, especially the United and Confederate states," not to enter Kentucky or to occupy Kentucky soil without express invitation from the state's legislative and executive authorities.[6]

In the long run this policy was bound to fail, and throughout the summer both sides prepared methodically for the day of failure. They began simply by seeking Kentucky recruits, carefully establishing camps outside of the state for their reception—Union camp near Cincinnati, just north of the Ohio River; Confederate camp near Clarksville, Tennessee, just below the Kentucky-Tennessee line. Inside the state there was the Kentucky State Guard, some 4000 militiamen strongly pro-Confederate in sympathies, commanded by Brigadier General Simon Bolivar Buckner—a solid West Pointer who had many friends in the Old Army, including both George B. McClellan and Ulysses S. Grant, and who was correctly believed to be ready to enter the Confederate service whenever neutrality should come to an end. As a counterweight, Unionists formed a militia of their own, naming it the Home Guard, and centering it at Camp Dick Robinson, not far from the state capital, Frankfort. The Home Guard was led by a burly ex-lieutenant in the Navy, William Nelson, a three-hundred-pound giant whom Mr. Lincoln made a brigadier general of volunteers and entrusted with a substantial quantity of arms and ammunition.[7] Nelson had influence in Kentucky. He also had much drive, and a flaming temper which one day would be the death of him; and now he worked hard to prepare the loyalists for the coming fight.

Governor Magoffin wrote letters of protest—to Mr. Lincoln, complaining about Nelson's force at Camp Dick Robinson, and to Mr. Davis, protesting the presence of Confederate troops in Tennessee, close to the Kentucky line. Lincoln replied blandly that the men at Nelson's camp were all Kentuckians, menacing nothing and attacking nothing; he did not think most Kentuckians wanted them removed, and he would not remove them. Davis replied with equal blandness, saying that his troops in Tennessee were there solely to protect that state from invasion.[8] Things went on as they had been, with Washington and Richmond raising troops, bringing in arms and lining up leading Kentuckians, no overt acts being performed but nothing being done in complete secrecy. During the summer Kentucky held a state election, sending a solid Unionist slate to the Federal Congress and increasing the Unionist majority in both houses of the state legislature.

The stakes were high. In Confederate hands, Kentucky would effectively blockade the Ohio River and deprive the Federals of any feasible base for a large-scale offensive in the Mississippi Valley, fundamental in the Union's grand strategy; if Mr. Lincoln felt that to lose Kentucky was to lose everything there was good reason for it. Conversely, if the state were held by the Union the Confederacy had no good way to save Tennessee, hold the Mississippi, and stave off a drive into the deepest South. Neither side could afford to lose, and neither side dared risk losing by moving prematurely; Kentuckians were notably touchy, and as far as anyone could see in the summer of 1861 they might go either way. Much would depend on which side first angered the Kentucky majority.

It was into this situation that General Frémont had thrust his proclamation about freeing the slaves of people who supported the Confederacy. The effect could have been a major Union disaster, except for two things—Mr. Lincoln's disavowal of the proclamation, and the abrupt appearance on Kentucky soil of a full-fledged Confederate Army, which on September 3 crossed the Tennessee line, occupied the towns of Hickman and Columbus, and began to plant heavy guns on the bluffs which overlook the Mississippi River at the latter point. Kentucky's neutrality was ended forever.

The occupation of Hickman and Columbus was accomplished by soldiers under contentious Brigadier General Gideon J. Pillow, but the movement had been ordered by Pillow's superior, Major General Leonidas Polk. Polk was a close friend of Jefferson Davis, a West Point graduate who years ago had left the Army to take holy orders, becoming at last a bishop in the Episcopal Church, as grave and as lacking in impetuosity as any bishop need be; a man who had returned to the Army when the war came, who had been given a general's commission by his old friend the President, and who somewhat against his will had been entrusted with the top Confederate command along the central portion of the Mississippi.

Polk knew as well as anyone that Kentucky needed very careful nursing, but he also believed that the Federals were going to send armies into the state any day now, and the immense weight of military necessity was on him. General Grant was moving to Cairo, building up forces which obviously would come down the river sooner or later, and there was no better place to stop such forces than Columbus. Armed Federals had recently appeared at the Missouri hamlet of Belmont, just across the river from Columbus, apparently designing a seizure of the Columbus bluffs, and a Federal gunboat had anchored off the town, looking menacing and sending a party ashore to tear down a Confederate flag which some incautious civilian had hoisted; and, altogether, General Polk believed that it was time for him to act. Grant had in fact been told by Frémont in complete disregard of Kentucky's neutrality that he was to take possession of Columbus as soon as he conveniently could, and although Polk did not know about these orders he could easily see what Grant's next move was likely to be, and as a soldier he was bound to beat his enemy to the punch if he could. On September 1, Polk wrote to Governor Magoffin, saying that it was "of the greatest consequence to the Southern cause in Kentucky or elsewhere that I should be ahead of the enemy in occupying Columbus and Paducah"; and not long after that he got Pillow's men in motion. He sent a hasty wire to President Davis, telling what he had done and explaining the reasons for it, and asserting that now that he had a force in Columbus he proposed to keep it there.[9]

There was an instantaneous dust-up; naturally enough, because the horizons of the war had been pushed out beyond calculation. The Confederate Secretary of War, L. P. Walker, ordered Polk to withdraw at once, and Governor Isham G. Harris of Tennessee wired that both he and President Davis were pledged to respect the neutrality of Kentucky: could not General Polk get his troops out of there immediately? (A neutral Kentucky was a perfect shield protecting Tennessee from invasion; with Kentucky in the war Tennessee was wide open, as Governor Harris could not help but realize.) Secretary Walker assured Governor Harris that Polk's movement was wholly unauthorized and that the prompt withdrawal of the Confederate force had been ordered, but Mr. Davis quickly overruled him, telegraphing to Polk that "the necessity justifies the action." Polk wrote to Harris explaining that the invasion had been ordered "under the plenary powers delegated to me by the President," adding that he knew of no especial commitment to honor Kentucky's neutrality and closing with a polite expression of regret that he could not concur with the governor's views.[10]

The first consequence was a brisk move by the Federals; the man Frémont had stationed at Cairo was capable of acting quickly. Learning what had happened, General Grant put all the infantry and artillery he could spare on steamboats and, with gunboats for escort, moved fifty miles up the Ohio to take possession of Paducah, Kentucky—another of those strategically important little cities, like Cairo, whose possession could mean so much. Having occupied the place on September 6, Grant hurried back to Cairo to round up reinforcements for the Paducah contingent, to get Frémont's approval of what he had just done—he had sent Frémont a telegram, earlier, proposing the seizure of Paducah, but had gone ahead and made the move without waiting for a reply—and to send a telegram to the Kentucky legislature announcing that the Confederates had violated the state's neutrality.[11] The legislature had just convened with a strong Unionist majority—27 out of 38 Senators, and 74 out of 100 in the House—and it reacted as might have been expected, requesting Governor Magoffin to call out the militia "to expel and drive out the invaders," meaning Bishop Polk's Confederates, and inviting the United States government to give Kentucky "that protection against invasion which is granted to each one of the states by the fourth section of the fourth article of the Constitution of the United States."[12]

This invitation actually asked the United States government to do nothing that it had not been planning to do anyway, but it did put a heavy load on a soldier who had already been overtaxed—Robert Anderson, who as a major in the Regular Army had had to take the heat at Fort Sumter, and who now was a brigadier general charged with the Federal command in Kentucky. Anderson was in wretched health. Fort Sumter had taken much out of him, and the summer had been even worse. As a native Kentuckian who had strong ties and deep sympathies with the South but who was also completely loyal to the Union, he had been torn two ways by powerful emotions, and he lacked the cold inner hardness to endure such a strain; apparently he was on the edge of what would now be called a nervous breakdown. When Polk made his move Anderson was in Cincinnati, conferring with eminent Kentuckians, just as he had been doing for months, on the delicate business of getting control over a state whose virginal neutrality was still intact. It was undoubtedly a relief to come to the end of these under-the-counter deals and to be able to make war out in the open, but in order to make war General Anderson was going to need more troops than were anywhere in sight. Thus far, the troops raised by the Middle Western states had mostly been sent either to Washington or to St.

Louis; the general had to occupy a large state, expelling invaders, and he did not have very many soldiers.

He did have two valuable subordinates whom he had persuaded the War Department to assign to him, men who were to play large parts in the war; two West Point-trained brigadier generals, William Tecumseh Sherman and George H. Thomas. Anderson sent Sherman off to get help from Frémont, if possible, and to urge the Governors of Illinois and Indiana to send along any troops they had, and he dispatched Thomas to take command of Camp Dick Robinson. He himself established headquarters in Louisville and set about recruiting Kentuckians for the Federal service.[13]

Meanwhile, the citizens of Kentucky began to get grim evidence that they were in a civil war, with strange new rules, or perhaps no rules at all, to govern them. United States marshals were going about arresting people on broad charges of disloyalty, and the legalities ordinarily involved in arrests and imprisonments were wholly lacking. As a sample there was the case of former Governor Charles S. Morehead, who was lodged in a cell in Fort Lafayette, far off in New York, after a marshal accused him of treason. Morehead could get no formal arraignment or hearing. His son-in-law appealed to President Lincoln, who presently told Secretary Seward that it would be all right to release Morehead, and others arrested with him, provided the release was approved by James Guthrie and James Speed. Guthrie and Speed were private citizens of Kentucky—estimable men, who had worked hard for the Union but who could not (under any statute readily brought to mind) legally say whether or not suspected traitors must stay in prison. Reuben T. Durrett, acting editor of the Louisville *Courier*, was arrested because some of his editorials seemed disloyal, and Joseph Holt, who had been Secretary of War in the last weeks of James Buchanan's administration, warned Lincoln that even if the man took the oath of allegiance he ought not to be freed: "I say that he would take the oath if necessary on his knees, and would stab the Government the moment he rose to his feet." An Associated Press correspondent, Martin W. Barr, was suspected of using his position "to advance the insurrectionary cause"; marshals came to his house at night and took him away, and from a cell in Fort Lafayette he gave his wife a fairly correct appraisal of his situation when he wrote: "I am here beyond the reach of law or liberty or juries." Bitterly, he added: "There remains but one outrage—to cut my head off."[14] Correspondent Barr was spared that final outrage, but he did not immediately get out of prison, either. The war had been slow in reaching Kentucky, but once it arrived it was rigorous. Kentucky's neutrality may have been an unrealistic venture, but from mid-April to September it had spared the people something. . . .

No doubt General Polk had blundered; the Confederacy lost much more than it gained when Kentucky went to war. Yet it may be that Polk's real blunder was that his drastic action was not quite drastic enough. Driven by military necessity, he had occupied Columbus; if at the same time he had also occupied Paducah, instead of leaving that place for General Grant to take, he might have put the Federals in a most uncomfortable box.

In one way this war in the West was going to be unlike any other war in history: it was going to be fought along the rivers, amphibious as no war had ever been before, and the generals were going to have to learn the rules as they went along. One of the rules was the unanticipated fact that in such warfare the defensive can be much more difficult than the offensive. It seemed obvious that guns on top of a high bluff could keep gunboats, transports, and supply steamers from getting past; Columbus had very high bluffs, and that was why General Polk had had the place occupied. But an invader blocked at Columbus could still invade if he could float south on some other stream that would put him close enough to the stronghold's rear to enable him to snip its lifelines. A Yankee general stopped at Columbus was bound to realize that he could send a force up the Tennessee River, which comes north across the state of Tennessee a little less than one hundred miles east of the Mississippi; if he went up that river far enough the Confederates would have to evacuate Columbus, even though their works there were wholly impregnable to assault. No Yankee general could ascend the Tennessee unless he first took Paducah, which is where the Tennessee flows into the Ohio. Holding Paducah, the Confederates could hold the

Tennessee and hence could hold Columbus and the Mississippi itself; losing Paducah, they could hold Columbus only until the Federals saw what the Tennessee River could do for them.

Polk had intended to take Paducah, but he was doing the job one step at a time, and Grant got into Paducah ahead of him. General Buckner promptly pointed out that this neutralized the possession of Columbus, which meant that the Confederacy had gained very little by its seizure of that place. As a result, Buckner believed that it would pay to get out of the state altogether, leaving the Yankees as the only invaders and trying to rally the citizens against them.[15] The idea was probably impractical, but Buckner had seen one thing clearly enough; taken by itself, Columbus was not worth what it cost. Polk should have gone for everything, but his hand had been forced; he had had to make a quick decision at a time when any choice he made was quite likely to turn out to be wrong. He confessed that the Confederates really should have moved into Columbus months earlier, "If we could have found a respectable pretext," for he believed that during all the time of neutrality "Kentucky was fast melting away under the influence of the Lincoln government."[16] In any case, another man now had the responsibility. Albert Sidney Johnston was on the scene at last, over-all commander for everything the Confederates had in the West.

Johnston was fifty-eight, a courtly man with a singularly winning personality, a famous veteran of the Old Army and in the opinion of some Southerners at that time the ablest soldier on either side. He had been in command for the United States Army on the West Coast when the war began; had stayed there, making no secret of his intention to side with the South but faithfully carrying on with his duties until Washington could send out a replacement; then he had resigned, traveling by horseback across the rough mountains and plains of the Southwest all the way to Texas, and going on to Richmond in the hope that President Davis could find something for him to do. He was cheered wherever he made an appearance, and no one received him more eagerly than Jefferson Davis, who immediately gave him a full general's commission. ("I hoped and expected that I had others who would prove Generals," Mr. Davis said a bit later, "but I knew I had *one*—and that was Sidney Johnston.") Johnston reached Nashville on September 14, to be received at the State Capitol by Governor Harris and an enthusiastic crowd. Called on to say a few words to the multitude, he instinctively touched the right note, addressing his civilian audience as "Fellow Soldiers!" and explaining: "I call you *soldiers* because you all belong to the reserve corps."

Polk was devoutly glad to see him. Before Johnston ever got to Richmond, Polk had written to Mr. Davis to urge Johnston's appointment to the top spot in the West; he had known Johnston since boyhood, had roomed with him at West Point, and had himself been persuaded to take the Western command only on the understanding that the job would eventually go to Johnston. Now Johnston was on hand, taking a look at the field that would occupy him for the rest of his life.[17]

What he saw was enough to dismay any general: much to do, and not enough to do it with. He warned Mr. Davis, two days after his arrival, that "we have not over half the *armed* forces that are now likely to be required," and he pointed out that although there were plenty of recruits there was no way to arm them. Whether faulty War Department planning or the tightening of the Federal blockade was responsible, the Confederacy was already pinched for weapons, and no one felt the pinch more than Albert Sidney Johnston. In addition to being responsible for Confederate operations in Missouri and Arkansas, he had to defend a line more than 300 miles long, from the Cumberland Gap in the east to Columbus in the west, and he had fewer than 30,000 men all told. The Yankees had nearly twice that many, and although every Federal commander was complaining bitterly about the lack of proper arms their situation was infinitely better than Johnston's.[18] He could do nothing but put on a bold front, acting as if he planned to move north to the Ohio River and hoping that the Federals could be bluffed into inaction. If he could stave off invasion during the fall and winter, Richmond might be able to help him by spring. It seemed to General Johnston that the war was going to last for at least seven years.

5: *Mark of Desolation*

Kentucky's war had grown out of Missouri's, a product of the shock waves that came surging east from the Mississippi; and these waves met others which rolled in from the south and the east, from Tennessee and Virginia, making a bewildering turbulence. While the rival governments in Washington and Richmond settled down to the slow and methodical business of training and equipping armies according to the professional pattern, in the heart and center of the land the war got away from them and made its own demands, creating unsuspected perils and opportunities. The fire was running down to the grass roots. Somewhere between the too vivid realities of slavery and abolitionism and the fine-spun abstractions of states' rights and Unionism, the war was becoming something which men could interpret in terms of wrongs done by their neighbors, of old grudges and local feuds, of farm prices and the cost of living and the pestilent inequities of courthouse politics. Flames burning so could be hard to control and hard to put out.

In western Virginia the mountain folk were trying to secede from secession, paying off old scores with the tidewater aristocracy and bringing on a series of fights that went sputtering from farm to farm and from town to town in the remotest highland valleys—mean little fights, altogether unromantic, in which generals lost reputations while private soldiers and assorted private citizens lost their lives. When Virginia left the Union, a majority of her people west of the Alleghenies dissented vigorously. Delegates from the western counties convened, orated, passed resolutions and, on June 11, announced that they had nullified the ordinance of secession and had established something which, they insisted, was henceforth the legal government of the state, with one Francis Pierpoint as governor. This expedient seemed useful, and Washington agreed to pretend—for a while, at any rate—that this creation was indeed Virginia; and the westerners prepared to carry their dissent to its logical if unconstitutional conclusion by wrenching the whole mountain district away from the Old Dominion and creating an entirely new state—a state which, they believed, might be called Kanawha, but which eventually would enter the Union as West Virginia.[1]

So Union and Confederacy fought for title to this land, believing that much was at stake. A Confederacy which held western Virginia could squelch the mountaineer Unionists and could also carry the war to the Ohio River; furthermore, by seizing the western half of the Baltimore & Ohio Railroad it could cut Washington's only direct railway line to the west. The Federals for their part felt that western Virginia offered both a back-door approach to Richmond and a prime chance to cut the line of the vital Virginia and Tennessee Railroad, which connected Richmond with Memphis and the Mississippi Valley. Eastern Tennessee, in addition, seemed to contain as many Unionists as western Virginia, and Union victories in Virginia might lead them to rally around the old flag to very good effect. Campaigning in the mountains was extraordinarily difficult, but the winner stood to get great advantages.

Things went badly for the South from the start. During the spring a remarkably brilliant and personable young major general, a former West Pointer turned railroad man, George Brinton McClellan, led a Federal Army of Middle Westerners in from Wheeling and Parkersburg, clearing the line of the B & O and smashing a small Confederate Army which guarded the mountain passes where the great turnpike from the Ohio River ran southeast to Staunton, in the Shenandoah Valley. McClellan did this with a flair and a competence which made him famous, and after the Federal disaster at Bull Run he was called east to reorganize and lead the shattered Army of the Potomac. He turned the mountain department over to his second-in-command, Brigadier General William S. Rosecrans, and went where opportunity called him. It was up to Rosecrans to hold what had been won and to add to it if possible.

Not much could be added. It seemed, just at first, that a victorious Federal Army ought to be able to march straight through to tidewater or to the deep South, attaining glory either way. This was possible, according to the maps. But the maps did not show how terribly bad the roads were, or how barren was much of the country they crossed; the central mass of the Alleghenies was an impossible spot for a major offensive because no army which made a really lengthy advance could supply itself.[2] Besides, in August the Confederates undertook a strong counteroffensive, and Rosecrans found that simply to hold the line would keep him busy enough.

This counteroffensive was conducted by General Robert E. Lee.

Lee was already famous—General Scott had rated him the best man in the army, and many of the Old Army crowd doubtless would have agreed—and he was on his way to military immortality, but what happened in the Alleghenies gave no hint that one of history's greatest soldiers was here commanding troops in action for the first time. If he had disappeared from view at the end of 1861 he would figure in today's footnotes as a promising officer who somehow did not live up to expectations. His western Virginia campaign, in short, was a failure. Most of the failure, to be sure, was due to circumstances over which Lee had no control, but part of it was his own. In this, his first campaign, he was still learning his trade.

He had spent the spring and summer in Richmond, most of the time as President Davis's principal military adviser—an important post, which he filled creditably, but devoid of real authority and, to a man with Lee's taste for action, woefully unexciting. Mr. Davis sent him to the mountains in the hope that "he would be able to retrieve the disaster we had suffered . . . and, by combining all our forces in western Virginia on one plan of operations, give protection to that portion of our country."[3] It was probably the most thankless assignment of Lee's career.

The Federals had about 11,000 soldiers in western Virginia. Detachments held the Baltimore & Ohio line, in the north, and some 2700 under Brigadier General Jacob Cox were off to the southwest in the Kanawha Valley, apparently meditating an advance along the Lewisburg Pike in the direction of Clifton Forge. The rest were in the center, in the general vicinity of Cheat Mountain, on the road that led to Staunton, guarding the country which McClellan's victories had won. The Confederates in western Virginia could muster more men, but for a variety of reasons—ranging from the bad health of the soldiers to the incompetence and jealousy of some of their commanders—they would not be able to put all of them into action.[4]

The principal Confederate force was a loosely knit army of perhaps 10,000 stationed at the town of Huntersville in the valley of the Greenbrier, south of the Staunton turnpike. It was led by Brigadier General W. W. Loring, stiff, touchy and experienced, a competent officer who unfortunately could never forget that he had ranked Lee in the Old Army. He was clearly vexed at Lee's arrival, and Lee carefully refrained from assuming direct command of the army; his own charter of authority was a little vague, and he contented himself with setting up his headquarters tent near Loring's, assuming apparently that the man was soldier enough to accept a superior's guidance if he were allowed to save a little face.[5] Farther south, theoretically operating against the Federal General Cox but actually contending furiously with each other for authority and public favor, were two politicians who had become brigadiers—Henry A. Wise, former Governor of Virginia, who had been sent here with his "legion" in the belief that his popularity with western Virginians would be an asset to the cause, and former Secretary of War John B. Floyd, whose military incompetence had not yet been made manifest.

Conditions for campaigning were bad. It began to rain in mid-August and kept on raining for weeks, making the rough mountain roads almost impassable; a supply wagon carrying six or eight barrels of flour would be dragged along inches at a time, the wagon bed scraping the ground, wheels axle-deep in mud. Typhoid fever, measles, and other diseases went through the Confederate camps so that in a short time nearly a third of the army was out of action; a North Carolina regiment, which came in with 1000 men, was down to a strength of 300 in a few weeks, although it had not been in combat at all. One of Lee's staff officers, writing after the war, said that although he saw the Army of Northern Virginia in all of its desperate trials he never felt as heartsick "as when contemplating the wan faces and the emaciated forms of those hungry, sickly, shivering men" whom Lee commanded in western Virginia in the summer and fall of 1861. A weary private wrote, "I am of opinion that we are near the jumping off place," and concluded that people who talked ecstatically about the beautiful mountain country "never had the extraordinary pleasure of wearing their feet out to their ankles walking over the mountains to see the romantic scenery"; he recalled "short rations, thin and ragged clothing, rain, mud, water and measles, all mixed up together."[6]

The same rains fell on the Federals, who had to tramp the same roads and contend with the same camp maladies; yet there seemed to be a difference. As sardonic an individual as Ambrose Bierce, who served here with the 9th Indiana Volunteers, wrote long afterward that he looked back on western Virginia "as a veritable realm of enchantment" and said that boys raised in the flat country of the Middle West found the mountains inspiring and picturesque. "How romantic it all was!" he cried. "The sunset valleys full of visible sleep; the glades suffused and interpenetrated with moonlight; the long valley of the Greenbrier stretching away to we knew not what silent cities." He and his comrades, he recalled, still felt that early, innocent patriotism "which never for a moment doubted that a rebel was a fiend accursed of God and angels—one for whose extirpation by force and arms each youth of us considered himself specially 'raised up.'"[7] Soldiers could stand almost anything, it seemed, when they knew they were winning.

And the Federals were winning. Early in September, Cox's column was endangered by the approach of wrangling Wise and Floyd, and Floyd's men had routed an Ohio regiment on August 26 in a sharp little fight at Cross Lanes, not far from the mouth of the Gauley River. But Wise and Floyd just could not work together—Cox wrote that Wise "did me royal service by preventing anything approaching unity of action between the two principal Confederate columns"—and Rosecrans marched down to the rescue, leaving a brigade under Brigadier General J. J. Reynolds at Cheat Mountain and on September 10 attacking Floyd at Carnifix Ferry, on the Gauley River, forcing that general to beat a speedy retreat. Wise and Floyd drew back to the mountains west of Lewisburg, each accusing the other of failing to come to his aid; and Lee, seeing an opportunity in the weakening of the Cheat Mountain contingent, moved up to attack Reynolds.[8]

The opportunity was there, if it could be grasped. Reynolds's Federals were spread out over a wide area, with a force at Cheat Mountain pass, another on the summit of the mountain, and the rest ranged along the valley of the Tygart River all the way to the town of Elkwater. The Confederates had an advantage in numbers; despite all the sickness, Lee probably had 6000 men ready for action. On September 8, after a conference with General Loring, Lee drew up his battle plan; in substance, it called for the convergence of several columns in Tygart River valley, with one force striking for the top of the mountain in order to turn the position in the pass. If all went well, Reynolds's whole force could be hemmed in and destroyed.

Nothing went well. The battle plan itself was far too elaborate, calling for co-ordinated operations by five separate columns in a country so rough and tangled that contact between the moving columns was impossible; even veterans led by veteran generals would have had trouble with it, and later in the war Lee rarely tried anything quite so intricate. The rains continued, completing the ruination of roads which had been atrocious enough to begin with. Through September 11 and 12 the soldiers floundered along, wet and tired, dimly aware that things were going wrong. One detachment lost its sleep, on a night of especially heavy rain, when a bear blundered into camp and set the men caroming into one another in the dripping blackness. The detachment that was supposed to carry the mountaintop—the movement on which all the other movements hinged—found the place too strongly held and too well fortified to be carried; the Federals were alerted, the surprise which Lee had counted on was gone for good, the men ate the last of their food and could get no more without returning to camp: and, all in all, the elaborate plan fizzled out in dismal failure without ever producing a battle at all. Sensibly, Lee called everything off and took the army back to its starting point.[9] Never again would Confederates try to regain the Cheat Mountain fastness.

Lee had no leisure to brood over misfortune. The mess that Wise and Floyd had concocted seemed likely to let Rosecrans advance as far as his resources of supply would permit, and it was up to Lee to provide a solution. Ordering Loring to leave enough men to watch Reynolds's brigade and to bring the rest down to the Lewisburg Pike, Lee went on in advance to see what could be done.

Having retreated from Carnifix Ferry, Floyd had dug in, some twenty miles to the southeast, at a spot called Meadow Bluff, and he had ordered Wise to join him. Floyd had the rank, and was entitled to issue orders, but Wise refused to obey. Instead, he built entrenchments ten miles nearer the enemy, on Little Sewell Mountain, and demanded that Floyd come up to support him. The situation was fantastic. Between them, Wise and Floyd had fewer than 4000 men, and the advancing Rosecrans had substantially more than twice that many. Yet the two Confederates were flatly refusing to join hands against him, each man staying doggedly where he was and calling on the gods, the government, and General Lee to witness how stiff-necked and perverse the other man was. The situation was complicated, as Lee quickly discovered, by one final oddity. By military law General Wise was as wrong as a man could be, but tactically he was dead right; the position he had chosen was far better than the one Floyd had selected, and if Rosecrans was to be stopped the place to stop him was obviously Little Sewell Mountain. Lee ordered all hands to concentrate there, and quietly notified Richmond that one of these two generals would have to be relieved. Mr. Davis recalled Wise, and a semblance of harmony descended on the Confederate camp while Lee got ready for the Federal assault.[10]

The assault never came. Rosecrans moved up to Little Sewell Mountain, examined its defenses, endured another torrential rainstorm, concluded that Lee's position was too strong to be carried and that a real advance through this mountain land was impossible anyway, and presently drew his army back to Gauley Bridge.[11] Lee found it impractical to pursue, and soon after Mr. Davis called him back to Richmond. From a Confederate viewpoint the campaign had been a distressing failure, and most of the blame was ascribed to Lee. E. A. Pollard, the hypercritical Richmond editor, wrote angrily that the losing campaign had been conducted by a general "whose extreme tenderness of blood induced him to depend exclusively on the resources of strategy, to essay the achievement of victories without loss of life."[12] (Of all the criticisms ever made of Lee, this one probably has the least validity.) Lee quietly accepted the criticism and made no public reply, but he was stung and he wrote to Mrs. Lee: "I am sorry, as you say, that the movements of the armies cannot keep pace with the expectations of the editors of papers. I know they can regulate matters satisfactorily to themselves on paper. I wish they could do so in the field. No one wishes them more success than I do and would be happy to see them have full swing."[13]

Altogether, the Federals had gained something significant, and a youthful Confederate confessed: "A decided reaction had taken place since the wonderful battle of Manassas. It had not been followed up by the extermination of 'the Yankees,' as I expected it would be."[14] The Northern government now held western Virginia permanently; it would be West Virginia just as soon as the formalities could be attended to, and a good third of the Old Dominion had been sheared away forever. The Federals were not yet beginning to win, but they were taking the ground on which they could begin to win a bit later. Imperceptibly, the scales were being weighted in their favor.

It was hard to see, at the time, because the summer and fall looked like a period of unbroken Confederate successes. There had been Bull Run, overshadowing everything, and there had been Wilson's Creek, with the unforgettable Lyon killed and his army driven into a long retreat. Before September was over there was another sharp Confederate victory in Missouri, bringing further discouragement to Unionists and giving General Frémont a new portion of woe.

Shortly before Lyon met his fate, a Union force had been thrust far up into the northwestern corner of the state to occupy Lexington, an attractive little town on high ground bordering the Missouri River, once a noted outfitting depot for trading expeditions to the Rockies. This force was commanded by Colonel James A. Mulligan of the 23rd Illinois—a regiment composed largely of Irish from Chicago, known at the time as "the Irish brigade"—and included Mulligan's own regiment, additional Illinois infantry, a regiment of cavalry, detachments of the Missouri militia and a little light artillery;

probably 3000 or 3500 men, altogether. Mulligan was to hold the line of the upper Missouri, and also prevent the state's secessionist government-in-exile from seizing specie held by banks in that area. He seized the specie himself so that he could protect it adequately, fortified a little hill on the edge of Lexington and awaited developments, which came promptly in the shape of General Sterling Price and a substantial army of Missouri state guards fresh from their triumph at Wilson's Creek. Kept from destroying Lyon's beaten army by Confederate McCulloch's refusal to campaign any longer in Missouri, Price had come up to pinch off this isolated Union outpost. He had 18,000 men and unless Federal reinforcements came up fast he could do exactly as he proposed to do.

The nearest Union base was at Jefferson City, more than one hundred miles away, commanded by a colonel with the unlikely name of Jefferson Davis. Learning about Price's advance, Frémont, in St. Louis, tried to get a relief column in motion, but Davis lacked transportation equipment, the Rebels had obstructed the river, and Price had all the time he needed. As he approached Lexington some of Mulligan's officers proposed a speedy retreat, but Mulligan was scornful. "Begad, we'll fight 'em!" he cried. "That's what we enlisted for, and that's what we'll do." Price hemmed Mulligan's camp in closely, cutting off its water supply and ingeniously devising a set of movable breastworks out of water-soaked bales of hemp. After two days of fighting, Mulligan was compelled to surrender, on September 20. He had suffered about one hundred casualties, he and all of his men were prisoners of war, and the Missourians had recovered $900,000 in cash.[15] They also, to all appearances, had won full control of all of the western part of the state.

Coming as it did on the heels of Wilson's Creek this looked to Union men like a setback of shocking dimensions. General Scott curtly notified Frémont that the President "expects you to repair the disaster at Lexington without loss of time," and Frank Blair (whom Frémont had put under arrest for insubordination) fumed that Frémont had an ample force but that "he simply lacked the capacity of wielding it."[16] But Price could not stay in Lexington and his "control" over western Missouri dissolved before the month was out. He marched south, and by late October he had got all the way to Neosho, in the extreme southwest corner of the state—farther from the center of things, actually, than he had been before the battle of Wilson's Creek. He had made a dazzling raid, disheartening Northern patriots, depriving the Union army of several good regiments and driving one more nail in General Frémont's coffin, but that was all.

Price led no more than 7000 men to Neosho. He had furloughed a number of people so that they could go home and provide for their families—after all, nobody in particular was supporting his army—and a good part of the force which he commanded at Lexington appears to have been local talent, minuteman types who would turn out for a fight in their own neighborhood but could not be counted as part of a permanent field army. At Neosho, Price touched base with his government. Claiborne Jackson was there, convening a fragment of the state's legislature—the minority that favored the Southern cause—in extraordinary session; and on October 31 this legislative fragment passed an ordinance of Secession, carefully complying with all of the forms and electing Senators and Representatives to the Confederate Congress. To the extent that they could speak for Missouri, Missouri at last was in the Confederacy.[17]

It was no more than a gesture, because these men could not now speak for Missiouri. Victorious in two battles, the Confederates had nevertheless lost the state. Seeming to win, they had been defeated; even while the vote was being taken, Frémont—on the move at last!—was bringing an army of 40,000 men down to the very town of Springfield which the Federals had had to evacuate six weeks earlier. Governor and legislators decamped, their flight the visible symbol of the shape affairs had taken.

There were other symbols—guerrilla warfare at its ugliest flaming up and down the western border, and a black and desolate path that marked Frémont's line of march. A correspondent for the New York *Times* who was with Frémont's army felt that "the country through which we pass seems weighed down by something like a nightmare," with all the landscape wearing "that same mark of desolation which is upon everything in this state." The people seemed not so much hostile as apathetic. Many houses were deserted, and a strange silence seemed to prevail; even the ring of the village blacksmith's anvil was stilled, largely (the correspondent felt) because the soldiers had stolen all of the blacksmith's tools.[18] To the west, the whirlwind had cut a sharper swath. Here were the "Jayhawkers"—Federal troops from Kansas, composed largely of frontiersmen who had learned to hate slaveholding Missourians beyond all reason during the wild times of the fifties, when newspapers a thousand miles away had printed columns about Bleeding Kansas, the Border Ruffians, and the fearful doings of Osawatomie John Brown. The Jayhawkers had been making war out on the fringes of the country Price had marched through, descending on town after town to ferret out Confederate sympathizers and confiscate their goods and chattels. They were followed, as often as not, by non-military Kansans with wagons who would glean where the soldiers had reaped, returning with wagons full of plunder. Price's irregulars behaved in the same way whenever they had the chance, and there were enough beatings, burnings, robberies, and shootings along the Kansas-Missouri border to satisfy the most vengeful.

Chief of the Jayhawkers—as far as any one man was chief—was a singular character named James H. Lane: a tall, lean, red-haired demagogue whom the good people of Kansas had chosen to represent them in the United States Senate and to whom Abraham Lincoln had given a brigadier general's commission and authority to recruit Kansas regiments for the Union. Lane was out from under anyone's effective control, although he did share Frémont's views about the need to emancipate secessionists' slaves. "Confiscation of slaves and other property which can be made useful to the Army should follow treason as the thunder peal follows the lightning flash," he asserted, and wherever his troops went confiscation took place—not merely of slaves, but of anything valuable which could be carried off. Lane was said to have told his men that "everything disloyal from a Shanghai rooster to a Durham cow must be cleaned out," and his men did their best to obey orders. Swooping down on the town of Osceola, where Price had left a quantity of supplies under guard, Lane shot up the town, carried off or destroyed everything it contained, and then set fire to the houses, ignoring the fact that much of the property thus laid waste was owned by Loyalists. A newspaperman who saw Lane in action said that he looked like "some Joe Bagstock Nero fiddling and laughing over the burning of some Missourian Rome."[19]

There was not very much to laugh at. A band of Jayhawkers would descend on a farm home, carrying off Negroes, horses, and wagons, returning a few days later to sweep up all the cows and sheep the farmer had, coming back still later to carry away the bed-clothing from the house. Farmers thus molested formed armed bands to protect themselves, laying ambushes in the dark by country roads and touching off fights that never got recorded because they had not the least military significance but which nevertheless took their steady toll of deaths. A woman living near Westport, who had seen her once-prosperous home completely despoiled, wrote despairingly: "Our property is all taken from us and I am left without a home with four little children to take care of . . . what will become of us God only knows . . . Times here are very hard; robbing, murdering, burning and every other kind of meanness on every side."[20] Without any question the Jayhawkers made Confederates out of many who had not been Confederates originally. The Jayhawkers' motives were mixed but their minds were simple. They were moved by patriotism, by old grudges and by a desire for loot, and when they made war they followed an uncomplicated rule: the man who owned slaves was no doubt a Rebel, and so he was an enemy, and it did not matter what happened to him. Like Ambrose Bierce's Indianians, the Kansans considered the Rebel "a fiend accursed of God and angels," and they behaved accordingly.

6: *The Road to East Tennessee*

It worked both ways, depending on geography. In western Missouri the country folk were harried by Jayhawkers, and the smoke of their torment went up to the impassive heavens; and far away in eastern Tennessee other country folk were getting the same treatment from Confederate troops, whose methods were equally rough except that they ran off with no slaves. East Tennessee was highland country, and like the people of the Virginia highlands the Tennessee mountaineers were Unionists. Slavery had never taken root in the mountains, and the people cared little for states' rights, and when the state went out of the Union they lost no time declaring themselves.

In mid-June there was a Union convention at Greeneville, home town of Senator Andrew Johnson—an exceedingly hardheaded man who was proud of his plebeian origins, hated the cotton aristocracy, and considered himself still a member of the United States Senate no matter what his state had done—and this convention adopted a bristling declaration of grievances. The "disunion government," this declaration said, had obstructed the right of free suffrage, fired on flags, and sent in "a merciless soldiery" which insulted people, broke into their homes, shot down women and children and arrested large numbers of people. This soldiery was accused of foraging its horses in cornfields, of stealing hay and provisions, and—according to a contemporary Northern account—of "offering the people, male and female, every indignity that ruffian bands are capable of." Because of all of this the convention named a committee to petition the state legislature to let east Tennessee have a separate government of its own.[1]

Such a step the state legislature did not dream of taking, and when the voters of Tennessee ratified the ordinance of secession the people in east Tennessee grew slightly more quiet, with Andrew Johnson taking off for Washington to argue his people's cause at the White House. But the lull was only temporary. A Knoxville secessionist warned Governor Harris that he must act at once "to repress a most fearful rebellion," and the Confederate authorities began arresting Unionists, their most noteworthy prisoner being a fiery itinerant preacher named William Gannaway Brownlow who had become editor of the Knoxville *Whig*, denouncing secession in every issue and keeping a United States flag flying over his own house. His paper was suppressed, its type and presses destroyed, and Brownlow was lodged in jail. General Polk wrote to President Davis from Nashville saying that east Tennessee was held by 2000 Southern troops but that it needed a good 10,000, and a Mississippian told Mr. Davis that agents of the Lincoln government had been dismayingly active, preaching sedition and arousing hatred to such an extent that "the people only await the occasion to rise in revolt against the Confederate government."[2]

New regiments were sent in, from Nashville and from Richmond, and Brigadier General Felix Kirk Zollicoffer was put in general command of the troubled area. Zollicoffer was one of Tennessee's leading citizens; a newspaperman and a politician, who had served in Congress and had edited the influential Nashville *Banner*, and who had had some military experience during the Seminole War. He was quiet, frail and unassuming, just turning fifty, a former Whig who had voted for the mildly Unionist Bell-Everett ticket in 1860 and had turned down command of the state's troops in the spring, taking a commission from the Richmond government a bit later. He hurried to the mountain country, found that until the reinforcements arrived he would have only thirty-three companies of infantry and six companies of cavalry, most of them untrained, to cover a large tract of wild country and overawe a most intractable populace. Understandably, General Zollicoffer felt that the assignment was a hard one.[3]

Washington would have been delighted to do for east Tennessee precisely what it was doing for western Virginia; the trouble was that east Tennessee was very hard to get at. It was shielded, to begin with, by Kentucky, which throughout the summer was a neutral no man's land not to be crossed by Federal troops. It was shielded even more by its own peculiar geography—by the great mass of mountains which lay over it like a turtle's shell, sealing it off from the North, complicating the long miles of bad roads with an almost impenetrable tangle of peaks, valleys, and forests. As a practical matter, people usually got into this part of Tennessee from due east or due west, or they stayed out. Unless some extraordinary effort could be made, Lincoln's soldiers would have to stay out.

But it was most important to get them in, because east Tennessee promised a great deal to the Union cause. Here was the asset President Lincoln had looked for in vain elsewhere in the South—a solid nucleus of Unionists who would rally around a Federal army the moment such an army appeared. The highland people were loyalists, and the central highlands ran over into North Carolina and down into northern Georgia and Alabama as well; establish a Union army in the upper Tennessee Valley, and the Confederacy might well begin to disintegrate at the core. Mr. Lincoln had believed—often rather against the evidence—that the Confederacy was not the monolithic unit its leaders said it was. Here was one place where he could prove it.

Whatever had really driven the people of the South to secede, it was undeniable that loyalty to the old Union ran strong wherever the slave population was small. In the Southland, as a whole, there was one slave to every two white people; in east Tennessee there was one slave to twelve whites. Most people were small farmers, poor, cut off from the main currents of Southern life, feeling no kinship whatever with the wealthy slaveowning class. In his distrust of the plantation aristocracy, Andrew Johnson accurately reflected the viewpoint of his own people. Most of them, probably, were willing to submit passively to Confederate authority, but they would do nothing whatever against the Union and they would rejoice openly if Confederate authority were removed.[4]

There was another matter of great practical importance. The most significant railway line in the South was the one that threaded the length of Tennessee, giving Richmond its connection with the west. If a Union army could be planted permanently across that railroad line the Confederacy would be in a dire fix; as a Richmond editor pointed out, in such case "the empire of the South is cut in twain and we become a fragmentary organization, fighting in scattered and segregated localities, for a cause which can no longer boast the important attribute of geographical unity."[5] Before Bull Run, President Lincoln had been aware of the strategic possibilities here, and late in September he wrote that he wanted an expedition "to seize and hold a point on the Railroad connecting Virginia and Tennessee, near the mountain pass called Cumberland Gap."[6]

Cumberland Gap meant the old Wilderness Road, the historic highway of pioneer America. Daniel Boone had blazed the trail long ago, and the slow caravans had followed, peopling Kentucky and opening half a continent to the young American nation. Now the flow would be reversed, with strange new caravans coming down to the gap from the north and west to restate the notion of a continental destiny. During the summertime of Kentucky's neutrality nothing very concrete could be done, but the administration and the east Tennesseeans could make certain arrangements—a strategic plan or a dark conspiracy, depending on the point of view.

These plans were devised in Washington at about the time General Polk was ending Kentucky's neutrality (which of course opened the way for direct action in respect to Tennessee). One of the most active of the Tennessee Unionists, William B. Carter, went to Washington and met with President Lincoln, Secretary Seward, and General McClellan, and promised to set up what a later generation would have called a fifth column. At a given moment during the fall (it was agreed) armed bands of east Tennesseeans would go swarming out to destroy all of the bridges on that vital railroad line; simultaneously, Washington would send an army under General George H. Thomas down through the gap to protect these guerrillas (whom the Confederates otherwise would unquestionably obliterate) and to occupy Knoxville and the surrounding area. Federal money was provided to finance the uprising; it was arranged that the numerous mountain men who had fled into Kentucky to escape Confederate arrest would be organized into Federal regiments, and Carter's brother Samuel, hitherto a lieutenant in the Navy, was made colonel and acting brigadier general to command them. William Carter was to go back to Tennessee shortly after the middle of October to get his people in motion, and General Thomas was to begin his march within a week thereafter.[7]

So ran the plan. If it had worked it might have affected the course of the war most materially, but it did not work; instead it went off half-cocked, disastrously, causing some of Carter's patriots to get hanged and bringing profound discouragement and renewed oppression to all east Tennessee loyalists.

To begin with, General Zollicoffer moved forward through Cumberland Gap as soon as he learned about the Confederate advance in western Kentucky, and he established his troops at a ford on the Cumberland River, thirty miles inside of Kentucky, by the middle of September.[8] General Zollicoffer, to be sure, could eventually be taken care of; was taken care of, quite effectively, a few months later. More important was a singular combination of factors which the planners in Washington had not been able to take into account—the ill health of General Robert Anderson, the excellence of the bluff staged by General Albert Sidney Johnston, and the nervous uncertainty which almost incapacitated that supposedly self-assured soldier, General William T. Sherman.

It began with Anderson. The hero of Fort Sumter had been living on his nerves for months, and it had been too much for him. While Kentucky was still neutral Anderson's doctors warned him that his brain might be affected if he remained on duty, and he spent part of the summer at Cresson, Pennsylvania, trying to restore his strength. The rest and the mountain air helped, but the doctors insisted that it would be dangerous for him to return to active duty before the end of the year. He had no sooner received this verdict, however, than a delegation of Tennessee Unionists led by Andrew Johnson and Congressman Horace Maynard came to put pressure on him. He testified later that they insisted that if he resumed active command along the border, "20,000 mountain boys would rally to my flag and follow me anywhere." He told them what his doctors had said, and added: "If I break down as they threaten me I cannot break down in a better cause," and he went back to his post just in time to witness the end of Kentucky's neutrality.

Anderson made his headquarters at Louisville and tried to cope with the situation, but it was too much for him. He went through the motions but he accomplished nothing, and friends at last induced his brother, Larz Anderson of Cincinnati, to come and tell him bluntly that the breakdown the doctors spoke about was actually taking place. He consulted the doctors afresh, and at last—on October 6, in a carefully worded telegram from Winfield Scott—he was relieved of his command and told to report for duty in Washington "as soon as you may without retarding your recovery." Anderson turned the command over to Sherman, expressing the hope that Sherman could destroy "the marauding bands who, under the guise of relieving and benefiting Kentucky, are doing all the injury they can to those who will not join them in their accursed warfare."[9] Then he went off stage, seeking the recovery that never came. He had seen the war begin, on the ramparts of Fort Sumter, and in a sentimental finale, four years later, a wreck of a man in a ruined fort, he would hoist his flag there again; but except for that his part in the war was finished.

The Sherman who replaced him was by no means the conquering hero of later days. He was gloomy, utterly lacking confidence in the raw volunteers entrusted to his command, hag-ridden by memory of the disaster which he had seen overtake similar volunteers at Bull Run, unable to realize that though his own problems were grave those of General Johnston were a good deal worse. He complained that he had been "forced into command of this department against my will," and in a mood of uncontrolled pessimism he estimated that it would take 300,000 men "to fill half the calls for troops" that were being made on him.[10] In plain English, Sherman had lost his nerve; temporarily he was a setup for the bold measures which General Johnston adopted.

Johnston had a long line to defend east of the Mississippi and he was badly outnumbered. He was getting recruits (although they were not so numerous as he had hoped, and the anticipated rising of Kentuckians to the Confederate cause was not taking place) but finding weapons for them seemed impossible and he believed that as soon as the Federals advanced they would discover the inadequacy of his force. His left was on the Mississippi, at Columbus, strongly held by Bishop Polk; Zollicoffer anchored the right, in front of Cumberland Gap; and Forts Henry and Donelson were being built just below the Kentucky line to command the Tennessee and Cumberland Rivers. To block the line of the Louisville & Nashville Railroad, which any Federal Army invading western Tennessee would certainly want to use, Johnston had put General Buckner, with just under 10,000 men, at Bowling Green; and Buckner was industriously sending out raiding parties, behaving like a man who was about to march north to the Ohio River, convincing Sherman that an army of 20,000 Confederates would soon capture Louisville,[11] and putting loyalist civilians in the back country into a state of wild panic. One roving Confederate detachment was commanded by a tough Irish veteran of the British Army, Colonel Patrick Cleburne, and as this outfit entered the hill country along the upper Cumberland the inhabitants ran and hid, anticipating massacre and destruction. One old woman astounded Cleburne by tottering out to meet him, an open Bible in her hand, announcing that she was prepared to die and implying that they might as well do their worst at once; the colonel had a hard time persuading her that no harm would come to her, and he wrote that he doubted the valor of male Kentuckians because of "the alacrity with which they fled from this strongly defensible country, leaving their wives, daughters and children to the tender mercies of supposed ravishers, murderers and barbarians."[12] From backwoodsmen to the commanding general, Kentucky Unionists were alarmed. If the essence of successful strategy is the ability to compel one's opponents to accept one's own appraisal of a situation, Albert Sidney Johnston was being a very good general this fall.

All of this fatally handicapped the plan to get east Tennessee back into the Union. William B. Carter left Camp Dick Robinson for the highlands on October 18 or 19, and a few days after that General Thomas set out for Cumberland Gap. Thomas had half a dozen fairly well-trained regiments, along with two new regiments of Tennessee refugees, and although he was short of equipment he believed he could carry out his assignment.

Thomas meant business. Like Lee, he was a Virginian who had had to choose between conflicting loyalties. He had made the choice Lee did not make, and for a century to come his native state would regard him without warmth. He was massive, sedate, with a deceptive air of unhurried calm; he had hurt his spine in some pre-war accident and to ride at a gallop pained him, so people called him "Old Slow-Trot." The nickname created a totally false picture, for Thomas was not a slow-trot general at all. He could move fast and he could hit with pulverizing impact, and when the Union Army got him it gained very nearly as much as it had lost when it failed to get Lee.

Thomas started out briskly enough. He brushed aside a Confederate outpost at Rockcastle Hills, fifty miles south of his starting point, occupied the town of London, and sent back word that he proposed to move on to a place called Somerset, where he believed he could pick a favorable time and route for going all the way to the Cumberland Gap and thence to Knoxville. The east Tennessee Unionists, informed that he was on the move, began their uprising, burning five railroad bridges, fighting with Confederate patrols and effervescing so freely that the Confederate commander in Knoxville reported that "the whole country is now in a state of rebellion"; the railroad authorities doubted that they could move any more army supplies, and a Confederate commissary officer wrote that the expected approach of the Federals has so inflamed the insurrectionists that "there is no telling how much damage they may do."[13]

What the east Tennessee people did not know, however, was that just when the uprising was beginning the Federal advance was canceled and that Thomas was compelled to take his army back to its original point of departure.

General Sherman had grown completely despondent. He believed that there was about to be a great Confederate offensive all across Kentucky, from the Mississippi to Cumberland Gap, which was exactly what General Johnston wanted him to believe, and just when the Confederates in east Tennessee were gloomily anticipating the worst Sherman was writing that "the future looks as dark as possible." He considered the east Tennessee project a sideshow anyway, and now he abruptly called it off so that he could concentrate all of his forces in defense of Louisville and the Ohio River. He had recently assured the Secretary of War that the Union ought to have at least 200,000 men in Kentucky, and a Pennsylvania politician who visited the War Department at this time was confidentially told "Sherman's gone in the head." On November 15—with Carter's fifth columnists neck-deep in hot water, and with Thomas's east Tennessee recruits angrily laying down their arms because they could not march in to redeem their home land—

Sherman was relieved of his command and ordered to a relatively quiet job in Missouri. An Ohio newspaper announced that Sherman was insane.[14]

Sherman was replaced by an officer who was not so extensively fooled by the game General Johnston was playing but who was unable to make good use of his own enlightenment: Brigadier General Don Carlos Buell, whom the War Department had sent to see Anderson in Fort Sumter, while the nation was still at peace, on a confidential mission of vast delicacy. Buell was a close friend of McClellan, one of the officers whom men of the Old Army labeled "brilliant"; a conscientious, methodical soldier with a strong body, a trim beard, and deep vertical lines (of heavy thought, or of astigmatism) between his eyes. The change in command did not help the east Tennessee people, because Buell had even less use for the thrust at Cumberland Gap than Sherman had. Buell believed that he must get his troops thoroughly organized, outfitted, and drilled before he could do anything at all, and he did not think the wilderness road to Knoxville offered anything worth a second thought; if he did anything at all there it would simply be a gesture to assuage the President. Neither Mr. Lincoln nor McClellan could ever budge Buell from this position.[15]

So the east Tennessee uprising went unsupported, and it collapsed, and men died because it was so. Confederate authority was restored with a hard hand. Troops were moved in, and there were raids, innumerable arrests, quick military trials with the head of a drum for the presiding officer's desk and a running noose for the unlucky; some men were hanged, and a great many were sent South to prison. Property of those who had risen in revolt was confiscated, sometimes by due process, sometimes by citizen-soldiers who had personal hatred for the property's owners. A secessionist observer confessed that "old political animosities and private grudges have been revived" and said that "bad men among our friends" were hunting down the insurrectionists "with all the ferocity of bloodhounds."[16] President Davis did his best to keep the repressive measures within bounds, but civil war in the backwoods is hard to restrain; like the immense national conflict of which it was a part (and to which it was giving certain characteristics) it was more easily started than controlled, and it could be extremely destructive. The Richmond editor's notion that "the enemy must be made to feel the war" stated a rule which the border people considered most sensible.

Sherman and Buell may have been right. The road to east Tennessee was long and hard, and the Union armies needed more equipment, more training, more of everything, before they campaigned in such difficult country. The whole scheme was probably just as erratic and impractical as those two officers thought it was. And yet . . .

Lyon and Price had shown that even the most grotesquely unready armies could do a great deal if the men in command insisted on it. This war had not yet become regularized, and it offered amazing possibilities to the determined irregular. (Tucked away in Johnston's army there was a Tennessee cavalry colonel who would demonstrate this point repeatedly in the years just ahead: an untutored planter and slave trader named Nathan Bedford Forrest.) As U. S. Grant later pointed out, when both sides were equally untrained and ill-equipped, the general who waited until he had everything in textbook trim simply permitted his opponent to do the same. Quick action might very well leave the fields and highways littered with the fragments of armies made to campaign before they were ready for it, but it might also win great victories.

East Tennessee must be reached through Kentucky, and if the Federals did not use the direct road they must go roundabout. This they at last did, taking two years and fighting terrible battles, moving by way of such places as Shiloh and Vicksburg, Stone's River and Chickamauga, losing more men in the process than the entire force they had in Kentucky when this protective caution was being exercised.[17] The man who finally got them there, General Grant, was as it happened one who believed thoroughly in the possibility of accomplishing things with untrained volunteers. Grant had hardly taken command at Cairo, at the beginning of September, before he was planning to attack General Polk at Columbus. Overruled, he kept looking for a way to take the offensive even while he was still trying to organize, arm, and provision his raw troops, and early in November he believed that he had found an opening. Actually, the opening was a bad one and Grant was unable to exploit it, but the trouble was the unreadiness of Grant himself rather than the unreadiness of his men.

General Frémont was marching into southwestern Missouri to drive out Price. He had heard that Polk was sending troops to Price, and so he ordered Grant to make a hostile demonstration at Belmont, the steamboat landing just across the river from Columbus. This should lead Polk to keep his troops at home, and it might also help to curb an annoyingly active commander of guerrillas, Jeff Thompson, who had been running wild in the country back of New Madrid, Missouri. The assignment was somewhat muddled and it was based on faulty information: Polk had no intention of sending men to Price, Thompson had temporarily withdrawn from the warpath, and there really was not much for Grant to do. But Grant saw a chance for action, and on the night of November 6 he put 3100 men on steamboats, with two wooden gunboats for escort, dropped down the Mississippi, and on the morning of November 7 took his men ashore a few miles upstream from Belmont and went looking for trouble.

He found it without delay. Polk had been warned that some kind of move was coming, and when his scouts told him about the approach of Grant's flotilla he sent Gideon Pillow with some 2500 men across the river to support the small Confederate garrison in Belmont. By midmorning Grant's men were fully engaged with these troops and a small but red-hot battle was on.

Grant had things all his own way, during the morning. The Confederates were driven out of their position, detached fragments huddling in the lee of the river bank while the Federals went roistering through the captured camp, seizing military equipment, picking up souvenirs, listening to speeches by their officers, and in general celebrating a glorious victory before the battle was half over. Polk had supposed that another column was going to attack Columbus itself, but nothing of the kind happened, and before long he sent reinforcements across to rally the beaten men and to cut off Grant's line of retreat; meanwhile, his heavy guns opened a sharp fire on the captured camp, and Grant's gunboats, totally unarmored, were unable to move in and make a stand-up fight of it. In the end, the Federals had to fight their way out, leaving all of the loot and many of their own wounded behind; they reached their transports late in the afternoon and got away for Cairo, but the Confederates could and did boast that Grant's men had been routed. Pillow reported that in the pursuit his troops found quantities of "knapsacks, arms, ammunition, blankets, overcoats, mess-chests, horses, wagons and dead and wounded men," and a Louisiana soldier said that most of his regiment was outfitted after the battle with captured blankets, coats, and rifled muskets. Grant had lost more than 600 men and he had accomplished nothing whatever, aside from inflicting equal losses on his foe and giving his men some combat experience. His case was curiously like that of Robert E. Lee: the first engagement under his command was not a success. Confederates who read their Bibles noted that the Union troops came down from southern Illinois, which was known locally as Egypt, and were beaten by Confederates, many of whom came from Memphis, and they cited a Scriptural prophecy: "Egypt shall gather them, and Memphis shall bury them."[18]

Belmont, in short, might as well not have been fought at all. It meant nothing and it depressed the spirits of many Northern patriots, one officer writing bitterly that "it is called a victory, but if such be victory God save us from defeat." It greatly encouraged the Southerners, who felt that they had won a significant triumph; General Polk believed that he had beaten off a serious attempt to take Columbus, and he got formal congratulations from President Davis and General Johnston, along with a resolution of thanks from the Confederate Congress.[19] But nothing had been changed. General Johnston's bluff had not yet been called. Until it was called, at Cumberland Gap, along the river, or somewhere else, by a soldier whose will to fight outweighed his instincts of caution, Tennessee would remain in Confederate hands.

A Vast Future Also

1: *Magazine of Discord*

Along the border all the fires were burning, producing a heat that made the war expand and an evil light that made the expansion visible. In the two capitals, posted so close together at the eastern end of the border country, the heat and light had strange effects. The men of government had to move slowly, for they were trying to organize and direct chaos itself; yet there was upon them a growing necessity to move quickly, to act even as they sought to prepare the means of action, to assert mastery over this war before it imposed its own monstrous rules.

The impulse which had forced the soldiers to fight at Bull Run before they were ready to fight had by no means spent its force, and it seemed clear that simply to drift could be ruinous. Whether one stood for the North, for the South, or for some vanished middle ground that once had room for both, the situation as it existed was intolerable. Every man had to look to the future, and no matter what he hoped to see there he had to work desperately to bring it into existence. It was a time when every American was impatient.

Among the impatient were these two excellent professional soldiers, Generals Joseph E. Johnston and P. G. T. Beauregard, who commanded the Confederacy's armed forces in northern Virginia. Between them these two had won at Bull Run, had found themselves unable to pursue the routed Federals when that battle ended, and for weeks thereafter had held their army in camp north and east of Centreville with outposts thrown forward so far that on bright days the vedettes could look across the Potomac and see the unfinished dome of the United States Capitol in Washington. They were dissimilar types, and they lived these days in a state of courtly, unostentatious rivalry—Johnston first in command, Beauregard second, the ranking somewhat fogged by Beauregard's glittering reputation and his native inability to understand that he had an immediate superior. Early in August Beauregard had proposed that they move forward, attack the Federal outposts, and see if they could not provoke the Yankees into fighting a battle in the open, outside of the Washington lines.[1] Johnston, cautious by nature and conscious that his army was very little stronger than it had been at the time of Bull Run, rejected the idea; but as fall came the two men agreed that it was time to strike a blow instead of waiting passively to see what the enemy might do, and at the end of September they sat in conference with Jefferson Davis at Johnston's Fairfax Courthouse headquarters to project a decisive offensive. With them was the third man in their army's hierarchy, Gustavus W. Smith, a Kentucky-born West Pointer who until recently had been commissioner of streets in New York City, now a Confederate major general.

All four men could see one thing readily enough: the Federal Army in front of Washington was growing faster than their own was growing, and if there ever was to be a Confederate offensive it had better take place quickly. Johnston remarked that "decisive action before the winter was important to us," and none of the others disagreed; the question was how such action could be made possible.[2] The soldiers believed that their army ought to be strongly reinforced, and they proposed in substance that Davis raise it to a strength of 60,000 men—nearly double its present size—by arming new recruits and by bringing in troops from every point in the deep South that was not actually under attack. With such an army, they argued, they could cross the Potomac, bring on a battle northwest of Washington, and win a victory that would virtually establish Southern independence. They believed that the Virginia theater was all-important. Smith spoke for the trio when he declared, "Success here at this time saves everything—defeat here loses all." No one, said Smith, questioned "the disastrous results of remaining inactive throughout the winter."[3]

This was true enough; and yet the generals were asking for the impossible. There were plenty of recruits to be had, but the weapons for them simply were not at hand. The War Department had placed contracts for the manufacture of weapons but Southern manufacturing facilities were wholly inadequate and so far the results had been negligible. Arms contracts had also been placed overseas, but very few arms had actually arrived; the procurement program was poorly managed, and also the derided Federal blockade was beginning to be somewhat effective. Mr. Davis, who was conscious of the deficiency, remarked sadly, long afterward: "The simple fact was, the country had gone to war without counting the cost." It was quite true, as the Richmond *Examiner* was insisting, that "the idea of waiting for blows instead of inflicting them is altogether unsuited to the genius of our people," but blows could not be inflicted without guns; for the moment the genius of the people was sadly crippled.[4]

There were, to be sure, numbers of troops at various points in the South who were not at the moment menaced by advancing Federals, and the generals felt justified in demanding that the Confederacy concentrate its available strength at the point of greatest danger. But the kind of concentration they wanted was, at the moment, a political impossibility. The Confederacy was still as much an association of independent and equal states as it was a nation, and the governors who insisted (with the full support of their constituencies) that proper garrisons be maintained in places which were not then under attack, but which conceivably would be as soon as the Yankees bestirred themselves vigorously, had to be heeded. Mr. Davis had to exercise his authority within the limits of a system under which the wishes of the separate states were all but sacrosanct. He had written recently to Virginia's Governor John Letcher that he would adhere to "my fixed determination not to have conflict with the Governors of the States and in all things to seek for that cordial cooperation with them which alone can enable us to succeed in our present struggle,"[5] and although in the years ahead he would be violently wrenched away from this program he could not at this particular stage of the war follow any other.

This fact was crippling to the Confederacy, but it was unavoidable. The Southern people might in truth be all fire and ardor, but they were bound by the rigid limits of the theorem on which they had seceded. The same law of state sovereignty which had kept Washington from touching the institution of slavery now kept Richmond from defending the institution effectively; and although Mr. Davis saw what lay ahead he was tied by what lay behind. So his conference with the generals ended with gloomy agreement that nothing in particular could be done. The army at Fairfax Courthouse would remain inert, waiting for the blockade runners to bring the essential weapons over the sea from England, waiting for the South's own rural mills and blacksmith shops to meet their contracts, waiting for the restless thousands of recruits to be armed and equipped for combat—waiting, as well, for the enemy to strike a blow and for demonstration of the fact that the Federal power could arm even more men and that the odds against the South would constantly grow longer. The cost, as Mr. Davis remarked, had not been counted, and the longer payment was deferred the worse the final settlement was going to be.

Reality as seen in Richmond, in other words, was not quite like the roseate visions that had inspired the founding fathers at Montgomery half a year earlier; and indeed some of the original Montgomery crowd were drifting away now, unable or unwilling to go on with the roles Montgomery had given them. Blustery Robert Toombs was no longer Secretary of State. He had resigned in July, at odds with Jefferson Davis, disgusted with the outside world for its refusal to recognize his foreign ministry, perhaps disgusted with the war itself for its failure to make more prominent use of Robert Toombs; the real trouble probably being that the cabinet just did not offer scope for his turbulent energies. Perhaps the army could use him. The army would soon find out, for Toombs had taken a brigadier's commission and was in command of a brigade of Georgia troops in Johnston's army; a soldier in spite of his own lack of military experience and his outspoken contempt for West Point, its teachings and its graduates. He was replaced in the cabinet by the distinguished Virginian, Robert M. T. Hunter, one-time member of the United States Senate, a conservative suspected of being willing to consider overtures regarding peace.[6]

Toombs was not the only man who found Army service preferable to a cabinet post. Leroy Pope Walker had been neither happy nor effective as head of the War Department. Frail, a poor administrator and a man who knew very little of military affairs, he had been a natural target for every complaint arising from the inaction of Southern armies and the nonappearance of the munitions of war, and although he had perhaps done just about as well as anyone had a right to expect he was under mounting criticism. He resigned in mid-September, solaced with a pleasant letter from Mr. Davis and an appointment as brigadier general, and went to the Gulf Coast for duty. In looking for a successor, Mr. Davis apparently considered the appointment of Robert E. Lee, and gave some thought as well to his friend Leonidas Polk; awarded the post at last, first on an "acting" basis and then definitely, to Judah P. Benjamin, who had been his attorney general and who, before secession, had been United States Senator from Louisiana.[7] Benjamin was suave, subtle, intelligent, deviously brilliant, and in the end Mr. Davis considered him indispensable; but to be Confederate Secretary of War called for just the qualities which Benjamin lacked—blunt frankness in counsel, and an instinct for being disarmingly candid with the electorate. Frankness and candor were needed on the issue that had driven Walker from the cabinet—the fact that the new nation was not yet armed for vigorous offensive warfare. Instead, the administration tried to shield the country from an unpleasant truth and put itself in the position of justifying inaction as a chosen policy. It at least seemed to argue that it was fighting a purely defensive war in which it would defend every acre of Southern soil but would commit no aggression and attempt no invasions, and in this thesis lay the seeds of a crippling estrangement between government and the people.

The estrangement was not yet visible. On November 6, indeed, there was a stirring demonstration of wholesome unanimity. Going to the polls to name a regular constitutional government to replace the provisional regime set up at Montgomery, the people of the

Confederacy unhesitatingly named Jefferson Davis for a six-year term and designated Alexander Stephens as Vice-President.[8] There had been no opposition, no campaigning, no dissenting voices, and no contest. As far as an election could say so, all was harmony.

Yet there was dissent. General Beauregard had a grievance, and so did Joe Johnston, and Vice-President Stephens and his friends were beginning to realize that they also had grievances. The reasons for these grievances were dissimilar and inadequate, not to say ridiculous, signifying perhaps little more than the fact that both professional soldiers and professional politicians can be very hard to get along with. But their existence was a bad omen. This government was new and small, and it might not have room for the inner turbulences which are characteristic of American administrations.

Beauregard's case seemed to reflect little more than Napoleonic vanity on the loose. It had begun more or less harmlessly, with Beauregard publicly criticizing Confederate commissary arrangements, drawing a mild and even-tempered rebuke from the President, and subsiding gracefully enough. Then Beauregard submitted a report on the Bull Run campaign, making it appear that interference at Richmond had kept him from executing a grand offensive design which could have captured Washington; and a summary of this document unfortunately appeared in the press before the report itself reached the President. Davis composed another rebuke, much less even-tempered than the first, began to assemble evidence to show that it was not he who had kept Confederate soldiers from winning the war, and suggested that Beauregard's report "seemed to be an attempt to exalt yourself at my expense." Beauregard countered, on November 3, by sending a letter to the editor of the Richmond *Whig* —an astounding epistle, which was headed "Centreville, Virginia,—within hearing of the Enemy's guns," and which blandly remarked that "my attention has been called to the unfortunate controversy" arising out of his Bull Run report for which the President had just reprimanded him. The letter then went on to remark: "If certain minds cannot understand the difference between *patriotism*, the highest civic virtue, and *office seeking*, the lowest civic occupation, I pity them from the bottom of my heart." In case anyone had missed the point, Beauregard added that he was not and never would be a candidate for any office; once independence was won, he just wanted to retire to private life.[9]

Beauregard's grievance grew from nothing much more solid than a simple inability to get along with the President who had appointed him. So, as a matter of fact, did Johnston's grievance, although it came out in a different way. Johnston, who seemed to be so courtly and self-effacing, unexpectedly displayed an abiding concern over rank, which unhinged him almost as badly as Beauregard had been unhinged by the realization that his fame had to be shared and controlled. On August 31 the Confederate Congress confirmed the appointments of the men Mr. Davis had nominated as full generals—Samuel Cooper, the Adjutant and Inspector General of the army; Albert Sidney Johnston, Robert E. Lee, Joseph E. Johnston, and P. G. T. Beauregard. These nominations stipulated that the appointments would be effective as of different dates, and under military law the commission of earliest date outranked the others. Reading this list and the accompanying dates, Joseph E. Johnston discovered to his horror that the date of his commission made him junior to Cooper, Sidney Johnston, and Lee. Of the five generals, he ranked fourth.[10]

According to Joe Johnston, this was insulting and illegal. Confederate law said that generals of identical commissions would have relative rank according to rank held in the Old Army—the United States Army, that is, from which one and all had resigned. In that army Joseph E. Johnston had been Quartermaster General, with brigadier's rank, and none of the other four had ranked higher than colonel. Therefore, said the aggrieved general, he was entitled to top rank in the Confederate Army: if he did not get it, both justice and he personally would be outraged. (The controversy actually was over the relative merits of staff and line commissions. The determining factor, in Mr. Davis's opinion, was the command an officer had held in the line. As a pre-war brigadier, Johnston of course had had a staff appointment.)

For a general to argue for higher rank is nothing new, but rarely has anyone submitted a longer or a more impassioned argument than the one composed now by General Johnston; nor, in the opinion of Mr. Davis and his Secretary of War, the astute lawyer Mr. Benjamin, did any sort of argument often rest on a weaker base. Mr. Davis coldly gave Johnston a two-sentence reply: "I have just received and read your letter of the 12th instant. Its language is, as you say, unusual; its arguments and its statements utterly one-sided, and its insinuations as unfounded as they are unbecoming."[11] With this, General Johnston had to be content. His rank remained number four.

All of this actually had done no immediate harm. Davis's and Johnston's angry exchange took place a fortnight ahead of the Fairfax Courthouse conference, without affecting their ability to have a reasoned exchange of views. What was significant about both the Beauregard and Johnston cases was the indication that the Confederate President was not going to try very hard to accommodate himself to a proud and touchy general; and Southern characteristics being as they were, he was likely to have to deal with a large number of proud and touchy generals before the war ended. Furthermore, even though the Confederate nation was set up under a one-party regime, there would inevitably develop, sooner or later, some sort of anti-administration party. Here was clear warning that when that happened, at least two of the five ranking generals in the Confederate Army might become allies of such a party.

As Vice-President, Alec Stephens had no more day-by-day responsibilities than any other American who occupies that office. Yet he represented something—if nothing more, that part of the South which had believed most fervently in states' rights and a simple pastoral society—and he was becoming more and more the confidant for people who were vigorously in opposition to everything the administration was doing. Robert Toombs, surly as a bereaved bear, was writing to him from Camp Pine Creek, near Fairfax Courthouse, complaining that Joe Johnston was "a poor devil, small, arbitrary and inefficient" and by implication denouncing Mr. Davis for keeping such a man in power. The trouble, Toombs believed, was West Point, where both Mr. Davis and General Johnston had been educated, an institution whose graduates seemed unable to appreciate military capacity in those who had merely been to the United States Senate.

"The army is dying," wrote Toombs. "I don't mean the poor fellows who go under the soil on the roadside, but the army as an army is dying and it will not survive the winter. Set this down in your book, and set down opposite to it its epitaph, '*died of West Point.*' We have patched a new government with old cloth, we have tied the living to the dead . . . we are lying down here rotting."

From another correspondent in the same army camp, Thomas W. Thomas, Stephens got even bitterer words. Less than a month before the election in which Davis and Stephens were running together as a ticket, Thomas was telling Stephens: "All governments are humbugs and the Confederate government is not an exception. Its President this day is the prince of humbugs and yet his nomination for the first permanent presidency meets with universal acceptance, and yet I do know that he possesses not a single qualification for the place save integrity. . . . Imbecility, ignorance and awkwardness mark every feature of his management of this army. He torments us, makes us sick and kills us by appointing worthless place-hunters to transact business for us on which depends our health, efficiency and even our lives. . . . He is king, and here where we are fighting to maintain the last vestige of republicanism on earth we bow down to him with more than eastern devotion."[12]

What Thomas Thomas might think of the administration in the fall of 1861 would not be worth recording, except for its revelation of the kind of talk which Mr. Davis's Vice-President and running mate was willing to listen to at the very moment when the administration was asking election for a six-year term. Mary Boykin Chesnut, mistress of a great South Carolina estate and wife of one of President Davis's intimate associates, wrote that "there is a perfect magazine of discord and discontent in that Cabinet; only wants a hand to apply the torch and up they go."[13] September had hardly begun before Secretary of the Navy Stephen R. Mallory was noting that "there was an opposition in Congress to the Administration"; Davis agreed with him, although Benjamin thought the case was not that bad. Thomas Bragg, the administration's new attorney general, felt that the governors from the deep South were "giving trouble about troops and not acting in harmony with the Administration," and he believed that the situation was going to get worse.[14]

Part of this, to be sure, represented little more than the growing pains of a new government whose leaders were unhappily discovering that it was possible to be sorely vexed by their own friends as well as by Yankees. But more of it came out of a dawning realization that the first summer of the war, even though it had been marked by glorious victories, had not in fact been going very well. The blockade was beginning to hurt, and the ardent recruits who could not be armed were impatient witnesses to the pain; and the Southern coast lay all but naked to the gathering Federal fleets. The North was settling down for a long pull, and although it had not yet mustered its power it had already won the border, from Virginia all the way to Kansas. The offensives that lay just ahead would be conducted by Federals, not by Confederates, and the more a man knew about Confederate strength the less confident he was that these offensives could be beaten back. To the average Southerner the war had hardly begun, but the leaders could see ominous signs in the sky. Time was passing, and it was working for the wrong side.

The editor of the Richmond *Whig* darkly noted that "our past inaction, whether constrained or voluntary, by enabling the enemy to organize his whole strength, will render necessary a vast deal of terrible fighting on our side, to battle his assaults and make good our independence." The *Daily Examiner* called attention to the fact that "the peace party of the North, like the Union party of the South, has entirely disappeared," and predicted that unless the Southern government could place the army on a completely new footing, "its chance next year will be bad."[15] President Davis closed a gloomy letter to General G. W. Smith with the cry: "Oh, that we had plenty of arms and a short time to raise the men to use them."[16]

Underlying everything, perhaps, there was an uneasy feeling that the war was threatening to take the South where the South did not want to go. The unhappiness of the men who were writing such angry letters to Alexander Stephens was symptomatic. Secession had been a valiant attempt to preserve not merely a fragment of the past but a concept of a society wherein the individual was everything and the government was next to nothing. This concept had a fatal limitation: it based a noble ideal of freedom upon a belief in slavery. In a short war, in which hot courage swept everything before it, this crippling contradiction might be evaded. It would have to be faced squarely in a long war.

2: *Struggle for Power*

When George B. McClellan reached Washington on the afternoon of July 26 to take command of the capital and its army, he was the living symbol of the Northern demand for speedy action. He may not consciously have meant to be anything of the kind, and in the end the role was a little too heavy for him, but that was how it was in the beginning. He was the North's first great hero, and for a little while he made the sky look brighter.

McClellan was a perfectionist, driven by an authentic vision and also by an ambition that soared on an updraft of public acclaim. He was a man who had great talents; he knew that he had them and he proposed to use them to the fullest, and at first he was in an immense hurry. During the year that lay just ahead he would finally come to seem the most maddeningly deliberate of men, but in the beginning he was impatient—impatient with incompetence, with pomposity and its fumbling ineptitudes, with the techniques of delay. He knew what was wrong with the Federal war effort and he knew how to set it right, and neither the President, the general-in-chief nor anyone else could stand in his way. To the restless men who wanted the rebellion put down at the earliest possible moment McClellan briefly appeared to be the very embodiment of the spirit that would win the war.

It fitted neatly with his position as national hero. He reached the capital when the military relics of the Bull Run disaster were still being collected and sorted out, and he brought with him the record of victory in the western Virginia mountains—the proof that

Northern soldiers could beat Southern soldiers if they were just led by the right man. He had a cool self-assurance, a winning manner, and a jaunty readiness to accept unlimited responsibility, and to a capital and a nation grown disillusioned with militiamen he seemed to be all soldier. His first steps were to sweep the stragglers off the streets, to police the barrooms, to get the innumerable stray officers back on duty, and to create an organization which looked like business. He not only made the capital safe; he made it look and feel safe, and when he rode about the camps on his business he was greeted by cheers.

On July 27 McClellan was formally welcomed by the President and was invited to come back to the White House in the afternoon and meet the cabinet. This was somewhat displeasing to General Scott, who felt that this new commander ought to stay within prescribed channels and approach the Chief Executive only through the commanding general, but after touring the city, making note of its defenseless condition and remarking that drunken soldiers and officers made the downtown section "a perfect pandemonium," McClellan shook hands with the top brass and, in the evening wrote to his wife to tell her all about it. Apparently the experience had been somewhat dazzling.

"I find myself in a new and strange position here: President, cabinet, General Scott and all deferring to me," he wrote. "By some strange operation of magic I seem to have become the power of the land. I almost think that was I to win one whole success now I could become dictator or anything else that might please me—but nothing of that kind would please me—*therefore* I *won't* be Dictator. Admirable self denial! I see already the main causes of our recent failure."[1]

For a man who had been in town hardly more than twenty-four hours these were strong words; yet it is easy to see how McClellan came to write them. He *had* become the power of the land, and everybody *was* deferring to him. He had come on the scene at that magical moment (which, for an ambitious man, may lead either to apotheosis or to downfall) when people long so desperately for a miracle worker that they take their appointed hero on faith, so that for a time he can do nothing wrong and can have, quite literally, anything he wants. All of the deep determination to wipe out the shame of Bull Run and go on to victory was expressing itself just now in the feeling toward McClellan. As far as Washington could speak for the country, the nation was putting itself unreservedly in his hands, and McClellan could not help knowing it . . . nor could he help being affected by the knowledge.

On August 2 he wrote to his wife full of confidence. He had just given the President "a carefully considered plan for conducting the war on a grand scale," and he went on: "I shall carry this thing on *en grand* and crush the Rebels in one campaign. I flatter myself that Beauregard has gained his last victory. We need success and must have it. I will leave nothing undone to gain it." But he must have a free hand: "Gen. Scott has been trying to work a traverse to have Emory made Inspector General of *my* army and of *the* army. I respectfully declined the favor and perhaps disgusted the old man. . . . He cannot long retain command I think—when he is retired I am sure to succeed him, unless in the mean time I lose a battle—which I do not expect to do."[2]

He had been in Washington no more than one week, and not for two more days would he even be ready to organize the regiments of his army into brigades; yet already he was fiercely possessive regarding that army, and he was looking ahead to the day when Scott would be removed from his path and he himself would be general-in-chief. If this was largely due to the simple fact that he had a good professional's pride in his job and resented anything that might delay him in its performance, it might have been heightened just a little by the kind of talk that was being poured into his ears. The attention he was getting was enough to test any man's poise.

On the night of August 4 there was a state dinner at the White House, given in honor of Prince Napoleon of France, who had come over to have a look at America and at the war. McClellan and Scott entered together, Scott leaning on McClellan's arm—swollen, gouty age, stumping along with vigorous, handsome young manhood—and McClellan felt correctly that "many marked the contrast." At the dinner table a lieutenant colonel on Prince Napoleon's staff, Camille Ferri Pisani, found himself seated between McClellan and the British minister, Lord Lyons. The officer talked with McClellan at some length; then, during a lull in the conversation, Lord Lyons asked him: "You are aware that you are talking with the next President of the United States?" Ferri Pisani repeated the remark to McClellan, who "answered with a fine, modest and pleasant smile."[3]

When a newcomer in Washington finds, after no more than ten days on the job, that he is being spoken of casually as the next President, his self-esteem is apt to grow beyond manageable proportions. Yet it seems clear that at this time what was driving McClellan was chiefly an intense desire to get on with the job. In his memorandum to the President, written on the day of that White House dinner, McClellan had recognized that this war was not going to be like other wars, in which the object usually was "to conquer a peace and make a treaty on advantageous terms." There could be no treaty here: what was necessary was not merely to beat the enemy in the field but "to display such an overwhelming strength as will convince all our antagonists, especially those of the governing aristocratic classes, of the utter impossibility of resistance." The contest "began with a class; now it is with a people," and only decisive military success could settle things. McClellan urged a comprehensive war plan: tighten the blockade, open the Mississippi, invade eastern Tennessee, establish a force of 38,000 men to protect the upper Potomac, the line of the Baltimore & Ohio and the capital itself, and then form a field army of 225,000 men to smash Confederate strength in Virginia and roll on "into the heart of the enemy's country, and crush out the rebellion at its very heart." Possibly a smaller force could do the job, but speed was essential; "the question to be decided is simply this: shall we crush the rebellion at one blow, terminate the war in one campaign, or shall we leave it for a legacy to our descendants?"[4]

In a Washington which had come increasingly to feel that General Scott's famous Anaconda Plan represented an inert defensive policy and foreshadowed an unendurably long war fought at a leisurely pace, this sort of talk was like a breath of fresh air. Crusty Gideon Welles summed up Scott's policy by saying that the old lieutenant general wanted only to enforce "non-intercourse with the insurgents, shut them out from the world by blockade and military frontier lines, but not to invade their territory," and he felt that this was unwise for the country.[5] He noticed, as did others, that Secretary Seward, still active as a policy-maker, quickly transferred his support from Scott to McClellan. The two men conferred almost daily, and it presently developed that Seward knew more about McClellan's plans and his disposition of troops than Scott himself knew. If, in his memorandum to Lincoln, McClellan had stepped far out of his sphere as army commander to outline grand strategy for the entire nation, he was unquestionably getting Seward's energetic support.

On August 8, McClellan wrote a letter to his wife that showed how things were going: "Rose early today (having retired at three a.m.) and was pestered to death with senators, etc, and a row with General Scott until about four o'clock; then crossed the river and rode beyond and along the line of pickets for some distance. Came back and had a long interview with Seward about my 'pronunciamento' against General Scott's policy. . . . How does he (Seward) think that I can save this country when stopped by General Scott—I do not know whether he is a dotard or a traitor! He cannot or will not comprehend the condition in which we are placed and is unequal to the emergency. If he *cannot* be taken out of my path I *will* not retain my position but will resign and let the admin. take care of itself."[6]

The row with Scott grew out of a letter which McClellan had that same day sent to the general-in-chief, saying that military intelligence indicated a threatened offensive by Beauregard, that Washington was woefully insecure, and that it was necessary to reinforce Washington at once to a strength of at least 100,000 men "before attending to any other point." Scott became indignant, telling Secretary of War Cameron that he had been unable to get McClellan to discuss the matter in person, that he himself did not think Washington was in any danger at all, and that he was tired of being bypassed and overridden by his junior—as a result of which, Scott urged that the President "allow me to be placed on the officers' retired list, and then quietly to lay myself up—probably forever—somewhere in or about New York."[7] President Lincoln intervened, and at his request

McClellan withdrew the letter, "with the most profound assurance for General Scott and yourself," but the old general was not appeased. He refused to withdraw his own letter, asserting that McClellan persisted in discussing with various members of the cabinet matters that he should properly be discussing with the general-in-chief, and adding: "With such supports on his part, it would be as idle for me as it would be against the dignity of my years, to be filing daily complaints against an ambitious junior who, independent of the extrinsic advantages alluded to, has unquestionably very high qualifications for military command."[8]

The pace was getting faster. On the same day that he withdrew the offending letter, McClellan wrote to his wife: "Gen. Scott is the great obstacle. He will not comprehend the danger. I have to fight my way against him. Tomorrow the question will probably be decided by giving me absolute control independently of him. I suppose it will result in enmity on his part against me; but I have no choice. The people call upon me to save the country. I must save it, and cannot respect anything that is in the way. I receive letter after letter, have conversation after conversation, calling on me to save the nation, alluding to the presidency, dictatorship, etc. As I hope one day to be united with you forever in heaven, I have no such aspiration. I would cheerfully take the dictatorship and agree to lay down my life when the country is saved. I am not spoiled by my unexpected new position. I feel sure that God will give me the strength and wisdom to preserve this great nation; but I tell you, who share all my thoughts, that I have no selfish feeling in this matter. I feel that God has placed a great work in my hands. I have not sought it. I know how weak I am, but I know that I mean to do right, and I believe that God will help me and give me the wisdom I do not possess. Pray for me, that I may be able to accomplish my task, the greatest, perhaps, that any poor, weak mortal ever had to do."[9]

Three days after this letter, McClellan wrote that "Gen. Scott is the most dangerous antagonist I have," adding that "our ideas are so widely different that it is impossible for us to work together much longer," and on August 16 he summed it up: "I am here in a terrible place—the enemy have from 3 to 4 times my force—the Presid't is an idiot, the old General is in his dotage—they cannot or will not see the true state of affairs." He enlarged on this slightly: "I have no ambition in the present affairs; only wish to save my country, and find the incapables around me will not permit it. They sit on the verge of the precipice and cannot realize what they see. Their reply to everything is, 'Impossible! Impossible!' They think nothing possible which is against their wishes."[10]

Three weeks in Washington: the general-in-chief was either a dotard or a traitor and in any case was "the most dangerous antagonist," and the President was an idiot; and talk about the presidency and a dictatorship was fluttering through the heated air. Yet the real problem was not so much General McClellan's troubles with his superiors and with himself as it was the fact that the Washington atmosphere was clouding his vision.

To begin with, he was losing sight of military realities. He believed that Beauregard was about to attack him, and in mid-August he assured his wife: "Beauregard probably has 150,000 men—I cannot count more than 55,000!"[11] At this moment the Confederate Army in his front (commanded, to be sure, by Joseph E. Johnston) had a total present-for-duty strength of just over 30,000, and six weeks later Johnston and Beauregard would abandon all plans for an offensive when they were told that their strength could not possibly be raised to as much as 60,000. McClellan believed that when he arrived on the scene Washington was all but totally defenseless, and although he wanted to take the offensive he must begin by taking massive precautions against disaster. Actually, the city had never been open to a sudden Confederate thrust, and although he had moved efficiently and swiftly to perfect the city's defenses he had after all had a moderately good foundation on which to build; and the defensive effort, which he properly put first, had begun to warp his understanding of the real situation.[12]

Even worse, in some ways, was his inability to understand the political currents that were swirling about him. He was engaging in an all-out struggle with General Scott for control of the Army, and he wanted political support. Understanding that the men who had made the Republican party and had put Lincoln in office wanted a vigorous prosecution of the war, he courted their help. He had been in Washington no more than a fortnight before he was inducing Senator Charles Sumner to urge the Governor of Massachusetts to rush more troops to Washington; he told Sumner that Scott did not share his own feeling of urgency and that Scott, in fact, was an embarrassment to him.[13] But McClellan did not quite understand just what the Republican leaders really wanted. They were demanding a hard war because they believed that to destroy the Confederacy must also mean destruction of the slave power and the slave system. They were as impatient with "the incapables" as McClellan was, because they feared that the incapables would fumble and stumble their way into some sort of a South-saving compromise. If they helped to create a new commanding general, they would expect hard-driving action and an end to all delays and all fuzziness of purpose; and if the commanding general did not give this to them they would turn on him without mercy.

Viewing the matter from London, Charles Francis Adams in mid-August wrote that the nation had already gone through three stages of "this great political disease." First, he said, there was "the cold fit, when it seemed as if nothing would start the country." Then came the hot fit, "when it seemed almost in the highest continual delirium." Now there was the third stage, when the country was in the process of "waking to the awful reality before it." He did not know what the fourth stage might be, but he felt that there must be a high principle to contend for; "I am for this reason anxious to grapple with the slave question at once."[14] John Bigelow, who stopped this month in Washington to accept appointment as United States consul in Paris, regretfully saw "a certain lack of sovereignty" in President Lincoln, and wrote that he seemed to be "a man utterly unconscious of the space which the President of the United States occupied that day in the history of the human race." David Davis, the stout Illinois jurist who had managed Lincoln's presidential campaign, heard from a pessimistic friend in Washington that the cabinet was incapable and that Seward was "leading Lincoln into a pit," and the correspondent gave a blunter phrasing to Adams's thought: "I am no prophet, but it appears to me we are only at the beginning of a mighty revolution."[15]

The summer weeks passed. The army constantly grew larger, showing its increased size and its improved drill in periodic reviews which encouraged soldiers and spectators alike. The chain of forts protecting Washington was made stronger, the task of piling up the innumerable things which the new army would wear or eat or shoot made progress despite woeful deficiencies in Secretary Cameron's organization . . . and the contest for control between the young general and the old general went on without a moment's letup, McClellan quietly contemptuous, Scott coldly furious. In September there were new rumors of a Confederate offensive, and Cameron—apparently forgetting that there was such a person as Scott—sent McClellan a fatuous note begging him to say how the War Department could be of service. McClellan asked for heavy reinforcements, including 25,000 of Frémont's men and the whole of the Regular Army, saying that the Army of the Potomac must be increased to 300,000 men even if this meant going on the defensive everywhere else in the United States. He added that he wanted sole control over the assignment of officers in his command.[16]

Scott protested in vain. He decreed that a general could communicate with a cabinet minister only through channels—that is, through his superior officer—and he was ignored. He formally ordered McClellan to give him a complete report on "the positions, state and number of troops under him," and to submit day-by-day reports on new arrivals and assignments. McClellan let the order lie for three weeks, then casually sent over an inadequate reply. Scott thought of having McClellan arrested and court-martialed, but concluded that "a conflict of authority near the head of the army would be highly encouraging to the enemies and depressing to the friends of the Union," and at length (having heard that 40,000 troops were being moved across the Potomac to the Virginia front) the general-in-chief found himself writing to the War Department to ask if he might be told "the meaning of the extraordinary movement of troops going on in the city."[17]

Nothing like this would have been happening if Scott had not been slated for early retirement. He knew this as well as anyone, and he was hanging on during the early fall in the hope that a man of his own choice rather than McClellan might succeed him. He had settled on Henry Wager Halleck, another of the studious officers whom Old Army people labeled "brilliant," a West Pointer who had won a Phi Beta Kappa key at Union College, who had published a work called *Elements of Military Art and Science*, and had translated Jomini's classic four-volume *Vie Politique et Militaire de Napoléon*. Halleck had resigned from the Army in 1854 and had settled in California, prospering mightily as a corporation lawyer. Late in August, Scott had had him appointed a major general in the Regular Army, and when Cameron went to Missouri in October to examine the decaying Frémont situation at firsthand Scott agreed to stay on the job until the Secretary's return, hoping that Halleck would be with him by that time.[18]

It was a vain hope. By this time no one could possibly replace Scott but McClellan. To the soldiers and to the Washington public, McClellan was the martial spirit incarnate. William Howard Russell of the *London Times* noted that the young general had gone to elaborate lengths to make himself known to the soldiers and especially to their officers. He was seen in the camps or on the parade grounds every day, appearing in the morning and not disappearing until after dark, seeing everything, being seen by everyone, playing to the fullest the part of the general who carried the fate of the Republic on his shoulders; and he did this, Russell felt, "either to gain the good will of the army, or for some larger object."[19] The good will of the Army he had won, beyond question; if a larger object was in view, McClellan had only to wait.

He did not have to wait much longer, for the Army of the Potomac was about to suffer one more public disgrace, and the shock of it would force a change—and, in the end, would arm and perpetuate a bitterness that would be felt to the last day of the war and beyond. On October 21 a small Federal detachment was routed in an engagement at Ball's Bluff, on the Virginia side of the Potomac thirty-five miles upstream from Washington. The engagement had little military significance, but it was one more dreary licking. The Confederates inflicted heavy losses and they killed, in hot battle action, a prominent Union commander—Colonel Edward D. Baker, an unskilled soldier but an orator and politician of much renown, a member of the United States Senate and for years an intimate friend of Abraham Lincoln.

Ball's Bluff represented a fumble. Earlier in the summer the Confederates had occupied Leesburg, Virginia, a few miles inland from Ball's Bluff, with a brigade under the same Brigadier General "Shanks" Evans who had fought so well in the opening hours of the Bull Run battle. There had been intermittent skirmishes up and down the Potomac between Confederates and Federals, and early in September Jeb Stuart's cavalry had won laurels by beating a party of Federals near the Virginia hamlet of Lewinsville. On October 19, McClellan sent a division under Brigadier General George A. McCall forward on the Virginia side to Dranesville, fifteen miles below Leesburg, to find out what Evans was doing. McCall was to send patrols out to tap at Evans's lines, and McClellan ordered Brigadier General Charles P. Stone, commanding a division at Poolesville, Maryland, to keep a sharp lookout along the river and see whether McCall's advance made the Confederates evacuate Leesburg. He closed with the suggestion: "Perhaps a slight demonstration on your part would have the effect to move them." At the same time he told McCall to return to camp as soon as his reconnaissance was finished.[20]

Out of all of this came tragedy. On October 21, McCall completed his work and withdrew. At the same time Stone, to make the "slight demonstration" that had been called for, had Colonel Baker take his 1700-man brigade across the river at Ball's Bluff to threaten Evans's left. Baker obeyed enthusiastically but inexpertly. He floundered forward from the top of the bluff, ran into Evans's main body, and got into a battle which he was unable to handle. His force was routed, with some 200 men killed or wounded and more than 700 captured, he himself was shot dead, and the survivors came straggling back to the Maryland side of the Potomac in woeful disorganization and dejection.[21]

Exactly three months had passed since Bull Run—three months of sober rededication, of immense effort, of hope rising from the ashes: and the harvest of those months seemed to be this ignominious defeat. It did not even have the stature of the earlier disaster. Bull Run at least came as the result of an honest effort to strike a blow; Ball's Bluff was just a blunder, the sort of thing which—in the judgment of men whose impatience was rising like a flood tide—came logically out of a timid defensive policy. It was not to be endured, and some of the most forceful Republicans in the Senate promptly undertook to bring about a change.

Their immediate target was old General Scott, the living symbol of inaction and delay. (Scott, to be sure, had nothing whatever to do with Ball's Bluff, but he was general-in-chief and if the Army was not being used properly the fault must be his.) Less than a week after the battle the opposition was in full cry.

Spearhead was a triumvirate of three Senators—Lyman Trumbull of Illinois, Zachariah Chandler of Michigan, and Benjamin Franklin Wade of Ohio. Trumbull, the mildest-mannered of the three, was a former Democrat just nearing fifty, a man who had become a Republican during the anti-Nebraska fight, a member of the Senate since 1855, an all-out war man always alert to uphold the authority of Congress. Chandler, a wealthy merchant who had helped found the Republican party and who had a dictatorial control over the party organization in Michigan, was Trumbull's age but tougher and more rough-hewn, a man who had declared during the spring that the Union would never be worth a rush without a little bloodletting and who was working furiously now to bring that bloodletting to pass. Wade, in his early sixties, was one of the most determined of the anti-slavery men in Congress—he had tried, in 1852, to repeal the fugitive slave law outright—and in the smoky Senate debates of the late 1850s he had been ostentatiously defiant of the slave-state spokesmen; wholly grim, wholly determined, altogether one of the rockiest men in Washington.

These three called on Lincoln, and then on Lincoln and Seward, insisting that it was time for action to drive the Rebels away from the vicinity of Washington. They also went to see McClellan, in a meeting held at Montgomery Blair's house and lasting for three hours, and McClellan convinced them that Scott was the great obstacle. To his wife, immediately after the conference was over, McClellan summed it up: "They will make a desperate effort to have Gen. Scott retired at once; until that is accomplished I can effect but little good. He is ever in my way, and I am sure does not desire effective action. I want to get through with the war as rapidly as possible." Once Wade remarked that even an unsuccessful battle would be better than continued delay, because "swarming recruits" would come in to make good any losses; to which McClellan quietly replied that he would rather have a few recruits before a victory than a flock of them after a defeat. This was sober good sense, to be sure, but sober good sense was not quite what these Republican "radicals" were looking for, and Mr. Lincoln warned McClellan that this demand for action was a political reality that had to be taken into account, adding: "At the same time, General, you must not fight until you are ready." McClellan was confident. "I have everything at stake," he replied. "If I fail, I will not see you again, or anybody."[22]

Chandler recorded his own thoughts in a letter to Mrs. Chandler the next day.

"If Wade and I fail in our mission, the end is at hand," he wrote. "If we fail I *may* take my seat in the Senate this winter, but doubt it." He told about the meetings with McClellan and with Mr. Lincoln, and went on: "If we fail in getting a battle here now all is lost, and up to this time a fight is scarcely contemplated. Washington is safe now, and that seems to be all they care for. . . . If the South had one tenth our resources Jeff Davis would today be in Philadelphia and before a month in Boston."[23]

In the end, the mission succeeded. The Senators apparently were just a little skeptical about McClellan's willingness to make a quick move, but they had reached something of an understanding with him and for the moment they were backing him. Scott's resignation was formally accepted on November 1, his attempt to get Halleck as his successor was ridden down, and McClellan was announced as the new general-in-chief, with authority over the entire United States Army. Mr. Lincoln and cabinet paid a formal call on General Scott, and when Scott left the city McClellan and his staff went to the railroad station to see him off: a dark, rainy morning, the two soldiers preserving the amenities and parting with courteous farewells, McClellan inwardly touched by this melancholy close to "the career of the first soldier of his nation." Then McClellan assumed his new responsibilities and the capital prepared for action.

How the whole business looked to the radical Republican element is set forth in a confidential letter which the editors of the Chicago *Tribune* got from their Washington correspondent shortly after this change took place.

"Matters have a better look," wrote the *Tribune* man. "Scott is squelched and with him those who have been using his *disloyalty* to further and veneer their schemes for deadening the progress of the war. A stormy week in the counsels of managers of affairs here sees McClellan placed at the head of affairs. The people should be made to thoroughly acquit him of the Edwards Ferry affair." (By "Edwards Ferry," the writer referred to the Ball's Bluff business.) "That, and the proposition to go at once into winter quarters here, and suspend hostilities, broke the back of the opposition to him in the Cabinet and the Army."[24]

3: *The Hammering of the Guns*

There were dimensions to national strength which the impatient men in Washington were slow to recognize. The armies perhaps could do it all, if they could be recruited, organized, equipped, and properly led, but getting them into action was a long process. Meanwhile, there were the ponderous black-hulled ships of the United States Navy, growing obsolescent as they swung to their anchor chains, inviting dry rot while lying "in ordinary"—vessels which before long would be as archaic as Noah's Ark but which at the moment represented a hitting power which the Confederacy could not possibly match. Even while McClellan and Scott wrestled for mastery of the Army, this force went into action and began to constrict the windpipe of the South: moving, if anyone had noticed it, according to the design sketched out in Scott's Anaconda Plan.

3: *The Hammering of the Guns*

Late in June, 1861, the Navy Department convened a board of officers to consider how the rebellion might best be stifled, and this board first of all cast its eyes on a 350-mile section of neglected coastline—the long, lonely, windswept strip of sand that ran down from the Virginia peninsula to the south of Cape Hatteras, cutting the North Carolina sounds off from the sea, pierced by irregular tidal inlets: "sterile and half-drowned," the board felt, cursed with abominable gales, protecting a series of marshes and cedar swamps, protecting also a number of small seaports which were ideal havens for Rebel blockade-runners. It seemed to the Navy people that this long sandy emptiness ought to be possessed by the Federal authorities without delay.[1]

Accordingly, on August 26 a flotilla left Hampton Roads bound south. It included five steam warships and one ancient sailing frigate, a revenue cutter, two chartered merchant ships carrying 900 seasick soldiers, and a tugboat named *Fanny*, sent along to be helpful wherever possible. The warships had a good deal of muscle. The leaders were the steam frigates *Minnesota* and *Wabash*, built of wood, until recently supposed to be able to lie in the line of battle against anything afloat; 3000-ton craft armed with twenty-eight 9-inch guns, fourteen guns of 8-inch caliber, and two 10-inch pivot guns. Next in line was *Susquehanna* mounting fifteen 8-inch guns and a few smaller pieces. The other craft were lighter, although they were a good deal stronger than anything the Confederates had afloat, and the whole was under the command of Flag Officer Silas Stringham, a lean sailor with clean-shaven face, a lengthy upper lip, cold eyes, and a stiff sense of duty. Army commander was Major General Benjamin F. Butler, the one-time pro-slavery Southern sympathizer from Massachusetts, whose recent suggestion that fugitive slaves be considered contraband of war was proving highly corrosive to the peculiar institution. Warships and transports, along with a couple of ancient hulks which were supposed to do duty as landing craft, headed for a place known as Hatteras Inlet, where the long sandy strip had been broken open by tidal currents and the force of strong southeast winds—a shallow gap leading into Pamlico Sound ten miles below Cape Hatteras, guarded by two makeshift forts, Forts Clark and Hatteras. On the morning of August 28 Stringham pulled his big steam frigates up and opened a bombardment.

The Confederates were so woefully overmatched that it was really no contest, although bad weather and Federal inexperience with the intricacies of a combined operation stretched the job out through twenty-four hours. Fort Clark was a mere outwork containing five guns, wholly unfit to stand up to the fire of a strong fleet. Hatteras was bigger, well-designed, containing perhaps a score of guns, but the guns were too light, the supply of powder was defective, and Stringham kept his ships cruising in a long oval which made it impossible for the Rebel gunners to register on their targets. Toward evening an easterly gale came up and the warships drew offshore for the night. Federal troops were sent ashore, with difficulty, the two hulks drifting in through the breakers in imminent danger of shipwreck; after some three hundred soldiers were landed the hulks pulled out into deep water and the three hundred were left rationless and unprotected on the beach, and out in the fleet men feared that during the night this landing party would be gobbled up. Nothing happened, however, better weather came with the dawn, and the warships returned to reopen their bombardment.

It did not go with complete efficiency. One of the ships vigorously bombarded a herd of beef cattle under the impression that it was firing on Confederate cavalry. The soldiers moved into Fort Clark, which had been abandoned during the night, just in time to come under fire from their own fleet; a soldier in the 9th New York was wounded in the hand by a Federal shell fragment, and so became the only Federal casualty of the entire operation. But these were mere incidents. Confederate guns were quite unable to reach the warships, the volume of Navy gunfire was devastating, and by noon the Confederate commanders did the only sensible thing and surrendered. (There was a little mix-up, here; the Confederates refused to surrender to the Army, which was at the gates, arguing that they could have held out against mere soldiers all year and that it was the big guns of the Navy which had beaten them. It was agreed at last that they would surrender to the "armed forces" of the United States, without specifying which arm of the service had done the job.) The

Federals found that they had won two forts, 670 prisoners, a thousand stand of small arms and upwards of two dozen guns. The victory had been complete, inexpensive and speedy.[2]

Hatteras Inlet did not contain enough depth of water to admit the big warships, and thus it appears that the expedition had originally planned simply to block the passage by sinking stone-laden schooners so that Confederate blockade-runners and privateers could no longer use it. But both Butler and Stringham could see that this was an important entrance to a stretch of water which offered striking opportunities to the Federals. They detailed two regiments of infantry to garrison the captured forts, together with some of the smaller warships to look after them, and sailed back to Hampton Roads at once to arrange for supplies and reinforcements and to induce the authorities to revise their plans.[3] Mindful, no doubt, of the merit automatically gained by the bearer of good news, Butler hurried on to Washington, called on Montgomery Blair, and with Blair and Assistant Secretary of the Navy Gustavus V. Fox paid a midnight visit at the White House. Lincoln got out of bed and (according to Butler) received the callers in his nightshirt, and found the news so good that he and Fox, who was a good head shorter, danced gaily around the room together, the presidential nightshirt all a-flutter.[4] . . . However all of this happened, Washington agreed to exploit the victory. Reinforcements were ordered to Fort Hatteras, and the War and Navy Departments began planning for operations inside the Carolina sounds.

The victory was worth a White House jig. The Navy had found a soft spot, and there was no way for the Confederates to repair the damage or to avert more trouble. A Southern newspaperman at Raleigh, North Carolina, asked dolefully: "What does the entrance of the Yankees into our waters amount to? It amounts to this: The whole of the eastern part of the State is now exposed to the ravages of the merciless vandals. New Berne, Washington, Plymouth, Edenton, Hertford, Elizabeth City, are all now exposed, besides the whole of the adjacent country. . . . Our state is now plunged into a great deal of trouble."[5] As soon as they got around to following up their victory the Federals would in effect control a good third of North

Carolina and a sizable portion of the Confederate seacoast; they would eventually command the back door to Norfolk, the Dismal Swamp Canal which came up from Elizabeth City, they would stop water communication between Virginia and the South, and if they bestirred themselves they might even cut the main railroad line that went south from Richmond. If Jefferson Davis felt that he could not strip the southern coast of troops in order to reinforce Johnston and Beauregard, what happened at Hatteras Inlet could only confirm him in his belief.[6]

But Hatteras Inlet was just the beginning. It was followed by a much heavier blow which put the Confederacy at a permanent disadvantage—a stroke which might even have inflicted a mortal wound except for the ironic fact that the men who were almost tearing the government apart with their demands for speedy action were quite unable to see that such action did not necessarily have to take place under their eyes, in northern Virginia.

The naval strategy board which had seen the possibilities at Hatteras Inlet had also given thought to the matter of tightening the blockade all along the line. The problem here was not that there were so many seaports to be closed: actually, as Minister Adams pointed out to the British Foreign Secretary, who had asked whether the United States really meant to blockade everything from the Chesapeake to the Rio Grande, there were hardly more than ten harbors in all those 3500 miles that needed to be plugged. The real problem was the lack of bases. Vessels patrolling off Charleston or Savannah, for instance, had to go to Hampton Roads or even back to New York to get their coal; as a result they spent most of their time simply going and coming, and a cruiser no sooner reached its station than its captain had to begin to think about leaving.

In addition, the coast below Cape Hatteras was more intricate than it looked, all honeycombed by bays and sounds behind a series of swampy islets. A blockade runner rarely needed to approach the main entrance of the seaport to which he was bound; if his craft did not draw too much water he could slip in through any one of a dozen little inlets and reach his destination by a side door, letting the big cruisers lie-to in the deepwater channels to their hearts' content.

(One Federal skipper remarked that when blockade-runners were caught, in those early days, "it was due rather to the stupidity of the persons attempting to run the blockade than to the effectiveness of the force employed to prevent it.")[7] The Navy needed a swarm of shallow-draft gunboats that could prowl into every river, creek and tidal marsh between Florida and North Carolina; and these boats, being fragile and often quite unseaworthy, could not stay at sea indefinitely but needed a convenient place to make minor repairs and escape bad weather.

All of this meant that the South Atlantic coast could not be sealed off with even moderate effectiveness until the Navy had a satisfactory base right in the middle of the area that was being blockaded—a harbor of refuge big enough to hold fleet, colliers, supply ships, subsidiary craft and the innumerable facilities for repair and maintenance, held with so much strength that the Confederates could not recapture it. The naval board consulted its charts and its collective experience, and finally—early in August: a fortnight or so before the Hatteras Inlet expedition sailed—drew up plans which were quickly embodied in formal orders. A powerful amphibious expedition, comprising the heaviest warships the Navy could spare and at least 12,000 soldiers, would go south as soon as it could be organized and equipped, and it would take possession of Port Royal Sound, in South Carolina—the sound, its interlocked arms and tentacles, and as much of the adjacent shoreline as might be needed to make everything secure.

Port Royal Sound lay in the heart of the fabulous sea island region, and it was potentially one of the best harbors on the Atlantic coast. Lying sixty miles beyond Charleston and thirty miles short of Savannah, and offering a shallow-draft inland waterway approach to both places, it was roomy enough for any imaginable fleet. The main entrance from the Atlantic was two miles wide, and deep enough for the big steam frigates, and the extensive shoreline offered convenient places for all of the docks, wharves, warehouses, barracks, and hospitals that could ever be needed. There was no city of any commercial importance here; the nearest town was Beaufort, a pleasant residential community, cooled by ocean breezes, a favorite place of resort for wealthy planters during the hot summers. The Confederates were known to have fortified the entrance strongly, and it seemed likely that Port Royal would be a much tougher proposition than Hatteras Inlet.

To handle this operation the Navy chose a man who had served on the naval strategy board—Captain Samuel Du Pont, until recently in command of the Philadelphia Navy Yard, an officer who had experience with blockade work in the war with Mexico. He was equipped with high priority orders, the cumbersome title of "Flag Officer"—the Navy at that time did not have any admirals and could not give the admiral's title to a man doing admiral's work—and a note from Gideon Welles to the effect that "no more effective blows can be inflicted on those who are engaged in this causeless and unnatural rebellion than by naval expeditions and demonstrations on the coast."[8] Du Pont was given the big steam frigate *Wabash* for flagship and he went to work at once to get his armada together.

To command the troops the War Department appointed Brigadier General Thomas W. Sherman, a West Pointer who had fought Indians and Mexicans and who had been employed this summer on the Washington fortifications; big, blue-eyed, with a good martial bearing and a great barracks-square voice, gifted apparently with all the talents a general needs except a knack for understanding and making himself understood by the American volunteer.[9] Early in August he and Du Pont went to New York, Du Pont to get ships lined up, Sherman to bring together, organize, and train the 12,000 men who were to be assigned to him.

He did not get far before he was singed by the fire that was being interchanged between Scott and McClellan. The Port Royal move had Scott's warmest blessing, but McClellan did not like it, and, in September, McClellan was warning the War Department of an imminent Rebel invasion and was demanding that every available soldier be put into the Army of the Potomac. For a time he got Sherman and Sherman's new regiments. On September 18 Mr. Lincoln had to intervene, with orders to Cameron and Scott: "To guard against misunderstanding I think fit to say that the joint expedition of the Army and Navy agreed upon some time since, and in which

Gen. T. W. Sherman was and is to bear a conspicuous part, is in no wise to be abandoned, but must be ready to move by the first of, or very early in, October. Let all preparations go forward accordingly."[10] The President's will prevailed, but McClellan remained obdurate. In mid-October he was asked to send the 79th New York to Sherman, and he made formal protest to the War Department: "I will not consent to one other man being detached from this army for that expedition. I need far more than I now have to save this country and cannot spare any disciplined regiment. Instead of diminishing this army, true policy would dictate its immediate increase to a large extent. It is the task of the Army of the Potomac to decide the question at issue. No outside expedition can effect the result. I hope I will not again be asked to detach anybody."[11]

Despite this protest the work of preparation went forward; and so, in the end, did the 79th New York, in spite of McClellan. Sherman got his men assembled at Annapolis, loaded them on a wonderfully varied lot of transports—vessels ranging from regular ocean liners down to harbor ferry boats—and late in October the whole expedition lay at anchor at Hampton Roads, ready to go.

Altogether there were fifty ships, counting the transports. They were headed by the Navy's best fighting ships, the powerful steam frigates and the lighter steam sloops that were to prove so handy in the years just ahead; there were converted merchant vessels which Du Pont, somewhat skeptically, had hurriedly armed for duty as men of war (turning a merchantman into a warship, he wrote, was "like altering a vest into a shirt"); there were even four of the light new warships that were known as "90-day gunboats" because only three months had elapsed from the laying of their keels to their actual commissioning; and all in all here was the largest fleet ever assembled under the American flag, up to that moment. Ready to go with it were twenty-five schooners loaded with coal. Sealed orders were distributed among the ship masters, and on October 29 the entire fleet got its anchors aboard and put to sea; with considerable confusion a double line was formed off Cape Henry, and the armada moved down the coast in the general direction of Cape Hatteras, bucking a rising sea and a stiff easterly wind.

It seemed for a time that the expedition might be heading straight into disaster. The easterly wind swung around to the southeast and blew up into a furious gale, and, on the afternoon of November 1, Du Pont signaled that each ship should look after itself; if the convoy was scattered captains could open their sealed orders and find out where they should reassemble. Next morning Du Pont could see only one vessel besides his own *Wabash*. However, the gale at last subsided and on November 4 most of the fleet got together off the bar at the entrance to Port Royal Sound. One transport carrying six hundred Marines had foundered, with a loss of seven lives: another transport full of army stores had gone down, and the warship *Isaac Smith* had had to throw her broadside guns overboard to stay afloat.[12] But the damage had been surprisingly minor. The fleet was ready for business.

Du Pont lost no time getting down to work. The fleet crossed the bar, which lay ten miles offshore, and anchored near the entrance to the sound. The gunboats went in close to brush off a little squadron of improvised Confederate warships under Flag Officer Josiah Tattnall, small boats were sent out to buoy the channel, and the warships cleared for action. Another day was lost when a stiff wind from the south made proper maneuvering impossible, but, on the morning of November 7, Du Pont hoisted a signal and the Navy went at it in earnest.

Port Royal was tougher than Hatteras Inlet. The Confederates had two good forts—Fort Beauregard, on Bay Point at the northern side of the entrance, and Fort Walker, on Hilton Head Island on the southern side—and they were solidly built, armed with heavy guns and plenty of them, a two-mile channel between the forts. Du Pont sailed straight down the middle, sprinkling each fort with long-range fire; then, just past the entrance, he led his ships in a swing to the south and came back close inshore, six hundred yards from Fort Walker, steaming slowly, throwing in heavy-duty shell as fast as his gun crews could service their pieces. Fort Walker replied stoutly; *Wabash* and other ships were hit, rigging was cut and spars came down, men were killed, and splinters flew from the wooden sides of the ships; but Fort Walker was plastered with a barrage heavier than the Confederate gunners had dreamed of, the jarring detonations of the big guns coming, as a Federal officer wrote, "as fast as a horse's feet beat the ground in a gallop." Explosive bursts of sand shot up in the air as the big shells exploded in the sand revetments; guns were dismounted, the flagstaff was knocked down, men were dismembered, and *Wabash* steamed in close, hardly moving, a man in the fore chains calmly taking soundings, broadside guns firing with the swift unhurried precision of professionals at target practice.[13]

Tattnall tried to come out, once, to make a fight of it. He had been a good friend of Du Pont in the old Navy days, and when he steamed up to open fire he dipped his flag in salute, and exchanged broadsides with *Wabash*. But he was tragically overmatched. His ships were river steamers, undermanned and wholly unprotected. *Wabash* loosed two-dozen heavy guns at him, the shot flying high but promising to blow him out of the water once the gunners corrected their range, and he could do nothing else but turn around and flee deep into the sound, pursued by Yankee gunboats, powerless to affect the issue of the battle.[14] The Federal fleet swung past Fort Walker three times, pounding hard, and a newspaper correspondent riding with the fleet saw a prodigious spectacle in the flashing guns, the innumerable white clouds of bursting shell, the incessant racket and the steady, methodical precision of the advance. Fort Walker's fire slackened, then stopped, and from the ships men could see soldiers running out of the works and heading for safety in the rear. Du Pont pulled up and sent a boat's crew ashore; the officer in charge found the fort empty, everything smashed, nobody on hand to offer surrender. He hoisted a United States flag on what remained of the flag staff, reporting proudly that he was "first to take possession, in the majesty of the United States, of the rebel soil of South Carolina"; the warships anchored and sounded off with their whistles, the crews cheered, and on the transports the bands broke out their instruments and played "The Star-Spangled Banner." A slightly impressionable war correspondent wrote that at this moment "I felt an enthusiasm, a faith in the might and the power of the Government to vindicate itself . . . such as I never before experienced." A thoughtful reporter for the Cincinnati *Gazette* consulted whatever sources were available and estimated that the victory had cost the Federal government approximately $4,903,000, including the value of the two ships lost in the storm.[15]

The Marines landed to take full possession, followed by Sherman's troops. Fort Beauregard, whose people had been front-row spectators of the whole affair, was abandoned when Fort Walker fell, and early next morning a landing party took possession. It found everything in good order, tents full of soldiers' gear and personal effects, a flock of turkeys strutting around in a pen; found that the departing Confederates had booby-trapped a frame building formerly used as headquarters, with a mine which blew up when a sailor tripped over a wire. The sailor was stunned and the house was wrecked, but there was no other damage. Sherman's troops went ashore, the turkeys were all eaten, and the Navy's gunboats went ranging far into the sound to see how the victory might be exploited.

Residents of the area had panicked, most of them having fled when the troops fled. One gunboat found three deserted forts, and in his examination of the surrounding countryside the skipper could meet no one but Negro slaves, abandoned by their owners, luxuriating in their unexpected freedom: they were "perfectly demoralized, are doing nothing, and seem to be perfectly convinced that we have come to free them, and are in consequence most friendly." Another naval officer got up to Beaufort, where the slaves were plundering the houses, loading rowboats and scows with their loot. He found only one white man, who "appeared to be suffering from some strong excitement or the effects of liquor," assured him that the United States forces would protect life and property, and sent him off to spread the word. Hundreds of Negroes came out to the fleet in boats, hailing the Federals as heaven-sent deliverers, and a refugee camp was set up on the southeast end of Edisto Island, with a gunboat detailed to stand by and keep a watchful eye on things.[16] And Du Pont and Sherman took counsel regarding the next step on the program.

As befitted men who have just won a great deal more than they had expected to win, the two commanders were in good spirits. Sherman considered Du Pont's handling of the fleet "a masterpiece of activity and professional skill" and told the War Department that the performance had been "a masterly one" which could hardly be appreciated by anyone who had not actually seen it. Du Pont a little later wrote that the action had been "like driving a wedge into the flanks of the rebels" and reflected that if the nation had kept up an adequate Navy in the first place and had relied on it instead of on politicians and money it might have nipped the rebellion in the bud.[17] Sherman went about establishing a camp on Hilton Head Island, and after a day of meditation he composed and issued a proclamation, in which he reminded the South Carolinians of the grievous error of their ways and invited them to return penitently to the Union.

He began by announcing that he himself had spent much time in South Carolina and that he and the soldiers and the warships "have come amongst you with no feelings of personal animosity; no desire to harm your citizens, destroy your property or interfere with any of your lawful rights or your social and local institutions." This was all very well, except that the entire countryside within a fifty-mile radius was in a turmoil, social and local institutions had been turned upside down, and animate property was taking its ease in the sun and living off of Old Massa's riches, precisely because the Federal soldiers and warships had appeared; and anyone who doubted that a general overturn was coming in with the huge black ships and the uneven ranks of blue-coated soldiers did not know what was going on. However, the general continued in the same vein . . . "I implore you to pause and reflect upon the tenor and the consequences of your acts. . . . We have come among you as loyal men, fully impressed with our constitutional obligations to the citizens of your state. . . . The obligation of suppressing armed combinations against the constitutional authorities is paramount to all others. If in the performance of this duty other minor but important obligations should be in any way neglected, it must be attributed to the necessities of the case."[18]

No doubt this was excellent, but it meant nothing. The time for soft words had gone. The hammering of the guns was all that mattered now, and General Sherman's vision failed to detect two things. The first was that where his army and Du Pont's ships came, the white people ran away and the black people stayed to raise hosannas: the revolutionary upheaval which Secretary Seward saw germinating in this war was taking place wherever the war actually touched bottom. The second thing that went unobserved was that for the moment Sherman and his men could go just about anywhere they wanted to go. Du Pont said it: a wedge had been driven into the Confederate flank, and for the immediate future there was very little the Confederates could do about it. A woman in Savannah saw it more clearly than the Federal general could see it. The day after Sherman issued his proclamation she wrote: "The fleet was hourly expected & the decision with most was to burn their dwellings & let the Yankees have smoking ruins to welcome them. . . . The panic on Saturday cannot be described, & the cars twice a day are loaded down with women & children bound to the interior. . . . At the present time the enemy by the land route could walk into our city without let or hindrance."[19]

4: "*We Are Not Able to Meet It*"

As it was to do so many times in the future, the Confederacy at this moment of crisis called on General Robert E. Lee. It did not yet recognize the full stature of the man on whom it would finally load everything, but the emergency was urgent and Lee was at least available. He had been ordered back to Richmond after the failure in the western Virginia mountains, and when Jefferson Davis realized that the Federals meant real harm in South Carolina, Lee was within reach. Mr. Davis created the Department of South Carolina, Georgia and East Florida and put Lee in command, thus making him responsible for the defense of all of the Atlantic coast below North Carolina, and Lee set out for the new task just as Du Pont was preparing to open his unanswerable bombardment.

As Lee himself doubtless realized, this job was much like the one which had meant trouble beyond the Blue Ridge: an assignment in which things had begun to go irretrievably wrong, and where a good man could lose much through little fault of his own. Here at Port Royal the Federals held high cards, and if they played them expertly they were likely to win. Still, they might make mistakes; the initial victory opened so many opportunities that it automatically increased the number of things which might be done wrong, and within a year or two it would be evident that Federal generals who were opposed to Lee usually *did* make mistakes, at substantial cost to themselves.

Lee made his headquarters at Coosawhatchie, a little station on the Charleston & Savannah Railroad some twenty miles inland from Port Royal. It was the nearest point on the railroad to the scene of action, but the action was over by the time Lee arrived. Forts Walker and Beauregard had been taken, and Lee could do no more than try to save the troops and perfect the defenses of Charleston and Savannah. His first report to the War Department was gloomy: "The enemy having complete possession of the water and inland navigation, commands all the islands on this coast and threatens both Savannah and Charleston, and can come in his boats within four miles of this place. . . . We have no guns that can resist their batteries, and have no resource but to prepare to meet them in the field." This would be difficult, because there was nothing much to meet the Federals with: "I fear there are but few state troops ready for the field. The garrisons of the forts at Charleston and Savannah and on the coast cannot be removed from the batteries while ignorant of the designs of the enemy. I am endeavoring to bring into the field such light batteries as can be prepared." Inhabitants of the coastal area were in a panic, there were few troops at hand, arms for new recruits seemed to be almost non-existent, and many weeks later Lee had to confess: "The strength of the enemy, as far as I am able to judge, exceeds the whole force that we have in the state; it can be thrown with great celerity against any point, and far outnumbers any force we can bring against it in the field." To his daughter Lee wrote that this assignment was "another forlorn hope expedition—worse than West Virginia."[1]

From their new base the Federals could attack Charleston or Savannah or they could cut the vital railroad line anywhere between the two cities. The country was ideally adapted for amphibious operations, and the Federals had an overwhelming fleet and substantially more land forces than could be brought against them. Clearly, Lee could not hope to hold any point on the interconnected sounds and rivers which could be reached by the Yankee gunboats. His only course was to strengthen the defenses of the two important cities and to draw an interior line, out of the Navy's range, which might save the railroad.[2]

As he had written, it was hard to make a good plan without knowing what the enemy meant to do. Fortunately for the Confederacy, the enemy at this moment did not really mean to do much of anything. Having won a much bigger victory than they had expected to win, the Federals were slightly baffled. They had hoped to seize a good harbor as a base for the South Atlantic blockading squadron; they had won a full half-dozen harbors, a protected inland waterway controlling half of the South Carolina coastline, and a spot from which the heart of the South was open to invasion. Port Royal was not so much a conquest as a point of departure, but Sherman expressed the full truth about the situation when he frankly confessed that "we had no idea, in preparing the expedition, of such immense success."[3] He had the opportunity and the means, but he had no instructions, beyond a rather generalized order that he and the Navy ought to move farther south if they could do so conveniently and occupy the harbor at Fernandina, Florida.

He was quite aware that something more ought to be done, and he seems to have suspected that it ought to be done rather quickly, but there were a great many details to be attended to. The army of occupation had to lay out and fortify its camp, the islets and coastal settlements must be overrun, provision had to be made for the masterless slaves who seemed to be sole occupants of most of the countryside–and, all in all, Sherman was very busy. Young James Harrison Wilson, a restless lieutenant of topographical engineers on Sherman's staff, fumed that "the army did practically nothing but sit down and hold the sea islands which the navy had captured for it":[4] a complaint which, besides being tinged with the perfectionism of youth, was written much later in the clear light of after knowledge. Sherman began to come in for bitter criticism in the North, although the men in Washington who wanted direct action so much never touched him with their spurs. In the end he devoted himself to planning a movement which would be executed during the spring, although by that time another general would be in charge: the bombardment and capture of Fort Pulaski, at the mouth of the Savannah River.

Sherman can be blamed too much. It was only the Confederates who realized (as they could hardly help doing) that if the Yankees followed up their advantage with energy it would be extremely hard to stop them. Two months after Du Pont's ships had overwhelmed the forts, Lee wrote that all along he had been expecting Sherman to send one column inland to cut the railroad while he used the fleet and the rest of his troops to isolate and capture either Charleston or Savannah: in Lee's opinion "this would be a difficult combination for us successfully to resist." As a matter of fact the entire Confederate coastline was vulnerable, both on the Atlantic and in the Gulf, and General Braxton Bragg, who commanded coastal defenses beyond the Florida peninsula, saw the danger. If the Federals struck hard at Mobile, he said, he did not see how the place could be defended, and he added significantly: "Our strength consists in the enemy's weakness."[5] Weakness of intent, that is; the Federals had all the power they needed if they used it vigorously.

In the Confederate capital the hypercritical Richmond *Examiner* believed that the Federals would fritter away their big chance. The editor did not think much of professional soldiers anyway, and he wrote petulantly: "There cannot be much bloody work where a LEE is opposed by a SHERMAN; and a SHERMAN confronted by a LEE. These generals are true scions of West Point, and both will take time before they go into action. When West Point meets West Point, spade meets spade, then comes *not* the tug of war. . . . West Point *Sherman* does not mean to fight until he gets perfectly ready." Because of this, the *Examiner* believed the blow at Port Royal might be a blessing in disguise: "It is much to be desired that something should occur in this latitude to rouse the people to energy and tear the speculating mandrakes bleeding from their spoils. . . . The effect of these grand demonstrations of the Yankees at various points will be admirable upon the Southern people, government, army and generals. All had grown over-confident and had consequently relapsed into listlessness and inactivity. The enemy are curing all of this for us."[6]

No eloquence matches that of an editor who finds that his readers, despite his best efforts, have grown hopeful; at which time bad news becomes a welcome stimulant, and editorial vision grows keen enough to find a silver lining in almost any disaster. And now, suddenly, the silver lining became real enough for any Southern eye to see, and there were a few weeks of wild surmise in which it was possible once more to credit the hoariest of the myths that had preceded secession—the theory that the outside world just would not let the Yankees win the war.

This came because U.S.S. *San Jacinto*, one of the Federal Navy's serviceable steam sloops of war, slipped in past the Virginia Capes on November 15 and anchored in Hampton Roads, bearing an exultant skipper, two important prisoners and an incalculable load of trouble.

The skipper was Captain Charles Wilkes, one of the best-known men in the Navy and one of the most self-willed. Opinionated and contentious, Wilkes was a lean man in his early sixties who had won fame for explorations along the Antarctic coast twenty years earlier, mapping 1600 miles of bleak shoreline and leaving Wilkes Land as an enduring name on the charts. (Characteristically, the feat that made him famous brought him also a court-martial and a public reprimand for inflicting illegal punishments on the enlisted men who served under him.) Wilkes was to have commanded U.S.S. *Merrimack* this summer, but that ship had been scuttled when the Navy Yard at Norfolk was lost, and he had been given *San Jacinto* instead and had gone down to cruise off Cuba.[7] Returning now from this cruise, he was in high spirits. He had given the tail of the British lion a vigorous twist (he did not like the British, although their Royal Geographical Society had once given him a medal) and he had also, as he believed, done much harm to the Southern Confederacy.

His prisoners were much more famous than their captor; were, indeed, two of the most prominent leaders of the South, men who, like himself, had reached their sixties trailing records of achievement —James Mason of Virginia and John Slidell of Louisiana. These elderly veterans of Democratic politics had slipped out of the country in October to go abroad as Jefferson Davis's commissioners to the governments of England and France, traveling with a dignity derived both from their own eminent positions and from the letters of instruction given them by Secretary of State R. M. T. Hunter. They were to make clear, said Hunter, that the Confederate states "are not to be viewed as revolted provinces or rebellious subjects seeking to overthrow the lawful authority of a common sovereign." The South was making no revolution; on the contrary it was simply trying to get away from a revolution which aggressive Northern sectionalists had tried to make "in the spirit and ends of the organic law of their first union." Withdrawing from that first union, the South had set up a government "competent to discharge all of its civil functions and entirely responsible both in war and peace for its action."[8] In simple justice, full recognition ought to follow.

Reaching Havana on a blockade-runner, Mason and Slidell on November 7 had taken passage on the British mail steamer *Trent*, a regular liner plying between the West Indies and the United Kingdom. Wilkes, whose ship was in Havana at the time, heard about it, sailed on ahead to lie in wait at a suitable spot in the Bahama Channel, and on November 8 boldly extracted the two men from the *Trent*, compelling that vessel to heave to by firing a shot across its bows, and compounding the indignity thus offered to the British flag by sending armed men aboard to make the arrests. For the first time the Federal power had laid its hands on two leading secessionists, and Wilkes felt that this was a substantial achievement. What he did not see was that it might also cause Great Britain to declare war.

Wilkes came into Hampton Roads to get coal, to tell his government what he had done, and to learn what he should do with his prisoners. He was ordered to go on to Boston and turn the men over to Army authorities at Fort Warren, which he promptly did, reaching Boston on November 24 to find that he was a national hero. Secretary Welles wrote a letter of commendation, pointing out that Mason and Slidell had been most "conspicuous in the conspiracy to dissolve the Union" and assuring Wilkes that his action "has the emphatic approval of this department." The city of Boston gave him a great banquet, bombarding him with oratory. The House of Representatives a little later passed a vote of thanks, editorial writers exulted, and all in all the people of the North showed much more enthusiasm for Wilkes's capture of two men than it had shown for Du Pont's capture of two forts.[9]

In the South the news brought expectant optimism. At first nothing was clear except that this Yankee skipper had committed an outrage which the British were likely to resent, and Mary Boykin Chestnut, the South Carolina diarist, felt that "something good is obliged to come from such a stupid blunder,"[10] but as the weeks passed it appeared that this "something good" might be fabulous indeed—might even take the form of a British fleet scouring the Southern coast clear of blockaders and invaders and presenting the Confederacy with immediate and permanent independence. The disaster at Port Royal began to look insignificant. Southern valor and British sea power could make an unbeatable combination.

For the British reaction to what Captain Wilkes had done was quick and spirited—inevitable, in a nation conditioned to believe that no outlanders could ever molest a merchantman flying the British flag. *Trent* reached Southampton on November 27, and when its news reached London a wave of indignation ran from the cabinet through Parliament and the newspapers to the man in the street. Earl Russell considered the seizure "an act of violence . . . an affront to the British flag and a violation of international law," and Lord Palmerston informed Queen Victoria that her government "should be advised to demand reparation and redress." The British admiral on the North American station was warned to get ready for trouble, and 8000 soldiers were ordered off to Canada. (It was reported that as one transport left the Mersey a regimental band played "Dixie.") There was uproar in the dignified Reform Club when the news came in; members became "violent, demonstrative and outrageous," and an ordinarily peaceful member of Parliament declared that if the insult were not atoned for "he would recommend the British colors to be torn to shreds and sent to Washington for the use of the Presidential water closets." One Englishman wrote to Seward that if the country were polled "I fear that 999 men out of 1,000 would declare for immediate war."[11]

Charles Francis Adams was not in London at the time. He was spending a few days at Frystone, the home of Richard Monckton Milnes, one of the few upper-class Britishers who was showing friendship to the American minister, and, on November 27, Mr. Adams and his host, with others, had gone forth in a chilly drizzle to inspect Pomfret Castle, historic scene of the murder of Richard II. Around midday Adams received a telegram from the American Legation, announcing the news, and he retained his correct Bostonian composure even though his reflections on what might come of Captain Wilkes's act "prevented me from thinking much of historical associations." His host offered to get him back to London at once, but Mr. Adams replied that all things considered he would like to stay at Frystone a day or two longer; right at the moment London was the last place on earth where he wanted to be. Until he heard from Seward and found out what his government was doing, the American minister must be both quiet and inconspicuous. Fortunately, there was no Atlantic cable, and it took about three weeks for London to send a message to Washington and get a reply. There would be a breathing spell in which the current excitement might die down slightly, in which somebody, on one side of the Atlantic or the other, perhaps even on both sides, might have sober second thoughts. The minister would be reserved.

Mr. Adams had no real idea what was happening. He knew that an American warship had been sent to the English channel to intercept the Confederate cruiser *Nashville*, on which, according to rumor, Mason and Slidell had planned to sail. That a British merchantman instead of a Southern warship had been used, and stopped, struck the minister as calamitous, and it seemed quite likely that the whole thing was in line with Mr. Seward's aggressive foreign policy, about which the American minister had worried earlier. It was perfectly conceivable that the Secretary now was actually reaching out for that foreign war which had obsessed him so much in the spring. It also seemed to Mr. Adams that American naval officers brought trouble no matter what they did; it was bad when they were too sluggish but it was even worse when they were too active. . . . Mr. Adams presently returned to London, where he warned the Legation staff that they probably would not be in London more than another month.[12]

Some of the thoughts which had come to Mr. Adams had occurred also to the British government. It was known that the American naval power had been most anxious to seize Mason and Slidell; it was known, as well, that Mr. Seward was a man of expedients who gained domestic political advantage by being, or by at least seeming to be, strongly anti-British. (It was asserted that when the Prince of Wales visited America in the fall of 1860 Seward had told the Duke of Newcastle that he expected to hold high office very soon and that "it will then become my duty to insult England, and I mean to do so.") Mr. Adams's son Henry doubtless reflected general opinion at the Legation when he wrote to his brother: "I consider that we are dished and that our position is hopeless." The British, he said, certainly meant to make war if it developed that Wilkes's act reflected the fixed policy of the American government, and he added: "What Seward means is more than I can guess. But if he means war also, or to run as close as he can without touching, then I say that Mr. Seward is the greatest criminal we've had yet." The minister himself remarked that one big reason for the excitement in London was the myth that "Mr. Seward is an ogre fully resolved to eat all Englishmen raw."[13]

Actually, Mr. Seward meant no harm. Even before he learned about the stormy times in London he wrote to Mr. Adams pointing out that Wilkes's act was entirely unauthorized. He also called in General McClellan, the recently appointed general-in-chief, and asked him what the possibilities were in case America should find itself at war with Great Britain. McClellan unhesitatingly replied that if the nation were to fight Great Britain it might as well give up all hope of winning its war with the Southern Confederacy: and Mr. Seward, accepting this professional opinion, remarked that "if the matter took that turn, they" (Mason and Slidell) "must at once be given up."[14] But it might not be easy. Too many Americans applauded the seizure. To climb down would be hard at best, and it would be wholly impossible if the British were too arrogant about it.

Seward's legal mind was fascinated with the interesting theory by which Captain Wilkes justified the captures. Wilkes pointed out that under international law a nation at war could properly halt a neutral ship in order to seize enemy dispatches. Such dispatches, by general agreement, were contraband of war. Mason and Slidell had carried no dispatches, to be sure, but it seemed to Captain Wilkes that they themselves were the very embodiment of dispatches, since they were charged to the ears with instructions, messages, arguments, and high state secrets. As living dispatches, then, they were, by a curious inversion of Ben Butler's reasoning in respect to fugitive slaves, contraband of war, and they could in consequence be removed legally from a neutral ship on the high seas. If this theory were accepted, Captain Wilkes had made only one mistake: he should have seized the *Trent* and brought the ship into an American port for adjudication by a prize court. The convolutions of this part of the argument led Mr. Adams to remark dryly that "Great Britain would have been less offended if the United States had insulted her a great deal more."[15]

The whole *Trent* affair was a sea lawyer's dream anyway. Not only was there this fascinating theory put forward by Captain Wilkes; under everything there was a fact which was bound to embarrass both governments if they let themselves think about it. Half a century earlier they had made war upon one another, at least partly because Great Britain then insisted on doing what America had done now and because America then fought to uphold the position now taken by the British. The whole business of the right of search and seizure at sea was mixed up in it; as the world's greatest sea power, Britain might not be too happy to fight in order to restrict that right. (France and other nations were openly disapproving Captain Wilkes's act because they did want that right restricted.) On the other hand, America's historic defense of the freedom of the seas simply did not have room for a defense of the sort of thing Captain Wilkes had done.

Dangerous as the situation looked, and was, both governments were in fact anxious to keep the crisis below flash point. On November 30 Lord Russell sent to Windsor Castle drafts of the dispatches which the cabinet proposed to send to Washington, the most important of which was a tart demand for reparations and apology, which Lord Lyons must give to Secretary Seward. The Royal Consort, Prince Albert, was unwell; was in fact sickening with the malady which two weeks later would kill him. He studied the drafts that evening, and early the next morning, unable to sleep, he considered their revision. Queen Victoria wrote in her diary that "he could eat no breakfast and was very wretched," but he composed a memorandum for her (although he felt almost too weak to hold the pen) and this memorandum greatly changed the tone which the government was about to use. It was in fact an attempt to make it easier for the United States to descend from Captain Wilkes's high horse if the United States really wanted to remain at peace.

In substance, Prince Albert suggested a rephrasing so that the British ultimatum would express confidence that Captain Wilkes had not acted under instruction, that the United States had not really meant to insult the British flag, and that on due reflection Washington would "spontaneously offer such redress as alone would satisfy this country, viz., the restoration of the unfortunate passengers and a suitable apology." The note remained stiff enough, to be sure: Mason and Slidell must be released and Washington must say that it was sorry about the whole affair; but there was a strong "let's not fight" twist to it, an absence of the dictatorial, angry tone which would have made it impossible for any American political leader to give ground. As Seward himself remarked later, when Lord Lyons told him he had a dispatch for him, everything depended on the way it was worded.[16]

The cabinet accepted the revisions, apparently with a feeling of relief, and the Prince in his turn was happy that the dispatch was to be shorn "of everything which could irritate a proud and sensitive nation." Lord Russell privately notified Lord Lyons that "the disposition of the cabinet is to accept the liberation of the captive commissioners and to be rather easy about the apology"—adding, however, that an apology by itself would not be enough: the prisoners must also be freed. Lord Lyons, in turn, behaved just as Mr. Adams had been behaving; that is, he kept very quiet. He sent to Lord Russell copies of American newspapers (which were praising Captain Wilkes and generally uttering defiance) with the remark that "to a person accustomed to the strong language of the American press, these articles appear moderate and even subdued in tone." The London *Times* man in Washington, the now-famous Bull Run Russell, did report that Mr. Seward was talking in warlike vein, saying "We will wrap the whole world in flames," but a Washington friend told him to pay no attention: "When Seward talks that way he means to break down. He is most dangerous and obstinate when he pretends to agree a good deal with you."[17]

Old General Scott was in Paris, his work in Washington finished, his health atrocious; but he sat down with Thurlow Weed, Seward's political guide, who was also visiting Europe, and with John Bigelow, the American consul, to pour oil on the troubled seas. Over Scott's name they produced a public statement saying that America certainly would "regard no honorable sacrifice too great for the preservation of the friendship of Great Britian," and predicting that Washington would happily free its captives if that would help to "emancipate the commerce of the world." Scott had a massive reputation in Europe, and the statement helped to reduce the tension. But if his country was to fight the British, Scott wanted to be back home; he broke off his visit and took ship for New York, writing to Seward that "I am returning home to share in perils, without the least hope of being useful," and adding: "I hope for peace with England, on honorable terms, & a speedy suppression of the rebellion. If not, O that I were 10 or 15 years less aged!"[18]

In the end it was all settled peaceably. Lord Lyons received the softened dispatch from the British cabinet, consulted Seward, assured him that the document did not breathe forth fire and slaughter, and gave it to him, and on Christmas Day there was a long cabinet meeting at which President Lincoln and his advisers finally agreed that the only thing to do was to free the prisoners. Mr. Lincoln confessed later that "it was a bitter pill to swallow," but he seems for some time to have felt that Mason and Slidell were white elephants, more difficult to hold than to liberate, and Attorney General Bates stated the obvious truth: to hold the prisoners meant a war with England, and "we must avoid it *now* and for the plain reason that *now* we are not able to meet it." Secretary Seward prepared an elaborate dispatch to be sent to London; it argued the case at substantial length, but pointed out that Wilkes had acted without orders (disavowed, the act need not be apologized for) and closed by announcing that the prisoners "will be cheerfully liberated." Lord Lyons wrote to Lord Russell saying that in his opinion the British government's demands had been substantially complied with, and Lord Russell replied that the American words and actions "constitute the reparation which Her Majesty and the British nation had a right to expect." Mason and Slidell and their secretaries, J. E. MacFarland and George Eustis, were liberated, H.M.S. *Rinaldo* called at Provincetown, Massachusetts, to pick them up and take them to England, and the case was closed. When the news reached London, Mr. Adams and Mrs. Adams soberly congratulated one another, and the Secretary at the Legation noted that the news was announced between the acts at most London theaters "and the audiences rose like one & cheered tremendously."[19]

So it was over, and the moment when Britain might intervene to make the Southern Confederacy independent passed. No one had watched it more closely than Robert E. Lee, who was still trying to find some way to keep the Federals from taking full advantage of what they had won in South Carolina, and he wrote thoughtfully: "We must make up our minds to fight our battles ourselves. Expect to receive aid from no one. Make every necessary sacrifice of Comfort, money and labor to bring the war to a successful issue & then we will Succeed. The cry is too much for help. I am mortified to hear it. We want no aid. We want to be true to ourselves, to be prudent, just, fair & bold. I am dreadfully disappointed at the spirit here. They have all of a sudden realized the asperities of war. . . . If I only had some veteran troops to take the brunt they would soon rally & be inspired with the great principle for which we are Contending."[20]

5: *Revolutionary Struggle*

The silver lining slowly disappeared, and as 1861 drew toward its end the Confederate capital showed a queer blend of lingering optimism and rising pessimism. On the surface things still looked good, and Varina Davis noted that most politicians, taking eventual European recognition for granted, were planning to join in the scramble for high office which would follow the attainment of full independence. The Richmond *Examiner*, mixing bile with insight, remarked that the Confederacy had passed its hour of greatest peril, the time in which it might have been overwhelmed before it could raise an army or prepare its defenses, and asserted: "If we are conquered at all now, it must be done by the regular and ordinary means of war, and not by the rush of a vast mob." Its enemies were contemptible: "The Yankee, always held in supreme contempt abroad as a swindling, low-bred huckster, is now regarded as destitute of courage," and no British Grenadier or French Zouave could ask for better sport than "hunting the swift-footed antelopes of McClellan." Still, trouble lay ahead. The Northern peace party had vanished, and Yankee recruits, "however vile and cowardly they may be," would be dangerous when drilled, organized, and equipped in large numbers. The armies the Confederacy must fight next year would be different from the hordes that had been routed at Bull Run. All in all, the Confederacy must reorganize its own army: "Unless it places it on a different footing from the present, its chance next year will be bad."[1]

The same thought had occurred to President Davis. So far, what had been done had been makeshift. Incomplete returns showed that the Confederacy now had 209,000 men under arms, present for duty; 258,000 for an "aggregate present," which was how the War Department tabulated things when it counted all of the extras. This was an extremely good showing, to be sure; but the Yankees had more than twice that many, and the sobering thing about the Confederate total was that a good half of the soldiers had signed up for twelve-month terms and would be going home in the springtime, when the Yankee hordes would be advancing. It was true that 1861 had brought dazzling victories, but the landscape nevertheless had been darkening. Missouri and western Virginia had been lost, most of the Carolina coast was gone, much of Kentucky was held by the Federals and Tennessee itself was in grave danger. Washington was preparing new amphibious expeditions—one of them, according to indications, aimed at New Orleans, largest city in the South—and the blockade undeniably was beginning to bind. Arms were short, and so was money, and a government of sharply limited powers, resting on a jealously guarded concept of states' rights, might easily find the whole situation hard to control. A friend of the President wrote in his diary: "I have not seen the President apparently so gloomy."[2]

As always, Mr. Davis showed a cheerful face to the public. Late in November he assured Congress that what had been done so far "has checked the wicked invasion which greed of gain and the unhallowed lust of power brought upon our soil"; the Confederate States "are relatively much stronger now than when the struggle commenced," and although privations lay ahead the people could be sustained by "the strength that is given by a conscious sense, not only of the magnitude but of the righteousness of our cause."[3] Yet the President had a special vantage point, from which he could see much which he could not talk about in public; only to his intimates could he discuss the picture in detail.

During the summer the President and his family had moved into the Brockenbrough mansion, on Clay Street at 12th, a tall, pillared dwelling known thenceforward as the White House of the Confederacy. Here, one evening early in December, there was a formal dinner, and after it was over Mr. Davis and a few friends adjourned to a retreat which the President called his "snuggery"—a book-lined room where, relaxing in easy chairs, the men could accept Presidential cigars and could listen to frank talk. In this quiet, pleasant hideaway, Mr. Davis revealed his worries.

The biggest concern was the volunteer army. Not only were many enlistments about to expire; even this early it was obvious that a good many regiments—including, Mr. Davis confessed, some from his own state of Mississippi—would refuse to remain in service. Governors and generals could be blamed, here: governors, because some of them would not co-operate with Richmond on troop recruitment and maintenance, and generals because so few of them were able to handle volunteer soldiers. (Attorney General Thomas Bragg, one of the men present at this little meeting, proudly noted that his brother, Braxton Bragg, was named by Mr. Davis as the only army commander who knew how to manage volunteers and retain their love and respect—a judgment which would call for revision before the war was over.)

Missouri and Kentucky offered problems, too. In Missouri, Price and McCulloch were on most evil terms, Price anxious to fight, McCulloch anxious to retreat; it seemed to Mr. Davis that he ought to send an outsider in to take top command, but if that happened Price's whole army would probably disband, in which case the theory that Missouri had recently entered the Confederacy would remain a thin theory and nothing more. Kentucky's situation was baffling. The legislature was firmly Unionist, and Governor Magoffin, who earlier had sounded like a secessionist, apparently was under the legislature's influence now, or under the influence of the Union generals; in either case he was hardly a man the Confederacy could count on. Secessionist Kentuckians wanted to wrench at least a part of Kentucky loose from its old moorings and bring it into the Confederacy—an attractive idea, but most irregular, since it was the precise counterpart of the illegal game the Yankees were playing in western Virginia. Something of the sort probably would have to be done, however, because the Kentuckians "are in a state of revolution."

Finally, there was the problem of money. Secretary of the Treasury was earnest Christopher Memminger, a careful lawyer who had served in the South Carolina legislature and whose fiscal horizon until recently had been bounded by routine Charleston philanthropies and the peacetime budget of a small and thrifty state; responsible now for balancing apparently limitless expenditures, like an inverted pyramid, on narrowly restricted means. He said that the Confederate treasury could carry on through April, but he did not know what would happen after that; somehow, the cost of fighting the war must be reduced. Both Mr. Davis and Secretary of War Judah Benjamin immediately assured him that this was out of the question. . . . Gold was being hoarded, there was a flood of paper money, and Mr. Bragg gloomily wrote: "By and by the crash will come, do what we may. It is to be hoped the war will end first —we could then recover after no great while."[4]

. . . The money question was unnerving, and yet it was a source of grim comfort, in a certain sense, because it did at least seem to impose a limit on a business which was getting more and more out of hand. On both sides there were sober men of affairs who believed that the war must end before long simply because it was moving beyond its financial base. Not long after Mr. Bragg saw the inevitability of trouble, Charles Francis Adams, surveying the aftermath of the Mason-Slidell trouble, wrote to his son about "the crushing nature of our expenditure, which must stop this war if something effective does not follow soon."[5] It was still possible, at the end of 1861, to believe that if all else failed war might flicker out because it had grown too expensive. . . .

The trouble was not so much the money problem, nor even the manpower problem, as it was the extent of the power which Mr. Davis's government had or could assert. Men could be made to enter the Army, or to stay in once they had entered; spending could be made to go far beyond the point where business prudence would set a limit; worthless pieces of paper could be made to serve (for a time, at least, and at a certain cost) as valid tools of exchange—*if* the government which controlled such matters insisted that these things be done. One man who was thinking along these lines was Robert E. Lee, who not long after the White House meeting wrote to Governor Letcher of Virginia to express concern about the problem of re-enlistment of the twelve-month men in the spring.

"I tremble to think of the different conditions our armies will present to those of the enemy at the opening of the next campaign," said General Lee. "On the plains of Manassas, for instance, the enemy will resume operations, after a year's preparation and a winter of repose, fresh, vigorous, and completely organized, while we shall be in the confusion and excitement of reorganizing ours. The disbanding and reorganizing an army in time of peace is attended with loss and expense. What must it be in time of active service, in the presence of an enemy prepared to strike? I have thought that General McClellan is waiting to take the advantage which that opportunity will give him. What then is to stand between him and Richmond?"

Like the impatient Republican radicals in Washington, Lee felt that the Army of the Potomac was being held in its camps beyond its time; unlike the radicals, he thought that the army's commander must have some sensible reason for his inaction. . . . Returning to the Confederacy's difficulty, Lee remarked that he knew of no way to hold the short-term regiments in service "except by the passage of a law for drafting them 'for the war' unless they volunteer for that period." Then he went on to state the feeling of the dedicated soldier and patriot, to put into simple words the incredible paradox which made revolutionists out of profound conservatives:

"The great object of the Confederate states is to bring the war to a successful issue. Every consideration should yield to that; for without it we can hope to enjoy nothing that we possess, and nothing that we do possess will be worth anything without it."[6]

In these words General Lee demanded and defined all-out war. Victory was all that mattered, and no price for it could be too high. No matter what changes war brought they would be accepted: in all-out war they have to be accepted; fixing their gaze upon victory itself, men become unable to see more than a millimeter beyond it, thereby putting themselves at the mercy of the implacable future. Three years from this fall the Confederate officer who ran the Bureau of Conscription—an agency which would come into being because of the truth voiced by General Lee—tried to describe the kind of war the Confederacy had been fighting. It had become, he said, one of those wars "in which the whole population and the whole production of a country (the soldiers and the subsistence of armies) are to be put on a war footing, where every institution is to be made auxiliary to war, where every citizen and every industry is to have for the time but one attribute—that of contributing to the public defense."[7]

The pressure was felt by both Presidents, by the man in Washington as well as by the man in Richmond. Two thirds of a year had passed since they had said the words which set the guns firing around Fort Sumter; so far, neither man had finished the task of preparing to fight the war which had then begun; yet each man was beginning to see that this war might presently become something that had not been bargained for in the springtime. Mr. Davis was being compelled to think about what the war was going to do; Mr. Lincoln, in equal perplexity, was being compelled to think of what the war was going to mean. Each man was beginning to see things that had not been visible in April.

On December 3, Mr. Lincoln was obliged to send his regular message to the Congress. He began almost as if there were no war at all, pointing out that the land had been blessed with good health and abundant harvests; he discussed certain vacancies on the Supreme Court, suggested changes in the Federal judicial system, proposed that the nation's industrial interests be represented at an exhibition which was to be held in London, and told how territorial organization was progressing in Colorado, Dakota, and Nevada. Then, at last, he got down to it.

"The war continues," said Mr. Lincoln. "In considering the policy to be adopted for suppressing the insurrection, I have been anxious and most careful that the inevitable conflict for this purpose shall not degenerate into a violent and remorseless revolutionary struggle. I have therefore, in every case, thought it proper to keep the integrity of the Union prominent as the primary object of the contest on our part, leaving all questions which are not of vital military importance to the more deliberate action of the legislature." Everything that needed to be done to save the Union would of course be done, but "radical and extreme measures" would be avoided, if possible. For the time being the President would stand on the policy previously announced: the war was being fought for reunion and would not be waged so as to interfere with any domestic institution.

Yet the business was infernally complicated, with ominous overtones. In Richmond it was beginning to be seen that a Confederacy militantly dedicated to states' rights might have to ignore its basic doctrine and embrace the very centralism it was fighting to avoid, if it wished to live; and in Washington the domestic institution which was not to be touched was being touched every time the war itself was touched. The war which was not being fought to end slavery was somehow *about* slavery; or, at the very least, slavery lay underneath everything, ready to be turned up whenever the plowshare cut through the thin sheltering crust. This meant that the remorseless revolutionary struggle which Mr. Lincoln was so anxious to avoid lay likewise just beneath the surface. How could it be avoided?

So far, the President had done his best. General Frémont had proclaimed freedom for the slaves in Missouri and had been quickly overruled; was, by this time, altogether on the sidelines, a general without a command, removed by Presidential order just after Scott himself had resigned, replaced (after a brief interval) by the General Halleck whom Scott had groomed as his own replacement. Not long after that, Secretary of War Cameron inserted in his annual report a flat statement that the government had the right to turn slaves into soldiers and would exercise that right whenever it needed to do so; Lincoln made him recall the report and remove the offending statement, substituting for it a platitudinous paragraph about the government's obligation to protect slaves who had been abandoned by their masters, as in the area around Beaufort, South Carolina.[8] The radical and extreme measures which were forever being proposed had not yet been adopted.

Yet these were expedients. Like President Davis, President Lincoln had to realize that what had been done so far was makeshift. The hard reality was that if the Federal government waged war to destroy a government based on slavery it could not, by any imaginable maneuver, keep the war from revolving about the fundamental concept of human freedom. This concept is dangerous; it takes fire, like phosphorus, whenever it is exposed to the air, and the war was exposing it to the winds of heaven. No disclaimer could hide the fact that a class which lived by the slavery of one group of people, on the acquiescence of another group which enjoyed personal freedom, had taken up arms to maintain its privileges. Here was the inescapable dilemma, and President Lincoln had to look at it.

He brooded on the fact, as he continued with his message to Congress.

This "insurrection," he said, was fundamentally a war on "the first principle of popular government—the rights of the people." (As the ineffable Ben Butler had pointed out, slaves somehow were people, and if they were people they had rights, from which it followed that the rights of those who were more widely recognized as people were also involved.) Somewhere, said Mr. Lincoln, far down in the struggle, there might be at stake the whole idea of a classless society in which the ordinary man was truly independent, free to rise as far as his talents and industry would take him. This ordinary man owned his own labor and he relied on it, and labor (said Mr. Lincoln, following this elusive idea) was superior to capital; it came first, and its rights deserved "much the higher consideration." A few men, owning much capital, either hired or bought men to labor for them, but they were in a minority. Most men—most men even in the slave states—neither worked for others nor had others working for them. They worked for themselves, on farms or in little shops, "taking the whole product to themselves, and asking no favors of capital on the one hand or of hired laborers or slaves on the other." Their position was not fixed. The world was open to them, and this independence was, just possibly, what finally was at stake in this war. So Mr. Lincoln had a word of warning for the free white Americans who thought that their blessings were from everlasting to everlasting: "Let them beware of surrendering a political power which they already possess, and which, if surrendered, will surely be used to close the door of advancement against such as they, and to fix new disabilities and burdens upon them, till all of liberty shall be lost."

It could not be seen very clearly, and the words which could express the things so dimly seen had to be groped for: but here in fact was the remorseless revolutionary struggle, stated as clearly as might be by a man who felt the immense values that were involved.

And Mr. Lincoln closed by saying: "The struggle of today, is not altogether for today—it is for a vast future also."[9]

Yet the future was hidden in a blinding mist. Both Richmond and Washington were reaching out for the future with uncertain hands, unable to see what they groped for, unable to know that the very act of reaching was going to create unending change. In his sketch of an ideal America where most people neither owned nor were owned, Mr. Lincoln was describing the country he knew, the magically lighted, subtly fading land of small farms and village industries, simple, uncomplicated, transitory, the breeding ground for the homeliest and loveliest of virtues. Far ahead, beyond the vision of any living man, lay Pittsburgh and Detroit, Gary and Los Angeles, the industrialized American empire with all of its greatness and infinite complications, a society in which no man could ever again be an island, something which Mr. Lincoln could neither foresee nor prevent: something endurable only if the loss of the kind of independence the President was talking about could be accompanied by the everlasting acquisition of a moral and political freedom broad enough to preserve somehow the concept of a society in which the unattached individual was the man who really mattered.

Mr. Lincoln could no more see how this would come out of the war than Mr. Davis could see that before the war ended he himself would be calling on his government to embrace the very thing his government had gone to war to prevent—emancipation. Each President was trying to project the present into the future, and each man was compelled to do things which would send the present back into the abandoned past. Perhaps each man was haunted by a dim awareness that this might be so.

For each President had to listen to a categorical imperative: "Get on with the war." This could not be escaped. This made each man a prisoner. The time of preparation was over, and now the war itself, with its imperious demands on all Americans, was about to take charge.

The Attorney General of the United States, the same Edward Bates who had contested with Mr. Lincoln for the Republican presidential nomination early in the summer of 1860, closed this year's entries in his diary on December 31 by lamenting the slowness of Federal military movements. Enormous efforts, Mr. Bates believed, were being made, and great battles undoubtedly were about to take place, yet there seemed to be no central direction; Mr. Bates recalled that he had recently warned Mr. Lincoln that it was time for the President to take effective control.

"I insisted," wrote Mr. Bates, "that being 'Commander in Chief' by law, he *must* command—especially in such a war as this. . . . If I were President, I *would* command *in chief*—not in detail, certainly—and I would know what army I had, and what the high generals (my Lieutenants) were doing with that army."[10]

At about the same time Judge David Davis, out in Illinois, got a letter from a friend in Washington who had been digesting the President's message and who felt that it was not nearly belligerent enough. Things around the capital, said this man, looked and felt much as they had just before Bull Run, with the same desperate eagerness for action raising war's demands to an unendurable pitch: "There is springing up again both in Congress & the country a good deal of restlessness & impatience, at the apparent inactivity of the immense army we have in the field. And you need not be at all surprised if there should be in a very short time another tremendous 'On to Richmond' cry."[11]

Always there was the Army, growing larger, covering the fields and roads all about Washington, moving toward no one knew quite what, looking for a definition of what it would soon be doing. People who saw its moving columns on the march were stirred by feelings that clamored to be put into words, and a woman who had seen these parading battalions sat by her hotel window early one morning and got some of the words down on paper. She wrote about a fiery gospel writ in burnished rows of steel, of the trampling out of the winepress of the Almighty, of the terrible swift sword which was flashing a fateful lightning, and it seemed to her that God was on the march . . . marching on through the cloud that hung over Presidents, soldiers, and all the people everywhere.

6: *The Want of Success*

As the old year ended Mr. Greeley's *Tribune* remarked that Washington was dirty, sickly, and possibly done for. Streets and alleys were "reeking," deep with mud and other matters. The army was very slow about removing the dead horses and mules which littered the encircling camps, typhoid fever was common not merely with the military but in the homes of the wealthy—even General McClellan had come down with the disease, bringing strategy to a standstill—and it struck the editor that if Congress did not quickly get things cleaned up "then typhus, and not Beauregard, will ere long force the Government and the inhabitants generally to abandon the doomed city."[1]

Mr. Greeley, to be sure, was the most mercurial editor in the history of American journalism, alternating between soaring enthusiasm and the most abysmal panic, and the year seemed to be opening brightly enough. New Year's Day, in 1862 as always, saw a big reception at the White House. Cabinet members and Justices of the Supreme Court attended, and Secretary Seward's daughter Fanny saw Mrs. Lincoln as "a compact little woman with a full round face," noted that she wore "a black silk, or brocade, with purple clusters on it," and discovered happily that the first lady was most cordial. The foreign diplomats were present, all a-glitter in bright uniforms, and they were followed by a great many Army and Navy officers, also in full regalia. When these eminent folk left the police opened the gates to the general public and an immense throng came in. Senator Orville Browning discovered when the crush subsided that his pocket had been picked and that he was out between $50 and $100 in gold, and Attorney General Bates wrote that the people were "overwhelming the poor fatigued President."[2]

The attorney general was not alone in feeling that Mr. Lincoln was carrying a heavy load. Some weeks earlier Mr. Russell of the London *Times* had gained the same impression. Mr. Russell went around one evening to see General McClellan and was told that the general, being tired, had gone to bed and would see no one; he learned that a night or two before this the same message had been given to the President, who had dropped in to discuss the war with his general-in-chief, and when he reflected on the load the President was carrying the newspaperman saw something both ludicrous and pathetic in the man's plight. "This poor President!" he mused. "He is to be pitied; surrounded by such scenes, and trying with all his might to understand strategy, naval warfare, big guns, the movements of troops, military maps, reconnaissances, occupations, interior and exterior lines, and all the technical details of the art of slaying." Mr. Lincoln, he reflected, was compelled to run "from one house to another, armed with plans, papers, reports, recommendations, sometimes good-humored, never angry, occasionally dejected, and always a little fussy." It involved a great deal of lost motion, and at times the President seemed a figure of fun, but it occurred to Mr. Russell that there had been Presidents who looked more dignified but somehow accomplished a good deal less.[3]

The war was moving, and Mr. Lincoln felt that the men whom he had appointed to direct it ought to be moving with it. This they were not doing. General McClellan could hardly be blamed for contracting typhoid fever, but the fact remained that he had been general-in-chief for two months and the Federal war effort was still going by piecemeal. In Missouri, General Halleck was methodically restoring order to the administrative chaos left by General Frémont, but if he had any plans for waging vigorous war no one knew what they were, least of all General Buell, who commanded in Kentucky and who would inevitably be concerned in any offensive General Halleck might undertake. General Buell, in his turn, was as busy as a man could be making preparations, but he did not seem ready to do anything and neither Mr. Lincoln nor McClellan himself had been able to persuade him that there was any merit in the plan to invade eastern Tennessee. Almost desperately, Mr. Lincoln had written to Halleck and Buell, asking them if they were "in concert"; each man had replied, in effect, that he had no idea what the other man was doing. General Buell added that he supposed

General McClellan would look after all of this, and General Halleck warned the President that "too much haste will ruin everything"; and Mr. Lincoln found as the New Year began that he was running three separate wars—in Missouri, in Kentucky, and in Virginia—and that there was no apparent connection between any two of the three.[4]

Missouri and Kentucky were a long way off, to be sure, but Virginia was right under the President's eyes. It was the showcase, watched by Congress and the press and the country, and although the Army of the Potomac had grown large and had begun to look and feel like a real army, displaying excellent drill and high morale in an endless series of colorful reviews, the fact remained that it was not actually doing anything. The worst part of this was that although the army was inactive a good charter for action seemed to exist, and action by this charter had been promised. The promise, unhappily, had never been fulfilled.

Early in November, General McClellan had assured Secretary Chase that he planned a bold swift movement. He would (he said) move 50,000 men to Urbanna, a little town near the mouth of the Rappahannock River some fifty miles east of Richmond. Once this advance was made, the general went on, he would send 50,000 more men to the same place, and with the two forces combined he would march west and capture Richmond before the Confederate Army around Manassas could get back to defend the place. Inasmuch as Mr. Chase was Secretary of the Treasury and the financial problem was massive, General McClellan asked how soon this advance ought to be made. Chase told him that "I could get along under existing arrangements until about the middle of February," and McClellan assured him that there was no problem; the whole thing would be done by February 1.

This was not just a scheme airily expounded to soothe a cabinet minister. Early in December, McClellan discussed the project soberly with Brigadier General J. G. Barnard, chief of engineers, and Barnard offered a couple of ideas for his consideration. It would take a good deal of time, said Barnard, to move the big army down the Chesapeake Bay by water, and Joe Johnston might very well slip in and capture Washington while the move was being made. Since Washington must be protected no matter what happened, it would thus be necessary to leave at least 100,000 men in the lines around the capital. Furthermore, this water-borne campaign against Richmond necessarily involved as a first step the capture of Norfolk. If McClellan was going to move via Urbanna the operation against Norfolk should be begun at once.

. . . thus General Barnard. The whole business was most interesting, but the fact remained that nothing whatever had come of any of it. What McClellan had said would be done by February 1 was not being done and nobody was preparing to do it, and it was beginning to be clear that it was not just the attack of typhoid fever—which, fortunately, was rather a mild case—that was causing the delay.[5]

There were men in Congress who were starting to complain bitterly, and they were men to whom a Republican President was obliged to listen. The Army was immobilized, these men were saying, because the men who could order it to move did not have their hearts in their work. The professional leadership of the Army must be at fault. In the Senate, Lyman Trumbull opposed a bill to increase the number of cadets at West Point, asserting bluntly: "I believe that it is owing to the West Point Academy that this war has languished as it has," and in the House, Owen Lovejoy cried that "we are afraid that we shall hurt somebody if we fight; that we shall get these rebels and traitors so exasperated that they will not return to their loyalty."[6] It was of course true that Mr. Lovejoy was a whole-souled abolitionist, and hence in a minority, but it was also true that more and more men were beginning to value zeal for the cause above professional competence. (The Senate by a vote of 25 to 12 killed the bill to enlarge the cadet corps.) Furthermore, the demand for hard blows struck quickly and vigorously was increasingly being coupled with a demand that the war be directed against slavery as well as against disunion. Grim Thaddeus Stevens, Republican leader in the House, called on the administration to recognize the magnitude of the crisis and to realize that "this is an internecine war in which one party or the other must be reduced to hopeless feebleness." The Federal power could never win such a war, he declared, until it got a revolutionary determination inspired by "the grand idea of liberty, equality and the rights of man." As things stood, "we feel that while we are fighting for a compact we are fighting to rivet still stronger the chains of slavery." Give to each general, he urged, a sword for one hand and "the book of freedom" for the other, and the army would soon "sweep despotism and rebellion from every corner of this continent."[7]

The President still saw the war as a fight to restore the Union, and he wanted to keep it that way. The most important fact about such a war, however, was that it had to be won, and the President was being forced to see that it had better be won quickly. If the professionals could do this for him, well and good. If they could not, men like Stevens were giving clear warning that the remorseless revolutionary struggle (against which Lincoln had warned, in his message to Congress) would soon become a reality. The professional might indeed find the book of freedom a troublesome bit of baggage, but it would be thrust into his hand if he did not win without it. Abraham Lincoln knew no more of military matters than any other small-town lawyer, and his efforts to educate himself were (as Mr. Russell had observed) both frantic and ungainly; but he could see that he would win no war unless the massive power of the Federal government could be brought to the points of contact and unflinchingly applied, and early in January he tried to get some action.

McClellan was sick and could not be consulted. The President had written to Halleck and Buell, urging that they join hands and break Sidney Johnston's line, getting in return from each man the bland confession that there were not even the haziest of plans for co-operation. Halleck went so far as to read the President a little lecture on the military art, pointing out that if he and Buell tried to mount simultaneous offensives they would simply be operating on exterior lines against a centrally placed enemy, a thing which "is condemned by every military authority I have ever read." On this letter the President wrote: "It is exceedingly discouraging. As everywhere else, nothing can be done."[8]

What followed was both pointless and odd, testifying to nothing except the President's desperation.

On the night of January 10, Mr. Lincoln held a White House meeting, talking to General Irvin McDowell, who in a way was McClellan's second-in-command in the Army of the Potomac, and to General William B. Franklin, a sober regular who commanded one of the divisions in that army; inviting also Secretary Seward, Secretary Chase, and the Assistant Secretary of War, Mr. Thomas Scott. Mr. Lincoln bluntly admitted that he had to do something—he at least had to talk to somebody—and he remarked quaintly that if General McClellan, sick or well, did not plan to use the army right away he would like to borrow it, provided he could find out what ought to be done with it. The two generals, subordinates of the absent McClellan but answerable also to the President, seem to have been more or less embarrassed: understandably enough, since in the history of the Republic no White House conference quite like this one was ever held, before or since.

They made constrained suggestions: flank Joe Johnston out of Manassas, take the army down to York River to move on Richmond direct, organize the troops into regular army corps for better ease of movement, assemble a siege train, get water transportation lined up, and so on; and the Quartermaster Corps was asked how long it would take to get the steamboats ready. (Quartermaster General Montgomery Meigs reported that it would take quite a time—four to six weeks, at the least.) Mr. Seward remarked that the important thing was to win a victory, and a victory at Manassas would be just as good as one on York River; and after this had gone on through three meetings McClellan himself got wind of it, found that he was well enough to attend conferences, and showed up at last, pale, still rather weak, full of dignity and reserve, casting a spell on his subordinates. Mr. Lincoln said that if the general-in-chief could function once more he himself would be glad to let go of the controls, and when Secretary Chase applied pressure McClellan said that he had a plan and a time schedule but that he would prefer not to talk about them at a meeting as large and (though he did not say it quite this way) as disorganized as this one. The business flickered out, finally, with the President saying that he would adjourn the meeting. Everyone's feathers had been ruffled and nothing much had been done, and the President went back to letter-writing.

On January 13, the final day of this unique series of conferences, Mr. Lincoln wrote to Halleck and Buell, trying to tell them what his notions of strategy were. He pointed out that he was giving no orders; these would come (no doubt) from McClellan; he was just trying to show how his mind was working.

"I state my general idea of this war to be that we have the *greater* numbers, and the enemy has the *greater* facility of concentrating forces upon points of collision," he wrote; "that we must fail, unless we can find some way of making *our* advantage an overmatch for his; and that this can only be done by menacing him with superior forces at *different* points, at the *same* time; so that we can safely attack, one, or both, if he makes no change; and if he *weakens* one to *strengthen* the other, forbear to attack the strengthened one, but seize and hold the weakened one, gaining so much."[9]

What the two generals thought of this is not on record, but the fact remains that Mr. Lincoln had been doing his homework. He had got, after nine months of war, a good grasp of the basic strategic principle that would have to guide him, and although nobody in Richmond saw his letter it got a strange, corroborative echo from that city in the very week that he wrote it.

There were anxious men in Richmond as well as in Washington this winter, the cause of the anxiety being not so much the inaction of generals as the strange conduct of state governors. Federal operations along the exposed Atlantic coast had created much alarm, and governors of seacoast states were demanding that weapons and men which had been sent to the Virginia theater be returned at once so that the coast could be defended. This impressed Jefferson Davis as a recipe for certain disaster, and Attorney General Bragg wrote in his diary: "The President was much irritated and declared if such was to be the course of the States toward the Government the carrying on of the war was an impossibility—that we had better make terms as soon as we could, and those of us who had halters around our necks had better get out of the Country as speedily as possible." Mr. Bragg added that the President seemed even gloomier now than he had been in December, and he remarked wistfully: "I wish he was dictator."

It seemed to Mr. Bragg that the Confederacy had been saved, so far, only because the Federal government did not press its advantages—"we profit more from their blunders and want of spirit to use the great advantages they have, than from our own feeble means and good conduct"—but he did not think this was going to go on much longer, and he confessed: "The plan of the enemy seems to be to attack us at many points simultaneously and thus preventing our sending aid to any given point, they outnumbering us at every point of attack. If they now fail, they can hardly make another such effort— But will they fail? or if they partially succeed now, what is to be the effect? It is vain to disguise the fact that we are in imminent peril. . . . A few days *may* decide our fate. God be with us and help us—"[10]

Like President Lincoln, Mr. Bragg lacked a military education. But he did know what could defeat the Confederacy, and he saw it precisely as Mr. Lincoln saw it. What he feared most was what Mr. Lincoln was trying to get his generals to do, and if neither General Buell nor General Halleck could quite get the President's point Mr. Bragg would have got it perfectly. What Mr. Lincoln had said he had said, using slightly different words.

The two men knew what they were talking about. The Federal government had at last reached the point where it could apply an unendurable pressure. At Hampton Roads it had assembled a strong amphibious expedition—15,000 soldiers on transports, with assorted gunboats to lead the way—and just when General McClellan's subordinates were trying to explain what might be done with the Army of the Potomac this expedition sailed out past the Virginia Capes, bound for Hatteras Inlet. It would enter the North Carolina sounds, break up Confederate installations there, occupy the mainland and repeat the Port Royal thrust at a point much closer to the Confederate capital. At the same time an even stronger expedition was being made ready to attack New Orleans itself, largest city in all the South, and the foundries at Pittsburgh were casting a score of big mortars and 30,000 shells to batter in the forts which defended that place; and on January 20 a wiry, elderly naval officer, Flag Officer David Glasgow Farragut, was given his orders for this force. Finally, parts of the western armies were on the move at last. A division of Buell's troops under General George Thomas was laboriously marching along the muddy Kentucky roads, through cold rains, to attack Confederate Zollicoffer's force which anchored the eastern end of Sidney Johnston's undermanned defensive line. General Grant, at the same time, was moving south from Cairo to menace the western end of that line, while Federal gunboats were prowling up the Tennessee River to see whether Confederate defenses there were as strong as they were supposed to be. (They would discover that they were not, and much would come of the discovery.) Slowly but surely the war was getting off of dead center.

As a matter of fact, the Federal government had been losing less time than ardent patriots supposed. What was being lost was more serious: understanding between the civilians who were running the government and the professional soldiers who were running the government's armies. The notion that the civilians should leave military matters to military men was dissolving. With this there was the beginning of a corrosive suspicion: might it not be that a general who moved slowly or ineffectively was not so much incompetent as disloyal? The professionals were being isolated and they were feeling their isolation; the messages they got from Washington were beginning to look like outrageous interference on the part of the politicians (who were responsible for all failures), and it would presently be easy for generals in their turn to question the motives of the men from whom their orders came. On January 20, General Halleck spoke his mind in a letter to General McClellan.

Writing as one professional to another, General Halleck said that the war so far had been conducted "upon what may be called pepperbox strategy." As he had tried to explain to President Lincoln, Federal forces were out on the rim of a circle and the Confederates were inside the circle: "We cannot expect to strike any great blow, for he can concentrate his forces on any one point sooner than we can ours." And the general voiced his lament: "I take it for granted, general, that what has heretofore been done has been the result of political policy rather than military strategy, and that the want of success on our part is attributable to the politicians rather than to the generals."[11]

Like everyone else General Halleck was feeling frustrated, which led him to see things as they were not. The Federal government had lost certain battles, to be sure, but it had won advantages that were of vast importance. Missouri and western Virginia had been gained, the border was in hand, the southern seacoast had been broken open and was about to be broken still further; and General Halleck and General Buell, bedeviled by a politically minded President, were at last being driven to begin the operations that would open the Mississippi Valley and push the Confederate frontier down below the southern border of Tennessee. The political policy which General Halleck was deriding was in fact justifying itself. Out on the rim, the Federals were starting to do exactly what Mr. Bragg was afraid they would do—put the heat on in so many places that the weaker power could not successfully resist. Albert Sidney Johnston was viewing the Federal war effort as a methodical preparation "to carry on the war against the Confederacy with a purpose as inflexible as malignant," and he could see no hope except to "convert our country into one vast camp of instruction for the field of every man able to bear arms." Just before the end of the year 1861 he had notified the Governor of Tennessee that to defend the vital center of his line he could count on hardly more than 17,000 men.[12]

As professionals, Mr. Lincoln's generals were falling short in their own field of competence; they were failing to see that they had gained a great advantage and that it was supremely important to press the advantage while it still existed. On top of this they were quite unable to realize that the political reasons for energetic action were irresistible. General McClellan had been helped into his position as general-in-chief by the very men who now were most insistent on action; he had taken office, in short, on the implicit understanding that he would make things happen quickly. In addition, the war was not being fought in a vacuum. There was Europe to think about.

The administration right now was being warned that British intervention—so narrowly averted by the settlement of the Trent affair—was highly probable unless the North began to win decisive victories.

From London, Mr. Adams had written early in January that "one clear victory at home might save us a foreign war," and on January 24 he amplified the warning in a letter to Secretary Seward: "I will venture to say that the course of events in America during the next six weeks must in great measure determine the future of the Government of the United States. For it is they and they only which can control the manner in which foreign nations will make up their minds hereafter to consider them. And in this sense the absence of action will be almost equally decisive." From far-off St. Petersburg, Minister Cassius Clay wrote that Prince Gortchakoff had warned him that a decisive reverse would quickly lead England to make common cause with the South, and he said: "Nothing but quick and effective success will save us from foreign enemies." Washington, Mr. Clay concluded, ought to prepare for war with England "as an inevitable result of any reverses which would prevent a subjection of the South before the 1st of April next."[13]

That these diplomats may have been taking too dark a view is beside the point. This was the advice Mr. Lincoln was getting, and if he was impatient with generals reluctant to strike hard and quickly there was reason for it. Back of his clumsy White House conferences and his almost frantic messages to the generals in the west lay the conviction that time was running out. The government could win the war if it struck immediately. If it did not, the future was all but unimaginable.

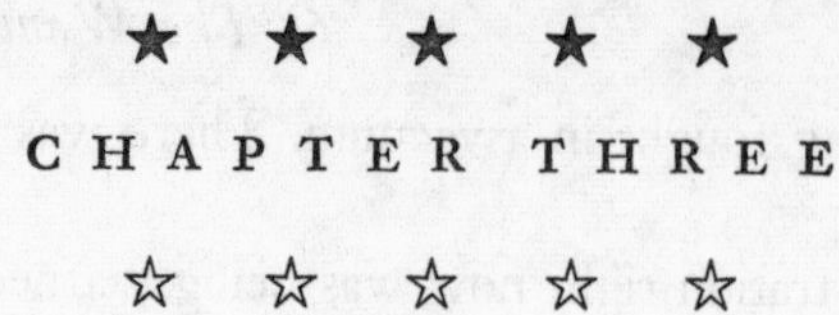

The Military Paradox

1: *Decision in Kentucky*

A year later the march could have been made in half the time, with a third of the equipment. Now the soldiers were learning their trade, and they gained wisdom by doing things the hard way. When General Thomas marched his division out of its camp at Lebanon, Kentucky, to go down to the Cumberland River and attack General Zollicoffer's Confederates, he had nearly one hundred miles to go; the way went roundabout through the hills, and as the cold January rains continued the roads grew very bad indeed so that the little army moved at a crawl. General Thomas had some 5000 men in his column, each regiment had thirteen baggage wagons, the mud was axle-deep, and the march went on for more than two weeks—it took eight days to cover the last forty miles. Boys who had not yet been hardened to march and sleep in the winter rain fell sick, many of them died, many more were sent home with medical discharges; an officer in the 2nd Minnesota estimated after the war that this march cost the army 20 per cent of its numbers.[1] But the men who were not sick kept on going, and, shortly after the middle of January, Thomas had his troops in camp near Logan's Cross Roads, ready for battle.

Zollicoffer's Confederates were camped on the north side of the Cumberland, six or eight miles away, in a bad spot—a swollen river at their backs and the enemy in their front, no room to maneuver, no good way to retreat if things went badly. More than a month earlier General Zollicoffer, who had been guarding Cumberland Gap seventy miles to the southeast, had moved up to the town of Mill

Springs, safely south of the river, so that he could keep an eye on the Federals, whom he suspected of planning to march into eastern Tennessee. Being both zealous and inexperienced he had ignored General Johnston's warning and had come north of the river, and when Richmond, worried by this move, sent Major General George B. Crittenden down to take top command Zollicoffer talked him into holding the exposed position now threatened by the Federals.

Crittenden was a West Pointer, who had fought for Texas in the days of the Lone Star Republic, had served in the Mexican War and had campaigned against the Indians on the frontier; a good man who had made a good record but who did not, in this month of January, have any luck at all. He was son of the famous John J. Crittenden, who had tried to work out a compromise to avert war just a year ago, and his younger brother, Thomas Crittenden, was now a brigadier general in the Union Army; the divided sentiments which tore Kentucky apart had split the compromiser's own family. As the Federals neared Logan's Cross Roads, Crittenden planned to stay where he was and await attack, but the unending rains led him to change his mind. A Union division under Brigadier General Albin Schoepf was known to be posted at no great distance from Logan's Cross Roads, on the far side of a stream known as Fishing Creek, and it seemed likely that the rains would have made this stream impassable, so Crittenden concluded to move out and smash General Thomas while Schoepf was immobilized. In the pre-midnight blackness of the night of January 18 he and Zollicoffer got their men into column and moved forward to make a surprise attack at dawn.

It was a bad night to march with inexperienced troops. The roads were almost impossible, the artillery got hopelessly mired down, and the infantry floundered inexpertly along in the downpour, moving with nightmare slowness. It was daylight before the advance guard stumbled up to the Yankee picket line, and only two Confederate regiments were on hand, the rest being far behind. No surprise was possible; the advance regiments got into line of battle as best they could (while the Federal drums beat Thomas's sleeping men out of their bivouacs) and the battle began.

Right at first, the Federals gave ground. But Thomas was able to get his men into position quickly, and a great many of the Confederates were armed with old-fashioned flintlock muskets which could not be fired in the rain; and just as the battle became general, Zollicoffer was killed. (Pathetically nearsighted, he had ridden up to a Union regiment under the impression that it was one of his own, and he was shot dead before he could get away.) News of his death demoralized the Confederates, whose spirits had been badly dampened anyway by the miserable night march, and just then Thomas struck with a massive counterattack. The Confederates resisted briefly, then broke and ran for it, with the Federals in full pursuit. By midday, Crittenden's army simply dissolved. Most of the fugitives managed to get back across the river, but they had to abandon their artillery, their wounded, their camp with all of its supplies, their wagon train, and the body of the lamented Zollicoffer. For the immediate future this army was out of existence, and when the depressing news reached Tennessee the unhappy Crittenden found that he was being blamed for everything. It was charged that he had been drunk, which was not true at all, and his reputation, like his army, evaporated.[2]

It had been a small battle, as such things went—each side probably brought about 4000 men to the field—but it was of much importance. The right end of Albert Sidney Johnston's line had been destroyed, once and for all; the actual casualty list had not been excessive, but for the time being at least he had lost 4000 men whom he could by no means afford to lose, and as a Tennessee patriot wrote to Mr. Davis, "there is now no impediment whatever but bad roads and natural obstacles to prevent the enemy from entering East Tennessee and destroying the railroads and putting East Tennessee in a flame of revolution."[3] For future reference, too, it might have been noted that General George Thomas, who looked so ponderous, could strike swiftly and powerfully once battle had been joined. His whole campaign, as a matter of fact, had been well handled, despite the wastage of the hard march down from Lebanon. Far from Washington, the Union Army had come up with one very solid soldier.

So the North had something to cheer about, and from the War

Department there came a formal note of congratulation, issued, "by order of the President," by the Secretary of War, praising the troops for their courage and fidelity and going on to underline the moral: "The purpose of the war is to attack, pursue and destroy a rebellious enemy, and to deliver the country from danger menaced by traitors. Alacrity, daring, courageous spirit and patriotic zeal on all occasions, and under every circumstance, are expected from the Army of the United States."[4] This of course was routine. What made the bulletin notable was the name signed at the bottom: Edwin M. Stanton, Secretary of War.

Mr. Lincoln had made the first change in his cabinet. Simon Cameron was out: Cameron, with the unhappy reputation and the face of a sad, rather sensitive fox, who had pressured his way into the cabinet and now was pressured out by the intolerable demands of war. His departure surprised no one and apparently pleased everybody except Cameron himself. Richard Henry Dana, Jr., wrote that "the relief of getting rid of Cameron is unspeakable," and predicted that the stock market would go up. Thaddeus Stevens, who had feuded with Cameron for years and had a low opinion of the man's integrity, grunted sardonically when he learned that Cameron was to be the new Minister to Russia, and remarked: "Send word to the Czar to bring in his things of nights."[5]

Cameron's trouble was much like the trouble that had befallen General Frémont in Missouri. He had been responsible for the spending of enormous sums of money, under circumstances which made it inevitable that there would be a good deal of graft, and he had neither the administrative ability to run the business efficiently nor the personal standing that would induce people to overlook the inevitable wastage and corruption. As a matter of fact the huge new armies were by now fairly well supplied and armed, and the flagrant abuses in purchasing (which Congress had already started to look into) apparently never enriched Cameron personally; but it had been obvious for some time that if the government proposed to win the war it had better get a new head for the War Department, and Cameron's last-minute attempt to win abolitionist support by urging the use of Negro troops had done no more than harden Mr. Lincoln's determination to replace him.[6] Now Stanton was in his place, his appointment confirmed by the Senate on January 15.

Stanton brought to the War Department everything Cameron lacked—executive ability of a high order, much driving energy, a hound dog's nose for tracking down irregularities and a furious insistence on removing them when they had been found. He was rude, dictatorial, abusive, a man who could be outrageously blunt and incomprehensibly devious at the same time. When he chose to be (which was not often) he could be charming. Fanny Seward felt that he had a cheery manner, a merry twinkle in his eye and an air of hearty warmth, and Charles A. Dana, the newspaper editor who later would become an assistant secretary of war, wrote that "Stanton had the loveliest smile I ever saw on a human face" and felt that he was most companionable.[7] Not many people saw him this way, and before the winter was out there would be many who felt that they had been profoundly deceived by him.

Among these would be General McClellan. When Stanton took office McClellan considered him one of his best friends. Stanton went around to see McClellan the day his appointment as Secretary of War was announced, saying that if he took the job it would be solely on McClellan's account: Did McClellan want him to take it? McClellan assured him that he did, writing to his friend S. L. M. Barlow that "Stanton's appointment was a most unexpected piece of good fortune," and Barlow in turn assured Stanton that "nothing since the war began with the exception of your appointment & that of General McClellan has seemed to me to be *right*."[8] During the fall, when the struggle to replace Scott was going on, McClellan had found Stanton his most trusted counselor. Once, when President Lincoln was more than usually a burden to him, McClellan wrote that he had taken refuge in Stanton's house "to dodge all enemies in the shape of 'browsing' Presidents, etc." At that time the general felt that the most unfortunate thing about Stanton was "the extreme virulence with which he abused the President"; he never spoke of him, McClellan said, except as "the original gorilla."

In other words, Stanton was typed as a good conservative Democrat, taking office at a time when the abolitionists badly needed curbing. In December, Barlow had written to him, predicting that "the whole abolition pack" would soon be snapping at McClellan's heels and remarking that this might be just as well; sooner or later the Democrats, the reasonable and responsible men who could fight for the Union without running a fever over slavery, would have to take control of the government's war policy, and the more rapidly the abolitionists discredited themselves, the better off everyone would be. Ward Hill Lamon, the good friend whom Lincoln had made marshal of the District of Columbia, feared that the anti-slavery faction would presently be attacking the President, and to a friend back home he was writing dolefully: "I wish you and some other honest men from Illinois would come here and go with me away down on the banks of the old Potomac and there sit down on a moss covered log and help me God Damn these Abolitionists—for if they ever get hold of the reins of this Govt the Govt is gone to Hell by a very large majority."[9]

What Stanton might have done if he had entered the war at a quieter time is an open question. He did come in, however, just when the hinges were turning. His temper fitted the requirements of the moment: he would be a dynamic Secretary of War, and he would begin by setting a new pace for his old friend General McClellan.

Journalist Donn Piatt, an intimate of Stanton, asserted after the war that he talked with the new Secretary at the time of the appointment and asked him what he was going to do in his new job. "Do?" cried Stanton. "I intend to accomplish three things. I will make Abe Lincoln President of the United States. I will force this man McClellan to fight or throw up; and last but not least I will pick Lorenzo Thomas up with a pair of tongs and drop him from the nearest window." (Lorenzo Thomas was Adjutant General of the Army, a crusty old paper-shuffler who was widely considered a substantial handicap to the war effort. Oddly enough, he turned out to be Stanton-proof; he never was removed, serving in his high position to the end of the war and beyond.) Piatt's understanding of the declaration, "I will make Abe Lincoln President" was that the new Secretary intended to teach all generals that they were subject to the orders of the civil authorities. The President was commander-in-chief: this, the Army must understand, was a statement to be taken literally.[10]

It would be taken literally, to begin with, by the President himself, and before long this was made clear.

Whether on Stanton's urging, on someone else's, or on his own initiative, Mr. Lincoln on January 27 issued a strange, comprehensive and rather baffling paper which bore the heading, "President's General War Order No. One." It began: "Ordered that the 22nd. day of February 1862, be the day for a general movement of the Land and Naval forces of the United States against the insurgent forces." It directed that the armies in Virginia, in western Virginia, in Kentucky and in Illinois, along with the gunboat flotilla on the Mississippi, be ready to move on that day, and that all other contingents stand by in a condition of expectant readiness; and it specified that the general-in-chief and all of his subordinates "will severally be held to their strict and full responsibilities, for the prompt execution of this order." A supplementary order, four days later, said that the Army of the Potomac would march down to cut the railroad southwest of Manassas Junction.[11]

On the surface, this accomplished nothing whatever. When February 22 came the various armies went on doing just what they had been doing before, even (in some cases) to the point of continuing to do nothing at all. It is possible that the order was not really intended to get specific action. It was a goad for the sluggish and a warning to the heedless, it reflected Secretary Stanton's belief that "the armies must move or the Government perish," and it was a reminder that the threads of power ran finally to the White House.[12] In any case, it quickly drew from General McClellan a detailed, carefully reasoned statement of his own immediate plans. On the final day of January, McClellan signed a lengthy letter to Secretary Stanton, telling the Secretary and the President exactly what he proposed to do and how he proposed to do it.

He began by arguing vigorously against the movement on Joe Johnston's position at Manassas Junction. He reverted to the Urbanna plan, and he projected this with a wealth of detail which showed that the idea had been getting some careful study. In substance, McClellan wanted to flank the Rebels out of northern Virginia and to carry the war at once to the region of the Confederate capital. This thrust would be co-ordinated with advances by Buell and Halleck in the west; further, McClellan saw all of these steps, in Virginia and in Kentucky alike, as parts of a great encircling movement by which the Confederacy would be hemmed in and constricted by a huge crescent, going counterclockwise all the way from Port Royal around to New Orleans. In each segment of this crescent the Federals would be on the offensive.[13]

It was a solid program, not altogether unlike the essence of old General Scott's Anaconda Plan, if anyone had stopped to think about it; surprisingly in harmony with the strategic concept which Mr. Lincoln had tried so vainly to impress on General Buell and General Halleck; and General McClellan presented it persuasively and with much clarity. In the end the general would have his way; that is, he would take the water route when he moved against Richmond, although he would find it necessary first to make at least a token advance toward Manassas Junction. But in presenting this paper he had in effect endorsed the demand that the Army of the Potomac move at once. He had outlined a program which called for concerted movements, and in the west the movements were already under way. Any army which lagged would call attention to itself in the most unmistakable way. Henceforward all generals were apt to be judged by comparison with the one who had the most energy.

When Thomas won his fight at Logan's Cross Roads the era of static warfare came to an end, and if the point was still missed in Washington it was visible from end to end of Kentucky. Farther west, while Thomas was making his campaign, the Federals had confirmed their earlier suspicions that there was a soft spot in the Confederate line, where the Cumberland and Tennessee Rivers came north across the Kentucky-Tennessee border, and this soft spot demanded attack: an attack which was also demanded by the men who had discovered it and who must eventually do the fighting, General Grant and the rugged sailor who represented the salt-water navy on the rivers of the Middle West, Flag Officer Andrew Foote. Even Halleck had seen it; he had written to Washington about it, and just as McClellan was signing the excellent letter which called for concerted action Halleck was telling Grant and Foote to start up the Tennessee and do the things they had said they could do. In mid-January McClellan had warned Buell, "You have no idea of the pressure brought to bear here upon the Government for a forward movement." Now the pressure was being wondrously intensified, and McClellan himself was the man who would feel it first.[14]

War Department thinking abruptly changed: evidenced by a singular trip through the Middle West made at the end of January by Assistant Secretary of War Scott.

Scott was an old crony of Cameron's, and as vice-president of the Pennsylvania Railroad had been associated with Cameron in railroad operations. On this western trip he devoted himself to a study of the way in which a major part of the Army of the Potomac could be moved to Kentucky and used to complete the smashing of General Johnston's line there. This project of course involved a complete reversal of all plans for an offensive in Virginia, and it was clearly worked out on Stanton's orders and with at least the passive approval of General McClellan. On February 1, Scott sent Stanton his preliminary findings. By combining the rolling stock of four railroads, he said, it would be possible to send soldiers from Washington to Pittsburgh at the rate of 15,000 men a day. Within six days, 60,000 men and their equipment—artillery, cavalry, baggage, tents, munitions, and rations—could be placed on the Ohio River somewhere west of Pittsburgh. Next day he amplified it: in just over five days, using steamboats for the journey west of Pittsburgh, the army could be deposited at Covington, Kentucky, across the river from Cincinnati. As a railroad man, Scott had worked out the logistics with much care. He had talked to the Middle Western governors, and he had also discussed the business with General Buell, whom he considered "a very superior officer—calm, prudent and with great power to control."

Buell told Scott that a column of "from 30 to 50,000 good soldiers from the Army of the Potomac" would enable the Federals to take and hold a good position between the Tennessee and Cumberland Rivers at a point which would cut the railroad line connecting

Johnston's central position at Bowling Green with the Mississippi River stronghold at Columbus, Kentucky. Once this was done, Buell could destroy the Confederates at Bowling Green while Halleck disposed of the Rebel force at Columbus; meanwhile the Potomac column could advance up the rivers, Nashville could be occupied, and "with Nashville for a base of operations the so-called Southern Confederacy could be effectually divided, and with reasonable facilities our armies could soon be able to accomplish great work south and east of that center."[15]

McClellan was interested. His friend Barlow warned him, on February 8, that Stanton definitely felt that McClellan ought to go to Kentucky, "*if* there is to be action there & none for the present in Va."; it was Barlow's belief that Stanton wanted McClellan to distinguish himself before the abolitionists pushed some other general into the limelight. Stanton told Scott that he had not really been able to impress the importance of the move on McClellan, but he hoped the man would come around before long; and McClellan was definitely warming up to the idea. Apparently early in February, McClellan wrote to Stanton: "Have you anything from Scott as to the means we can command in the way of moving troops westward by rail & water. My mind is more & more tending in that direction, tho' not fully committed to it. But there should be no delay in ascertaining precisely *what we can do* should it become advisable to move in that direction. Please put the machinery in motion to ascertain exactly how many troops we can move per diem to Kentucky, how many days the transit would occupy, etc. Should we change the line I would wish to take about 70,000 infantry, 250 guns, 2500 cavalry—at least 3 bridge trains." The words "I would wish to take" indicate clearly that McClellan was thinking of going west in person.[16]

The project hung in the air for a short time and then dissolved and was heard of no more. It dissolved because it suddenly became unnecessary, and for the best of reasons: someone else had already done what was being planned so elaborately. On the day when Scott talked with Buell about the great things that could be done if a Federal army moved up the rivers and cut the Columbus-Bowling Green railway line, General Grant and Flag Officer Foote captured Fort

Henry, the Confederacy's sole stronghold on the Tennessee, and Grant notified Halleck that he would move twelve miles cross country and take the Rebel fort at Dover, on the Cumberland. As an immediate result, Albert Sidney Johnston ordered his subordinates to prepare for the evacuation of both Bowling Green and Columbus. Before the month was out he would move to regroup his outnumbered forces in the state of Mississippi, just below the southern border of Tennessee.

2: *Unconditional Surrender*

A Belgian who traveled across Kentucky at the end of 1861 wrote that the Confederates who held Albert Sidney Johnston's line were fantastic. They had nothing much in the way of uniforms, their weapons were antiquated, it was hard to tell officers from privates and equally hard to tell soldiers from civilians, and the visitor shuddered when he looked at these characters who brandished "their frightful knives" and who went about uncombed, unshaven, and unwashed. It seemed to the Belgian's orderly European soul that they belonged to "a state of society but little to be desired," and in their camps he saw more sickness and less discipline than he had seen among the Federals; yet somehow the men looked dangerous, for "their determination is truly extraordinary, and their hatred against the north terrible to look upon, there is something savage in it." They believed that they were fighting for their homes, their families and their own precious lives, and they might be extraordinary fighters.[1]

The capabilities of these soldiers would be shown in many battles, and they would be just as dangerous as the Belgian imagined. But in this month of January they were in a desperately bad fix and General Johnston did not quite see how he was going to get them out of it.

General Johnston saw disaster coming. From the beginning he had had too much territory to defend and too few men to defend it with, and now the pay-off was at hand. Late in January he had predicted that the Federals would soon attack Fort Henry and Fort Donelson and then would move on Nashville, and there was not much he could do to stop them. The two forts were unfinished and undermanned, with no more than 4000 men between them; Johnston had only 23,000 men at Bowling Green, the strong point which marked the center of his line, and he felt compelled to send 8000 of these off to the vicinity of Clarksville, where the all-important railroad from Columbus crossed the Cumberland twenty-five miles upstream from Fort Donelson. He believed that Buell, who was obviously about to take the offensive, had 80,000 men; an estimate that was only a little too high, although more than a third of Buell's men were by no means ready for action. Bowling Green was well fortified, and Johnston thought he could hold the place if Buell made a frontal assault, but there was little chance that Buell would do anything so foolish. He was much more likely to flank the Confederates out by coming up the Cumberland, and Johnston simply did not have the manpower to stop him.

The general complained, correctly, that "our people do not comprehend the magnitude of the danger that threatens," and he begged Richmond to send him more troops. This, for a variety of reasons, most of them excellent, Richmond felt quite unable to do; it did, however, send him General Beauregard, who reached Bowling Green on February 4 and learned to his amazement that General Johnston had no more than half the men Beauregard supposed he had.[2]

As always, Beauregard was preceded by a great deal of tall talk, and when the Federals heard about his new assignment they understood that he was bringing fifteen Virginia regiments of infantry with him. This, to be sure, was not the case; but the fact that this false report came on ahead of him was one of the things that triggered the Federal offensive in Kentucky. If Beauregard, who was a host in himself, was bringing strong reinforcements, it would be well to strike before the reinforcements arrived; and this was an element in the thinking that sent Grant and Foote up the rivers into Tennessee.

At this distance that thinking is rather hard to trace. General Halleck, who commanded everything west of the Cumberland, had patiently explained to President Lincoln that too much haste would be ruinous, and he was not by nature impetuous. Still, he had sent Grant and Foote out to investigate the western end of General Johnston's line, and Grant and Foote had seen weakness there and had been clamoring for action. Halleck did not especially want to act, he had a reserved opinion of General Grant (who had been typed as a rough-hewn man who drank too much) and he did not really have to listen to Foote, who was, although a naval officer, Halleck's own subordinate, responsible for certain strange auxiliaries called gunboats. But Halleck had a sensitive ear and he had heard what the President and the Secretary of War were saying, and when he learned that Beauregard was bringing reinforcements he felt that something ought to be done quickly. So he told Grant and Foote to go ahead and try their luck.

Their luck was in. Grant and Foote came up to Fort Henry on February 6 and found that the place was a sham. It was inexpertly built on low ground and the Tennessee River was in flood; the high ground across the river, which the Confederates should have fortified in the first place, was largely unoccupied, its hillsides furrowed by the beginning of trenches but wholly harmless to invaders. Grant had brought 15,000 soldiers, and he put them ashore and marched up the two sides of the river to invest the fortifications and prepare for an assault, and Foote steamed up against the current and opened a preliminary bombardment. The fort collapsed almost at the first touch. Its commanding officer, Brigadier General Lloyd Tilghman, knew that the place was indefensible, and before Grant drew his lines Tilghman sent most of his men off to Fort Donelson, twelve miles to the east, staying himself with the handful retained to work the guns. He and the gunners made a good fight, putting one of Foote's gunboats out of action, causing men to die amid flying splinters and scalding steam; but the Navy's big guns broke his parapets, dismounted his guns and dismembered some of the gunners, and by early afternoon Tilghman could see that it was time to quit. He hauled down his flag and surrendered to the Navy while Grant's army was still getting into position, and the Federals had gained one of the easiest and most significant victories of the entire war. The victory surprised its authors. Grant had supposed that his men would have to do a good deal of hard fighting, and Foote mildly confessed to Secretary Welles: "I made a bold dash at Fort Henry to inspire terror, & it succeeded." A newspaper correspondent remarked acidly that "Gen. Grant evidently did not understand that Commodore Foote . . . believes in energetic action at close quarters," and an infantryman said the soldiers "really felt sore at the sailors for their taking of the fort before we had a chance to help them."[3]

The fall of Fort Henry left General Johnston in a desperate situation. The railway line was gone forever, the Tennessee River now was an undefended highway for the Federal invader, running all the way to northern Alabama—Foote sent Lieutenant S. L. Phelps and three unarmored gunboats ranging up the river as soon as the fort surrendered, to spread alarm all through the South—and General Johnston's army, always inadequate, was broken squarely in half. When he consulted his lieutenants the day after the fort was taken, Johnston had no illusions about his prospects.

Johnston met with Beauregard, who was still appalled by his discovery of the essential weakness of the western army, and with his second-in-command at Bowling Green, Major General William J. Hardee, a solid officer who had written a textbook on tactics before the war: in Northern and Southern armies alike, untrained company officers were desperately trying to learn their new trade by studying Hardee. The Confederates found that they could do one of two unsatisfactory things—concentrate at Fort Donelson immediately and try to destroy Grant before he could be reinforced, or evacuate the fort at once and beat a speedy retreat to some place in southwestern Tennessee. The first looked a little too much like putting all of the eggs in one insecure basket—if this eastern half of Johnston's severed army were lost the Confederacy itself would probably be lost shortly afterward—and yet the other choice was not inviting either. To retreat meant, unquestionably, the loss of Nashville, capital of Tennessee, a supply depot of vast importance and an industrial center of considerable consequence. Nashville had never been fortified, and even if it had been a Federal advance up the Tennessee would quickly make it untenable; if it was to be saved, the only place to save it was at Fort Donelson. Johnston had held his line, from the beginning, largely because he had convinced the Federals that he was much stronger than was actually the case. Unfortunately, the Confederacy also had come to believe the same thing. If it now lost Tennessee simply because a few gunboats had spent one morning bombarding one lonely fort, the shock to public morale would be disastrous.

He did what he thought was best, and the people who came around a bit later to complain that he was wrong never had to carry the load he was carrying on February 7, 1862; and it might be added that when the whole thing blew up in his face he did not offer excuses or blame somebody else. Johnston tried to go down the middle. He would put about half of the men he had available (starting with the 8000 at Clarksville) into Fort Donelson, in the thin hope that they could somehow beat Grant, Foote and the terrible gunboats—those gunboats, black monsters with slanting sides, slow-moving, fearfully armed, apparently irresistible—and with the rest he would retreat as fast as he could and as far as he had to. He told Beauregard to get over to Columbus and take charge of the western half of the army, to leave enough men to hold the Mississippi River forts and to take everybody else south in the hope that there could be a reunion somewhere along the southern border of Tennessee. Then he struck his tents and marched.

So the Confederates evacuated Bowling Green, while cautious Buell drew nigh to this empty stronghold with powerful misgivings. Of the fearsome fighting men whom he commanded, Johnston sent nearly half into Fort Donelson—not enough to defeat Grant, too many for his army to lose—and with the rest he went unhappily down to Nashville, looking for a haven and hoping for the best. The shadow of dark wings was over him. He was moving toward a place he had never heard of, a stumpy clearing on high ground above the Tennessee River near a bleak country meetinghouse known as Shiloh Church, where he had an appointment with a Yankee bullet: a collective appointment, so to speak, which he shared with thousands of others. When he rode out of Bowling Green he had just two months to live.

On the Federal side, General Grant waited for the infamous roads along the Tennessee to dry out a bit, and then he marched east to the tangled ridges overlooking the Cumberland River, where Fort Donelson and its inadequate trench system awaited him. The weather was warm and his men were jubilant, and as they got out of the mud and hit the good roads on high ground they went along brightly, tossing overcoats and blankets into the dead grass by the roadside, supposing that the weather would always be mild.

The whole business was just a little more than the Federal high command could digest. When General Buell learned that Halleck's people were going to move up the rivers he wrote that the idea was strategically sound but that it was premature, poorly organized, undertaken without his consent. He sensed as well that the war might be moving out from under him. He had just explained to Washington that it was not possible to go through Cumberland Gap into East Tennessee, because the roads were so bad and the country was so devoid of forage; yet even while Grant and Foote were on their way to Fort Henry he had sent a strange telegram to General Thomas, off to the east, asking impatiently: "What now is the condition of the roads? How soon could you march and how long do you suppose it would take you to reach Knoxville? Are your supplies accumulating in sufficient quantity for a start? How is the road in advance likely to be affected by the passage of successive trains? What dependence can you place in supplies along it, particularly forage? Do you hear of any organization of a force there?" (Nothing whatever came of this.) Halleck meanwhile was bombarding both Buell and McClellan with anxious messages saying that the crisis of the war was at hand, that he needed support, and that the whole western theater of operations ought to be under one man, who obviously should be General Halleck.[4] And Grant moved on to Fort Donelson, while Foote took his ironclads back to the Ohio and came plugging up the Cumberland to attack the fort's water batteries.

Grant was doing no more than follow a soldier's instinct to get at the enemy and hit him. Originally, Fort Henry had been the objective. Once taken, it was to be fortified and held, and the blow at Fort Donelson was incidental; when he left Cairo to go up the Tennessee, Grant expected to be back at the base in a few days, and after Fort Henry surrendered Grant airily wired to Halleck: "I shall take and destroy Fort Donelson on the 8th and return to Fort Henry." None of the Federals quite understood that the Confederate works on the Cumberland amounted to much, and the pre-battle planning, such as it was, usually mentioned the town of Dover rather than the fort itself.[5] There was no way to know that Grant's twelve-mile march from the Tennessee to the Cumberland was one of the epoch-making movements of the war.

It might have been better if Grant had moved faster. On February 8, Donelson was weakly held, and Grant's 15,000 could have overrun the place without much trouble. But it took much longer than Grant had supposed to get the march organized, and it was February 12 before his troops got to the scene and prepared to fight; and by this time Johnston had sent in powerful reinforcements, so that Fort Donelson was held by 16,000 men or more—a larger force, on that day, than Grant had with him, although more Federal troops were on the way to join him. Instead of pushing over an insignificant outwork Grant's army was moving into the biggest battle yet fought in the west.

But war goes by a strange logic, and in the end the delay helped the Federal cause mightily simply because it enormously increased the value of the prize that could be won. Instead of taking a fort which sooner or later must fall anyway, Grant now had the opportunity to destroy a significant part of Johnston's army—a much larger part than Johnston could afford to lose. Quite unintentionally, Grant had permitted his opponent to make a huge mistake; if he could take advantage of it he could win one of the war's greatest victories.

Fort Donelson had originally been laid out as a work to keep Yankee steamboats from coming up the Cumberland, and its core was a set of water batteries overlooking a long stretch of the river; a dozen guns, or thereabouts, only two of them really heavy enough to fight armored gunboats, manned by enthusiastic but poorly trained gun crews. To protect these batteries against attack by land, the Confederates had dug a long, irregular line of enclosing trenches which ran for several miles along the inland ridges, and these trenches now were very strongly held. When the Federals got ready to fight, their obvious tactic was to use what they had learned at Fort Henry:

surround the place with troops and then bring up the gunboats to hammer the fort into submission. With the water batteries destroyed and the fleet in control of the river, and with Union troops blocking all the exits by land, the Confederates could do nothing but surrender.

That put it up to Flag Officer Foote. He was a hardhead who followed his own rules: Regular Navy to the core, a little fussy—it was recalled that when the Navy subdued certain Chinese forts in the fifties Foote had led a storming party across rice fields and over ditches under heavy fire, carefully holding a big umbrella over his head against the oppressive Oriental sun. He believed in total abstinence, the abolition of profane swearing, and a strict observance of the Sabbath, and he had somehow been able to make Old Navy shellbacks abide by these principles without mutiny. He had misgivings about this attack at Fort Donelson, because he knew that his ironclads were not really as strong as people thought, but the army was in a hurry so he went into battle somewhat against his better judgment.[6] He came up the river on the afternoon of February 14 with four ironclads, *Pittsburgh*, *St. Louis*, *Carondelet*, and *Louisville*, followed by the unarmored gunboats *Tyler* and *Conestoga*, and when he was about a mile from the water batteries he opened fire. He had a megaphone and he kept popping in and out of the pilothouse on *St. Louis*, shouting instructions to his captains.

At long range he had all the advantage, since the Confederate guns were too light to do much damage at any distance, and if he had stayed far away and kept on firing he probably could have put the water batteries out of action. But the Fort Henry lesson had been learned a bit too well. He had won there by coming in close and so he came in close now, steaming up to a mere 400 yards, and here the Rebel guns could hurt him. *St. Louis* was struck fifty-nine times and drifted downstream out of action, steering gear smashed, pilothouse wrecked, pilot killed, Foote himself wounded. *Louisville* also was disabled and drifted after the flagship, and then the two other ironclads collided, *Pittsburgh* was struck along the waterline and seemed ready to sink, and before the day ended the whole squadron had retired and the bombardment had been an expensive failure. Fort Donelson was going to be an Army fight.

Grant had three divisions in line—reinforcements came up the Cumberland in transports, just behind Andrew Foote's gunboats—and he had them strung out in a long semicircle facing the Confederate trenches. On his right was Brigadier General John A. McClernand, a good war Democrat from Illinois, inexpert but valiant, thirsting for military distinction; in the center was Brigadier General Lew Wallace, also ardent for fame, destined to be remembered because years later he would write a novel, *Ben Hur;* and on the left there was a stiff-backed old regular with long white mustachios, Brigadier General Charles F. Smith, who had been commandant of cadets at West Point when Grant was an indifferent student there. According to the newspaper correspondents the private soldiers whom these officers commanded were eager for battle; actually, they seem to have been numb and very much subdued, for the weather had suddenly become abominable. After several days of unseasonable warmth which led heedless boys to abandon overcoats and blankets it had blown up a storm, with a wind bringing rain that turned to sleet followed by snow, the thermometer dropping to 10 degrees above zero. There had been skirmish-line fighting, and some of the wounded men froze to death; at places the underbrush took fire, so that others died in flames; and on each side boys who were first drenched and then chilled caught colds that would bring pneumonia and death no matter how the battle went.[7] Both sides had active sharpshooters, and the men in the front lines were not allowed to have campfires for warmth at night.

In the Confederate lines there had been depression when the gunboats came up, because it was widely supposed that these ugly vessels were unbeatable, but after the boats were driven off and it was seen that they had really done very little harm the soldiers' spirits rose. Their generals, however, were pessimistic. They could not be sure that the gunboats would not soon return to the fight, they knew that Grant had been strongly reinforced, and they began to see Fort Donelson for what it was, a trap in which the army could easily die; and although they had got the bulk of their troops into the fort less than forty-eight hours ago they concluded, on the night of February

14, that at daybreak they must make an all-out fight to break Grant's lines so that they could lead a general retreat to Nashville.

All things considered, the decision was sensible enough. But it did underline two things: the folly of occupying Fort Donelson in strength in the first place, and the even greater folly which had governed the selection of the fort's commanding officers.

The man in charge was John B. Floyd, one-time Secretary of War for President Buchanan, a wholly untrained soldier who had come from the East bearing a brigadier general's commission and a record of utter failure in the western Virginia campaign; a famous man and a devout patriot, but a leader without personal force or any idea of the responsibilities that go with leadership. Second to him was Brigadier General Gideon J. Pillow, opinionated and cantankerous, who had fought in the Mexican War and so knew something about military matters. Bishop Polk had found him a difficult subordinate, and he was the one Confederate in all the war for whom U. S. Grant would voice outspoken contempt; and his concept of a commander's responsibilities was no better developed than Floyd's.

The number three man was more of a soldier and more of a man: Brigadier General Simon Bolivar Buckner, who had commanded secessionist home guards in Kentucky during the period of that state's neutrality, and to whom Lincoln had once offered a generalship in the Union Army. (He was a friend of Grant's, and had given Grant a life-saving loan when Grant showed up in New York, broke, after resigning from the Army on the west coast in 1854.) Unfortunately for the Confederacy, both Floyd and Pillow ranked him.

The battle plan was simple. At daybreak Pillow would lead most of the garrison in an attack on the right of the Federal line. Buckner would leave a small contingent to hold the entrenchments and would follow Pillow with the rest. Once the Federal line was opened, everybody would march southeast. Arrangements were hastily completed, and at dawn the fight began.

It had snowed again during the night, but the day came in clear with a wintry sunlight lying on the white hills. Pillow's men struck with fury, crumpling McClernand's line, driving his brigades back in disorder, capturing six guns and putting some 2000 Federals out of action. There was bitter fighting in the woods and ravines, but the Confederate attack had taken the Federals by surprise; by a little after noon the escape route was wide open, and Buckner (who had distrusted the whole Fort Donelson business from the beginning) supposed that it was time to start the retreat.

Grant had ridden downstream before the fighting began, to confer with the wounded Foote, and he did not return to the battlefield until after midday, when he found the right half of his army in full retreat. He ordered Lew Wallace, who on his own initiative had marched to McClernand's support, to advance, and with McClernand hastened to reorganize the beaten brigades for a counterattack; he sent an almost frantic message to the Navy to ask for a renewal of the bombardment by the shattered gunboats, and he ordered Smith to attack the Confederate right. As quickly as he could, he restored order and prepared to recapture the ground that had been lost, but his work almost certainly would have gone for nothing if he had not been immeasurably aided by a singular action on the part of General Pillow. For that officer, having done exactly what he had set out to do, now ordered all of the Confederates back into their trenches, and the door that had swung open so wide was about to be slammed shut again.

Apparently Pillow felt that the fort could be held. Apparently, also, he believed that the attacking column had been so disorganized by the hours of hard fighting that an orderly retreat was impossible; and he may have been moved by the thought that the soldiers were hungry, all but exhausted and in no physical condition to begin a hard march over bad roads. (It is also possible that his reasoning simply went beyond rational analysis.) In any case, he gave the orders. Buckner protested vigorously, Floyd hesitated and at last upheld Pillow, and the advantage that had been won was thrown away. By night all of the Confederates were back in their trenches, bewildered by the way victory had turned to defeat. To increase their gloom, C. F. Smith had seized a part of their lines and held a position from which he could make a shattering attack the next morning.

Floyd, Pillow, and Buckner went into conference. The first two had sent jubilant telegrams to Johnston, who by now was in Nashville, announcing that they had won a great victory, and Johnston naturally passed the word on to Richmond; but after darkness came these two generals could think of little except saving their own skins. Grant apparently had reoccupied his lines, and (as Buckner pointed out) the fort and all it contained would have to be surrendered. Neither Floyd nor Pillow wanted to be the first Confederate general captured: after all the Federal talk about treasonous rebellion, it seemed possible that captured generals would be hanged. So Floyd incredibly abdicated, passing the command to Pillow, who unhesitatingly abdicated in his turn and passed it to Buckner. A couple of steamboats still lay at the river front, and Floyd got himself aboard, with a few regiments of his troops, and incontinently sailed upstream to safety. Pillow fled in a small boat and eventually joined Floyd. Buckner, who had the soldierly belief that a general who surrendered his troops ought to stay with them and share their fate, wrote and sent through the lines a note to General Grant asking the Federal what terms he could give.[8]

Commander of cavalry in this Confederate Army was Colonel Nathan Bedford Forrest, the one-time planter and slave-trader who was much more of a soldier than men like Floyd and Pillow knew how to use. Like Buckner, he had felt trapped in Fort Donelson, and during the gunboat bombardment he met a chaplain and told him: "Parson, for God's sake pray! Nothing but God Almighty can save this fort!" Forrest had no intention of letting his men share in the doom of the fort, and when he learned what was going to happen he called his officers and said: "Boys, these people are talking about surrendering, and I am going out of this place before they do or bust hell wide open." He got his troops together, found that Grant's lines were less tight than his superiors thought, and led his men off through the night, cavalrymen floundering through ice-cold water in the swamps but getting out alive.[9]

In his cabin behind the Union lines, General Grant was aroused and given the dispatch his old friend Buckner had written. His reply was simple and direct: "No terms except unconditional and immediate surrender can be accepted. I propose to move immediately upon your works."

And an unconditional surrender was made, first thing next morning.

3: *The Disease Which Brought Disaster*

The news from Fort Donelson struck Nashville into a blind panic which was all the worse because everybody had been so confident. General Johnston had brought Hardee's 17,000 men in a few days earlier, but although his evacuation of Bowling Green had been dismaying he seemed to feel that Nashville could be held and no one had been in a mood to doubt. The public optimism had even interfered with his military plans. He wanted to block the Cumberland River by mooring an immense raft in the steamboat channel, but there had been much passive resistance; the steamboat men opposed a move that would stop the flow of ordinary commercial traffic, nobody supposed that the Yankee gunboats would ever really get this far, and when Floyd and Pillow sent word that they had won a great victory the project died. On Sunday morning, February 16, the churchgoing crowds were in high spirits.

Johnston knew the worst before anybody went to church. An aide aroused him at daybreak with a dispatch from Buckner saying that the fort and everybody in it were being surrendered. Johnston sat up in his camp cot, asked the aide to reread the dispatch, muttered grimly, "I must save *this* army," and summoned his staff to prepare the troops for an immediate departure. He would get his army out of Nashville, marching southeast to the vicinity of Murfreesboro, sending a contingent to hold Chattanooga and then awaiting developments and a hoped-for junction with Beauregard and Bishop Polk's troops from the Mississippi Valley; and the citizens who had been ready to celebrate saw the long columns tramping across the river and plodding south in undisguised retreat. Nashville was doomed, and by evening everybody knew it.[1]

No large Confederate city had yet been occupied by a Northern army. Wartime propaganda had portrayed Federal soldiers as brutes inclined to rapine and murder, shamefully undisciplined; no one knew what horrors the Yankee invader would inflict but everyone seemed to expect the worst, and one soldier wrote years later that in all the war he never saw such frantic, unreasoning fear as he saw now in Nashville. There was a great rush to get out of town. Southbound trains were jammed, with extras running. People who owned horses and carriages set off by road in a cold rain, often with no clear destination in mind, and others started out on foot, lugging valises and carpetbags. Many people who were not trying to go anywhere wandered up and down the streets in a daze, adding to the general confusion. Swarming mobs began to sack government warehouses and steamboats, carrying off immense quantities of bacon, salt pork, flour, blankets, and clothing, roughly commandeering horses and wagons to help remove the plunder; a newspaper correspondent, properly shocked, noted that these mobs included "Negroes, Irish laborers and even genteel-looking persons." One crowd filled the street in front of Johnston's headquarters—he had moved into Nashville from nearby Edgefield when the retreat began—demanding angrily to be told whether the army planned to defend the city or to abandon it; dispersing only after soothing oratory by assorted generals. Johnston had his hands full, trying to get river-side batteries planted so that the gunboats might at least be delayed, supervising the details of the retreat, advising the Governor of Tennessee to get the state archives off to safety.[2]

Johnston kept his personal equanimity, and when those egregious fugitives, Generals Floyd and Pillow, showed up on Monday he greeted them courteously and named Floyd temporary commandant of the city, with responsibility for keeping order and removing military stores. This responsibility, like the ones which had preceded it, Floyd found beyond his powers. Not until Tuesday, when Bedford Forrest and his cavalry reached Nashville, was anything effective done. Forrest was put in charge of the military depots, and he charged the plundering mobs with his tough troopers, sabers swinging and much profane shouting going on, and the looting came to a stop.

Forrest organized army wagon trains to remove such stores as remained; he reported bitterly that millions of dollars' worth of supplies had been lost, adding that "with proper diligence" all could have been saved, and he finally got the city back on an even keel. By February 23, one week after Donelson had surrendered, Johnston had his troops in camp near Murfreesboro, and Forrest and the rear guard escorted the wagon trains out of town to join him. Groggy and half empty, Nashville awaited the arrival of the Federal Army.[3]

As it happened, the Federal power was in no great hurry. There were in the Kentucky-Tennessee area two men who believed in crowding a beaten foe—General Grant and Flag Officer Foote—and they did their best. Wounded in one leg and one arm, Foote found that he could still get around, and on February 19 he took two gunboats upstream from Donelson and captured the town of Clarksville, where there was a railroad bridge; after which he and Grant agreed that the thing to do was to get troops and gunboats up to Nashville as fast as possible, and by daybreak on February 21 they had an expeditionary force afloat at Fort Donelson, ready to go, capable of reaching Nashville the same day. At this point the high command intervened. General Halleck telegraphed Grant not to let the gunboats go beyond Clarksville; after which he telegraphed to Secretary Stanton saying that there existed "a golden opportunity to strike a fatal blow" but that the blow could not be struck unless he, Halleck, could control Buell's army. Buell, meanwhile, had got his army into Bowling Green, and, while Forrest was pulling the rear guard out of Nashville, Buell began an overland advance toward that point, begging Halleck to send some gunboats up the Cumberland for protection. Crippled and badly off balance, the Confederates had just time to get away to safety. Buell's advance guard reached Edgefield, on the opposite side of the river from Nashville, on the evening of February 24, barely twenty-four hours after Forrest got the last Confederate soldiers out of there.[4]

As a matter of fact everybody was off balance, victors and defeated alike. The capture of the two forts stunned everyone. Both Federals and Confederates had to adjust not merely their plans but their ways of thinking about their plans: the Federals because they had won, with a single stroke, something which they had thought needed the most elaborate organization and preparation; the Confederates because they suddenly found themselves losing the whole western half of the war. The war which had been moving so slowly had abruptly passed the first of its great turning points. Now it was going at full speed, pulling men along with it, setting a pace which would be ruinous to all who could not themselves move with equal speed. Its entire climate had changed.

In the North there was much rejoicing. Here at last was a victory to make men forget about Bull Run, and with the victory there was a new hero whose appearance was all the more refreshing because up to now no one had paid much attention to him. Grant's laconic "unconditional surrender" note touched precisely the right key—men played with his initials and began to call him "Unconditional Surrender Grant"—and Secretary Stanton asserted that the aggressive spirit that would win the war seemed to him to be expressed perfectly in Grant's threat, "I propose to move immediately on your works."[5] President Lincoln made Grant a major general of volunteers, and the Senate quickly voted confirmation; now Grant outranked everybody in the west except Halleck himself.

There were off-stage mutterings that the man had simply been lucky, and although Halleck had recommended his promotion he had reservations about him. Halleck assured Stanton that C. F. Smith was the real hero of Fort Donelson, and he urged that the elderly Brigadier General Ethan Allen Hitchcock be promoted and sent west, because "an experienced officer of high rank is wanted immediately on the Tennessee line"—the line, that is, where Grant was commanding. Hardly a fortnight after Fort Donelson surrendered, Halleck complained angrily that Grant was ignoring his orders and failing to make proper reports: "Satisfied with his victory, he sits down and enjoys it without any regard to the future." (This was an odd complaint, in view of the fact that Grant would have had Federal troops and gunboats at Nashville while Forrest was still trying to remove commissary and quartermaster stores, if Halleck had not immobilized him.) Then Halleck told McClellan that rumors said Grant "has resumed his former bad habits," and for a time—although the general public knew nothing about it—Grant was under a cloud.[6]

Grant unquestionably had been lucky. After all, it was Foote who had made Fort Henry surrender and Grant who got most of the credit for it. Grant's delay in getting from Fort Henry to Fort Donelson had actually worked out in Grant's favor, and, at Fort Donelson, Grant's opponents had committed the most fantastic blunders. Nevertheless, the fact remained that Grant had displayed a trait which, as the coming years would show, he shared with Robert E. Lee—the ability to take immediate and devastating advantage of his foe's mistakes; and in any case no one in Washington was prepared to find very much fault with a soldier who had just captured the largest bag of prisoners in American military history.[7] The War Department presently quieted Halleck by curtly telling him that if he had anything against Grant he must file formal charges and make them stick, and Halleck dropped the matter. (Apparently the man did not really want to get rid of his subordinate; he was just being petulant, and once he had blown off steam he was ready to forget about it.) In Thomas, the western armies had produced a soldier who could fight and win; now, in Grant, they had come up with another. And there was also Flag Officer Foote.

The Confederates found much reason for gloom. There had been a disastrous failure in generalship, and no amount of explanation could gloss over the strange performance at Fort Donelson; President Davis removed Floyd and Pillow, Floyd was never again employed in a field command, and Pillow was used only sparingly. Johnston came in for severe criticism, which he took in soldierly silence. He could have argued that even if he had been mistaken in putting so many men into a fort that could not be held, things would have gone well enough if his subordinates had been equal to their opportunities, but he felt that this was no time to make excuses and he stoutly told President Davis: "I observed silence, as it seemed to me the best way to serve the cause and the country."[8] He had been beaten, but he would offer no alibis.

Yet defective generalship was not the real trouble. The dreadful truth which the Fort Donelson affair revealed was that the Confederates in Kentucky were simply overextended. Johnston had been compelled to try to do too much with too little, and even if the abysmal mistakes had been avoided his line was due to break whenever the Federals really hit it hard. Halleck, Buell, and the United States Navy had the power to repossess Kentucky and conquer Tennessee whenever they nerved themselves to use it, and the fact that Grant and Foote had forced the hands of their reluctant superiors was incidental; the break was bound to come sooner or later.

Upheld by Mr. Davis, Johnston undertook to serve cause and country as best he could. He prepared to reassemble his army and make ready for a new fight farther south, and his task was extraordinarily difficult. He had 17,000 men near Murfreesboro, and Beauregard, then at Jackson, Tennessee, was finding that there were some 21,000 along the Mississippi. Even when these forces got together the army would be much weaker than the force which the Federals could be expected to bring south, and getting them together would be hard. They were 300 miles apart, and before February ended Halleck was preparing to get Grant and the gunboats over to the Tennessee and drive upstream; if this move was made with vigor, Johnston and Beauregard might not be able to get together at all. Beauregard was in poor health, and from Jackson he wrote: "I am taking the helm when the ship is already on the breakers . . . How it is to be extricated from its present precarious position, Providence above can determine." He brightened up when he reached the Mississippi Valley, and February 23 worked out an ambitious scheme to regain the offensive. If the governors of Tennessee, Mississippi, Louisiana, and Arkansas could raise from 20,000 to 40,000 new troops, and if reinforcements could be brought over from west of the Mississippi, Beauregard believed he could march north, take Paducah and Cairo and threaten St. Louis . . . This plan, however, was wholly impractical, and it died in its cradle. Beauregard had written that the loss of Fort Donelson would bring "consequences too lamentable to be now alluded to," and these consequences were upon him. He could do nothing but leave garrisons to hold a few forts on the Mississippi north of Memphis and take his field force down to Corinth, Mississippi, while the War Department ordered 15,000 men sent up from Mobile, Pensacola, and New Orleans.[9] Johnston might be able to reconstitute an adequate army provided the Federals gave him plenty of time.

This, it developed, the Federals would do. To organize, equip, and move a proper army of invasion took time. There were a thousand details to arrange; tangled lines of command must be set straight; what was done here must be co-ordinated with what was done elsewhere; and above everything else it was necessary to be prudent, lest all that had been gained be lost through front-line rashness. Altogether, displaying an admirable capacity for taking infinite pains, the careful men at headquarters took a good deal of time—and, quite unintentionally, presented it to General Johnston.

The commanders at the front could see that this was the moment to push ahead, ready or not, the moment to drive the enemy into a corner before he could regain his footing or recover his wind. But there is an unformulated military law by which understanding of urgency and front-line reality diminishes with each mile of distance to the rear echelon; so that it was actually possible for a department commander to tell Washington that he had a golden opportunity to strike a blow, and in the same breath to restrain the subordinates who were on the verge of striking it. It was at this time that Secretary Stanton began to reflect that in choosing top commanders he would probably pick men who went personally where their troops went: "I am very much inclined to prefer field work rather than office work for successful military operations."[10]

Yet the respite which Johnston was about to get was of no immediate comfort to worried folk in the South. Things were bad no matter where they looked. In southwestern Missouri, Union Brigadier General Samuel R. Curtis had reoccupied the town of Springfield and had driven Price all the way into Arkansas; he apparently had completed Federal reconquest of Missouri and he seemed to be about to attempt an invasion of Arkansas as well, and he had already crossed the border of that state with something over 10,000 men, his numbers rising to 30,000 or 40,000 in the panicky rumors that went rippling eastward. On the Gulf Coast, northeast of the separated mouths of the Mississippi there was a barren sand patch known as Ship Island, once held by Confederate troops, abandoned in September as untenable; the scene just now of a steady, ominous build-up of Federal troops and an in-gathering of many supply vessels, while black-hulled warships cruised off the entrances to the big river and sent light craft up to Pilot Town and the Head of the Passes. Flag Officer Farragut himself arrived on February 20, and Major General Benjamin Butler would presently be there as Army commander, and the two officers obviously meant to attack New Orleans—which unhappy metropolis, by no means ready for an attack, was at precisely this moment compelled to send troops north to strengthen General Johnston.

These were the threats. There was also another actual defeat. Just when Forts Henry and Donelson were being lost, the Federals struck hard inside the North Carolina sounds, moving at last to exploit the Hatteras Inlet breakthrough, threatening to overrun the entire coast from Chesapeake Bay to the vicinity of Wilmington. This thrust was costly in itself and even worse in its implications, for it pointed again to the grim moral underlined in Tennessee: the South's defensive line was too long and too thin, and it could be broken whenever the Federals came down hard. (Mr. Lincoln's strategic concept was getting a certain verification this winter.) Roanoke Island illustrated the matter perfectly.

Roanoke Island was haunted: the place where England's first American colony, planted at the gateway to the unknown darkness, had vanished forever, leaving the dim memory of little Virginia Dare and the ominous word "Croatan" for an eerie, tragic legend. The island was flat, swampy, ten miles long, lying at the meeting place of North Carolina's inland seas, Pamlico Sound and Albemarle Sound; if the Federals could occupy it they could control both sounds, the cities that lay on their shores, the rivers that came into them, and a feasible back-door approach to Norfolk. Roanoke Island, in other words, was a place the Confederacy had to hold, but it was just one of a great many places that had to be held and when the blow fell Roanoke Island was not prepared.

The place was commanded by Brigadier General Henry A. Wise, who was given the post in December 1861, when it seemed advisable to get him out of western Virginia. Wise had had no military training whatever but he had been learning things about warfare, and he had abundant energy; he did his best to set matters right, but he was fatally handicapped not only by the basic lack of resources but by his inability to make the high command see that this case was important. His immediate superior was the department commander, Major General Benjamin Huger, a first-family career soldier from Charleston, grown rigid and unimaginative in long years of Army routine, an aristocrat described by an irreverent kinsman of Wise as "one of those old West Point incompetents with whom the Confederacy was burdened." Wise notified Huger that he desperately needed reinforcements, only to be told: "I think you want supplies, hard work and coolness among the troops you have, instead of more men." As a former governor of Virginia, Wise knew how to pull political strings, so he hurried to Richmond to appeal to Secretary of War Judah Benjamin, but Benjamin also was unresponsive; he simply told Wise to get back to Roanoke and do the best he could with what he had. Haggard and in poor health, Wise obeyed, anticipating disaster; then, early in February, he came down with pneumonia and had to take to his bed in a shore-side hotel, leaving the island and its 2500 defenders in command of Colonel H. M. Shaw.[11]

If the Confederates left everything to the man on the spot the Federals gave Roanoke Island top-level planning and support. Back in September the War Department had organized an oversized division with the idea that it could be used, with gunboats and small craft, to clear the Confederates out of the eastern shore of the Chesapeake. Then McClellan scented larger possibilities inside Hatteras Inlet and concluded that this force could accomplish a great deal more if it went into the Carolina sounds. President Lincoln backed the idea, the Navy named Flag Officer L. M. Goldsborough to handle the gunboats, and the Army's part of the program was entrusted to Brigadier General Ambrose E. Burnside, a West Pointer who had left the Army to go into business before the war and who had commanded Rhode Island's three-months recruits at Bull Run.

Before the war ended the Northern people would hear a great deal of Burnside, much of it bad, for it was his evil fate to be tested far beyond his strength, which was moderate; but this first assignment was just his size and he did very well with it. He was a likable sort—big, florid, friendly, his handsome face adorned by a beard which was elaborate even by Civil War standards—and he always recognized his own limitations even if he was never able to surmount them. He had 11,500 men, and in mid-January he and Goldsborough sailed from Hampton Roads with a fleet of more than sixty vessels—shallow-draft gunboats, transports, tugs, open barges designed for use as landing craft and a number of ferryboats never intended for work on blue water. They ran into a southeast storm that gave them a vicious tossing, wrecking two ships and almost bringing the whole expedition to grief, but they reached Hatteras Inlet at last and after waiting a week for the seas to moderate they came inside. Burnside put about a third of his men ashore there and made ready to attack Roanoke Island, forty-five miles to the north.

The business was well organized. Burnside had three brigades afloat, and for each brigade there was a steam transport towing twenty landing craft. Goldsborough put the fighting ships up in front, and on the afternoon of February 7 the fleet came up Pamlico Sound in a line two miles long, while a cold wind whipped a spatter of rain out of a leaden sky and the pine trees on the low shores looked as if they grew directly out of the water. Transports and landing craft remained at the southern end of the island while the warships steamed up the western side to force their way through Croatan Channel, which was narrow, obstructed by sunken hulks and pilings, guarded by forts, batteries, and a small Confederate fleet; a defensive layout which looked tough but which quickly turned out to be extremely weak.[12]

Goldsborough came in close to the shore of the island, thus avoiding the fire of most of the batteries, which had been built so that their guns could play on the middle of the channel and on nothing else. His guns were much heavier than anything the Confederates had, and they quickly overpowered the nearest defensive work, Fort Bartow, silencing its guns and setting its barracks on fire. The Confederate fleet comprised seven tugboats and river steamers, mounting a total of eight guns, and this collection—a "pasteboard fleet," as one Southerner remarked bitterly—could make no more than a token resistance. C.S.S. *Curlew* went to the bottom from a direct hit by a 100-pound shell, another vessel was disabled, the little fleet drew off, returned for a second encounter, and then took off for the far end of Albemarle Sound, completely out of the fight. There were other forts on the Roanoke shore north of Fort Bartow, and these took comparatively little damage, but as the day ended it was evident that they could be left to the army, which would be on hand very shortly.

For while the bombardment was going on Burnside had put his brigades ashore at the southern tip of the island, and on the morning of February 8 the troops came up the island's one road to the main defensive line, a redoubt mounting three inadequate fieldpieces and flanked on each side by a quarter of a mile of entrenchments, manned by perhaps 1500 men. If Wise had had enough men, guns, and time he might have made this place impregnable, for the island was narrow here and the cramped approach to the redoubt had a tangle of swamps on each side, but his line was too short and too thin. Burnside sent flanking columns along through mud and waist-deep water, and he had a prodigious advantage in numbers. His men stormed the place with moderate loss, and by afternoon his column moved on up the island to take the forts in the rear. The Confederates could do nothing but surrender; Burnside had the island, with upwards of 2000 prisoners, thirty-two guns, 3000 stand of small arms and stacks of supplies, and the Federals had the whole area of the Carolina sounds at their mercy, with ample time to remove the obstructions from Croatan Channel and plenty of soldiers and warships to mop up all of the isolated forts on the mainland.[13]

The unhappy General Wise, recuperating from his illness, moved off to Currituck County, North Carolina, and wrote an indignant letter to President Davis, declaring that the island could have been held if a proper effort had been made and complaining bitterly: "The North Carolina troops had not been paid, clothed or drilled, and they had no teams or tools or materials for constructing works of defense, and they were badly commanded and led, and, except a few companies, they did not fight." If this was less than just to the unlucky soldiers who had been trapped on the island, the general's feeling that he had been badly let down by the higher authorities was understandable, and when Congress appointed an investigating committee to hold hearings on the matter he exploded: "I intend to 'accuse' General Huger of nothing! nothing!! nothing!!! That was the disease which brought disaster at Roanoke Island." The committee eventually agreed with him, reporting that blame for the loss ought to be divided between General Huger and Mr. Benjamin.[14]

Wherever the blame belonged, the moral was clear enough. Like Fort Donelson, Roanoke Island had been lost because the Confederacy had not quite been able to make an adequate defense of a vital strong point, and although mistakes had been made the underlying trouble was a simple lack of resources. The Confederate domain was so big that it could not be defended everywhere. During the next few weeks Burnside and Goldsborough methodically overran all of North Carolina's inland seaports, from Elizabeth City on the north to Beaufort on the south, and although they at last repeated the Port Royal story, failing to exploit their gains aggressively, they had sliced off one more piece of Southern territory and had clamped one more constrictive grip on the new nation. Middle and western Tennessee were gone, the Atlantic coastline was going fast, the trans-Mississippi was crumbling, New Orleans was facing a dire threat; if the Federals now moved on Richmond with all their strength, the war might be approaching its end.

4: *Time for Compulsion*

The weather in Richmond was as bad as the news from the fighting fronts. There was a cold, relentless rain which turned unpaved streets to mud, and February 22, which was to witness the inauguration of Jefferson Davis for his six-year term as President of the permanent Confederate government, struck Attorney General Bragg as "one of the worst days I ever saw." The bad weather and bad news had turned the attorney general into a pessimist. He wondered if the Confederacy would live to inaugurate another president, and in his diary he recorded a skeptical verdict: "Time alone can answer–but I fear not." A furloughed soldier in town to see the sights wrote that he fortified himself by buying an umbrella but that most of his comrades bought whiskey, and Capital Square, where the inaugural address would be delivered from a canopied wooden platform, was all bobbing with umbrellas as the crowd assembled.[1]

In the Confederate White House, Mr. Davis retired to his room to kneel in long prayer "for the divine support I need so sorely," and at noon he went to the Capitol, to greet the new Congress in the Hall of Delegates and to sit by while Vice-President Stephens took the oath of office. Mr. Davis was gaunt and pale, for his health had not been good of late, and the committee on arrangements suggested that it might be better if the ceremonies were held indoors, but he insisted on going through with the program as originally planned; there was a high symbolism to this affair, marking the transition from a provisional government to one which was to last forever, and none of the formalities would be slighted. The procession formed and moved out into the rain, and when Mr. Davis mounted the platform he seemed to Mrs. Davis "a willing victim going to his funeral pyre." He was sworn in, bending to kiss a Bible which a Nashville publisher had proudly presented as the first Bible to be printed in the Confederacy; then, bareheaded, with rain coming down on the expectant crowd, he began his address.[2]

The Southern people had floated to war on oratory, but the war had changed and the only eloquence that mattered now was the terrible eloquence of the thing done, and most of the things done lately had been done by Yankees. More than any of those who listened to him, Jefferson Davis was aware that this nation which was now proclaiming its permanence might die before summer unless battles were won, and the means by which battles could be won were not immediately visible. Joe Johnston, immobilized at Centreville by rains which turned the Virginia roads into impassable troughs of wet clay, had fewer men in camp now than he had had two months ago, and the Federals in his front outnumbered him by three to one. Sooner or later they would advance–this very day, as a matter of fact, was the one specified in Mr. Lincoln's order as the date for a great forward movement everywhere. Burnside could move up to Norfolk almost any time he chose, and the great Federal fleet could strike anywhere; and the Yankee armies that were starting up the Tennessee and down the Mississippi could be stopped by nothing much short of a military miracle. None of this could be said in public. Mr. Davis could do little but recite inspiring generalities.

Within limits, he was frank enough. He pointed out that the last hopes for reunion and a solution of sectional differences "have been dispelled by the malignity and barbarity of the Northern states in the prosecution of the existing war." Civil liberties in the North had vanished, the jails were full of men arrested without due process, for opinion's sake, and the men who reigned in Washington, "feeling power and forgetting right, were determined to respect no law but their own will." The South had won victories and it had suffered defeats—"the tide for the moment is against us"—but no patriot could doubt that the final outcome would be victory. It had to be victory, because "nothing could be so bad as failure, and any sacrifice would be cheap as the price of success in such a contest." Perhaps Providence meant that the Southern people must learn the real value of liberty by paying a high price for it; they were contending, after all, against "the tyranny of an unbridled majority, the most odious and least responsible form of despotism." Men must deserve the aid of a higher power; "With humble gratitude and adoration, acknowledging the Providence which has so visibly protected the Confederacy during its brief but eventful career, to Thee, O God, I trustingly commit myself, and prayerfully invoke Thy blessing on my country and its cause."[3]

The message seemed to be well received. The furloughed soldier who had bought the umbrella wrote that people listened as attentively "as if it had been beautiful spring weather," and a War Department clerk believed that the candid comment on recent defeats bespoke a more effective policy for the future and said stoutly: "We must all stand up for our country." Wispy Alec Stephens commented that "the country must work out its own deliverance," adding: "Our new government is now in its crisis: if it can stand and will stand the blow that will be dealt in the next eighty or ninety days, it may ride the storm in safety."[4]

The cabinet had gone over the speech with care, in the two or three days preceding the inauguration, striking out words and putting words in until Mr. Bragg concluded that this must be "the best seasoned document surely that ever was issued"; but although he had made certain contributions of his own Mr. Bragg confessed that the whole business had seemed like a waste of time—"I was thinking of how we were to escape the storm which threatened to overwhelm both Gov't and people." The Confederacy, he believed, needed good luck, good management, and a great deal of energy, and he concluded: "Too much has been left to our generals." This remark was one the Republican radicals in Washington would gladly have taken for their own. (For a good footnote, add Halleck's complaint to McClellan that too many decisions were being made by politicians.) In any case, while the speech was in preparation Mr. Davis told the cabinet that the Confederacy must shorten its lines. Specifically, Joe Johnston would have to leave northern Virginia and get closer to Richmond, which would be in grave danger of capture as soon as spring came.[5]

Plans for retreat were top secret, of course, but Mr. Davis discussed the worsening military situation in a message which went to Congress three days after the inaugural. He confessed frankly that the government had tried to do more than it could do and that it had run into trouble as a result. The army was not big enough, and it was in bad shape because the expiration of the short-term enlistments was forcing it to reorganize under the most difficult conditions. The policy of short-term enlistments, like the government's overoptimistic estimate of its own capacity, simply reflected the original belief that the war would be short. Mr. Davis pointed out that he had opposed the policy and that Congress, inspired by the people, had adopted it, but he was not disposed to be censorious.

"It was not deemed possible," he recalled, "that anything so insane as a persistent attempt to subjugate these states could be made, still less that the delusion would so far prevail as to give the war the vast proportions which it has assumed." But the delusion had prevailed—had perhaps even grown somewhat in recent weeks—and the army now was in such an unsettled condition that it was hard to say just how big it actually was. (Mr. Davis would have a concrete suggestion for Congress on this point before long.) A War Department official was admitting privately that the Confederacy now was weaker than it had been in July 1861, and was darkly noting that "the enemy are rapidly acquiring the character of being better soldiers than ourselves." Joe Johnston's troop returns were dismayingly eloquent. In December he had had, at Centreville, in the Shenandoah Valley and along the Potomac, 62,000 effectives, present for duty; in February he had but 47,000.[6]

General Johnston had in fact been having a most unhappy winter, the ordinary problems of Army command having been intensified by two special factors—an unwise act of Congress, and the unusual personality of the Secretary of War, Judah Benjamin.

At the end of 1861 Congress had tackled the one-year enlistments and in a laudable effort to help the Army had almost ruined it. Congress passed a law providing a $50 bounty and a 60-day furlough for any soldier who re-enlisted for three years or the duration of the war, and it specified that if he wanted to he could shift from his own branch of the service to another—from infantry to artillery, for instance—or move to a different company in his old branch. Furthermore, after the re-enlistees got settled in their new units they could elect new company and regimental officers, which of course meant that most of the good disciplinarians would be replaced by army-politician types who would no more speak harshly to the men under them than a Congressman would offend his loyal constituents. So there was a general coming and going and shuffling about such as front-line military camps rarely see or dream of; and the crowning difficulty was that the furloughs which sent so many soldiers home were issued, not by the army commander but by the Secretary of War.

Mr. Benjamin was a wealthy lawyer-politician from Louisiana, in some ways the most brilliant man in the cabinet, unquestionably the one who best knew how to get along with Jefferson Davis. He was of unshaken equanimity, always smiling and yet not really easygoing either; sharing with Edwin M. Stanton the belief that generals must be kept in their place by the civil authorities. He distributed furloughs to General Johnston's soldiers with the easy grace of a good politician, despite the general's complaint that "the discipline of the army cannot be maintained under such circumstances," and he had a way of issuing orders to Johnston's subordinates without regard for the normal chain of command. In January Mr. Benjamin in this way nearly drove Stonewall Jackson out of the Army.

Jackson, who by now was a major general, and a difficult man to handle in his own right, commanded under Johnston in the Shenandoah Valley, and around the first of the year he marched west to maneuver the Federals out of the town of Romney. Having done this he returned to Winchester, leaving Romney occupied by a division under the Brigadier General Loring whom Lee had found so touchy during the fall campaign. The winter was cold and snowy and things at Romney were dull, and Loring and his officers were discontented; they sent a round robin complaint to the War Department, and Benjamin promptly wired Jackson that Loring's command was in danger of capture and must be withdrawn. Jackson at once obeyed, after which he sent in his resignation, explaining that "with such interference in my command I cannot expect to be of much service in the field." In the end, largely because of the active intervention of General Johnston and Virginia's Governor Letcher, the business was smoothed over, Jackson withdrawing his resignation and Benjamin tacitly agreeing that the Secretary of War ought not to issue direct tactical instructions to officers in the field. (Benjamin had never really meant any harm; he simply wanted to be accommodating to some unhappy constituents.) But the affair remained in General Johnston's little black book as one of many points of complaint against the Secretary.[7]

Now, with the crisis of the war approaching, there began a steady deterioration in the relationship between General Johnston and President Davis.

In the summer Johnston had made, and lost, a sharp argument concerning his proper rank, since which time his attitude toward Mr. Davis had been correct but somewhat distant. His acrid disagreements with Secretary Benjamin had made his attitude toward the President still more reserved; after all, Mr. Davis supported Mr. Benjamin in these disputes. Now the question of the best way to use Johnston's army caused the President and the general to drift still farther apart. Each man was a bit thorny, ready to take offense and to meditate on the offense after taking it, and although their basic ideas about the military problem were much the same they differed about the ways in which those ideas should be expounded and put into effect. They began to misunderstand one another, and misunderstanding presently bred mistrust; and before spring came General Johnston and his government were under the same sort of cloud that was settling down upon General McClellan and the government in Washington.

In mid-February Mr. Davis asked Johnston to come to Richmond to confer on a matter so highly secret that it could not be discussed by mail. Johnston came down and met with the President and cabinet on February 19 and 20, and Mr. Davis told him what he had just told the cabinet—that the army in northern Virginia must be withdrawn: McClellan would advance before long, and Burnside would doubtless come up through Norfolk, and all available troops must be within supporting distance of the capital. Johnston had already written that his position was dangerously exposed and inadequately manned, and he agreed to the withdrawal readily enough; but he argued that before he could retreat he must send to the rear a number of heavy guns, a great quantity of supplies, and an inordinate amount of camp baggage and equipment, and the water-soaked roads were so abominable just now that it was impossible to move even field artillery, to say nothing of siege guns and a huge wagon train. For the moment he was totally immobilized, and he did not see how he could move at all until winter ended and the roads became dry.[8]

Apparently misunderstanding began here. Johnston wrote that although no formal order was issued there was a general understanding that "the army was to fall back as soon as possible," and a few days later he wrote to the President about "the progress of our preparations to execute your plans." But Mr. Davis was not at all sure that the plans were his; he felt that they were, in fact, General Johnston's, and he had a different idea as to what they actually called for. He hoped that when Johnston got rid of his heavy equipment he might even move forward on the offensive (provided, of course, that his army could be reinforced) and the President evidently believed that Johnston was not to retreat without first consulting Richmond. Some time later Mr. Davis wrote that when the retreat was made Johnston was so poorly informed about the terrain in his rear that he did not know how to select a new position—which, said Mr. Davis, "was a great shock to my confidence in him" and indicated that "he had neglected the primary duty of a commander."[9]

General Johnston, meanwhile, got a shock of his own. The projected retreat was of course the gravest of military secrets; but when Johnston returned to his hotel, immediately after leaving the office of the President on February 20, he met a colonel who gave him an interesting rumor he had just picked up in the lobby: the cabinet was talking about moving the army back from Centreville. The next day Johnston met another acquaintance—an unfortunate who, the general explained, was too deaf to overhear anything not intended for his ears—who had picked up the same story the same evening. Thus the strategic discussion which was so highly confidential that the President had not even wanted to write a letter about it in advance had leaked out of the White House with miraculous speed; so that the substance of it was circulating in a hotel lobby before Johnston himself got there.[10]

This may have had long-range consequences. One of the items about which Mr. Davis complained the most, as he and General Johnston drew farther apart, was the fact that General Johnston was so very reticent about his military plans. He would not discuss these, except in the broadest and most general terms, and this reticence was one of the things which finally made it impossible for the two men to work together at all. Johnston was a reserved sort to begin with, and it seems altogether likely that his experience in Richmond on February 20 confirmed him in the instinctive belief that it just was not safe to discuss military secrets with civilians—not even with the civilian who was at the head of the government.

But all of that was for the future, and what mattered immediately was different. Confidential news might go all across town on the first winds that blew, President and general might disagree on what was to be done and on the reasons for doing it, storing up much personal bitterness, one man against the other; yet underneath all of this the Confederacy, blindly but effectively, was this winter making up its collective mind that it would go on with the war in spite of recent disasters. What the people of the North had done after Bull Run the people of the South were doing now: drawing new determination out of humiliation and defeat, discarding unthinking arrogance and preparing to see the war as it actually was and not as it had been ignorantly imagined.

The editor of a newspaper called *The Telegraph*, in the town of Washington, Arkansas, called the turn when he summed up the lesson that had been taught by the disaster at Fort Donelson. The people of the South, he said, had committed the classic error of those who go to war overconfidently: "We have despised the enemy and laughed at their threats, until, almost too late, we find ourselves in their power." He went on: "We have allowed our chivalry to cool most wonderfully, while we have been pluming ourselves on being 'the superior race,' and when our wives or sisters did some noble, self-sacrificing act, wondering 'if such a people could ever be conquered.' The wonderment has been expressed again and again even *ad nauseam*, and now it is answered. *They may be*. Not by force of arms, but from decay of chivalry and innate love of ease." He suggested that it was time to buckle down to it.[11]

In years to come, some Southern patriots would complain that Mr. Davis was too stiff-necked and unyielding to admit that he had made mistakes or to correct mistakes once they took place, but at this time he was humble and thoughtful. To a correspondent in Alabama he wrote, "I fully acknowledge the error of my attempt to defend all the frontier, seaboard and inland," but he pointed out that the lack of men and munitions had made an offensive policy impossible; "necessity, not choice, has compelled us to occupy strong positions and everywhere to confront the enemy without reserves." Everyone had supposed the Confederacy stronger than it actually was, and it had not been possible to correct this delusion because "an exact statement of the facts would have exposed our weakness to the enemy." The thing to do now was to avoid vain recriminations and get down to the task of raising a bigger army and using it aggressively.[12]

Mr. Davis began by reorganizing his own cabinet. He would keep Mr. Benjamin, whose counsel seemed indispensable, but Mr. Benjamin obviously could not remain in the War Department: Congress and the public were blaming him for the loss of Roanoke Island, and it was clear that the man could not get along with the generals—Joe Johnston was widely quoted as having remarked, at a Richmond dinner table, that the Confederacy could not succeed with Mr. Benjamin as Secretary of War. So Benjamin was made Secretary of State—R. M. T. Hunter had left the cabinet to enter the Senate—and George W. Randolph, a grandson of Thomas Jefferson, a former officer in the United States Navy, and a successful lawyer and politician, went to the War Department. Thomas Bragg, who had grown so deeply discouraged of late, was asked by Mr. Davis to resign as attorney general, and was replaced by Thomas Hill Watts of Alabama, who had supported the Bell-Everett ticket in 1860 but who was generally believed to be a follower of William L. Yancey. Congress confirmed the new appointments, with some grumbling—it did not like Benjamin at all, and a good many Congressmen would have been happy to see Stephen Mallory replaced as head of the Navy Department—and then Congress made its own contribution by passing a bill to provide the Confederate states with an active general-in-chief to run all of the armies. Mr. Davis immediately vetoed this bill, on the ground that it undercut the President's constitutional powers, but he bent to the wind by calling General Lee to Richmond and giving him, "under the direction of the President," control of military operations. Final control, of course, would remain with Mr. Davis, and no one who knew the man doubted that he would exercise it, but the move at least brought the South's best soldier back to the capital. Lee wrote to his wife that he could see neither "advantage or pleasure" in the new assignment, but he accepted uncomplainingly, comforting himself with the belief that it would eventually lead to an active command in the field. Robert Toombs said tartly that the arrangement simply meant that Davis and Lee together would be Secretary of War no matter who nominally held the office.[13]

Congress had not finished. On March 11 it adopted a bristling resolution "declaring the sense of Congress in regard to reuniting with the United States." The sense of Congress clearly was that such reunion was out of the question, no matter what defeats might be suffered: "It is the unalterable determination of the people of the Confederate States, in humble reliance upon Almighty God, to suffer all the calamities of the most protracted war, but that they will never, on any terms, politically affiliate with a people who are guilty of the invasion of their soil and the butchery of their citizens."[14] This gesture of defiance was followed not long after by a sweeping enactment which put the waging of the war on an entirely new footing and in effect remodeled the substructure of the whole Confederate government. Congress passed a conscription law, and the Richmond government, founded on the most unwavering faith in states' rights, suddenly found itself empowered and directed to reach into the sovereign states and compel citizens to enter the Army—a power which even the government at Washington did not then have and did not especially want to have.

Mr. Davis requested this in a special message sent to Congress on March 28. The Constitution, he pointed out, gave Congress the power to raise armies, and what was needed was a better and simpler way of doing it. The Federal advance had aroused among the people a spirit of resistance which "requires rather to be regulated than to be stimulated," and conscription was the best way to regulate it. After a debate which—considering the nature of the change—was comparatively brief, Congress agreed, and on April 16 it adopted a draft act giving the President the power to call out, for three years or the duration, all white male citizens between the ages of eighteen and thirty-five. Furthermore, the new law provided that the twelve-months men whose terms were expiring would be drafted too; their terms now were three-year terms, no matter what the original enlistment papers said. There would be no more shifting from one arm of the service to another. The men could elect their own officers, once the drafting and re-enlisting was over, but they would stay where they were, and men not in the Army would be drafted if they did not speedily volunteer. A few days later a supplementary act provided for innumerable exemptions, and in the months ahead its provisions would raise some very difficult problems, but the big step had been taken. The disintegration of the Confederacy's armies would stop. The nation would no longer try to wage war as a loose assemblage of self-sufficient states.[15]

Naturally, this provoked certain outcries. Georgia's Governor Joseph E. Brown, whose manifold duties never kept him too busy to write extensive letters of protest to the President of the Confederacy, complained that the act was subversive of Georgia's sovereignty and "at war with all the principles for the support of which Georgia entered into this revolution," and declared that he could have nothing to do with "the enrollment of the conscripts in this state"; nor was he soothed by Mr. Davis's rejoinder that the cause was lost forever if the central government could do no more than ask the states to send in militia regiments which could be called out only to repel invasion. Alec Stephens, drifting into a shadowland where hard facts had to be adjusted to vaporous doctrine, considered conscription "very bad policy" and complained that it was all the fault of the West Pointers, in whom lay no salvation. "If the Southern volunteer," said Stephens, oddly, "should ever come to forget that he is a gentleman (and that is what the West Point men say he must do) then it will be merely a struggle between matter and matter, and the biggest and heaviest body will break the other." Inasmuch as the point of the whole business was the undeniable fact that the weaker body was on the verge of being broken forever because of its weakness, Mr. Davis let this ride; his attitude doubtless stiffened by facts called to his attention by the War Department. During the last thirty days, the Department disclosed, the terms of service of 148 regiments expired. Most of the men in these regiments were not re-enlisting, and most of those who did re-enlist "entered corps which could never be assembled, or, if assembled, could not be prepared for the field in time to meet the invasion actually commenced."[16] The volunteer spirit was not enough. It was time for compulsion.

But Jefferson Davis understood that the draft, by itself, was not enough either. The government could raise large armies, but it must also learn how to use them. Its forces would always be outnumbered, and if they were to win the men who led them must surpass material limitations. In a thoughtful letter to General Johnston, Mr. Davis tried to explain the necessities of the case, writing soberly: "The military paradox that impossibilities must be rendered possible had never better occasion for its application."[17]

5: *Contending with Shadows*

The terrible pressure of time was upon both Presidents. Mr. Davis was compelled to act by the closing circle of the Federal armed forces; Mr. Lincoln, by the rising momentum of the war itself. Facing the imminent peril of defeat, Mr. Davis tried to reorganize his Army; facing the danger that the war might become altogether unmanageable, Mr. Lincoln sought to reorganize his country's whole mental attitude. On the evening of March 5, Mr. Lincoln called his cabinet into consultation, and on the next day he sent a special message to Congress.

In this message the President urged adoption of a joint resolution: "Resolved, that the United States ought to co-operate with any state which may adopt gradual abolishment of slavery, giving to such state pecuniary aid, to be used by such state in its discretion to compensate for the inconveniences public and private produced by such change of system."

The Northern government was neither making war on slavery nor asserting any power to interfere with slavery in the states. Yet slavery was the indigestible lump, after all, the one thing that had made compromise impossible, and perhaps there still was time to deal with it rationally. Mr. Lincoln believed that if slavery died in the border states it had no real hope for survival anywhere else on the continent, and to kill that hope, he felt, "substantially ends the rebellion." He clung as well to his primary article of faith: the states which said they were out of the Union were really still in it, and this proposed act of co-operation would apply to them if they chose to accept it. And there was one other point: the tremendous sums being spent to fight the war "would purchase, at fair valuation, all the slaves in any named state."

In December, Mr. Lincoln had warned that all indispensable means to restore the Union would be used. Now he insisted that the war would continue as long as resistance to reunion continued, and "it is impossible to foresee all the incidents which may attend and all the ruin which may follow it." The act of Congress, to be sure, would not by itself accomplish much, but it might initiate a great deal; and so, "in full view of my great responsibility to my God and to my country I earnestly beg the attention of Congress and the people to the subject."[1]

The President had assembled some figures. In a letter to the editor of the New York *Times* he pointed out that the government was spending about $2,000,000 a day to fight the war. To buy and free all of the slaves in all of the border states at a price of $400 per head would cost less than three months more war would cost. If the action shortened the war by three months, then, there would be some sort of gain. He went into more detail in a letter to Senator James McDougall of California, who opposed the plan. Delaware, for instance, contained 1798 slaves; they could be freed for $719,200—less than half of one day's war costs. In all of the border states put together there were 432,622 slaves; they could be freed for $173,048,000, which was a little bit less than the cost of eighty-seven days of war.

He explained that the thing could be done gradually. "Suppose, for instance," he wrote to Senator McDougall, "a state devises and adopts a system by which the institution absolutely ceases therein by a named day—say January 1st, 1882. Then, let the sum to be paid to such state by the United States be ascertained by taking from the Census of 1860 the number of slaves within the state, and multiplying that number by four hundred—the United States to pay such sum to the state in twenty annual installments, in six per cent bonds of the United States. The sum thus given, as to *time* and *manner*, I think would not be half as onerous, as would be an equal sum, raised *now*, for the indefinite prossecution of the war; but of this you can judge as well as I."[2]

A few days later the President discussed the proposal with a delegation of border state leaders. He insisted that the government did not want "to injure the interests or wound the sensibilities of the slave states." Still, the government was making war, and to make war it had to put armies in the slave states; and just because they were there these armies made the institution of slavery more acutely troublesome than it had ever been before. Abolitionists complained because the armies did not destroy the institution and slaveholders complained because the armies did not protect it, and altogether there was increasing turmoil, a great comfort to secessionists. He believed that if his resolution were adopted by Congress and accepted by the states, this trouble would cease "and more would be accomplished toward shortening the war than could be hoped from the greatest victory achieved by the Union armies." Emancipation, he went on, was entirely up to the people of the states affected, and yet it was a national matter also. "Slavery existed, and that, too, as well by the act of the North as of the South," he explained, "and in any scheme to get rid of it the North as well as the South was morally bound to do its full and equal share."[3]

In due time the resolution was passed by both houses of Congress, but no state followed the lead, and the response Lincoln had hoped to get was not forthcoming. The extremists were unmoved. Thaddeus Stevens was openly contemptuous: "I think it is about the most diluted, milk and water, gruel proposition that was ever given to the American nation." Congressman C. A. Wickliffe of Kentucky, viewing the plan from a position diametrically opposite to Stevens', cried out in the House: "Let us alone; permit us to do our duty in the pending struggle and we will attend to our domestic institutions."[4] The war was not going to be shortened; the nation was not going to save money or lives, but would have to fight the war to a finish regardless of "all the ruin which may follow it." As a practical matter, Mr. Lincoln's attempt had no effect.

Yet it was enormously significant. For the first time the President of the United States had discussed emancipation, not as a lofty abstraction which a happier age might some day embrace, but as an immediate measure aimed at reunion and a shorter war. Disclaiming all intent to use the Federal power to interfere with slavery, he had at the same time reiterated that "all indispensable means" to win the war would be used, and here was the clearest indication that emancipation might soon look indispensable. In effect the President was warning that unless final victory were won quickly, emancipation would be adopted as an essential war measure.

Of all the men in the North the one who most vitally needed to heed this warning was General George B. McClellan.

McClellan was a conservative Democrat who sincerely and openly detested abolition. When he became general-in-chief he wrote to his friend Barlow begging him to "help me dodge the nigger," declaring: "I am fighting to preserve the integrity of the Union & the form of the Govt.–and no other issue. To gain that end we cannot afford to mix up the negro question–it must be incidental & subsidiary. The Presdt. is perfectly honest & is really sound on the nigger question. I will answer for it now that things go right with him."[5] Now there was this writing on the wall, cryptic but still readable: if the Confederacy fell within the next few months, the infinitely complicated, infinitely tragic problem in human sorrows and destinies which McClellan knew as "the nigger question" could still be dodged; or at least the effort to dodge it could continue, which might come to the same thing. But if victory did not come soon the problem would become central to everything the nation did and the time for dodging would end forever.

So far, General McClellan's winter had been no happier than General Johnston's. He had been helped into his high place by hard men who believed in hard war, and they wanted immediate action. They wanted it so badly that General McClellan had been in General Scott's place for no more than a week when Mr. Russell of the

London *Times* made a note about it: "The inactivity of McClellan, which is not understood by the people, has created an undercurrent of unpopularity, to which his enemies are giving every possible strength." Before December ended, Senator Ben Wade, hardest and most impatient of them all, was complaining that the nation would soon be $600,000,000 in debt with very little to show for it. "All this," said the senator, "is hanging upon one man who keeps his counsels entirely to himself. If he was an old veteran who had fought a hundred battles, or we knew him as well as Bonaparte or Wellington was known, then we could repose upon him with confidence. But how can this nation abide the secret counsels that one man carries in his head, when we have no evidence that he is the wisest man in the world?"[6]

A basic trouble of course was that General McClellan refused to take the Republican radicals into his confidence; they were giving every sign of a strong desire to run the war, and the general was keeping them at arm's length. Yet Ben Wade did speak for the increasing restlessness of a vigorous people who had gone to war without realizing that wars are not always won quickly. In spite of victories elsewhere this restlessness was growing day by day because of the inactivity of the Army of the Potomac. Until that army moved and won victories of its own McClellan was going to be the target for the deadliest sharpshooters in Washington.

McClellan thus was in an exceedingly strange position. Unless he could win the war quickly it was likely to turn into the last thing he wanted it to be, a war for emancipation; yet at the same time the greatest pressure for speed—a pressure which could break him if he resisted it too long—was coming from the men he despised most, the militant emancipationists. McClellan could best thwart them by doing exactly what they wanted him to do, a point which probably no one except Mr. Lincoln himself was subtle enough to grasp.

Call them emancipationists, radicals, or radical Republicans; all the words apply. They believed firmly in immediate and uncompensated emancipation; they were radicals in that they bluntly favored the revolutionary struggle which Mr. Lincoln wanted to avert; and they were Republicans of an intense partisanship, working night and day to win political advantage for themselves and their party. Their motives were mixed but their goal was clear; they wanted immediate action, and they believed this could come only from generals who felt as they felt. Senator Wade's recent remarks indicated that they might very soon go on the warpath against General McClellan himself. McClellan seems to have sensed this, and a few days after the senator had spoken Mr. Lincoln tried to reassure the general.

"I hear that the doings of an investigating committee give you some uneasiness," the President wrote. "You may be entirely relieved on this point. The gentlemen of the Committee were with me an hour and a half last night, and I found them in a perfectly good mood. As their investigating brings them acquainted with the facts, they are rapidly coming to think of the case as all sensible men should."[7]

The investigating committee the President was talking so hopefully about was the Joint Committee on the Conduct of the War, and "the case" was the bungled fight at Ball's Bluff which had wrecked a brigade of the Army of the Potomac and had killed Colonel Edward D. Baker, close friend of Mr. Lincoln and a prominent member of the Senate. Reacting to this disaster, Congress in December had created this investigating committee, with Ben Wade as its chairman. Other members were Senators Zachariah Chandler of Michigan and Andrew Johnson of Tennessee, along with Representatives Daniel W. Gooch of Massachusetts, John Covode of Pennsylvania, George W. Julian of Indiana and Moses F. Odell of New York. The committee had broad powers and relentless determination; in effect it was the action arm of the militant radicals, largely controlled by Wade and Chandler; a fearsome committee if ever there was one. Right now it was methodically ruining Brigadier General Charles P. Stone, who had commanded the troops that fought at Ball's Bluff. Stone was blameless but unlucky, a professional who did not understand how violently this war departed from the professional soldier's tradition. He was about to learn.

General Stone was caught in the middle. A West Pointer who had been entrusted with security of the capital in the anxious days just before Mr. Lincoln's inauguration, he commanded a division along the upper Potomac in the summer and fall of 1861, and this division contained three regiments from Massachusetts, strongly tinged with abolitionist sentiment. Fugitive slaves kept coming into his lines, pursued by indignant masters, and General Stone followed his orders in respect to all such: that is, he promptly returned the fugitives to their owners, who were residents of Maryland and presumably loyal Unionists. The New Englanders complained bitterly, and before long General Stone was involved in hot arguments with the Governor of Massachusetts, forceful John A. Andrew, and with the even more forceful Massachusetts Senator Charles Sumner. Then on October 21 came Ball's Bluff, in which battle these same New England regiments suffered heavy losses.

Less than a week after the battle, Bull Run Russell made a little note: "It is whispered that General Stone, who ordered the movement, is guilty of treason—a common crime of unlucky generals—and at all events is to be displaced and will be put under surveillance." *Harper's Weekly* said that "somebody must be sacrificed on the altar" and remarked that General Stone's reputation was under attack, and Senator McDougall asserted later that rumor, "that great manufacturer of falsehoods," had been calling the general a traitor throughout the fall and winter. When the Committee on the Conduct of the War began to hold closed-door hearings on Ball's Bluff, Stone was squarely on the spot.[8]

He got no help from his superiors. Called before the committee early in January to explain why his troops had gone into action at Ball's Bluff, General Stone was flying blind. As far as he knew, all that was going on was a clumsy attempt by uncomprehending civilians to examine the military plans and orders under which he had been operating. The case was fairly clear; he had been instructed to make a demonstration toward Leesburg, Virginia, to see what the Confederate forces there were doing and if possible to induce them to go elsewhere, and whether he had done well or poorly he had at least done what he had been told to do. Yet he could not really explain it, because Army headquarters put him under wraps just before he testified. Some time later he said: "I was instructed at General McClellan's headquarters that it was the desire of the general that officers giving testimony before the committee should not state, without his authority, anything regarding his plans, his orders for the movements of troops, or his orders concerning the position of troops."[9] That left General Stone in the position of assuming all of the responsibility for an action taken at the direction of the high command. He could pass the buck to no one.

General Stone knew very well that his military competence was under attack, and about the time of the hearings he did what any professional soldier would do in a similar case; he asked for a court of inquiry, at which the record would speak for itself under the examination of fellow professionals. A court of inquiry, however, he could not get. A staff officer at McClellan's headquarters warned him not to apply, pointing out: "Your military superiors are under attack, and that consideration involves the propriety of abstaining just now."[10] The only inquiry would be this one by the Committee on the Conduct of the War, and what General Stone did not know was that the committee proposed to show, not merely that he had made mistakes but that he was actively disloyal to his country.

After it heard General Stone the committee heard others, all in closed session, and it got some rather odd testimony. It appeared that General Stone had exchanged letters with Confederate officers across the Potomac. There had been many flags of truce, with mysterious emissaries passing back and forth. Camp gossip said that if Union guns damaged Confederate civilians' property General Stone would see that it was paid for. Escaped slaves were too willingly restored to men who claimed them. Encouraged by leading questions, various officers and enlisted men said that they doubted General Stone's loyalty, considered him a secessionist at heart and did not want to fight for him. He had let the Rebels plant batteries when he could have prevented it. (It turned out later that the batteries specifically complained of simply did not exist.) This went on and on, through 260 pages of the committee's records.[11] It was not exactly evidence, as a lawyer would understand the word, but it was at least testimony, and the committee passed it along to the Secretary of War (first Cameron, and then Stanton) and suggested that General Stone be called to account.

On January 28, Secretary Stanton sent McClellan a written order to relieve General Stone from his command and put him under arrest. McClellan removed him, but suspended execution of the order for his arrest, saying that Stone ought to have a chance to answer the charges, and, on January 31, Stone went before the committee for a second time and learned that he was in serious trouble. He was told that the committee had evidence which "tends to prove that you have had undue communication with the enemy," and for the first time he realized that the committee really took this fantastic talk of treason seriously. Instead of being asked to explain a military mistake he had been supposed to prove that he was not a Benedict Arnold.

He did not know who had accused him or specifically what he was accused of. He could do nothing but make a general statement of innocence, which he did, with hot eloquence: "This is a humiliation I had hoped I should never be subjected to. I thought there was one calumny that could not be brought against me. . . . This government has not a more faithful soldier; of poor capacity, it is true, but a more faithful soldier this government has not had. . . . If you want more faithful soldiers you must find them elsewhere. I have been as faithful as I can be."[12]

He might as well have saved his breath. He was no longer Charles P. Stone, a man with honor to defend and a life to live. He was just a counter on the board where an intense struggle for power was going on; he had been played, and the contestants were about to remove him and drop him in the box. Senator Wade was out to prove that lack of drive on the field of battle probably came from an over-tolerant attitude toward slavery and slaveholders, and that this in turn might well bespeak treason. He was sounding a grim warning for all Army officers who were lukewarm on slavery and who also were failing to win victories.

Among these officers was General McClellan, who apparently did not at once get the true drift of things. Colonel J. H. Van Alen, an officer on the headquarters staff, told Attorney General Bates that when it was learned that the committee wanted Stone removed from command, McClellan remarked, "They want a victim," to which Colonel Van Alen replied: "Yes—and when they have once tasted blood, got one victim, no one can tell who will be next."[13] McClellan evidently failed to see that the committee wanted not so much a victim as an object lesson. This object lesson, indeed, was being set up primarily for the instruction of the general-in-chief himself.

Anyway, Stone's destruction proceeded without any protest from Army headquarters; which, at last, piously lined up with the men who were destroying him. A week after General Stone's second appearance before the committee, while the order for his arrest was still in abeyance, McClellan's intelligence agents laid hands on a refugee from Leesburg who had a tale to tell, and they sent McClellan a report. As McClellan described the report later: "There were in it statements which the refugee said he had heard made by the Rebel officers, showing that a great deal of personal intercourse existed between them and General Stone. I think it was also stated that General Evans, then the Rebel commander there, had received letters from General Stone; and there was a general expression on the part of those Rebel officers of great cordiality towards Stone—confidence in him." General McClellan doubted that this statement by itself was enough to justify the arrest of General Stone, but he talked to the refugee and felt that the man was sincere and so he took the report and showed it to Secretary Stanton—who ordered him to arrest General Stone at once and send him to Fort Lafayette, in New York Harbor.

Accordingly, on February 8, McClellan sent an order to the provost marshal directing him to arrest General Stone, retain him in close custody, and send him under guard to Fort Lafayette for confinement, with the injunction: "See that he has no communication with any one from the time of his arrest."[14] So it was done. General Stone was locked up. There were no formal charges against him anywhere. Try as he could, he was unable to get a hearing, or even a plain statement of the reasons for his arrest; he simply stayed in prison, not to emerge until many months had passed, his reputation a ruin.

Early in March, General McClellan himself discussed the Ball's Bluff affair before the committee. He really knew nothing about the disastrous move across the river, he said, except what General Stone had told him. He himself had ordered a demonstration, and he insisted that he had not meant that troops were to be sent across at Ball's Bluff; General Stone might have met his instructions simply by moving troops down to the river bank and displaying them there. For the rest, General Stone had given discretionary orders to Colonel Baker, and to judge the matter by General Stone's report Colonel Baker was responsible for the result. General McClellan added that he knew of no good reason why General Stone could not have sent troops to Colonel Baker's relief from the force he had at Edwards Ferry, a few miles downstream from the scene of the action.[15] And that closed the case. No matter how the committee allocated the blame, it was not going to be able to award any of it to General McClellan.

It was time for the Army of the Potomac to move, and when it moved there were in the background these two seemingly unrelated factors: President Lincoln's desperate attempt to get the slavery issue settled before it changed the character of the entire war, and the radicals' implacable determination to destroy any general who, being unsound on "the Negro question," was not waging war with ruthless speed and effectiveness. Taken together, these factors would affect every move the Army made and every decision its commander reached. Unless he understood their implications the Army commander, like General Stone himself, would be contending with incomprehensible shadows.

6: *Forward to Richmond*

Mr. Lincoln had formally ordered a general advance by all of the armies for February 22. On that day Mr. Davis addressed a rain-drenched crowd in Richmond, while Bedford Forrest was getting the last wagonloads of supplies out of Nashville and Joe Johnston was reflecting on the folly of telling elected officials about military plans; and the Army of the Potomac remained in its camps, idle except for the firing of Washington's Birthday salutes. Two days later Mr. Lincoln went to a funeral. His eleven-year-old son Willie had died, victim of the typhoid fever that was so prevalent, and Mr. Lincoln rode out to the Oak Hill Cemetery in a carriage with his oldest son Robert and the two Senators from Illinois. Mrs. Lincoln, too broken to leave the White House, kept to her room, and a February gale—a fragment of the same weather that had spoiled the Confederate inauguration—ripped at the bunting with which patriotic merchants had decorated the downtown streets of Washington. Then, a few days after this, McClellan put part of his army in motion, taking approximately 40,000 men up the Potomac to Harper's Ferry; a promising move which drew much attention and which by unlucky chance came to look like a humiliating fiasco.

Before descending on Richmond (as he planned eventually to do) McClellan wanted to re-establish and protect the western line of the Baltimore & Ohio Railroad. To do this he proposed to move a large force up the Shenandoah Valley, and to supply this army it was necessary to have new bridges over the Potomac at Harper's Ferry. His engineers quickly laid a pontoon bridge there, and on February 26 the advance guard crossed the river, troops cheering, bands playing "Dixie," McClellan and his staff looking on, all hands bubbling with enthusiasm. Then the engineers got ready to build a second and more important bridge, big enough to carry all of the traffic involved in the movement and supply of a substantial army; a semipermanent bridge, designed to rest on a number of canal boats, which had been floated up the Chesapeake and Ohio Canal and were now to be moved over into the river so that they could serve as piers.[1]

Everything had been carefully organized. Working parties were ready to begin. The long column of troops was moving up the Maryland side of the river, and it was time to get the boats out of the canal—at which moment it was discovered that the boats were just a few inches too wide to go through the locks that would bring them to the place where they were needed.

A high wind came up, endangering the pontoon bridge, the approaches to which were already clogged by wagon trains. The ponderous canal boats lay below the locks, as useless as if they had never left Washington. The engineers and their working parties were able to do nothing, and since they could do nothing the Army itself could not do very much, and it was all most embarrassing. McClellan rode forward as far as Charles Town, where old John Brown had been tried and hanged less than three years ago, and he made up his mind to hold this town and the country roundabout. The advance guard was moved forward, and arrangements were made to build up supplies at Harper's Ferry so that this one-bridge army could eventually move on to Winchester; with the lower end of the Shenandoah Valley held the Baltimore & Ohio people could at least rebuild their own railroad bridge. The general and his staff and all the rest of the army then went back to Washington, which was chuckling over a new joke: this expedition, people told one another, had died of lockjaw.[2]

Mr. Lincoln got the news about all of this from Secretary Stanton, who strode into his study, locked the door behind him, and showed the President the telegram about the canal boats. When the President asked him what this meant, Stanton replied: "It means that it is a d——d fizzle. It means that he doesn't intend to do anything." Mr. Lincoln then sent for Brigadier General Randolph B. Marcy, a long-service regular who was a member of General McClellan's official family and of his personal family as well; that is, he was General McClellan's chief-of-staff and also his father-in-law, warmly loyal to the man in each incarnation. Mr. Lincoln now blew up at him with an anger few men ever saw him display.

"Why in the nation, General Marcy," demanded the President, "couldn't the general have known whether a boat would go through the lock before spending a million dollars getting them there? I am no engineer, but it seems to me that if I wished to know whether a boat would go through a hole, or a lock, common sense would teach me to go and measure it." General Marcy tried to explain—after all, the general-in-chief didn't go around with a yard-stick in his hands, measuring things personally—but he was cut short. Mr. Lincoln told him sharply that this failure had just about destroyed the prestige won at Fort Donelson, and said there was a rising impression that General McClellan did not really intend to do anything anyway. At last he dismissed the unhappy chief-of-staff with a curt "I will not detain you any further now, general." Secretary Nicolay recalled later that this was just about the only time he ever saw Mr. Lincoln lose his temper.[3]

Actually, the Harper's Ferry expedition looked worse than it was. The Baltimore & Ohio was able presently to resume train service to the West; Federal troops occupied Winchester; and General McClellan eventually argued that despite the misfit canal boats the expedition had had important strategic consequences.[4] But it does seem to have convinced the President that either he or Mr. Stanton must henceforth have much more to say about the organization, movements, and general direction of the Army of the Potomac. He quickly acted on this conviction.

It began with the situation along the Potomac River below Washington. (Upstream or downstream, the Army's luck on this river was bad.) The Confederates had batteries on the lower river, closing the stream to merchant vessels and actually putting the capital under a partial blockade, which did little real harm but made the Federal government look impotent. The Army of the Potomac could always go down and open the river, but as long as General Johnston held his position at Centreville and Manassas the Confederates could easily close it again, because with the main Confederate Army in northern Virginia the right bank of the lower Potomac was Confederate territory no matter what anybody did. General McClellan thus felt that the big thing was to get Johnston out of northern Virginia; once that happened the lower Potomac would open itself.

Just here, however, the case began to grow very complicated.

McClellan wanted to take his army by water to the town of Urbanna, near where the Rappahannock River entered Chesapeake Bay; and he wanted Johnston's army to stay exactly where it was until this move was made, because Urbanna was much nearer Richmond than Centreville was. Once the Army of the Potomac reached Urbanna, Johnston would have to retreat in a hurry, and there was every prospect that the Federals could destroy him as he did so. Then Richmond could be taken, and the war no doubt would end. Furthermore, since the Potomac would remain closed until Johnston fled, McClellan's army would go to Urbanna by way of Annapolis, where its transports could descend the broad, unblocked Chesapeake. It would begin its "forward to Richmond" move, in short, by marching off to the north of east, attacking neither the batteries which isolated Washington nor the Confederate Army which menaced it. It occurred to Abraham Lincoln that this was altogether too much to expect an impatient public to understand. It would look like outright retreat, and the administration could not quite explain publicly that this was the first cunning move in a campaign against Richmond. Before he could consent to this program the President must confer with his cabinet, with General McClellan, and finally with General McClellan and all of the general's principal subordinates.

To the cabinet and military leaders, Mr. Lincoln said that the march to Annapolis would probably be acceptable if McClellan could just send one or two divisions down the Potomac first. There were, of course, those batteries, but the Navy could silence them until the transports had passed, which was all that mattered. The Navy had just commissioned a new warship named *Monitor*, some sort of ironclad with a revolving turret, about to leave New York for Hampton Roads. Might not *Monitor* lead a flotilla up the Potomac to silence those batteries? The business would be considered.

Next came General McClellan. Talking to him in private on the morning of March 8, Mr. Lincoln appears to have been blunt. Not only did the move to Annapolis seem to leave Washington in danger, he said, but men who had to be listened to were beginning to say that that was the purpose of it—that it reflected a treasonous design looking toward defeat by prearrangement. McClellan, of course, grew angry (just as General Stone had grown angry) and demanded an immediate retraction. The President tried to explain that the accusation was not his and that he was simply imparting some unwelcome information which was bound to affect the general's course of action, but McClellan was not appeased.[5] He undoubtedly realized the President was talking about the radical Republicans. It was no secret that the members of the Committee on the Conduct of the War were demanding an immediate opening of the lower Potomac, and their pertinacity in sniffing out traitorous intent was a matter of recent record. McClellan's friends had just warned him of "a powerful cabal that will overthrow him if he does not move within a few days," and now the President was trying to tell him that the business was extremely serious.[6] But when he looked back on it, all McClellan could remember was that the President had used insulting language.

Then came a meeting of the President with McClellan and a round dozen of McClellan's generals, at which the generals were polled on the question of the move to Urbanna. Of the twelve who were questioned, eight favored following McClellan's plan and four were opposed, two with reservations; which led Mr. Stanton to remark bitterly, "We saw ten generals who were afraid to fight."[7] Any comments Mr. Lincoln may have made at the time are not recorded, but as soon as the meeting was over he composed and issued two General War Orders which showed precisely how the whole affair impressed him.

General War Order No. 2 directed that the Army of the Potomac be at once organized into army corps, and named the officers who were to command the corps. The officers named were Generals Irvin McDowell, Edwin V. Sumner, Samuel P. Heintzelman, and Erasmus D. Keyes. The first three of these had voted against the move to Urbanna, and Keyes, who had voted for it, had done so with the proviso that the Rebels should first be driven away from the lower Potomac. In addition, the troops around Harper's Ferry were designated a fifth corps, command of which was given to Major General Nathaniel P. Banks, former member of Congress and former governor of Massachusetts, a good Republican but a soldier whose military capacities were wholly untested. To top it all, the troops that were to be retained in Washington to defend the capital were put under command of Brigadier General James Wadsworth, a wealthy Republican who was designated Military Governor of the District of Columbia.

Close on the heels of this came General War Order No. 3, which directed that the Army of the Potomac must depart on no campaign without leaving in and around Washington a force large enough—in the opinion not only of the commanding general but also of all of his corps commanders—to keep the city perfectly secure. Not more than two of the new corps could be moved until the lower Potomac was entirely clear of Confederate batteries; and no matter what move the army made, it must begin to make it not later than March 18, ten days hence.[8]

All in all, the President had had a busy day. He had given McClellan the warning about the political dangers which surrounded him; he had attended the council of war, which went as if no warning had been given; he had then reorganized the Army of the Potomac, naming the men who were to be McClellan's principal lieutenants; and, finally, he had ordered the army to move and had set up the conditions under which the movement was to be made.

This had no sooner taken place than the bottom fell out of the Urbanna plan, once and for all. Joe Johnston evacuated his position at Centreville on March 9 and marched south to a new position below the Rappahannock River.

Johnston had been making his preparations ever since his Richmond conference with Mr. Davis and the cabinet, just before Washington's Birthday. He had in the Centreville area some 36,000 effective troops, with 11,000 more divided between the Shenandoah Valley and the lower Potomac, and he had no intention of waiting for McClellan to attack him or of letting McClellan steal a long march and get between him and Richmond. He spent a little more than two weeks moving his supplies to the rear; then, at the end of the first week in March, he concluded that this chore could never be completed and ordered the army to burn everything that was not already on the road—food, camp equipment, private baggage, and all. His troops began to move on March 7, and two days later the fortified lines which had been held so long were empty.

The bonfires were spectacular. At Thoroughfare Gap, not far behind Johnston's lines, the commissary department had built a huge meat-packing plant—much too far forward, General Johnston had always insisted—and this, with more than a thousand tons of bacon, was burned. One soldier remembered piles of bacon "as high as a house" sending up queer yellow and blue flames, spreading a smell of fried bacon for twenty miles around. In the camp itself mountains of baggage went up in flame and smoke. Johnston complained that in the easygoing days when the army first established itself at Centreville every private soldier had brought a trunk full of clothing, and all of these trunks were burned; a serious loss, since many of the men had enough clothing there to last the rest of the war if they could have saved it. There was spirited complaint, especially by the commissary department, and Mr. Davis wrote that the destruction made "a painful impression on the public mind," but Johnston was relentless. He had at least got his army down to marching trim, and now he established it on a line running from Rappahannock Bridge to Culpeper Courthouse, just south of the Rappahannock River, and awaited developments.[9]

These came without delay. News of the retreat reached Washington on a Sunday evening, March 9, while McClellan was in conference with the President and the Secretary of War, and the general hurried off to headquarters and began issuing orders. Couriers went spattering through the muddy camps around Washington, and the next morning the Army of the Potomac was in motion—making, at last, the advance to Centreville which the President had been urging all winter long—and immense columns of infantry and artillery crossed the Potomac and went slogging forward along muddy roads. A cold rain came down, dampening the enthusiasm of the crowds that looked on; dampening also, it seemed, the spirits of the commanding general, who was moving from one anticlimax to another. An aide who saw McClellan riding to the front felt that the man looked glum, and wrote afterward: "He who could that day have read the General's soul would have seen there already something of that bitterness which subsequently was to accumulate so cruelly upon him."[10]

At Centreville there was plenty to see: long lines of trenches, flimsy enough (a newspaper correspondent felt) but obviously laid out by engineers who knew their business; mounting, in many redoubts, imitation cannon made of painted wood. The pervasive whiff of scorched bacon floated in from Thoroughfare Gap, and the camp itself held a dull odor of smoke and wet ashes. At Manassas Junction storehouses were still smoldering, machine shops had been destroyed, a wrecked locomotive and some half-burned boxcars stood on a siding, and there was an indescribable mess caused by the breaking-up of hundreds of barrels of flour, vinegar, and molasses. A plant which had been built to render tallow had been burned and gave off its own dismal odor, and broken casks of beef and pork lay all about. The soldiers poked around amidst all of the rubbish and seemed to feel let down; they had nerved themselves for a great march into battle and had written their last letters home, and now they faced nothing but this abandoned camp with its Quaker guns and its malodorous combination of scents. General McClellan set up headquarters at Fairfax Courthouse and called in those new corps commanders to talk about what ought to be done next.[11]

The field of choice was narrow. The Urbanna plan was dead beyond recall. There did not seem to be much point in just sitting down at Centreville, and nobody cared for the idea of taking to the muddy roads in direct pursuit of the absent General Johnston; clearly there was nothing to do but leave a guard to look after the Centreville-Manassas area and get the army back to Washington, bring up the transports, and move down the Potomac for a campaign against Richmond along the sandy peninsula that lay between the York and James Rivers.

While the generals reflected on this there was still another change in the picture. On March 11 Mr. Lincoln issued one more War Order, removing McClellan from his position as general-in-chief and reducing him to the post of commander of the Army of the Potomac. Until further notice there would be no general-in-chief; all Army commanders would report directly to the Secretary of War—in effect, to Mr. Lincoln himself—and the order specified that "prompt, full and frequent reports will be expected of each and all of them." In addition, the order enlarged the responsibilities of General Halleck, the one Department commander who seemed to be getting a little action, giving him control of everything west of a north-and-south line through Knoxville, Tennessee, thus making cautious General Buell a Halleck subordinate. Also, and significantly, it resurrected the somewhat shopworn hero of the abolitionists, General John Charles Frémont, giving him command of a newly created Mountain Department roughly comprising western Virginia and eastern Tennessee.[12]

This order was no sooner issued than the President heard from General McClellan, getting an outline of the projected move down to

Hampton Roads. Back to General McClellan from the White House came this prompt reply, dated March 13:

"The President having considered the plan of operations agreed upon by yourself and the commanders of army corps, makes no objection to the same but gives the following directions as to its execution:

"1st. Leave such force at Manassas Junction as shall make it entirely certain that the enemy shall not repossess himself of that position and line of communication.

"2nd. Leave Washington secure.

"3rd. Move the remainder of the force down the Potomac, choosing a new base at Fortress Monroe, or anywhere between here and there; or, at all events, move such remainder of the army at once in pursuit of the enemy by some route."[13]

On January 24, Mr. Adams in London had warned that what happened during the next six weeks would probably be decisive, adding that if nothing happened that also would be decisive: European recognition could hardly be averted unless the Federal government by spring looked like a winner. The six weeks were up, and the warning was being heeded. The command system had been reshuffled, with promotion for a general whose armies were in action and demotion for generals who seemed unhurried; an encouraging gesture had been made to the abolitionists; and General McClellan had been told bluntly to put his new base wherever he chose but at all events to get moving and chase the foe.

General McClellan learned about his demotion through the newspapers, which got to Fairfax Courthouse before the official dispatches did, and long after the war he wrote that this "proved to be one of the steps taken to tie my hands in order to secure the failure of the approaching campaign."[14] This, to be sure, was one way to look at it, but at the time McClellan saw it quite differently. To his friend Barlow he wrote: "I shall soon leave here on the wing for Richmond—which you may be sure I will take. . . . *The President is all right*—he is my strongest friend."[15]

There were political angles to this business, on both sides. The abolitionists were openly moving to assume direction of the war.

What they had done to General Stone was one illustration of the fact; another was an act of Congress approved on March 13 which had an unmistakable anti-slavery cast. It read:

"All officers or persons in the military or naval service of the United States are prohibited from employing any of the forces under their respective commands for the purpose of returning fugitives from serivce or labor, who may have escaped from any persons to whom such service or labor is claimed to be due, and any officer who shall be found guilty by a court-martial of violating this article shall be dismissed from the service."[16]

Conservative Democrats like Barlow were rallying behind McClellan; whether he liked it or not, the general was in politics. If the President sustained him, the abolitionist surge might expend its force harmlessly. In December, Barlow had written Stanton that the abolitionists must sooner or later discredit themselves and that the Democrats could then assume control of the government's war policy. Now, even though the President had been acting with a good deal of severity, he still stood between McClellan and the radicals. The demotion mattered little. McClellan still commanded the country's most important army. There was some reason for him to assure Barlow that the President was still his strongest friend.[17]

Yet the ground under his feet was getting shaky. Attorney General Bates was a conservative, who was warning Mr. Lincoln to watch out for the machinations of the radicals and to stand firm against "the pressure brought to bear for the entire prostration of McClellan." But Mr. Bates was getting badly disillusioned about General McClellan, feeling that the advance to Centreville and the return therefrom was not unlike the uphill-downhill march of the noble Duke of York, and in his diary he made the wry comment: "Upon the whole it seems as if our genl. went with his finger in his mouth on a fool's errand and that he has won a fool's reward."[18]

On March 17, one day ahead of the deadline set by Mr. Lincoln, the advance elements of McClellan's army embarked at Alexandria for Hampton Roads.

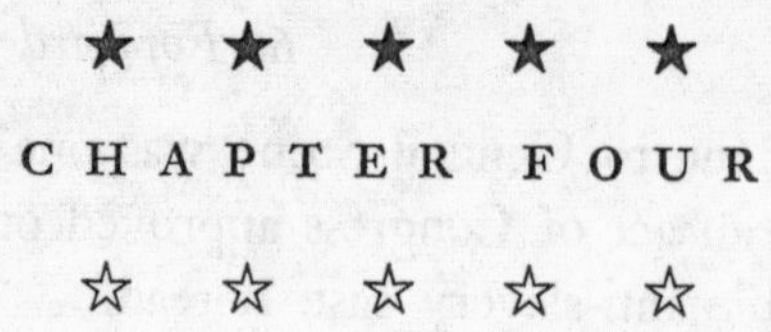

Stride of a Giant

1: *The Ironclads*

The two warships swung to their cables off Newport News Point, riding easily to the incoming tide at the three-fathom line. The spring sky this morning held neither wind nor clouds, and men who saw these ships said that they made an unforgettable picture. Their black hulls had the final buoyant perfection of the last designs before steam; their raked masts, going aloft just off the perpendicular, carried yards precisely squared, with tarred rigging making unobtrusive India ink patterns against the blue. U.S.S. *Cumberland* and U.S.S. *Congress* were enforcing the blockade at the mouth of the James River, and if the job was important it was also simple. It could be done at anchor, lower booms swung out, a cluster of small boats alongside, crews indolently busy with odd jobs. On *Cumberland* the men had been doing their washing, and they hoisted long fore-and-aft lines of scrubbed clothing to add a homely touch to this naval picture.

Before the day ended a good many people looked at these ships, because each ship was about to die, dramatically and in the center of the stage. This was the last morning: last morning for the ships, for many of their people, and for all that the ships represented—a special way not merely of fighting on the sea but of moving on it and understanding it, of combining grimness and grace in one instrument. In a war that destroyed one age and introduced another, these ships stood as symbols of the past.

They had no engines and they were made all of wood, and of course they were entirely out of date. But even obsolete warships can be useful as long as they are stronger than anything the enemy has, and the rickety Confederate flotilla that lived somewhere up the James was far too weak to come down and fight. So *Cumberland* and *Congress* rode the tide, on a morning so still that *Cumberland* loosed her sails and let them hang for a thorough drying. The morning was warm, and inshore some soldiers from the 20th Indiana infantry stripped off their uniforms and went splashing about in the shallows: it was not every year that an Indiana boy could go swimming as early as the eighth of March. Noon came, and the warships piped their crews to dinner: roast beef and potatoes, and very good, too, an old salt on *Cumberland* remembered.

While the men ate, lookouts scanned the horizon, for routine, and just as the messcloths were being put away they saw something: a businesslike pillar of black smoke going skyward over the Craney Island flats at the mouth of the Elizabeth River, five miles off to the southeast. There was a film of haze over the water and the low shores that day, making a mirage, and officers studied this development carefully with their telescopes. The pillar of smoke looked stationary, at first, but at last it could be seen that it was moving north out of the mouth of the river and into the wide reach of Hampton Roads, and the base of the pillar rested on a black hull. *Cumberland's* dangling sails were brailed up and the lines of washing came down, the small boats were dropped astern and the booms were rigged in. The drummers beat to quarters, and officers passed the word along the decks: *Merrimack* is coming out![1]

Merrimack had been a legend all winter, and the lower deck had grown somewhat skeptical. It was known that the burly steam frigate which had been burned and scuttled the previous spring, when Gosport Navy Yard at Norfolk was abandoned, had been raised, rebuilt, and renamed; she was now C.S.S. *Virginia,* she had been remodeled so radically that she looked like no ship that had ever floated before, and she was sheathed all over in iron so that it just might be that there was not a warship in the United States Navy that could do her any harm. Now she was coming out, and the matter would be put to the test. *Cumberland* and *Congress* cleared for action and stood by.

The new warship was as big a riddle to her own people as to anyone else. She was completely untested. About all anyone could say of her, for sure, was that she would float if the water were calm enough, and that she was abominably uncomfortable. (Crowded quarters and lack of ventilation caused much sickness; during her two months of life her crew of three hundred always had been between fifty and sixty men in hospital ashore, besides the ordinary sicklist aboard ship.) She was as sluggish as a dismasted hulk on the verge of foundering, could steam at little more than five miles an hour, needed at least thirty minutes to turn around, and drew between 22 and 23 feet of water. On a 275-foot hull she had a central superstructure, or citadel, 160 feet long, with rounded ends and slanting sides; anyone who had ever looked upon a river in flood was instantly reminded of a barn drifting downstream, submerged to the eaves. Her citadel had wooden walls two feet thick covered with four inches of iron, and the decks before and after it were completely awash. She carried ten guns—four rifles, and six nine-inch Dahlgrens—and at her bow, under water, she wore a massive cast-iron beak. While she was being remodeled citizens who strolled up to watch told her constructor that she would either capsize as soon as she left the docks, suffocate all hands, or deafen everybody by the concussion of guns fired inside that cramped citadel. Now she was going to fight, and Confederates as well as Yankees would learn something.[2]

Her skipper was Franklin Buchanan, a stalwart in his early sixties, a man of distinction in the Old Navy. He had been an officer since 1815, had been made first superintendent of the new Naval Academy at Annapolis in 1854, and carried one of those odd tag-lines that sometimes cling to a man: he was said at one time to be the third-strongest man in the Navy. He came from Maryland, and in April of 1861 he resigned, believing that Maryland would quickly secede; he tried unsuccessfully to withdraw the resignation when he found that the state would not secede. If this indicated a lack of original fire for the Southern cause no sign of it remained. He had become a captain in the Confederate Navy in September and now was a flag officer commanding the James River Defenses, with his flag in *Merrimack-Virginia*.

He wanted to find out about his crew as well as his ship. Most of his men were out-and-out landsmen—he had told the Secretary of the Navy that two thirds of them had never even been seasick, and one gun crew was composed entirely of a draft from a Norfolk artillery company. As the ship came slowly out into the roads Buchanan called all hands for a traditional now-hear-this pep talk. The eyes of the nation were upon them; every man must do his full duty, and more; the Yankee warships must be taken, "and you shall not complain that I do not take you close enough. Go to your guns!"[3] *Virginia* came out into Hampton Roads, made a ponderous left turn, and steamed up toward the two sailing ships, while flag hoists blossomed at the yardarms of every Federal warship within sight. The Indiana swimmers hurried back to camp to get their clothing and their muskets, and the gunners in the batteries on the mainland prepared to open fire.

Anchored close inshore, two or three miles to the east of *Congress* and *Cumberland*, were two of the most powerful warships in existence, U.S.S. *Minnesota* and *Roanoke;* huge steam frigates rated at 3500 tons, mounting 44 heavy guns, sister ships to the old *Merrimack* herself. *Roanoke* was helpless with a broken propeller shaft that had been under leisurely repair for weeks, and she signaled now for tugs to tow her into action, opening on *Virginia* at long range with such guns as would bear. *Minnesota* slipped her cable and prepared to steam into the fray, but ran ingloriously aground and could do no more than call for tugs and fire ineffectually at a distance of more than a mile.

Virginia came on, inexorably, in slow motion, ignoring this fire and the fire from the shore batteries; drew abreast of *Cumberland*, then turned and came in bows-on, tricing up one of her forward gunports, running out a seven-inch rifle, and opening fire. Her first shell smashed through *Cumberland's* bulwarks, spraying jagged splinters all about, and exploded amidships, killing nine Marines. *Virginia's* gunport blinked shut, and the big steamer came on; then the port-lid went up again, the black muzzle of the rifle reappeared, and a second shell was fired. This one knocked *Cumberland's* forward pivot gun out of action, and killed or wounded the entire gun crew. (The gun captain, John Kirker, was carried below with both arms gone at the shoulder. As he was laid on the deck in the sick bay he begged a shipmate to draw his sheath knife and cut his throat.) *Virginia* came still nearer, firing with deadly regularity, proving the grim truth of a point long suspected by naval men: a wooden warship simply could not stand shell fire. Before long *Cumberland's* gun deck was so littered with dead bodies that details worked frantically to stack the corpses somewhere out of the way of the gun carriages. But this helped very little; fighting bows-on, *Cumberland* could bring hardly any of her guns to bear no matter how she disposed of her dead.

Closer and closer came *Virginia*, ugly and black and irresistible, coming in for collision; and at last, with a jarring, splintering crash she struck *Cumberland* in the starboard bow, breaking a huge hole below the waterline. For a moment the two ships hung together; then they broke apart, *Virginia's* iron beak was wrenched off, and water came surging into *Cumberland's* orlop deck in a torrent. Wounded men on the berth deck gaped at a sudden rush of odd-looking fugitives, men in red smocks, swarming up the ladders from below, hurrying aft; powder-handlers, driven from the forward magazine by the rising water. *Cumberland's* bow dipped lower; the two ships lay side by side, a hundred yards apart, and a sudden cheer went up from *Cumberland's* gun deck—at last the guns could be trained on their target.

Cumberland fired three broadsides, breaking the muzzles of two of *Virginia's* guns, exploding one shell in her smokestack with an ear-splitting clang that made the Confederates think a boiler had blown up; yet doing no really serious damage. The exasperated Federal gunners could see the 80-pound shot they were firing bouncing high off the ironclad's sides and arching off to the west to drop in the oyster beds on the far side of the James River, a mile away. Even with her entire broadside in action at point-blank range, *Cumberland* could not seriously harm her opponent.[4]

The Federal warship sagged lower and lower, with water knee-deep on the berth deck, wounded men calling for someone to help them; and from *Virginia's* upper deck Buchanan shouted a demand for surrender—getting a defiant "No!" for answer, followed by a shot from one of *Cumberland's* guns. But if this defiance was gallant it was also useless. *Cumberland* was sinking fast by now, and at last one of her officers bawled an order down a hatchway—"Every man for himself!" The most anyone could do was carry a few of the wounded men up to the gun deck; *Cumberland's* boats were all adrift, far astern, and men too badly hurt to swim had no hope. The ship lurched heavily to starboard, hung briefly with her stern in the air, and then went to the bottom like a stone, most of the wounded going down with her. The tip of one mast remained above water, flag still flying.[5]

Virginia moved up the James, and men on *Congress* cheered, thinking the iron monster was out of the fight. But Buchanan was simply getting room to make an ungainly turn, and presently the ironclad came back, heading straight for *Congress*. This ship spread her sails to get into shallow water where *Virginia* could not follow and ran hard aground, and *Virginia* took station astern and opened a pitiless fire that wrecked the big frigate and set it ablaze. Federal shore batteries hammered at the ironclad, and even the infantry opened fire; Buchanan, going out on the open deck for a better view, was wounded by a minié ball and had to be carried below. But *Congress* was helpless, and the ironclad kept on pounding. The captain of the Federal ship was killed, the flames were out of control, and at last *Congress* struck her flag in surrender. The Confederate James River flotilla—wooden gunboats *Yorktown*, *Jamestown*, and *Teaser* —had come down to join Buchanan's flag, and now they steamed up to seize *Congress* and remove her crew, but the Federal batteries ashore opened a heavy fire on them, happy to find targets that could be hurt. An officer in one of these batteries, a lawyer in civil life, raised a point: *Congress* had surrendered, and therefore were not the Confederates legally entitled to board her? This meant nothing to old Brigadier General Joseph K. F. Mansfield, who growled: "I know the damned ship has surrendered, but *we* haven't," and the fire was continued; the Confederate ships drew away, *Yorktown* under tow with a disabled boiler and four men dead; and *Virginia*, now commanded by her executive officer, Lieutenant Catesby ap R. Jones, steamed out of range, accompanied by her consorts, and drifted with the tide, surveying the situation.

From Lieutenant Jones's point of view the situation could hardly have been better. The Union fleet was out of action, two ships gone, *Minnesota* stranded, *Roanoke* immobile; the frigate *St. Lawrence*, which had tried to come up and join the fight, had followed the strange Federal habit of that disastrous afternoon and gone aground. *Virginia*, to be sure, had taken a hammering. Two men had been killed and eight had been wounded, everything above decks had been riddled, the flagstaff had been shot away and the colors were fastened to the perforated smokestack, there was a leak forward where the iron beak had been wrenched off, and the vessel looked more like a homemade derelict than ever. But her armor was still intact, her wheezy engines were working about as well as they ever did, and she was fully operational; and as the sun went down she was unchallenged mistress of the waters.[6]

Far to the north, President Lincoln's cabinet got the news and met in a mood close to despair. Secretary Stanton believed that *Virginia* would immediately steam up the Potomac and bombard the capital, and wanted to sink barges in the channel to block the way; was dissuaded, at last, when Secretary Welles convinced him that *Virginia* drew too much water to make the trip, but feared that the ship might instead head for New York and bring catastrophe to New York Harbor. (This too was a needless worry; Buchanan could have told him that the last thing *Virginia* would dare try was a voyage in the open sea.) What seemed indisputable was that *Virginia* might proceed at leisure to destroy every Federal warship in the lower Chesapeake, and if that happened General McClellan's plan for an advance up the peninsula between the James and York Rivers would need immediate revision. No Yankee transport would dare visit Hampton Roads as long as this ironclad was unchecked.

Nothing more could be done tonight. The tide was ebbing, and there was danger that *Virginia* would go aground along with everybody else, so at dusk the ironclad and her gunboats drew off to a safe anchorage at the mouth of the Elizabeth River, under protection of Confederate batteries, to send dead and wounded ashore and make emergency repairs. After dark the flames from burning *Congress* made a red glow in the night by Newport News Point. Toward midnight the flames reached the frigate's magazines and she blew up with a great burst of fire and sparks and a heavy concussion that went echoing off across the still water. With morning, *Virginia* would come out again to finish the job.

Then, at the last possible moment, hope for salvation returned to the Federal Navy; U.S.S. *Monitor* came steaming in past the Virginia capes after sunset, moved up into Hampton Roads, and anchored near *Minnesota*, which was still struggling to get afloat like a man trying to wriggle out of a straitjacket. Now the Federals had an ironclad of their own. With it they could turn overwhelming disaster into a face-saving, life-saving stalemate. When morning came, ironclad would fight ironclad . . . and every navy in the world would have to rebuild.

As a matter of fact the rebuilding had already begun. Both the British and the French navies already had ironclads in commission, with more under construction and still others under design; and Foote's gunboats on the western rivers were armored, even though they were armored too lightly. *Virginia* had simply dramatized the fact that an unarmored ship could not possibly fight an armored ship, and when the smoke from the burning frigate fogged the sunset on the evening of March 8 that lesson had been driven home once and forever. The next day's fight between *Monitor* and *Virginia* would supplement it; putting on display not the world's first ironclads, but just the world's first fight between ironclads.

In all of this there was acute embarrassment for the United States Navy, if the Navy had had time to reflect. Its professionals had been completely outthought and outmaneuvered by the underrated civilian who served as Jefferson Davis's Secretary of the Navy, Stephen R. Mallory of Florida. Mallory had seen what the experts failed to see and he had acted on what he saw, and the United States Navy was extremely lucky to be getting out of this fix at all.

Less than a month after Fort Sumter, Mallory had seen the need for ironclads. Sadly deficient in shipyards, shipwrights, and naval architects, the South could not hope to build a seagoing fleet that would match the Federal fleet, and Mallory knew it. He knew, too, that wooden warships were obsolete anyway. Firing shell, he said, wooden ships would destroy one another so quickly that a sea fight would be nothing more than a contest to see which ship would sink first; and early in May he had urged the Congress to meditate on "the wisdom and expediency of fighting with iron against wood." When *Merrimack* was raised and rebuilt he saw to it that she was heavily armored, and the job was well under way before Secretary Welles's people got around to consider the question of using armor at all. Not until October did the Federal government contract for the building of *Monitor*, and the only thing that saved the day for the United States Navy was the fact that the North had an industrial plant that could handle a job like this with impressive speed.

In her own way *Monitor* was just as odd as *Virginia*. A heavily armored turret carrying two 11-inch guns stood amidships on a long, armored hull that had no more than a foot or two of freeboard; there was a little knob of a pilothouse forward and a smokestack aft, and nothing more. If the Confederate ship looked like a half-submerged barn, the Federal looked (as men said) like a tin can on a shingle. Built after the designs of the irascible genius John Ericsson, *Monitor* was as hard to live in as *Virginia*, and very little more seaworthy—she had come close to foundering, on her trip down from New York—but she drew much less water and answered her helm better; and, all in all, here she was in Hampton Roads on the morning of March 9, and Ericsson's idea would quickly be put to the test.[7]

Skipper of *Monitor* was Lieutenant John Worden. He reported to the senior naval officer present, Captain John Marston of *Roanoke*, who sensibly ignored Washington's orders to send the ironclad up the Potomac and told Worden to stand by *Minnesota*. Worden cleared for action and his crew turned in for the night, while tugboats continued their unavailing efforts to get *Minnesota* afloat. Dawn brought a fog, which thinned out toward eight o'clock to reveal once more that moving pillar of smoke down by the mouth of the Elizabeth; here was *Virginia*, ready for another battle. *Monitor's* men were called to battle stations, and Worden steered down to meet his opponent. The two vessels got to close range and opened fire, and for the next two hours the world's first fight between armored ships was on, the two ships so wreathed with clouds of coal smoke and powder smoke that they could hardly see each other.

It was a strange fight. Neither ship could really hurt the other. Solid shot clanged against the iron plates and ricocheted far across the bay; shell burst with spectacular but ineffective explosions against iron turret and slanting citadel; *Virginia* tried to ram, but was far too sluggish, and gave *Monitor* no more than a nudge. In each ship the seamen quickly learned to refrain from leaning against the bulkheads; if a shot struck the armor while a man was touching the wall just inside the man could be killed or stunned. One of *Monitor's* men was knocked unconscious for ten minutes because his knee touched the turret wall when shot hit the armor outside.

Once *Virginia* hit a corner of *Monitor's* pilothouse with a heavy shell, breaking ironwork and leaving the structure somewhat insecure; and a moment later a shell exploded against the face of the pilothouse, driving flecks of paint, iron and powder in through the sighting slit, stunning and blinding Lieutenant Worden and putting him out of action. Until the youthful executive officer, Lieutenant Samuel Dana Greene, could be called from the turret *Monitor* was without a commander, and she drifted off into the shallows, temporarily out of the fight. *Virginia* promptly turned on *Minnesota* and opened a fire which set that luckless frigate ablaze and sank one of the tugs that had been trying so unsuccessfully to get the ship afloat.

Captain G. J. Van Brunt, *Minnesota's* commanding officer, suddenly found that he had the ironclad where every gun would bear, at easy range, and he fired an enormous broadside–two 10-inch guns, fourteen 9-inch and seven 8-inch: a weight of shot and shell which, as he said, would have blown any wooden ship clear out of the water. The missiles struck *Virginia* and bounced away, and Captain Van Brunt suddenly realized that the day of ships like his was over forever. When he came to make his report on the fight he wrote, as if bemused: "Never before was anything like it dreamed of by the greatest enthusiast in maritime warfare." It seemed to him that *Minnesota* was not merely out of date but immediately doomed, and he made preparations to destroy the ship and abandon it; but then *Monitor* got back into action, and it was ironclad against ironclad once more.

Once *Virginia* ran aground, but her engine room crew tied down the safety valves, piled oil-soaked rags into the furnaces, raised a perilous head of steam, and the ungainly fighting machine floundered off into deeper water.[8]

Somewhere around noon the fight died down as if by mutual consent. Because she had lost her ram and had consumed so much fuel, *Virginia* was riding higher at the bow than she normally would, and Lieutenant Jones was well aware that if the Yankees fired at her unarmored waterline, forward, they could riddle her. Her leak was troublesome, and the channel where she fought was narrow, and there was always the danger that she would become stranded again and hang there helpless. *Monitor*, in her turn, was in no mood to insist on a finish fight. She was under command of a junior officer, and orders were to play it safe and take no chances; *Monitor's* assignment today was strictly to save *Minnesota* from destruction, and this had been done, by the narrowest margin. In addition, Greene feared that if another shot hit the pilothouse where the first one had struck, the ship's steering gear would be disabled—Worden had always believed the pilothouse was *Monitor's* most vulnerable spot. So when at last *Virginia* steamed back to her base, *Monitor* stayed close to *Minnesota* and made no attempt to pursue.

The battle was over. It had been a complete stand-off, and Assistant Secretary of the Navy Gustavus V. Fox said the most that could be said when he telegraphed McClellan that night that the battle showed "a slight superiority in favor of the *Monitor*." He added that the Confederate ironclad "is an ugly customer, and it is too good luck to believe that we are yet clear of her"; and a few days later he warned the Navy Department that although *Monitor* was more than a match for her opponent she might easily be put out of action in her next fight and it was unwise to place too great dependence on her. *Monitor's* chief engineer, Alban C. Stimers, was more optimistic, and he telegraphed congratulations to Ericsson, telling him that "you have saved this place to the nation by furnishing us with the means to whip an ironclad frigate that was, until our arrival, having it all her own way with our most powerful vessels."[9]

In a way, *Monitor* had won something important; she had at

least restored the status quo. As long as she remained afloat, McClellan could bring his army down in transports and put men and supplies ashore near Fort Monroe. The army's campaign against Richmond could go ahead, even though *Virginia's* presence would impose certain handicaps. But the weight of the whole campaign rested on this queer, mastless warship with the revolving turret. *Monitor* could not be risked; she could neutralize *Virginia*, but she could do nothing more than that; dared do nothing more, because of all the ships in the United States Navy this was the one that must not be lost.

Meanwhile, Mr. Mallory had a nice answer for the impatient men in the Confederate Congress who had been demanding that he leave the cabinet because he had not given the Confederacy a navy.

2: *The Vulture and the Wolf*

Major General Braxton Bragg found the Mississippi town of Corinth badly overcrowded and wholly lacking in proper control. Troops were swarming into the place, disorganized and without supplies; the weather was atrocious, with rain and cold wind, and no one had made any arrangements for the sick, who were numerous. The one hotel was in danger of being sacked by hungry soldiers who crowded into the dining room in defiance of military restraint and even went into the kitchen to snatch hot meats off of the stoves, threatening to slaughter the hotel proprietor when he tried to stop them. Part of this disorder was probably due, as General Bragg now and then remarked, to the fact that these were raw troops led by untrained officers, which in turn could be blamed on "universal suffrage, the bane of our military organization"; a deeper reason was the fact that this little railroad junction town in northern Mississippi had suddenly become the Confederacy's most important troop center west of Richmond—the place from which General Albert Sidney Johnston would try to regain all that had been lost and chase the invading Yankees back to the Ohio River.[1]

Driven out of Kentucky and middle and western Tennessee,

General Johnston had discovered that his government would give him in disaster that which he had never been able to get in more prosperous times: reinforcements and some attention to his problem. He commanded more men now than he had ever had before, despite the heavy loss at Fort Donelson; by the final weeks of March he had between 40,000 and 45,000 men in Corinth, in addition to possibly 8500 who held New Madrid and Island Number Ten, on the Mississippi. Beyond this he could use, if he could get them across the river, the 20,000 Confederates now operating in Arkansas.

General Bragg had brought 10,000 men up from Mobile and Pensacola, and 5000 more had come from New Orleans, under Brigadier General Daniel Ruggles. (These would go under Bragg's command, and Mrs. Bragg assured her husband, by letter, that Louisiana troops were "obedient, good marksmen, habituated to exposure, and free from the besetting sin of our Confederacy, *drunkenness*.")[2] Leonidas Polk had brought down approximately 10,000 men who until March 2 had been stationed at Columbus, Kentucky, and, on the long march over from Murfreesboro, General Johnston had brought 17,000 and odd who had been at Bowling Green. All in all, there were plenty of soldiers at Corinth. The trouble was that they were not yet an army, but the raw materials of an army; putting them together and giving them the indefinable combination of training and inspiration which would make them feel and act as a unit would take time, which the Yankees might not allow.

In a sense, everything depended on whether or not the Federal invaders would come on with energy. If they did, neither General Johnston nor anyone else would have a chance to turn this convocation of soldiers into an army. Moving up the Tennessee River were 40,000 men under General Grant, their advance guard no more than twenty miles away. Coming overland from Nashville were 35,000 more under General Buell; they were a good deal farther off, and it seemed unlikely that they would move very rapidly no matter where they were. On the Mississippi, trying with the Navy's help to destroy all Confederate installations north of Memphis, were 25,000 men led by John Pope, a man with much raw energy, engaged now in an effort to isolate the strong mid-river fort at Island Number Ten. And from the far side of the Mississippi, because of recent events in the Arkansas foothills, the Federal power could draw reinforcements whenever it chose.

Yet the dominant factor might be General Johnston himself. General Johnston refused to feel that he was licked. Even as he led his dejected troops southeast from Nashville late in February, a storm of bitter criticism swirling about his head, winter rains and gales tormenting the soldiers, Johnston kept thinking about how he was going to beat the Yankees rather than about how they were beating him. He had been outgeneraled and he had been beaten, and he was woefully outnumbered, but his one thought was to regain the initiative. He planned not merely to check the invader but to win back everything that had been lost, and each day given him by the slow advance of the opposing armies was a day he would use to the utmost. As he rebuilt his army at Corinth he still had a chance, and it was a chance he did not propose to miss.

To wait was to lose. Grant had as many men as he had, and Grant had come up the Tennessee River almost to the Mississippi line, his headquarters at the town of Savannah, most of his troops thrust forward to the high ground back of Pittsburg Landing on the west bank of the Tennessee, around a country meetinghouse known as Shiloh Church. Once Buell joined Grant, Johnston would be compelled to use 40,000 to beat 75,000; the task would be impossible, and Johnston knew it. His only hope was to destroy Grant before Buell reached the scene. If he could do this he could turn the war upside down.

The chance was thin, of course. By any reasonable standard Johnston's army was no more ready to take the offensive than McDowell's had been at Bull Run. General Bragg was gloomily saying that few of the regiments had ever so much as made a full day's march and that most of the rank and file had never done a day's work in their lives,[3] and although General Bragg was a dour pessimist who usually believed the worst the situation was not promising. If the army did not come unraveled when it marched up to Pittsburg Landing it might very well fall apart when it made its attack. A cautious general, naturally, would wait until he had the army in better shape; yet a cautious general, waiting thus, getting everything ready before he moved, would simply condemn himself to fight a little later against overwhelming odds. General Johnston could not afford to be cautious.

He was greatly helped by the fact that General Halleck, who commanded all of the foes that were coming in on him, was the very embodiment of caution. Halleck had sent Grant up the Tennessee but had ordered him to be extremely careful; whatever happened, Grant was not to stir up a fight until Buell joined him. This was playing it safe: it was also giving General Johnston several priceless weeks of time which might have been denied him. Most of Grant's troops reached Pittsburg Landing by the end of the third week of March, and if they had moved on to Corinth at once they could have torn Johnston's army apart before its diverse elements had fully assembled. Such an advance, of course, would have been a bit risky, and Halleck would permit no risks. Grant must keep his army in its camps until Buell's men arrived. Then, no doubt, they could do something about getting on with the war.

It must be said in General Halleck's behalf that he had had other things to think about, and that one of his armies had in fact effectively disrupted a part of General Johnston's plan for a great counteroffensive.

Johnston planned to advance on both sides of the Mississippi River—to regain western Tennessee and Kentucky with his own army while with another army he drove the Yankees out of Missouri, going up to Cairo and beyond, perhaps even to St. Louis. West of the Mississippi there was a fairly substantial number of Confederate soldiers, and in January the Confederate government had sent out a new man to take command of these, to weld them into an army, and to use them under Johnston's direction. This new man was Major General Earl Van Dorn, a slim, elegant little soldier with curly hair, charming manners and a strong taste for fighting. A West Pointer in his early forties, Van Dorn had an excellent record. He had been an Indian fighter of note, with four wounds received in action on the western plains, and he had done well in the Mexican War, taking another wound and winning promotion for gallantry. He had dash and energy, and he seemed just the man to carry out Johnston's plan for action beyond the Mississippi.

Van Dorn had to begin by getting Ben McCulloch and Sterling Price to work together. President Davis wanted no repetition of the Wilson's Creek business, where a victory had lost most of its value because these soldiers could not agree, and he had given Van Dorn authority over both. Armed with this authority, Van Dorn conferred with Johnston shortly before the evacuation of Bowling Green, and worked out a bold plan for leading Price and McCulloch up through Missouri to St. Louis and thence eastward into Illinois—a move which, if it worked, would unquestionably hamstring the Federal thrust up the Tennessee River. Then he set out to cross the Mississippi and take over his new command.

He was met by a letter from General Price which convinced him that he had better hurry. The Confederates were about to retreat from Missouri to northwestern Arkansas, and Price and McCulloch were arguing more bitterly than ever. They could not agree about who ranked whom or what ought to be done next, and altogether it was time for someone to take charge. Van Dorn found the antipathetic generals camped, with their respective commands, in the Boston Mountains in northwestern Arkansas, seventy miles below the Missouri line. He was struck by the physical contrast between the two men. Price was tall, handsome, his ruddy face fringed by silvery hair and whiskers, his bearing courtly; Van Dorn's chief of staff remembered that Price housed his visitors in some luxury and gave them kidneys stewed in sherry for breakfast. McCulloch was spare, wiry, a little stoop shouldered, with sharp eyes peering carefully out from under shaggy brows, a man who looked and was a tough frontiersman. Texas to the core, with a Texan's flair for gaudy costumes, he had for battle a suit of black velvet, with high-topped patent leather boots and a broad-brimmed Texas hat. Jefferson Davis regarded him highly, and wrote long after the war of his "vigilance, judgment and gallantry."[4]

Van Dorn was what the two men needed. Simply because he had superior authority and was present, the quarrel over rank and planning ended. Price and McCulloch grew enthusiastic about the scheme for a counteroffensive, and Van Dorn presently notified Johnston that he had close to 20,000 men ready for action. Among these was a contingent unusual even for this western army, in which the extraordinary was routine: a brigade of two regiments of Cherokees and one of Creeks from the Indian Territory led by Brigadier General Albert Pike, an Arkansas lawyer with a benign eye and a flowing beard, a reputation as a Masonic poet and philosopher, and a knack for persuading red men to go along with the doctrine of states' rights. Van Dorn believed that more troops could be raised without difficulty and he was confident that the western half of the revived offensive would move on schedule.[5]

The first step was to whip the nearest Federal Army, a hard-fighting, hard-foraging outfit of fewer than 12,000 men, led by Brigadier General Samuel R. Curtis, who in the last few weeks had ended the long stalemate in southwestern Missouri, driving Price's Missourians out of Springfield and chasing them all the way into Arkansas. Curtis would have brought more men except for the fact that he was such a prodigious way from home—300 miles from St. Louis, 200 miles from the nearest railhead at Rolla, Missouri—and he had to make numerous detachments to protect this long supply line. He was in fact a good deal farther from his base than any other Union general had yet gone, and in rough winter weather he had made one of the longest marches of the war. His advance had a spectacular quality that was lost to sight because bigger armies elsewhere were getting most of the attention.

Curtis was halfway through his fifties, a quiet West Pointer who had left the Army a few years after graduation to work as a civil engineer. He had built railroads and levees, had been chief engineer in St. Louis and mayor of Keokuk, and late in the 1850s he had been elected a Republican Congressman from Iowa, resigning in the summer of 1861 to take a brigadier's commission. Proud of the advance his army had made, he was deeply disturbed by the horrors war inflicted on civilians. Many of these horrors, he was aware, came from his own troops. He had Franz Sigel's German regiments, which had earned a reputation for relentless foraging, and his native-American regiments really were not much more orderly; when his soldiers lost touch with their own supply trains they plundered farm and homestead with grasping hands. Price's retreating Missourians had done a good deal of looting and burning, too, and there were guerrilla bands to carry on where the soldiers left off; all the countryside had been ravaged, and was pock-marked with the blackened timbers of burned homes, barns and mills—"a sickening sight," Curtis wrote, "which for the sake of humanity I could pray were effaced from the record of events." Back of the pomp and glitter of war, he said, there was so much misery that "all should forever more earnestly implore Heaven to deliver us from 'war, pestilence and famine.'"[6]

Van Dorn got his army under way on March 3, Pap Price and his men at the head of the column, McCulloch's division following, Pike and the Indians bringing up the rear; altogether, there were nearly 15,000 Confederates in the line of march. (This was one of the few times when a major battle saw the Confederates with a substantial advantage in numbers.) Curtis lay to the north, with part of his army, under Sigel, thrust forward to the town of Bentonville, and Van Dorn tried to cut this force off and destroy it. Sigel was alert, fended him off, and got his command away unscathed; and a measure of the evil nature of Van Dorn's luck in this campaign is the fact that during this one important week Franz Sigel behaved like a competent general . . . Van Dorn pursued and found the Union Army drawn up south of Pea Ridge, back of Little Sugar Creek, facing south.

Curtis's troops were astride of the main road into southwestern Missouri—the road to Springfield, the one both armies had used on their recent march down, known locally as the Telegraph or Stagecoach Road. This road ran north from Curtis's camp past a country inn called Elkhorn Tavern, went on over Pea Ridge, dropped down into Cross Timber Hollow, and in its progress through these back-country names and places went on to the Missouri line and then continued up to Springfield. Van Dorn proposed to make a wide detour to his left, marching at night along a byroad that would bring him into the Telegraph Road north of Elkhorn Tavern first thing in the morning. He would then be in Curtis's rear and squarely across his supply line and his only avenue of escape, and if the Confederates moved smartly he ought to disperse or capture the whole Union

Army. Van Dorn put his troops in motion on the night of March 6; by his timetable, the battle would open shortly after dawn on March 7.

However, there were delays. Curtis had suspected that something of this kind might be done, and he had had parties out obstructing the road which Van Dorn had to use—hard-working details directed by a man skilled at road work, an Iowa colonel named Grenville Dodge, who would be famous a decade later as one of the chief builders of the Union Pacific Railroad. Dodge had this byroad pretty well blocked, the march took a good deal longer than had been planned, and it was midmorning or later before the Confederates had reached their chosen position. The long column somehow broke in half during the night, and when Van Dorn and Price were ready to make their attack by Elkhorn Tavern it developed that McCulloch and the other half of the army were miles in the rear, only halfway around the long semicircle of the flanking route. Curtis, meanwhile, had had just time enough to swing his army around and get ready to meet this attack on his rear; and when McCulloch attacked along the western end of Pea Ridge, two miles or more from the scene of Price's attack, Curtis sent divisions under Colonel Peter J. Osterhaus and Colonel Jefferson C. Davis over to handle him.

If Van Dorn had had a fully trained army with a competent staff and a little more professional leadership he probably would have won his battle, but he had none of those things and he did not get a victory. McCulloch's cavalry and Pike's Indians attacked first, captured a three-gun battery, and then came under artillery fire, which the tribesmen found strange and terrifying: they took to the woods, where each man got behind a tree in the old wilderness-fighting tradition, and the Indians were of little more account on this battlefield. McCulloch rode far to the front to get his division into action and was shot dead by a Northern sharpshooter; his chief brigadier was killed, another one was captured, his attack broke up in disorder, and by late afternoon the battle centered around Price's assault along the road by Elkhorn Tavern. The fight was a hard one, and at sundown the Federals had been forced to retreat half a mile or more, but their line was unbroken and Van Dorn in effect was fighting with hardly more than half his army.

The bruised armies spent an uneasy night on the field, the Federals who had fought McCulloch came up, and in the morning Curtis ordered a counterattack toward Cross Timber Hollow. Van Dorn, whose men were just about out of ammunition, discovered that through some misunderstanding his wagon master had sent the ammunition train off fifteen miles to the east. He ordered a retreat, part of his line broke under Federal pressure, and before noon the Confederates were swarming away from the field in disorder, pursued with only moderate diligence by an exhausted Union Army which had narrowly escaped destruction. Each army had lost some 1300 men in killed, wounded, and missing: Curtis still held the road to Missouri, to the railhead and to safety; Van Dorn's army would need to be reorganized before it could be used again, and it was no longer possible for its general to contemplate an invasion of Missouri.[7]

It had been a near thing. Curtis wrote that during the battle, while his men were wrestling for the ground around Elkhorn Tavern, time had seemed to stand still—"I watched the minute hand of my watch a thousand times"—and he confessed that when the battle ended his army was just about out of provisions and low on ammunition; if the final Union counterattack had not cleared the Telegraph Road, the army would have been almost helpless. But if the victory had been won by a painfully narrow margin, it was decisive when it came. Missouri would be Federal territory for the rest of the war, subject to alarms and excursions but not seriously contended for, and Johnston's plan for a counteroffensive astride the Mississippi would have to be modified. Few Federal officers ever averted more trouble than Curtis did when he spun his army around and won his fight at Pea Ridge.

The man had no eye for glory. When he looked out over the field where so much had been won he could see only the price that had been paid, by his own men and by his enemies. A few days after the battle he spoke his mind in a letter to his brother, writing about "the bold rocky mountain . . . under whose shadow so many fell," and he brooded thoughtfully: "The scene is silent and sad. The vulture and the wolf now have the dominion, and the dead friends and foes sleep in the same lonely graves."[8] Every general moved to victory across long rows of graves in the trampled earth. Curtis was one who had to look back afterward and think about how those graves had been filled.

So Albert Sidney Johnston had lost the first round, far away in the Ozark foothills. His great counteroffensive could not be won by a swift, dazzling thrust at the Federal rear; whatever was done would have to be done in the lonely fields and thickets around Shiloh Church. But it was only the first round that had been lost. Johnston's big opportunity remained, narrowing day by day but still open. The Federal move up the Tennessee was marking time, losing time, permitting the armies of Grant and Buell to remain separated while the Confederates they had to beat worked desperately to strike them before they were ready; and as the month of March ended Johnston had in fact performed a minor miracle. He had created an army, which had come to believe in itself. It lacked a great many things but somehow it had acquired an immense capacity to fight, and General Johnston proposed to use it without further delay.

Late in the month he made formal announcement of his new organization—three army corps, somewhat undersized but nevertheless duly organized, led by Polk, Hardee, and Bragg, with a small reserve corps under an impressive new officer who only a few months earlier had resigned from the United States Senate, John C. Breckinridge of Kentucky. In addition to leading one corps Bragg was acting as chief of staff, and he was a skilled and relentless disciplinarian. He complained that the Army was still "an heterogeneous mass" containing "more enthusiasm than discipline, more capacity than knowledge and more valor than instruction," and he noted distressing shortcomings in equipment: in most regiments some men had regular percussion rifles, others had smooth-bore flintlocks and some were armed with nothing better than country shotguns. Johnston had tried to increase the number of men in combat assignments by hiring slaves from local planters to serve as cooks, teamsters and so on, but he had had little luck, and he mused that the ways of prosperous civilians in wartime are strange: "These people have given their sons freely, but it is folly to talk to them about a Negro or a mule." He remarked that one additional brigade might make the difference between victory and defeat, and he wondered what the planters thought their precious slaves would be worth if his army should be beaten.[9] Yet even though the deficiencies in supply and training were obvious, an enormous amount of work had been done. Jefferson Davis sent an encouraging message: "You have done wonderfully well, and now I breathe easier." And from General Lee came the appreciative comment of a fellow professional:

"No one has sympathized with you in the troubles with which you are surrounded more sincerely than myself. I have watched your every movement, and know the difficulties with which you have had to contend. . . . I need not urge you, when your army is united, to deal a blow at the enemy in your front, if possible before his rear gets up from Nashville. You have him divided, keep him so if you can."[10]

General Johnston did not need to be urged. His army was not really in proper shape, and if he could wait another ten days he would get strong reinforcements from beyond the Mississippi—he had ordered Van Dorn to come to Tennessee with all speed, the march was long and the roads were bad, and the move was taking a good deal of time—but 40,000 men could do now what 60,000 men could not do a fortnight from now, and the time of preparation was over. Buell's men would join Grant's by the end of the first week in April, at the latest . . . and, on the night of April 2, Johnston ordered plans drawn up for an immediate advance against Grant's army at Pittsburg Landing.

3: *Pittsburg Landing*

Almost everything that could go wrong went wrong when Johnston's army marched from Corinth to Pittsburg Landing. The soldiers did not know how to make a cross-country hike and most of their officers did not know how to direct them. The orders governing the march were imperfectly drafted and poorly executed, and General Johnston quickly learned what General McDowell had learned on the way to Bull Run—that the one thing an untrained army cannot possibly do is to move from here to there efficiently. The soldiers were in good spirits, and whenever they saw the commanding general ride by they cheered loudly, but they spent most of their time stumbling into bewildering traffic jams and waiting for somebody to untangle them, and in the end it took them three days to go twenty miles. During this time they ate the last of the five-days' rations they had in their haversacks. General Beauregard was so discouraged that at last he wanted to cancel the entire movement, go back to base, and start over again.

General Beauregard was the Army's second-in-command. He suffered from ill health; also, from a subtler ailment which impelled him to make grandiose plans for an army which needed exceedingly simple plans. When he drew up the order of attack for Johnston's signature, he behaved as if these troops were veterans, used to intricate movement and the shock of battle, and he asked them to do more than they could do. They were to leave Corinth on April 3, moving by two roads which converged near a farmhouse a few miles short of the Federal position. Cavalry had learned that Grant's men were camped in a loose grouping three miles wide, occupying the high ground inland from Pittsburg Landing, facing generally toward the west, with the swampy lowland of Owl Creek on the north and the equally swampy valley of Lick Creek on the south. Hardee's corps, in the lead, was ordered to march for sixteen or seventeen miles and bivouac for the night a mile or two away from the Federal outposts. Before dawn on April 4 this corps would form line of battle, covering the whole Federal front. Half a mile behind it Bragg's corps would form a similar line, with Polk's corps and Breckinridge's reserves forming behind Bragg. Then the army would attack, hoping to break the Federal left and drive the whole Federal Army away from the Tennessee River and into the Owl Creek bottomlands, where it could be destroyed.

For a professional army that could move smartly and hold its formation, the scheme might have been sound enough, but for this army it was just too much. Hardly a handful of Johnston's 40,000 had ever seen a battle or made an ordered march to a battlefield, and the chance that they could stick to this tight schedule was remote; it was even less likely that the fragile corps organizations, which had existed for less than a week, could hold together once those long battle lines moved in through woods and ravines on each other's heels. Johnston seems to have supposed that the three corps would attack side by side, which would have been much simpler. Apparently he and Beauregard misunderstood each other; with a slight excess of courtliness, Johnston was giving Beauregard a good deal of scope in his second-in-command function. In any case, as issued the orders embodied Beauregard's ideas, and much confusion attended their execution.[1]

Getting out of Corinth was bad enough. Hardee's corps, which was to move first, got tangled up in the streets with other troops and with wagon trains and was unable to leave town until the afternoon of April 3; instead of reaching its destination that night it had to camp along the road, getting to the designated point long after daybreak on April 4. Bragg's corps fell far behind, its road blocked by units that were supposed to follow it, one entire division temporarily lost; Johnston himself had to ride back, dig the missing unit out of Bishop Polk's corps, into which it had strayed, and get the road cleared. On the night of April 4 there was a heavy rain—by this time the attack had been postponed for twenty-four hours—and not until late in the afternoon of April 5 was the army at last in the spot it was supposed to have reached thirty-six hours earlier. The battle lines were drawn, and at dusk Johnston and his corps commanders had an informal conference.

To General Beauregard it was clear that the opportunity had passed. The whole battle plan rested on the belief that the army would make a quick march and take the Yankees by surprise. The march had been unconscionably slow, and it had been so noisy that a surprise seemed out of the question. After the rain the men had blithely fired their muskets to see whether the powder charges had been dampened, so that there had been a constant *pop-pop* of small arms fire through the late afternoon and early evening. There had been much cheering and yelling: loud cheers for General Johnston, wild shouts when a startled deer jumped out of a thicket and bounded along the line of troops; enough noise, altogether, to arouse the most unobservant foes. Rations were almost exhausted, much food having been thrown away by boys who felt themselves overloaded. In addition, Buell surely must have arrived by now. The Federals would be on the alert, and the attack ought to be canceled.

Johnston would not hear of it. If rations were low, the Federal camp contained abundant supplies which victorious Confederates could eat. The cavalry said that Buell had not yet appeared. From President Davis there had just come a telegram: "I hope you will be able to close with the enemy before his two columns unite. I anticipate a victory." What President Davis anticipated General Johnston would try to give him. He remarked, "I would fight them if they were a million," and he ended the conference by saying, "Gentlemen, we shall attack at daylight tomorrow." Later that evening he calmly told an aide, "I have ordered a battle for daylight tomorrow, and I intend to hammer 'em!" Many things had gone wrong, but the men in the ranks were keyed up for a fight and so was the commanding general, and a fight there would be as soon as the sun came up on April 6.[2]

By all logic Beauregard ought to have been right. Yet the astounding fact was that the Federals were woefully, incredibly unready. They were not entrenched (as Beauregard believed they surely must be) and they were not even arranged in line of battle; they were simply in camp, waiting for orders from headquarters, waiting for Buell, waiting for the time when they could march down to Corinth and finish the job that had been begun at Fort Henry and Fort Donelson.

Many things had worked together to create this condition. Halleck's repeated orders to delay the offensive had led Grant and his lieutenants to think of nothing except the restrictions which headquarters had imposed. Impatient to get on with the war, Grant was overlooking the possibility that his rival might get on with it ahead of him. (Those earlier battles unfortunately had led Grant to feel that Johnston's army was discouraged and ready to quit: a point on which he was about to get a world of enlightenment.) Grant himself was still at Savannah, seven miles downstream, waiting for Buell, whose approach was extraordinarily slow. Buell's army had begun leaving Nashville on March 15, impelled by no sense of urgency. It had waited for ten days, rebuilding a bridge—a twenty-four-hour job, if someone had been driving the Engineer Corps to hurry—and it was coming on as if it had all the time in the world. The Federals, in short, had got into a dangerous state of mind, in which it seemed to them that nothing would happen until they themselves made it happen.[3]

In addition, the camp at Shiloh was under the immediate command of William T. Sherman, who had recovered all too well from an abject loss of nerve. During the previous fall, in Kentucky, he had considered Johnston's army much more numerous, aggressive, and dangerous than it really was, and had worried himself into a nervous breakdown and removal from command. Regaining his poise, he had recently been restored to combat duty: and in this first week of April he probably was the last man in the army to take alarm because of enemy activity in his front. He flatly refused to believe that Johnston's army was about to attack (six months earlier, because he did believe it, he had been published to the world as a lunatic) and when his patrols warned him that something ominous was building up, off beyond the tangled forest, he dismissed the warnings with contempt. At the very moment when Johnston was insisting that the attack would be delivered even if all of Lincoln's Yankees were alarmed and ready, Sherman was assuring Grant that although there was a good deal of shooting along the picket lines "I do not apprehend anything like an attack on our position." Some of Sherman's officers certainly knew better, but what they knew did not matter. Up to a certain point, in any army, the thoughts of the principal generals are the only thoughts that count.[4]

Thus Sherman's caution, which should have been awake but was sound asleep, ran across Beauregard's, which should have been justified but was not; and the battle itself began on this characteristic note of conscientious confusion, which accurately reflected the state of the armies and of the divided nation that had raised the armies. These early battles of the Civil War were not like the ones that came later except in the pain and agony they inflicted. Not only were the officers and men who fought these battles untrained, doomed to make errors which would not be repeated once experience had been gained, the nation itself was in these battles colliding violently, at last, with the reality which it had so long refused to face. It had risked war gaily, had threatened war jauntily, had accepted it with a wild, half-hysterical sense of relief, and it had done all of these things simply because it had known nothing whatever about war. Now–at Shiloh, and at one or two other places–it was going to learn. Here was where (as the saying then went) it would see the elephant. No wonder there was something unreal about the genesis and development of such encounters. Anything else would have been a miracle.

The first sounds of battle came to the Confederate Army like enchanted, beckoning notes of promise. April 5 was bright, clear, and springlike after the storm, and men in the 38th Tennessee, striding along in the woods where new leaves, half-opened, put moving shadows on the roadways, heard gunfire far ahead and "could hardly be restrained from rushing up to the fray." Men looked at one another, laughed, cheered, and remarked that the fun was at last beginning. Fatherless rumors sped down the marching columns–the Yankees had been whipped and were taking to their boats, some of them had been cut off and were fleeing through the woods, this very column would presently go and round up these cowardly fugitives.[5] . . . Battle was still nearly twenty-four hours away. These boys were hearing the racket that bothered Beauregard so much, the firing of innumerable muskets by soldiers who wanted to know whether these weapons, after a heavy rain, could in fact be fired at all. (A good deal of this came from within the Yankee lines, where equally innocent soldiers, equally soaked by the same storm, were making the same sort of test.)

Give the innocents credit. When the reality came, next day, most of them went into it with the same enthusiasm and stayed in it as long as they were asked to stay. Whatever finally determined the outcome of the battle of Shiloh, the end did not come because either army took fright and ran away or got weary and dogged it. Johnston's soldiers had all of the savage, frightening determination which the Belgian visitor had noted early in the winter; they were no more ready for battle than the Bull Run mobs had been, but when they struck the Federal line of battle they struck it, as Beauregard himself remarked, "like an Alpine avalanche," curing U. S. Grant forever of his notion that the Confederate soldier's heart was not in this fight. Long after the war, when he talked with friends in the Army of the Potomac about such grim fights as Gettysburg and the Wilderness, tough Sherman used to say: "So help me God, you boys never had a fiercer fight than we had there."[6]

Sunday, April 6, was clear and cool as the day before had been, and just at dawn there was a timeless quiet which reminded one young Confederate of the small-town Sabbath back home, so that he half-expected to hear church bells calling the faithful to worship. Johnston's first line began to move as soon as the light came, and the general was just finishing breakfast when the first spatter of small-arms fire sounded along the front—real shooting, this time, not just the aimless firing of boys testing their powder charges. Various officers were urging him to go back to Corinth and begin all over again, but he swung into the saddle with the comment: "The battle has opened, gentlemen; it is too late to change our dispositions." He rode to the front to take general charge of the assault, while Beauregard went to the rear to see that the support troops came up properly, and the great, shapeless army began to advance through the thickets for its first battle. Men in Breckinridge's reserve corps were told to pile their knapsacks and leave squads to guard them, and men detailed for this noncombatant assignment objected to being kept out of the fight; one soldier offered to give all of his hardtack to any man who would let him have a place in the front line. The sporadic firing up ahead became heavier, solidified into long rolling volleys, expanded with the crash of artillery, and became a consuming, bewildering uproar that would go on without a break all day long.[7]

The Federals were not ready, but they were not exactly caught asleep in their tents, either. They had sent patrols forward at dawn, and these collided with the Confederate skirmishers in the woodland twilight and formed tough knots of resistance. They were pushed back as Hardee's main line came up, but they had given the alarm, and battle lines were formed in front of the camps. The real trouble was that of the six divisions in Grant's army, only two were up in front when the fighting began, and nobody had told them to entrench. Sherman had his division around Shiloh Church with his right touching the Owl Creek Valley, and off to his left, somewhat out of touch with him, was a new division under Brigadier General Benjamin M. Prentiss, a former militia colonel who was about to display a talent for determined fighting. Farther back were three more divisions—McClernand's, which had learned its trade at Fort Donelson; another set of Donelson veterans belonging to C. F. Smith, who was absent with an infected leg and had turned his command over to W. H. L. Wallace, an Illinois lawyer who had served in the Mexican War; and three brigades led by still another Illinois lawyer-politician, Brigadier General Stephen A. Hurlbut, South Carolina born, a friend of Abraham Lincoln. Several miles north of these, posted downstream as a sort of flank guard, was the division of the future novelist, Lew Wallace, who never did manage to get his men into action this day. Of the six divisional commanders only Sherman was a West Pointer.

So the Federal front was sketchy, and it remained so even when the troops in the rear were moved forward, because as they moved up the men in front were being pushed back, and there never was a really connected front. There were many battles but no one line of battle; Shiloh was a grab bag full of separate combats in which divisions, brigades, and even regiments fought on their own, each one joined by fragments of other commands that had fallen apart in the shock of action, most of them fighting with their flanks in the air, knowing nothing of any battle except the fragment which possessed them—great waves of sound beating on them, smoke streaking the fields and making blinding clouds under the trees, advance and retreat taking place sometimes because someone had ordered it and sometimes on the impulse of the untaught soldiers who were doing the fighting.

On the Confederate side there was equal confusion. Bragg's second line advanced through Hardee's first line so that the elements of the two commands were completely intermingled, with the men of Polk and Breckinridge coming up to infiltrate the disordered lines. Command arrangements dissolved entirely, and at last the corps commanders made spur-of-the-moment plans: Bragg would take the right, Polk the center, and Hardee the left, with Breckinridge operating wherever he seemed to be needed. Troop movements were utterly disordered. One soldier wrote after the battle that "we fooled around for 5 or 6 hours before we got to see a Yankee, although the battle was raging not more than half a mile from us." He added that when his regiment at last did get into action "I tell you they made us fight a while before they let us quit."[8]

This was happening, remember, to men who (save for the Donelson veterans in Grant's army, and a scattering of Polk's men who had been at Belmont) had never fought before and who were most inadequately trained for fighting, and whose company and regimental officers were in no better case than themselves. Many of them, naturally, cut and ran for it without delay. Part of Sherman's division simply disappeared, and by noon there were thousands of Union fugitives glued to the ground on the river bank at Pittsburg Landing, men so overwhelmed by terror that no conceivable effort could get them back into action: Grant estimated later that at no time during the day were more than 25,000 Federals actually fighting. Many Confederates were beguiled by the fact that the camps they captured had abundant food lying ready to hand, the breakfasts which the Yankees had not had time to eat; hungry soldiers paused to fill their bellies and drifted out of any man's control. A nephew of Varina Davis, an officer in a Mississippi regiment, told about finding a crowd of 300 men or more lounging about in the rear. These men explained that "we are all smashed," although they had lost no more than three or four killed and two dozen wounded, and he wrote angrily: "These are the kind of troops of which you read gallant deeds and reckless conduct, they lose half a dozen, retire in time to save their haversacks and are puffed accordingly."[9]

Yet the stragglers and the incontinent foragers and the faint-hearts were, incredibly enough, in the minority. Sherman's division broke, retreated, and reformed its fragments with McClernand's men, but the records showed that it had 1900 casualties, which proves that it did a good deal of fighting. If many Confederates left the ranks to sack the Yankee camps, more of them stopped only long enough to pick up modern muskets to replace their own antiquated weapons; the rear was disorder raised to the nth power, but on the firing line everything was strictly business, and men who were frightened almost out of their wits managed to keep on fighting. Wholly characteristic was the breathless comment in one Confederate's letter: "It was an awful thing to hear no intermission in firing and hear the clatter of small arms and the whizing minny balls and rifle shot and the sing of grape shot the hum of canon balls and the roaring of the bomb shell and explosion of the same seaming to be a thousand every minute . . . O God forever keep me out of such another fight. I was not scared I was just in danger."[10]

All morning the Federals were pushed back. Johnston's plan was working . . . except that there was one hard core of Federal resistance, Prentiss's men and some of W. H. L. Wallace's, who took their stand at last in an old country lane that ran along the crest of an almost imperceptible little rise in the ground, with briar patches and underbrush all along the front: the famous "sunken road" of postwar memories, although in actual fact it was not sunken at all and was held, apparently, just because it was a handy place to form a line and because the men who formed the line did not want to go back any farther. Grant rode up once and told Prentiss to hold the line at all hazards, and, after Grant left, the lawyer-soldier and his men obeyed orders literally. This place and the ground in front became known as the hornets' nest; the men beat off repeated Confederate assaults, and hugged the earth grimly when Rebel artillerists put many guns in line and pounded the lane and the trees around it and everything to the sides and in the rear . . . and the Federals stayed and shot the next Confederate attack to bits, and noon passed and the afternoon grew long and the sun dipped down toward the smoky skyline, and but for the stand that was made here General Johnston might have driven Grant's army into the river or into Owl Creek swamp or straight into perdition itself and the victory he wanted so desperately would have been won.

Johnston himself had been up in front all day, riding from this place to that, keeping the attack moving; and at last he came up near a peach orchard, a little to the east of the hornets' nest, and tried to get a new assault organized. The air was full of bullets, and one bullet ripped away the sole of one of his boots: he waggled his foot, laughed, told an aide that this had come pretty close but that he was unhurt; then a bullet struck him in the leg, cutting an artery, and he reeled in the saddle, growing faint from loss of blood before he knew that he had been hit. He was laid on the ground, somebody went to find a surgeon, nobody thought of applying a tourniquet . . . and then, apparently in no pain, speaking no word, he looked up at the sky and died.[11]

Hope of victory died with him: or, to be more exact, died a little before he died. The stand at the hornets' nest had gained Grant just the respite he had to have. From the beginning, Johnston's only hope had been that he could overwhelm the Federal Army in one shattering assault, and he had not quite made it. Grant's army had been mangled, it had been driven back almost to the edge of the Tennessee, much of it had been put entirely out of action . . . but the hornets' nest had held firm, hour after hour, and as the afternoon passed the Confederacy's dazzling opportunity grew narrower and narrower and at last vanished altogether. Far to the rear, on high ground commanding the steamboat landing, Grant put together an immense rank of artillery, with a reorganized infantry line behind it and on the flank. Farther back, Lew Wallace at last overcame the confusion that had grown out of garbled orders and unfamiliar roads and got his division of 8000 men on the road to the Federal right; they would be on hand shortly after dark, and when they arrived Grant would have the advantage in numbers. Most important of all, Nelson's division of Buell's army had arrived—at last—and the steamboats were bringing his advance guard across the Tennessee, the men kicking the skulking fugitives at the landing as they tramped up to take their place in the new battle line. When Johnston died the Confederacy assuredly lost a soldier it desperately needed, but it had already lost its chance to win the battle of Shiloh.

. . . except, perhaps, for the intangible that cannot be accurately appraised. Just possibly, this man's capacity for firing the spirits of tired soldiers might have been enough to send one final, triumphant assault through the shouting twilight, capturing guns, breaking the last infantry line, destroying the heads of the reinforcing columns and achieving the impossible in the smoky darkness above the deep river. Probably it would not have happened so, but the one man who might conceivably have made it happen was dead.[12]

The hornets' nest was taken at last. All the rest of the Federals had retreated, and the men who had saved Grant's army were cut off, surrounded and made helpless. By five o'clock or thereabouts General Prentiss surrendered, giving the Confederates 2200 prisoners and an empty country lane. It took time to get his men off to the rear and to reorganize the Southern battle line, and when these things had been done it was too late to fight any more that day. Grant's guns were in action, the new line had been formed, and in the river Federal gunboats were throwing huge shells into the ravines and gullies where the exhausted Confederates were sorting themselves out. Sensibly enough, Beauregard (who had succeeded to the command when Johnston died) pulled his leading units back a few rods and ordered the troops to make the best bivouac they could for the night.

It was a dreadful night. Toward midnight there was a hard thunderstorm, with a downpour to soak the soldiers who slept among so many dead and wounded. Sudden flashes of lightning illuminated hideous scenes—dead men everywhere, pools and creeks given a ghastly tint by the blood of wounded men who had crawled down to drink and had died with their faces in the water, brambly fields carpeted with torn bodies, helpless wounded men lying in the downpour chanting weak calls for help: the memory of it leading one Confederate to write: "O it was too shocking too horrible. God Grant that I may never be the partaker in such scenes again . . . when released from this I shall ever be an advocate of peace."[13]

But things are seldom all of one pattern. There were men who ate well and slept well that night. After all, the Federal camps were there to be looted, and many of the tired Confederates feasted and told one another that there would be nothing to do tomorrow but bury the dead and finish raking in the Yankee supplies; no doubt the enemy had all gone across the river. A Tennessee soldier recalled that "our mess had that night all the tea, coffee, sugar, cheese, hard-tack and bacon they could want," and remembered that wine and liquor were found among the surgeons' stores; in the morning one stout foot soldier tried to go into battle with a huge cheese impaled on his bayonet. Some men became so interested in the spoils that they forgot about the unfinished battle, and one Confederate officer wrote bitterly that if the high command had had the sense to burn all of the captured stores that night the army might have won the fight next day. All through the Federal camps, he said, Confederate soldiers were picking up valuables, and by midnight "half of our army was straggling back to Corinth loaded down with belts, sashes, swords, officers' uniforms, Yankee letters, daguerreotypes of Yankee sweethearts, likenesses of Grant, Buell, Smith, Prentiss, McClellan, Lincoln, etc., some on Yankee mules and horses, some on foot, some on the ground prostrate with Cincinnati whiskey." General Bragg told his wife that Shiloh was lost because of lack of discipline and lack of good officers, concluding savagely: "Universal suffrage, furloughs & whiskey have ruined us."[14]

That looting, straggling, and lack of discipline harmed the army is beyond question, but the plain fact is that regardless of these things the army had had it. That it had done as much as it had done was one of the marvels of the war; to do anything more was wholly out of the question. Grant's army had been shaken to its shoetops but it had never quite been broken; Grant himself had never had any notion of retreating, even when things were at their worst; Lew Wallace's division reached him not long after dark, and during the night 20,000 of Buell's soldiers came across the river—and when the morning of April 7 came there was nothing Beauregard could do but get his men back to Corinth as best he could.

He did not do this at once. The fighting began all over again soon after sunrise, and for most of the morning it was a hard, stubborn battle, the Federals attacking now, the Confederates disputing every inch of the ground. Not until after noon did Beauregard accept the inevitable and order a retreat, and when his army withdrew the Federals made no more than a gesture of pursuit. Grant's army had been fought out. Buell's troops were fresh enough, but Buell was only partly under Grant's orders, the relationship between the two generals was exceedingly delicate, and each man apparently felt that it would be just as well to let the soldiers catch their breath and think about going after this Confederate Army at some later date.

It is clear enough now that a hard, vigorous pursuit might have destroyed Beauregard's army. But the controlling fact undoubtedly was that this battle had brought utter exhaustion to the victor as well as to the defeated. The Unionists had lost upwards of 13,000 men, the Confederates more than 10,000, and the figures call for a little reflection. The armies that met on April 6 were larger than the armies that met at Bull Run, but—it can stand one more repetition—they were hardly in the slightest degree better trained or organized. They had fought three times as long as the Bull Run armies had fought, and had suffered approximately five times the losses, and although there had been heavy straggling on both sides there had been no actual rout.[15] If in the end they drifted apart, it is no wonder. In all American history, no more amazing battle was ever fought than this one.

Nor have many battles been more decisive, in their effect on the course of a war. Shiloh represented a supreme effort on the part of the Confederacy to turn the tables, to recoup what had been lost along the Tennessee-Kentucky line, to win a new chance to wage war west of the Appalachians on an equal footing. It failed. After this, the Southern nation could do no more than fight an uphill fight to save part of the Mississippi Valley—the great valley of American empire without which the war could not be won.

4: *Threat to New Orleans*

When General Beauregard pulled his men away from Shiloh Church and took them stumbling back toward Corinth, on the afternoon of April 7, a door which the Confederacy for its life's sake had to keep open began to swing shut. The hinge was Pittsburg Landing, where more than 20,000 Americans had been shot, where Albert Sidney Johnston looked at the sky and died; and the final, echoing slam of the door's closing sounded just a few hours later, 110 miles to the northwest, when other Confederates surrendered their stronghold at Island Number Ten and gave the Federal invader, once and for all, the means to control the middle Mississippi River.

Island Number Ten no longer exists. Long ago the Mississippi rolled over it, washed part of it away, joined what was left to the Missouri shore and cut a new channel elsewhere; as if when the guns were stilled the place was no longer worth preserving. In 1862 the island was a two-and-one-half-mile-long mud patch lying in a great loop of the river, rimmed with strong ramparts and heavy guns, so menacing that even Flag Officer Andrew Foote was afraid of it. It blocked the river. The island and the army together kept the Confederate west alive. But the army was beaten and the strong point was taken, and on the day these things happened the Confederate west began to die. The fall of Island Number Ten was the essential postscript to Shiloh.

Running south from Columbus, Kentucky, where a Confederate Gibraltar had been abandoned because of the loss of the forts on the Tennessee and the Cumberland, the Mississippi in 1862 crossed the Tennessee-Kentucky line, turned sharply to the west, and then doubled back in the beginning of a huge S-curve, flowing due north for five or six miles, going west once more, and then flowing south toward Memphis and the Gulf. Island Number Ten lay at the bottom of the first loop; at the top of the next loop, Madrid Bend, on the Missouri shore, was the town of New Madrid, and fifteen miles downstream, on the Tennessee side, was the unremarkable town of Tiptonville. The country all about was low and marshy, half-drowned in the spring of 1862 by high water in the big river. To support Island Number Ten the Confederates had two routes: they could go up the river by steamer, or they could go by land along the river bank from Tiptonville. No other approach was feasible. The long peninsula that ran north from Tiptonville to Madrid Bend, with the bristling island as an anchor on its eastern side, was almost completely isolated by a chain of swamps and ponds at its base. To hold the river route the Confederates had to hold New Madrid and the

Missouri shore to the south of it; to keep the land route open they had to hold Tiptonville; and to do all of this they had upwards of 7000 soldiers, a large number of heavy guns, and a little flotilla of wooden gunboats which were not very formidable. Shortly after the fall of Fort Donelson, Halleck sent an amphibious expedition down to take the river away from them.

The expedition consisted of 20,000 men led by John Pope and was supported by Flag Officer Foote, who had seven iron-plated gunboats and a fleet of barges mounting big mortars. Pope put his men ashore at Commerce, Missouri, forty miles above New Madrid, marched down the river without opposition, and began to lay siege to New Madrid on March 3. It developed that this place was neither strongly fortified nor well manned, and Pope captured it in ten days, after which he moved some of his infantry and artillery ten miles downstream to Point Pleasant to keep the Confederates from sending men and supplies up the river by steamboat. He had finished the first half of his assignment. Now he had to get across the river, occupy Tiptonville, isolate Island Number Ten and compel it to surrender.

The second half of the job was not going to be easy. To get over to the Tennessee shore Pope had to have transports, and to protect the transports he had to have gunboats, and to reach him these vessels would have to steam past Island Number Ten, which was obviously impossible. Foote, stumping about on crutches—the wound he had taken at Fort Donelson was refusing to heal—held his flotilla just upstream from the island, moored his mortar boats along the bank, opened a long-range bombardment, and studied his problem with rising pessimism. He was as tough as any man in the Navy, but he refused to run in close and hammer these fortifications the way he had hammered the forts on the Tennessee and the Cumberland. Island Number Ten was far too strong; furthermore, the river ran in the wrong direction. At Fort Henry and Fort Donelson, Foote's fleet had fought facing upstream, and a disabled boat would drift back to safety. Here the fleet would be facing downstream, and a disabled boat would drift down to certain capture—a thing which seemed all the more likely because the gunboats were sadly underengined, so that even moderate battle damage could make it impossible for them to steam against the strong current of the Mississippi. Foote devoted himself to the bombardment; it went on for three weeks and was most spectacular to see and hear, but it did the Confederates little real damage. Meanwhile, General Pope kept on calling for gunboats and transports.[1]

At this point Pope's engineer officers had a bright idea. The place where Foote's fleet was lying was twelve or fifteen miles from New Madrid by water, but it was not half that distance in an air line, and the long peninsula that lay between the fleet and the army was half a marsh, covered with second-growth timber and cut by innumerable sluggish bayous. It ought to be possible (said the engineers) to make some sort of waterway across this peninsula, so that shallow-draft steamers could leave the river and go cross-lots to New Madrid. Since there appeared to be no other way to get transports, Pope accepted the proposal, sent back to Cairo for tugboats, barges, and incidental equipment, and put six hundred men to work to create a canal. While Foote went on with his bombardment, Pope's engineer troops went off into the bayous and got to work.

They dug a ditch across a cornfield, came up to a submerged forest, and began felling trees. Here they had to work afloat, devising ingenious ways to cut through the tree trunks four and one half feet below the surface of the water, rooting out stumps, hoisting submerged logs and snags out of the way, pulling and chopping and digging and sawing all at the same time. While they labored, other details worked to convert empty coal barges into floating batteries, hoping that if the gunboats could not get downstream Pope could be given something that would float and carry guns. Day after day the work on the waterway continued: a non-military job done by energetic Westerners who knew how to improvise and who were exercising the national aptitude for changing the face of the landscape. In a little less than three weeks the work was done, and there was a waterway six miles long, fifty feet wide and a little more than four feet deep. Now Pope could have his transports.[2]

He still could not have his gunboats, as they drew too much water for this canal, and without the gunboats the transports would be of no use. (The business of making floating batteries out of coal barges was a forlorn hope, at best.) The Confederates had planted batteries along the Tennessee shore of the river above Tiptonville, covering every feasible landing place, and the river here was a mile wide. Federal guns on the Missouri shore could not hope to silence these batteries, and unless one or two sturdy fighting ships could come in and pound them the transports would have to stay at New Madrid. Desperately, Pope wired Halleck asking that Foote be required to give two of his gunboats, minus crews, to the Army; Pope would man them with soldiers and try to run them past Island Number Ten in spite of the odds.[3]

Perhaps if Andrew Foote had been well he would have been bolder, but his health was atrocious and much of his old drive was gone. He was impatient with his enforced inaction, however, and the idea of turning his ships over to the Army and letting soldiers try to do what sailors could not do was altogether too much; and so when Commander Henry Walke, skipper of the gunboat *Carondelet*, insisted that he could take his boat down the river Foote told him to go ahead. Walke had felt all along that it ought to be possible to run past Island Number Ten. He wanted just two things: a barge loaded high with bales of hay, to lash to the portside for protection against gunfire, and a night dark enough to give him a fair chance to go down the river unseen. He got both, presently, and on the night of April 4 *Carondelet* left her moorings and drifted downstream to run the gantlet.

She was moving slowly, just fast enough for steerageway. The high-pressure engines of river steamboats normally fed their exhaust into the smokestacks, making a noisy, locomotive-like *puff-puff* which could be heard miles away; to muffle the sound Walke had his engineers rearrange things so that the exhaust went into the paddle box, and he would not try to make any speed until the Confederates discovered him. Slipping down with the current, ungainly with the clumsy barge fastened to her port side, *Carondelet* went on toward Island Number Ten.

Carondelet had been afloat for less than four months, but she was a veteran; had fought at Fort Henry, had opened the bombardment at Fort Donelson, and had been hit so hard there that she had to go back to Cairo and go into drydock for repairs; all in all she had seen about as much close action as any vessel afloat. Walke was ready for anything. If the boat should run aground or become disabled he would resist boarders: cutlasses and muskets were served out, and hoses were attached to the boilers so that scalding water could be directed at hostile parties, and if worse came to worst he was prepared to scuttle his vessel rather than let the Confederates have her. The night was dark as the inside of his pocket, with a thunderstorm building up, and *Carondelet* reached the upstream end of Island Number Ten without being seen.

Then the storm came, and the midnight blackness suddenly dissolved into vivid moments of daylight as enormous flashes of lightning broke out of the clouds, throwing river and gunboat into startling relief: black boat on a glistening river, spectral green trees for a background, blue-white lightning winking on and off like an erratic spotlight in some prodigious theater. The Southern lookouts saw it, and, on *Carondelet*, Walke could hear the Confederate drums beating the long roll, calling the gunners to their stations, and rockets arched up into the sky as Island Number Ten notified batteries on the Tennessee shore that there was a Yankee gunboat on the water. Walke cracked on steam, and *Carondelet* surged ahead, dragging the heavy barge, running heavily like a man in a nightmare. The dry soot in the gunboat's stacks, ordinarily kept damp by the exhaust steam, took fire and sent tall jets of revealing flame high out of each pipe: and with these flares as beacons, while great sheets of lightning lit the river and the rockets shot up toward the dripping clouds, *Carondelet* kept on coming.

The Confederates manned their guns and opened fire, the crash of the guns mingling with the crash of thunder, deafening noise and the constant off-and-on of the lightning flashes bewildering everybody. Walke had his pilot steer close to the shore of the island, hoping that the Confederate gunners would overshoot their target; *Carondelet* almost ran aground as a result but sheered away just in time, the heavy shells passed overhead, flash of the guns and flash of bursting shell punctuating the thunderstorm—and at last, in spite of everything, *Carondelet* passed the island unhurt and went pounding down the reverse stretch of the big bend in the river. A couple of solid shot hit the hay barge, minié balls spattered here and there without harm, and then the firing ended and *Carondelet* came steaming down to New Madrid at midnight, the thunderstorm tapering off, Pope's troops lining the waterfront to cheer. The gunboat drew up to a mooring, Army officers came aboard to offer congratulations, and Walke as an Old Navy man issued the traditional order: Splice the main brace. Nobody on his boat had been hurt, the thing that he thought could be done had been done, and from this moment on, Island Number Ten was helpless.[4]

Nothing remained now but to pick up the pieces. On the morning of April 5—the beautiful spring day when the soldiers around Shiloh were firing their guns to see how rain had affected loaded muskets—Pope had transports and one gunboat on the river below New Madrid and he could get on with the job, which he promptly did. Troops went aboard the stern-wheelers that had come down through the cutoff, Walke discarded his hay barge and his hot-water hoses, and the Federals went down to cross the river. *Carondelet's* guns knocked the Confederate river batteries to bits, and before long John Pope had soldiers over on the Tennessee shore around Tiptonville and Island Number Ten had been cut off. The Confederates along the river took to the brush to escape capture, Foote sent U.S.S. *Pittsburgh* down to join *Carondelet*—once Walke had done it, everybody could see how simple it was—and late on the evening of April 7 Island Number Ten surrendered and the victory that had just been won at Shiloh was made complete. To all intents and purposes, the Confederacy had lost the middle Mississippi.

Which is to say that they had lost the one stretch they had a chance to hold. They still possessed a strong point called Fort Pillow, on a Tennessee bluff forty-five miles above Memphis, and ever since the fall of New Madrid they had been strengthening the place; and Pope and Foote made plans for an Army-Navy assault. But Fort Pillow could be allowed to die on the vine. Once Beauregard was driven out of Corinth, Fort Pillow would be cut off and would fall of its own weight, just as the great fort at Columbus had fallen after the conquest of Fort Henry and Fort Donelson. Halleck correctly judged that there was no point in fighting for Fort Pillow, and he ordered Pope to put his army on transports, steam back to Cairo, and come up the Tennessee to join Grant and Buell at Pittsburg Landing. The major effort would be the advance on Corinth, and Halleck would have more than 100,000 men; the Navy could be left to clean up the fragments along the Mississippi. Shortly after Pope left, Andrew Foote was compelled to go on sick leave,[5] which would be followed by undemanding shore-side assignments in the east. He had fought his last fight, contributing mightily to Union victory in the west, burning himself out in the process, and he had just over a year to live. Welles sent in another good man, Captain Charles Henry Davis, to replace him, and the fleet and the mortar boats dropped downstream and began a desultory bombardment of Fort Pillow. In effect they were marking time until the advance of Halleck's army one hundred miles to the southeast made its effect felt.

John Pope had done a first-rate job, and the human cost of it had been remarkably low. From first to last, Pope had had fewer than a hundred casualties; he had been fighting the river rather than the Confederates, and he had fought it with much skill and intelligence. He had captured several thousand prisoners, had taken many heavy guns and a great deal of ammunition, and he had opened all of the upper half of the Mississippi River; vastly aided by the fact that the Confederate defense had been most inept. Beauregard wrote after the war that the attempt to hold New Madrid was "the poorest defense made of any fortified post during the whole course of the war," and late in March he had sent in a new man, Brigadier General W. W. Mackall, replacing Brigadier General John P. McCown, to pull things together. Mackall reported that the undersized army which was trying to hold the river was in deplorable shape: "One good regiment would be better than the force I have. It never had any discipline. It is disheartened—apathetic."[6] If Pope had done well it must be added that he had not had much besides the river itself to beat.

Here was one more symptom of the ominous weakness that was disturbing Jefferson Davis so greatly. The Confederacy was discovering it could not meet all of its vital commitments. To hold that segment of the big river which lies one hundred miles north of Memphis was essential, and the high command in the west knew it perfectly well. In February, Beauregard had told Polk that New Madrid was all-important and must be "watched and held at all costs," and a month later Polk wrote that "it is of the highest importance to hold Island Ten and Madrid Bend to the last extremity. It is the key of the Mississippi valley."[7] But the high command had been compelled to meet two essential needs with means adequate for only one. The major effort had gone to the attempt to regain the offensive in the Tennessee Valley, and the Mississippi had had to take what was left. What was left was not nearly enough. As Mr. Lincoln had foreseen, when the Federal power put on the pressure everywhere something was bound to collapse.

Ominous symbol of this fact was the presence in the middle river of five unarmored Confederate gunboats from New Orleans commanded by Commodore George N. Hollins. Everybody understood that the Federal drive down the river was finally aimed at New Orleans, largest city in all the South, and New Orleans was under threat from two directions—from upstream, where Grant and Pope and Foote were pressing their offensive, and from the Gulf, where Flag Officer Farragut had been assembling a powerful fleet of deep-water vessels backed by 10,000 soldiers under Ben Butler, who were roosting uncomfortably on a Gulf Coast sandspit named Ship Island. Between New Orleans and the mouth of the river were two strong forts, Fort Jackson and Fort St. Philip, which were supposed to be powerful enough to stop Farragut. Butler might try to come up by land, but his force was not very large and anyway Butler was no soldier; he was just an old-time Democratic politician, who less than two years earlier had tried to get Jefferson Davis made President of the United States, and the Confederate Army commander in Louisiana remarked that Butler was "a harmless menace," explaining: "A Black Republican dynasty will never give an old Breckinridge Democrat like Butler command of any expedition which they had any idea would result in such a glorious success as the capture of New Orleans." This appeared to make sense, although the Confederacy then had much to learn about Butler's extreme adaptability to the demands of Black Republicanism; and the people at Richmond, who had many worries anyway, made up their minds to defend New Orleans in Tennessee, most of the troops were sent north to fight at Shiloh, and Hollins was ordered to take his flotilla along to stop Foote.[8] If the Federals did try to come up from the Gulf the Confederates would rely on the two forts, on a collection of converted river steamers in which nobody had much confidence, and on two ironclads which were being built at New Orleans and which, if the Yankees just waited long enough, might some day be formidable warships.

Hollins believed this was a serious blunder. His ships were not strong enough to stop Foote's river squadron, but with the aid of the river and the forts they might be able to stop Farragut. Hollins was in his sixties, a veteran of nearly half a century in the Old Navy, and he understood both the deep-water steam sloops of war which were Farragut's principal reliance and the troubles Farragut was likely to have getting these ships over the oozy sandbars which lay at the mouth of the Mississippi.

Nearly a hundred miles below New Orleans, as the winding river ran, there was a place known as the Head of the Passes, where the river forked and sent a number of separate outlets down through the muddy delta to the open sea. Three of these passes were deep enough to be used by shipping—Southwest Pass, South Pass, and Pass a Loutre, which angled off to the east—and at the mouth of each one there was a sandbar, offering problems to ships of deep draft. To get over these bars, no matter which pass he used, Farragut would have to take guns and stores out of his biggest ships and bring the ships in unarmed, towed by lesser craft, inching along one at a time, moving arms and equipment up in barges and putting the ships back into fighting trim after they had reached the Head of the Passes. Hollins believed that his little flotilla, if it hovered in the lower river ready to make a quick dash down to the shallows, could greatly interfere with this tedious operation, could perhaps make it impossible. As an alternative, he believed, he could keep his vessels up by the forts in a position where they could get a crippling raking fire on the Federal fleet if it tried to bombard or run past the forts. Either way, he argued, his little flotilla would be of some value if it stayed below New Orleans; if it went north of Memphis it would be wasted.[9]

Hollins may have overstated the case, but his argument illustrated the dilemma which confronted the authorities at Richmond. No matter where they looked, this spring, they saw a crisis. Added together, these crises had overwhelming weight. It was not possible to deal with all of them at once. They had to be met one at a time, with a harassed President and cabinet trying desperately to guess which one should be met first. In this case they guessed that the Federal offensive in the upper river was more dangerous than the one at the river's mouth, and they acted accordingly. It developed finally that they had guessed wrong, but they would have been just about as wrong if they had guessed the other way. No good guess was open to them.

Basically, they were gambling on the assumption that Forts Jackson and St. Philip were strong enough to keep the Federal fleet from coming up to New Orleans. These forts were of prewar construction, solidly built of masonry; good enough, apparently, to justify the belief that wooden ships could not make a stand-up fight with first-class forts. The stronger of the two, Fort Jackson, lay west of the river, twenty miles upstream from the Head of the Passes. Fort St. Philip was on the opposite bank a few hundred yards farther up the river. If the fleet came up to attack these forts it would be under fire from both sides at once. The forts could stand a great deal of hammering and the wooden warships could not. As long as the forts held out the lower river was closed to anything but a hit-and-run raid, and if one or two ships did slip through they would be isolated and could offer no real threat to New Orleans. If the new ironclads were finished in time the river would be sealed beyond any question, but even without them the defenses ought to hold.

The trouble was that everything depended on the forts, and they were not actually as strong as the people in Richmond thought they were. Their construction, to be sure, was solid enough. Fort St. Philip had been built by the French in 1746, had been strengthened by the Spanish in the 1790s, had been brought up to date by the Americans in 1812, and had withstood a British bombardment in 1815, when General Pakenham tried to take New Orleans and failed, making an undying legend out of Andrew Jackson and the Tennessee riflemen. Fort Jackson was more modern, having been finished in 1831, a solid brick pentagon surrounded by a moat, with enclosed casemates, and with a water battery close to the edge of the river. Between them these forts mounted more than a hundred guns, with seventy-five or eighty arranged so that they would bear on the river passage. Unfortunately, most of these guns were not nearly heavy enough. More than half of the total were mere 24-pounders, and there were hardly any of the ponderous Columbiads, the ship-killers whose immense shells could break a wooden warship into fragments.[10]

In addition, there was Flag Officer David Glasgow Farragut. Farragut was an old-timer: born in Tennessee in 1801, he had gone to sea at the age of nine as midshipman under one of the half-forgotten heroes of the War of 1812, the Commander David Porter who took U.S.S. *Essex* on her famous cruise into the Pacific. Farragut was a veteran of battle action before he reached his fifteenth birthday and had stayed in the Navy ever since, but the half-century of naval routine which had been his life had never fossilized him; now, in his early sixties, he was supple, buoyant, a kindly man with an imagination and a sense of humor, owning both a veteran's understanding of the uses of sea power and a young man's willingness to risk everything on one sudden thrust. He had no intention of playing this game the way the Confederates expected him to do. As he saw it, the forts did not need to be beaten into submission; they simply needed to be passed. A determined man, he believed, could run his fleet by the forts without taking crippling damage—the engagements along the Carolina sounds had taught that much—and once the fleet was beyond the forts, New Orleans, which had practically no garrison at all, would be at his mercy. When New Orleans fell the forts would be cut off and could do nothing but surrender even though they might still be in perfectly good fighting trim.

Farragut had been given a ponderous flotilla of schooners carrying enormous mortars which could throw terrible 13-inch shells, this flotilla being led by a pushing, ambitious junior, Commander David Dixon Porter, son of the man under whom Farragut had served as a boy in *Essex;* and the general understanding, supported vigorously by Porter, was that a proper bombardment by these mortars would blast the forts into helplessness before Farragut made his advance. But Farragut took very little stock in this. He had been given the mortar flotilla against his will and he strongly doubted that it would accomplish anything. He would let Porter make his bombardment, but he understood that in the end everything would depend on his own ability to rush past the forts, taking a pounding but banking on the faith that he could get most of the fleet upstream.[11] Now, in mid-April, he was assembling and refitting his vessels at the Head of the Passes, preparing for the big moment.

He was full of confidence, and he sent home a wholly characteristic letter: "As to being prepared for defeat, I certainly am not. Any man who is prepared for defeat would be half defeated before he commenced. I hope for success; shall do all in my power to secure it, and trust to God for the rest."[12]

So, before long, he would strike the blow that would either lose a fleet or win the largest city in the Confederacy.

5: *Fire on the Waters*

The Confederate defenders at New Orleans faced a simple problem. They had to make Farragut stop and fight when his fleet reached the forts. There were two ways to do this, and both would be tried. If either way worked the city would be saved.

One way was to block the river itself. If a huge raft, bound together with heavy chains, firmly moored to the banks and anchored to the river bottom, could be placed in the waterway between the forts, the fleet would have to stop under fire and clear the channel. It would be pinned down, compelled to take the prolonged shelling that no wooden warships could endure, and its fighting craft would be splintered long before the obstruction could be removed.

The other way was to follow Secretary Mallory's new book: build, man, and equip one or more invulnerable ironclads which could come down between the forts and do to Farragut's ships what *Virginia* had done to *Cumberland* and *Congress*. Farragut had no Monitors and it would be a long time before he could get any, and this would be checkmate.

Two chances, then, and either one might work; yet the odds really were very bad. To block the river the defenders had to conquer the Mississippi itself, so that the floating barricade would stay where it was supposed to stay despite the great twisting current and the unending succession of floating logs which came down like battering rams; and to get the ironclads into action the Confederacy had to overcome its own profound industrial weakness and do an intricate job of manufacturing without enough materials, machine shops, skilled workers, or time. In the end, the defenders did their devoted best on both of these attempts, and failed. If their problem was simple, it was also insoluble. What they needed was a man who could work miracles, and they had no such person.

The man who was appointed to try to work miracles was Major General Mansfield Lovell, a thirty-nine-year-old West Pointer with pleasing manners who had fought in the Mexican War, taking two wounds and winning a brevet promotion for gallantry, and who had left the Army in 1854, to go into business in New York. He had become, a few years later, deputy Commissioner of Streets in New York City, his superior there being the Gustavus W. Smith who now was one of Joe Johnston's principal subordinates in Virginia. During the months after Fort Sumter, Lovell had concluded that his ties ran South rather than North. He resigned, went to Richmond, got a major general's commission from Jefferson Davis, and, in October 1861, he was given the top command in New Orleans, replacing the aged Major General David E. Twiggs whose years and failing health had rendered him incompetent.

When Lovell first reached New Orleans he was appalled to see how little had been done to put the city's defenses into shape. Conditions were so bad, he said later, that he was afraid to give the War Department all of the details for fear the news would leak out and encourage the Yankees. Guns were lacking, ammunition was scanty, subsidiary equipment was in bad shape, and although New Orleans was aflame with patriotism there were hardly any arms for recruits. Lovell took hold with vigor, arranging with New Orleans foundries to cast some heavy guns, building a powder factory to make ammunition, harassing Richmond with demands for everything from saltpeter and rifles to a little attention, and making unending tours of inspection of his forts and military camps.[1]

Before coming to New Orleans Lovell had stopped in Manassas to talk with General Beauregard, who urged him to get busy on the job of blocking the river, and when Lovell saw how few heavy guns were in the forts he concluded that this job must have top priority. He got busy, and by the beginning of the winter he had an immense raft in place—a formidable affair of forty-foot cypress logs bound together by chains, crisscrossed with heavy timbers, firmly moored to each bank, with as many anchors as Lovell could find used to tie it to the bed of the river, which at this place was 130 feet deep with a bottom of soft mud. As long as this raft stayed in position no ship could pass, but the raft's security after all was up to the Mississippi, which was rising constantly, pressing on it with increasing force, pounding it day after day with the tons of driftwood that came down on its boiling current.

Early in March the raft gave way, anchors tearing out of the river bottom, chains snapping like so much thread, logs and timbers coming apart and floating harmlessly downstream. A new barricade was hastily created, with the help of $100,000 voted by the New Orleans city council, and the gap was closed; but the river kept on rising, Farragut was hauling his big ships over the shallows at its mouth, and just as the defenses in Tennessee caved in this second raft also collapsed and the waterway was clear again. Lovell rounded up a number of schooner hulks, tied them together with chains as well as might be, moored them in midstream, and hoped for the best.[2]

The best began to look worse, week by week. It was impossible to get Richmond to realize how much pressure was on here. The Tennessee line was being lost, McClellan's huge army was in front of Yorktown, there were half a dozen urgent calls for every man and gun the Confederacy possessed, and Lovell would have to look out for himself. He called for heavy guns, over and over, without getting them. Almost all of the infantry he had was up in Tennessee. Lovell's only solace was that the Yankees were going to attack by water rather than by land, which meant that he could not do very much with infantry even if he had it. Hollins and his gunboats were long gone, and when Hollins came back alone, looked at the situation, and frantically wired the Navy Department for permission to bring his little fleet back he was curtly ordered to report to Richmond for duty on a shore-side board which was inquiring into naval matters on the James River. The people of New Orleans, feeling the cold shadow of Farragut growing longer and darker, reflected that this General Lovell was after all a Northerner and that the city had been denuded of soldiers, and began to complain that something must be wrong with the man's loyalty. Early in March he told Richmond that he was being accused of "sending away all troops so that the city may fall an easy prey to the enemy."[3] Rarely has a conscientious soldier been more frustrated.

A good deal was going to depend, obviously, on the ironclads, and the big question here was whether they could be finished in time. The desperate attempt to create them illustrated the crippling handicaps which beset the Confederate Navy Department. In its original decision to upset the naval balance by building ironclads the Department had shown courage and ingenuity, and it had acted with commendable promptness; by the time General Lovell reached New Orleans, in October, the Department had contracted for the construction of two ironclads there, *Louisiana* and *Mississippi*, and by the middle of the winter these were shaping up as powerful monsters, stronger even than *Virginia*, fully capable of wrecking Farragut's entire fleet. With any luck at all, the Department should be able to put them into action by the time Farragut was ready to rush past the forts.

Unfortunately, the Department had not one shred of luck at

any time. There were two contractors—E. C. Murray, for construction of *Louisiana*, and the brothers Asa and Nelson Tift for *Mississippi*—and these men quickly found that they were living in the exact center of a contractor's nightmare. Every day brought new delays. It was even hard to get the white pine timber out of which the hulls were to be built; the South had plenty of lumber, to be sure, but not much of it was in New Orleans, the river was closed at the mouth and in Tennessee, and the mere business of getting lumber transported to the shipyards was infernally difficult. It was even harder to get iron for armor. Murray used railroad rails—Richmond made a special dispensation permitting the tearing-up of railroad tracks—and the Tifts, after much difficulty, finally contracted with a mill in Atlanta for iron plates; and agents went all across the South to round up bolts, angle irons, and other bits of hardware. It was hard to find shops capable of building machinery and even harder to find skilled mechanics to work in them, and it was almost impossible (as the Tift brothers learned) to find, anywhere in the Confederacy, a shop that could make suitable propeller shafts. Money was an unending problem. Approved bills for materials and services went unpaid for months, some shops flatly refused to accept government orders because of this, and when the Navy Department did attend to the financial end it usually sent, instead of cash, drafts for Confederate bonds payable in Richmond, which were not acceptable in New Orleans. (This was not the Navy Department's fault; these drafts were all it could get from the Treasury Department, which had troubles of its own and which in any case was under orders to give Army claims priority over those of the Navy.) A citizens' committee raised some money to pay workers and satisfy the most pressing of the other demands, and (except for a five-day strike for higher wages, in November) work never actually came to a standstill, but it went with maddening slowness. When Farragut had his fleet ready for action and Porter was about to open his bombardment of the forts, *Louisiana* and *Mississippi* were still unfinished.[4]

This was especially trying to General Lovell because this major element in the defense of the city was entirely out of his control. When he urged Richmond to find some way to speed the work on the ironclads he was informed by the President and the War Department that he had no jurisdiction over naval matters and must not concern himself with such things. The government did, however, present him with a white elephant. In mid-winter Congress voted $1,000,000 for an oddly conceived river-defense fleet, a strange assortment of ordinary tugboats and river steamers which were to be bought, entrusted to veteran steamboat captains with civilian crews, piled with cotton bales to protect their engines, and used as rams, pure and simple, to butt the Yankee warships out of the river; and all of this was to be under the Army's direction. (The same idea had occurred to Secretary Stanton, in Washington, and a similar collection of Federal rams was getting ready to go into action above Memphis; and it can only be said that Stanton had much better luck with this unorthodox variant than Lovell ever had.) The money was spent, the steamboats were bought and were considered weapons, the steamboat captains proved too individualistic and unmilitary to respond to anybody's control, and in the end this flotilla was of no use at all. But it was an idea, no doubt. . . . Early in April Richmond sent stern orders: *Louisiana* was to go upriver to fight the Federal gunboats that had just passed Island Number Ten. Lovell protested vehemently, and so did the governor of the state, T. O. Moore, and they were icily informed by President Davis that although the Federals in the lower river had nothing but wooden ships, which the forts could handle, they had ironclads up above Memphis and only *Louisiana* could stop them. Since *Louisiana* still lacked motive power, and could not move one foot under her own steam, she stayed at her wharf, with workmen swarming around to get her propulsive machinery in order, and nothing came of this: but the fact that the order was issued shows how Richmond was thinking.[5] Doom was building up just ninety miles to the south, but the authorities were really concerned about the remote threat hundreds of miles to the north.

Part of this was Lovell's fault. Commander William C. Whittle, ranking naval officer at New Orleans, told Secretary Mallory that from his chats with Lovell he was convinced that the Army believed it could stop Farragut at the forts. Late in March, Lovell assured the

War Department that Farragut's thrust looked like "a diversion for the column descending from Cairo," and even by April 15, when Porter's mortars were testing the ranges and Farragut's big ships were getting ready for the crucial test, Lovell wrote that "if we can manage to obstruct the river so as to retain them thirty minutes under our fire I think we can cripple the fleet." Nobody quite saw how deadly Farragut's fleet was going to be. The extenuating circumstance is that nobody could have done much about it even if there had been better foresight.[6]

The real problem was Farragut himself. If he had given the Confederates one more week, they would have had *Louisiana* ready for him, and in another week or so they would have had *Mississippi* ready too, and he would have been a dead duck. But Farragut was in a hurry. After half a century of service he commanded a fleet and he was going to use it. He wrote to his wife: "I have now attained what I have been looking for all my life—a flag—and having attained it all that is necessary to complete the scene is a victory. If I die in the attempt it will be only what every officer has to expect. He who dies in doing his duty to his country, and at peace with his God, has played out the drama of life to the best advantage." His flagship was U.S.S. *Hartford*, a steam sloop of war, square-rigged with auxiliary steam, a wooden ship that could easily kill the flag officer and everybody else on board if enemy shell fire lasted very long, but *Hartford* was going to go upstream just as soon as the flag officer could manage it and the extra week or two that the Confederacy needed so desperately was not going to be available. It appears that *Hartford* was what sailors call a taut ship. An enlisted Marine made note that on a day when the flagship took on coal, any Marine who showed up for duty with a soiled white belt was going to answer for it next morning.[7]

Farragut was on the spot, although it does not seem to have bothered him. His orders from Secretary Welles said that he was to reduce the defenses and take New Orleans, and added: "As you have expressed yourself satisfied with the force given you, and as many more powerful vessels will be added before you can commence operations, the Department and the country will require of you success."[8] It was laid on the line, in other words. Farragut had no room for an alibi if anything went wrong. (The river between the forts was 130 feet deep, after all: plenty of room there for a flag officer who could not quite make it.)

He was not just an old man full of dash; he was a good executive and a careful planner, and his final instructions to his captains were detailed. The captains were to strike their topgallant masts and land all spars and rigging except what was needed to operate under topsails, foresail, jib, and spanker; one or two guns must be mounted on poop and forecastle to fight enemy gunboats, because the ships would fight head-to the current and broadside guns could not hit targets more than three points forward of the beam. Grapnels must be handy to hook on to fire rafts and tow them away if necessary. All ships must be trimmed slightly by the head so that if they ran aground they would not swing bows-on down the river; if a ship's machinery should be disabled the captain must drop anchor and let his vessel drift slowly downstream: in no case could anyone turn around and steam back for the Head of the Passes. Spare hawsers must be ready so that if a captain had to tow another ship he could do it. No matter what happened, no ship could pull out of action without the flag officer's permission. And, finally: "Hot and cold shot will no doubt be freely dealt to us, and there must be stout hearts and quick hands to extinguish the one and stop the holes of the other. I shall expect the most prompt attention to signals and verbal orders."[9]

He had another problem, although he did not know about it. Commander Porter, who had the mortar flotilla, was persistently undercutting him in letters to Assistant Secretary of the Navy Gustavus V. Fox, with whom he was on familiar terms. Porter worked methodically to damn the flag officer with faint praise: Farragut was probably the best man of his rank, but after all he was an old man and "men of his age in a seafaring life are not fit for the command of important enterprises, they lack the vigor of youth" (which Porter, obviously, had in great measure). Farragut, said Porter, failed to say what his plans were, and indeed "he talks very much at random at times, and rather under-rates the difficulties before him, without fairly comprehending them." It was really hard for a man of Farragut's years, finding himself in command of a large fleet for the first time in his life; "he is full of zeal and anxiety, but he has no administrative qualities, wants stability, and loses too much time in talking."[10] In the end this did Farragut no harm, but the ambitious junior was getting plenty of edged words on the record for ready reference in case the expedition failed.

Although Porter was not above angling for his superior's job he was an efficient operator on his own hook, and by the middle of April he had his twenty mortar schooners moored along the river banks about a mile and a half below Fort Jackson, with coastal survey experts triangulating the ranges; the fort could not be seen from the schooners' decks, and everything must be done by indirect fire, with observers at the mastheads spotting the fall of the shells. For camouflage, the masts were dressed with leafy branches. A couple of days were used for sporadic firing to test the ranges and to see whether the return fire from the forts would be damaging. (Mostly, it was not: Porter lost one schooner, and his attendant gunboats suffered minor casualties.) On April 18 everything was ready and the flotilla began its bombardment in earnest, throwing 200-pound shells in high, arching parabolas and dropping a fair percentage of them inside Fort Jackson, the principal target.

The bombardment was spectacular, and it went on day and night, at the rate of more than a thousand shells every twenty-four hours. Porter had boasted that he would reduce the forts in two days, and at first it looked as if he might have been right: woodwork in Fort Jackson caught fire and sent up dense clouds of smoke, parapet gunners took refuge in the protected casemates, and so many shells burst inside the works that optimistic sailors in the rigging of the Federal ships felt that the end must be near. But although the bombardment was a sore trial to the nerves of the Confederates in the forts, it never came close to putting the forts out of action. Their return fire was inaccurate but it was always spirited. At night they sent flaming fire rafts downstream, putting an eerie flickering light on the river, causing Farragut's gunboats *Sciota* and *Kineo* to collide, with crippling damage, when they tried to evade one of these blazing drifters. The bombardment went on and on, past Porter's forty-eight hours, drawing out at last to six full days, the forts still full of fight. Ben Butler came aboard *Hartford* once to watch, and wrote of "that superbly useless bombardment," and Farragut grew more and more impatient. He had never believed that the forts could be reduced in this way, and he grew tired of waiting. He made up his mind, at last: enough was enough, the fleet would go up regardless.[11]

On the night of April 20 he sent Commander Henry H. Bell upstream with gunboats *Pinola* and *Itasca* to blast an opening in the floating barrier. They found the barrier to consist of six floating hulks, anchored about a hundred yards apart, supporting a huge chain which blocked passage; but the line of hulks ended some distance short of the right bank, the gap being filled by a raft which could be drawn aside to create an opening in case of need. The forts opened fire, shooting wildly in the darkness; Bell's men went aboard one of the hulks and planted powder charges, but the charges failed to explode, one of the gunboats ran aground and had trouble getting off, and in the end all that could be done was to cut loose the raft. Bell got his two vessels back unharmed, but most of the barrier was intact. The place where the raft had been was open, but the opening was too narrow to let the fleet do more than go up in single file close to Fort Jackson. Furthermore, lookouts in the fleet next morning reported that a new chain had been strung across the opening, and Farragut sent a boat up late one night to find out. The boat rowed through the opening, took soundings, found no chain, came back and reported; and finally, at two in the morning of April 24, *Hartford* hoisted two red lanterns to the mizzen peak and the big fleet got under way.[12]

It was a black night, with no wind to ripple the water, and although the moon was about to rise there would be smoke to hide it, coal smoke from the ships' funnels, powder smoke from scores upon scores of great guns, with deadly flashes of light from guns and shells and fire ships to break the darkness; and there was a four-mile current in the river so that a crippled ship (or a ship whose captain faltered) would drift downriver, helpless. Here was the old sailor who did not propose to waste the chance his flag had given him, a man whose chief underling had warned that he "lacked the vigor of youth" and whose superior had warned that success would be expected, and who in his own turn had told his wife that death coming out of duty well done would make a good end to life's drama—and ship after ship brought its anchors up and steamed north against the river, with the silent forts waiting beyond the chained hulks. The fleet would be sunk if it had to stand and fight, but it was not going to stop. It had certain advantages; the barrier had been broken, the ironclads were not quite ready, and on *Hartford's* poop deck it had a lanky flag officer, stalking up and down on springy legs, knowing exactly what he was going to do and what he was going to make other people do—and, altogether, this was it.

One by one the ships went through the gap in the barrier. One or two missed their bearings and crashed into the chain itself, hung in midstream briefly, then broke loose and went on; and the Confederate gunners discovered what was happening and opened fire, long ranks of guns on parapet and in casemate flashing incessantly on the rim of the night. On *Hartford*, Farragut had the gun crews lie down until their guns would bear, and the men sweated it out while shell and solid shot snapped shrouds and backstays and splintered the bulwarks. The fleet drew abreast of Fort Jackson, and Fort St. Philip was just upstream on the other side, and the gun crews sprang into action. Then the whole fleet was firing broadsides to port and to starboard while the forts slammed back with everything they had, and the heavy smoke rolled and coiled over the river to blind everybody. Far downstream Porter's mortars opened an all-out bombardment, and a few men whose duties allowed them to look aloft saw a terrifying marvel—red glow of the lighted fuses of the great shells soaring high into the night, blinking on and off as they revolved slowly, hanging motionless for a moment and then coming down fast to explode in blinding light and stupefying noise over the forts and the water and the echoing marshes.

Men could see too much and too little. Gunners could make out their targets only as quick bursts of fire, and the Confederate cannoneers could do little more than blaze away at what they supposed was the middle of the river. Ship captains had to steam up a channel that had no shores and no beacons, nothing visible anywhere except the stabbing flames from gun muzzles and bursting shell. One of Butler's staff officers, on the flagship, said later that the business was like "all the earthquakes in the world and all the thunder and lightning storms together, in a space of two miles, all going off at once." Captain Thomas T. Craven, on U.S.S. *Brooklyn,* confessed that he never expected that he or his ship or the fleet itself would live through it, and old Farragut wrote that the fight "was one of the most awful sights and events I ever saw or expect to experience."[13]

In mid-passage *Hartford* ran aground under the guns of Fort St. Philip, a doughty Confederate tug captain rammed a fire raft hard alongside, a sheet of flame ran up *Hartford's* bulwarks and rigging, the fort's gunners fired as fast as they could handle their pieces, and for a moment it looked as if flagship and flag officer had reached the end of the run. But tug and raft were driven off, the flames were put out, the Confederate gunners fired just a little too high, and at last *Hartford* wrenched her hull out of the mud and went on with minor damage. There was a Confederate ram in the river—*Manassas,* a converted tugboat with a flimsy turtleback covering of thin iron plating—and this craft rammed both *Mississippi* and *Brooklyn,* hurting them but not crippling either one; was driven away and finally was sunk by gunfire. U.S.S. *Varuna* got safely above the forts, fought two unarmored rams, *Governor Moore* and *Stonewall Jackson,* and was sunk, the only Federal ship casualty of the night; her two assailants were disposed of as the rest of the fleet came up. Three gunboats failed to make the passage: *Itasca,* disabled by a round shot through her boilers, and *Kennebec* and *Winona,* which got entangled in what remained of the floating barrier, were badly shot up, and had to go back to the original anchorage. But the fleet as a fighting unit never stopped moving, and as daybreak came in over the swamps Farragut had thirteen warships safely past the forts, a fleet that was somewhat cut up but perfectly capable of doing everything it was supposed to do.

He had his ships anchor a few miles upstream from the forts, at the old quarantine station, to bury the dead, attend to the wounded, wash down the decks, make hasty repairs, and count losses. Altogether he had lost thirty-seven men killed and 149 wounded, all of his ships had been hit hard, and the forts themselves had suffered only minor damage—but he done exactly what he had believed he could do, the big danger had been met and passed, and New Orleans was entirely at his mercy. All he had to do now was go on and take it.[14]

He went on and took it. One of his gunboats achieved the improbable by overawing and then capturing a battalion of infantry near the quarantine station, and just below New Orleans there were men with field pieces prepared to make a fight. A few blasts from the heavy guns dispersed them; and then the fleet came up to the New Orleans waterfront in a drizzling rain, saw angry crowds shaking fists and uttering impotent curses in front of lifeless warehouses, cowed them with the threat of the terrible guns, anchored—and New Orleans was gone, United States flag flying, mayor stoutly refusing to surrender but confessing that if the Yankees wanted the city they had it, General Lovell leading a handful of third-rate troops off into the hinterland, the greatest city in Dixie caving in while the scarred black warships anchored in the river just offshore.

Lovell was helpless. When the ships passed the forts he had fewer than 3000 troops to defend New Orleans, and the troops were of no use to him. He had certain militia regiments drawn up on the "inner line" of defenses just below the city, but he gave them no ammunition, and he explained why. They could not fight warships no matter how they tried, and anyway "they had in some regiments manifested such an insubordinate disposition that I felt unwilling to put ammunition in their hands";[15] and whatever Lovell did, Farragut could and would bombard the city unless it gave in, so Lovell took his useless handful out of town and let the Federals have it. Farragut saw the United States flag run up and then, still somewhat shaken, wrote a letter to his wife: "I am so agitated that I can scarcely write & shall only tell you that it has pleased Almighty God to preserve my life & limb, through a fire of 2 days, that the world has scarcely known—I shall return publicly my thanks as well as all those of our Fleet for his Goodness & mercies." Along the waterfront great stacks of baled cotton were burning, not to mention ranks of steamboats which nobody wanted the Yankees to have, and the old man felt a sailor's grief over it: "all the beautiful Steamers & Ships were set on fire & consumed."[16]

There were, of course, the Confederate ironclads, and the fight had come just a little too soon for them. Lacking the ability to move, *Louisiana* had been towed downstream and tied to the bank near Fort St. Philip, where she had been able to do no more than add a few guns to that fort's battery; her crew blew her up and sent her to fragments a few days after Farragut had gone by. At a New Orleans wharf there was *Mississippi*, two of her three propellers still lying on the dock, her iron armor not yet fastened, no guns aboard, workmen fighting for time that had been denied them. The naval officer who had been sent down to fit her out and fight her confessed, desperately, that when Farragut passed the forts "I did not know, in the name of God, what to do with her"; in the end he did the only possible thing and set the hulk on fire, and the blazing wreck drifted harmlessly down past Farragut's grim fleet while the city's fate was being settled.[17]

Farragut's final point proved itself. Once he had New Orleans it was the forts and not the Federal fleet that were isolated; distracted by the long bombardment, hopeless because everything else was gone, the garrison in Fort Jackson mutinied, and not long after Farragut had taken New Orleans the forts surrendered and everything was finished. The Federal power held both ends of the Mississippi, and the old flag officer had won. After the news got to Washington, Farragut was made rear admiral, first of that grade in the U. S. Navy.

6: *Brilliant Victory*

The movement of the Army of the Potomac to Hampton Roads was an impressive display of the irresistible strength of the North. More than 400 transports were on the water—ocean liners, bay and harbor steamboats, schooners, laboring tugs hauling heavy barges—going from the Potomac wharves at Alexandria to the landing stages under the guns at Fort Monroe. The business had been organized by men who knew exactly what they were doing, and although at times two dozen ships anchored in the lower bay, awaiting their turns to unload, there were no real delays. In the final weeks of March the North moved more than 75,000 soldiers and an almost infinite variety of equipment that embraced everything from siege guns to observation balloons and the apparatus to generate hydrogen gas, and did it without accident or confusion. (Without serious accident, anyway: eight mules were lost when a barge foundered.) Never on earth had anyone seen a water-borne military movement so prodigious. An admiring British writer remarked later that the whole affair had been "the stride of a giant."[1]

But there was no second stride. Having made the first, the giant paused, irresolute, muscle-bound, anxious to avoid a fall. The war was about to take a strange turn.

As far as any Northerner could see in the middle of April, 1862, the war was almost won. The Confederacy was losing the Mississippi River and all of the west, its Atlantic coastline was being sealed off, and it was obviously hard pressed. Secretary Stanton was so confident that on April 3 he closed the Army's recruiting offices and ordered all recruiting details back to their regiments.[2] Now the North's largest army, carefully trained for eight months and equipped with everything an army could use, was coming down to crush a Confederate capital whose outnumbered defenders were still trying to reorganize their troops all the way down to company and regimental levels. This, surely, would be the final blow. It had to be.

And yet . . . four months later, after this army had done its level best, the war had turned topsy-turvy and it was the North rather than the South which seemed to be in danger of defeat. Once the Army of the Potomac went into action the tide began to flow in the other direction. The beginning of the long war—the all-out, all-destroying, disastrous war that finally went beyond control—dates from this army's advance up the Virginia peninsula.

Did this happen because the Army of the Potomac advanced, or in spite of it?

Cause and effect are curiously mixed, and the area of sheer coincidence has vague boundaries. It was coincidence, for example, which determined that when the campaign approached its climax the army would have to fight a military genius immeasurably more skillful than its own leadership. But other troubles were home-grown. The army had stayed too long in Washington. It had the touch of the parade ground; it had known too many grand reviews and too little reality. It would presently be remarked that although this was the best-drilled of all the Union armies, its regiments straggled most atrociously on a route march, so that sometimes the drifters by the roadside visibly outnumbered the plodders in the ranks.[3] During the months in Washington the army had almost come to seem less a military instrument than a tool of politics, the means by which one faction or another would control the destiny of the nation. Its strategy might be less significant than its political philosophy. Its commanding general was beset by uncertainties and misunderstandings, some of them his own, some of them not his own.

The army's very name was significant. It was the *Army of the Potomac*, the river of the national capital. It might campaign to the gates of Richmond, but all that it did would be controlled by what it had left behind. Of all the country's armies, this was the one—as everyone knew, all too clearly—that could most quickly and certainly lose the war: and so at times it was hard to see that this was the army, also, which could most quickly and certainly win it. A general who took the offensive with this army needed to be bold, determined, and uncommonly clear-minded.

A hint of the way things were going to work came on March 23, in the battle of Kernstown.

Ever since the unhappy canal boat expedition McClellan had kept an army corps in the lower Shenandoah Valley, and the commander of this corps, General Nathaniel P. Banks, had been having a pleasantly uneventful war. He had 25,000 men and the Confederates in his front numbered hardly 4500; decisive odds, surely, except that the Confederates were led by Stonewall Jackson, about whose singular capacities neither General Banks nor the rest of the world knew as much just then as they would know a little later. Jackson's little force had been pushed out of Winchester and had gone, apparently, far to the south, and could be nothing more than a minor nuisance;

so when McClellan began his move to Fort Monroe and needed a garrison for the area around Manassas he naturally thought about General Banks. Banks was ordered to leave a division at Winchester and prepare to bring everybody else east of the Blue Ridge, and he promptly obeyed. At Winchester, with its principal advanced line at Kernstown, a few miles south, he posted the division of Brigadier General James Shields; 11,000 men, approximately, whose chief function was to keep the lower valley clear of Rebels so that the rebuilt line of the Baltimore & Ohio Railroad could operate without interruption.

Shields came from County Tyrone by way of Illinois and the west coast; a lean, combative man who had the odd idea that Stonewall Jackson was afraid of him, and who had once challenged Abraham Lincoln to fight a duel, but who otherwise was competent and well-balanced.[4] He had led troops with distinction in the Mexican War, and when Banks went east of the mountains Shields stayed on the alert and kept his troops alert also, maintaining as good a lookout as any general could considering the fact that at this time, in Virginia, the Federals were using some of the world's worst cavalry against some of the world's best.

Jackson had heard about Banks's withdrawal, and he seems to have believed that the man was leaving fewer troops around Winchester than was actually the case. Joseph E. Johnston had just warned him to keep close to the Yankees—the sort of order no one ever needed to give Jackson twice—and anyway Jackson considered Winchester his own private bailiwick and wanted to drive the invaders out for personal reasons. On the morning of March 23 he sent Johnston a characteristic message: "With the blessing of an ever-kind Providence I hope to be in the vicinity of Winchester this evening."[5] Then he made his word good by moving in to make a savage attack on the Federal lines at Kernstown.

Probably the least important thing about the battle of Kernstown is that Jackson tried to do the impossible, and failed. Shields had more than twice Jackson's numbers, and these Federals were good soldiers—Westerners, mostly, plus a few Pennsylvanians, with some regiments which would eventually be listed with the best combat units in the Union Army. Jackson's line was halted and at last it had to give ground, and by dark its dour commander, furious over the reverse, was leading it up the valley in full retreat. He had lost some 700 men, and Shields (who himself was wounded) had had smaller losses and was entitled to claim a victory.[6] For the rest of the war, Shields's men bragged that they were the only ones who had ever beaten Stonewall Jackson.

But the victory meant nothing at all, whereas the mere fact that the battle had been fought meant a great deal.

The lower Shenandoah Valley was an extremely sensitive area. When a hostile army touched it the Federal government would react vigorously, almost automatically. Kernstown revealed this fact, and both Jackson and Robert E. Lee made note of it for use later on. What followed Kernstown was most instructive to both of these soldiers.

It seemed clear to the Federals that Jackson was much stronger than anyone had supposed—otherwise he would hardly have dared to attack Shields—and there was a hasty reshuffling of troops. Banks was sent back to Winchester, horse, foot, and guns, to drive Jackson away and keep him away. It seemed necessary also to reinforce Pathfinder Frémont, who was just assuming command in West Virginia and who must protect the western segment of the Baltimore & Ohio. (If the Rebels were strong enough to attack Shields they no doubt contemplated aggression a little farther west, as well.) So the division of Brigadier General Louis Blenker was detached from McClellan and sent to Frémont, with orders to tarry a while in the lower valley until Banks had finally disposed of Jackson.

Meanwhile McClellan was trying to get the Army of the Potomac down to Fort Monroe. At the end of March his move was well under way. In the four army corps commanded by General Keyes, Heintzelman, Sumner, and McDowell—those commanders whom he had not chosen but who had been thrust upon him by the President—he had 126,000 men, present for duty. Keyes and Heintzelman were already on the peninsula, Sumner's corps was in transit, and McDowell's was ready to leave. Now this disturbance at Kernstown knocked McClellan's arrangements slightly out of line and led to a major miscalculation.

President Lincoln had consented to the peninsula move with grave misgivings, and had laid down two firm conditions to govern it. First, there must be a strong force around Manassas to keep the Confederates out of northern Virginia; second, there must be, in Washington and its circling camps, a garrison powerful enough to make the city secure against any sudden Confederate thrust. The arrangements by which McClellan made provision for these two requirements while he also moved his army men to the lower Chesapeake were necessarily intricate, and Kernstown deranged them; revising them, McClellan invited trouble and speedily got it.

Departing for Fort Monroe, McClellan sent Secretary Stanton a tabulation of his strength, pointing out that he was leaving Banks with 35,000 men to hold northern Virginia, and that General Wadsworth, commanding in Washington, had 20,000 more. The total thus remaining to meet President Lincoln's stipulation was, accordingly, 55,000 men, which struck McClellan as ample and was only 10,000 short of the number which the council of corps commanders had fixed as proper to defend the capital.[7] Accordingly, on April 1, McClellan himself left for Fort Monroe, and Stanton took the figures to the White House to show them to the President.

When the President and the Secretary of War examined the figures they felt that there were serious holes in McClellan's arithmetic. The 55,000 who were to hold northern Virginia had originally been figured as being in addition to General Banks's corps. Now it developed that this corps made up the larger part of the whole, and Banks had nearly all of his men over in the Shenandoah, moving down west of the Massanutten Mountain far from the vital area east of the Blue Ridge. To be sure, McClellan had told Banks to bring everybody but Shields back to the vicinity of Manassas "the very moment the thorough defeat of Jackson will permit it," but that moment had not arrived; as far as Mr. Lincoln could see, the region which he had ordered held in force was hardly being held at all. To make things worse, the 20,000 left with Wadsworth included some levies that were already ticketed to go elsewhere and in any case were made up largely of untrained troops, imperfectly equipped. Joe Johnston was known to have his army somewhere below the Rappahannock, and it struck Mr. Lincoln that what had been done would present to Johnston "a great temptation . . . to turn back from the Rappahannock and sack Washington." He had accepted the plan McClellan gave him, but it seemed to him now that "that arrangement was broken up and nothing was substituted for it."[8]

It seemed, in short, that McClellan had simply disobeyed clear orders, and the President acted promptly. On April 3 he ordered Stanton to have either McDowell's or Sumner's corps held in front of Washington, to operate in the Manassas area. Since Sumner's corps was already on the move, Stanton chose McDowell, and McClellan was notified that this corps—33,510 men present for duty, by the latest returns—was detached from his command and would not join him on the peninsula. McDowell henceforth would get his orders not from McClellan but from the War Department.[9] As far as McClellan was concerned, McDowell was an independent operator, and the Army of the Potomac had just lost a quarter of its strength.

. . . which might not have been so serious if anyone at army headquarters had been able to say how strong the army really was, either before or after this loss. But it is just here that one begins to encounter that fantastic uncertainty about numbers which was to hang over the Army of the Potomac like a fog too heavy for the winds to lift. McClellan's headquarters was handicapped by a singular inability to determine the size either of this army or of the army which it was about to fight: a shortcoming which made victory impossible and which bewildered no one as long or as profoundly as it bewildered the commanding general himself—with whom, indeed, much of it originated.

On April 7, three days after he had begun to move up the peninsula, McClellan was unable to come within 17,000 of stating the number of men he actually had with him. He told Brigadier General John E. Wool, the white-haired veteran of the War of 1812 who commanded at Fort Monroe, that he had just 68,000 men present for duty; on the same day he sent to President Lincoln a telegram stating that "my entire force for duty only amounts to about 85,000."[10]

To be sure, this need not have mattered much, because the Army of the Potomac just now had a prodigious advantage over its opponent. When McClellan's divisions marched up from Fort Monroe there were fewer than 15,000 Confederates on the scene (fewer enemies, altogether, than the margin of McClellan's doubt about the size of his own army) and more than a week would pass before that number could be increased to any great extent. Yet this was of little help, because army headquarters always credited Confederate commanders with having from two to four times as many men as was actually the case. In addition to fighting the tough Confederates who were physically on the scene with loaded weapons in their hands, the Army of the Potomac had also to contend with scores and scores of thousands of enemies who never existed. As a result, it tended to move very slowly.

The business began with the Army intelligence section—Secret Service, as it was known then. McClellan had confided his Secret Service to a man who was carried on the books as "E. J. Allen," but who in real life was Allan Pinkerton, the first and most famous of America's great private detectives.

Pinkerton was a diligent detective and a first-rate organizer, and he set up a network of spies, messengers, and observers all over Virginia, submitting to McClellan periodic reports which were highly convincing because they contained such a wealth of detail. Running through each report that went to McClellan would be revealing thumbnail comments: "coffee getting scarce . . . plenty of lead . . . salt scarce . . . a good supply of tents and camp equipment except camp kettles . . . plenty of wagons and teams, generally impressed . . . on an average arriving at Richmond 3 companies daily." Here would be a note on the number of shooting galleries in and around Richmond and on the extent to which Confederate soldiers used them; there, a remark that Southern regiments averaged from 700 to 800 men in strength; next, a statement that almost all fortifications were built with slave labor. From each area came just the sort of detail that would show that methodical observers had been taking notes on the spot.

With these comments, of course, came the estimates of troop

numbers. These were based on the reports from the Pinkerton operatives, on the examination of Confederate prisoners and deserters, and on things said by contrabands, the figures finally presented being drawn up by Pinkerton himself. Pinkerton carefully worked out percentages so that the totals assembled for any unit could be reduced to a proper present-for-duty level, following his percentages so faithfully that now and then this or that Confederate general would be credited with having "6,346⅔" men in his division. When he drew up his grand totals Pinkerton arbitrarily raised the numbers slightly, on a system previously discussed with McClellan, to make certain that there was a margin for error to cover new arrivals or units that somehow had been missed.

He gets credit, nowadays, for having been worse than he was, and some of his estimates indeed were grotesquely unreal—such as an autumn report that Beauregard's command contained 100,000 men, and that the Confederates had thirty-three regiments on the peninsula. But at times his carefully calculated totals were fairly close to the mark. On November 15, 1861, for instance, Pinkerton worked it out that there were in Virginia, from Norfolk all the way to the western mountains, approximately 117,100 armed Confederates. The official returns for December 31 (six weeks later, in other words) show an "aggregate present" for all Confederate forces in the state of 118,306. On the face of it, Pinkerton late in 1861 was keeping very fair track of Confederate numbers in Virginia.[11]

Yet the result was disaster. The "aggregate present" figure, which came so close to the Pinkerton total, actually had very little relation to the number "present for duty": the number, that is, that would be of use in battle. It was always substantially higher, including sick men, men under arrest or on noncombat details, men from disorganized units awaiting reassignment, men without weapons —all the multitude of military extras who had to be fed, paid and reported on but whom no foe would ever have to face. Even when he came closest to accuracy, Pinkerton made a paper army look real. In addition, his reports got worse instead of better as time went on, and his estimates of the numbers McClellan would have to face finally lost all touch with reality. In the end Pinkerton was persuaded that the Confederacy had between 100,000 and 120,000 soldiers on the peninsula, and that their available forces around Richmond came to more than 180,000.[12]

These wild guesses would have done less harm, however, if there had not been at army headquarters (where such matters can be cross-checked) a will to believe them. This will McClellan had and never lost. Long after the war, when the truth about Confederate Army strengths in Virginia was clear to everyone, he clung to the belief that he had been beset everywhere by superior numbers: a belief which had no base in fact or in logic but which, if held hard enough, might perhaps justify the paralyzing indecision which governed the direction of the Army of the Potomac.

Yet this indecision was more than the simple result of a belief that the enemy was the stronger. It preceded that belief, displaying itself in a baffling lack of capacity to drive a chosen plan through to its conclusion, and it became visible before the spring campaign was a week old.

On March 19, McClellan had sent Secretary Stanton an outline of his strategic design. He would go up the peninsula to make an advanced base at West Point, where the Pamunkey and Mattapony Rivers meet to form the York, fifty miles northwest of Fort Monroe. Somewhere between West Point and Richmond, he said, the Confederates would concentrate to fight the great, decisive battle, and so it was all-important for him to reach West Point as quickly as possible. About one third of the way up the river was the historic town of Yorktown, where Cornwallis had come to grief, and Yorktown was powerfully fortified by the Rebels. It could be taken by siege, of course, but that would involve a delay of weeks, and there were no weeks to spare; no days to spare, even. At all costs, Yorktown must be taken at once. This, said McClellan, could be done by a joint Army-Navy attack. The Navy "should at once concentrate upon the York River all their available and most powerful batteries." If it did, Yorktown should fall in a few hours; if not, the business might take weeks. Since speed was essential, McClellan insisted, full naval co-operation was "an absolute necessity"; Yorktown was the key to the entire campaign.[13]

What McClellan was talking about, of course, was an operation after the Fort Henry model—a pulverizing naval bombardment, with the Army coming in when the dust settled to mop up pockets of resistance and take full possession. The plan was definite enough and it made perfectly good sense—and nothing was ever done to put it into effect.

McClellan appears to have assumed that the President or the Secretary of War or somebody would tell the Navy that its warships were supposed to reduce the fortifications at Yorktown, but nothing of the sort happened. Assistant Secretary Fox insisted afterward that the Navy had never been asked to bombard Yorktown, and he added that the Confederate works there were so strong, and were situated on such commanding ground, that they could not have been reduced by naval gunfire anyway. Flag Officer Louis Goldsborough, commanding at Hampton Roads, understood that Washington simply wanted *Monitor* to keep *Virginia* away from the transports and the disembarkation area around Fort Monroe. Goldsborough talked to McClellan the morning the general reached Fort Monroe, and McClellan said nothing to him about any bombardment. Instead, he asked the Navy to help in the reduction of a Confederate fort at Gloucester, which lay on the north side of the York just opposite Yorktown.

Between Yorktown and Gloucester the York is only 1000 yards wide, and with forts in both places the Confederates had the mouth of the river firmly closed. McClellan told Goldsborough that he wanted to land troops on the banks of the Severn River, a few miles north of Gloucester. Gloucester then could be stormed from the rear, and if that was done nobody would need to bombard anything. If Gloucester fell, Yorktown might fall also; or, at the very least, warships would be able to enter the York and harass the flank of the Confederates on the peninsula. At any rate, Goldsborough assigned seven gunboats to help with the Severn River operation and believed this was all the Army wanted. Apparently he was right; on April 3 McClellan notified Stanton that he had talked to the flag officer and was confident that the Navy would crush *Virginia* if the ironclad came out, adding that he hoped to advance the next day and that "my only trouble is the scarcity of wagons."

The Federal advance began, as anticipated, on the morning of April 4, and it was keyed neither to a bombardment of Yorktown nor to the capture of Gloucester but to the belief that the troops could simply force their way past Yorktown and isolate it by getting into its rear. McClellan sent Heintzelman and the III Corps straight up to Yorktown to pin the Confederate garrison in the fortifications there, while Keyes and the IV Corps swung to the left and headed for a place known as Halfway House, four and one half miles beyond Yorktown on the road to Williamsburg, at the narrowest part of the whole peninsula. Once Keyes reached Halfway House, Yorktown would be cut off and must fall. As his army reached the Confederate outposts McClellan sent word to Stanton: "I expect to fight tomorrow, as I shall endeavor to cut the communication between Yorktown and Richmond."[14]

But tomorrow brought no fight. Getting abreast of Yorktown, Keyes met an unexpected obstacle—the Warwick River, a pesky, inconsiderable stream which had been thought to lie somewhere off to the left, well clear of the Army's line of march. Keyes found that the Warwick rose near the Yorktown fortifications and lay squarely across his road; the Confederates had built a series of little dams which turned much of the low ground into gummy swamps, and they had put up trenches, rifle pits, and batteries to bar the way. The advance came to a halt, while McClellan studied the situation and took thought.

To study the situation the Army command had an untried military instrument—an observation balloon, with Professor T. S. C. Lowe, aeronaut, as airborne military observer. The "aeronautic train," consisting of four wagons carrying the deflated balloon and the apparatus for generating hydrogen gas, was trundled forward to the hamlet of Cockletown, the apparatus was unloaded, and early in the evening the balloon was inflated and sent aloft. From an altitude of one thousand feet Professor Lowe found that he could see a good deal, and on the following day there were more ascensions, with Army officers making maps and taking copious notes. Confederate

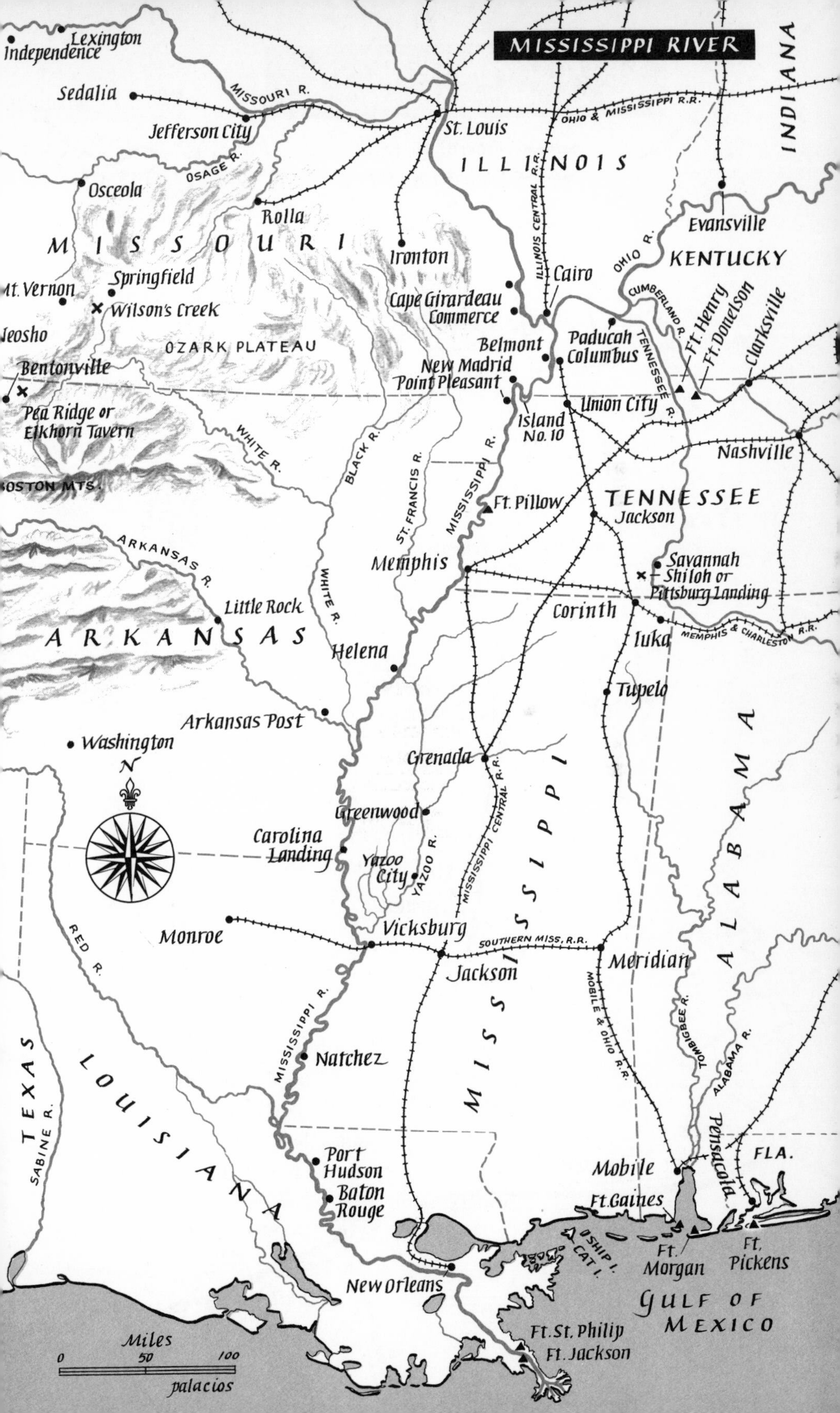
MISSISSIPPI RIVER
Lexington
Independence
Sedalia
MISSOURI R.
Jefferson City
St. Louis
OHIO & MISSISSIPPI R.R.
INDIANA
ILLINOIS
OSAGE R.
Osceola
Rolla
ILLINOIS CENTRAL R.R.
Evansville
MISSOURI
Ironton
OHIO R.
KENTUCKY
Cairo
Mt. Vernon
Springfield
Wilson's Creek
Cape Girardeau
Commerce
CUMBERLAND R.
Ft. Henry
Ft. Donelson
Clarksville
Neosho
OZARK PLATEAU
Paducah
Belmont
Columbus
Bentonville
New Madrid
Point Pleasant
TENNESSEE R.
Pea Ridge or Elkhorn Tavern
Union City
Island No. 10
WHITE R.
BLACK R.
MISSISSIPPI R.
ST. FRANCIS R.
Nashville
BOSTON MTS.
Ft. Pillow
TENNESSEE
Jackson
ARKANSAS R.
Memphis
WHITE R.
Savannah
Shiloh or Pittsburg Landing
Little Rock
Corinth
ARKANSAS
Iuka
MEMPHIS & CHARLESTON R.R.
Helena
Tupelo
Arkansas Post
Washington
N
ALABAMA
Grenada
MISSISSIPPI
MISSISSIPPI CENTRAL R.R.
Greenwood
Carolina Landing
Yazoo City
YAZOO R.
RED R.
Monroe
Vicksburg
SOUTHERN MISS. R.R.
Jackson
Meridian
MISSISSIPPI R.
MOBILE & OHIO R.R.
TOMBIGBEE R.
ALABAMA R.
TEXAS
LOUISIANA
Natchez
SABINE R.
Port Hudson
Pensacola
FLA.
Mobile
Baton Rouge
Ft. Gaines
SHIP I.
CAT I.
Ft. Morgan
Ft. Pickens
New Orleans
GULF OF MEXICO
Ft. St. Philip
Ft. Jackson
Miles
0
50
100
palacios

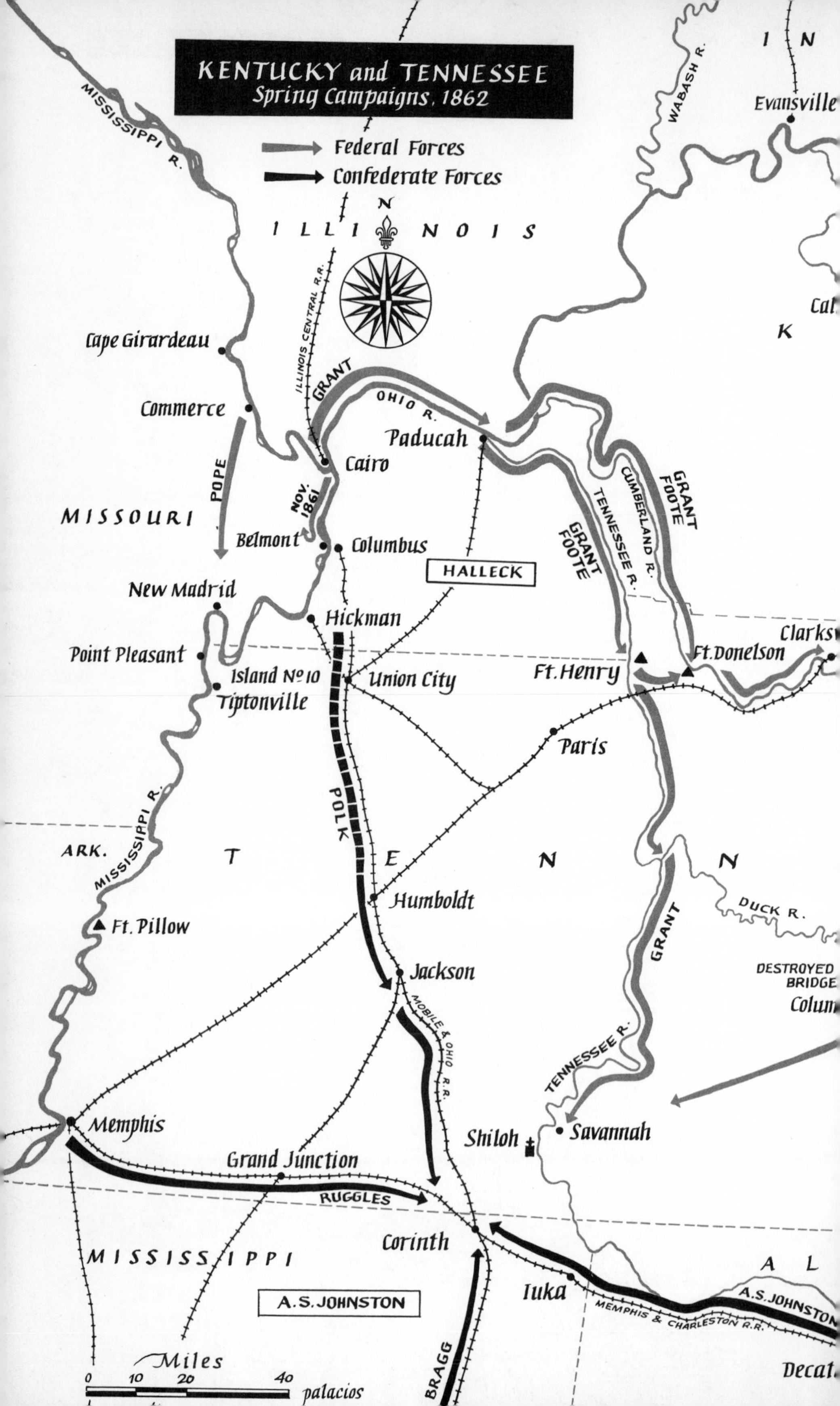

KENTUCKY and TENNESSEE
Spring Campaigns, 1862
Federal Forces
Confederate Forces
N
ILLINOIS
IN
Evansville
WABASH R.
MISSISSIPPI R.
ILLINOIS CENTRAL R.R.
Cape Girardeau
Commerce
GRANT
OHIO R.
Paducah
Cairo
POPE
NOV. 1861
MISSOURI
Belmont
Columbus
HALLECK
New Madrid
Hickman
TENNESSEE R.
CUMBERLAND R.
GRANT FOOTE
GRANT FOOTE
K
Point Pleasant
Island No 10
Tiptonville
Union City
Ft. Henry
Ft. Donelson
Paris
POLK
ARK.
MISSISSIPPI R.
T
E
N
N
Humboldt
Ft. Pillow
DUCK R.
GRANT
Jackson
DESTROYED BRIDGE
MOBILE & OHIO R.R.
TENNESSEE R.
Memphis
Shiloh
Savannah
Grand Junction
RUGGLES
Corinth
MISSISSIPPI
A L
A.S. JOHNSTON
Iuka
A.S. JOHNSTON
MEMPHIS & CHARLESTON R.R.
BRAGG
Miles
0 10 20 40
palacios

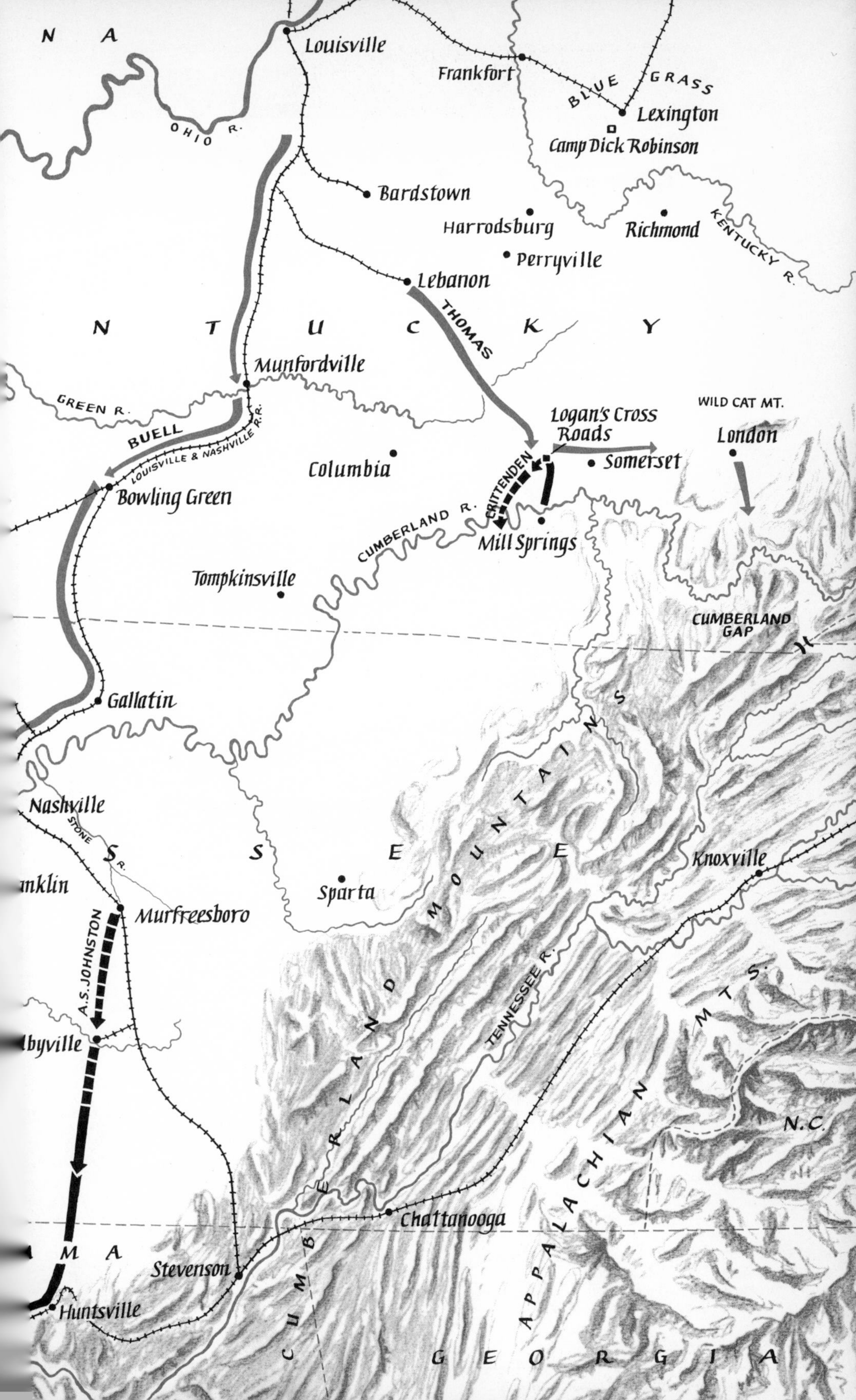
N A
Louisville
Frankfort
BLUE GRASS
Lexington
Camp Dick Robinson
OHIO R.
Bardstown
Harrodsburg
Richmond
KENTUCKY R.
Perryville
Lebanon
THOMAS
N T U C K Y
Munfordville
GREEN R.
WILD CAT MT.
Logan's Cross Roads
London
BUELL
LOUISVILLE & NASHVILLE R.R.
Columbia
Somerset
CRITTENDEN
Bowling Green
CUMBERLAND R.
Mill Springs
Tompkinsville
CUMBERLAND GAP
Gallatin
Nashville
STONE R.
S S E E
nklin
Murfreesboro
Sparta
Knoxville
CUMBERLAND MOUNTAINS
A.S. JOHNSTON
TENNESSEE R.
lbyville
APPALACHIAN MTS.
N.C.
Chattanooga
M A
Stevenson
Huntsville
G E O R G I A

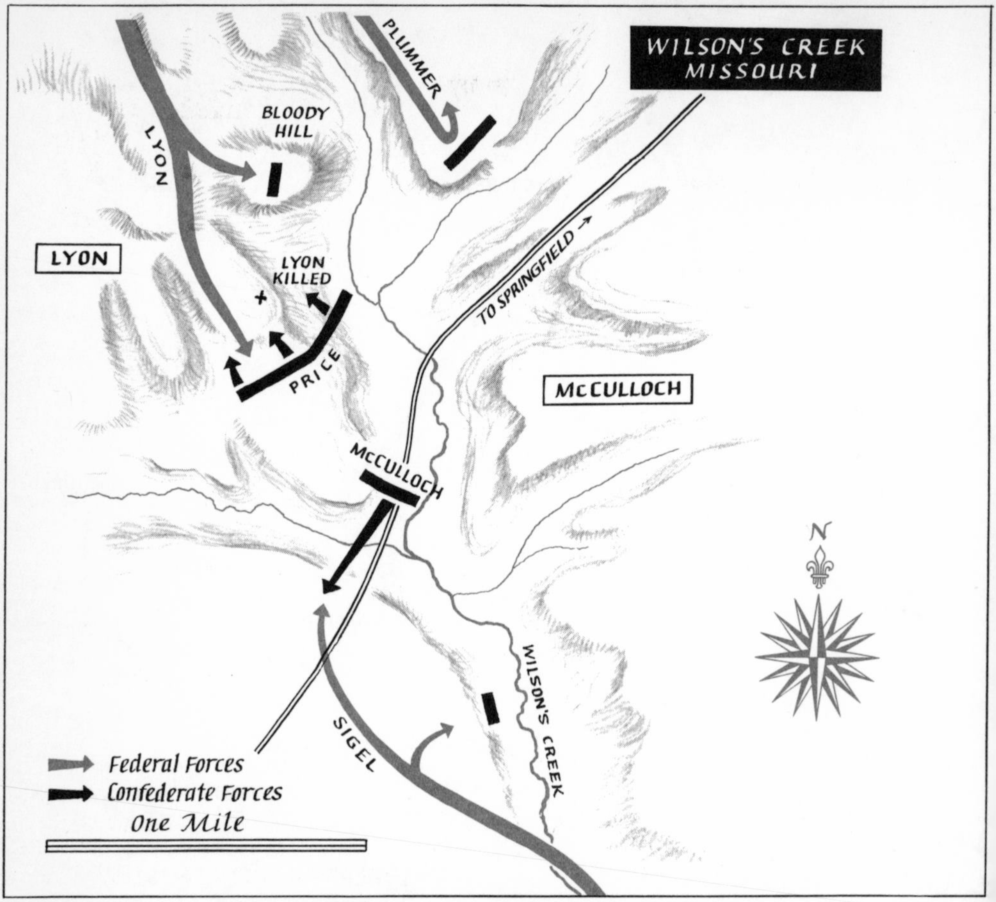

WILSON'S CREEK
MISSOURI
PLUMMER
BLOODY
HILL
LYON
LYON
LYON
KILLED
TO SPRINGFIELD →
PRICE
McCULLOCH
McCULLOCH
N
WILSON'S CREEK
SIGEL
Federal Forces
Confederate Forces
One Mile

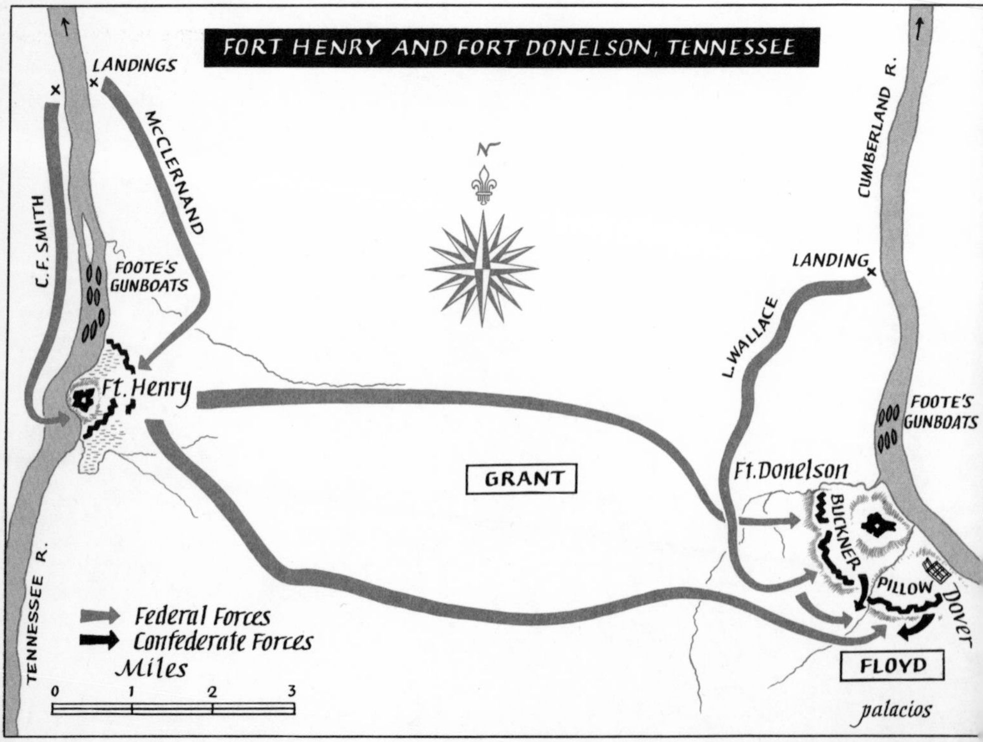

FORT HENRY AND FORT DONELSON, TENNESSEE
LANDINGS
McCLERNAND
C. F. SMITH
FOOTE'S
GUNBOATS
Ft. Henry
N
CUMBERLAND R.
LANDING
L. WALLACE
FOOTE'S
GUNBOATS
GRANT
Ft. Donelson
BUCKNER
PILLOW
Dover
FLOYD
TENNESSEE R.
Federal Forces
Confederate Forces
Miles
0
1
2
3
palacios

Richmond
Fort Monroe
HAMPTON ROADS
CAPE HENRY
JAMES R.
Petersburg
Norfolk
Portsmouth
Suffolk
DISMAL SWAMP
Currituck
Lynchburg
VIRGINIA
ALBEMARLE & CHESAPEAKE CANAL
Elizabeth City
RICHMOND & DANVILLE R.R.
Weldon
Hertford
ROANOKE I.
Fort Bartow
Edenton
ALBEMARLE SOUND
CROATAN SOUND
anville
ROANOKE R.
Plymouth
CAPE HATTERAS
HATTERAS INLET
Washington
Forts Hatteras and Clark
PAMLICO SOUND
Raleigh
Greensborough
Goldsborough
NEUSE R.
ATLANTIC & N. CAROLINA R.R.
New Berne
NORTH CAROLINA
Morehead City
Fort Macon
WILMINGTON & WELDON R.R.
CAPE FEAR R.
ATLANTIC
WILMINGTON & MANCHESTER R.R.
Wilmington
Fort Fisher
OCEAN
CAPE FEAR
Florence
N
PEE DEE R.
SOUTH CAROLINA
SANTEE R.
Branchville
SOUTH CAROLINA R.R.
EDISTO R.
Charleston
Fort Sumter
THE CAROLINAS
CHARLESTON & SAVANNAH R.R.
Coosawhatchie
EDISTO I.
Beaufort
Fort Beauregard
PORT ROYAL
Fort Walker, HILTON HEAD I.
Miles
0
100
GA.
Fort Pulaski
Savannah
palacios

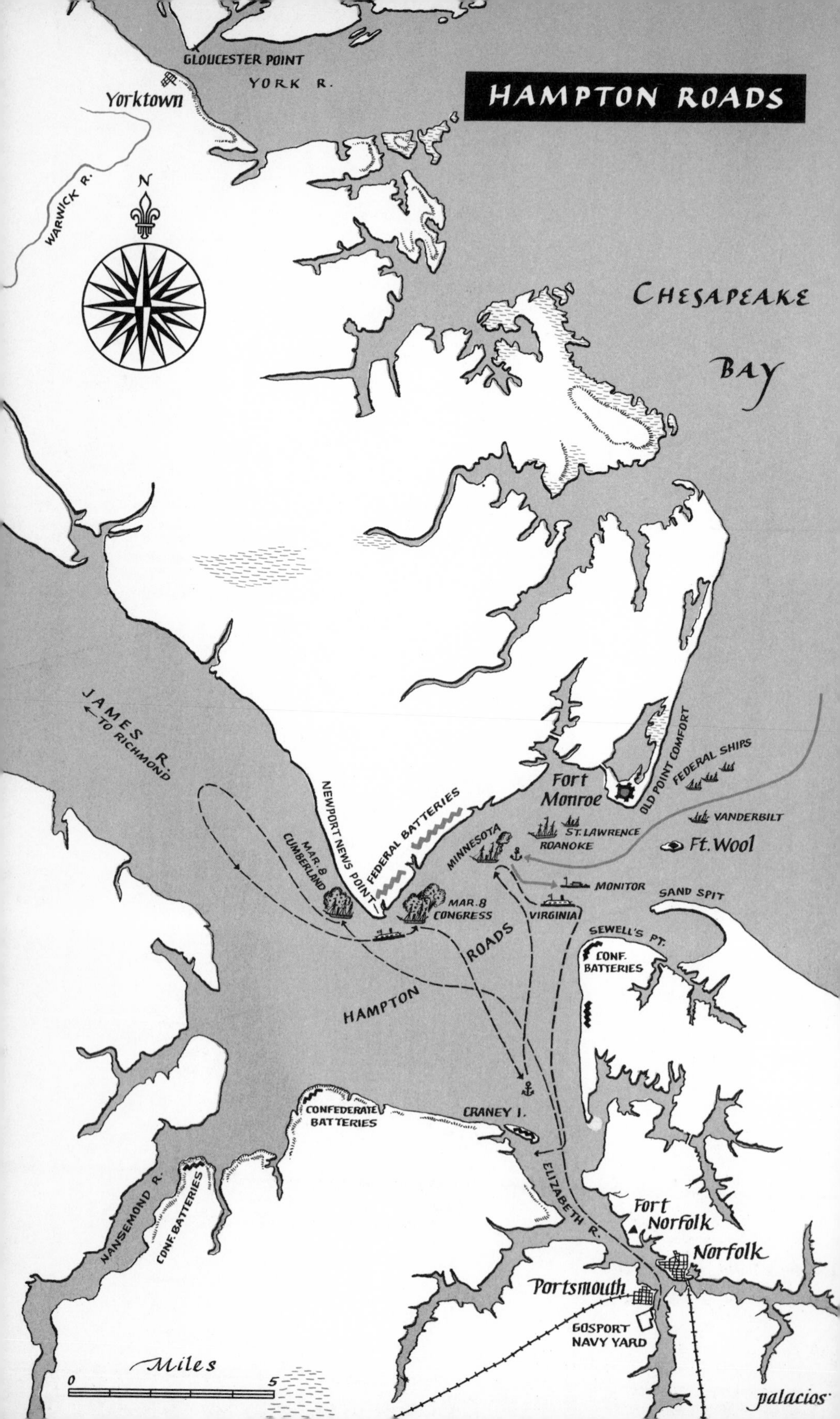
HAMPTON ROADS
GLOUCESTER POINT
YORK R.
Yorktown
WARWICK R.
N
CHESAPEAKE
BAY
JAMES R.
← TO RICHMOND
NEWPORT NEWS POINT
FEDERAL BATTERIES
MAR. 8
CUMBERLAND
MAR. 8
CONGRESS
Fort
Monroe
OLD POINT COMFORT
FEDERAL SHIPS
VANDERBILT
ST. LAWRENCE
ROANOKE
MINNESOTA
Ft. Wool
MONITOR
SAND SPIT
VIRGINIA
ROADS
HAMPTON
SEWELL'S PT.
CONF.
BATTERIES
CONFEDERATE
BATTERIES
CRANEY I.
ELIZABETH R.
NANSEMOND R.
CONF. BATTERIES
Fort
Norfolk
Norfolk
Portsmouth
GOSPORT
NAVY YARD
Miles
0
5
palacios

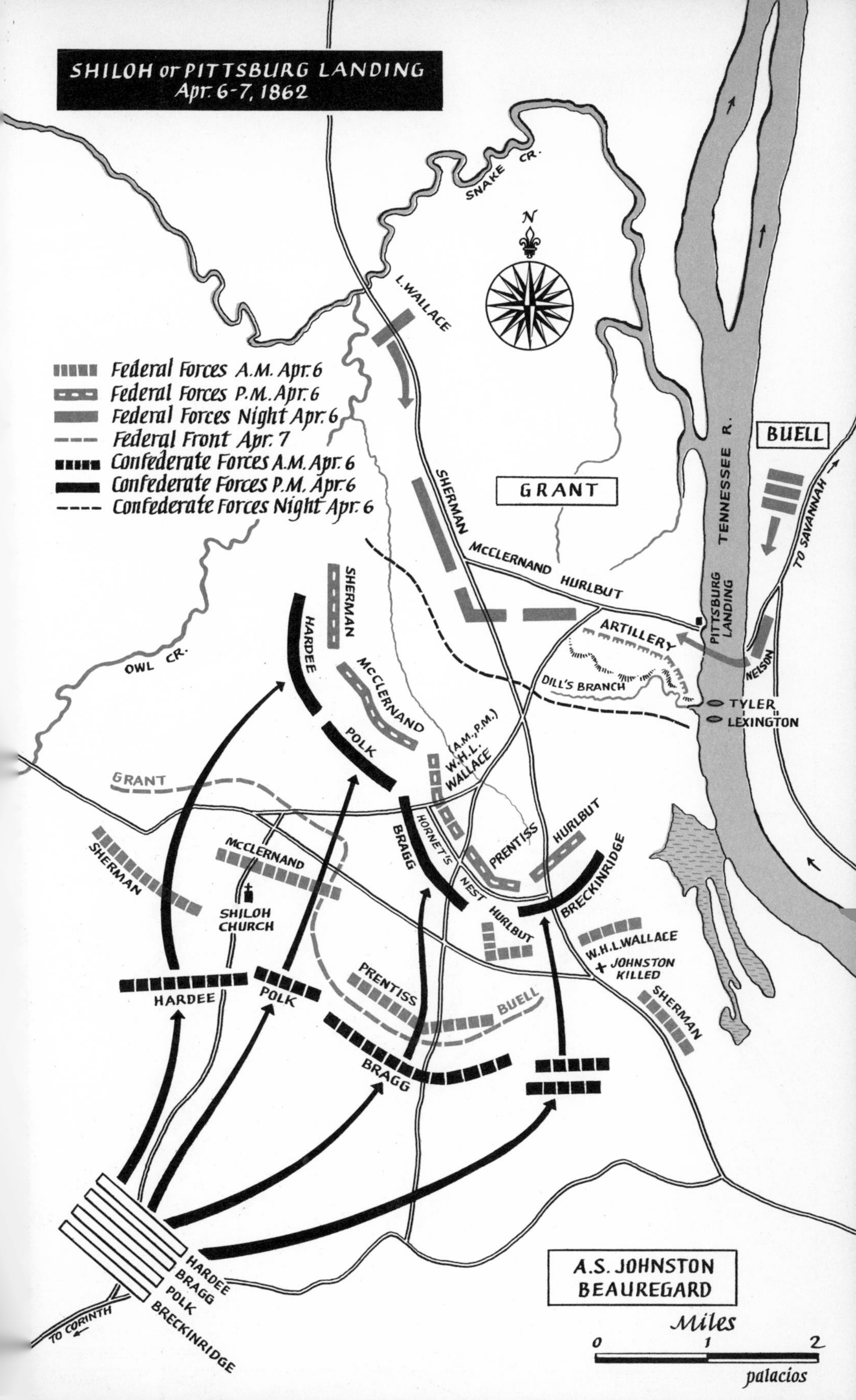
SHILOH or PITTSBURG LANDING
Apr. 6-7, 1862
Federal Forces A.M. Apr. 6
Federal Forces P.M. Apr. 6
Federal Forces Night Apr. 6
Federal Front Apr. 7
Confederate Forces A.M. Apr. 6
Confederate Forces P.M. Apr. 6
Confederate Forces Night Apr. 6
SNAKE CR.
N
L. WALLACE
SHERMAN
GRANT
BUELL
TENNESSEE R.
TO SAVANNAH
McCLERNAND
HURLBUT
PITTSBURG LANDING
ARTILLERY
NELSON
DILL'S BRANCH
TYLER
LEXINGTON
OWL CR.
SHERMAN
HARDEE
McCLERNAND
POLK
(A.M., P.M.) W.H.L. WALLACE
GRANT
BRAGG
HORNET'S NEST
PRENTISS
HURLBUT
BRECKINRIDGE
SHERMAN
McCLERNAND
SHILOH CHURCH
HURLBUT
W.H.L. WALLACE
JOHNSTON KILLED
HARDEE
POLK
PRENTISS
BUELL
SHERMAN
BRAGG
HARDEE
BRAGG
POLK
BRECKINRIDGE
TO CORINTH
A.S. JOHNSTON
BEAUREGARD
Miles
0
1
2
palacios

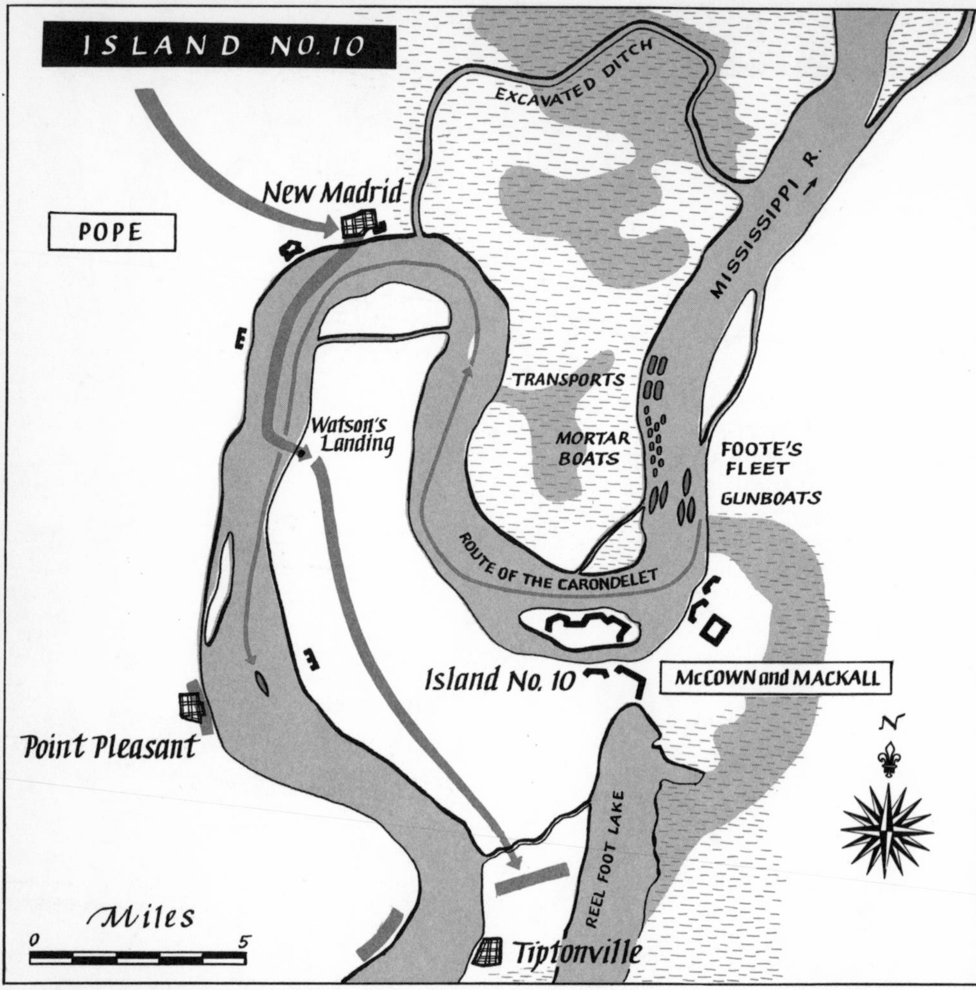

ISLAND NO. 10

POPE

New Madrid

EXCAVATED DITCH

MISSISSIPPI R.

Watson's Landing

TRANSPORTS

MORTAR BOATS

FOOTE'S FLEET

GUNBOATS

ROUTE OF THE CARONDELET

Island No. 10

McCOWN and MACKALL

Point Pleasant

REEL FOOT LAKE

Tiptonville

Miles

0 5

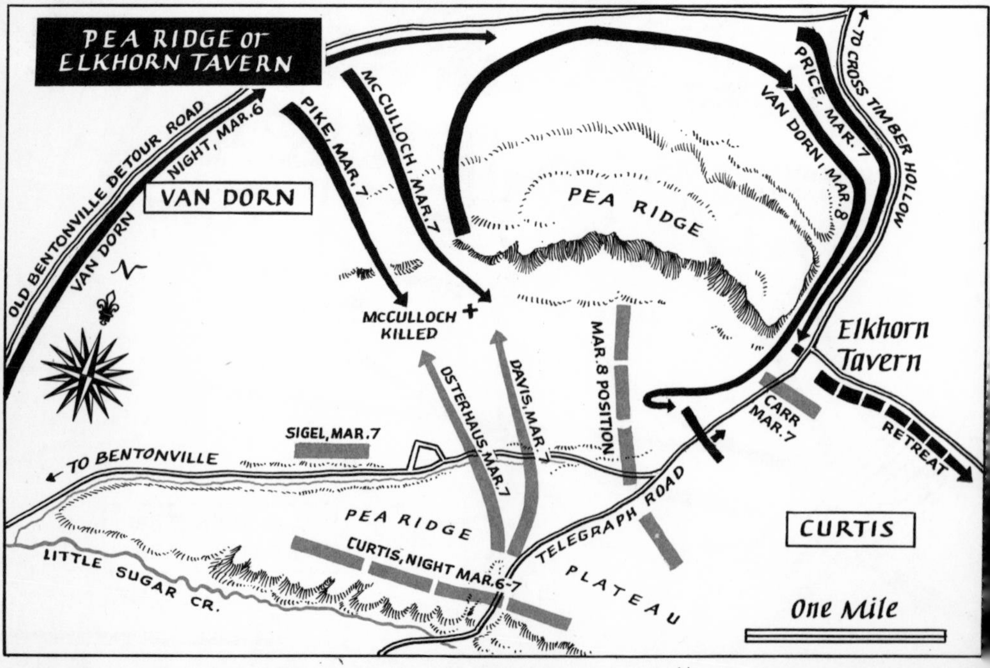

PEA RIDGE or ELKHORN TAVERN

OLD BENTONVILLE DETOUR ROAD

VAN DORN NIGHT, MAR. 6

VAN DORN

PIKE, MAR. 7

McCULLOCH, MAR. 7

PRICE, MAR. 7

VAN DORN, MAR. 8

TO CROSS TIMBER HOLLOW

PEA RIDGE

McCULLOCH KILLED

OSTERHAUS, MAR. 7

DAVIS, MAR. 7

MAR. 8 POSITION

Elkhorn Tavern

CARR MAR. 7

RETREAT

SIGEL, MAR. 7

TO BENTONVILLE

TELEGRAPH ROAD

PEA RIDGE

CURTIS, NIGHT MAR. 6-7

PLATEAU

CURTIS

LITTLE SUGAR CR.

One Mile

NEW ORLEANS

Covington
PEARL R.
MISSISSIPPI
LOUISIANA
Mississippi City
Biloxi
SHIP I.
CAT I.
LAKE PONTCHARTRAIN
Fort Pike
LOVELL
Fort Macomb
LAKE BORGNE
New Orleans
Proctorsville
CHANDELEUR SOUND
CHANDELEUR IS.
ERROL IS.
N
MISSISSIPPI R.
Old Quarantine Station
Fort St. Philip
Fort Jackson
BARATARIA BAY
Fort Livingston
GULF OF MEXICO
Pilot Town
PASS A LOUTRE
NORTH EAST PASS
WEST BAY
HEAD OF THE PASSES
SOUTH PASS
SOUTHWEST PASS
FARRAGUT
Miles
0 5 10 15 20
palacios

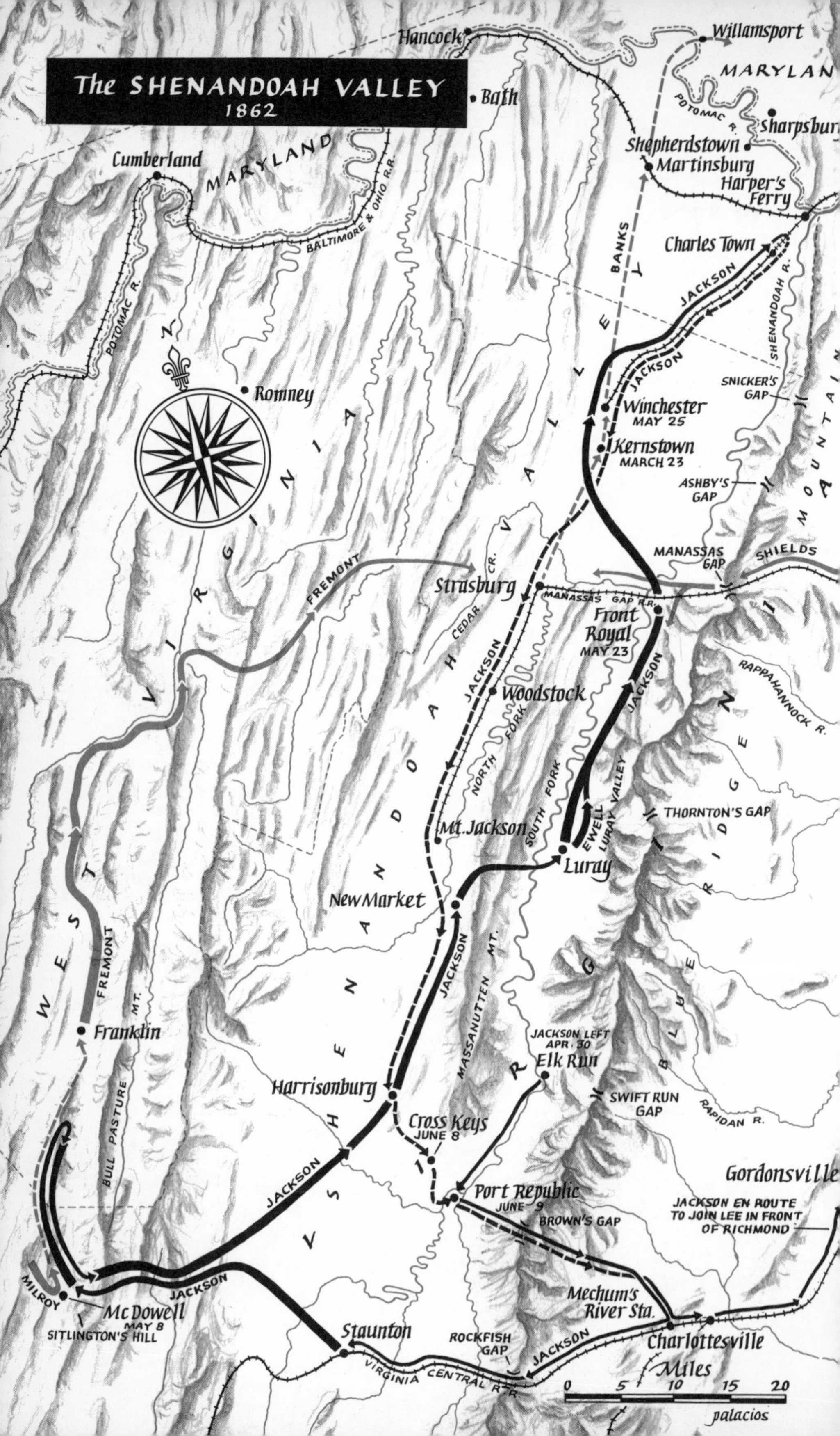

The SHENANDOAH VALLEY
1862
Hancock
Willamsport
MARYLAN
Bath
POTOMAC R.
Sharpsbur
Shepherdstown
Martinsburg
Harper's Ferry
Cumberland
MARYLAND
BALTIMORE & OHIO R.R.
POTOMAC R.
Charles Town
BANKS
JACKSON
SHENANDOAH R.
Romney
Winchester
MAY 25
Kernstown
MARCH 23
SNICKER'S GAP
ASHBY'S GAP
MANASSAS GAP
SHIELDS
FREMONT
Strasburg
CEDAR CR.
MANASSAS GAP R.R.
Front Royal
MAY 23
RAPPAHANNOCK R.
Woodstock
NORTH FORK
SOUTH FORK
LURAY VALLEY
EWELL
THORNTON'S GAP
Mt. Jackson
Luray
New Market
MASSANUTTEN MT.
FRANKLIN
Franklin
BULL PASTURE MT.
JACKSON LEFT APR. 30
Elk Run
SWIFT RUN GAP
RAPIDAN R.
Harrisonburg
Cross Keys
JUNE 8
Gordonsville
Port Republic
JUNE 9
BROWN'S GAP
JACKSON EN ROUTE TO JOIN LEE IN FRONT OF RICHMOND
MILROY
McDowell
MAY 8
SITLINGTON'S HILL
Mechum's River Sta.
Staunton
ROCKFISH GAP
Charlottesville
VIRGINIA CENTRAL R.R.
Miles
0 5 10 15 20
palacios
WEST VIRGINIA
SHENANDOAH VALLEY
BLUE RIDGE MOUNTAINS

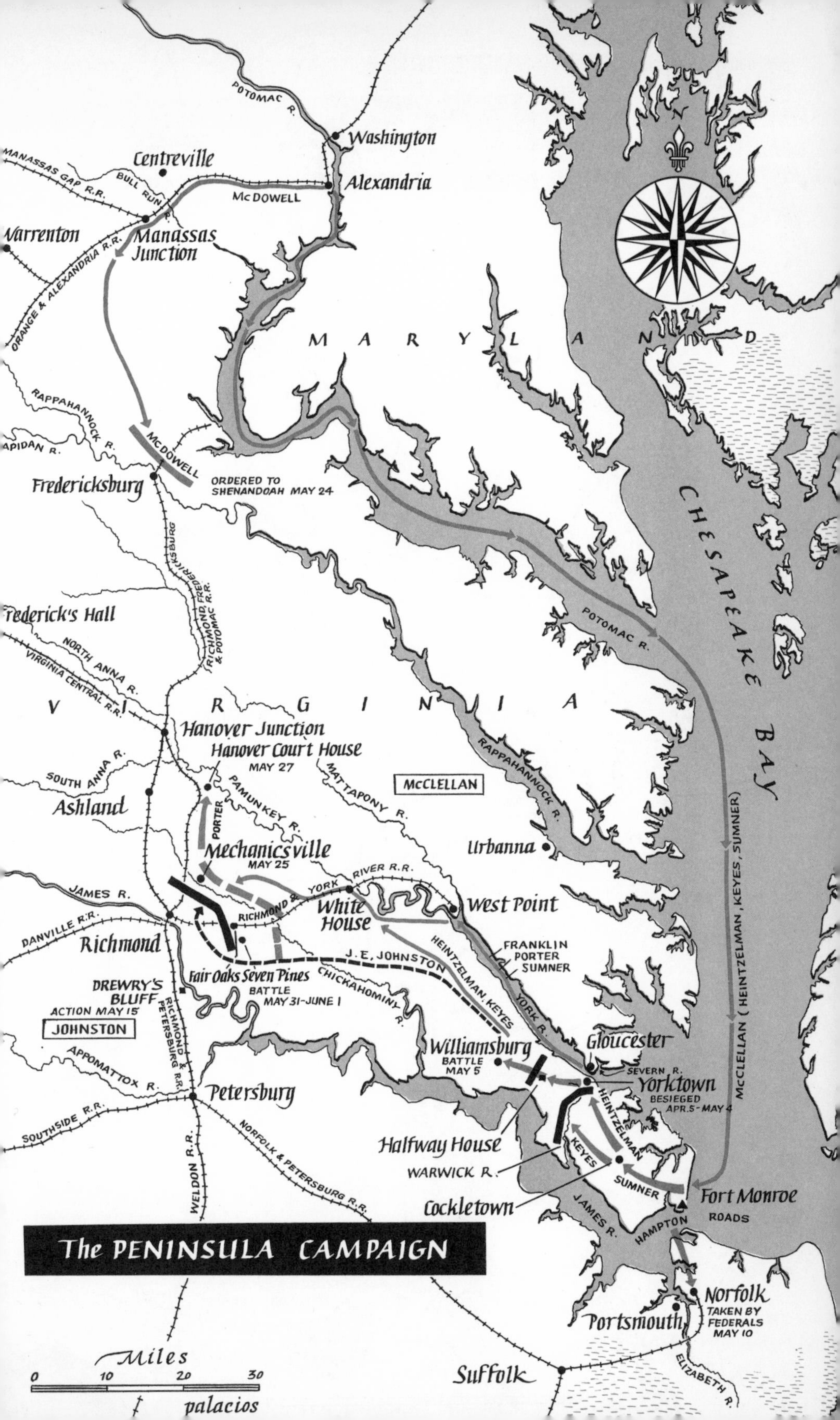

POTOMAC R.
Washington
Centreville
Alexandria
MANASSAS GAP R.R.
BULL RUN
McDOWELL
Warrenton
Manassas Junction
ORANGE & ALEXANDRIA R.R.
N
M A R Y L A N D
RAPPAHANNOCK R.
RAPIDAN R.
McDOWELL
Fredericksburg
ORDERED TO SHENANDOAH MAY 24
CHESAPEAKE BAY
RICHMOND, FREDERICKSBURG & POTOMAC R.R.
Frederick's Hall
NORTH ANNA R.
VIRGINIA CENTRAL R.R.
POTOMAC R.
V I R G I N I A
Hanover Junction
Hanover Court House
MAY 27
SOUTH ANNA R.
MATTAPONY R.
McCLELLAN
Ashland
PAMUNKEY R.
PORTER
RAPPAHANNOCK R.
Mechanicsville
MAY 25
Urbanna
McCLELLAN (HEINTZELMAN, KEYES, SUMNER)
JAMES R.
RICHMOND & YORK RIVER R.R.
White House
West Point
DANVILLE R.R.
Richmond
FRANKLIN
PORTER
SUMNER
J. E. JOHNSTON
HEINTZELMAN, KEYES
Fair Oaks Seven Pines
BATTLE MAY 31-JUNE 1
CHICKAHOMINY R.
DREWRY'S BLUFF
ACTION MAY 15
JOHNSTON
RICHMOND & PETERSBURG R.R.
YORK R.
Williamsburg
BATTLE MAY 5
Gloucester
SEVERN R.
APPOMATTOX R.
Petersburg
Yorktown
BESIEGED APR.5-MAY 4
HEINTZELMAN
SOUTHSIDE R.R.
Halfway House
KEYES
WARWICK R.
SUMNER
WELDON R.R.
NORFOLK & PETERSBURG R.R.
Cockletown
JAMES R.
Fort Monroe
HAMPTON ROADS
The PENINSULA CAMPAIGN
Norfolk
TAKEN BY FEDERALS MAY 10
Portsmouth
Miles
0 10 20 30
Suffolk
ELIZABETH R.
palacios

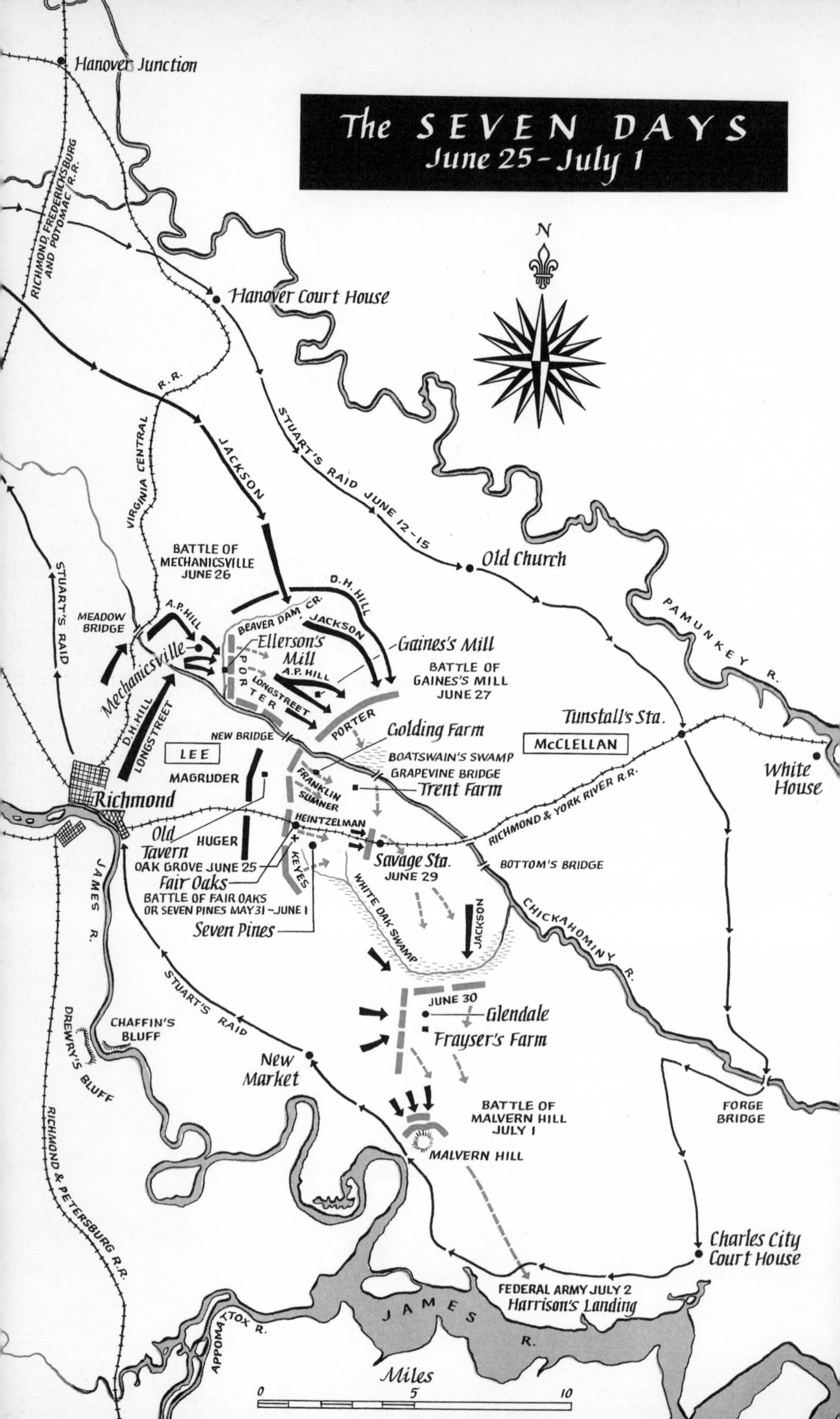

The SEVEN DAYS
June 25 - July 1
N
Hanover Junction
Hanover Court House
RICHMOND FREDERICKSBURG AND POTOMAC R.R.
VIRGINIA CENTRAL R.R.
JACKSON
STUART'S RAID JUNE 12-15
Old Church
PAMUNKEY R.
BATTLE OF MECHANICSVILLE JUNE 26
STUART'S RAID
MEADOW BRIDGE
A.P. HILL
D.H. HILL
BEAVER DAM CR.
JACKSON
Ellerson's Mill
Gaines's Mill
BATTLE OF GAINES'S MILL JUNE 27
Mechanicsville
PORTER
LONGSTREET
A.P. HILL
D.H. HILL
LONGSTREET
NEW BRIDGE
Golding Farm
Tunstall's Sta.
McCLELLAN
LEE
BOATSWAIN'S SWAMP
GRAPEVINE BRIDGE
White House
MAGRUDER
FRANKLIN
SUMNER
Trent Farm
RICHMOND & YORK RIVER R.R.
Richmond
HEINTZELMAN
Old Tavern
HUGER
KEYES
Savage Sta.
JUNE 29
BOTTOM'S BRIDGE
OAK GROVE JUNE 25
Fair Oaks
BATTLE OF FAIR OAKS OR SEVEN PINES MAY 31 - JUNE 1
Seven Pines
JAMES R.
WHITE OAK SWAMP
JACKSON
CHICKAHOMINY R.
STUART'S RAID
JUNE 30
Glendale
Frayser's Farm
CHAFFIN'S BLUFF
DREWRY'S BLUFF
New Market
BATTLE OF MALVERN HILL JULY 1
MALVERN HILL
FORGE BRIDGE
RICHMOND & PETERSBURG R.R.
Charles City Court House
FEDERAL ARMY JULY 2
Harrison's Landing
JAMES R.
APPOMATTOX R.
Miles
0
5
10

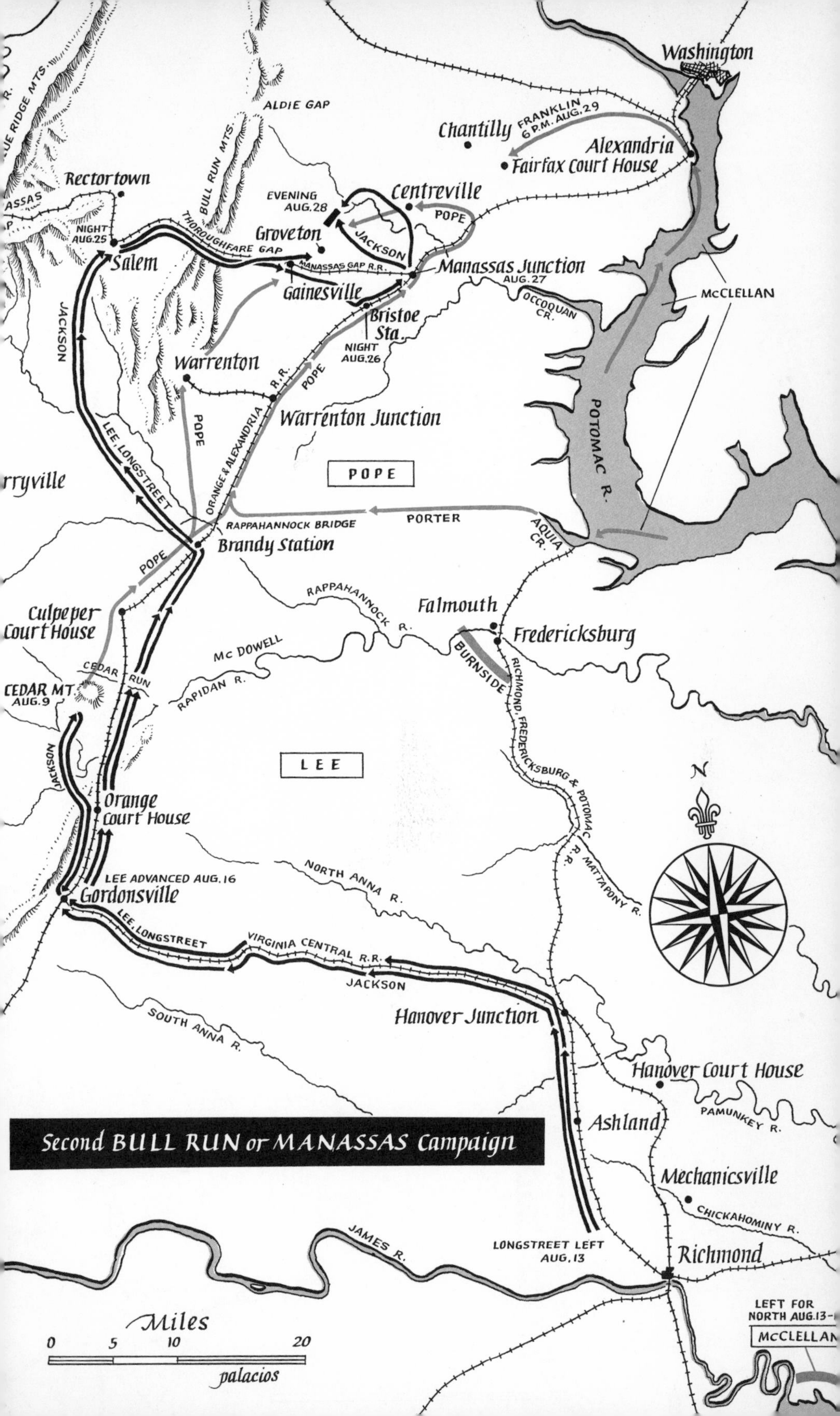

Second BULL RUN or MANASSAS Campaign
Washington
Alexandria
Fairfax Court House
Chantilly
FRANKLIN 6 P.M. AUG.29
ALDIE GAP
BULL RUN MTS.
BLUE RIDGE MTS.
Rectortown
NIGHT AUG.25
Salem
THOROUGHFARE GAP
EVENING AUG.28
Centreville
POPE
JACKSON
Groveton
MANASSAS GAP R.R.
Gainesville
Manassas Junction
AUG.27
Bristoe Sta.
NIGHT AUG.26
OCCOQUAN CR.
McCLELLAN
JACKSON
Warrenton
POPE
ORANGE & ALEXANDRIA R.R.
Warrenton Junction
POTOMAC R.
POPE
LEE, LONGSTREET
RAPPAHANNOCK BRIDGE
PORTER
AQUIA CR.
Brandy Station
RAPPAHANNOCK R.
Falmouth
Fredericksburg
Culpeper Court House
CEDAR RUN
CEDAR MT. AUG.9
Mc DOWELL
RAPIDAN R.
BURNSIDE
RICHMOND, FREDERICKSBURG & POTOMAC R.R.
LEE
JACKSON
Orange Court House
N
LEE ADVANCED AUG.16
NORTH ANNA R.
MATTAPONY R.
Gordonsville
LEE, LONGSTREET
VIRGINIA CENTRAL R.R.
JACKSON
Hanover Junction
SOUTH ANNA R.
Hanover Court House
PAMUNKEY R.
Ashland
Mechanicsville
CHICKAHOMINY R.
JAMES R.
LONGSTREET LEFT AUG.13
Richmond
LEFT FOR NORTH AUG.13-
McCLELLAN
Miles
0 5 10 20
palacios

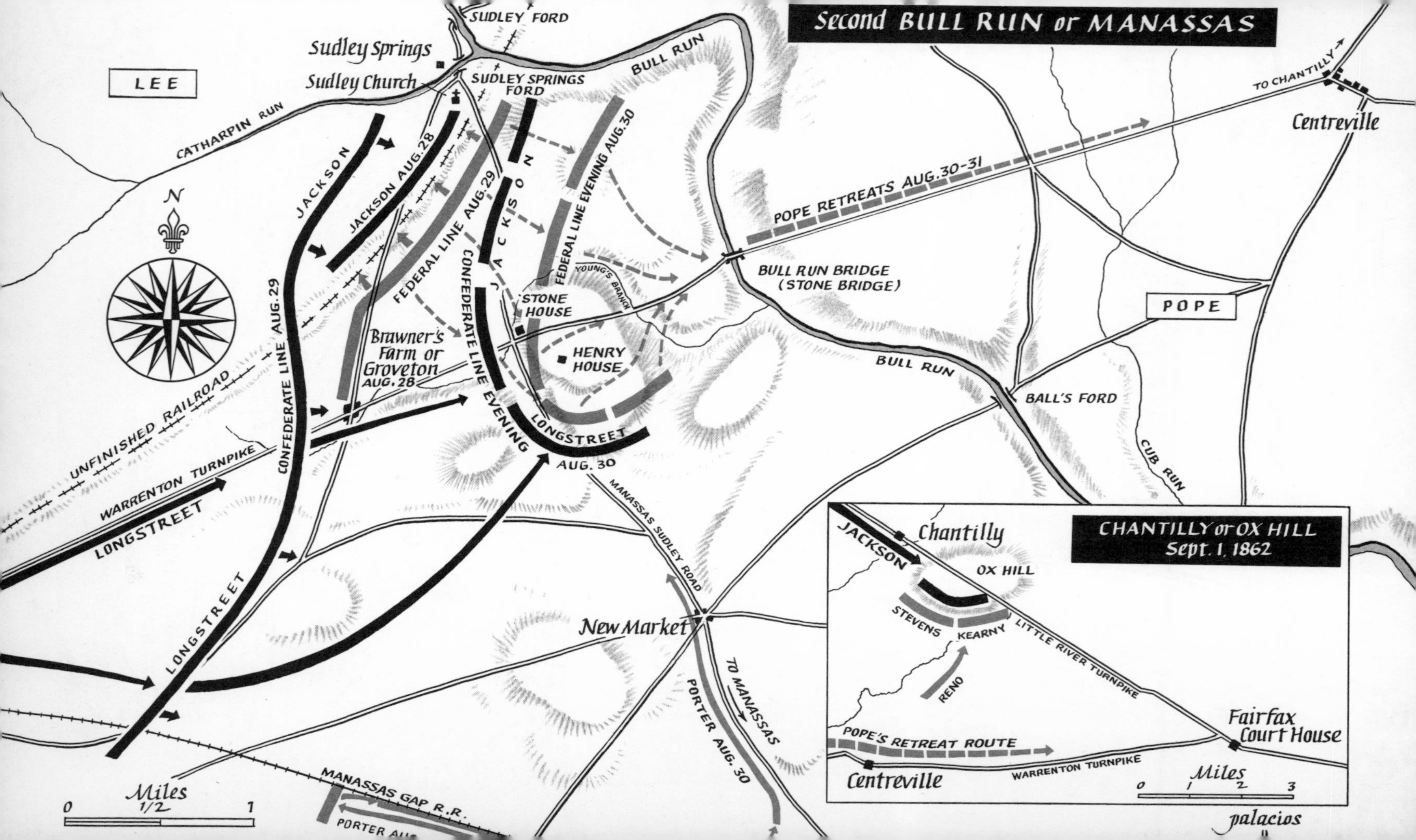
Second BULL RUN or MANASSAS
LEE
N
Sudley Springs
Sudley Church
SUDLEY FORD
SUDLEY SPRINGS FORD
CATHARPIN RUN
BULL RUN
JACKSON
JACKSON AUG. 28
FEDERAL LINE AUG. 29
JACKSON
FEDERAL LINE EVENING AUG. 30
CONFEDERATE LINE AUG. 29
CONFEDERATE LINE EVENING
UNFINISHED RAILROAD
WARRENTON TURNPIKE
LONGSTREET
LONGSTREET
LONGSTREET
AUG. 30
Brawner's Farm or Groveton
AUG. 28
STONE HOUSE
HENRY HOUSE
YOUNG'S BRANCH
POPE RETREATS AUG. 30-31
BULL RUN BRIDGE (STONE BRIDGE)
BULL RUN
BALL'S FORD
CUB RUN
POPE
TO CHANTILLY
Centreville
MANASSAS SUDLEY ROAD
New Market
TO MANASSAS
PORTER AUG. 30
MANASSAS GAP R.R.
Miles
0
1/2
1
CHANTILLY or OX HILL
Sept. 1, 1862
JACKSON
Chantilly
OX HILL
STEVENS
KEARNY
RENO
LITTLE RIVER TURNPIKE
POPE'S RETREAT ROUTE
WARRENTON TURNPIKE
Centreville
Fairfax Court House
Miles
0
1
2
3
palacios

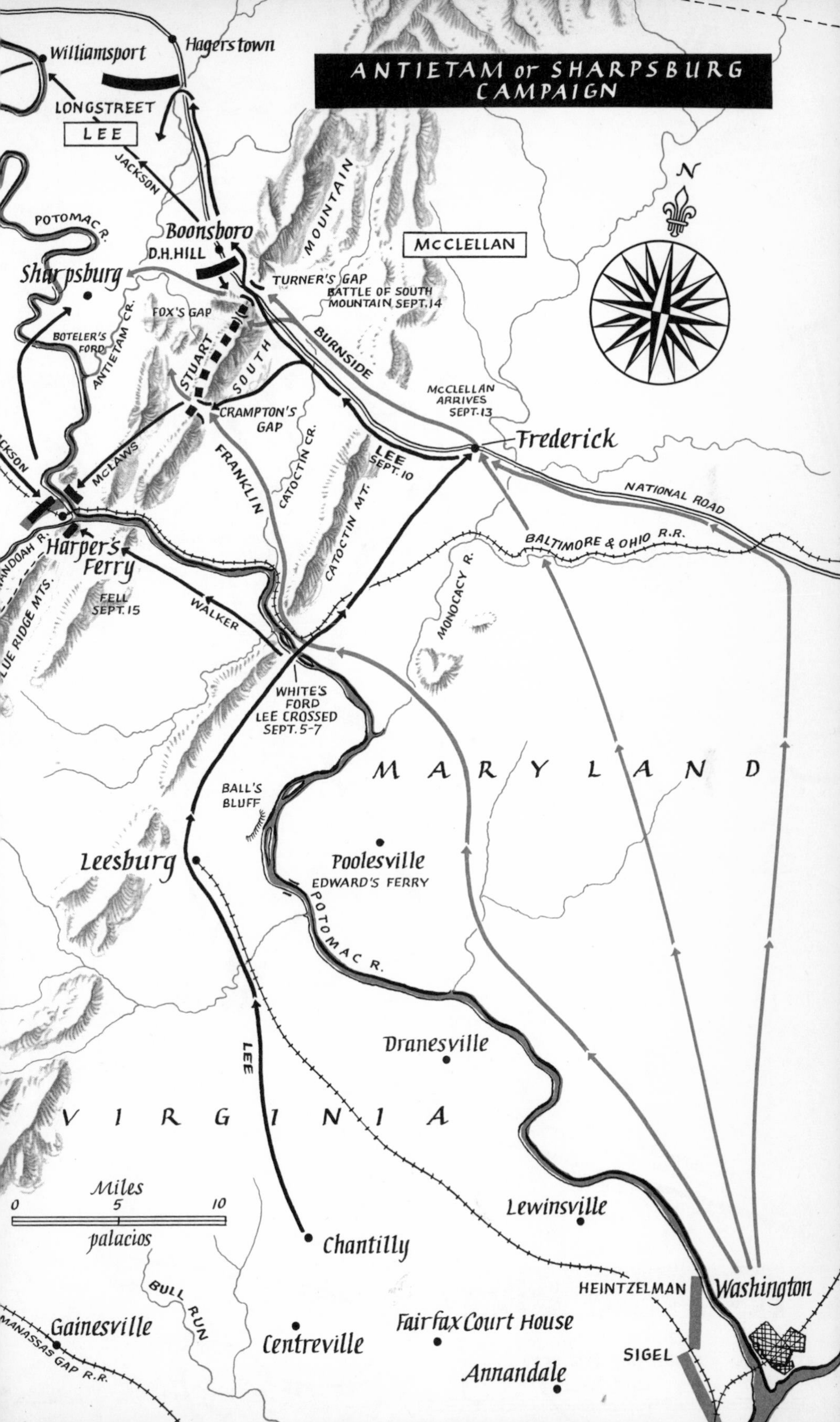

ANTIETAM or SHARPSBURG CAMPAIGN
Williamsport
Hagerstown
LONGSTREET
LEE
JACKSON
POTOMAC R.
Boonsboro
D.H.HILL
MOUNTAIN
McCLELLAN
Sharpsburg
TURNER'S GAP
BATTLE OF SOUTH MOUNTAIN SEPT.14
FOX'S GAP
BOTELER'S FORD
ANTIETAM CR.
STUART
SOUTH
BURNSIDE
CRAMPTON'S GAP
McCLELLAN ARRIVES SEPT.13
Frederick
McLAWS
FRANKLIN
CATOCTIN CR.
LEE SEPT. 10
CATOCTIN MT.
NATIONAL ROAD
BALTIMORE & OHIO R.R.
Harper's Ferry
FELL SEPT.15
WALKER
MONOCACY R.
WHITE'S FORD LEE CROSSED SEPT. 5-7
MARYLAND
BALL'S BLUFF
Leesburg
Poolesville
EDWARD'S FERRY
POTOMAC R.
LEE
Dranesville
VIRGINIA
Miles
0
5
10
palacios
Lewinsville
Chantilly
HEINTZELMAN
Washington
BULL RUN
Gainesville
Fairfax Court House
Centreville
SIGEL
Annandale
MANASSAS GAP R.R.

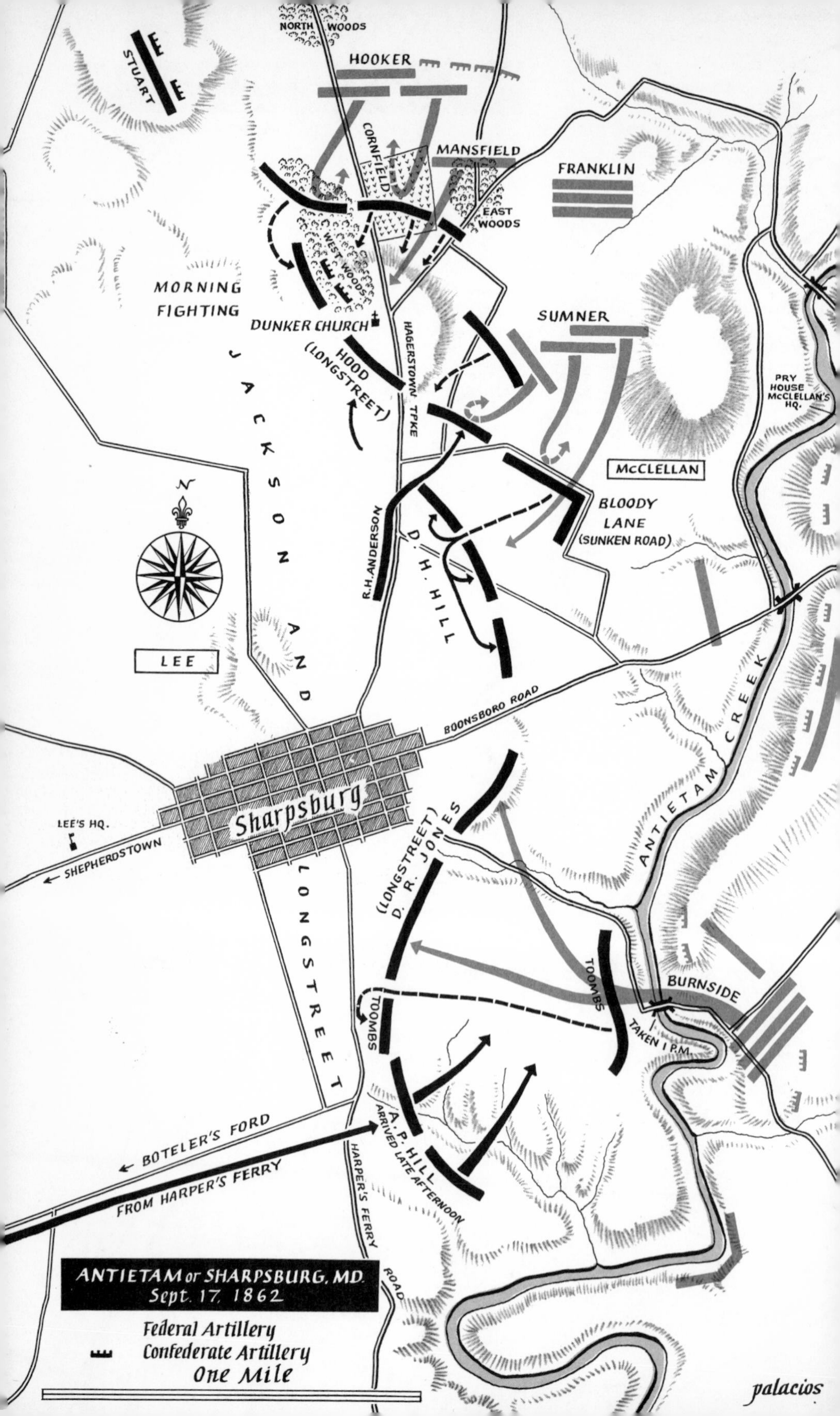

NORTH WOODS
STUART
HOOKER
CORNFIELD
MANSFIELD
FRANKLIN
EAST WOODS
WEST WOODS
MORNING FIGHTING
DUNKER CHURCH
HOOD (LONGSTREET)
HAGERSTOWN TPKE
JACKSON AND
SUMNER
PRY HOUSE McCLELLAN'S HQ.
McCLELLAN
BLOODY LANE (SUNKEN ROAD)
R.H. ANDERSON
D. H. HILL
LEE
BOONSBORO ROAD
ANTIETAM CREEK
Sharpsburg
LEE'S HQ.
SHEPHERDSTOWN
LONGSTREET
(LONGSTREET) D. R. JONES
TOOMBS
BURNSIDE
TAKEN 1 P.M.
A. P. HILL ARRIVED LATE AFTERNOON
BOTELER'S FORD
FROM HARPER'S FERRY
HARPER'S FERRY ROAD
ANTIETAM or SHARPSBURG, MD.
Sept. 17, 1862
Federal Artillery
Confederate Artillery
One Mile
palacios

artillery, of course, fired at the balloon repeatedly, but without effect; the gunners had to invent the whole science of antiaircraft fire on the spot, and anyway they had no high-angle guns.[15]

McClellan concluded that the Confederate works along the Warwick were too strong to be carried by assault. He appears to have reached this conclusion quickly. On April 4, before the aerial observations were finished, he notified McDowell (of whose detachment he had not yet been informed) that he was going to have to move forward to "invest" Yorktown, which meant siege operations; and the next morning he sent back to Fort Monroe for his heavy guns and siege mortars. He also told McDowell that he was going to bring McDowell's corps down to attack Gloucester by way of the Severn River.

It was precisely at this point that McClellan was told by Washington that McDowell's corps was no longer his to command. Its 33,000 men could not be included in any strategic design pursued by the Army of the Potomac. Bitterly, McClellan wrote later that this "left me incapable of continuing operations which had begun. It compelled the adoption of another, a different and less effective plan of campaign. It made rapid and brilliant operations impossible. It was a fatal error."[16]

McClellan would have been more than human if he had not complained. Yet his assertion that the withdrawal of McDowell compelled him to adopt "a different and less effective plan of campaign" and "made brilliant and rapid operations impossible" is obviously a rationalization devised after the event. It finally took him a month to take Yorktown, instead of the hours specified in his March 19 letter to the Secretary of War, but this delay cannot be ascribed to the fact that he learned, after his army had made contact with the Confederates around Yorktown, that he could not use McDowell's corps.

For the clear fact is that when this news reached him McClellan had already consented to delay. He had sent back for his siege train and was preparing to shatter the Confederate works by bombardment, and the one thing certain about this operation was that it would take a great deal of time.

McClellan's siege train then included seventy-one pieces of ordnance, ranging from a few imported Whitworth rifles and some ordinary 20-pounders and four and one half inch rifles all the way up to immense cannon which could fire 200-pound projectiles, and a large number of 10-inch and 13-inch siege mortars. The lighter pieces would go by road, horse-drawn, much as field artillery moved, but the heavy ones—the really important pieces—were altogether too ponderous to be handled that way. They had to be brought up by water, in barges, with derricks, sling carts, rollers, jacks and specially built wagons to move them into position at the end of the trip; and then they had to be placed on wooden firing platforms, in massive earthen emplacements, with ramps of log-and-earth construction leading up to the platforms, before they could be put into action. Simply to get these pieces into position was a long and laborious process, never resorted to unless the army was prepared to sit down in front of a fortified position and be spendthrift of time.

It took the army, thus, five days simply to make the necessary reconnaissances and pick the sites for the batteries; after which it took more than three weeks to prepare the emplacements and get the guns and mortars into position. (Along with everything else, it was necessary to haul more than seven hundred wagonloads of powder, shells, equipment, and small stores from the tip of the peninsula to McClellan's lines.) Inevitably, the program was a certified time-killer.[17] The notion that the delay in front of Yorktown was due to McClellan's last-minute discovery that he could not use McDowell loses most of its gloss when it is matched against two things—what was originally planned with respect to McDowell, and what was actually done about him.

McClellan's schedule called for McDowell's corps to be brought down to the peninsula last of all. This corps was to tarry in the Washington area (as McDowell explained the scheme to President Lincoln) "until it was ascertained that the whole of the enemy's force was down below; and then, when he" (McClellan) "had their whole force in hand down below, this remaining corps was to go down also."[18] It undoubtedly made conservative good sense to hold back this fourth of the army until the enemy had been made to display his hand, but it undeniably had a wait-and-see quality; there was nothing in it to make anyone suppose that the army could not act until this last segment of it reached the scene.

Furthermore, McDowell's corps was between one and two weeks away from McClellan in any case. If the President and the Secretary of War had kept their hands off altogether, McClellan would not have had these troops before the middle of April at the very earliest. What he would then have done with them is a matter for speculation, no doubt, but the record is eloquent.

As soon as he learned that this corps was being withheld, McClellan wrote asking Mr. Lincoln to reconsider. The Gloucester move, he said, was crucial; if he could not have all of McDowell's corps, could not he have two divisions from it—or, if no more could be done, just one division? If he had to, he said, he could make do with one.

One division he got, at last—12,000 men, under Brigadier General William B. Franklin; and, as Mr. Lincoln pointed out afterward, it took ten days for this division to make the trip. In addition, when the division reached the lower bay, on April 20, McClellan was not ready to use it. After its arrival the division stayed on transports for two weeks while McClellan, his staff, and the Navy people steamed about making arrangements to get it ashore in rear of Gloucester.

In the end, just as things were about to begin to happen, the unfeeling Confederates evacuated the entire Yorktown line and marched off up the peninsula, leaving McClellan free title to Yorktown, to Gloucester, and to everything else. The Prince de Joinville, that stoutly loyal French ornament on McClellan's staff, wrote mournfully: "The Confederates had vanished, and with them all chance of a brilliant victory."[19] Once again, Joseph E. Johnston had confounded McClellan by beating a retreat. But the chance for a brilliant victory had vanished long before.

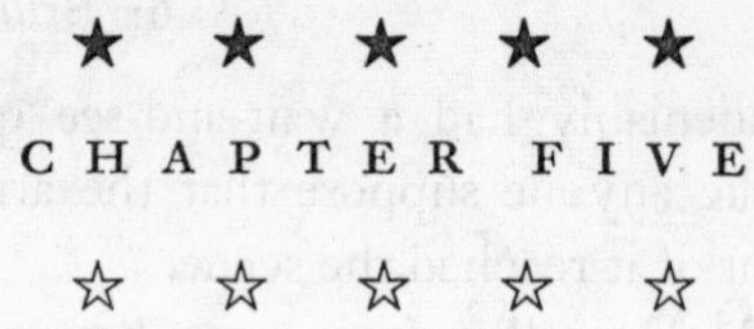

Turning Point

1: *The Signs of the Times*

There had been a good deal of artillery fire along the Yorktown lines during the night, and there had also been a good deal of rain, but both died out before dawn; and although the morning of May 4 was undeniably damp it was strangely and disturbingly silent. Joe Johnston had gone, leaving empty trenches, a number of abandoned cannon, and a set of live shells with trip-wires attached buried in the works to discourage Yankee patrols. Although his retreating army moved slowly in the heavy mud it had plenty of time. The Army of the Potomac had at last made itself ready to bombard—it had, this morning, forty-eight heavy guns and mortars in six prepared batteries, and a few of these had already opened fire—but it was not ready to pursue. The situation was both pleasing and embarrassing.

General McClellan sent a wire to the War Department announcing that he now possessed Yorktown, and when Secretary Stanton sent congratulations, spiced with the remark that he hoped soon to hear that General McClellan had taken Richmond as well, the general replied that "our success is brilliant," said that its effects would be of great importance, and declared that he would pursue with fervor and would in fact "push the enemy to the wall."[1]

The rain began afresh, the bad roads grew worse, and the army's advance guard went with difficulty toward Williamsburg, where the Confederate rear guard might possibly be overtaken. The rear guard, it developed, was waiting, protected by a series of modest field fortifications, and on May 5 there was a savage, costly, and rather pointless battle which went on until twilight, at which time the Confederates resumed their retreat. The Union Army lost some 2200 men, the Confederates lost perhaps 1700, and the battle might as well not have been fought except that it gave part of each army some combat experience, which may conceivably have been worth the price paid. McClellan was in Yorktown during the fight, embarking troops to go to the head of the York River, and before the day ended Johnston went riding up the peninsula to prepare to meet such a move, and to a large extent the battle fought itself.[2]

President Lincoln, meanwhile, was getting busy.

It struck him now that when the Confederates lost Yorktown and the peninsula they also lost all chance to hold Norfolk, and if they lost Norfolk they would automatically lose that fearsome ironclad, *Virginia*, whose existence had made it impossible for McClellan to use the James River; and so on May 6 the President came down the Chesapeake accompanied by Secretary Stanton and Secretary Chase and went into conference with Flag Officer Goldsborough and with Major General John E. Wool, Army commander at Fort Monroe. In his original campaign plan McClellan had remarked that Norfolk would fall when Richmond fell, which was true enough, but Mr. Lincoln did not want to wait that long and so he was on the scene to try his own hand at running a campaign.

The task presented only moderate problems, because once Yorktown was gone the Confederates were quite ready to leave Norfolk as soon as somebody hustled them. The President got the Navy to bombard the Confederate batteries at Sewell's Point, with the two cabinet members he went here and there on a tugboat looking for a good place for troops to disembark and march toward Norfolk, and a fascinated Army officer wrote about seeing the President giving orders to somebody from the deck of Goldsborough's flagship: "dressed in a black suit with a very seedy crape on his hat, and hanging over the railing he looked like some hoosier just starting for home from California with store clothes and a biled shirt on." Norfolk was abandoned, Union troops marched in on May 10 to find the business district stagnant and the old navy yard destroyed; and the Confederate Navy realized that there was nothing on earth it could do with *Virginia*. The famous ironclad was much too unseaworthy to go out into the open ocean and drew too much water to go up the James to Richmond. In the end her own crew blew her up, on May 11, and McClellan—who told Stanton that if this happened he could base himself on the James—telegraphed his congratulations and remarked that this would enable him to make his own movements "much more decisive."[3]

Decisive movements were just what Mr. Lincoln wanted, and McClellan would have been well advised to pay a little more attention to these energetic civilians who bustled about on gunboats and tugs, giving orders to Army and Navy officers and looking at times like remnants from the gold rush. To be specific, he would have been wise to go down to Fort Monroe to confer with them as soon as they got there. He was told of their arrival by Secretary Stanton and was invited to come down for a talk, and on May 7 he replied that this unfortunately was impossible. He was then at Williamsburg, making arrangements for a continued advance toward the head of the York, and he notified the Secretary that "in the present state of affairs . . . it is really impossible for me to go to the rear to meet the President and yourself." He repeated the substance of this later in the same day: "I regret that my presence with the army at this particular time is of such vast importance that I cannot leave to confer with the President and yourself."[4] The distance from Williamsburg to Fort Monroe is approximately thirty miles.

If there was in this refusal a faint echo of the evening in November when McClellan had returned to his Washington headquarters and had gone straight to bed, leaving the President (who had come to headquarters to see him) to cool his heels in the waiting room on the ground floor, nobody commented on it; and the most that can be said is that McClellan now lost an excellent chance—possibly his last chance—to improve his relations with his superior officers. This relationship had been deteriorating for months; here and now, with the army ready to resume its march on Richmond, the general might have welcomed an opportunity to sit down with the President and the Secretary of War, explain his plans and problems, listen while they explained theirs, and restore mutual understanding and faith.

It seems a pity that McClellan could not find time for it. An

Army commander who is about to undertake a climactic campaign needs above everything else the confidence of his government. If he lacks this he is tragically isolated and his army is dangerously handicapped. The Lincoln government's confidence in McClellan, to say nothing of his own confidence in the government, had been fading for months, and the long delay in front of Yorktown had made matters worse. Early in April Mr. Lincoln had written to McClellan, trying to explain that forces which neither President nor general could long resist made determined action necessary. "Once more let me tell you," the President had written, "it is indispensable to *you* that you strike a blow. *I* am powerless to help this. . . . I beg to assure you that I have never written you, or spoken to you, in greater kindness of feeling than now, nor with a fuller purpose to sustain you, so far as in my most anxious judgment I consistently can. *But you must act.*"[5] That letter had been written on April 9. Now, a month later, the general and the President could sit down together and talk things out; could do this in the light of the occupation of Yorktown, the seizure of Norfolk, the death of the *Virginia*, the rising surge of Federal victories on other fronts—could do it, in short, under circumstances which might have made it possible for civilians and soldiers to understand one another and to work together in harmony. But it did not happen.

The tragedy of the long delay at Yorktown was that attitudes and habits of mind developed earlier had begun to harden; in the mind of the commanding general, and in the collective mind of the army itself. The unique separateness of this Army of the Potomac, like that of no other American army either then or later, was becoming fixed; a separateness reflected partly in a nervous irritability that would respond instantly to any real or imagined slight. Four days after his army took possession of Yorktown, McClellan found it necessary to chide his wife for her failure to appreciate what a great thing he and his army had done.

"Your two letters of Sunday and Monday reached me last night," he wrote. "I do not think you over much rejoiced at the results I gained. I really thought that you would appreciate a great result gained by fine skill & at little cost more than you seem to. It would have been easy for me to have sacrificed 10,000 lives in taking Yorktown, & I presume the world would have thought it was brilliant. . . . I am very sorry that you do not exactly sympathize with me in the matter."[6]

It is necessary to emphasize that this was not just the outburst of a spoiled egotist. McClellan had begun to reach a point at which his own government looked like an enemy. It wanted him to fail; it was playing politics with the war, trying to turn a war for reunion into an abolitionist crusade. When he won something, he won because pure military skill had triumphed over sordid political scheming; to doubt the genuineness of his achievement was to line up, however unintentionally, with the enemy. This attitude was being instilled in him by the men in whom he had most confidence. S. L. M. Barlow, the New York lawyer and financier who was immensely influential in Democratic politics, sounded the keynote in a letter he sent McClellan during the first fortnight at Yorktown: "The dastardly conduct of those in Washington, who seek to drive you from the Army, or into a defeat, to serve their own selfish ends, is beginning to be understood and when the people know the facts, as they will, when it becomes necessary, the ambitious scoundrels in Washington will wish they had never been born."

Writing thus, Barlow simply reflected a thesis which Democratic party leaders were more and more beginning to embrace. While the Yorktown siege was still going on, Barlow got a letter from Samuel Ward, Washington lobbyist and financier, suggesting that Secretary Stanton ought to be impeached for treason "in having interfered with the progress of the war, & its organization by competent authority, to the detriment & probably the destruction of the north." Ward advised him: "Circulate the story or rumor of bets that Stanton will be in Fort Lafayette in less than 60 days." (Fort Lafayette was the prison for men suspected of disloyalty. It was where General Stone was lodged.) When Yorktown at last fell, Barlow wrote McClellan jubilantly: "I cannot express to you the intense satisfaction caused by your triumphant success at Yorktown & on the peninsula. I feel like laughing & crying alternately. The hounds who had pursued you so bitterly are now in despair and they know it. The most noisy abolitionists now fear to say anything openly & the politicians among them are trying to get on your side without delay."[7]

This would not have been so bad if it had concerned McClellan alone. But the officer corps of the Army of the Potomac was tied closely to him, and the point of view of the commanding general went down through brigadiers, colonels, and field officers, like a subtle infection running into the bloodstream, to all ranks. Above all, it affected the Regular officers; the professionals, who wanted to have as little as possible to do with Washington politics and now found that General McClellan stood for everything they stood for and that his political enemies stood for everything he and they were against. A glimpse of the way this went is afforded by a letter which Barlow got in April from Brigadier General Thomas F. Meagher, commander of the Irish brigade in Sumner's II Corps. Meagher was an Irish patriot—a man just under forty who had been born in Waterford, had been condemned to death in 1848 for sedition, had seen his sentence commuted to transportation to Tasmania, had escaped from that lonely place and had come at last to New York, where he became an American citizen and the recognized leader of the New York Irish. Ten days before Yorktown was taken he wrote to Barlow telling how things looked to the Army of the Potomac.

"With regard to the rumors you mentioned to me as intimating a serious difference between our general in chief and the Government," he wrote, "I heard of such (or something like such) a day or two after we disembarked. Since then have heard nothing—I understood that McDowell had played what the officers of the Regular Army and General McClellan's friends regarded as a 'scurvy trick' in his taking advantage of the latter's absence in this quarter to get a Corps d'Armee, and so withdraw some 50,000 men from this critical field of operations. . . . The officers of the Regular Army who spoke to me on this subject seemed greatly excited and indignant at what they considered to be 'foul play' on the part of General McDowell and the Administration, and one of them informed me that although General McClellan said nothing . . . yet that it was his determination after the siege and battle of Yorktown to resign his command."[8]

This attitude had a profound political coloration. New York

banker August Belmont, a power in the Democratic party, wrote to Barlow late in April: "The conduct of the Administration against McClellan is really disgraceful & wicked, it shows once more that instead of patriots & statesmen we have only partizans at the head of government." Belmont foresaw "the most calamitous results" from the fact that "the chief command of the army was taken from the hands of the most unquestionable capacity to be put upon the weak shoulders of civilians." McClellan's most trusted subordinate in the army was Brigadier General Fitz John Porter, handsome, affable, well-born, a West Pointer with a good Mexican War record, now a division commander in Heintzelman's III Corps. Porter was vigorous on the Democratic side. Some time in April he wrote to Manton Marble, editor of the strongly Democratic New York *World*, putting himself and the McClellan officers generally right in the middle of the political fight. "This army will cause a revulsion of opinion on its return home," Porter wrote. "I hear that the most conservative opinions" (anti-abolitionist opinions; in short, conservative Democratic opinions) "are expressed everywhere and the few abolitionists in the armies of the U.S. are not looked upon as friends to the Union. The conservative element throughout the army will make itself felt at the next election." A few weeks later he assured Marble: "Our men wish to go home—and wish the war to cease—but they say they will whip the abolitionists when they get home especially for trying to prolong this unnatural war. Our men will speak, and good-bye to the abolition traitors, who try now to defend themselves by publishing falsehoods." A fortnight after Yorktown was occupied, a young New York officer asserted stoutly: "If McClellan is defeated it will be the fault of the administration, not his own."[9]

McClellan and his devoted followers, obviously, had got themselves neck-deep in politics. They had a perfect right to do this, but it left them no room for complaint if the political pressures became irksome; and it was bound to have a crippling effect on the army itself. For the hot anti-slavery men—the Ben Wades, Zach Chandlers, and the rest, to whom the gauntlet was being thrown down—were precisely the men who had felt all along that an officer's professional training and capacity mattered less than his zeal for the cause. Knowing precisely how all of the political currents were flowing, these men now could consider their old suspicions confirmed. The anti-West Point faction and the anti-slavery faction were tending to become one group; and at the same time the ardent Democrats were becoming pro-West Point, and the inevitable rivalry between regulars and volunteers was becoming a political rivalry as well. Benjamin Stark, one of Barlow's correspondents in Washington, was telling Barlow that it was up to "us of the reasonable party" to persuade the people that "war is a science which requires time and means for its successful development."[10]

Meanwhile the slavery issue continued to assert itself. Mr. Lincoln was doing his best to keep it under control, but the task was getting harder. It had been made acute this spring by the action of a general named David Hunter, who commanded Federal troops along the south Atlantic coast and who abruptly conceived it his duty to proclaim emancipation in his domain. Without consulting Washington, General Hunter announced that all slaves in Georgia, Florida, and South Carolina were now free; and this news reached Washington just when Mr. Lincoln was trying patiently, with scant success, to persuade the border state leaders to accept gradual and compensated emancipation. General Hunter's proclamation was, to be sure, an indication that the institution was apt to be shattered forever by brute force if it were held onto too tenaciously, but it was not the sort of thing that helped Mr. Lincoln's negotiations. On May 19 the President announced that whatever Hunter's proclamation might consist of it was null and void, and that no general anywhere had been or would ever be authorized to end slavery by pronunciamento. He then went on to turn his rebuke of Hunter into a direct appeal to slave-holders.

Congress, he pointed out, had voted for compensated emancipation; would not the slave-holding states go along with this, of their own free will? "I do not argue," he wrote. "I beseech you to make the arguments for yourselves. You can not, if you would, be blind to the signs of the times. I beg of you a calm and enlarged consideration of them, ranging, if it may be, far above personal and partizan politics. This proposal makes common cause for a common object, casting no reproaches upon any. It acts not the Pharisee. The change it contemplates would come gently as the dews of heaven, not rending nor wrecking anything. Will you not embrace it?"[11]

The signs of the time were not everywhere visible: the signs of the terrible times of the spring of 1862, which said clearly that slavery was dying and that the only question for anybody was whether it should die quietly, in bed, with mourners tearfully consenting, or by unmitigated violence on the field of battle. McClellan read Mr. Lincoln's proclamation, and wrote to his wife: "I am very glad that the Presdt had come out as he did about Hunter's order—I feared he would not have the moral courage to do so."[12]

It may have taken moral courage to rescind General Hunter's proclamation: what General McClellan could not see—could not, in his most thoughtful moments, get so much as a glimmering of—was that it also took moral courage for a President beset by the strongest men in his own party to sustain a general who clearly, and to every politician's knowledge, was the active favorite of the strongest men in the opposition party. McClellan could see only that the administration was reducing his status, taking away parts of his army and listening too attentively to politicians whose ideas were unlike the ideas of the politicians to whom he himself was listening. He could understand neither Mr. Lincoln's deep desire to win the war before it became the kind of war in which victory itself might be indigestible, nor the fact that Mr. Lincoln was under an irresistible compulsion, which no general could lighten, to insist upon the absolute safety of the city of Washington. And it was everybody's hard luck that these two points were of dominant importance during the campaign on the Virginia peninsula.

The time element had always been a sore point. McClellan had been given the supreme command largely because the administration wanted quick and decisive action, and he had lost it because he seemed too cautious; he could not move until everything was ready, until every possible mischance had been discounted in advance. But the same administration that wanted him to be swift and daring was itself the very soul of niggling caution as far as the capital was concerned. Risking everything with one hand, it would with the other risk nothing whatever; and the things that took place that spring make no sort of sense unless the reason for this extreme conservatism is understood.

The security of the national capital meant more than anything else. The Federal government was not fighting a foreign war, in which temporary loss of the capital could be atoned for later; it was fighting to prove that it could maintain its own political integrity, and loss of the capital city would be taken as the unmistakable sign that it had failed. The sign would be read abroad as quickly as at home. It would almost certainly lead Britain and France to recognize the Confederacy, and recognition was likely to end everything. So here was a point on which President Lincoln would take no chances at all. He had to be *certain* that Washington was safe, and he could take no general's word for it—unless that general had won the last ounce of his unreserved confidence, which no living general had yet done.

McClellan had collided with this fact before—after all, that was how he had lost McDowell's corps—and he collided with it again, painfully, as he moved in pursuit of Joe Johnston.

The roads on the peninsula were bad, the maps were worse and the weather itself was not favorable, and army headquarters still believed that the Confederates had a great advantage in numbers; but in the fortnight following the battle of Williamsburg, McClellan's advance went smoothly and with reasonable diligence, and there seemed to be good understanding between the general and the administration. When McClellan, who had little use for his corps commanders, asked permission to make new arrangements, Stanton told him that the President did not want the existing organization broken up but that since big battles were impending McClellan could do as he chose, at least on a temporary basis. McClellan reshuffled his troops and created two new army corps, giving one to his friend Fitz John Porter and the other to the General Franklin who had brought that division down from McDowell.[13] McClellan also asked that the Navy open the river route to Richmond, after the Farragut manner, and the Navy at least tried; sent *Monitor*, a new ironclad named *Galena* and three gunboats steaming up the river to

Drewry's Bluff, a bit of high ground on a sharp bend in the James just seven miles below Richmond. Here the Confederates had hastily built a fort, with *Virginia's* gunners to handle the heavy ordnance, and they had driven piles and sunk hulks in the river to block the channel, and if they lost this fort they lost everything because the Federal flotilla then could go straight to the Richmond wharves.

The fort held, and on May 15 the Navy got a bloody nose. The Confederate batteries were one hundred feet above water-level, *Monitor* could not elevate her guns enough to hit anything, the wooden ships dared not come to close quarters, and *Galena* turned out to be unexpectedly fragile. Her armor was not strong enough to stop heavy shot at close range, and what happened to her demonstrated an unhappy truth about naval warfare in the age of iron: inadequate armor was worse than no armor at all, because broken bits of iron flew about the decks like shell fragments. She was hit forty-three times, took heavy casualties, and was reduced almost to a wreck, and after a few hours the Federal flotilla drifted off downstream out of range. (When *Galena* reached dry dock her armor was stripped off and she eventually went back into service as an ordinary wooden gunboat.) It was clear that the Navy could not do below Richmond what Farragut had done below New Orleans.[14]

Still, this was no more than a check. The James at least was an open highway to within ten miles of the Confederate capital, and if General McClellan wanted to move his base over to that river he was able to do so. He considered the idea, but concluded that at least for the present he would move from the York, and by May 16 he had established a supply depot at a place called White House, on the Pamunkey, twenty-two miles due east of Richmond, on the Richmond & York River Railroad. And now, with Johnston pulling his men into the Richmond defenses behind the Chickahominy River, which meandered sluggishly from northwest to southeast a little more than half of the way from White House to Richmond, McClellan made an urgent call for reinforcements.

On May 8 he had written to Stanton pointing out that the Confederates would unquestionably mass their forces to defend Richmond and that the Federals ought to concentrate also; "all the troops on the Rappahannock and if possible those on the Shenandoah should take part in the approaching battle . . . All minor considerations should be thrown to one side and all our energies and means directed toward the defeat of Johnston's army in front of Richmond." On May 14 he reiterated this in a direct appeal to Mr. Lincoln. He would not be able to put more than 80,000 men into battle, he would have to fight perhaps double his own numbers, and he needed every man he could get. He went on, eloquently, the only general in American history who felt moved to assure his President that the country's principal army, on the eve of battle, was actually loyal to the government:

"Any commander of the re-enforcements whom Your Excellency may designate will be acceptable to me, whatever expression I may have heretofore addressed to you on that subject. I will fight the enemy, whatever their force may be, with whatever force I may have, and I firmly believe that we shall beat them, but our triumph should be made decisive and complete. The soldiers of this army love their Government and will fight well in its support. You may rely upon them. They have confidence in me as their general and in you as their President."[15]

The reinforcements McClellan wanted were McDowell's men, recently strengthened to something like 40,000 by the addition of Shields's division, which had just been moved over to the Rappahannock from Banks's domain in the Shenandoah Valley; and the commander who would be acceptable in spite of past remarks was of course McDowell himself, whose headquarters at this time were at Falmouth, across the river from Fredericksburg, fifty miles north of Richmond. There was just one difficulty. McClellan hoped that "all minor considerations" would be ignored in the use of this force, and the chief of these considerations was Mr. Lincoln's rigid insistence that McDowell, whatever else he did, remain at all times between the Confederate Army and Washington. As early as April 11, McDowell had been told that he was to consider the protection of Washington his essential responsibility and was to "make no movement throwing your forces out of position for the discharge of this primary duty."[16] In his appeal for McDowell's corps McClellan was specifying that it ought to be sent to him by water, which would effectively take it off the board for a fortnight. Mr. Lincoln had McDowell come to Washington for a quick conference, and on the next day, May 17, Stanton sent a reply to McClellan.

The President, said Stanton, would not uncover Washington entirely, and thought that McDowell could reach the peninsula more quickly if he went by land. But McDowell definitely would be sent; he had been ordered to march down from Fredericksburg by the shortest route, keeping himself always in position to protect the capital but joining McClellan's right wing as rapidly as possible. He would retain full command of his own troops, and although when he made contact he would come under McClellan's control, McClellan was instructed to "give no orders, either before or after your junction, which can put him out of position to cover this city."[17]

Rather more than half a loaf, presumably much better than no bread at all; McClellan was to get what he had asked for, although it would be given in a way he did not want, with attached conditions which he considered objectionable. And the fact that these conditions were attached, and that the reinforcements would move by road instead of by water, suddenly became new evidence of villainous bad faith on the part of the administration. To his wife, on the day after he received Stanton's dispatch, McClellan burst out:

"Those hounds in Washington are after me again. Stanton is without exception the vilest man I ever knew or heard of."[18]

2: *Do It Quickly*

The situation between Jefferson Davis and Joseph E. Johnston was strangely like that between Abraham Lincoln and General McClellan. Mr. Davis felt that his Army commander was unpredictable, hard to guide and much too secretive; General Johnston felt that the President gave him no support, nagged him with petty directives and opposed a politician's deviousness to a soldier's honest competence. The two men did not exactly distrust each other, but each man certainly looked at the other with a wary eye. If there had been a time for such a thing, the two Presidents doubtless could have sympathized with one another. The two generals could have done the same thing.

In all of this Mr. Davis had one advantage which Mr. Lincoln lacked.

Mr. Lincoln spoke to General McClellan (when he did not address him directly) through Secretary Stanton: an arrangement which originally was excellent and was at any rate unavoidable, but which by the middle of the spring of 1862 was unfortunately quite certain to increase the difficulty of communication. Mr. Davis, on the other hand, spoke to General Johnston for the most part through General Lee, and this made all the difference in the world. General Lee had the complete confidence of both the President and the Army commander, he took elaborate pains to retain it, and he had a professional capacity of his own which neither man ever called in question. Although the Federal government all but lost touch with its principal army, a similar thing did not happen on the Confederate side.

As a matter of fact there never existed between President Davis and General Johnston the profound difference in fundamental attitudes which did so much to cut President Lincoln off from General McClellan. General Johnston was extremely cautious, defensive-minded, reluctant to put everything to the touch—as a soldier, indeed, he was in many ways somewhat like General McClellan—but up to a certain point any Confederate general defending Richmond had to have those qualities, and they were never the basis for his disagreements with Mr. Davis. These two men were estranged more by little things than by big ones. Each man was proud, touchy, quick to take offense and slow to forget about it afterward, and their bitterest exchanges came over comparative trivialities. They quarreled acridly, not over the sort of commitment the nation had made when it went to war, or over the way in which the war might best be won, but over such matters as why General Johnston ranked fourth instead of first among Confederate generals, and whether regiments from the same state should or should not be brigaded together. They might agree that the old lines at Centreville and Manassas could not be held, but they would wrangle at great length about who actually ordered the lines abandoned and who ought to be blamed for the loss of all that bacon. When Johnston at last evacuated the Yorktown lines (which he had never wanted to enter in the first place) Mr. Davis was disturbed not by the retreat but by the general's tight-lipped refusal to say where the retreat was going to end. Both men believed that the ideal way to defend Richmond, once the peninsula was given up, was to assemble all the troops that could be found and boldly go north of the Potomac (a thing, incidentally, which formed the basis for Mr. Lincoln's worst nightmares); when it proved impossible to do this, Johnston darkly suspected that the President refused to do for him what he might have done for another man.[1]

Standing between these two men, Lee could prevent a complete estrangement. He could assuage Johnston's feelings when they were hurt, could call the man to time when necessary without making him feel that bumbling civilians were outraging blameless soldiers, and on occasion could deflect to himself complaints which otherwise would have gone direct to the President. Snubbed by McClellan, Mr. Lincoln once remarked that he would hold the general's horse if that would help win the war; Jefferson Davis would never conceivably have said anything of the kind, but General Lee might have held the horse in his stead—or, more probably, might have seen the snub coming and found a way to smother it.

Lee's position in all of this was difficult. He held a position which Mr. Davis had invented at a time when it seemed necessary to veto an act of Congress creating the position of general-in-chief: a necessity arising from Mr. Davis's conviction that the President's constitutional function as commander-in-chief must not be infringed upon by any such act of Congress. Lee had much authority and no authority, all at the same time. He was charged, "under the direction of the President," with conducting the military operations of the armies of the Confederacy; his orders, in other words, were binding on one and all, but on matters of any consequence he could speak only at the President's direction.[2] Perhaps the most revealing measure of his capacity as a man is the fact that this spring, even thus limited, he found and used a device that confounded Mr. Lincoln, Secretary Stanton, General McClellan, and all of the Federal armies in the state of Virginia.

By the first of May, when McClellan was almost ready to open his bombardment at Yorktown and Johnston was almost ready to foil him by departing, the general Confederate situation in Virginia was desperate. On the peninsula, Johnston with 55,000 men faced an army approximately twice that large. At Norfolk, which was about to be abandoned, the Confederate Major General Benjamin Huger had 10,000 soldiers, who presumably would join Johnston; they were balanced by 12,400 Federals under old General Wool at Fort Monroe, who would eventually be put under McClellan's command. In northern Virginia, from the Shenandoah Valley to the tide-water city of Fredericksburg, there were some 75,000 Federal troops in the separated commands of McDowell and Banks and in the Washington lines. In addition, Pathfinder Frémont had upwards of 17,000 scattered up and down the mountain valleys of western Virginia; he was beginning to pull them together and was contemplating a move south to break the railroad line that connected Virginia and Tennessee. To meet this immense array—which, for all anyone in Richmond knew, might at any moment be welded into one army—the Confederacy had 13,000 men under Brigadier General Joseph R. Anderson, below the Rappahannock watching McDowell; 6000 or more under Stonewall Jackson in the upper Shenandoah; 2800 under Brigadier General Edward Johnson west of Staunton, to keep an eye on Frémont; and 8500 under Major General Richard Ewell, poised at one of the gaps in the Blue Ridge, ready at need to join Jackson against Banks or to move east and join Anderson against McDowell. Since the Confederate authorities had a fairly accurate count on Federal strength, a simple exercise in addition was all anyone needed in order to understand the inadequacy of Confederate manpower in Virginia.

If the Federals had moved with speed, beginning in April, there would have been nothing for the Confederacy to do except call all of these detachments to Richmond, fold them into Johnston's army, and prepare for a backs-to-the-wall fight at the gates of the capital. If McClellan had broken through the Yorktown lines in the first week of April and moved swiftly up the peninsula he would have forced his opponents to make such a concentration. The supposed threat to Washington would have disappeared, the bulk of the Federal forces would have joined McClellan, and the final showdown—the battle which, if won by the North, would have brought the war nearly to an end—would have taken place under conditions giving all the advantages to the Union.

It did not happen so. McClellan spent a month at Yorktown, and the month thus lost was a free gift to the Confederacy. Early in April, Mr. Lincoln warned McClellan that the Confederates "will probably use *time* as advantageously as you can," and Lee set out to prove that Mr. Lincoln was correct. On April 25 he wrote to Stonewall Jackson, suggesting that "in the present divided condition of the enemy's forces" a blow could be struck. Banks, thought Lee, would make a good target, and perhaps Jackson, Ewell, and Edward Johnson could join forces and hit him. Lee added: "The blow, wherever struck, must, to be successful, be sudden and heavy." Jackson, who was just the man to see the possibilities in such a maneuver, proposed that Frémont's hesitant advance be knocked back first and that Banks then be attacked, and on May 1 Lee authorized him to go ahead. The initiative, surrendered during the long siege operation at Yorktown, had been picked up by hands that would use it most effectively.[3]

It would be necessary to use it quickly. McClellan was coming up the peninsula, and if his progress looked slow in Washington it looked ominous enough to General Johnston, who knew perfectly well that if the Northerner were allowed to play the game in his own way the Confederacy would be beaten. McClellan would leave nothing to chance. He had not merely the stronger battalions, but also the great siege guns, the mortars, and the field artillery to blast any line of entrenchments to bits, and he would make no attack until he was prepared to use all of these assets to the full. Just before leaving Yorktown, Johnston had given Lee his pessimistic appraisal of the situation: "We are engaged in a species of warfare at which we can never win. It is plain that General McClellan will adhere to the system adopted by him last summer and depend for success upon artillery and engineering. We can compete with him in neither."[4] This judgment was realistic. McClellan's plan would work, inevitably, provided he were given time enough to execute it; the one qualifying factor was that it was going to be a very slow process. If, by seizing the initiative, the Confederate strategists could rob the man of the unlimited time he had to have, something might be done.

Johnston continued to retreat, going at last all the way behind the Chickahominy and drawing his lines almost in the suburbs of Richmond, and the gloom which had pervaded the Confederate capital all spring became deeper than ever. President Davis was quite unable to find out when or where, or even *whether*, the army would offer battle; the Confederate government uneasily prepared to ship its vital papers out of the city; and bristling Robert Toombs, a strangely uninfluential brigadier in Johnston's army, voiced his despair and his disgust with professional soldiers in an angry letter to Vice-President Stephens: "This army will not fight until McClellan attacks it. Science will do anything but fight. It will burn, retreat, curse, swear, get drunk, strip soldiers—anything but fight." To round out the picture, he added: "Davis's incapacity is lamentable."[5] Both Mr. Davis and General Johnston were uneasily aware that General McDowell was very likely to bring 40,000 men down to join McClellan in the near future, and they knew that if this host marched down to the Chickahominy from Fredericksburg the cause was lost. . . . And far off in the Shenandoah Valley, Stonewall Jackson put his troops on the road, heading east through a gap in the Blue Ridge, doubling back to Staunton, and disappearing entirely from the ken of all Federal patrols, scouts, and military thinkers.

The military planner who becomes lost in the fog of war rarely notices the onset of the fog. It comes on gradually, the sum total of many small uncertainties which hardly seemed worth a second thought. There is a little patch of mist here, another patch over yonder, a slow thickening of the haze along the horizon, the sky turning gray and sagging lower over the woods, sunlight fading out imperceptibly . . . and then, suddenly, the horizon has vanished altogether, there is fog everywhere, and the noises that come from the invisible landscape are unidentifiable, confusing and full of menace; at which point it is mortally easy to give way to panic and do one's self great harm.

So it was with the Federals after the occupation of Yorktown. Little doubts came into being; seeming, at the time, of no great consequence; hanging in the air and waiting for some quick shock to jar all of them together into one disastrous uncertainty.

When the Confederates moved up the peninsula to get away from McClellan, the War Department in Washington tried to appraise the general situation, learning nothing to cause great uneasiness, learning indeed nothing at all for certain, sensing only that the Rebels were up to something. From his station in the North Carolina sounds area, where he had been exploiting the advantages gained by the occupation of Roanoke Island, General Burnside sent word that some of the Rebel troops in his front seemed to be moving north to Virginia. Peering across the Rappahannock at Fredericksburg, General McDowell reported that there appeared to be some sort of build-up of the Confederate forces in his front; it was rumored that Stonewall Jackson would appear before long to take over-all command. From the western mountain valleys, General Frémont sent word that Brigadier General Robert Milroy, commanding Frémont's advance in the foothills thirty miles west of Staunton, was menaced by advancing Rebels led by Jackson in person. Banks reported that whatever Jackson was doing he had at least disappeared from Banks's front. And, at Fort Monroe, Secretary Stanton, who was helping Mr. Lincoln capture Norfolk, picked up the rumor that the Confederate Army which had just left Yorktown would be reinforced and sent north to threaten Washington. He also heard that Jackson was to be reinforced.

There was not, in all of this, anything more than the mild uncertainty as to enemy movements and intentions which is normal in time of war. The Federal government reflected and went on with its plans. McDowell was to be strengthened for the projected advance on Richmond. Banks was to make certain that Jackson had actually departed, and having done so was to detach Shields's division—the outfit which had beaten Jackson at Kernstown, earlier in the spring —and send it off to join McDowell at Fredericksburg. Banks then was to get his own troops back to a safer position. His advance guard was at the town of Harrisonburg, barely twenty-five miles north of Staunton; it must retreat, and Banks must concentrate at Strasburg, eighteen miles south of his main supply base at Winchester. If Jackson had gone a-roving, and if McDowell was going to march down to the Chickahominy, there was no need for the Federals to do anything in the Shenandoah Valley except guard the lower end of it.[6]

Everything was under control, and there were just two small areas of doubt: Jackson's whereabouts and intentions, and the revival of Washington's ancient fear that the Rebels were scheming to invade across the Potomac. Neither of these seemed very important; they were just there, two hazy spots in the landscape. If the two grew, blended into one, turned the haze into a real fog, there might be trouble. For the moment things looked serene enough.

Vanishing from the sight of Banks, Jackson moved roundabout to Staunton, where on May 5 he picked up the little force of Edward Johnson and got a telegram from General Lee, who filled him in on the situation as Richmond saw it. Lee had heard about Banks's retreat, and he had drawn the proper deduction: Banks was sending troops to McDowell, which could only mean that McDowell was about to come down to join McClellan. The entire point of current Confederate strategy was to prevent this—the Confederacy's sole hope for survival depended on it—and Jackson must do something effective and do it without the slightest delay. Lee's telegram was explicit: "Object of evacuating Harrisonburg may be concentration at Fredericksburg. Watch Banks movements. If you can strike at Milroy do it quickly."[7]

Do it quickly . . . the words Mr. Lincoln had been repeating over and over, all spring, all winter and all spring, all fall and all winter and all spring, without getting any especial response; used now by a general on the other side, directed to the one soldier of all soldiers who would understand and respond. (It is permissible to suspect that Mr. Lincoln would have found General Lee a good man to work with, if fate can be imagined as having put them on the same side.)

From Staunton, Jackson marched west to strike General Milroy. (Moderate confusion, quickly dispelled, developed when Washington, hearing that Jackson had been joined by a General Johnson, assumed that Joe Johnston was on the scene. For additional brief bewilderment, Milroy was near a town named McDowell, and Jackson's plan to attack McDowell was translated into a plan to fall upon the general of that name.) Anyway, with perhaps 9000 men Jackson on May 8 appeared in Bull Pasture Valley, near this town of McDowell, and found that Milroy (who had been joined by a detachment under Brigadier General Robert C. Schenck, and who by now may have had 4000 men in all) was most belligerent. Outnumbered though they were, the Federals attacked Jackson's position on a height known as Sitlington's Hill, part of Bull Pasture Mountain; failed, were driven off, and at the close of the day retreated northward toward the town of Franklin, where Frémont had his headquarters and where he was trying to assemble a striking force. Jackson sent Richmond the slightly cryptic message that "God blessed our arms with victory at McDowell" and set out in pursuit.[8]

The pursuit was slow—nobody could move very fast on those atrocious mountain roads—and Jackson was never able to force his opponents to stand and give battle again. Probably he did not especially want to. It was Banks, not Frémont, who was really on Jackson's mind, and, after following Milroy and Schenck for three days, Jackson left them to their own devices, wheeled his own column about, and got back to the Shenandoah Valley as rapidly as he could. He had done Frémont's army no particular harm, but he had taken it out of the play. That was all that mattered.

When Jackson returned to the Shenandoah the Federal inability to see just what was going on grew slightly deeper. Jackson seemed to be coming down the valley, with evil designs on General Banks's force, but nothing was quite certain except that Banks and his people were becoming anxious. Banks's strength had been whittled thin. He had had to detach forces, earlier, to watch the upper Rappahannock, and now Shields and 11,000 men had marched out of the valley to join McDowell; when he reached Strasburg, Banks had no more than 8000 men, who were unhappy because they had to retreat. A retreat in hostile territory was no fun; one infantryman noted that every dooryard was full of "jeering men and sneering women," and said there even seemed to be more dogs, all of them barking at Federal soldiers. (Some of the men asserted that secessionist-minded roosters perched on fence posts and crowed derisively.) Brigadier General Alpheus Williams, one of Banks's division commanders, wrote to his daughter that "if the amount of swearing that has been done in this department is recorded against us in Heaven I fear we have an account that can never be settled." Williams blamed the withdrawal on ignorant civilians in Washington, and mused darkly: "I sometimes fear that we are to meet with terrible reverses because of the fantastic tricks of some vain men dressed in a little brief authority." Banks himself was disturbed. He had warned Stanton that the Confederates would undoubtedly concentrate against any small force left in the valley, and from Strasburg he wrote that Jackson's return to the valley worried him: "I am compelled to believe that he meditates attack here."[9]

The horizon was beginning to be a little blurred. Still, the situation did not seem really ominous. Shields and his men reached Falmouth, and McClellan was notified that McDowell's host would march down to join him well before the end of the month. McClellan sent Fitz John Porter and the newly-formed V Corps off on a foray toward Hanover Junction, to clear McDowell's path of Confederate infantry, and then anchored his right wing near Mechanicsville north of the Chickahominy to await the promised reinforcements. At the distant mountain town of Franklin, Frémont was trying to weld his somewhat mixed brigades into an army, taking the better part of two weeks for the job. Banks was at Strasburg, his forces drawn up in a defensive line astride the Valley Pike, the main road that came northeast from Staunton through Strasburg to Winchester. As far as Banks knew, Jackson was thirty miles away, at New Market; if the man planned to attack Strasburg, the Valley Pike was obviously the road he would use. To protect his flank against marauding guerrillas Banks had posted a thousand men under Colonel John R. Kenly at Front Royal, ten miles to the east, on the Manassas Gap Railway.

Now Jackson disappeared again. Screening his front with cavalry, he side-slipped to the east, crossing the Massanutten Mountain ridge and getting over into the valley of the South Fork of the Shenandoah, picking up General Ewell and Ewell's 8000 men en route. On the night of May 22, Jackson had his entire force, thus increased to 17,000 men, in camp ten miles from Front Royal, with the massive bulk of the Massanutten ridge between himself and Banks. He was now on a direct road to the big Federal base at Winchester, with no one in his path but Colonel Kenly, who had no reason to suppose that Jackson was anywhere in the neighborhood. And over at Strasburg, Banks continued to gaze attentively to the southwest, waiting for Jackson's advance to take solid form behind the shifting Confederate cavalry patrols on the Valley Pike.

Then Jackson struck, and the blow disrupted the entire Federal strategic plan in Virginia.

On May 23 he drove suddenly down on Colonel Kenly, sweeping through Front Royal, capturing Kenly and most of his men, pausing long enough to pick up prisoners and captured goods, and then moving straight on for Winchester. As Banks had supposed, Jackson was going to move along the Valley Pike; the trouble was that he was going to reach it eighteen miles in Banks's rear.

Fugitives from Kenly's shattered command brought the news to Strasburg that night, and there was nothing Banks could do but order an immediate retreat. Evacuating his lines, he set off for Winchester, pushing a bulky wagon train along with him, and Jackson swung his leading elements toward the west to strike the ungainly column on the march, hoping to break it and destroy Banks's army outright. He came close to success, but not quite close enough, one difficulty being that his infantry was almost exhausted. These Confederates had been marched hard, the last few days—not for nothing did Jackson's infantry bear the unofficial title of "foot cavalry"—and the weather was hot and their feet were sore, and they knew nothing about the high strategy involved; as they struggled along, constantly goaded to move more rapidly, they complained bitterly that Jackson was "marching them to death to no good end." Banks just managed to escape destruction, reaching Winchester and drawing a defensive line to check the pursuit.[10]

He escaped destruction but he could do no more than that. On May 25, Jackson attacked the Federal line at Winchester and broke it, and Banks's shattered army continued its desperate flight to the Potomac. Temporarily, at least, a good part of the army was disorganized, and although a measure of order was restored once the battlefield was left behind, the retreat was little better than a rout. Jackson pressed hard, trying to force one more battle and turn retreat into destruction, but his men were exhausted, and the cavalry which had screened him so well tarried in Winchester to loot the rich stores the Federals had abandoned. Banks got away, reached the Potomac at Williamsport, and got his frazzled army across the river to safety. Jackson accepted the situation, moved his own army up to the outskirts of Harper's Ferry, and let his men pause for breath. A perfectionist, he regretted that any of the Federals had escaped, and he wrote grimly: "Never have I seen a situation when it was in the power of the cavalry to reap a richer harvest of the fruits of victory."[11] But if the harvest seemed incomplete it was nevertheless extremely rewarding.

Jackson's soldiers suddenly realized that the general whom they had accused of marching them to death had been leading them to a dazzling triumph, and their confidence in him rose high, along with their pride in themselves. The people of Winchester looked on them as saviors and gave them a hysterical greeting, seeming to be "demented with joy and exhibiting all the ecstasy of delirium." From the captured Federal supply dumps the needy Confederates could acquire unimaginable riches, which one man tabulated breathlessly: "Brand new officers' uniforms, sashes, swords, boots, coats of mail, india rubber blankets, coats and boots, oranges, lemons, figs, dates, oysters, brandies, wines and liquors, the choicest hams and dried meats and sausages, all the contents of a large city clothing establishment and miscellaneous grocery and confectionery."[12] All in all, it was a great day in the morning.

But the real effect was felt in Washington, where the gathering fog became absolute. Nothing was clear except that the Federal force which had been holding the Shenandoah Valley had been knocked off the board, and that a Confederate Army of unknown size but aggressive intent had reached the Potomac. The counterstroke aimed at Washington had been anticipated for months: this, possibly, was it, taking form in the wake of Banks's desperate flight. McDowell was ordered to suspend his movement on Richmond and to get at least 20,000 men over to the valley as rapidly as possible. Lincoln notified McClellan that "the enemy are making a desperate push against Harper's Ferry and we are trying to throw Frémont's force and part of McDowell's in their rear." Frémont was ordered to move east to Harrisonburg and get into Jackson's rear. McDowell ordered Shields to head back to the valley, notifying Mr. Lincoln that he was doing what he had been told to do but that the move was a bad one and that "I shall gain nothing for you there and I shall lose much for you here." Mr. Lincoln sent a slightly amplified report to General McClellan, saying that he believed the enemy thrust at the Potomac "is a general and concerted one, such as could not be made if he was acting upon the purpose of a very desperate defence of Richmond." He added: "I think the time is near when you must either attack Richmond or give up the job and come to the defence of Washington."[13]

Shields's men began their countermarch, beset by rumors that Jackson with twenty, thirty, or even forty thousand men was about to attack Washington. They had made a hard march to reach McDowell, and now they were retracing their steps with even greater speed, they understood perfectly well that somebody was panicky, and as before they swore vigorously. One of their number wrote: "I trust that the Recording Angel was too much occupied to make a note of the language used in Shields's division when we learned, with mingled feelings of rage and mortification, that we were to return to the valley by forced marches."[14]

3: *The Last Struggle*

The panic which Stonewall Jackson inflicted on Washington was really rather brief, and not all of its effects were bad.

To be sure, it killed the prospect that McDowell's troops would reinforce McClellan, and it led Secretary Stanton to send a tense message to the governors of the Northern states, urging them to send forward all available volunteers and militia as rapidly as possible. But it also led the War Department to correct an earlier error. The recruiting stations which had been closed so fatuously at the beginning of April were reopened, and steps were taken to round up the vast number of absentee soldiers and get them back to their regiments.[1] In addition, Mr. Lincoln and Secretary Stanton soon recognized Jackson's thrust for what it was—a daring maneuver rather than the beginning of a massive invasion of the North—and they realized that when he marched to the outskirts of Harper's Ferry, Jackson actually took a very long chance. If the available Federal troops were handled properly he could be cut off and destroyed; and so these two civilians—who at the moment were in their own persons the Army's high command, board of strategy, and general staff, all combined—undertook to bring this about.

In a way this was the beginning of wisdom, and Mr. Lincoln here came to see something which he never forgot. The Southern Confederacy lived by its armies. While they lasted it would last and if they died it would die, and so whatever it did with them it could not afford to lose any of them outright. But any Confederate Army which moved out of its own territory must always face superior numbers. If it invaded the North, or even moved out into the border area to threaten an invasion, it gave the Federal power the chance to make the best possible use of its greater resources—to fight the kind of war in which the Federals held all of the advantages. When it sent its armies north the Confederacy risked more than it could bear to lose and presented its enemies with a rich opportunity.

This much Mr. Lincoln was beginning to see. But to see an opportunity is one thing and to take advantage of it is something quite different, as the President and the Secretary of War presently discovered.

They worked out a good series of moves, and if wars were fought on chessboards with pieces that would infallibly go to the precise squares chosen for them, Stonewall Jackson would have come to grief quickly. As soon as they heard about what had happened to Banks, they ordered Frémont with something under 15,000 men to march at once to Harrisonburg, to cut off Jackson's retreat, while McDowell brought three divisions to Strasburg, the town from which Jackson had just flushed Banks. Since the Potomac itself was held by 15,000 or more, all of the exits would be blocked and Jackson could be rounded up and defeated.

This chessboard, however, was full of mountains and atrocious roads and it was swept by heavy rains, and some of the pieces had minds of their own. Frémont, at the town of Franklin, faced muddy going, he was short of supplies, the mountain roads between Franklin and Harrisonburg had been blocked by Jackson's engineers, and Frémont felt that he ought to use his discretion; instead of marching east to Harrisonburg he chose to go roundabout to Strasburg, which was much farther away but which somehow seemed easier to reach. McDowell's troops also encountered rain and muddy roads, and although McDowell did move toward the place he had been told to move toward the going was slow, and there was further delay when Shields, who led the advance, paused at Front Royal because of a wild story that Confederate James Longstreet was coming down the valley of the South Fork of the Shenandoah from Luray with a large force. Still, the combination nearly worked. On May 30, for instance, both Frémont and Shields were much closer to Strasburg, which Jackson would have to pass through on his retreat, than Jackson was himself. But Shields took a wrong road when he left Front Royal next morning, and time was lost while the column was pulled back and redirected, and Frémont's advance was most hesitant about driving on into Strasburg; and in the end Jackson just made it. Pushing 2300 unhappy Federal prisoners ahead of him, plus a wagon train loaded with booty captured at Winchester, Jackson got his rear guard out of Strasburg just as the first Yankee patrols entered the place, and thereafter the Federals could do nothing but chase him. Frémont followed along the Valley Pike, and McDowell sent Shields up the Luray Valley on the chance that he might head Jackson off or strike his flank somewhere beyond the Massanutten Mountain . . . but the big opportunity was gone.[2]

Yet if the attempt to destroy Jackson had been a humiliating fizzle, the President and the Secretary of War might well have felt hopeful about the general military situation at the end of May. Jackson, after all, had at least gone away, and the invasion scare had gone away with him; and on the two principal fighting fronts, in the east and in the west, the news was good and the prospects were even better. McClellan was edging forward beyond the Chickahominy, apparently in excellent spirits, full of confidence: notified that McDowell would not be joining him and that he would have to take Richmond with what he had, he replied stoutly: "The time is very near when I shall attack Richmond." To protect his right flank in preparation for this great event he sent Fitz John Porter to drive Rebel infantry away from Hanover Court House, north of Richmond. Porter did the job handsomely on May 27, and McClellan sent a jubilant telegram to Stanton saying that this was "a glorious victory" and that "the rout of the Rebels was complete." He reported that he had two army corps across the Chickahominy and that the other three were ready to cross as soon as the necessary bridges were finished. The roads would soon be dry enough for artillery, and he spoke confidently of "closing in on the enemy preparatory to the last struggle."[3]

It was good to find the commander of the Army of the Potomac talking so hopefully, considering all of the things that had gone wrong; it was even better to learn what had been happening in the west. General Halleck's powerful army had at last taken the Mississippi town of Corinth, on May 30. Beauregard and his Confederate Army had fled to the south, and it was briefly possible to believe, in Washington, that final conquest of everything the Confederacy had west of the Alleghenies was imminent.

Corinth by itself was nothing in particular; a railroad junction town, the base from which Albert Sidney Johnston had led his troops up to fight at Shiloh and to which the beaten army had returned after he and his high hopes had died. It had almost been swamped with wounded men after the battle, and there was a great deal of sickness; one dejected Confederate described the town as "the worst place I have ever been in," said that the drinking water was foul, and asserted that 17,000 sick men had been sent away from the place in the weeks following the big battle on the Tennessee.[4] Corinth was important partly because it was the place where the one railroad line directly connecting the Mississippi with Virginia crossed the north-south line of the Mobile & Ohio, and even more because as long as it was held by a Confederate Army the Confederacy had protection for Fort Pillow, Memphis, Vicksburg, and that segment of the Mississippi River which the Federals had not yet taken. Grant's move up the Tennessee early in the spring had been aimed at Corinth, and after Shiloh had been won Halleck assembled a huge army at Pittsburg Landing and resumed the offensive.

He resumed it with great deliberation. He began by bringing together the separate armies of Grant, Buell, and Pope for a total of better than 100,000 effectives—an army more than twice as large as anything Beauregard could bring against him—and he took the supreme command himself, making Grant his second-in-command and turning Grant's troops over to George H. Thomas. This actually put Grant on the shelf, giving him an impressive title but nothing at all to do, it almost drove Grant out of the Army, and it doubtless reflected Halleck's feeling that Grant had been careless at Shiloh.[5] Buell, Thomas, and Pope became in effect corps commanders; Halleck insisted that the army remain concentrated when it moved, and ordered these officers to maintain constant touch with him. Every segment of the army was kept under his direct control.

Halleck reached Pittsburg Landing on April 11, spent a little more than three weeks perfecting his army's organization, and during the first week in May he set out for Corinth, twenty-four miles away. The army took two days to move the first fifteen miles and twenty-four days to move the last six. When it marched, front and flanks were protected by clouds of pickets and scouts; when it halted, it entrenched to the eyes. This advance was the most defensive-minded offensive imaginable, and it took that form not merely because Halleck was ultracautious by nature—a born office worker, he felt ill at ease as a field commander—but also because his whole operation was aimed primarily at Corinth rather than at the Confederate soldiers who held the town. He did not try to make Beauregard fight and he did not try to surround and capture him; he simply wanted Corinth, and if Beauregard would get his army out of there and go away Halleck would be happy.

There was nothing else for Beauregard to do. The heavy Confederate losses at Shiloh had been more than made good when Van Dorn and Price finally crossed the Mississippi and came to Corinth with some 12,000 men who had fought at Pea Ridge, but the camp at Corinth was unhealthful and there had been a steady wastage; when the Federals reached the Confederate lines Beauregard had approximately 50,000 effectives of all arms. On May 25 he called his subordinates into council: Bragg, the pessimistic martinet, the studious Hardee, Bishop Polk, former Vice-President Breckinridge, and the two westerners, Van Dorn and Price—and explained the situation. To give up Corinth would be to lose an important strategic position—it was especially important to hold on as long as possible because the task of fortifying Vicksburg was just getting under way—but to stay too long would be to risk loss of the entire army, and so it was time to leave. The generals could do nothing but agree, and Beauregard ordered the army withdrawn to Tupelo, a town on the Mobile & Ohio fifty miles to the south. Sick men and wagon trains were sent on ahead, various devices to make the Federals anticipate a Confederate offensive were worked out, and on the night of May 29 the army left Corinth and moved south. The Federals were completely fooled; just when the last Confederates were getting out of Corinth, General Pope advised Halleck that he would probably be attacked as soon as morning came, and when the first Northern troops entered Corinth no one knew where Beauregard had gone. Halleck sent Pope down the railroad to examine the situation and pick up stragglers, and dispatched a triumphant telegram to Stanton.

Beauregard, he said, had given up a fortified position of surpassing strength, had abandoned great quantities of stores and baggage and was in headlong flight: Pope was "pushing the enemy hard" and had taken 10,000 prisoners, and "the result is all I could possibly desire."[6]

This report was greatly exaggerated. Beauregard had executed a most orderly withdrawal, he had lost little property, and few prisoners had been taken. (To do Pope justice, he never said he had taken many prisoners; he had simply estimated that 10,000 stragglers were trailing Beauregard's army and had predicted, erroneously, that most of them would soon surrender. The exaggeration was largely Halleck's own, although the blame went to Pope and Halleck did nothing to set the record straight.)[7] But one sentence in Halleck's report was entirely correct. The result of this methodical, glacial campaign was indeed all that Halleck could desire, even though the opposing army had got away unharmed.

For Halleck was no more pugnacious than McClellan. He was campaigning by the map and by the textbooks. He had set out to take a strategic point and he had taken it, and, as long as Beauregard remained in Tupelo, Halleck had no intention of following him. He had Corinth, and Corinth was the most he had wanted to get. As a chess player, he now had a definite positional advantage; a winning advantage, if properly exploited.

With a compact, well-equipped army of 100,000 men, Halleck held a key railroad center and could move in any direction he chose, and there was little the Confederates could do to stop him. They had Beauregard and his 50,000 at Tupelo, scattered details along the Mississippi from Fort Pillow to Vicksburg, 12,000 at Knoxville under Major General Edmund Kirby Smith, 2000 at Chattanooga, detachments in Louisiana watching Ben Butler at New Orleans—and nothing much else. The Federals could open the Mississippi all the way to the mouth if they chose; they could march straight south and take Mobile; they could swing east, take Chattanooga, and possess all of eastern Tennessee—something Mr. Lincoln wanted just about as much as he wanted the capture of Richmond itself. All they had to do was get at it.

Certain fruits fell into their hands at once. With a Federal Army in Corinth both Fort Pillow and Memphis were doomed. Beauregard ordered the former place evacuated at once, and its garrison moved down to Grenada, Mississippi; and on June 6 Federal rams and gunboats under Flag Officer Davis came downstream to Memphis, destroyed a Confederate fleet there in a brisk battle watched by most of the townspeople, who lined the bluffs to see the spectacle, and forced the defenseless city to surrender. The Mississippi was open now all the way down to Vicksburg; and as a matter of fact it was open from the south all the way *up* to Vicksburg as well, Farragut having sent seven of his ocean-going bruisers upstream in May to tap the defenses and see if the Navy could crack them without help. The Vicksburg fortifications at this time were not nearly as strong as they became a bit later, but they were more than the Navy could manage; still, there were Federal gunboats above the city, the salt-water ships were just below it, Farragut himself was coming up in *Hartford*, followed by Porter and the mortars, and if 20,000 men from Halleck's army could be sent there in June or July the place would unquestionably be taken and the river would be open from Minnesota to the Gulf.

All of the possibilities were visible to everyone, and no one was more impressed by the extent of them than Jefferson Davis.

Mr. Davis was coldly furious over the fact that Halleck had been permitted to take Corinth without a battle, and he promptly sent a military aide to Tupelo with a set of icy questions to which Beauregard was ordered to reply in writing. Why had the army retreated from Corinth? What plans were there for recovering the lost territory? Why had the camp at Corinth been so sickly, why was not a stronger defensive line chosen, could not Halleck's communications have been cut, what if anything had been done to hold the Mississippi and Memphis—and, in general, how about the whole sorry business anyway?

Beauregard replied in writing, answering the questions with dignified formality, pointing out that the retreat had been approved by all of his chief subordinates. As to future plans, they would depend largely on what the enemy did. If Halleck divided his forces, Beauregard would move against one of the separated contingents; if Halleck tried to keep his army together, every effort would be made—by demonstrations along his flanks, and by the spreading of false reports in the newspapers—to induce him to split it up. Also (Beauregard told the aide) if the President thought the retreat a mistake Beauregard would ask for a court of inquiry; he himself considered the movement the equivalent of a brilliant victory.[8]

Whatever his army did next, Beauregard would not be directing its movements. His health had been bad all spring, and once his troops were established at Tupelo—the camp site was much better than the one at Corinth, the water was good, and the list of invalids immediately grew shorter—he took sick leave, on advice of his doctors, going to the noted watering place of Bladon Springs, Alabama, to recover his health. Mr. Davis considered that the general had deserted his post without getting War Department permission and he at once removed Beauregard from command, putting Braxton Bragg in his place. From Bladon Springs, Beauregard wrote to his trusted aide, Brigadier General Thomas Jordan, expressing himself about Mr. Davis in terms which sounded much like McClellan's more impassioned remarks about the Federal administration. "If the country be satisfied," wrote General Beauregard, "to have me laid on the shelf by a man who is either demented or a traitor to his high trust—well, let it be so. I require rest & will endeavor meanwhile by study and reflection to fit myself better for the dark hours of our trial, which, I foresee, are yet to come. As to my reputation, if it can suffer by anything that living specimen of gall & hatred can do—why it is not then worth preserving . . . My consolation is, that the difference between 'that Individual' and myself is—that if he were to die today, the whole country would rejoice at it—whereas, I believe, if the same thing were to happen to me, they would regret it."[9]

The situation in Mississippi was oddly like that in Virginia. Two Federal armies had made slow, methodical, and apparently irresistible advances, and each had reached a position from which a decisive victory might be won. Halleck had his army well in hand and was meditating an advance on Chattanooga; McClellan's army was more extended, the unpredictable Chickahominy flowing between its separated wings, the weaker wing lying nearer the enemy; but the river was being bridged, he had disposed of the threat to his right flank and rear, he would soon be able to wheel up his heavy guns, and he was preparing for what he himself had spoken of as "the last struggle."

It might be the last struggle in sober truth. At the end of May 1862, it was still possible (and for the last time) to believe that the war might be won, might be lost, might at least be *ended*, before it became all-consuming. Senator Sumner, in Washington, was musing darkly that "except at New Orleans the real strength of the Rebellion has not been touched,"[10] but now the Federal government had two immense armies placed where they could touch it directly and with decisive effect. Everything depended on what those armies did. They could end everything in a matter of weeks; could end it (and this would not be true much longer) while it was still possible to imagine the men of the contending sections making a peace that would contain saving compromises and evasions—a peace which could relieve the nation from the necessity of redefining its own meaning in the terrible heat of war. It might yet be that this war was an incident rather than an absolute.

What these great armies would do depended on many things: on the men at arms who composed them, on the limited mortals who commanded them, on the armies that stood against them, and their men at arms and commanders, on the accidents of wind and weather . . . and, it may be, on the wheeling stars in their courses, and on forces no man will ever understand. . . .

On the night of May 30 a violent rainstorm swept down the valley of the Chickahominy. An impressionable Northern newspaper correspondent wrote that "nature's artillery rolled and clashed magnificently, as if in stately mockery of the puny efforts of martial men," and spoke of the "tropical grandeur and sublimity" of the scene. A more matter-of-fact courier on General Johnston's staff called it simply "the worst night I ever saw." A Massachusetts officer remarked that the storm caused a flood in "the treacherous Chickahominy, of which it was hard to say at the best of times where its banks were, and of which no man could say today where its banks would be tomorrow." General Johnston concluded that this storm put McClellan at a grave disadvantage—with the banks flooded, the Army of the Potomac might be unable to use its bridges—and he ordered an attack.[11]

McClellan's position was awkward. He had two-fifths of his army, the corps of Keyes and Heintzelman, south of the river. Keyes held a mile-wide front from the station of Fair Oaks, on the Richmond & York River Railroad, to the crossroads of Seven Pines, southeast of Fair Oaks; Heintzelman had his two divisions several miles to the rear, guarding the flank at White Oak Swamp and the bridge by which the main road from Williamsburg crossed the Chickahominy. All the rest of the army—McClellan himself, and the corps of Porter, Franklin, and Sumner—was north of the river, the whole position was fifteen miles from flank to flank, and on the wet morning of May 31 it was quite likely that some or even all of the bridges would soon be out of service. Keyes and Heintzelman were temporarily isolated, and Johnston could hit them with vastly superior numbers.

The original plan had been to attack north of the river. President Davis, who was most impatient to have the Yankee Army beaten before it could impose siege warfare on Richmond's defenders, had urged this several days earlier and Lee had agreed with him; and so, for that matter, had Johnston, feeling that it was important to defeat that part of the Federal Army with which McDowell, whose advance was anticipated, would make contact. Then came the news that McDowell was marching to the Shenandoah Valley and not toward Richmond. Johnston quickly revised his plans. He would attack the soft spot, south of the river, and he would do it while the river was still rising. On the morning of May 31 he put his army in motion.

Johnston's battle plan was excellent, but its execution was sadly bungled. Orders were misunderstood, James Longstreet got his division on a road someone else was supposed to use, Huger's division ran into this roadblock and was crowded completely out of action, a number of Longstreet's brigades were unable to reach the firing line, and the pulverizing attack which was to have been delivered by overwhelming numbers turned into a straight slugging match in which much of the Confederate advantage was unused. McClellan ordered Sumner to take his corps across the river and get into the fight, and Sumner—a tough, literal-minded old-timer, who had been an Army officer before McClellan was born and who joined a complete lack of imagination to an unshakable belief in the overriding importance of obeying orders—got his men across on a bridge that was beginning to float away, and gave the shaken Federal lines the stiffening they had to have. Much of the fighting took place in a wooded swamp, where fighting men stood in water to their knees, and where details went along the firing lines to prop wounded men against trees or stumps to keep them from drowning. The Confederates gained a good deal of ground on May 31, lost most of it the next morning, and finally accepted a drawn battle which left things just about as they had been before the fighting started.[12] If things had gone well, they might have destroyed a large part of McClellan's army. Nothing went well. Seven Pines, or Fair Oaks—the battle went by both names—was a victory for no one.

But it had certain effects. Its casualty list was grimly instructive. Union losses ran to slightly more than 5000 and Confederate losses were about 6000—higher totals, for each side, than had been run up at Bull Run and Williamsburg put together. The war was getting tougher, and the hard fighting qualities of Northern and Southern soldiers had been tragically emphasized. Leadership had been defective—neither commander had really put his hand on the battle to exert firm control—but the men in the ranks had met the test magnificently. There had been little of the runaway panic that had marked Bull Run. For the two armies together, the "captured or missing" total, always high when shaky troops are in action, came to hardly more than 1000.[13]

In addition, this drawn battle served as a definite check on McClellan. He had apparently been nearly ready to begin his final offensive when this battle took place; more than three weeks passed, after it, before he considered himself ready to resume the advance. He did, to be sure, bring Franklin and Sumner south of the river, leaving only Porter's corps to guard his flank and his supply line, but the whole attitude of his army was defensive. There was no more talk about "closing in on the enemy preparatory to the last struggle." The battle was a stalemate and it was followed by a more extended stalemate.

Finally, there was one development of high importance in the story of the Civil War. On the evening of May 31 General Joseph E. Johnston was severely wounded. On the following day, Mr. Davis put Robert E. Lee in command of the Army.

4: *Railroad to the Pamunkey*

The Southern Confederacy had no gift for statecraft, and the ins and outs of domestic politics were always a snare for its feet, but it had a definite talent for making war which might in the end make up for all other deficiencies. This talent was manifest in various places—in the amazing pugnacity and endurance of the ordinary citizen, for one—but it was most strikingly and powerfully embodied in the person of General Lee.

When Lee took command of the army in front of Richmond—significantly, he immediately began calling it the Army of *Northern* Virginia, although its chance of ever seeing northern Virginia again seemed remote—he was the unknown quantity in the story of the Civil War: the incalculable, the factor no one could figure on in advance. This gray man in gray rode his dappled gray horse into legend almost at once, and like all legendary figures he came before long to seem almost supernatural, a man of profound mystery; but his basic approach to the war was quite simple. He seems to have worried not at all about the ultimate meaning of the war: he knew that he was a Southerner and he would fight to the end to bring victory to the South, and that was enough. But he understood the processes of war as few men have ever done. He knew, apparently by instinct, the risks that must be taken and the gains that can be won thereby, the way to impose his will on his opponent, and the fact that sooner or later a general must be willing to move in close for a showdown fight regardless of the cost. Because he was what he was, the war lasted much longer and was fought much harder than seemed likely at the beginning of June in 1862.

When Lee took command the army was moderately unhappy. It had had a costly fight and it sensed that the fight had been badly directed. The swampy bottom lands were hot and humid and stank fearfully from the debris of battle, there was a good deal of sickness, and some regimental surgeons were easy marks for malingerers who suffered from nothing worse than a desire to take it easy. Rations were ample, but poor; a Louisiana soldier said the bacon was strong and the bread was sour, and for good measure he added that he could not find one soldier whose pants were not worn out in the seat. Still, morale was good enough, in the main—General Longstreet insisted after the war that the chief result of Seven Pines had been to give the men greater confidence in their own fighting capacity—and the men in the ranks cocked a collective eye at the new commander and waited to see what he would do with them.[1]

What he would do first was put all hands to work digging trenches. The army had a long line to hold—it ran from Chaffin's Bluff on the James, crossed all of the main roads coming into Richmond from the east, touched the Chickahominy a little above New Bridge, and ran along the south side of that stream to Meadow Bridge—and Lee ordered this line strongly fortified. The soldiers grumbled a bit, considering day laborers' work with pick and shovel beneath the dignity of fighting men, and Jefferson Davis noted bitterly that "politicians, newspapers and uneducated officers have created such a prejudice in our Army against labor that it will be difficult until taught by sad experience to induce our troops to work efficiently."[2] But the men who complained nevertheless toiled as directed, and before long the field fortifications were impressive.

Creating these defensive works, Lee was actually getting ready to take the offensive. McClellan was busily fortifying his own lines, making them so strong that the blow which had been struck at Seven Pines could not be struck again. What Lee needed was a line of his own strong enough to be held for a short time by a small force. If he had that he could take the rest of the army out and compel Mc-

Clellan to fight in the open. Digging trenches, he was freeing his army for maneuver.

If he could not do this the war would probably be lost before the summer ended.

Everything McClellan had done so far indicated that he was getting ready for siege operations. Behind lines too strong to be attacked, he could prepare short advances which, in the end, would give him positions for his matchless siege artillery. With those terrible guns properly sited he could flatten the strongest fortifications, and then his infantry could do the rest; and the very fact that he overestimated Lee's numbers so greatly increased the probability that he would follow this course, because if Lee had as much infantry as McClellan thought he had this was the only course that made any sense at all. His siege train was the great equalizer, and if he were allowed to play the game in his own way it would inevitably win for him—as Joe Johnston had pointed out weeks earlier and as Lee himself quickly realized. Lee was taking the first step toward compelling McClellan to play a different sort of game, in which the equalizer could not be used.

The second step would involve Stonewall Jackson, who was just now finishing his spectacular valley campaign.

During the first week in June, Jackson retreated from Strasburg, pursued by Frémont and followed on a parallel course, east of the Massanutten Mountain, by Shields. At the southern end of this mountain, where Frémont and Shields could join forces, Jackson paused to rest his troops briefly at the hamlet of Port Republic, posting Ewell a few miles west at Cross Keys, in Frémont's path. On June 8 Ewell repulsed a rather spiritless attack by Frémont, and on June 9 Jackson at Port Republic had a much more severe fight with the advance regiments of Shields's division. If the entire division had been present Jackson might have had more than he could handle, but as it was the Federals were too weak to make serious trouble and Jackson finally drove them off in full retreat. Then he withdrew to a convenient gap in the Blue Ridge, from which point he could either strike the flank of any Federal Army which tried to continue on up the valley, or if his government wished could move to Richmond; and on June 13 he wrote to Lee, outlining the situation and asking what Lee wanted him to do next.

A little before this, Lee had considered reinforcing Jackson and sending him back to disturb the peace of the lower valley once more, but the time for this had passed. Jackson in his letter had said he did not think he ought to return to Winchester "until we are in a condition under the blessing of Providence to hold the country," and Lee sent his letter on to Mr. Davis with the significant note: "I think the sooner Jackson can move this way, the better—the first object now is to defeat McClellan. The enemy in the Valley seem at a pause. We may strike them here before they are ready there to move up the Valley—they will naturally be cautious and we must be secret & quick." Mr. Davis endorsed this, "View concurred in," and Lee set about making his arrangements.[3]

The preliminaries were already under way. Before he made final plans Lee needed to know where McClellan's right flank was anchored, how it was guarded, and what sort of protection there was for the all-important Federal supply route, the Richmond & York River Railroad line back to White House on the Pamunkey. He told his cavalry commander, the youthful, flamboyant, and highly gifted Brigadier General James Ewell Brown Stuart, to go and find out. With 1200 troopers Stuart on June 12 rode off on what quickly became one of the most spectacular missions of the war.

Stuart was storybook romance incarnate. He had a compulsive desire for the limelight and just the right combination of daring and military skill to get it, and along with his theatrical qualities he was a hard worker and an unusually competent cavalry commander. He rode far to the north, crossed the headwaters of the Chickahominy and swung east, went slicing down behind the Federal right flank, crossed the railroad near the great base at White House, and wound up by riding entirely around McClellan's army, recrossing the Chickahominy far downstream and returning to the Confederate lines on June 15 after days and nights of gaudy adventure. The ride made him famous, and was most embarrassing to McClellan—if a Confederate cavalry brigade could ride all the way around the army without even getting into a serious fight there must be something wrong with the Federal security arrangements—but the important thing was that Stuart gave Lee exactly the information Lee needed.[4]

The Federal right flank consisted of Fitz John Porter's corps, recently enlarged by the arrival of a good division of Pennsylvania infantry under Brigadier General George A. McCall, just brought down from McDowell's corps. Porter had McCall posted behind Beaver Dam Creek, facing Mechanicsville, six or seven miles northeast of Richmond, with the rest of the corps drawn up behind it. There were detachments of cavalry roving out toward the right and rear, but there was nothing solid either to guard Porter's flank or to protect the railway line. The right of the Army of the Potomac, in other words, was in the air, and the army's connection with its source of supplies could be snipped with one stroke . . . just the spot for Stonewall Jackson.

Now it was necessary to do two things: strengthen Jackson, and befuddle the Yankees. Lee found a way to gain both ends at once. He sent reinforcements to Jackson—an infantry division under Brigadier General William H. C. Whiting, which included a brigade consisting largely of Texas troops led by a bearded young giant named John B. Hood; a brigade which would soon be one of the world's most famous combat outfits—and he did it ostentatiously so that the news would be certain to reach McClellan. (It did reach him, and was passed on to Washington, where it caused a certain perplexity; leading Mr. Lincoln, at last, to remark that if 10,000 Confederates had left Richmond to join Jackson that was as good as a reinforcement of 10,000 for McClellan, and how about getting on with the offensive?[5]) And then, as he drew up the schedule for Jackson's descent on Porter's right and rear, Lee showed one of the qualities that made him such a deadly opponent—the readiness to risk everything in order to make a blow decisive.

McClellan had an effective force of approximately 105,000 men, of whom some 30,000 were with Porter, north of the Chickahominy, while all the rest were south of the river facing Lee's new fieldworks. When Jackson and Whiting joined him, Lee would have between 80,000 and 85,000. He proposed now to use no more than 25,000 of these to hold the Richmond lines—25,000 against approximately three times their number—while he struck McClellan's exposed right with all the rest. It was a battle plan which, if things went badly, could lose everything, for if McClellan caught on he could smash that thinly held trench line and go straight into Richmond; but it was also a plan which could win everything if it worked properly, because it contemplated nothing less than McClellan's total destruction. Lee was not merely trying to make his enemy retreat; he wanted to annihilate him, cutting him off from his base, driving him into the muddy pocket between the Chickahominy and White Oak Swamp and beating him to death before the Federal commander had a chance to figure out what was going on. It might accomplish much less than that, to be sure, and much less would be acceptable, but basically it was a shot at winning the war in one stroke, taken with a cool understanding of the fact that what could be won at one stroke might also be lost the same way.

Even Mr. Davis, who had the stoical self-control of an Iroquois Indian, felt the strain, and he wrote to Mrs. Davis that "the stake is too high to permit the pulse to keep its even beat." He took comfort in the thought that a total defeat of McClellan would solve the Confederacy's problems in the east, "and then we must make a desperate effort to regain what Beauregard has abandoned in the West." He would have had a certain grim amusement, perhaps, if he had known that a garbled version of Beauregard's departure from Tupelo had reached McClellan's desk in the form of a report that Beauregard and part of his army had just reached Richmond to help Lee in its defense.[6]

. . . Washington was a little harder to fool than it used to be. On the day Jackson turned back Frémont's assault at Cross Keys, Mr. Lincoln told Stanton that Richmond after all was the focal point, that Confederate activities elsewhere in the east were nothing more than attempts to divert attention, and that hereafter it would be wise to stand on the defensive in the valley; Frémont and Banks could hold that area, and McDowell, once he got his command reassembled, should be sent down to McClellan. A week later the President wrote to Frémont that "Jackson's game—his assigned work—now is to magnify the accounts of his numbers and reports of his movements, and thus by constant alarms keep three or four times as many of our troops away from Richmond as his own force amounts to. . . . Our game is not to allow this."[7] In the end, McDowell never did get down to join McClellan, yet by the time Lee opened his offensive McClellan had received, in reinforcements, rather more than the equivalent of what he had lost when McDowell's corps was taken from him early in April. He had been sent Franklin's and McCall's divisions (both originally of McDowell's corps) and the 11,500 men at Fort Monroe had recently been put under his command; in addition to which, seven regiments from Baltimore had been ordered to join him. Altogether, more than 35,000 men had gone to the Army of the Potomac since the day McClellan was informed that McDowell was no longer part of his command.[8]

McClellan was an emotional sort, 'way up one day and far down the next, but during the first few weeks of June he was rather consistently optimistic. A week after the fight at Seven Pines he notified Washington that he would be ready to advance and take Richmond as soon as McCall's division came down and the roads got dry enough to move the guns. Three days later, after reporting that Beauregard was said to be in Richmond, McClellan said that he would attack "as soon as the weather and ground will permit." McCall arrived on June 12, and on June 14 McClellan wired that the weather was "very favorable." The country remained most difficult, and it was necessary to perfect the defensive works because of the Federal inferiority in numbers, but the general remained hopeful, and he found time to say that he would like to have permission to lay before the President, by letter or by telegraph, his views "as to the present state of military affairs throughout the whole country."[9] Whatever those views might be, his opinion of his own situation seemed clear: he was just about ready to advance.

South of the Chickahominy his line was compact, running from White Oak Swamp to the Chickahominy in a big crescent whose convex side was toward the enemy. Keyes's corps held the left, by the swamp, with Heintzelman and Sumner next; at the right, Franklin was posted in a strong position on the Golding farm overlooking the river. On June 19, McClellan told Mr. Lincoln that his army was well over the river except for "the very considerable force necessary to protect our flanks and communications," and said that his picket lines were within six miles of Richmond. The Rebels were alert, ready for a fight at every point; a general engagement might take place at any hour, and a Federal advance would involve "a battle more or less decisive." The fact that the Confederates had sent upwards of 10,000 men to reinforce Jackson simply showed how strong and confident they were. Still, the Army of the Potomac was ready: "After tomorrow we shall fight the Rebel army as soon as Providence will permit. We shall await only a favorable condition of the earth and sky and the completion of some necessary preliminaries."[10]

Along the front south of the Chickahominy the Federal line was a mile or more from the Confederate trenches—out of sight, most of the way, with a good deal of timber in between the opposing lines. Each army had skirmishers and pickets in this no-man's land, and there was much sniping and sharpshooting—a wearisome, monotonous warfare, broken now and then by moments of fraternization between rival infantrymen. Like the Confederates, the Federals found this country hot and sickly. Typhoid fever was prevalent, scurvy had begun to appear in some units, good drinking water was hard to find, and McCall's soldiers found the arrival at White House depressing. A number of undertakers had set up shop there—business was good, and it was certain to be a good deal better very soon—and their signs on the wharves were the first things the soldiers saw when they disembarked; "Undertakers & Embalmers of the Dead—Particular Attention paid to Deceased Soldiers."[11]

On June 25, McClellan finally began his advance; a modest forward movement of Heintzelman's skirmish line, with elements from Sumner's and Keyes's corps coming in on each flank, the object apparently being to clear the way for a more powerful advance a day or two later by Franklin's corps in the direction of Old Tavern, a crossroads a mile or so west of Golding's farm. McClellan spoke of it as a preparatory move, and because of the prodigious fighting which took place during the week that followed it this affair has been more or less forgotten; it cost the Army of the Potomac some five hundred casualties, and it showed how this powerful host could inch forward in its quest for positions from which the great siege guns could operate.[12] If General Lee proposed to make McClellan play a different game the time was getting short.

Although General McClellan spoke of this advance with confident satisfaction he had reason to be somewhat uneasy.

In the first place, Stuart's ride had shown McClellan exactly what it showed Lee—that the Federal supply line, running back along the Richmond & York River Railroad to White House on the Pamunkey, was highly vulnerable—and McClellan had been giving thought to a possible change of base. The James River was perfectly safe, and a base at Harrison's Landing, fifteen miles south of McClellan's present position, would have been secure. Basing the army on the James had in fact been under consideration ever since the occupation of Yorktown, but during the leisurely pursuit of Johnston the Federal supply line had been anchored on the Pamunkey and the arrangements made then had never been changed. Now, however, it was necessary to prepare for an emergency, and McClellan ordered a temporary depot set up at Harrison's Landing; if the Confederates did break the line to the Pamunkey, Harrison's Landing could quickly be made the new base.

However, there was an immense catch to this. To transfer the base to the James would be to ruin the whole campaign, because if the army's supply line went by dirt road to Harrison's Landing, McClellan would never be able to use his big guns. Once he let go of the Richmond & York River Railroad it would be impossible for him to conduct siege operations. He could fight the kind of fight he wanted to fight—the kind at which the Confederates could not beat him—only if he operated from the Pamunkey.

This was so, simply because the most powerful weapons in his siege train could not be moved any appreciable distance except by rail or water.

McClellan's siege train at this time consisted of 101 pieces of ordnance.

Slightly more than half of these were weapons which, although they were too cumbersome to be used as ordinary field artillery, could nevertheless move slowly by road provided the roads were reasonably solid. These were the four-and-one-half-inch Rodman rifles, the 30-pounder Parrotts, the rifled Whitworths from England, and a few eight-inch howitzers and eight-inch mortars. They were good weapons and Lee had little to match them, but they were not the guns that made McClellan's siege train genuinely awesome.

The real rock-crushers, the huge weapons which could pulverize any defensive works they could reach—the equalizers, in short—were irresistible but hard to move. There were forty-eight of them: eleven 100-pounder Parrotts, two 200-pounder Parrotts, ten 13-inch sea-coast mortars and twenty-five 10-inch mortars. These could be transported by barge or they could be transported by rail, but they could not be transported any distance by road. (Lee had remarked, as early as June 4, in a discussion of McClellan's base at White House: "I think the only way the enemy can get his heavy guns up that way is by the railroad.") To move them at all, from wharf or from railroad siding, involved building special ramps and using derricks, sling carts, rollers and a prodigious amount of pully-hauly business; the lightest of them weighed four and one half tons and the biggest weighed twice that much. McClellan had been able to use some of them at Yorktown because of a convenient creek, deep enough to carry barges, and he would be able to use them in front of Richmond—once he had gained ground for suitable emplacements—because of the railroad; but at Harrison's Landing there were neither creeks nor railroads. To send this heavy ordnance to Harrison's Landing would be about as bad as sending it back to Washington.[13]

Thus McClellan had excellent reason for being sensitive about any threat to the railroad line which ran back to the Pamunkey; and to increase his unease he got news, on June 24—the day before he made his preparatory advance south of the Chickahominy—that Stonewall Jackson was coming his way. A Confederate deserter, picked up by Federal cavalry, asserted that Jackson's troops were moving to Frederick's Hall, on the Virginia Central Railroad, and would come on from there to attack the Yankee flank north of the river. McClellan passed this on to Stanton, asking if the War Department had any news regarding Jackson. Stanton could only tell him that all sorts of rumors, some of them obviously planted, were in circulation; the deserter's story might also be a plant, he said, but at the same time it would not be safe to disregard it entirely. It may be that McClellan considered the story unreliable; at any rate he went ahead with the movement the next day, and after the firing had stopped on June 25 he sent Stanton a confident telegram saying "we have gained our point fully and with but little loss" and adding that the whole front was quiet.[14]

The confident mood quickly died. At 6:15 that evening McClellan sent the Secretary another telegram in which he foresaw the worst. He was convinced, he said, that Jackson was about to attack his flank, that Beauregard had checked in with reinforcements and that the enemy's force was at least 200,000 men, and he went on in strange vein:

"I shall have to contend against vastly superior odds if these reports be true; but this army will do all in the power of men to hold their position and repulse any attack. I regret my great inferiority in numbers, but feel that I am in no way responsible for it, as I have not failed to represent repeatedly the necessity of reinforcements; that this was the decisive point, and that all the available means of the Government should be concentrated here. I will do all that a general can do with the splendid army I have the honor to command, and if it is destroyed by overwhelming numbers, can at least die with it and share its fate. But if the result of the action, which will probably occur tomorrow, or within a short time, is disaster, the responsibility cannot be thrown on my shoulders; it must rest where it belongs.

"Since I commenced this I have received additional intelligence confirming the supposition in regard to Jackson's movements and Beauregard's arrival. I shall probably be attacked tomorrow, and now go to the other side of the Chickahominy" (his headquarters were on the Trent farm, south of the river) "to arrange for the defense on that side. I feel that there is no use in again asking for reinforcements."[15]

But this hour of gloom also passed, and at 10:40 that night McClellan wrote the Secretary still another dispatch, from Fitz John Porter's headquarters:

"The information I received on this side tends to confirm impressions that Jackson will soon attack our right and rear. Every possible precaution is being taken. If I had another good division I could laugh at Jackson. The task is difficult, but this army will do its best, and will never disgrace the country. Nothing but overwhelming forces can defeat us. Indications are of attack on our front tomorrow. Have made all possible arrangements."[16]

5: *Seven Days*

Ever after, men spoke of the last week in June simply as The Seven Days; aptly enough, because during those days a pattern emerged from chaos, much after the manner described in the Book of Genesis. They were days of bitter fighting among wooded hills and ravines, of confused flight and pursuit past broken bridges in impassable swamps, with a final climax on a blazing slope where the great ranks of guns proved stronger than the great ranks of men who tried to take the guns by storm; one battle, seven days long and infinitely deep, changing the war and compelling the nation in the end to find new definitions for itself. The hope that the war could be something less than a revolutionary struggle died somewhere between Mechanicsville and Malvern Hill. And so, for the matter of that, did thousands of young men.

General Lee's battle plan was admirable, but there was a good deal of slippage when it was put into effect. Many things went wrong, and the Confederacy might have come to disaster except that all of its mistakes were balanced by the mistakes of its enemies. If, at last, Lee won less than he had hoped to win, he nevertheless won much more than had seemed possible three weeks earlier, and his victory kept the war alive for more than two and one half years. It was a dazzling achievement, even though it did not always go according to the script.

The left of Lee's line was held by an impetuous, hard-fighting officer who would become one of the Confederacy's most famous combat soldiers, a bearded young major general named Ambrose

Powell Hill, who commanded an oversized division of six brigades massed south of the Chickahominy to the north of Richmond. Next to Hill on the east, drawn up by the turnpike that ran to Mechanicsville, the modest village on the far side of the river where Porter's patrols guarded the Federal right flank, were two more large divisions also led by men who would win much fame in combat—James Longstreet, dogged, unbreakable, and opinionated, and D. H. Hill, sharp-tongued, dyspeptic (as used in the 1860s, the word apparently meant that he was plagued by ulcers), and distinguished, in an army where personal valor was commonplace, by his extreme bravery under fire.

Stonewall Jackson, with three divisions—his own, Ewell's, and Whiting's—was coming down from the valley by way of Gordonsville. The plan called for him to move southeast several miles north of the Chickahominy, following a route which would put him squarely behind Porter's corps. He was due to reach the scene on June 26. As soon as his outriders made contact with A. P. Hill's pickets, Hill would move to the north side of the Chickahominy at the Meadow Bridge, a mile or so above the place where the Mechanicsville turnpike crossed, would drive the Federals out of Mechanicsville, and move on to menace Porter's main line, which was solidly established, facing west, behind Beaver Dam Creek. Once Hill had cleared Mechanicsville, Longstreet and D. H. Hill would cross and form in his rear. The Federal position on the creek was exceedingly strong, but it would hardly need to be attacked frontally because Jackson's powerful force would be cutting in behind it, and Porter would be obliged to retreat to escape destruction. Then the entire force—Jackson, the Hills, and Longstreet, upwards of 55,000 men altogether—would sweep down the north bank of the river, breaking the railroad line once and for all, cutting McClellan off from his base and compelling him to pull his army together south of the Chickahominy with an aggressive foe in his immediate rear.[1]

This plan, to repeat, was risky, since if McClellan once bestirred himself he could smash his way into Richmond, letting his rear take care of itself. But it would be altogether out of character for McClellan to do anything of the kind, and one of Lee's strong points was his ability to assess the spiritual limitations of the men who fought against him. Besides, Lee felt certain that his Major General John B. Magruder could once again make McClellan believe in perils which did not exist.

Magruder would be responsible for the defense of Richmond while Lee was making his attack north of the river, and although he would soon reveal grave shortcomings as a field commander he had undeniable talents in the dramatic arts; in the Old Army he had been an enthusiastic dabbler in amateur theatricals, and he at least knew how to create an illusion. Magruder now was told to move his men about, making a big noise and a great to-do, causing his outnumbered battalions to look both aggressive and numerous, acting as if he were about to unleash a terrible offensive all along the line—and, if none of this worked, to hold the line with the bayonet, dying hard and slowly until either Lee or the end of everything came to him. Magruder had done this earlier with vast success. During the first few days at Yorktown he had sprinkled 5000 men along a 13-mile front, making McClellan believe that the position was much too strong for anything but the famous siege train; the whole operation leading Joe Johnston, when he reached the scene, to report that "no one but McClellan could have hesitated to attack."[2] What Magruder had done once he could doubtless do again. Lee was betting the Confederacy's life on it.

In the end Magruder played his role to perfection. The actor who put on such a poor performance that the entire production almost failed was, of all people, Stonewall Jackson himself.

Famous for the speed of his marches, Jackson here came in late. He was supposed to arrive opposite A. P. Hill on the morning of June 26; at 3 P.M. on that day neither Jackson nor any tidings of him had arrived, and the hot-blooded Hill went ahead without him: crossed the river, marched east through Mechanicsville, drew up his men in a broad battle line facing the Federal position behind Beaver Dam Creek, and without further ado opened his attack.

When Hill did this the entire operation was put in motion, irreversibly. Longstreet and D. H. Hill dutifully crossed the river in his wake, and Lee went with them, supposing that he would at once come in touch with Jackson, whose moving column ought to be just beyond A. P. Hill's left flank. Lee quickly discovered that no one had seen anything of Jackson; he was presumably on the way, but when he would show up was anyone's guess. Hill had made his move strictly on his own hook, and now Lee had two thirds of his army north of the Chickahominy and there was nothing in the world to do but go on with the assault even though it was exactly the sort of operation Lee had planned to avoid—a straight frontal attack on a position which was altogether too strong to be carried that way. Regardless of what had happened to Jackson, the offensive must be pressed hard; the thing that could not be forgotten for a moment was that McClellan right now was closer to Richmond than Lee was. If the Federal General were allowed to look up, even for a moment, he might see it.[3]

The Federal position was immensely strong, and Hill's men never had a chance. The attack was rebuffed with heavy loss—Hill's division sustained between 1300 and 1500 casualties, inflicting fewer than 400 on the enemy—and McClellan was elated. During the morning, when scouts confirmed the rumors that Jackson was approaching, he had sent Stanton an anxious wire: "There is no doubt in my mind now that Jackson is coming upon us, and with such great odds against us we shall have our hands full. No time should be lost if I am to have any more reinforcements." During the evening, while the fight was still going on, he telegraphed that "my men are behaving superbly, but you must not expect them to contest too long against great odds," but by nine o'clock at night he was full of confidence, reporting: "Victory of today complete and against great odds. I almost begin to think we are invincible."[4]

They might be invincible, but they were going to have to move. Jackson had finally arrived, and although he was twelve hours late he was at last precisely where Lee wanted him to be, massed just north of Porter's right flank. Porter's lines could never be carried by direct assault, but they would collapse as soon as Jackson advanced, which he was certain to do when daylight came. McClellan thus made up his mind to do two things—bring Porter back to a position where he could make an all-out defense of the supply line to the Pamunkey, and at the same time make preparations for a change of base to the James River in case Porter should be overwhelmed. At daylight, accordingly, Porter retreated, going back three miles or more, past Dr. Gaines's Mill to a long crescent of high ground behind a meandering watercourse called Boatswain's Swamp. The ground had been well chosen; the left flank was firmly anchored on the Chickahominy, there was a jungle of second-growth timber, brambly fields and intricate gullies to delay attacking troops, and along the crest there was abundant room for Federal infantry and artillery. While the infantry was countermarching, Porter's wagon train began its laborious movement toward the south side of the Chickahominy, while Major Elisha S. Kellogg of the 1st Connecticut Heavy Artillery moved ten of his big guns to the Golding farm, where they could fire on either bank of the river.[5]

These guns were the light heavyweights—five of the four-and-one-half-inch Rodmans and five 30-pounder Parrotts. They had long range and good hitting power and they would be most useful; but the forty-eight blockbusters were still aboard ship at White House, and unless Porter could hold his position they would stay aboard ship until a new campaign was launched. If the White House base had to be given up they could be carried around to the James easily enough, but it would be next to impossible to place them where they could be used in any attack on Richmond. No matter how it might be rationalized, a change of base would be a defeat—unless McClellan solved all of his problems by breaking Magruder's line and marching in to Richmond.

. . . Which is much easier to say, of course, than it could have been to do; the hardest part of all, perhaps, being to understand (in the midst of battle smoke, conflicting reports and universal confusion) even that the thing *might* be done. Staying at headquarters on the south side of the river, McClellan saw the battle through the eyes of his generals, accepting the distorted vision they gave him, not realizing that it was doubly distorted because most of them did not really know what they were looking at; and presently it seemed to him that he was being assailed, furiously and with overwhelming numbers, on both sides of the river at once. Magruder was putting on a show, as instructed, and he had his audience enthralled all the way. He staged mock charges, had artillery and infantry open sudden bursts of fire, shuttled men in and out of sight with a great deal of cheering and stentorian shouts of command—and, all in all, simulated a terrible fight which failed of realism only in that hardly anyone got hurt. All along the line, McClellan's subordinates assured him that they were hard pressed and could not spare a man.

North of the Chickahominy there was no fooling. After a long delay—it took time to get the real assault columns formed, and once again Jackson was strangely tardy in reaching his position—Lee struck Porter's lines on June 27 with everything he had, and by mid-afternoon an enormous battle was rolling and rocking up and down the tangled slopes and marshes of Boatswain's Swamp. There was deadly twilight in the ravines, where the trapped rifle smoke eddied in the hollows like heavy fog, and the Confederates who fought here recalled a half-blind advance through an unending din, and when they tried to tell about it they could speak only of isolated bits of action that had no particular sequence or meaning . . . riderless horses galloping off to nowhere, stretcher bearers stumbling in and out of vision, a long rank of cannon stabbing the darkness with bright jets of flame "fifteen feet long and large around as a barrel," officers waving swords and trying in vain to make their orders heard, a lone battalion running up hill, its colonel riding in front with the regimental colors, the men all cheering and waving their hats; and all the time, without ever a break or a pause, the crashing tumult of sound which at least one veteran, long afterward, called the most terrible noise he heard in the war except possibly for Spotsylvania Court House. In the rear, regimental surgeons met the ambulances and tried in vain to keep up with their duties. (One Confederate doctor said that the stretcher cases unloaded at his station filled a two-acre lot in no time; he and his fellows operated all night, and in the morning found many wounded men still awaiting attention.) Trying to sum it all up, a Southern gunner wrote to his wife: "Satan was holding his orgies on earth & death supped fat on the feast"—which, after all, may have been as good a way as any to describe it.[6]

Some fantastic freak of acoustics kept most of the racket from being heard at McClellan's headquarters, where for a time it was supposed that nothing more than an artillery duel was going on. (A mile or two downstream Professor Lowe had a balloon in operation. An officer from McClellan's staff went up in it and saw what was really happening, and when he came down he got his horse and went to McClellan all in a gallop to report; late in the day McClellan sent Henry Slocum's division from Franklin's corps and two of Sumner's brigades across the river to help.)[7]

Lee had trouble getting his attack co-ordinated. For a time A. P. Hill's division fought unaided, and it was badly mangled. Some of Jackson's units went astray on the winding country roads, so that Hood's brigade at last went into action with Longstreet's division, some distance to the right of Jackson's proper front. Not until dusk did all the gray divisions north of the river go forward together, but when they did they were irresistible and Porter's line finally collapsed. Twenty-two Federal guns and 2800 Federal soldiers were captured, and as darkness came Porter's broken divisions fled across the bridges to the south bank, with Slocum's men acting as rear guard. As the roar of battle died away an insistent crying filled the air; thousands of wounded men were calling for help, and all about there were unwounded Confederates trying to get their fragmented battalions together, chanting regimental numbers endlessly so that stragglers could know where their comrades were: "First South Carolina! Thirteenth Georgia! Fourth Alabama!" The darkness was flecked with shifting lights as stretcher bearers with lanterns probed the splintered underbrush.[8]

All through the battle, McClellan had done his best to keep the War Department advised. During the morning he wired that the whole army was "so concentrated that it can take advantage of the first mistake of the enemy," adding: "Success of yesterday complete." At noon he wrote that the Confederates were making a heavy attack north of the river, and that an attack was also anticipated on the south side, and an hour later he reported that things were going well but that the worst was yet to come: "If I am forced to concentrate between the Chickahominy and the James I will at once endeavor to open communication with you. . . . Goodbye, and present my respects to the President."

At 4:30 in the afternoon he sent an odd message across the river to the embattled Porter: "Send word to all your troops that their general thanks them for their heroism, and say to them that he is now sure that nothing can resist them . . . I look upon today as decisive of the war. Try to drive the rascals and take some prisoners and guns. What more assistance do you require?" Half an hour later he assured Porter that he was ordering up more troops, and instead of urging him to drive the rascals he warned: "You must hold your own until dark." Dark came, and defeat for Porter came with it, and at eight in the evening McClellan telegraphed Stanton that there had been a terrible battle. He specified: "Attacked by greatly superior numbers in all directions on this side; we still hold our own, though a very heavy fire is kept up on the left bank of the Chickahominy. The odds have been immense. We hold our own very nearly. I may be forced to give up my position during the night, but will not if it is possible to avoid it. Had I 20,000 fresh and good troops we would be sure of a splendid victory tomorrow."[9]

To avoid possible confusion, it should be remarked that "this side," which superior numbers had been attacking in all directions, was the south side of the Chickahominy, where nothing at all had been happening except General Magruder's game of bluff; and "the left bank," where the dogged Rebels still kept up a heavy fire, was the north side, where McClellan's whole campaign had just gone to ruin. When the wire was written there were three times the needed "20,000 fresh and good troops," lying ready to hand below the river. Nobody was giving them anything to do, and the vision of splendid victory flickered and died.

McClellan called in his corps commanders that night and issued his orders for a retreat to the James. His staff was busy, and the detailed schedules by which the ponderous army and its long wagon trains would move through the bottleneck between the Chickahominy and White Oak Swamp toward Harrison's Landing were carefully drawn; when the conference ended, the different commanders hurried off to put these orders into effect. McClellan sent a dispatch to

Flag Officer Goldsborough, the Navy's ranking officer in Virginia waters: "We have met a severe repulse today, having been attacked by greatly superior numbers, and I am obliged to fall back between the Chickahominy and the James River. I look to you to give me all the support you can in covering my flank as well as in giving protection to my supplies afloat in the James River."[10] Then, a little after midnight, he got off one more message to Stanton: possibly the most remarkable of all the dispatches he ever wrote.

". . . I have lost this battle because my force was too small. I again repeat that I am not responsible for this, and I say it with the earnestness of a general who feels in his heart the loss of every brave man who has been needlessly sacrificed today. I still hope to retrieve our fortunes, but to do this the Government must view the matter in the same earnest light that I do. You must send me very large reenforcements, and send them at once. I shall draw back to this side of the Chickahominy, and I think I can withdraw all our material." He returned to his earlier thesis: if he had 10,000 fresh men he could win a victory within twenty-four hours, and a few thousand more would have made the battle which had just been lost a victory instead of a defeat. Then came the peroration:

"As it is, the Government must not and cannot hold me responsible for the result. I feel too earnestly tonight. I have seen too many dead and wounded comrades to feel otherwise than that the Government has not sustained this army. If you do not do so now the game is lost. If I save this army now, I tell you plainly that I owe no thanks to you or to any other persons in Washington. You have done your best to sacrifice this army."[11]

The Seven Days Battle would go on for four more days, but its outcome was signed, sealed, and delivered when that dispatch was composed. Whatever might be true of the Army of the Potomac, its commanding general had been whipped into something close to hysteria. His gaze was fastened with such feverish intensity on the shortcomings of his superiors and on his own innocence that it was not possible for him to see the opportunity which Lee's daring maneuver had opened to him. The man who wrote that dispatch had given up the effort to win and was preparing for the post-mortem.

Ordinarily, a field commander who accuses the Secretary of War, to his face, of trying to destroy the country's most important army can expect nothing less than instant dismissal, and McClellan knew this as well as anyone. He told his wife, not long afterward: "Of course they will never forgive me for that. I knew it when I wrote it, but as I thought it possible that it might be the last I ever wrote it seemed better to have it exactly true. The President, of course, has not replied to my letter and never will. His reply may be, however, to avail himself of the first opportunity to cut my head off." What McClellan did not know, however, was that his dispatch was expurgated before it reached the President and the Secretary. Custodian of military telegrams at the War Department was Major A. E. H. Johnson, and when he read this wire he sent for his superior, Colonel Edward S. Sanford. Properly horrified, Sanford simply lopped off the last two sentences before sending the dispatch on to Mr. Stanton, and that choleric official never saw the final, furious accusation until some time after McClellan had been removed from command.[12] Unaware of this, McClellan naturally assumed that the Secretary of War either felt too guilty or lacked the courage to discipline him: an assumption which could only confirm the low opinion of Mr. Stanton which he already had.

In point of fact Mr. Lincoln did reply, on June 28. He told McClellan: "Save your Army at all events. Will send re-enforcements as fast as we can. Of course they cannot reach you today, or tomorrow, or next day." Then he and Mr. Stanton set about it to get those reinforcements. General Burnside, at New Berne, North Carolina, was told to send north all the men he could spare and to come with them himself. To Halleck, at Corinth, went a peremptory wire from Stanton telling him to send 25,000 men "by the nearest and quickest route by way of Baltimore and Washington to Richmond"; this was made necessary, the Secretary explained, "by a serious reverse suffered by General McClellan before Richmond yesterday, the full extent of which is not yet known." On the same day Lincoln notified Major General John A. Dix at Fort Monroe that they had lost touch with the Army of the Potomac, and ordered Dix to do everything possible to open communication with General McClellan and tell the War Department how things were going.[13]

Then, strangely, the President and the Secretary grew hopeful. They had heard no more from McClellan, but they had been looking at the map, rereading McClellan's original battle plan, and reflecting on the strategic possibilities, and they apparently concluded that everything that had happened so far was more or less incidental to McClellan's promised assault on Richmond. On June 29, Mr. Lincoln told Secretary Seward, "I think we have had the better of it," and Stanton agreed, adding the bright prediction that McClellan "will probably be in Richmond within two days." On the following day Mr. Lincoln said that as far as he could see things were going according to plan and that lack of news was the chief reason for worry, although he did remark that McClellan "had a severe engagement in getting the part of his army on this side of the Chickahominy over to the other side." Stanton notified General Wool at Baltimore that McClellan at last had his entire army across the Chickahominy, asserting: "The position is favorable and looks more like taking Richmond than any time before." When General Halleck reported that he would send the 25,000 men he had been told to send but that this would mean giving up his projected advance on Chattanooga, both the President and the Secretary told him to send nobody: to get into East Tennessee and possess the railroad line to Virginia was as important as taking Richmond itself. Obviously the intense anxiety created by McClellan's midnight telegram after the battle of Gaines's Mill had died down.[14]

It returned quickly enough. At 7 P.M. on June 30, McClellan got a telegram through to Stanton. He had reached the James and had boarded a gunboat, and his words made it clear that no attack on Richmond was anywhere in sight:

"Another day of desperate fighting. We are hard pressed by superior numbers. I fear I shall be forced to abandon my material to save my men under cover of the gunboats. You must send us very large re-enforcements by way of Fort Monroe, and they must come very promptly. My army has behaved superbly, and have done all that men can do. If none of us escape, we shall at least have done honor to the country. I shall do my best to save the army. Send more gunboats."[15]

The army was safe. General Lee, winning an improbable victory that was changing the current of the war, was in fact feeling somewhat frustrated. He was a perfectionist; he had had a chance to destroy McClellan's army and the chance had eluded him—chiefly, when all is said and done, because the military machine he was operating was still too new and too imperfectly fitted together to function smoothly. It could fight like all the furies, but it could not shift its weight quickly; its footwork was poor and its muscular co-ordination was defective, and so an enemy that might have been killed got away alive—bloodied, badly beaten, but nevertheless alive and capable of full revival.

On June 28, the day after the Gaines's Mill fight, McClellan got his army started on the march to Harrison's Landing, abandoning the base at White House, sending the transports off, destroying an immense quantity of supplies that could not be moved—a staff officer mentioned the loss of millions of rations and hundreds of tons of ammunition—and breaking the bridges that crossed the Chickahominy.[16] Temporarily, Lee lost contact with him, except for an unsuccessful assault made by some of Magruder's men on the Golding farm position, and for a time it was not clear whether McClellan was going to try to regain his lost base at White House, march down the Chickahominy to the lower peninsula, or move directly to the James. Altogether, the Army of the Potomac got a twenty-four-hour head start, and it was just enough. Lee's army was never able to make up for the lost time, and the great battle of annihilation did not take place.

Not quite . . . the opportunity was there. McClellan's army had to go along a narrow roadway, and the column was very long, encumbered by a wagon train and a shambling herd of 2500 beef cattle, unable either to retreat with speed or to turn and fight with all its strength. Theoretically, it was possible for part of Lee's army to circle around south of the Chickahominy and smite the head of this column while another part struck the flank and the remainder assailed the rear, and this is what Lee tried to do. If all had gone as he hoped, the Army of the Potomac would have ceased to exist. But nothing went quite right for him. Magruder proved an inexpert tactician, Huger moved much too slowly, and Jackson, most inexplicably, missed a crucial assignment. Although it had to fight on June 29 at Savage Station and on June 30 at Glendale—the latter engagement was as vicious a battle as either army ever fought, but Lee could not get more than two of his six divisions into action—the Army of the Potomac could not be brought to a stand. By July 1 the head of the column had reached Harrison's Landing and the protecting gunboats, and McClellan had Porter plant abundant infantry and an overpowering array of guns on high ground at Malvern Hill, overlooking the James, to indicate that the army was ready for one more fight.

One more fight it immediately got. The position at Malvern Hill was really far too strong to attack with any hope of success, but the Federals had been getting whipped and retreating day after day and if Lee suspected that one more battle would finish them it is easy to see why he felt that way. Besides, this would be the last chance to strike a blow, and Lee was a fighter; and that afternoon and evening saw one of the most tragic and hopeless attacks of the war, with Magruder's and D. H. Hill's divisions and elements from other commands trying heroically to do the impossible. Up the long slope they went, brigade after brigade, and the Federal guns knocked their lines all apart and covered the hillside with broken bodies; this was one of the few battles in the Civil War in which most of the casualties were inflicted by artillery. At Gaines's Mill an afternoon of failure had been followed by an almost miraculous moment when everything suddenly worked, and a victory had been gained, with the triumphant Rebel yell tingling across the twilight. That did not happen at Malvern Hill. Night came, the killing ended and the Federals were unshaken; and as the crash of the guns stopped the dusk throbbed with the pathetic cries of thousands of wounded men who wanted somebody to come out and help them.[17]

Victorious at last, but nevertheless beaten, the Army of the Potomac withdrew during the night and made its camp at the new base of Harrison's Landing, with warships in the river to stand guard.

CHAPTER FIVE: *Turning Point*

6: *Letter from Harrison's Landing*

A newspaper correspondent who reached Harrison's Landing on July 2 wrote that the Army of the Potomac seemed to be "more dead than alive." The soldiers who had been fighting and marching in the swamps for a week were unutterably dirty, plastered with mud from head to foot, and hundreds of them stood knee-deep in the James trying to scrape the clay off of their uniforms with sticks. At least one field hospital was so jammed that an army surgeon was unable to get inside and go to work, and the correspondent remembered seeing a wounded officer, his face streaked with blood and mud, wandering about offering five dollars to anyone who would give him something to eat and getting no takers. Yet when one talked to the soldiers they seemed to be in good spirits, all things considered, and most of them said they were ready to "go at them again" as soon as reinforcements arrived. They were not entirely sure what had happened, and one enlisted man doubtless spoke for many when he admitted that he did not know whether "we have made an inglorious skedaddle or a brilliant retreat," but at least the marching and fighting had ended and there was a chance for tired soldiers to get a little rest. McClellan wrote to his wife: "I have still very great confidence in them, and they in me. The dear fellows cheer me as of old."[1]

No one in Richmond had the least doubt what had happened: the Confederacy had won a mighty victory. General Lee wrote soberly that "under ordinary circumstances the Federal Army should have been destroyed," but he remarked that "regret that more was not accomplished gives way to gratitude to the Sovereign Ruler of the Universe for the results achieved," and he spelled these results out with unemotional accuracy: the siege of Richmond had been raised, the whole Federal campaign had been completely frustrated, thousands of prisoners had been taken, fifty-two pieces of artillery and more than 35,000 stands of small arms had been captured, and stores and supplies of great value had been taken although these were "but small in comparison with those destroyed by the enemy." Secretary Mallory assured his wife that the Seven Days made up "a series of the grandest Battles that was ever fought on the American continent," and exulted that "the Great McClelland the young Napoleon now like a whipped cur lies on the banks of the James River crouched under his Gun Boats."[2]

The cost of this achievement had been high. Lee's army had lost 3286 men killed and 15,090 wounded, with somewhere between 900 and 1000 men recorded as missing, for a total casualty list of slightly more than 20,000: very close to one fourth of all of the men Lee had in his command when the Seven Days began. (Federal losses had been smaller: 1734 killed and 8062 wounded, with the dismaying number of 6053 missing in action. Most of the "missing" had been taken prisoner, as had a great many of the wounded men.) Over the long pull, the Confederacy could not afford such casualties; there was a grim hint here that the aggressive strategy which had saved Richmond might be altogether too expensive for regular use.[3] From afar, Beauregard wrote that Lee's feat in concentrating forces against McClellan's exposed right was "a master-stroke of policy," although he considered that if McClellan had not "lost his presence of mind" he might well have broken through Magruder's carefully staged defenses and taken Richmond.[4]

McClellan was sorting out his own impressions. He was justly proud of the fighting his troops had done and he assured the President that once the men had had a little rest they would be as spirited and as vigorous as ever; his immediate plan was to make the camp on the James perfectly secure, but he believed that if he had more men he might make a new campaign. Early on July 1, before the fighting began at Malvern Hill, he telegraphed Adjutant General Lorenzo Thomas that if the government planned to reinforce him at all it should do so at once, and liberally: "I need 50,000 more men, and with them I will retrieve our fortunes. More would be well, but that number sent me at once will, I think, enable me to assume the offensive." Even a few thousand fresh men, if they came quickly, "will do much toward relieving and encouraging this wearied army." On July 2, after Mr. Lincoln and Secretary Stanton told him that moderate reinforcements were on the way, McClellan reported that he would have the army "ready to repulse the enemy tomorrow," and he assured the President that "every 1,000 men you send at once will help me much."[5]

Then the picture began to look darker. His chief engineer officer, Brigadier General J. G. Barnard, warned McClellan that "the only salvation is for this army to be ready promptly to resume the offensive"; it must advance speedily "or we are bagged." It could do nothing of the kind, however, unless it were greatly strengthened, and the administration (said General Barnard) was most unlikely to do much because if it revealed the size of the crisis it could not conceal its own blunders. Let McClellan, therefore, send a trusted emissary to lay the case before President Lincoln and Secretary Stanton; the mere fact that such a man was sent would show the country that something was wrong. In General Barnard's opinion, "We need 200,000 more men to fill up the ranks and form new regiments."

McClellan forthwith sent his chief-of-staff, General Marcy, off to Washington, notifying Mr. Stanton that Marcy would give him "a perfect understanding of the exact condition of this army." He was much more pessimistic now than he had been forty-eight hours earlier, and he explained that it was vital to get his army into proper shape "before the enemy can attack again." Then he gave the Secretary the bad news: "I doubt whether there are today more than 50,000 men with the colors. To accomplish the great task of capturing Richmond and putting an end to this rebellion re-enforcements should be sent to me rather much over than much less than 100,000 men. I beg that you will be fully impressed by the magnitude of the crisis in which we are placed."[6]

At this point General McClellan heard from President Lincoln, who wrote that the government just did not possess, east of the mountains and outside of McClellan's army, more than 75,000 men altogether.

"Thus," said Mr. Lincoln, "the idea of sending you fifty thousand, or any other considerable force promptly, is simply absurd. If in your frequent mention of responsibility you have the impression that I blame you for not doing more than you can, please be relieved of such impression. I only beg that in like manner you will not ask impossibilities of me. If you think you are not strong enough to take Richmond just now, I do not ask you to try just now. Save the Army, material and personal; and I will strengthen you for the offensive again, as fast as I can. The Governors of 18 states offer me a new levy of three hundred thousand, which I accept."[7]

The disaster in front of Richmond was bringing results that could be seen more clearly in Washington than at Harrison's Landing, and Mr. Lincoln was responding to them. He was moving very carefully, because an abrupt right-angle turn could not be taken at high speed and also because it was very hard to see what sort of road lay beyond the turn.

So far the Northern war effort had gone on its original momentum. Save-the-Union patriotism plus the fury born of defeat at Bull Run had put 637,000 men in the army and there had been an impressive list of victories; the order that stopped recruiting in April had been born of the general belief that the war would soon be won. But the old momentum was gone. The western army had gone to Corinth at a crawl, letting its opponent escape virtually unhurt. The eastern army had been equally slow in its approach to Richmond and had at last met cruel defeat. In May the War Department quietly urged Northern governors to raise some new regiments, and in June it reopened the recruiting stations, but the harvest was very thin. From western Virginia, where the response was more or less typical, Governor F. H. Pierpoint reported that the men who might enlist "have engaged in other pursuits for the season," and even the all-out-war stalwart, Governor John A. Andrew of Massachusetts, confessed that this unexpected plea for more men "finds me without materials for an intelligent reply."[8] The administration could not suddenly call for more volunteers without confessing error and ruinous defeat—General Barnard's appraisal had been tolerably acute—but more volunteers it had to have, and a slightly involved political approach had been devised.

Secretary Seward went off to New York at about the time the Seven Days fight was beginning. He was to take certain political soundings, and he bore a letter from Mr. Lincoln, to be shown wherever it might be helpful. Mr. Lincoln explained the military necessities as of that hour: hold all that had been won in the west, open the Mississippi, take Chattanooga and eastern Tennessee, and raise at least 100,000 new troops so that Richmond could be captured. This would substantially end the war, the President believed; and then, characteristically, he went on to adorn this instrument of political maneuver with a frank statement of his own bedrock determination:

"I expect to maintain this contest until successful, or till I die, or am conquered, or my term expires, or Congress or the country forsake me; and I would publicly appeal to the country for this new force, were it not that I fear a general panic and stampede would follow—so hard is it to have a thing understood as it really is. I think the new force should be all, or nearly all, infantry, principally because such can be raised most cheaply and quickly."

Using this, Secretary Seward persuaded the Northern governors to sign an appeal (which, most thoughtfully, he himself had drafted in advance) expressing the patriotic hope that "the recent successes of the Federal arms may be followed up by measures which must insure the speedy restoration of the Union." The time had come for "prompt and vigorous measures to be adopted by the people"; Mr. Lincoln accordingly was urged to call upon the states for such numbers of volunteers as might be needed to win final and lasting victory. This appeal, which won approval on June 30, was then pre-dated to June 28 and sent to the White House, and, on July 2, Mr. Lincoln made it public together with a formal call on the states for 300,000 more recruits.[9] Thus, as he told General McClellan, he had been "offered" a huge new body of men, and he had accepted the offer. The North would get on with the war.

It was hard, as Mr. Lincoln said, to get a genuine understanding of reality. The reality here was that the war had grown larger than it had been, and that a larger effort would be required to win it. This larger effort would come from a people who were just learning that the energy which had won part of the war was not enough to win all of it; and the effort would be called for by a President who had just defined his will to win as absolute. Here was the clearest possible warning that with this man in the White House there would not be a peace without victory, that a restored union would be fought for but not bartered for, that whatever needed to be done would be done. The device by which the 300,000 men were to be got might be a devious political trick, but the important thing was that the government was going to get them. In the end the shock of the Seven Days would be as significant a turning point as the shock of Bull Run had been a year earlier.

On July 8 Mr. Lincoln showed up at Harrison's Landing to have a talk with General McClellan.

The general's mood seemed to be good. On July 4 he sent a soldierly reply to the President's message about reinforcements: "I will do the best I can with such force as I have and such aid as you can give me. . . . If the capital be threatened, I will move this army at whatever hazard in such direction as will best divert the enemy." He went on to say that the whole army was drawn up for an Independence Day review, with bands playing and everything looking good; and on July 5 he notified Adjutant General Thomas that he had his army satisfactorily placed for all defensive purposes and that the position also "enables me at any time to resume the offensive, which I hope soon to be in a condition to do." This message crossed a letter from Mr. Lincoln, who said that he had talked with General Marcy and understood the whole situation, and that for the immediate future the defensive must be McClellan's primary concern. McClellan himself, said the President, must be the judge of what he could or could not do at Harrison's Landing, but a significant postscript gave the admonition: "If, at any time, you feel able to take the offensive, you are not restrained from doing so."[10] For the first time in weeks, the general and the President seemed to be in complete harmony.

There were occasional alarms. On July 6, McClellan told his wife that the enemy was massed in his front and that he was about to give battle. It was a solemn occasion, and he wrote: "I go into this battle with the full conviction that our losses make it necessary for me to chance the fate of my army. My men are confident & I have no doubt as to our success unless the Creator orders otherwise. I believe we will give them a tremendous thrashing. . . . Tomorrow will probably determine the fate of the country." Tomorrow, as it happened, brought no battle at all. Lee was not massing troops anywhere: he had just notified Mr. Davis that the Yankee gunboats made it impossible for him to attack the Union position with any hope of success, and that he would therefore leave a small force of infantry and cavalry to keep an eye on things, and take the rest of the army back to Richmond and let it get some rest.[11] Not being obliged to fight, McClellan spent at least part of July 7 composing a document which he gave to Mr. Lincoln shortly after the President reached camp.

Some time earlier the general had asked leave to submit a paper on the general state of military affairs, but this document—if indeed it had any connection with that request—was pure politics: advice from a general to a President on the kind of war the President ought to be conducting. It was in substance a flat restatement of the conservative Northern Democratic position on the war, submitted with the warning that if it were not made official government policy "our cause will be lost." Military power must not be used to upset "the relations of servitude," and "neither confiscation of property, political executions of persons, territorial organization of states or forcible abolition of slavery should be contemplated for a moment." Without a conservative policy it probably would not be possible to get new recruits for the Army, and "a declaration of radical views, especially upon slavery, will rapidly disintegrate our present armies." Of course, Mr. Lincoln would need a general-in-chief who was in thorough sympathy with such a policy; General McClellan did not ask for the appointment, but would happily serve "in such position as you may assign me." (There was a faint, quaint echo here of the position Mr. Seward had taken in the spring of 1861 when he gave Mr. Lincoln a note modestly offering to run the government for him.) The general reported that Mr. Lincoln read the paper, thanked him for it, and put it in his pocket.[12]

There were, of course, many things for the President to do. He reviewed the troops, looking at the soldiers, letting them look at him.[13] He talked with McClellan and with the corps commanders about the condition of the army and the intentions of the Rebels, trying to find out whether the army was safe where it was and whether if need be it could safely be withdrawn. He was especially struck by the great number of absentees from the army, and after he returned to Washington he wrote anxiously to McClellan on the subject. As far as he could learn, he said, at least 45,000 soldiers who belonged to the army were not with it, and there seemed to be no way to get them back; which was a pity, because if McClellan had them he could in the President's opinion, "go into Richmond in the next three days."

These absentees represented a problem the War Department never was able to solve. Comparatively few of the missing 45,000 were actually deserters; mostly, they were men who had fallen ill and had been transferred to hospitals in their home states, the theory being that they would recover more rapidly in familiar surroundings. The theory was sound enough, but the home-state hospitals were entirely under the control of home-state politicians, and the army had no way to reclaim a man who got into one of them. McClellan once estimated that not more than a tenth of the men who were sent to these hospitals ever returned to duty, and neither he nor any other army commander was able to do anything about it.[14] To the end, the army carried on its rolls the names of thousands of men who never fought.

But the paper on war aims was what really mattered now.

In place of the larger effort which Mr. Lincoln was demanding it called for a more moderate effort. In effect it proposed that the administration act as if somebody else had won the presidential election of 1860. (Define war, with Clausewitz, as a simple extension of politics: here was a bland proposal to make this war an extension of the politics of the losers rather than of the victors.) It rested on the assumption that the war had not, in 15 desperate months, changed the base for any man's thinking, and it was aimed at victory-by-consent and restoration of the status quo.

The paper meant more than it openly said, but its interpretation was no problem for anyone who knew how the conservative officers in the Army of the Potomac were talking. Quite openly, these men were saying that the administration wanted McClellan to fail so that d impose anti-slavery doctrines on the South. This, they said, final disruption of the Union, because no matter how badly the Southern states were beaten they would never come back into the Union unless the government promised not to touch slavery. The Union could not possibly be restored by sheer force. Secession needed a beating, but it also needed reassurance, kind words and a lot of coaxing.

The point of view is explicitly stated in a letter written just then by Colonel Gouverneur K. Warren, a Regular who commanded a brigade in Porter's corps and who would eventually be a hero of Gettysburg and a corps commander. Warren wrote that President Lincoln ought to "discard the New England and Greeley abolitionists entirely; this would remove the cause for resistance from the masses South, and we could crush out the Secession leaders." He went on to assert that the restored Union "is unattainable without allowing the Southern people their constitutional rights, for it is otherwise degrading them."[15]

McClellan shared this notion, and he had actually come to feel that his recent defeat might really have been a blessing. Writing to Mrs. McClellan on July 10, in a mood of rare humility, the general put it thus:

"I have not done splendidly at all—I have only tried to do my duty & God has helped me—or rather He has helped my army & our country—& we are safe. I think I begin to see His wise purpose in all this & that the events of the next few days will prove it. If I had succeeded in taking Richmond now the fanatics of the North might have been too powerful & reunion impossible. However that may be, I am sure that it is all for the best."[16]

What the general was telling his wife was of course a deep secret, although he believed that Secretary Stanton—"the most deformed hypocrite & villain that I have ever had the bad fortune to meet with"—was reading all of his private telegrams, and he remarked that the Secretary's ears would probably tingle if he could also read the letters to Mrs. McClellan.[17] But the existence in the officer corps of this kind of feeling was common knowledge. Not long before the beginning of the Seven Days, Porter wrote to Manton Marble, of the strongly Democratic New York *World,* with a pointed suggestion: "I wish you would put the question. Does the President (controlled by an incompetent Secy) design to cause defeat here for the purpose of prolonging the war?" And the effect of this train of thought on officers' attitude toward their own government comes out in an indignant letter written a few weeks after this by Alexander S. Webb, a rising young staff officer who was inspector general for the army's chief of artillery. Webb assured his father that "the fools in Washington" were determined that "General G.B. McC must be 'subalternized,'" and he burst out angrily: "Was there ever *such* a government, such fools, such idiots. I tell you father I feel as if every drop of blood I have should be poured out in punishing these men. I hate or despise them more intensively than I do the Rebels."[18]

This was a strange state of mind to be pervading general headquarters of the nation's most important army, and it led the commanding general into strange mental and emotional byways. The day after McClellan saw a disguised blessing in his defeat, he confided to his wife: "I have commenced receiving letters from the North urging me to march on Washington & assume the Govt!" He would of course do nothing of the kind, but the idea remained in his mind, and a little time after this he told her: "I have nothing as yet from Wash. and begin to believe that they intend & hope that I & my army may melt away under the hot sun–if they leave me here neglected much longer I shall feel like taking my rather large military family to Wash. to seek an explanation of their course. I pray that under such circumstances I should be treated with rather more politeness than I have of late."[19]

More often, his mood was one of resignation. He believed that he would be superseded and he did not care very much: "I have lost confidence in the Govt. & would be glad to be out of the scrape–keep this to yourself." The feeling deepened, and shortly afterward he wrote: "If things come to pass as I anticipate I shall leave the service with a sad heart for my country but a light one for myself. I am tired of being dependent on men I despise from the bottom of my heart. I cannot express to you the infinite contempt I feel for these people;–but one thing keeps me at my work–love for my country and my army." His feeling toward President Lincoln had curdled: "I cannot regard him in any respect my friend. I am confident that he would relieve me tomorrow if he dared to do so. His cowardice alone prevents it. I can never regard him with other feelings than those of thorough contempt."[20]

To his old friend Barlow he wrote in similar vein. He was sorry so many good soldiers had "fallen victims to the stupidity and wickedness at Washington which have done their best to sacrifice as noble an Army as ever marched to battle," but he was resigned: "I do not care if they *do* take me from this Army—except on account of the Army itself. I have lost all regard & respect for the majority of the Administration, & doubt the propriety of my brave men's blood being spilled to further the designs of such a set of heathen villains."[21] But the mood of resignation did not keep him from feeling angry, and he gave Mrs. McClellan his unvarnished opinion of Secretary Stanton:

"So you want to know how I feel about Stanton, and what I think of him now. I will tell you with the utmost frankness. I think that he is the most unmitigated scoundrel I ever knew, heard or read of; I think that (and I do not wish to be irreverent) had he lived in the times of the Savior, Judas Iscariot would have remained a respected member of the fraternity of the apostles, & that the magnificent treachery & rascality of E. M. Stanton would have caused Judas to have raised his arms in holy horror, & he would certainly have claimed & exercised the right to have been the betrayer of his lord & master, by virtue of the same merit that raised Satan to his 'eminence.' I *may* do the man injustice."[22]

Mr. Lincoln of course never saw this letter, but he did know that there was a bottomless chasm between his Secretary of War and his principal field commander, and he also knew that the general's letter of advice on war policy did not fit at all with his own determination to drive on for victory at any cost; and on July 11 he signed an order naming Major General Henry W. Halleck General-in-Chief of the armies of the United States and ordering him to report at once to Washington.

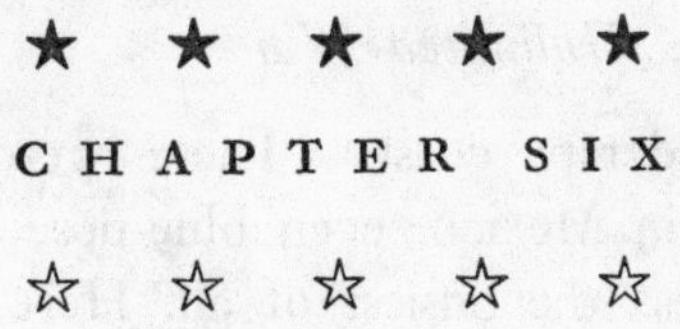

CHAPTER SIX

Unlimited War

1: *Trading with the Enemy*

In the old days, Nassau in the Bahamas was a sleepy colonial port where time stood still and nobody cared. Hardly anything ever happened. Once in a great while a tropical storm would drive some merchant ship on an offshore reef, and the more energetic inhabitants could go out, after the storm was over, to pick the bones. Once in a great while, too, one of the cruisers of Her Majesty's West Indian squadron would drop in for a visit, lying in port with deck awnings white under the sun while the commanding officer went ashore to confer with the governor on some item of empire business. Most of the time the place simply drowsed, and a visitor remarked that its whole air was "one of indolent acquiescence in its own obscurity."

Then came the American Civil War, and Nassau suddenly became the most important single way station on the sea road to the Southern Confederacy, which meant that for a brief, frenzied time it was the town where fortunes could be made more quickly than anywhere else on earth. The harbor was full of ships, the wharves were piled with freight, and the streets, inns, and drinking places were crowded with men who had much money to spend, not much time to spend it, and the reckless high spirits born of the knowledge that no matter how much they spent they would get it all back in a very few days. Nassau, in short, was the center of a hell-roaring boom, and one sailor wrote that what was going on here must have been like the scenes in the pirate havens in the days when the Spanish Main was beyond the law.

Nassau was like this because it was a neutral port within easy reach of the Confederate coast. (There were others—Bermuda, Havana, Matamoros in Mexico, even blue-nose Halifax far to the north—but Nassau was the busiest of all. Here the blockade-runners got their cargoes, which came over from England in complete security, and here they delivered the cotton which the outside world wanted so much; and no merchant had ever imagined anything like the profits that could be made here. Freight charges on Confederate imports could run to fifty pounds sterling per ton, sometimes to eighty or a hundred pounds, and a cargo of five hundred bales of cotton could earn fifty pounds for each bale. A ship that made two round trips between Nassau and the mainland paid for herself and showed a profit besides, and if she made more than two her owners grew rich. Sailors got the unheard-of wage of $100 a round trip, plus a $50 bonus, and there were desertions from the warships of the West Indies squadron as a result. A ship captain could earn $5000 for a round trip, and in addition he could carry a certain amount of freight on his own account, which was like owning a gold mine. One skipper bought a thousand pairs of corset stays in Liverpool for the equivalent of twenty-seven cents apiece, and sold them in Wilmington, North Carolina, for three dollars each. He also discovered that tooth brushes (of which a huge number could be carried in an ordinary carpet bag) could be sold in the Confederacy for seven times their cost.[1]

The business started rather slowly. During most of the first year of the war, cautious British shippers refused to run the blockade with anything but their oldest, least valuable vessels; wheezy, leaky steamers, and ordinary sailing craft—"unseaworthy slugs which we could well afford to lose," as one supercargo recalled. The blockade was very loose during 1861, and hardly ten per cent of the blockade-runners were caught; it was partially effective then only because fear of capture kept many ships in port and because the Confederate government was opposed to the cotton exports which were the only substantial means of paying for imports.[2] But by 1862 the United States Navy had learned its trade and had put many new cruisers on patrol, so that getting through called for faster ships; also, the cotton embargo was relaxed, and the fantastic profits that could be made were beginning to be clear to one and all. So British yards began to build ships especially designed for blockade-running—long, narrow, rakish vessels of shallow draft and low freeboard, painted gray to reduce visibility at night (one captain even made his crew wear white uniforms, believing that it was too easy for Yankee lookouts to see a man in dark clothing), burning anthracite coal which made little or no smoke, with short pole masts, and smokestacks that could be telescoped down to stubs. Some of these vessels were jerry-built, and racked themselves to pieces in short order, but most of them were sturdy enough to do their work, and although a good many were caught or driven ashore a great many more got through. They had little trouble with the dangerous offshore shoals and sandbars; the war had put scores of licensed coastal pilots out of work, and these men, lured by Southern patriotism and high wages, could take the blockade-runners in through channels the Federal cruisers dared not attempt.[3]

The number of harbors open to the inbound blockade-runners was limited. The Federal thrust which sealed off the North Carolina sounds closed a whole series of ports that could have been used, the occupation of Port Royal in South Carolina was even more effective, and in the spring of 1862 Savannah was virtually blocked when the Northerners bombarded and captured Fort Pulaski, at the mouth of the Savannah River. But Charleston remained, closely guarded though it was, and most important of all there was Wilmington.

Wilmington was on the Cape Fear River, the hardest river on all the coast to close. The river came slanting down to the sea behind a long sandy peninsula which was cut here and there by little inlets, some of them deep enough for a shoal-draft steamer. The principal entrance, protected by a dangerous shoal, was guarded by Fort Fisher, a work so strong that the Federals never tried to take it until the war was nearly over, and there were batteries to guard all of the little inlets. The blockading squadron had to patrol a sieve forty miles long, and the Confederates had signal stations all along the coast to tell blockade-runners where the patrol was weakest. Traffic here could be cut down but it could never be stopped, and so many blockade-runners went in and out that some Northerners believed that the blockade-running captains had made a deal with officers of the United States Navy. Secretary Welles never took any stock in these rumors, but the mere fact that they were in circulation showed how porous the blockade really was at the mouth of the Cape Fear River.[4] Like Nassau, Wilmington became a gold-rush town, a swaggering staggering little seaport that had suddenly become one of the busiest and most important places in all the Confederacy.

Staid and respectable before the war, Wilmington now was wide open. Speculators were drawn from all over the Confederacy by the weekly auctions of luxury goods, and there was a substantial influx of the kind of rogues who always appear in a boom town. The captain of one of the blockade-runners said that a breakdown in law enforcement made it unsafe to go about the streets at night; murders and robberies were common, and in daytime there were bloody fights between sailors from the merchant ships (whose pockets were full of money) and soldiers stationed in Wilmington. Agents and employees of the importing companies lived high, spending money so freely that food prices in the local markets went beyond the reach of ordinary citizens; most people who were not connected with the import-export business left town if they could, spurred on by the fact that in the summer of 1862 yellow fever broke out, due partly (it was supposed) to the non-enforcement of ordinary quarantine regulations. Convalescent soldiers from the Richmond hospitals who paused in Wilmington en route to their homes enjoyed the stopover very much. With all of the money that as floating around, the ladies' committee that had been organized to provide meals for soldiers on sick leave was better financed than any other committee in the Confederacy, and it had an infinite range of delicacies to choose from when it did its marketing. The soldiers who got meals at the long tables in the railroad station ate very well. On a marshy flat across the river from the city, steam cotton presses had been put up, and there the outward-bound steamers got their cargoes. The wharves where this was done were heavily guarded, to prevent the escape of men who were trying to dodge conscription, and vessels loaded with cotton were obliged to fumigate their cargoes before they left the river, to smoke out possible stowaways.[5]

. . . War is not just armies, and battles, and clever campaigns laid out on the map and then ratified in blood. It is a resort to force, to be sure, which is to say that men have temporarily abandoned the effort to exert a reasoned control over events; but it creates forces of its own as it goes along and then itself becomes subject to them, and goes where they drive it. From the moment of its beginning war contains, cruelly invisible, the shape of its unimaginable end product, much as a block of marble contains a statue before the chisel ever touches it. What was happening in Nassau and Wilmington and other places like them was a partial gauge of the forces that were now at work.

These forces were at work elsewhere—in Virginia and in Tennessee, along the Mississippi and in New Orleans: at almost every place where the fevered bodies of the estranged sections touched. They involved cotton, and gold, and the whole list of goods and services with which the Northern and Southern people had supplied each other before they went to war. They showed themselves first in easy money and the corruption that easy money brings, and good patriots in both sections denounced the base cupidity of profiteers. But what the profiteers were doing reflected not so much human baseness as the peculiar stresses generated by the effort to conduct a civil war according to the rules and standards conventionally applied to war with a foreign enemy.

There is, for instance, the age-old rule that one does not trade with the enemy in wartime.

One does not: but the two nations which had made this war were not foreign enemies, they were simply the estranged halves of an economic whole. They depended on each other, and the fact that they were making war did not end that interdependence in any degree. It simply compelled them to struggle against one of the most profound economic forces in American life—the necessity for an exchange of essential goods between the Northern and the Southern states. This force was too strong for them. The exchange had to go on. Even as they tried to build an impassable wall between themselves they were compelled to cut holes in it.

This became apparent in the summer of 1862—the strange summer when so many of the hidden compulsions of the war began to display themselves. Federal troops by now occupied a good deal of secessionist territory—part of Louisiana, various Carolina seaports, western Tennessee and a fringe of northern Mississippi, not to mention a certain amount of Virginia: this, plus such important commercial centers as New Orleans, Nashville, and Memphis. In these cities the intense Northern desire for cotton, sugar, rice, and tobacco suddenly encountered the even more intense Southern desire for everything from munitions to shoes, from corn and bacon to medicine and salt. Canny traders began to make deals, because unbelievable profits were involved; and governments began to wink at those deals, even to encourage them, because it seemed that they had to if they were to carry on the war, even though the deals gave direct aid and comfort to the enemy.

The Federal government outlawed trade with the Confederacy, but it believed that commerce followed the flag, which meant that traders followed the army. (Sometimes, being ardent men, they got slightly ahead of it.) The traders were accompanied by Treasury Department agents, who enforced intricate regulations governing the purchase, sale, and transportation of commodities in occupied areas, and who were empowered to seize and offer for public sale all cotton acquired by the army. Most business was done under Treasury permits, and Secretary Chase—who drew up the regulations, appointed the agents, and issued the permits—explained his general policy thus: "It is my wish to have just as much cotton, rice, sugar and tobacco brought out of the insurrectionary states as possible without . . . increasing the resources of the Rebels and thus prolonging the war." This ideal was lofty but unattainable, because it was humanly impossible to buy anything in or near an "insurrectionary state" without increasing the resources of secession; the impulses set in motion by circulating money can hardly be checked, and anyway one bale of cotton looks much like another. A busy Treasury agent remarked that he could not possibly "investigate the morals" back of any shipment of cotton, or concern himself very much with where the cotton had been, how it got away from there, or who had originally raised, owned and shipped it.[6] It goes without saying that these agents, who had power of life or death over business deals, came under great temptation. Some of them proved incorruptible, and some did not.

So the occupied cities began to revive. Nashville came first. Trade was dead when Buell's men arrived, in February; there was no cotton, and although there was a great hunger for Northern goods the Northern traders would not take Confederate money, and Tennessee bank notes were badly depreciated. But the traders went scouting around, baled cotton began to appear, United States currency started to circulate, and in two months some 3600 bales of cotton had gone north, at an average price of $100 a bale. (That price would go ever so much higher in another year; even so, it represented about two and one half times the prevailing price at the beginning of the war.) Confidence in the Tennessee bank notes revived, the market for Northern products became brisk, and it was estimated that before the summer ended Nashville would send out at least 18,000 bales.

It was the same in Memphis, only more so. This city was occupied on June 6, and Yankee merchants lost no time. Within a fortnight steamboats were unloading flour, coffee, pork, and salt along the levees; it was said that more than two hundred traders were in town, and Memphis merchants who wanted to do business either took the oath of allegiance or bribed a Treasury agent. More than 8000 bales of cotton had been sold by the first week in July, and before July ended the planters who had cotton to sell were refusing to take even United States currency, demanding payment in gold or silver. This infuriated U. S. Grant, who commanded in western Tennessee, and who uttered formal denunciation of "speculators whose love of gain is greater than their love of country." He remarked that U.S. paper money was legal tender all over the North and decreed that anyone who, owning cotton, refused to sell it for anything but specie would be arrested and forcibly dispossessed of his bales. The same thing, he added, would happen to any trader who paid out gold or silver. Grant's subordinate, bristly red-haired Sherman, who was in command at Memphis, complained that gold paid for cotton went immediately to Nassau to buy guns and ammunition, and cried: "We cannot carry on war and trade with a people at the same time."[7]

This was of no help. The Northern government was vigorously promoting the cotton trade, for a variety of reasons—to assuage the New England mill owners, to improve the position of the dollar in foreign exchange, and to persuade Southern planters that it was good to do business with the Old Union—and the protests of the soldiers had little effect. The War Department overruled Grant, and Sherman fumed that Memphis now would be more useful to the Confederacy than it was when the Confederates occupied it. Neither Bragg nor Van Dorn, he declared, could maintain his army without the meat that was preserved by contraband salt that came down from the North and the munitions that were bought with gold that was paid for cotton, and he wrote to the Adjutant General that "this cotton order is worse to us than a defeat."[8]

The case was intricate. In the spring of 1862 Confederate Secretary of War George W. Randolph warned Major General Samuel Jones, commanding the Confederate Department of Alabama and Western Florida, that although a military commander was authorized to destroy export cotton if he thought it was going to go to the enemy, it was necessary to use discretion: "He should bear in mind that it is good policy to exchange produce for arms and munitions of war with anyone willing to make such exchange." A few months later Mr. Randolph notified President Davis that the Confederate commissary general believed that "the Army cannot be subsisted without permitting trade to some extent with Confederate ports in possession of the enemy." As far as Mr. Randolph could see, the Confederacy could violate its policy of keeping cotton out of Yankee hands, or it could risk the starvation of its armed forces. He presented his own recommendation: "I advise that the commissary general be authorized to contract for bacon and salt, and the quartermaster general for blankets and shoes, payable in cotton, and that the general commanding on the Mississippi be instructed to permit the cotton delivered under these contracts to pass our lines." In the fall of the year, a French cotton broker in New Orleans wrote to Secretary Randolph offering a deal: he could forward 100,000 sacks of salt for the Confederate government if in return he could get 10,000 bales of cotton, to be sent out through New Orleans to France. He could also provide bacon, shoes, blankets, and flannel on the same terms. President Davis wrote his own comment: "The objection to this is the proposed shipment to a port in the possession of the enemy. If the supplies can be obtained free from this objection it should be done . . . As a last resort we might be justified in departing from the declared policy in regard to exports, but the necessity should be absolute."[9]

The trouble was that the necessity was absolute. By the winter of 1863 Mr. Randolph's successor as Secretary of War, James A. Seddon, was confessing that the Department had contracted for various things from suppliers inside the Federal lines; "the contracts were of course made reluctantly, but under a strong conviction of the necessity of resorting to such means of obtaining adequate supplies." Such deals, he agreed, tended to produce much more illicit trade, and sometimes demoralized good Southern civilians, but the armies had to be fed and clothed, and sometimes "irregular modes of supply" were the only recourse. It would probably be necessary to do more of this, and if so the army commanders in the field would have to get used to it.[10]

It was a two-way street. Cotton was well on its way toward a price of a dollar a pound in the Northern market; salt was rapidly climbing at the same rate in the South. Without salt, meat could not be preserved, armies could not be fed and even the slaves in the cotton fields would go hungry. The Confederacy had extensive saline wells in southwestern Virginia, and these were being exploited to the limit, but the South had never come close to providing all of its own salt; in the three years before the war, New Orleans alone imported about 700,000 sacks annually. Now the salt-cotton combination became too much for any government to control; military necessity was allied with an economic pressure that went beyond the possibility of restraint. One of Secretary Chase's Treasury agents explained how the pressure was felt in New Orleans:

A sack of salt could be bought in Federally occupied New Orleans for $1.25. On the far side of Lake Pontchartrain, in Confederate territory, each sack could be sold for anything from $60 to $100. A trader who could take a thousand sacks across the lake, therefore, could make $60,000 or more on an investment of $1250; and with the money thus made he could buy cotton at ten cents a pound with the certainty that he would get at least sixty cents for it as soon as he got it back within the Federal lines.[11] No government that ever existed could stop a trade which dripped money as copiously as that; and in this case the two governments which ostensibly wanted to stop it had their own reasons for hoping that at least some of it would continue.

There was not much the army commanders could do about it. Halleck, the new Federal generalissimo, told Grant in mid-August to do everything he could to kill the contraband trade, but he also tried to rationalize the matter of bringing in the cotton: the Army had to have cotton to make tents for those 300,000 new volunteers, and anyway the Confederates could buy munitions at Nassau with baled cotton just as easily as they could buy them with the gold they got by selling cotton to the Yankees. Sherman, who noticed that everytime he halted a southbound shipment of contraband at Memphis he heard anguished wails from the respectable merchants at Cincinnati, declared angrily that "Cincinnati furnishes more contraband goods than Charleston, and has done more to prolong the war than the State of South Carolina."[12]

Some soldiers protested and did the best they could; others adjusted themselves, and possibly did better—for themselves, at any rate, if not for the common cause. High priest of those who found adjustment pleasant was Major General Benjamin Butler, Federal commander at New Orleans.

At one time or another Butler was a thorn in practically everybody's side. He was a politician of subtle skills and excellent connections, a soldier of practically no military capacity, an opportunist alert to every shift in the wind, and a capable administrator who gave New Orleans a dictatorial military government as efficient as it was distasteful. He managed to win the hatred and contempt of

Southerners as no other Yankee ever did—their mildest epithet for him was "Beast," they accused him of everything from stealing teaspoons to insulting Southern womanhood, and Mr. Davis at last proclaimed him "an outlaw and common enemy of mankind" and directed that if he were ever captured he should be put to death without trial.[13] This grew out of the fact that when Butler first reached New Orleans he hunted down and hanged one William B. Mumford, a citizen who had torn down and mangled a United States flag hoisted by Farragut's men. Inasmuch as Mumford did this before the Federals formally took possession of the city he had committed no crime, under military law or any other kind of law, and good Southerners considered the hanging no better than plain murder.

Butler was in command at New Orleans just when people began to realize that there was something to be said for doing business with one's enemies. New Orleans, of course, was one of the chief places where such business was done, and a special odor hung over the cotton-sugar-salt-contraband traffic that took place under Butler's regime. Butler himself insisted that he was scrupulously honest throughout, and nobody ever proved anything to the contrary. Yet there always seemed to be a dead rat back behind the wainscoting somewhere. A frustrated Treasury agent reported that Butler "is such a *smart* man" that it would be very hard to find anything he really wished to hide, and said that "it is the general impression here that money will accomplish anything with the authorities." Certainly the general's brother, Colonel Andrew J. Butler, was making all kinds of deals, raking in profits which were estimated to run as high as $2,000,000. Despite his title, Colonel Butler was not in the Army; he was just *with* the Army, one of a number of enterprising merchants who had followed the Army into the cotton south. He traded in nobody knew quite what, up the Mississippi, shipping goods in boats which the Army had seized. He traded also across Lake Pontchartrain, in salt, and it was said that he had made a fortune sending sugar back to New York; and, all in all, he was typical of his time and place. The multiplicity of deals that were going on inspired a cynical wisecrack among Union men in New Orleans. They said that they wished Ben Butler was President of the United States: he would make millions for himself during the first three months of his presidency, but he would go on and win the war during the next three months.[14]

What happened in the west happened also in the east. A clerk in the Confederate War Department at Richmond wrote that "it is sickening to behold the corruption of the commercial men," and he said that the Confederate capital was infested with Baltimore merchants who were importing huge quantities of goods from the North and selling them in Richmond at fabulous prices; some of them, he was told, were making $50,000 a month clear profit. At the end of the year a Confederate enrolling officer asked permission to raise a force to squelch the contraband trade that was coming down the eastern shore of Maryland and across the Rappahannock; the "northern Neck" of Virginia, he said, was "worse than Yankeedom itself." But the War Department warned him that the case must be approached with much discretion: "All trade with the enemy is demoralizing and illegal and should, of course, be discountenanced, but at the same time, situated as the people to a serious extent are . . . some barter or trading for the supplies of their necessities is almost inevitable and excusable."[15]

The demoralization was real; it existed on both sides, and it was costly. A few months before the end of the war one of Bragg's officers who had been touring Mississippi turned in a somber judgment: "The fact is that cotton, instead of contributing to our strength, has been the greatest element of our weakness here. Yankee gold is fast accomplishing what Yankee arms could never achieve—the subjugation of this people." At that same time a committee of the Federal Congress, finishing a survey of the illicit trade, concluded that it had cost the North much more than it was ever worth, both physically and morally. Trade with the enemy, said this committee, had prolonged the war and had cost thousands of lives "and millions upon millions of treasure," and had gone far to support the Confederate armies in the west. Occupied New Orleans, the committee believed, had helped the Confederacy more than any of the Confederacy's own seaports with the single exception of Wilmington.[16]

In any war, the men who die for patriotism die also for the

enrichment of cold-eyed schemers who risk nothing, and every battlefield is made uglier by the greed of men who never fight. But what was happening here, although it included all of that, went far beyond it. This was the conclusive evidence that the warring states were tragically and mysteriously bound together. Fighting to destroy each other, the two nations still had to have each other's help.

2: *The Ultimate Meaning*

In the early part of the war Abraham Lincoln had warned that it might become a remorseless revolutionary struggle, and at the end of it he remarked that neither he nor any man had expected a result as "fundamental and astounding" as it finally brought; and he confessed that he himself had not so much dominated events as he had been dominated by them. In the year that began with the retreat from Bull Run and ended with the retreat from the Chickahominy, the war became too great for any man to manage. After the summer of 1862 one could hope only to understand it—and, understanding, to give meaning to it. When he returned to Washington from Harrison's Landing, Mr. Lincoln found this was his greatest task.

The war was going to run its course; that much was clear. In both the east and west the Federal government had lost the initiative, and even though much had been won it must nerve itself for a new effort greater than any it had made before. Presidential Secretary John Nicolay wrote that the second week in July was "a very blue week here," and went on to say: "I don't think I have ever heard more croaking since the war began than during the past ten days. I am utterly amazed to find so little real faith and courage under difficulties among public leaders and men of intelligence." Attorney General Bates admitted that it was hard to be cheerful, and he saw "no foresight, no activity, no enterprise, no dash" in what was being done. Thomas Scott, concluding a stint as Assistant Secretary of War, told Barlow that people felt gloomy and were losing confidence, and predicted that unless some military success were won soon "all will be lost and separation of the states become inevitable."[1]

This was not wholly the result of military failure. The war of late had gone badly, but it had also gone far: so far that men had to re-examine the basis on which they were fighting. This was what was really disturbing. The people of the North had formally declared that they were making war solely to restore the Union; and yet this war, which could not conceivably have occurred if slavery had not existed, was bound to become a war about slavery if it went on long enough, and that moment was now at hand. (Of all the miscalculations ever made by an American soldier, the greatest may well have been General McClellan's notion that victory deferred would leave the peculiar institution undamaged.) When Northern armies entered the South they touched cotton, and the government had to do something about it, even though what it did was unrehearsed, irregular, and quite unsatisfactory; they also touched slavery, and government was going to have to do something about that too, although nobody could be sure what effect this might ultimately have.

Whatever the effect might be, President and Congress knew that it was time to move.

On July 12 Congress passed a new confiscation act, providing sterner penalties for secession. Persons convicted of treason, said the act, would suffer death and their slaves would be freed, and people who joined in the rebellion or aided it in any way would be subject to fine or imprisonment and the loss of their slaves. Furthermore, any slaves who escaped from, were abandoned by, or were captured from people engaged in rebellion "shall be forever free of their servitude and not again be held as slaves." The fugitive slave law would be inoperative unless the fugitives belonged to loyal masters, and the President might use ex-slaves in any way he chose to help win the war. Finally, the President was authorized to make provision for the transportation and resettlement "in some tropical country beyond the limits of the United States" of any slaves thus freed who were willing to emigrate.

This was a declaration of intent rather than a solid piece of legislation. Enforcement of the act was left hazy, and Mr. Lincoln was startled to find Congress asserting its power to free a slave within a state; he even prepared a veto message, and was induced to approve the act only when Congress adopted a proviso that the slaves in question were war captives and, as such, government property. (If the government itself owned slaves it of course could free them without raising constitutional questions.) This bill plainly restated the fact that slaves were property, and it offered nothing at all to the Negro who was owned by a Unionist.[2]

Nevertheless, it was a step of great significance. If it did not quite mean emancipation it meant that Congress was prepared to accept emancipation. Property which would become non-property if the owner's political orientation was considered defective had a most uncertain future. The bill invited the President to go as far as he liked in using former slaves to fight slavery—a leaf, after all, from the book of old John Brown—and it rested on the unspoken assumption that the war itself was writing slavery's doom.

This assumption Mr. Lincoln shared. On the day Congress approved the confiscation bill he called Senators and Representatives from the border states to the White House and urged them to support the plan for compensated emancipation, and his plea amounted to a statement that slavery was dying and that in self-interest the slave states ought to realize what they could on an investment which eventually would be wiped out.

"If the war continue long," said the President, "as it must, if the object be not sooner attained, the institution in your states will be extinguished by mere friction and abrasion—by the mere incidents of war. It will be gone, and you will have nothing valuable in lieu of it." In their consultation with self-interest, he said, the border states need do no more than make up their minds: "I do not speak of emancipation *at once*, but of a *decision* at once to emancipate gradually."

It did no good. Of the twenty-seven border state men at this meeting, only eight would go along. The rest saw objections: the plan would cost too much, it would make the secessionists angrier than ever, it would probably lead in the end to unconstitutional emancipation all across the board—and in short they would have none of it.[3]

Behaving so, they played into the hands of the abolitionists.

If the slavery problem had to be touched at all—and by the summer of 1862 it obviously did—compensated emancipation represented the gentlest approach possible. Now Mr. Lincoln was informed that this gentleness would get no response from the very people it was supposed to please. If, thereafter, border state sensibilities meant much less to him it is not to be wondered at; border state support just was not there when he needed it most.

Broadly speaking, the border state men represented the moderates, the men who felt either that slavery was acceptable or at least that it must not be interfered with by any government in Washington. To carry moderate Northerners with him, Mr. Lincoln had overruled every Federal officer who tried to push the government into emancipation—first General Frémont, then Secretary Cameron, most recently General Hunter. The moderates had applauded, but their applause amounted to little more than a polite patter-patter of clapped hands. Now a larger, harder, longer war effort was needed, and Mr. Lincoln had to rally men who had iron in them, the men who were ready to be wholly immoderate in their backing of the Union cause. These included of course the abolitionists, who were vigorous and noisy but still a minority. Much more important, however, were the men who had been willing to let slavery alone as a matter of tactics, but who nevertheless had deep antislavery convictions. These men were in a majority in the North, and the war itself had come because the party which spoke for them had won the election in 1860; leaders of the cotton South had believed, probably correctly, that slavery must eventually die if that party controlled the government. To suppose now that these men would accept defeat and disunion rather than try to destroy slavery outright was simply to delude one's self.

Mr. Lincoln's attitude was hardening, and so was his language. Reverdy Johnson went to New Orleans on a mission for the State Department, and sent back word that Louisiana Unionists were falling away from the faith because they feared the Federal government was headed toward emancipation. Mr. Lincoln replied curtly that he doubted it, and he warned: "It may as well be understood, once for all, that I shall not surrender this game leaving any available card unplayed." When Cuthbert Bullitt, a Treasury official in New Orleans, turned in a report similar to Johnson's, the President asked him if the Louisiana loyalists really imagined that he would lose the war in order to save their slaves. Then he went on, with the tenseness of a man who has had all the argument he wants: "What would you do in my position? Would you drop the war where it is? Or would you prosecute it in future with elderstalk squirts charged with rose-water? Would you deal lighter blows rather than heavier ones? Would you give up the contest leaving any available means unapplied?" For himself, he said, he would not give up. He would do everything possible to save the Union, and he made but one qualification: "I shall do nothing in malice. What I deal with is too vast for malicious dealing." Some time after this he explained to the painter, F. B. Carpenter, that in this summer of 1862 he felt that he had "reached the end of the rope," and (with a return to the figure of speech used in the letter to Reverdy Johnson) that "we had about played our last card, and must change our tactics or lose the war."[4]

He changed his tactics and thereby changed the character of the war . . . and the future of America.

Ten days after he had his talk with the border state men the President held a cabinet meeting. To this July 22 cabinet meeting he presented a certain paper, saying that he did not want any advice on the substance of it, because he had made up his mind; he just wanted his cabinet members to know what was coming, and he would hear any comments that they might have to make. The paper was a document which has come down in history as the preliminary Emancipation Proclamation.

It began as a simple recital of the fact that Congress had passed a new confiscation act, and it warned all of the people who might be affected by that act to take note of its provisions and be guided accordingly. It served notice that at the next session of Congress the President would once again press for compensated emancipation, and it went on to say that the sole purpose of the war remained what it always had been—to restore and maintain "the constitutional relation between the general government and each and all of the states wherein that relation is now suspended or disturbed." Then came the meat of it:

"And, as a fit and necessary military measure for effecting this purpose, I, as Commander-in-Chief of the Army and Navy of the United States, do order and declare that on the first day of January in the year of Our Lord one thousand, eight hundred and sixty-three, all persons held as slaves within any state or states, wherein the constitutional authority of the United States shall not then be practically recognized, submitted to, and maintained, shall then, thenceforward, and forever, be free."[5]

In many ways this was an odd document. Clearly, the President had doubts about the legal basis for emancipation. He had always insisted that Congress lacked power to overturn slavery, and even stout antislavery men like Secretary Chase agreed with him; the whole thing now was pinned to the President's war powers—he would issue this proclamation in his military capacity, as a military measure. Even odder was the fact that the proclamation would apply to the embattled Confederate states but not to slave states like Kentucky and Maryland which were still in the Union, nor to those parts of the seceded states which were now under Federal control. This writ, in other words, would run only in those states where the Federal government had no power to enforce its writs; unless it were heeded by men who were already fighting like grim death to get entirely out from under the Federal government, it would be heeded by nobody. Finally, the proclamation did no more than announce that another proclamation would be issued later unless the war were won much more speedily than anyone anticipated.

It can easily be shown, in other words, that it was a singularly weak document. And yet . . . there was a war on, and thousands of men were dying for intangibles no more solid than the look of a flag adrift in the wind or the ring of a phrase; and between Canada and the Rio Grande there were more than three million people who were slaves and knew freedom only by hearsay; and when the President of the United States said with whatever qualifications that these people should be then, thenceforward and forever free his words would have the echoing reach of a great trumpet call in the night. Once said they could never be recalled. They would go on and on—then, thenceforward and forever.

The cabinet was somewhat taken aback, but it was receptive. Secretary Seward and Secretary Welles had had forewarning; a little more than a week earlier they had ridden in a carriage with the President on the way to funeral services for an infant child of Secretary Stanton, and the President had told them he believed emancipation was "a military necessity absolutely essential for the salvation of the Union." He asked their opinion, and both men had said that they felt the same way but that they would like to have time to think about it a little longer. Having thought, they now voiced warm support. Montgomery Blair was somewhat dubious, fearing the effect on the fall elections, on the money market and on morale generally—the Blairs, after all, were border state men. Secretary Chase was just a little nonplused. He had written a month earlier that when the armies advanced "slavery met us at every turn, and always as a foe," and had considered it obvious that either slavery or the Union must perish, but the President's proposal made him uneasy. He would support it, but he was afraid that it might lead to a slave insurrection, and thought it might be safer to let army commanders in the field take the lead.

In the main, the cabinet gave the President its backing. Secretary Seward did have a word of caution, however. Issued now, he said, the proclamation would come on the heels of military disaster and might sound like a despairing plea for the help of the slaves rather than a bold assertion that the slaves would be freed: would it not be better to wait for a victory so that the proclamation could rest on military success? Mr. Lincoln saw the point at once and the proclamation went into a pigeonhole, to stay there until somebody won a battle. Meanwhile, its existence would remain a deep secret.[6]

Among the millions who were not in on the secret was the eminent editor of the New York *Tribune*, Horace Greeley. With all of his eccentricities Mr. Greeley frequently spoke for the great body of Northern sentiment which the President was determined to hold in line, and as the summer waned Mr. Greeley felt it necessary to call the President to time. The August 20 issue of the *Tribune* contained an open letter to Mr. Lincoln, headed "The Prayer of Twenty Million," which complained bitterly that the President was losing the war because he was too soft in regard to slavery.

The President, said Mr. Greeley, was "strangely and disastrously remiss" in failing to enforce the emancipation provisions of the new confiscation act; he was unduly influenced by "certain fossil politicians" from the border states; the Union cause was suffering intensely from "mistaken deference to rebel Slavery," and loyal Northerners unanimously felt that "all attempts to put down the rebellion and at the same time uphold its inciting cause are preposterous and futile." It was time for the President to free the slaves, and Mr. Greeley wanted action now.[7]

Mr. Lincoln was prompt to reply, and on August 25 the *Tribune* printed his letter to Mr. Greeley—a letter which was aimed not so much at the editor himself as at the millions in the North who, in the end, would decide whether there would be an unbroken Union and whether slavery could endure.

His policy, said Mr. Lincoln, was very simple: he would save the Union—as quickly as possible and in a Constitutional way. Next:

"If there be those who would not save the Union unless they could at the same time *destroy* slavery, I do not agree with them. My paramount object in this struggle *is* to save the Union, and is *not* either to save or to destroy slavery. If I could save the Union without freeing *any* slave I would do it, and if I could save it by freeing *all* the slaves I would do it; and if I could save it by freeing some and leaving others alone I would also do that. What I do about slavery, and the colored race, I do because I believe it helps to save the Union; and what I forbear, I forbear because I do *not* believe it would help to save the Union. I shall do *less* whenever I shall believe what I am doing hurts the cause, and I shall do *more* whenever I shall believe doing more will help the cause." In closing, he wrote that this expressed his view of his official duty; as a person, he hoped as he had always done that all men could be free.[8]

One of the interesting things about this letter is that it was written exactly one month after Mr. Lincoln told his cabinet that he was going to proclaim freedom for the slaves: a fact of which the editor was given no faintest hint. Mr. Lincoln told him that he would do what the war made him do, but he did not tell him that he already knew what this would be and that he already had made up his mind to do it. The Emancipation Proclamation was not going to come out as a letter to the editor. It would come out when some victory in the field could give it life . . . life for words and an idea, bought by the deaths of many young men.

In these days when he waited for victory the President seemed to keep probing for the ultimate meaning of the thing which he was about to do. To change the Negro from a chattel to a man would have unending consequences. What were they going to be? How would the nation adjust to them? When a delegation of "Chicago Christians of All Denominations" called to present a memorial favoring emancipation, Mr. Lincoln responded with a brooding soliloquy. What practical effect would a proclamation have? Would it help the Union cause more than it hurt it? Might it not be well first to rally the people behind the idea that the constitutional government itself was at stake? This was "a fundamental idea, going down about as deep as anything." What about the slaves themselves? "Suppose they could be induced by a proclamation of freedom from me to throw themselves upon us, *what should we do with them?*"[9]

That question haunted him, as it haunted others. Was America ready for unlimited freedom? What *would* it do with the Negro? It had begun by making a slave of him, and whenever he managed to stop being a slave and tried to make his way as a free man in a free society it resented him, with the deep, illogical resentment we reserve for those whom we have wronged. Suppose the whole race suddenly came out of slavery: Was there a place for it in America?

There were discouraging signs. Wholly typical was a newspaper item which was printed within a fortnight of Mr. Lincoln's talk with the cabinet about emancipation. Irish dock workers in Cincinnati had rioted all along the waterfront, stoning and beating free Negroes who had been hired (at wages much lower than the wages the Irish had been getting) to unload steamboats, driving them through the city, clearing the wharves of them; it was done in broad daylight, and the police stood by and offered no interference.[10] The free Negro would come in on the very lowest level of the economic pyramid, and the people who occupied that level were uncomfortable enough already and did not want to be crowded; nor were the people on higher levels willing to concern themselves much with the implications of the turmoil beneath them. The majority in the North might dislike slavery, but it was by no means prepared for the seismic shock that would run through all society when millions of slaves tried to lay their hands on the benefits of freedom.

Perhaps there was a way out. If the freed slaves could be taken entirely out of the country and transplanted in some faraway land, America might avoid the distressing problems raised by universal freedom. The idea of colonization had been in Mr. Lincoln's mind for a long time, and in the middle of August he discussed it frankly with a committee of free Negroes at the White House. The discussion was moody, clouded, unhappy. The Negro race, said the President, suffered under the greatest wrong ever inflicted on any people, yet nowhere in America could Negroes hope for the equality which free men normally want; "go where you are treated the best, and the ban is still upon you." As President he could not alter this; he could only reflect that "there is an unwillingness on the part of our people, harsh as it may be, for you free colored people to remain with us." Without slavery and the colored race America would not be fighting this war, and "it is better for us both, therefore, to be separated."

So he urged the Negroes to embrace colonization. He was thinking about Central America. There was a country there (he did not name it) which ran from Atlantic to Pacific, with good harbors on both coasts, a fertile land endowed with deposits of coal, a place where political conditions were indeed rather unstable but a land without prejudice, eager for colonists—"to your colored race they have no objections." If a fair handful of free Negroes would make a start there, with their families, the United States government would give its support and protection: "If I could find twenty-five able-bodied men, with a mixture of women and children, good things in the family relation, I think I could make a successful commencement." Would these free Negroes put their minds on it for a while? The Negroes gravely assured him that they would think about the matter and let him know, and then they went away . . . and of course nothing at all ever came of it.[11]

Nothing could come of it. The freedom that was to be given, with such risks and at such cost, was to be given in America, and its effects would have to be faced there and not in some far-off colony. Also, a strange thing had taken place during the years of slavery, which hardly anybody had thought about. The people who were about to be freed were slaves and they were Negroes; but also, quite unexpectedly, they had become Americans, and Americans they would always be—then, thenceforward and forever. Having taken them, used them and shaped them, the country could discharge its responsibility only by taking on a new one of immeasurable dimensions. To define freedom anew for the Negro was to redefine it for everybody, and the act which enlarged the horizon of those in bondage must in the end push America's own horizon all the way out to infinity.

3: *A Long and Strong Flood*

When President Lincoln gave command of the nation's armies to General Halleck he supposed that he was rewarding diligence and promoting a soldier who had the secret of victory. It was quite a while before he realized that Halleck, although diligent, shared with General McClellan a singular genius for making war in low gear. Halleck understood everything except the need to be in a hurry. He carried moderation to excess, and he was aggressive only in theory. He could crowd a weaker opponent into a corner, but instead of exterminating him there he would give him a chance to get out; and in July of 1862, when he was called to Washington and placed in supreme command, he fully shared with General McClellan responsibility for the fact that the war's tide had turned and that the Confederacy's prospects were brighter than they had been for many months.

It was not easy to see this, because Halleck had been in command in the west and in the west the Federals had been winning decisively. The trouble was that what was won did not stay won. Victories were not spiked down and made permanent. The beaten foe always got a chance to get up and renew the fight. Since the foe had infinite determination, this chance was always accepted.

Federal armies had occupied New Orleans and Memphis, driven the foe from Missouri and western Tennessee, seized northern Alabama and Mississippi, occupied Cumberland Gap, paralyzed the Confederacy's vital western railway network and (working with the powerful Federal fleets) had opened all but a tiny fragment of the great Mississippi waterway. By the middle of July they had thus gained an advantage that the Confederacy could not possibly overcome without plenty of time to repair damages, harness unused resources and fight according to its own plan rather than to the plan of the invader. General Halleck let it have this time, just as General McClellan had done. If the consequences were less spectacular they were equally expensive.

After he took Corinth, General Halleck did exactly what beaten Beauregard hoped he would do. Instead of moving boldly on with a force too large for his opponents to meet he divided his army into halves, separated the two halves, and presently lost the initiative without even knowing he had lost it.[1]

Restored to his old command, Grant became head of an army of occupation, protecting the ground that had been gained but unable to do more than that. His troops were spraddled out from Memphis eastward to the Tennessee River, holding a belt of northern Mississippi, repairing and garrisoning the railway line that went all the way north to Columbus in Kentucky. He had plenty of men to do all of this, but he did not believe that he had enough to do this and in addition mount a real offensive; furthermore, what he did would be conditioned to a large extent by the doings of the other half of the victorious army, the half commanded by General Don Carlos Buell.

3: *A Long and Strong Flood*

While Grant held western Tennessee, Buell was instructed to go out and take eastern Tennessee. He would move almost directly eastward from Corinth, crossing the Tennessee River at Decatur and following that river and the Memphis & Charleston Railroad to Chattanooga; the project had such high priority that when Mr. Lincoln and Secretary Stanton called on Halleck for 25,000 men to reinforce McClellan after the Seven Days defeat they told him to send no one at all if to do so would delay or imperil Buell's move. Naturally enough, Halleck sent no one, but the all-important campaign west went slowly—apparently because both generals seemed to worry more about what Buell was moving away from than about his destination. His base of supplies lay at Louisville, far to the north, and when he began to move he had to repair and protect the Memphis & Charleston road so that these supplies (coming down from Louisville most roundabout) could reach him; difficult, because the road ran parallel to the Confederate front and could be broken easily. At Decatur, Alabama, he reached a north-south line from Nashville, and eighty miles farther east, at Stevenson, a second line from Nashville came down, and these routes seemed infinitely preferable, once he got to them; but during July, while his army inched its way toward Chattanooga, Buell learned something about the kind of cavalrymen the Confederacy had in its service and the lesson was so instructive that he never did get to Chattanooga.

The first teacher was a soldier who, like the Jeb Stuart who plagued McClellan, combined jaunty flamboyance with solid competence: a big Kentuckian named John Hunt Morgan, who left Knoxville early in July with nine hundred troopers and rode northwest into Kentucky. Here, for more than three weeks, he went rampaging about, destroying Federal supply dumps, dodging or beating the Federal cavalry detachments that came out to stop him, wrecking railroad lines, beating up the environs of Lexington and Frankfort and raising such a disturbance that the President notified Halleck: "They are having a stampede in Kentucky. Please look to it." Halleck in turn told Buell to suppress Morgan even if it delayed the advance on Chattanooga.[2] It was quite beyond Buell's power to suppress Morgan, but the Chattanooga expedition was unquestionably delayed.

Even worse was a simultaneous raid mounted by Nathan Bedford Forrest, the untaught soldier who made war with driving fury, and who had just been appointed a brigadier general. Forrest took a thousand men out of Chattanooga on July 9 and rode into middle Tennessee, picking up reinforcements along the way, capturing a whole brigade of Buell's troops, a live brigadier general and half a million dollars worth of supplies at Murfreesboro. He got away clean, destroyed three important railroad bridges near Nashville, and came so close to Nashville that the Federals there thought he was actually going to capture the place. He no sooner went away than Morgan came back, riding across Tennessee not far north of Nashville and making a serious break in the Louisville & Nashville line near the town of Gallatin; when Federal cavalry came out to fight him, Morgan beat and dispersed it and captured the commanding general. Federal reports on all of this bristle with complaints about disgraceful conduct on the part of Yankee cavalrymen, but the complaints do no more than prove that Morgan and Forrest knew how to find and hit the weak spots. They also knew how to show Buell that the north-south railroads in Tennessee were little safer that the east-west line in northern Alabama.[3]

But the real trouble was not with the supply lines. Buell's march was leisurely from beginning to end—one officer in Buell's army said it was "like holiday soldiering," with the average day's march beginning at dawn and ending long before noon—and the notion that it might be well to beat the Confederates to Chattanooga bothered hardly anybody. Buell left Corinth on June 10, came within striking distance of Chattanooga before July ended, and never struck; in effect his army went aground along the Alabama-Tennessee border and remained aground until late in August, stirring into active movement only when the Confederates at last assumed the offensive. Buell was an extremely deliberate soldier and Halleck could not hurry him. One of Halleck's defects was that he did not know how to spur a subordinate on: he could only nag at him, filling the record with warnings but never actually infusing a sense of urgency into anyone. A Lee or a Grant in Halleck's position that summer would have had faster movement on the Chattanooga expedition or a new commander; Halleck could only call for speed without getting it.[4]

So Chattanooga, which might have been taken, was not taken. The same was true of Vicksburg.

In the month of June 1862, Vicksburg was just waiting for someone to come and capture it. Hasty fortifications had been built, eighteen guns had been mounted, and 3600 infantry had been assembled, but the great fortress that was to block the Federal advance for a year had hardly begun to take shape. Just below the city was Admiral Farragut, with *Hartford* and ten other deep-water cruisers and Porter's mortar flotilla; just above was Flag Officer Davis, who had four armored river gunboats and some more mortars. With all of this naval power on hand, two divisions from Halleck's army could have taken the place with ease; and the three miles along the Vicksburg waterfront were at that time the only piece of the entire Mississippi River which the Confederacy really controlled.

But Halleck was still digesting Corinth. The Navy Department, in turn, inspired by what Farragut had done at New Orleans, believed that the old admiral and his squadron had unlimited capabilities, and without waiting for Halleck it told Farragut to go ahead and smash the Vicksburg batteries the way he had smashed Forts Jackson and St. Philip. Ben Butler had sent three thousand soldiers up the river with Farragut, under Brigadier General Thomas Williams; once Farragut had pulverized the defenses, these could go ashore and occupy the town just as Butler had occupied New Orleans.

Admiral Farragut was game but skeptical. His ships badly needed repair, it was hard to get coal, the river was falling and deep-draft ships might run aground, his crews were sickly, and anyway he had not actually smashed these lower-river forts; he had pounded them and passed by, and they had surrendered because once New Orleans was occupied they were hopelessly cut off. At Vicksburg the case was very different, because Vicksburg could not be cut off by water. It could never just be occupied; it would have to be fought for, and most of the fighting would have to be done by soldiers on dry land.

Farragut tried. On June 28, after Porter's mortars had bombarded the Confederate works without great effect, he took his burly ships up the river. There was a spectacular two-hour running fight, in which three of the Federal ships were turned back. The rest got through, with moderate losses to personnel, the Confederate batteries had suffered little damage—and Farragut, as he had anticipated, found that he had indeed got the bulk of his fleet past Vicksburg but that nothing noteworthy had been accomplished. Williams's brigade was altogether too weak to take Vicksburg by storm; lacking anything better to do, it went ashore on the Louisiana side of the river and began trying to dig a canal across the base of the long, narrow point of land opposite Vicksburg, in the hope that the Mississippi would cut a new channel there and leave Vicksburg high and dry. (It was a vain hope. The soldiers dug a huge ditch but it had been planned badly and the river refused to do its part. The scheme fascinated Federal planners for months to come, and hundreds of thousands of man-hours of hard work were expended in the steaming heat, but was all a wasted effort.) Farragut's fleet above the city was no better off that it had been below.[5]

Meanwhile, Vicksburg ceased to be an easy mark. Before June ended there were 10,000 Southern soldiers in the place, with energetic Earl Van Dorn to command them, and day by day the defenses grew stronger; and presently it was the Federals rather than the Confederates who were in difficulty. Visible sign of this change was a remarkable exploit by a remarkable warship, C.S.S. *Arkansas,* which came out on July 15 to the intense embarrassment of the United States Navy, and which eventually gave Admiral Farragut an excuse to go all the way back to salt water.

Like all of Secretary Mallory's ironclads, *Arkansas* faintly resembled *Merrimack-Virginia.* Her 180-foot hull was low in the water, with a central citadel for guns and machinery protected by an armor belt three inches thick, ingeniously but precariously made out of railroad rails bolted to stout wooden bulwarks. She had an iron beak for ramming, ten powerful guns, twin screws, and rickety machinery that was quite likely to break down just when a breakdown would be most damaging; with all her defects she was a most formidable antagonist, and that she existed at all was largely due to her commanding officer, Lieutenant Isaac N. Brown, who would have been an asset to anybody's navy.

During the winter and spring *Arkansas* had been under construction at Memphis, and after the fall of Island Number Ten, the unfinished craft was towed down the Mississippi and up the Yazoo, which enters the big river just above Vicksburg, and moored at the town of Greenwood, two hundred miles upstream. On May 28, Lieutenant Brown was ordered to go to Greenwood, finish the warship, arm and man her, and then take her out and fight the Yankees. He found that he had an empty hull, with disassembled machinery, no carriages for the guns, and most of the railroad iron lying at the bottom of the river in a sunken scow. Since the Yazoo was in a state of flood, the place where the *Arkansas* was moored was four miles from dry land, and Greenwood lacked machine shops and other manufacturing facilities. Somehow he got the hulk towed 150 miles downstream to Yazoo City, where there was high ground. He fished up the sunken railroad iron, got a detail of two hundred soldiers to toil as ships' carpenters, sent armed men around the neighboring plantations to seize fourteen forges and attendant blacksmiths, hired men to fell trees, cut green timber and make gun carriages (which had never before been made in the state of Mississippi) somehow kept the job going on a twenty-four-hour basis—and, in a little more than five weeks, got the thing done. *Arkansas* was given a crew—sailors from the river fleet that had been lost at Memphis, plus a number of volunteers from Jeff Thompson's Missouri command—and Lieutenant Brown was instructed to report to General Van Dorn for orders.

Brown wanted to stay in the Yazoo and hold that river for the Confederacy: an idea that made sense, for the Yazoo came down from some of the richest farming country in North America, and it would be well to keep out Yankee marauders. Van Dorn wanted him at Vicksburg, however, so Brown headed downstream—stopping for a day, en route, to make repairs and dry out damp powder, his wheezy engines having leaked steam into one of his magazines. On July 15, *Arkansas* came down to the mouth of the Yazoo looking for a fight.

The Federals had heard rumors about her, and this day they sent three warships up the Yazoo to investigate—two wooden craft and the armored gunboat *Carondelet*, which had run the batteries at Island Number Ten, and whose commanding officer, Henry Walke, had been a messmate and friend of Isaac Brown on a round-the-world cruise in the prewar Navy. *Arkansas* met the trio a few miles from the Mississippi and immediately opened fire; *Carondelet* was disabled and driven into shallow water, the unarmored gunboats fled at top speed, and *Arkansas* came out into the big river to find the entire Federal fleet, Farragut's and Davis's ships together, anchored in two long lines on opposite sides of the river. This probably would have been the end of it, except that the Federals were caught napping, with no steam up. Brown cruised past the combined fleets, firing as he went, taking a hammering but reaching the Vicksburg waterfront triumphantly and making fast to a wharf under the protection of Confederate batteries. Brown had been wounded twice, the armor on *Arkansas's* port side was almost ready to fall off, and the ship had a staggering casualty list, but she had unquestionably wiped the eye of the United States Navy.[6]

That night Farragut sought revenge. The spot where *Arkansas* had tied up was noted, and range lights were fixed on the opposite shore to mark the place; and after dark, while a thunderstorm raged, Farragut's squadron went steaming down past Vicksburg, each one firing a broadside at *Arkansas's* berth. This would probably have destroyed her if she had been there, but she was not: the Confederates had noticed the range lights and, guessing what was coming, had shifted *Arkansas* to a different position. The Federals made a huge noise and expended much ammunition but did no especial harm, and Farragut unhappily confessed his "great mortification" in a message to Secretary Welles, admitting frankly that the Confederates had taken him entirely by surprise. Welles testily told him he had better not leave Vicksburg until *Arkansas* was sunk; then, after a day or so, thought better of it, and telegraphed the admiral that he could leave whenever he chose. Farragut chose to leave at once and went steaming off to New Orleans, dropping General Williams and the troops at Baton Rouge as he went. A few days later Davis pulled his own fleet up to the mouth of the Yazoo, retiring shortly thereafter all the way to Helena, Arkansas, and the Confederates had Vicksburg all to themselves.[7]

Actually, they had a good deal more than that. Jubilant over Farragut's departure, Van Dorn ordered General Breckinridge to take five thousand men down the river and recapture Baton Rouge. Breckinridge tried, on August 5, and was beaten off after a fight in which General Williams lost his life, but although Breckinridge lost this fight the Confederacy had unquestionably won the campaign. In mid-June it had owned no more than three miles of the Mississippi; by mid-August it held several hundred miles of it—everything from Helena to Port Hudson, Louisiana, a few miles above Baton Rouge, where Breckinridge built a fort. It continued to have ready access via the Red River to all of its resources in the trans-Mississippi region, and the Federals were farther from opening the river than they had been at the end of the spring, when the job was all but completed. *Arkansas* presently ran hard aground because of an engine failure and had to be blown up, but she had served her purpose. Considering the fact that the southland contained hardly any sailors, mechanics, shipwrights, naval architects, or iron workers, Mr. Mallory and his men were showing an amazing aptitude for building and using armored warships.

Colonel Morgan, General Forrest, and Lieutenant Brown were the living signs that something was wrong with the Federal conduct of the war in the west. Three cavalry raids involving fewer than three thousand troopers all told, and one wild cruise by a square-cornered gunboat jerry-built by amateurs on the edge of a cornfield—these would have been no more than incidents, except that the Federal power had let the war get into a condition of unstable equilibrium in which mere incidents could jar it into a new shape. If blows so light would mean so much, a really hard blow might have prodigious effect.

A hard blow was in fact being prepared, and would be launched by General Braxton Bragg.

Bragg was a strange combination, a hard case with an unpredictable streak of irresolution; stern, angular, contentious, a man who would seem to have been utterly lacking in personal magnetism except that he remained a romantic hero to his wife, Elise Bragg, and to the end retained the affection and trust of Jefferson Davis, who was somewhat angular and contentious in his own right. Mrs. Bragg wrote sensitive love letters to her husband. Like any soldier's wife, she was haunted by the fear that he might be killed in action, and she comforted herself with the thought that his high rank would keep him away from the firing line. Then came Shiloh, where the army commander himself was killed, and she wrote pathetically: "I had taught myself to believe *you could not* be hurt, danger had so often surrounded you, your high rank in a measure protected you. The first awakening from this hope was the death of Johnston—his rank was higher—his poor wife had probably thought the same with me." She wanted his physical presence, and she could write: "Oh that you could come to your wife's arms for a few days, until soothed and calmed she could restore you to your country."[8]

Bragg got command of the Confederate Army at Tupelo, after Beauregard was removed, and he took hold with firmness, ordering the death penalty for stragglers and looters and enforcing his orders rigorously. A general who behaves so does not win the affection of his soldiers, yet this harshness—applied to an army which had been almost entirely out of hand on the short march up to Pittsburg Landing in April—seems to have improved morale. After one private was court-martialed and executed for shooting at a chicken, missing, and hitting a Negro, one of the man's comrades ruefully admitted that the army's discipline was improved "because it felt it had at its head a man who would do what he said and whose orders were to be obeyed." Bragg drove himself as hard as he drove anyone else, ruining first his digestion and then his temper by constant overwork; a fellow officer who admired his zeal and felt that he was getting good results confessed that his ways were so stern that he "could have won the affection of his troops only by leading them to victory." Bragg found Army command a strain, but at the moment his health was good and he told Mrs. Bragg that he hoped to "mark the enemy before I break down." He added that the tide had turned in favor of the Confederacy and he saw the prospect of "a long and strong flood."[9]

The turning tide would strike Buell first. With more than 40,000 men, that methodical officer was carefully getting ready to move on Chattanooga, but he was taking ever so much time about it and his own position actually was most insecure; he was a long way from his base, and if the Confederates could strike northwest from eastern Tennessee in strength they might cut him off and give him serious trouble.

When the summer began the Confederates had a little more than 15,000 men in eastern Tennessee. Most of these were at Knoxville, under the command of a solid Old Army soldier, Major General Edmund Kirby Smith, who had led a brigade at Bull Run, had been wounded in action, and enjoyed the full confidence of the authorities at Richmond. A small Union force had recently occupied Cumberland Gap, the difficult northern gateway to eastern Tennessee, but it was not yet an offensive threat and Kirby Smith was strong enough to contain it. He was not strong enough, however, to do anything about Buell, and in June he notified Richmond that Chattanooga would be lost unless strong reinforcements could be sent in. At the same time he wrote to Bragg, explaining that he was powerless to save Chattanooga. Bragg immediately sent three thousand men to Chattanooga as a stop gap, and then studied the situation to see if he could not do more.[10]

He found that he could do much more, and he did it with speed, efficiency and daring. He would leave Van Dorn with 16,000 men to hold Vicksburg, and he would leave General Price with 16,000 more at Tupelo to watch northern Mississippi; between them, these officers ought to be able to handle any offensive Grant was likely to make this summer, especially in view of the abrupt lessening in Federal naval pressure on the Mississippi. With the rest of his army, approximately 31,000 men, Bragg boldly set out for Chattanooga, planning not merely to protect that city but to join with Smith in an invasion of Kentucky that would compel Buell to retreat and might even drive him to destruction. Then the "long and strong flood" Bragg had hoped for would be a reality.

One thing Bragg understood clearly. This was a railroad war, the first one in history, and a general who knew how to use the rails could move armies faster and farther than armies had ever been moved before. To get from Tupelo to Chattanooga he had to take the long way around—776 miles, over six railroads, going south from Tupelo to Mobile, northeast to Montgomery and Atlanta and then northwest to Chattanooga—but the railroads could move the army much more quickly than it could go if it took the direct route and walked, and Bragg's headquarters understood logistics. The army began to move on July 23, and late in July Bragg and his 31,000 were coming into Chattanooga and Bragg and Smith were planning a campaign into Buell's rear. The whole complexion of the war in the west had changed.[11]

The Confederacy had regained the offensive; the lid was off, and infinite possibilities were in the air. Neither Chattanooga nor even Vicksburg, which the Federals could have had for the taking six weeks earlier, was in danger now; instead Buell was in danger, the whole Federal grip on the Mississippi Valley was threatened, a Confederate invasion of the North was taking form, and the war which had seemed so near to its end was beginning all over again.

4: *Triumph in Disaster*

Howell Cobb of Georgia, who was one of the founding fathers of the Confederate States of America, was putting in the summer as a brigadier general in the Army of Northern Virginia. As a military man he had but a modest position in the chain of command, but as one of the nation's most eminent political leaders he could talk to anybody on equal terms, and early in August he saw hard times coming and sent a brief warning to Secretary of War Randolph.

"This war must close in a few months, perhaps weeks," he wrote, "or else will be fought with increased energy and malignity on the part of our enemies. I look for the latter result."[1]

His forecast was sound, and the most obvious sign that he knew what he was talking about lay in the things which were being said and done just then by a new Federal Army commander in Virginia, Major General John Pope.

General Pope, who had made a first-rate record in the west, had been brought east by the Northern government late in June to make an army out of the luckless contingents which had suffered so much at the hands of Stonewall Jackson: the commands of Frémont, Banks, and McDowell. Frémont, who ranked Pope, considered the new arrangement an insult and resigned, his departure lamented by no one save the most ardent abolitionists. He was replaced by Franz Sigel, who had fought poorly at Wilson's Creek and well at Pea Ridge; a soldier who, if not exactly a hero to the abolitionists, was at least a hero to the German-American soldiers who had strong anti-slavery leanings. Sigel, Banks, and McDowell became corps commanders in the army which Pope put together: a force which numbered, at the outset, about 42,000 men and which Pope concentrated along the upper Rappahannock with aggressive intent. At the very least he could take the pressure off of McClellan's beaten army; with luck, he and McClellan together might stage a pincers operation that would capture Richmond and destroy Lee's army. The odds were against it, because Lee was squarely between them and was most unlikely to permit any such thing, but on paper at least the project was feasible.

Pope was energetic. He also was full of windy bluster, and although he actually was no more brutal than many other Federal generals he had a great talent for seeming to be so, and his appearance in the Virginia theater did symbolize a hardening of Federal policy, which presently became quite as malignant as Howell Cobb anticipated. In the end good Southerners hated John Pope almost as much as they hated Ben Butler.

Broadly speaking, Pope had been brought east to fight with the gloves off: to be aggressive, to live off the country as far as possible, and to teach the inhabitants of occupied Virginia that secession was a rocky road to travel. He began by issuing a singularly maladroit address to his troops, announcing that in the west Union soldiers usually saw only the backs of their enemies and declaring that he wanted to hear no more about defensive positions, lines of retreat and the like—an army that advanced and won battles did not need to worry about such things. This done, he spelled out his policy toward noncombatants in a series of orders which clearly indicated that the whole atmosphere of the war had changed.

Citizens of occupied territory would be held responsible for all damage done by guerrillas; the guerrillas themselves, if caught, would be executed and so would everyone who had aided them. If shots were fired at Union soldiers from any house, that house would be destroyed and the people who lived in it would be arrested. Disloyal citizens would be driven outside the army's lines, and if they returned they would be treated as spies. Inhabitants of occupied territory who did not leave home must take the oath of allegiance to the United States, and any who took this oath and then violated it would be shot. Furthermore, the United States Army would confiscate any forage or other foodstuffs that it needed when it was operating in secessionist territory.[2]

The bark was really worse than the bite. The harshest parts of the orders were not enforced, innocent noncombatants were not shot despite these rasped threats, and by the end of the war the policy thus laid down would be considered more or less normal for an army campaigning in hostile country. But these orders did not come at the end of the war; they came when the old illusion that some limit could be placed on mortal combat still lingered, when the phrase about "the war between brothers" might yet seem to connote romance and good sportsmanship rather than anger, bitterness and a deep desire to hurt. They outraged and shocked the Southern nation, which at once concluded that John Pope was a monster, but their real significance went far beyond Pope. They meant that the Federal government had at last abandoned the belief that it could make war dispassionately and without leaving scars and resentment. As Mr. Davis promptly pointed out to the Confederate Congress, these orders were perfectly in tune with the spirit of the Confiscation Act which the Federal Congress had recently adopted: they meant ruthlessness and a fight to the finish, and the Confederacy could respond only by "employing against our foe every energy and every resource at our disposal."[3]

If the shootings and imprisonments promised by General Pope failed to materialize, the orders did bring much suffering to Virginians who lived in the path of Pope's army. The Federal soldiers never were tightly disciplined, any long march meant extensive straggling, the stragglers always included the worst rowdies in the army, and the men now interpreted the new directive to mean that pillage and looting were more or less legal. Farms were stripped of livestock and grain, smokehouses were robbed, homes were entered, and one Federal officer ruefully admitted that "the lawless acts of many of our soldiers are worthy of worse than death." Most of the men rationalized their behavior: it was absurd to protect secessionist property when the men who were trying to put down secession were hungry. This feeling as a matter of fact existed in McClellan's army as well as in Pope's, and some of the Army of the Potomac units this summer ravaged the Virginia peninsula with a heavy hand.[4]

As an inevitable by-product, the soldiers became an antislavery force. An army which, by orders and on impulse, deprived secessionists of their property in order to win the war was not likely to make an exception in the case of human property. Soldiers who had not a trace of sympathy for the Negro would nevertheless set him free if his owner was an enemy who needed to be hurt. No matter what laws or proclamations might come out of Washington, the Union armies were certain to corrode the institution of slavery to the point of its collapse if they operated in slave territory long enough. The slaves themselves got the point before anyone else did, and the appearance of Federal troops sent waves of restlessness across every plantation. A few weeks after McDowell's regiments occupied Fredericksburg, Betty Herndon Maury noticed that the town was clogged with runaway slaves, who were "leaving their owners by the hundred and demanding wages." She added: "Many little difficulties have occurred since the Yankees have been here, between white people and Negroes. In every case the soldiers have interfered in favor of the Negroes."[5] Be it noted that this happened under McDowell, who was one Federal general who tried so hard to protect Southern property that his soldiers actually suspected him of being disloyal to the Union.

A ferment was working, and the only way to stop it was to stop the war, presumably by winning it. In Virginia the Federals had the manpower to win; McClellan and Pope had fully twice as many men as Lee had, and reinforcements were in sight. But McClellan was on the James and Pope was on the Rappahannock, and the victorious Army of Northern Virginia lay between them. Pope obviously would never be sent down to the peninsula, because the administration was as reluctant as ever to uncover Washington. He would unquestionably advance overland, striking at Richmond from the north, and his army was smaller than Lee's; if McClellan remained inert, Lee could slip out of Richmond, defeat Pope, and then get back and confront the Army of the Potomac in its lines at Harrison's Landing. So McClellan and Pope would have to work together and their moves would have to be precisely co-ordinated, and, early in July, Pope wrote to McClellan to find out what could be done.

McClellan's reply was cordial but not very helpful. He approved of Pope's decision to concentrate his forces, and he promised that if Pope advanced and was attacked by Lee, "I will move upon Richmond, do my best to take it, and endeavor to cut off his retreat." But he warned that "it is not yet determined what policy the enemy intends to pursue, whether to attack Washington or to bestow his entire attention upon this army"; for his own part, McClellan could only say that "I shall carefully watch for any fault committed by the enemy and take advantage of it." To this frank acknowledgment that Lee had the initiative, McClellan added the hope that Pope could at least advance his cavalry enough to divert Lee's attention from the Army of the Potomac.[6]

It would have been hard enough at best to get one harmonious offensive from these two separated armies; as things actually were it was simply impossible. McClellan and Pope disliked and distrusted each other intensely. McClellan expected Pope to fail and Pope expected McClellan to let him fail, and in the end each man was right. When Pope first reached Washington he told President Lincoln that McClellan ought to be removed, and not long afterward he assured

Secretary Chase that McClellan's "incompetency and indisposition to active movements" were so great that if Pope ever needed the help of McClellan's army he was not likely to get it. McClellan's opinion of Pope was unquestionably expressed (at least in part) by his close confidant, Fitz John Porter, who told a friend that in his address to his troops Pope "has now written himself down, what the military world has long known, an Ass," and said that the Army of the Potomac had no confidence in the man.[7] Only an alert and forceful general-in-chief could have made Pope and McClellan work together, and the general-in-chief at this point was Halleck.

Halleck assumed his new duties in Washington on July 23. Realizing that the first trouble spot to examine was at Harrison's Landing, he left immediately for that place to have a talk with McClellan. Six months earlier he had assured McClellan that the Federals' "want of success" came because politicians rather than soldiers were making mistakes;[8] now he and McClellan, two generals who had done much to prove that this appraisal was wrong, would see if they could somehow manage to get the Army of the Potomac back into action.

McClellan told Barlow that he had not been consulted about Halleck's appointment and that the move was undoubtedly "intended as 'a slap in the face'"; he believed that he himself was about to be relieved of his command, and since he was tired "of submitting to the whims of such 'things' as those now over me" he would be happy enough to go into retirement. He preserved the amenities, however, telling Halleck that he would have urged his appointment if he had been asked for his advice and assuring him that he felt not a particle of enmity or jealousy. This was perhaps stretching things a little, but at least the two generals conferred without striking sparks.[9]

The interview was fairly brief, and neither man got much out of it. Halleck was informed that the Army of the Potomac was badly outnumbered—its latest report showed 101,000 present for duty, but Lee had at least 200,000. (Halleck told Secretary Stanton when he got back to Washington that he had not been in the east long enough to know whether this estimate of Lee's strength was correct.) The army would advance on Richmond if it could be strongly reinforced; meanwhile it would be bad to withdraw it from the peninsula, because the true defense of Washington was there. McClellan in turn was told that it was impossible to reinforce him to any great extent; if he could not move on Richmond with very moderate additions to his strength it would probably be necessary to withdraw his army. (If the Army of the Potomac and Pope's army were made into one, Halleck wanted McClellan to command the whole.) Then Halleck returned to Washington, reflected that if McClellan was right about the size of Lee's army it was mortally dangerous to approach that army with divided forces, and on July 30 he sent word that "in order to enable you to move in any direction" McClellan should at once send away his sick men, of whom there were about 12,000.

Then, on August 3, the ax came down. Halleck formally notified McClellan that "it is determined to withdraw your army from the peninsula to Aquia Creek." McClellan protested vigorously, but Halleck was firm: the decision was his own, he would risk his reputation on it, and McClellan must hurry the movement as fast as he could.[10]

So the peninsula campaign was over, the first great campaign of the Army of the Potomac. It had lasted just about four months: a month at Yorktown, nearly a month spent moving from Yorktown to the lines along the Chickahominy, a month in front of Richmond ending in the agony of the Seven Days, and finally a month of dazed convalescence at Harrison's Landing. The army had fought hard and endured much, it had pride and self-pity at the same time, and it was developing its own legend, which—like the profound emotional attachment which it had for its commanding general—would always set it apart from the other Union armies. It was acquiring what can only be called a sort of dogged pessimism, a fatalistic readiness to expect the worst, as if it sensed that its best efforts would be wasted but was not thereby made disheartened; and now as for months to come it would have to keep step with its rival, the Army of Northern Virginia.

The Army of Northern Virginia was also developing its own distinctive character. It had a harder, more tragic fate, and yet there is more laughter in its legend—as if, in some unaccountable way, it worried less. Out of hardship, intermittent malnutrition, and desperately-won victories it was creating a lean, threadbare jauntiness. Beneath this was the great characteristic which it derived from its commander—the resolute belief that it could not really be beaten no matter what the odds might be. It had paid many lives for that conviction and it would pay many more before it reached the last turn in the road, but what it got seems to have been worth the price.

In the middle of July its situation did not exactly look promising. The invading Federals had been beaten but they had not been driven away, and they were still camped within twenty-five miles of Richmond. With a Federal fleet in the James, Lee had never seen any chance to attack the Harrison's Landing camp successfully, and for some weeks after Malvern Hill he believed that McClellan would be reinforced and would try again to capture Richmond. Pope's concentration along the upper Rappahannock contained the threat of final disaster, for it hinted that the Federals might at last be trying to bring their overwhelming numerical advantage to bear at close quarters. The figures told the story. Pope's strength had been raised to more than 50,000, although not all of these were at hand—one division lay far to the east, at Fredericksburg, and other units had not come down from the Shenandoah. Burnside was bringing 12,000 men up from North Carolina and would move to join Pope before long. Even if McClellan left 10,000 men to hold Fort Monroe, which was probable, it was clear that if he and Pope moved together the Federals could assemble more than 140,000 men at the gates of Richmond. Lee commanded fewer than 70,000 men of all arms. His only recourse was to put Pope out of action before the gigantic concentration could be effected.[11]

He could do it if he moved fast and boldly—provided, of course, that the Army of the Potomac, which was close enough to put the clamps on at any time, permitted him to move at all. On July 13 he took the first step, sending Stonewall Jackson with 12,000 men off to Gordonsville, where the Virginia Central Railroad crossed the line of the Orange & Alexandria. (If his army planned to go north or if Pope's army planned to come south, Gordonsville was a place the Confederacy had to hold.) This was bold enough, because Gordonsville was sixty miles from Richmond and if McClellan advanced suddenly Jackson could not get back in time; but anything was better than to remain inactive and await envelopment, and Lee took the risk. News of the move reached both Pope and McClellan, but nothing happened. Pope went on concentrating his army in the vicinity of Sperryville, twenty-five miles north of Jackson's position, and McClellan stayed at Harrison's Landing, demanding reinforcements. The first step having been taken successfully, Lee went on to take a longer one, sending A. P. Hill and his powerful "light division" off to join Jackson.

Lee was gambling, having coldly weighed the odds. When Hill reached him, Jackson had nearly 30,000 of the best soldiers in Lee's army. The Army of the Potomac, hardly two marches away from Richmond, now had a solid two-to-one advantage in numbers, and again if it saw its opportunity and acted on it the Confederacy might be ruined. Lee frankly told Mr. Davis that he disliked to reduce his own strength so drastically, but that Jackson's original force was not big enough to attack Pope and that Pope "ought to be suppressed if possible."[12] Whatever risks this action might involve, the worst risk of all for a general in Lee's situation was to try to play it safe; so Lee waited, with the controlled calm of a gambler who has everything riding on the next play, while Jackson marched north of the Rapidan to commence the suppression of General Pope.

For a few hours it looked as if General McClellan might spoil everything. On August 5 he sent an infantry division forward to occupy Malvern Hill, a move which might easily be the first phase of a massive advance on Richmond. Lee ordered out the troops and came down to give battle if necessary, but he soon concluded that McClellan was just reconnoitering and he calmly wrote to Jackson, "I have no idea that he will advance on Richmond now." Jackson's own move, he added, looked sound, and he hoped Jackson could attack Pope before long.[13] Lee's estimate of McClellan's intentions was correct. After spending twenty-four hours surveying the scene from Malvern Hill, the Federal column called in its skirmishers and went back to Harrison's Landing.

Having learned that Pope had posted two undersized divisions near the town of Culpeper, Jackson marched north to pounce on this force before it could be strengthened or withdrawn. He encountered it on August 9, drawn up along a little stream near a hill known as Cedar Mountain, and perhaps it was reminiscent of the great days in the Shenandoah Valley because these 8000 Federals were commanded by the General Banks who had played such a large and unhappy role in the Valley campaign. Banks had been beaten there, and now he must be beaten here; Jackson immediately ordered an attack.

He was just a little too immediate about it, as a matter of fact, because he attacked before half of his men were in position, and Banks's soldiers put up a stiff fight. They killed Brigadier General Charles S. Winder, who commanded what was formerly Jackson's own division, caught his men off balance, and drove the first Confederate assault back in disorder, routing the famous Stonewall Brigade which had won General Jackson a nickname at Bull Run. But Jackson rallied his men, brought up A. P. Hill's division, and late in the day launched an overpowering assault that swept the field. Once again, Banks had to retreat; Jackson followed him a short distance, found that Pope with most of his army was not far away, and then withdrew behind the Rapidan. The battle meant nothing in particular, except that it raised Confederate morale and further depressed the Yankees; but it did give clear notice that a large part of Lee's army was a long way from Richmond, and that a curious reversal of roles had taken place. Until this moment the focal point for all of the military activity in Virginia had been the city of Richmond; now it was the army of John Pope.[14] Lee was on the offensive.

Cedar Mountain was fought on August 9. On August 13 Lee sent James Longstreet and 25,000 men away from Richmond to Gordonsville, and two days later he departed for Gordonsville himself. He was leaving fewer than 25,000 men to protect the capital—infallible sign that he expected no trouble from General McClellan—and he was taking all the rest of his army, between 50,000 and 55,000 men, up to the Rapidan River. He had called his army the Army of Northern Virginia, and he was going to get it back to northern Virginia no matter what. The Federals could perhaps stop him, but time was running out on them; they had been prodigal of it all year, and they had used up their surplus; now they must act with speed. Specifically, they could keep Lee from doing what he intended to do—smash Pope and carry the war up to the Maryland border—only if the Army of the Potomac moved faster than it had ever moved before.

There is a might-have-been here. The operation against Pope—the strategic combination which transferred the war from the suburbs of Richmond to the environs of Washington—could have been broken up late in July by a vigorous advance by the Army of the Potomac. No such advance was made or seriously contemplated. On July 26, long after Jackson had been detached, McClellan told Halleck that reinforcements were "pouring into Richmond" and suggested that he should have Burnside's and Hunter's men plus 20,000 fresh troops from the west so that he could renew his campaign. Two days later he reported that this story about Confederate reinforcements had been confirmed. Lee's plans would never be interrupted by a general whose grip on reality was that infirm, and when McClellan finally realized what was happening and (on August 12) asked permission to advance on Richmond it was too late.[15] His own orders to come north were more than a week old; Washington had made up its mind. He might, just conceivably, have marched toward Richmond without orders, and Mr. Lincoln almost certainly would have upheld him, but he did not do it and it is almost impossible to imagine him acting so. The only thing to do now was to get the Army of the Potomac up to join hands with Pope for a new campaign.

The movement was made reluctantly. Eleven days passed between the receipt of orders and the beginning of their execution. To an extent this is understandable. To organize the withdrawal of a large army was an intricate business, and it took time to line up the transports, to schedule the embarkation of the various units and to arrange for debarkation along the upper Potomac. But under this there was the undeniable fact that the army command did not for one moment want to do what it was being forced to do, and it was moving with leaden feet, muttering furiously as it did so. The atmosphere around the headquarters tents was murky, with bitter resentment moving through sulkiness toward outright defiance. General Burnside visited Harrison's Landing while Halleck was there and Quartermaster General Montgomery Meigs remembered that the staff officers who sat around a campfire outside the tent where Halleck and McClellan conferred said openly that the army ought to march on Washington "to clear out those fellows"—an echo, although Meigs did not know it, of the dark thought McClellan had toyed with in a recent letter. Burnside, honest and uncomplicated, listened to this for a while and then got to his feet and said: "I don't know what you fellows call this talk, but I call it flat treason, by God!"[16]

Staff talk, to be sure, is often frothy; but it does reflect a state of mind. Army headquarters was haunted by a brooding suspicion that disaster might even be a good thing. If Pope's army came to grief, would not the policy of the Army of the Potomac (overruled by the malevolent incompetents in Washington) somehow be vindicated? Alexander Webb, a young staff officer, expressed this feeling bluntly in a letter written the day the first units of the army left for the north: "I have one hope left; when that ass Pope shall have lost his army, and when Washington shall again be menaced (say in six days from this time) then and only then will they find out that our little General is not in his right place and then they will call loudly for his aid."[17]

McClellan himself never put it quite that way, but he came fairly close to it. At the end of July he had expressed his gloom in a letter to Barlow: "If this army is retired from here I abandon all hope—our cause will be lost." Three weeks later, just before he himself left the peninsula, he was able to see good fortune for himself in disaster for another, and he wrote to Mrs. McClellan: "I believe I have triumphed!! Just received a telegram from Halleck stating that Pope and Burnside are very hard pressed."[18]

5: *The Pressures of War*

The letter from Lord Palmerston struck Charles Francis Adams as both irregular and ominous. It was irregular because the Prime Minister did not usually communicate directly with the representative of any foreign power; when he had anything to say to such a person he spoke through the Foreign Minister, Lord Russell. In addition, the letter was ill-tempered and unfriendly. Both in what it said and in the fact that it had been written at all it seemed to indicate that Her Majesty's government was looking for trouble, and when he finished reading it Mr. Adams tossed it across the table to his son and asked: "Does Palmerston want a quarrel?"

Dated June 11 and marked "confidential," the letter read as follows:

"I cannot refrain from taking the liberty of saying to you that it is difficult if not impossible to express adequately the disgust which must be excited in the mind of every honorable man by the general order of General Butler, given in the enclosed extract from yesterday's 'Times.' Even when a town is taken by assault it is the practice of the commander of the conquering army to protect to his utmost the inhabitants and especially the female part of them, and I will venture to say that no example can be found in the history of civilized nations, till the publication of this order, of a general guilty in cold blood of so infamous an act as deliberately to hand over the female inhabitants of a conquered city to the unbridled license of an unrestrained soldiery.

"If the Federal government chooses to be served by men capable of such revolting outrages, they must submit to abide by the deserved opinion which mankind will form of their conduct."[1]

The newspaper clipping, which had given upper-class England an exquisite case of the shudders, described the conduct of Major General Ben Butler, who was ruling occupied New Orleans with a maladroit and offensive efficiency. Not long after he got there Butler promised Montgomery Blair: "If I am let alone I will make this a Union city within sixty days."[2]

He was overconfident, because New Orleans was a big city with a deserved reputation for turbulence, and the occupation force was not large; still, he had restored order, and things had gone fairly well except that New Orleans did not in any sense become a Union city. General Butler had not been let alone. The women of New Orleans, who hated him and his soldiers and the whole Federal government, found a great many ways to show just how they felt, and the general feared that they might presently touch off a regular uprising. To prevent it he had issued, on May 15, General Orders No. 28, which reverberated near and far. This order announced that any woman who, by word or deed, insulted the Union flag, uniform, or army made herself liable to be treated as "a woman of the town, plying her vocation." Having issued this order, the general sat back to let the world digest it; one result being the angry letter sent to Mr. Adams by Lord Palmerston.

Admittedly, the situation had been difficult. Union officers had been spat upon as they walked along the sidewalks, household utensils had been emptied upon them, and there had been derogatory remarks and gestures. One woman was said to have rejoiced volubly when the funeral procession for a dead officer passed her house, and she had been arrested and given uncomfortable lodgings on desolate Ship Island, under guard; a scandalous punishment, for she was of gentle birth. An English merchant who was in New Orleans said that "a pretty Creole lady" told him: "Oh! How I hate the Yankees! I could trample on their dead bodies and spit on them!" Another lady wrote that Federal troops were by common report "the dirtiest, meanest-looking set that were ever seen—nothing at all of the soldier in their appearance," and one spunky young woman asked indignantly: "And how did they expect to be treated? Can a woman, a Southern woman, come in contact with one of them and allow her countenance to retain its wonted composure? Will not the scornful feelings in our hearts there find utterance?"[3]

There was no outlet for scornful feelings once Order Number 28 was published. Genteel womanhood could permit itself a certain leeway as long as the invader remained properly chivalrous, but Ben Butler did not go by the book and he had replaced chivalry with a lewd riddle: just how would a woman of the town who was plying her vocation be treated by occupation troops? Lord Palmerston (along with many others) feared that a licentious soldiery would do its dreadful worst; Butler himself argued that she would simply be ignored, her words and gestures disregarded; and no woman of New Orleans ever put the matter to the test. The icy silence of the carefully averted glance came down upon the city. No officers were insulted, and no women were molested, hatred grew deeper and quieter, and Mr. Adams had this letter from the Prime Minister of Great Britain to consider.[4]

He consulted Lord Russell, who knew nothing about the case and was himself vexed because the Prime Minister had edged over into the Foreign Minister's territory. There were conferences and exchanges of additional notes, all very dignified and very secret, and in the end things were smoothed over: Lord Palmerston had not meant to offend either Mr. Adams or the United States. Yet the whole affair had disturbing connotations. Mr. Adams wrote to Secretary Seward that "this unprecedented act of the Prime Minister may not be without great significance." His Lordship had been "hostile at heart" all along, and "it may be that he seeks this irregular method of precipitating us all into a misunderstanding." Mr. Adams would be on his guard.[5]

He would need to be. Lord Palmerston actually was seeking nothing in particular just then; yet his government was drifting slowly but perceptibly toward the point at which it would recognize the Confederacy, and Mr. Adams was quite right in considering the Prime Minister's touchiness an evil omen. The real trouble was not what General Butler had done in New Orleans but what General Lee had done in Richmond. Lee had laid his hands on a war that was about to end and had extended it into the indefinite future, and the American minister was compelled to reflect that a long war greatly increased the danger of foreign intervention. It could almost be laid out on a chart. If the line representing the available supply of cotton continued to drop, while the line representing the military outlook of the Confederacy continued to rise, the two would eventually cross—at precisely which moment Britain and France might very well see to it that the Confederate States of America became an independent nation.

This moment was getting much nearer. With Lee and Bragg swinging north the Confederacy's military prospects had never looked better; and with textile factories all across Lancashire closing and thousands of workers living on public charity, the cotton industry had never looked worse. Before July ended the London *Spectator* wrote despairingly about the rising darkness in the Midlands, where "first one town and then another is swallowed up in the gloom of universal pauperism," and the *Saturday Review* felt that the cotton famine was the saddest thing that had happened to England in many a year: "In the worst of our calamities there has seldom been so pitiable a sight as the manufacturing districts present at this moment."[6] There were in England more than 2600 cotton mills and nearly half a million textile workers, and by the middle of the summer they were deep in trouble. In September workers were going on the thin diet of parish relief at the rate of 6000 a week, adding to a relief roll which held more than 150,000 names when the month began. By the year's end half of all the textile hands in England would be entirely out of jobs, and most of the rest would be working half-time. The American Civil War was becoming a matter of dire concern to hundreds of thousands of men and women who had barely heard of Abraham Lincoln or Jefferson Davis and did not know Alabama from Michigan.[7]

These people were not going to take a dispassionate view of the war. Folk with leisure and means could if they pleased savor the elements of a romantic military drama, or weigh the opposing merits of secession and reunion. The average Englishman who worked for wages was going to interpret this war strictly in terms of its effect on him; and just now it was affecting him most painfully right where he lived. The Liverpool cotton broker who referred to the war as a serious labor disturbance in the Southern states was being perfectly logical.[8] To the workers and businessmen of England that was all the war amounted to—unless the people who were actually fighting it should manage to make it mean something transcendent, more important even than the struggle for daily bread and annual profits.

The people who were doing the fighting could see no farther than anyone else. They could only make out that the war was bigger than they were, bigger than anyone had planned or imagined, and that it was enforcing changes whose final significance was beyond analysis. They could do nothing except get on with the fighting, and as the war increased in size and scope they were more and more compelled to follow the one terrible rule: Do whatever needs to be done to *win*.

This rule was pointing Mr. Lincoln in the direction of emancipation, although he had doubts about his legal right to go there; and it was driving Mr. Davis, who had said that the Confederacy wanted nothing except to be left alone, to mount a full-dress invasion of the North.

Making this invasion, Mr. Davis wanted everyone to understand the necessity. Early in September he sent instructions to the leaders of the principal armies, Lee and Bragg and Smith. If they reached non-Confederate soil they were to issue proclamations explaining what the invasion meant. The Confederacy (they were to say) was fighting solely for peace, which would come when the United States abandoned its attempt to rule a people who preferred self-government, and the generals were to point out that "we are driven to protect our country by transferring the seat of war to that of an enemy who pursues us with a relentless and apparently aimless hostility." Southern fields had been laid waste, Southern people had been killed and Southern homes had been desolated, and "the sacred right of self-defense demands that if such a war is to continue its consequences shall fall on those who persist in their refusal to make peace."[9]

The trouble was that the consequences of the war were falling on everybody, including uncomprehending English factory hands 3000 miles away. The sheer weight of the armies was exerting a force of its own; under its pressure the societies which supported those armies were being profoundly transformed. This was hard to bear and hard to understand, especially in Richmond, capital city of a nation which had been created in order to prevent change. Even as he sent his armies north Mr. Davis was receiving letters and hearing complaints which testified to the pressure.

There was Governor Brown of Georgia, who was writing in heat and at length to insist that the conscription act was illegal. The Confederate constitution, said Governor Brown, was "a league between sovereigns," and in such a league the central government could draft nobody. Furthermore, conscription was wasteful; the governor believed that the Confederacy had drafted "tens of thousands" of men whom it was unable to arm and who therefore could do no fighting, but whose labor would be most valuable on the farm or in the workshop. Mr. Davis was curt in his reply. He was sure that conscription was legal; and, anyway, "I cannot share the alarm and concern about State rights which you so evidently feel but which to me seem quite unfounded."[10] He passed over the economic argument; and here, as a matter of fact, the governor was on fairly solid ground.

A little earlier in the year, the Confederate Quartermaster General A. C. Myers reported to the Secretary of War that supplies in his department were totally inadequate to meet the demand and that he was currently unable to fill requisitions to outfit 40,000 men. The reason for this, he said, was clear; the conscription act was pulling workers out of the very factories on which the Army was relying for its supplies, and manufacturers "have been rendered incapable of complying with the contracts made with this department." Not long after this, Secretary Mallory pointed out that the Navy was having great trouble getting armored warships built because of a dire shortage of skilled mechanics. To an extent, this shortage came because so many mechanics in Southern shops came from the North, and fled the country as soon as the war began; but of the mechanics who remained, many had been drafted, some shops were closed altogether, and contractors were unable to fill their engagements.[11]

The Southern railroads were suffering most of all. Indeed, their whole situation was complicated almost beyond understanding and ultimately beyond remedy.

When the war began the railroads foresaw outright ruin, not realizing that the war would mean more traffic rather than less, and so they did their best to retrench, encouraging their workers to enlist and reducing their workshop crews to a minimum. By the time they discovered that this was a mistake the conscription act was in force, holding the enlisted workers in the Army; now the roads were deteriorating badly, engines and cars and tracks were going unrepaired, carrying capacity was declining, and both the Army and the national economy were gravely handicapped. In addition, the government had exerted some control over the railroads but had not gone far enough with it; it moved engines and cars from one road to another, as military needs dictated, but made no provision for their return, so that the roads which originally owned the rolling stock lost it forever and could not replace it. (This was a sore point with Governor Brown, the Georgia railroads having been especially hard hit in this way. He objected to a strong central government, but he did want Richmond to reach out and compel people to send back that missing railroad equipment.) As a final factor, when the government arranged for the transport of soldiers and armaments it bargained so sharply that the railroads made little money out of such traffic; now they were widely suspected of preferring to haul goods for civilian account whenever possible. The Federal government's railroad director, Brigadier General D. C. McCallum, had a better understanding of the matter. He wrote that war demanded lavish expenditure rather than economy, especially where the railroads were concerned, and he summed it up with a remark which reveals one of the truly disturbing characteristics of modern war: "The question to be answered was not 'How much will it cost?' but rather, 'Can it be done at all, at any cost?'"[12]

It was impossible, apparently, to wage war conservatively; a point especially hard to accept in the Confederacy, which had everything to lose and nothing to gain except what it already had when the war began. The Confederacy was bound to be conservative, lest the mere act of making war destroy the things it was fighting for; furthermore, its resources in dollars and in men were strictly limited, and probable costs had to be reckoned with parsimonious care. Yet caution was not going to win. General Lee had seen that. He had taken hair-raising chances to drive McClellan away from Richmond, and he was taking chances equally startling in his present campaign against Pope, and he had paid, and would continue to pay, in casualties, a much higher price than he could really afford . . . but he had saved the capital and the cause and he had put the Yankees on the defensive, and if he had done otherwise the war would be over by now, the Southern dream gone forever. Like it or not, the civilian leadership had to behave in the same way.

A case in point was the plight of Mr. Memminger, the Secretary of the Treasury.

In every respect he was an ultraconservative man of finance, a most cautious reckoner of probable costs, a born counter of pennies, complete with pursed lips and coldly contemplative eyes: and he had given the Confederacy a fiscal policy which in its essentials was simply a dependence on paper money. This had come about, not because Mr. Memminger had suddenly become flighty but because his hand had been forced by events beyond his control. He later recalled that when he took office the Treasury Department did not even have money enough to buy him a desk; its first purchases abroad were made on his own private draft, and there was not in the entire country one sheet of bank-note paper on which money could be printed. This shortage of paper was soon remedied, and ever so much money was printed with nothing to support it except a general faith that the South would win the war: Mr. Memminger was already being blamed, and Robert Toombs had recently derided him for "attempting to carry on a great and expensive war solely on credit—without taxation." The complaint was sound but cruel, for Mr. Memminger had little choice.[13]

He had had an impossible assignment: to finance an all-out war in a land which contained almost no hard money and had no way to get any more. It was a land whose states, deeply in debt, were already emitting bonds and treasury notes in order to keep afloat; a land which not only detested the mere idea of a central government powerful enough to impose heavy taxes but also believed firmly that the war was going to be short; a land which neither could nor would follow a conservative financial policy. In the spring of 1861 Congress did vote a general property tax to support an issue of $100,000,000 in treasury notes. Since proper tax-gathering machinery did not exist, Congress stipulated that the several states could assume the tax for their citizens, at a ten per cent discount; all but two of the states promptly took advantage of this offer, issuing more treasury notes to make the payments, and the inflationary spiral was under way. Congress authorized more bond issues, and more treasury notes, and Mr. Memminger found himself lord of a realm of paper money, financing a war on credit with nothing solid for the credit to rest on.

There had not, actually, been anything else he could do. He

had adopted a desperate expedient to meet a desperate situation, and although inflation was beginning to get out of control—the increasing flood of paper money was running across an increasing shortage of all of the things money could buy—the country was still able to carry on the war. The problem was that while the financial structure would hold together for the immediate future, a really long war would bring it to collapse and ruin.[14]

Early in the year Mr. Davis had called Joseph E. Johnston's attention to "the military paradox that impossibilities must be rendered possible." Impossibilities were needed in industry, in transportation, in finance, in the administration of government itself. At the end of July, Mr. Davis was reminded that the states west of the Mississippi were far away, all but isolated and in dire need of help; and the kind of help they needed seemed to call for nothing less than a partial remodeling of the Confederate government.

The reminder came in a letter from Governor F. R. Lubbock of Texas, who spoke for the governors of Arkansas, Missouri, and Louisiana as well as for himself. The western states, said Governor Lubbock, needed three things—a general-in-chief, much more money, and a new supply of arms and ammunition. The general-in-chief must be a regular pro-consul, all but independent of direct War Department control, able to organize an army, to lead it in action, to shape strategy and to spend money on equipment; there should also be a special branch of the Treasury Department west of the river to provide the necessary money—western soldiers mostly were not paid at all, and some of them were getting mutinous. From twenty to thirty thousand stand of small arms ought to be forwarded at once. To all of this the President could do little more than reply that he had already sent west the best general he could spare, all the money the Treasury could provide, and all the small arms that were available. He would try to do more. The business of a Treasury branch was certainly illegal and probably impractical, but he would see about it[15] . . . and perhaps, in the end, this impossibility could be made possible along with all of the others.

It was necessary to do so many things that had not been counted on when the war began. Everything was changing, the changes welcomed by some and deplored by others but inevitable in any case. The editor of *DeBow's Review*, listing the new manufacturing plants that were springing up in the deep South, believed that the South would become truly independent, able to make for itself many things previously bought from Yankees, and he rejoiced: "This alone, if our people would look at it aright, would make the war a paying one to us."

Not all saw it that way. Another editor noted that if there was a new factory on every stream and in every valley the South would become a different sort of place. It would be overrun with factory workers, who were "sons and daughters of Belial," and he did not like the prospect. "No wonder," he mused, "that those who cling with love, which is often the highest form of reason, to the old framework of our society, shudder at the thought of a Lowell on the Appomattox or a Manchester in the Piedmont region."[16]

6: *Scabbard Thrown Away*

The New York correspondent of the London *Times* wrote late in July that the people of the North were getting tired of the war. Enlistments in the Army were lagging; wages were high and jobs were plentiful, "the first bloom of war excitement is over," and all of "the rum-shops and lager beer saloons" were buzzing with stories about the horrors of battle and the miseries of campaigning in Southern swamps. Disabled veterans back from the front were to be seen everywhere, mute evidence that soldiering was not always a lark—in sober fact, the war was a little more than anyone had bargained for. The English reporter felt that Northerners were having second thoughts: "They were ready for a short, sharp and decisive conflict. They were not ready for an obstinate struggle, to last for years."[1]

The falling off in enlistments was coming just when the Federal government was making an extra effort to increase the size of the Army. It had recently called for 300,000 volunteers but it was not getting them, and the news from the fighting fronts was so bad that no one was quite sure that 300,000 additional soldiers would be enough even if they did come forward. The one certainty seemed to be that the war would be lost if they did not come.

So popular enthusiasm was at a low ebb, and the war had grown so big and so heavy that simple enthusiasm was not going to be enough anyway. This discovery, made in Richmond at the beginning of the spring, was now being made in Washington, and Mr. Lincoln's government came to the same conclusion Mr. Davis's government had reached: if men would not go into the Army of their own free will they must be made to go. This meant death for one of the proudest traditions in the land. Americans had always believed that the volunteer spirit, the heartbreaking patriotism of youth responding to oratory and music and flags, would carry them through any dangers, and once this belief was struck down it would never revive; but there was no help for it. Gingerly, and with much less boldness and resolution than had been displayed in Richmond when the same problem arose, Washington reached out to embrace conscription.

The embrace was not quite complete, because there were legal ins and outs, not to mention political quaverings. As the law stood the President could not compel citizens to go into the United States Army. He could, however, draft the state militia for nine months, and by Constitutional theory the militia included all of the adult males in each state. This authority, cut and stretched to fit the emergency, was now put to use. On August 4 the President called on the states to enroll 300,000 militia, adding the proviso that if by August 15 any state failed to met its quota under the previous call for volunteers, men would be drafted from the militia to make up the deficiency.

This was a fairly roundabout approach. The volunteer regiments would be raised and organized by the states in the old familiar way, and if the Federal government drafted anybody it would do it at secondhand, using state machinery. A most intricate accounting system was devised, under which one three-year volunteer equalled four nine-months militiamen, and if a state met its full quota of volunteers none of its people would have to be drafted. This was rather an approach to conscription than conscription itself but it was an extremely powerful stimulus to volunteering, because no elected officials in state, city, town, or country cared to be part of a machine which dragged good voters by neck and heels into the Army. So official persons all over the land gave vigorous support to the recruiting program and saw to it that alluring bounties were offered regardless of expense. Cumbersome as it was, it worked—for a time, anyway—and, by December, Secretary Stanton was able to announce that he had 420,000 new soldiers, of whom 399,000 had volunteered. Implicit in all of this, of course, was the idea that if the war went on the government would use compulsion to the limit to keep its Army up to strength.[2]

This meant just what the more drastic Confederate conscription act meant, as devout states' rights theorists had noted with shock. It was a clear assertion of the power of the central government to reach clear inside a state and lay its hands on the individual citizen, and a government which could do this was no longer a government of limited powers. The change was inevitable, because this was no longer a limited war. Somewhere between Shiloh and Malvern Hill—or possibly at some point along a diagonal running between Mr. Davis's resort to the draft and Mr. Lincoln's decision to emancipate—it had become unlimited, and it had to be fought accordingly.

It was bewildering, and good men were disturbed. The very godfather of secession, William L. Yancey himself, was reported to have said in the Confederate Senate that he would prefer conquest by the Yankees to the despotism of President Davis: which may have been the sort of thing the President was thinking of when he wrote to his friend General Bragg that "revolutions develop the high qualities of the good and the great, but they cannot change the nature of the vicious and the selfish." General William T. Sherman looked about him in western Tennessee and confessed that he was "appalled by the magnitude of the danger that envelops us as a people," because rebellion in the South was accompanied in the North by a dismaying rise of democracy and anarchy[3] (it was always a bit hard for Sherman to tell the two apart). And in cotton plantations along the Mississippi there was so much raiding and counterraiding, so much burning of cotton and so much turmoil among the chattels, that good planters hardly knew which side they were on.

Planters were supposed to burn their cotton to keep the Yankees from getting it. Since his baled cotton represented his whole year's income the average planter hated to do this. He hated it even more if he lived where Yankee traders might come along and offer cash money for his crop. (It was unfortunately very hard to bargain with these traders, because if the price they offered was rejected a squad of Yankee soldiers was likely to show up and confiscate everything in sight, paying nothing at all.) The local Southern authorities therefore organized armed patrols and sent them up and down the river to burn all the cotton they could find. Here and there the planters offered resistance, and at a place called Carolina Landing, seventy miles above Vicksburg, a patrol was routed and forced to retreat; regular troops had to be sent up from Vicksburg, and the patrol at last burned the cotton behind a cordon of bayonets. A Chicago newspaper correspondent rejoiced that "this business of destroying the private property of citizens has done more to strengthen the national cause than all the victories our armies have achieved," and one resident wrote despairingly to the governor of Mississippi that many planters had simply abandoned their homes and moved away. Overseers were running off, the slaves were out of control, and unless something was done soon the Yankees would get 20,000 bales of cotton out of one county.[4]

Unlimited war meant that sort of thing, along with much else, and men tried in vain to restore the old limits. The New York banker, August Belmont, who was a conservative but stoutly Unionist Democrat, got a letter in August from a friend in New Orleans who begged him to work for a speedy compromise peace.

If the war went on much longer, said this friend, the South would be ruined. It was almost ruined now, but it was not going to stop fighting; the more it suffered the angrier and more determined it became, and it would sacrifice its last life to prevent Northern conquest. Could not sober conservatives in the North lead in a great movement to end the war on a simple basis of forgive, forget, and behave? Let both sides confess error, renew the old friendship and restore the prewar world in all its lost splendor. As the weaker side, the South could make no overtures, but the stronger North could do so, and if the government at Washington refused to go along a political party could perhaps bring it about—the Democratic party, which had always tried to "maintain the constitution as it was framed and interpreted for more than two-thirds of a century." If a chance for compromise existed it was utter madness to go on with the war.[5]

There was nobility in the idea that there ought to be a peace without victory; yet in August of 1862 America's tragedy was that it was caught between the madness of going on with the war and the human impossibility of stopping it. Secession had been a direct result of the outcome of the election of 1860. To restore the status quo would be to assume that either the North or the South had had a great change of heart—that the North would not again go Republican, or that the South would quietly acquiesce if it did. Neither Mr. Lincoln nor Mr. Davis was going to assume anything of the kind. Each man was fighting for a dreadful simplicity. Neither one could describe a solution acceptable to him without describing something wholly unacceptable to the other; neither man could accept anything less than complete victory without admitting complete defeat. Both sides had heard the trumpet that would never call retreat. The peace-makers could not be heard until the terrible swift sword had been sheathed; but the scabbard had been thrown away, and now the Confederacy was carrying the war into the enemy's country.

It was making, in fact, its one great co-ordinated counteroffensive of the war. The odds against this counteroffensive were forbidding but the thing just might work, and if it did the Confederacy could win everything it had ever wanted.

It would begin in the west. Braxton Bragg had stolen a long march on the Federals by getting into Chattanooga while Buell was still methodically perfecting his arrangements in central Tennessee. If Bragg and Kirby Smith together could get behind Buell, force him to battle and destroy him, both Tennessee and Kentucky could be regained, the Federals along the Mississippi would have to retreat, and the war would look very different. It would look like a final Confederate triumph if, while the westerners were doing this, Lee could go north of the Potomac and win a smashing victory on Yankee soil.

There were of course a great many "if's" in this, but it could happen; Mr. Davis told Bragg and Smith what was expected of them just as Lee was preparing to move away from McClellan and go after Pope; and in August the armies began to march.[6]

Bragg and Smith were optimistic. They respected each other, they were well aware that their enemies were temporarily off balance, and they believed that once they got into Kentucky they would be fighting a war of liberation, with enthusiastic popular support canceling the perennial Federal advantage in numbers. Unfortunately, Mr. Davis had given them a good idea rather than the blueprint of an actual campaign. Nobody had real over-all authority over what was about to be done except the President, who was much too far away to do more than block out the general objectives. Bragg could give no binding orders to Smith, and Smith could give none to Bragg. They were committed to cordial co-operation, but there was no boss. Bragg and Smith commanded separate armies, facing different foes under different conditions, and if at a crucial moment one man wanted to go one way while the other man wanted to go another way co-operation was likely to disappear.

Bragg and Smith met at Chattanooga early in August and apparently agreed on a plan. They had two Federal armies to consider. Buell's, which then numbered a little more than 30,000 and could quickly be made bigger, was spread out along the railroad that came southeast from Nashville to Stevenson, Alabama; if left alone, it would some day march on Chattanooga. A force of 9000 under Brigadier General George W. Morgan occupied Cumberland Gap, and presumably meant to come down eventually on Knoxville. The first step for the Confederates, obviously, was to dispose of those Federal armies.

Bragg understood that the campaign would begin with the recapture of Cumberland Gap, which would take care of the Federal General Morgan; after this, Bragg and Smith would join forces and fall on Buell. Beating Buell, they would clear central Tennessee of Federals, and then move into Kentucky—which, according to that spirited Kentucky cavalryman, John Hunt Morgan, would immediately throw out its Unionist governor and legislature and support the Confederacy enthusiastically with numerous recruits and abundant supplies.

Smith either understood the plan differently or changed his mind immediately after the conference. He marched out of Knoxville in mid-August, before Bragg was ready to move, left a division to mask Cumberland Gap, and went boldly north into Kentucky, getting farther away from Bragg at every step.

Thus co-operation had failed at the outset, and Bragg had to revise his own plan. Since Smith was entering Kentucky with hardly more than a third as many soldiers as Buell commanded, he had to be supported; and so, on August 21, Bragg got his army under way, crossing the Tennessee River at Chattanooga and striking northward into the tough mountain country in order to put his army between Buell's and Smith's. He made the move smartly, and Buell—whose grasp on the military initiative had been somewhat loose all summer—was forced to give up his cautious advance on Chattanooga and adjust his movements to those of his enemy. By September 5, Bragg had crossed the mountains and the Cumberland River and had gone all the way to the Kentucky line, entering that state at the town of Tompkinsville, while Buell was still concentrating his own forces at Murfreesboro, seventy-five miles to the south. Buell was being reinforced. He was gathering in his own scattered units, and in addition two of Grant's divisions were coming from western Tennessee to join him. Grant was warned to keep a third available; and it seemed to Buell that his best course was to leave an adequate force to hold Nashville and take everyone else into Kentucky in pursuit of Bragg. Since Bragg would go all the way to the Ohio River unless Buell overtook him, the pursuit was necessary; but to Andrew Johnson, the militantly Unionist Tennessee Senator who had been made military governor of the state, it looked like a ruinous retreat, and Johnson filed bitter complaints with Washington. Washington was not happy. When Buell sent a reasoned explanation of his proposed movements, Halleck gave him a cold reply: "March where you please, provided you find the enemy and fight him."[7]

Bragg and Smith were still a long way apart, and to get their armies and their ideas for using them into close harmony might be difficult; but their campaign undeniably was off to an excellent start, and it spread feverish alarm in the North. By August 30 Smith was approaching the town of Richmond in central Kentucky, roughly halfway between Cumberland Gap and Cincinnati, and at this place he virtually obliterated a scratch force of 6500 Federals which tried to stop him. The soldiers were mostly untrained Indiana recruits, hastily scraped together and sent to the front under one of Buell's trusted lieutenants, Major General William Nelson; Smith's veterans disposed of them with moderate effort, capturing 4000 unwounded prisoners. One immediate result of the victory was that the Federal General Morgan evacuated Cumberland Gap and made a prodigious two hundred mile retreat all the way to the Ohio River.

Smith marched on and occupied Lexington, where he got a heartwarming welcome: Confederate flags all over the place, women and girls crying a welcome from every window and garden, baskets of food and buckets of cold water at street corners for the refreshment of tired Confederates, everyone exulting (as an Arkansas soldier put it) that "Kentucky was at last about to be free." The town almost exploded with joy when John Hunt Morgan and his cavalry came through on the gallop; all the church bells rang, and people who had no flags waved their handkerchiefs, and laughed or wept or cheered as the spirit moved them. Smith sent a jubilant message off to Bragg. He was going to move on to Cincinnati, he said, all that was needed was to have the left of his army in touch with the right of Bragg's, and "if I am supported and can be supplied with arms, 25,000 Kentucky troops in a few days will be added to my command."[8]

Moving against Cincinnati, Smith was spreading himself just a bit thin. He commanded about 21,000 men, but 8000 of them were at Cumberland Gap and 3000 more were chasing Federal General George Morgan, and Smith had hardly more than 10,000 soldiers immediately at hand; not enough by half for an invasion of Ohio. But the long strong flood Bragg had talked about was moving, the Federals were obviously getting panicky, and in a panic anything can happen; so Smith's leading division went north through Cynthiana toward Covington, and all the Ohio country responded in a fever of patriotism, fright and overflowing energy. David Tod, Governor of Ohio, urged loyal men in each county to take up arms and prepare for the worst, declaring that "the soil of Ohio must not be invaded by the enemies of our glorious government." Major General Lew Wallace, who may have been just the man for the assignment, assumed command of the defenses of Cincinnati, suspended ferryboat service on the river, devised the slogan "Citizens for labor, soldiers for battle," and announced that all business would be suspended so that able-bodied men could go out and dig trenches, under police supervision. From the outlying precincts homespun citizens showed up with muzzle loaders, powder horns, and leather bullet pouches; 15,000 of them and more, by all accounts, men who were either backwoodsmen or could pass for such with citified reporters; and they prepared to man the trenches dug by less picturesque folk, in case armed secession drew nigh. They were said to be squirrel hunters and this was their great day, and they became legendary; shooting no Rebels, because no Rebels ever came within range. The final note about them is an anxious query sent to Wallace by a Regular Army officer a fortnight later: "Cannot I get rid of the Squirrel Hunters? They are under no control." In the end, Cincinnati was saved. Kirby Smith had just been making a feint.[9]

The danger looked real enough at the time. Bragg also was driving north, and Buell's men marched hard in a vain effort to overtake him. Bragg came up thirty miles east of Bowling Green, which had marked the center of Albert Sidney Johnston's line just a year earlier, and at Munfordville, where the railroad to Louisville crossed the Green River, he struck a Federal strong point held by 4000 men under Colonel John T. Wilder, who until recently had been an unassuming Indiana business man and who now was about to add a strange little footnote to the story of the Civil War.

Bragg's advance guard attacked the fortifications twice and was repulsed with moderate loss. Then Bragg brought up the rest of his army and sent in a demand for surrender, pointing out that the Federals were surrounded and that their case was hopeless. Through the Confederate lines that night came a flag of truce and a Yankee officer

—Colonel Wilder in person, seeking a conference with Major General Buckner, who led a division in Hardee's corps. In Buckner's tent Wilder became disarmingly frank. He was not, he said, a military man at all, but he did want to do the right thing. He had heard that Buckner was not only a professional soldier but an honest gentleman as well; and would Buckner now please tell him if, under the rules of the game, it was Colonel Wilder's duty to surrender or to fight it out?

Somewhat flabbergasted—he said later that he "would not have deceived that man under those circumstances for anything"—Buckner said Wilder would have to make his own decision. (He knew what a weight that was. Seven months earlier he had had to surrender Fort Donelson, his superiors having fled from responsibility, and when he sent a flag through the Yankee lines his old friend Grant had been merciless.) Buckner pointed out that Wilder's men were hemmed in by six times their own numbers and that Bragg had enough artillery in line to destroy the fort in short order; at the same time, if the sacrifice of every man would aid the Federal cause elsewhere it was Wilder's duty to fight. . . . In the end, Buckner took him to see Bragg, who was curt with him but let him count the cannon in the Confederate works. Wilder counted enough to convince him that the jig was up, and at last he surrendered: a well-meaning but bewildered citizen-soldier who had gone to his enemy for professional advice and, all things considered, had been fairly dealt with.[10]

Perhaps this was high tide, or something like it. It was September 17, and the advancing Confederates had canceled the threat to eastern Tennessee, had taken more than 8000 prisoners, and had compelled 50,000 Yankee invaders to head northward in unseemly haste for the Ohio River. They had caused happy crowds to go cheering through the streets of Lexington, and had forced other crowds to dig trenches at Cincinnati, while squirrel hunters held a muster. Bragg suddenly ceased to be the dour dyspeptic; for once in his career he actually seemed lighthearted, and he fairly bubbled with praise for the soldiers in his command.

"My army is in high spirits, and ready to go anywhere the 'old general' says," he wrote, in a letter to Mrs. Bragg. "Not a murmur escapes a man. . . . We have made the most extraordinary campaign in military history." One of his officers noted that two soldiers who had been sentenced to be shot for insulting Kentucky women (nature of the insult not specified) had been reprieved by the commanding general, and wrote: "We begin to think Bragg isn't nearly the inhuman, blood-thirsty monster that he has been represented to be." Colonel Wilder, having toured the camp, said that although Bragg's soldiers were terribly ragged and dirty, "I never saw an army in a more perfect state of discipline," and in a dispatch to the War Department Bragg asserted: "My admiration of and love for my army cannot be expressed." He spoke of its "patient toil and admirable discipline" and remarked that "the men are much jaded and somewhat destitute, but cheerful and confident without a murmur." He added hopefully: "We move soon on a combined expedition with General Smith."[11]

High tide; but possibly not quite as high as it looked. The men were, after all, very tired, for they had made a prodigious march across difficult country, and although Bragg held his enlisted men in high regard he had little use for most of his generals. (He had told Adjutant General Cooper earlier in the summer that some of these "are only incumbrances and would be better out of the way," and said that their weakness robbed his army of a quarter of its efficiency.)[12] Smith was still one hundred miles away, and although Buell had been badly outmaneuvered he was too strong to be beaten unless Bragg's and Smith's armies could be united. Near Munfordville Bragg hesitated, waited for Buell to attack him, found that he would not, and at last moved northeast to Bardstown, where he hoped that Smith would join him. (This move gave Buell a clear road to Louisville, whereas before the road had been blocked.) At Bardstown, however, Bragg found no Smith: just a letter from Smith urging him to destroy Buell as quickly as he could because the people of Kentucky would not support the Confederacy until Buell had been defeated.[13]

Bragg's pessimism began to return. He believed that the success of his whole campaign depended finally on an uprising of loyal Kentuckians; if they were not going to rise the campaign would be a failure no matter how brilliantly it had been conducted. When a cheering Bardstown crowd surrounded his hotel and called him out to the veranda for a speech, Bragg was frank. He had come north to enable Kentucky "to express her southern preference without fear of northern bayonets," but it was all up to the people themselves. If they would support him he would support them, but if they should "decline the offer of liberty" he would take his army away and leave the state to its own devices. He notified the War Department that "we are sadly disappointed at the want of action by our friends in Kentucky." Recruits thus far did not even equal the number of casualties that had been incurred, although casualties had been light; he had brought 15,000 stand of arms along but so far had found hardly anyone to use them, and "unless a change occurs soon we must abandon the garden spot of Kentucky to its own cupidity."[14]

The bright sky was slowly darkening; the unhappy fact being that although Bragg and Smith had outwitted and outmarched their opponents they had passed an invisible meridian and had moved into an area where time was on the side of the Federals. Simply to march into Kentucky was not enough, no matter how brilliantly it was done. The Yankees who held Kentucky had to be beaten—not in outpost affairs, but in a major battle—and the longer this battle was deferred the less chance did the Confederates have to win it, because the Yankee armies were getting stronger every day while the Confederate armies were not. Bragg and Smith were not exactly avoiding battle, but they were not driving on relentlessly to provoke a battle at all hazards; by this time the hazards were beginning to look too great. Smith was torn between a desire to occupy Frankfort, the capital of the state, and a fear that the Federals would strike him in the rear, and his moves were tentative and ineffective. Bragg was beginning to show the strange bleakness of spirit which sometimes came upon him in time of crisis, making him brood over a danger instead of striking it dead with one decisive blow. Growing uncertain, he was beginning to fumble.

The Yankees themselves were far from happy. Buell, who had been actively campaigning all summer without once encountering

Confederate infantry, was as deliberate as ever. He got up to Louisville while Bragg was occupying Bardstown, and he busied himself organizing the untrained reinforcements which Middle Western governors were frantically sending to him, but Washington was growing irritable. Before September ended, the War Department ordered him to turn over his command to George Thomas, suspending the order only when Thomas protested that it was unfair to change generals on the eve of a decisive battle. (Unfair to the man replaced; unfair, also, to the man who had to replace him.) Buell stayed in command, but his neck was in a noose and he would inevitably pass from the scene unless he won a victory.

But the real pressure was on the Confederates. Taking the offensive, they had obligated themselves to live beyond their means. All that they had won would be lost unless they got a victory in the open field. Unlimited war demanded an unlimited victory.

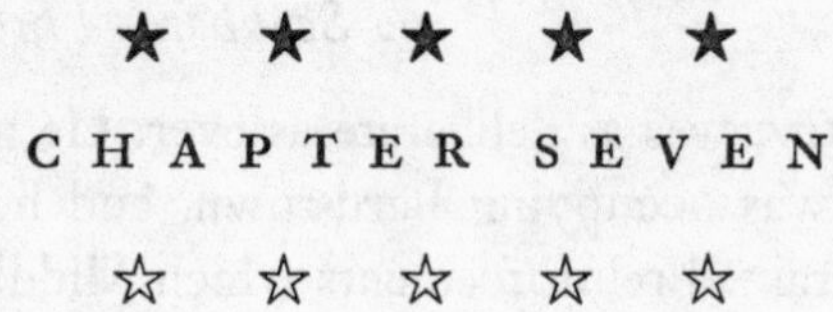

Thenceforward and Forever

1: *Recipe for Confusion*

In the West, John Pope had declared, Federal soldiers mostly saw the backs of their enemies, and the same thing ought to happen in Virginia. Whatever this statement lacked in accuracy—Buell's army right now was going north at top speed, the backs of its enemies out of sight in advance—it at least breathed the offensive spirit. Acting on this spirit, and recovering quickly from the embarrassing check at Cedar Mountain, General Pope in mid-August assembled his troops and set out to carry the war to the foe. He got as far as the Rapidan River, made ready to cross and campaign in true western style, and then began to learn that in Virginia things were different.

To begin with, he was facing Robert E. Lee, whose like he had not yet seen. In addition he was at the mercy both of his own shortcomings, which General Lee would cruelly expose and exploit, and of the high command of the Army of the Potomac, which expected him to fail and which in the end would be deliberate enough to make failure certain. Finally, General Pope was coming to the stage just when the nature of the war was changing.

Both sides had supposed originally that they fought to restore the past, the difference between them being largely a question of what the past really meant and how it could best be regained. Now something more fundamental was coming to the surface, compelling men to examine their ideas about the future. So the fighting would be different, hereafter, infinitely harder to control and understand than it had been before. The going was likely to be rough for a Federal Army commander unless he was either totally phlegmatic or exceptionally perceptive; and John Pope unfortunately was neither. He was just average, operating in a time and place where a strictly average soldier was likely to run into trouble. What happened to him was probably inevitable, and anyway he brought most of it on himself, but he could have been luckier.

By August 15, Pope had about 55,000 men under his immediate direction, including 8000 men of General Burnside's corps under Major General Jesse Reno. He was on the Rapidan—that fated river which almost seemed to be a boundary between Federal and Confederate Virginia—and Halleck had warned him to stay there until the Army of the Potomac joined him; and so Pope waited, guarding the river crossings and expecting that from 70,000 to 100,000 of McClellan's veterans would presently be lined up beside him. When that happened, Pope believed, General Halleck would come down from Washington to take field command, with Pope and McClellan as his chief lieutenants. Meanwhile Pope would hold the pivot.

He had picked a poor spot for it, because his position was potentially most dangerous. The Rappahannock River was behind him, and the railroad which was his life line ran back to that river on a long diagonal, from his right front to his left rear. If the Confederates should steal a march, side-step a few miles to the east and then move due north across the Rapidan, they could reach the Rappahannock crossing before Pope could—cutting off his supplies, closing his escape hatch, trapping him between the rivers and then disposing of him at their leisure. The inexpert Federal cavalry was hopelessly overmatched by Jeb Stuart's men, which meant that Lee almost certainly could steal a march or two if he tried, and Lee was exactly the sort who would try. He would try it soon, because time was running out. McClellan was still at Harrison's Landing but his troops would begin to reach Pope in ten days or less. Whatever Lee did must be done quickly.

His first attempt just missed. On August 18, Lee ordered a shift to the right followed by a quick drive across the river, and if things had gone as planned Pope's army very probably would have been crushed. But some of Stuart's cavalry missed an assignment and

Robert Toombs's infantry left unguarded a river crossing that was supposed to be sealed, and so a Federal patrol got south of the Rapidan and learned what was up by capturing an officer bearing Lee's orders. So Pope was warned; and although he had spoken freely about letting lines of retreat take care of themselves and acting always on the offensive he retreated now in great haste, and late on August 19 he had his entire force safely back behind the Rappahannock. He guarded the crossings with care, and for several days Lee could do nothing but spar with him and look for an opening.[1]

There was no opening, for Pope was on the alert; and with each passing day Lee's chance for victory grew smaller. On August 20 McClellan's V Army Corps, under Fitz John Porter, began landing at Aquia Creek, ten miles northeast of Fredericksburg, and started to move west toward the upper Rappahannock. On August 22 the III Corps, led by Samuel P. Heintzelman, reached Alexandria and began to march down overland. The rest of Burnside's men were coming up, and so was a detachment brought over from western Virginia, and, by August 25, Pope had 70,000 men within call, with more on the way. Lee was already outnumbered, and in another week his case would be hopeless.[2]

He would not give the Yankees that week. He had said that John Pope ought to be "suppressed"—quite as if the man were no soldier but a mere disturber of the peace on whom the law ought to descend—he proposed to do it personally, and if he could not break through Pope's line he would go around it. On August 25 he sent Stonewall Jackson with 24,000 men off on a long swing to the northwest. Jackson was to march entirely away from Pope's front, circling off behind the Bull Run mountains and then coming east through Thoroughfare Gap to strike Pope in the rear. Lee and Longstreet would tarry on the Rappahannock, to persuade Pope that the whole Confederate Army was still there, and in due time they would follow Jackson, join hands with him somewhere far to the north of their present position, and there compel Pope to fight a battle. Once Pope was beaten there would be time to see about the Army of the Potomac.

This of course was precisely the sort of move Stonewall Jackson liked. Something about the campaign in the Chickahominy swamps had baffled him, but he was over it now, thinking and acting like the Jackson of the Valley campaign; he was a panther once more, swift and stealthy and deadly, and he got his veterans on the road at dawn and set off on a typical Jackson march, driving his men relentlessly, discussing his plans with no one. Lee saw him off, and then—as calmly as if there was nothing on earth to worry about—he wrote to Mrs. Lee, giving her a modest summing-up of the plan that had been in his mind ever since he left Richmond.

"I think we shall at least change the theater of war from James river to north of the Rappk," he wrote. "That is part of the advantage I contemplated. If it is effective at least for a season it will be a great gain."[3]

To move the war from the vicinity of Richmond to the vicinity of Washington would, as he said, be very good; even if he failed to destroy Pope's army he would nevertheless have gained much. But Lee was really looking for a chance to win it all—to get the Yankees entirely out of Virginia and to win on Northern soil the victory that would end the war. The Confederate tide was rising, in the east and in the west, and the unearthly vision of independence achieved was something better than a mirage. Lee was not looking solely for a tactical advantage; he was leading the counteroffensive that sought nothing less than final triumph, and this move that risked so much had everything to gain.

The risk, to be sure, was immense. Already outnumbered, Lee was dividing his army in the immediate presence of his enemy, which is the sort of thing that all the books warn against, and for at least two days the halves of his army would be out of touch. If Pope discovered what was going on and acted with reasonable intelligence and energy he could bring Lee's entire campaign to ruin, holding those separated halves apart and dealing with each in turn under conditions which would give him all of the advantages. If he could even stall for another week or so, the two Federal armies would be fully united and no conceivable strategic brilliance would help the Confederacy. Once again, Lee was letting everything ride on the play of one card.

But the risks had been carefully figured. Lee had no higher opinion of Pope's military capacity than McClellan had. He knew that Pope's army was still a collection of unassimilated units, some of which were poorly led and were used to defeat. If Lee was trying to unite two separate armies on the field of battle, the Federals after all were trying to do the same thing, and Lee undoubtedly was able to see that smooth co-operation between Pope and McClellan was unlikely. Finally, the whole tone of the war just now was in his favor. The Yankees were at odds with themselves; a sudden shock might jar them apart. Secretary of the Navy Mallory expressed it, in a letter he wrote at the end of the month:

"We are stronger today than we have ever been, while our enemy is weaker. As our people have become firmly bound together for this war, those of the North have become discontented, and discord is now predominant in their counsels. Lincoln's cabinet dread a defeat, and hence their armies are everywhere retreating. . . . If we should defeat Pope decidedly, the backbone of the war will be over; for the opposition to the abolition party would shear it of its strength."[4]

Northern discord and discontent were very real, producing tangible military consequences. Among these (and this was much to General Lee's advantage) there was a distorting, paralyzing pressure on the central nervous system of the Army of the Potomac.

That army would fight heroically when the time for fighting came, but its military mind had been warped. There was that overwrought, emotional atmosphere at headquarters in which the government itself was seen as an enemy, individual members of the government were abominable villains, leaders of other Federal armies were stupid rivals; and a long-nursed sense of injury and isolation created a sensitivity so acute that the army could not be handled at all except by someone with the most delicate touch. Just when the outcome of the war might depend on the agility with which this army left its own chosen field to operate in a field selected by someone else (villainous superior or detested rival) the army was sluggish and petulant. It disliked the way Washington treated it; even more, it disliked the kind of war Washington obviously meant to fight, and it wanted to define what victory was going to mean even before it flexed its muscles to insure that the victory would be gained.

While he was preparing to send his sick away from Harrison's Landing, at a time when the order to withdraw his army had been foreshadowed but not yet received, McClellan explained to Halleck, by letter, that the Federal government must fight for a victory which the South would accept.

"The people of the South," he wrote, "should understand that we are not making war upon the institution of slavery, but that if they submit to the Constitution and the laws of the Union they will be protected in their constitutional rights of every nature. . . . I therefore deprecate and view with infinite dread any policy which tends to render impossible the reconstruction of the Union and to make this contest simply a useless effusion of blood." Halleck replied that he agreed entirely, and that Pope's venomous orders regarding Southern civilians in occupied territory were most injudicious: still (he said) it was necessary to bring the Army of the Potomac to Pope's side, and would McClellan please hurry the movement along?[5]

All things considered, the movement went slowly. Orders to leave the peninsula had been received on August 3, and the first contingents reached the upper Potomac nineteen days later. Those nineteen days added up to more time than the Federal government could afford to lose. They were time enough to enable Lee to shift the cockpit of the war from the valley of the James back to northern Virginia, and to compel the government at Washington to stop thinking about what the capture of Richmond would mean and to think instead about what would happen if Pope's army were lost. Perhaps, indeed, these were the days in which the last chance to keep the war within bounds faded and died. General Halleck grew impatient and told McClellan to move faster, and McClellan's feelings were hurt; and it was necessary to send down a sort of military ambassador to smooth his feathers.

The ambassador was General Burnside, who managed to convince McClellan that although the general-in-chief was more or less in a hurry he was not actually hostile, and McClellan at length wrote Halleck: "I am glad to say that Burnside has satisfied me that you are still my friend." Halleck replied almost apologetically, admitting that in the heat of the moment, what with the crisis of the war at hand and all, he may have been a trifle brusque: "It is very probable that my messages to you were more urgent and pressing than guarded in their language. I certainly meant nothing harsh, but I did feel that you did not act as promptly as I thought the circumstances required." Then, as delicately as possible, Halleck again called for speed:

"There is enough and more than enough for all of us to do, although none of us can do exactly what we would wish. That Lee is moving on Pope with his main army I have no doubt. Unless we can unite most of your army with Burnside and Pope, Washington is in great danger. Under these circumstances you must pardon the extreme anxiety (and perhaps a little impatience) which I feel. Every moment seems to me as important as an ordinary hour."[6]

In all of this General Pope was caught in a squeeze. He understood very well that the Army of the Potomac was moving deliberately, and he knew what this meant; but he did not yet see that the Army of Northern Virginia was moving with lightning speed, and to understand what this meant was altogether beyond him. Beset in front and in rear, he was simply in over his depth, and he continued to think that he had the initiative even after Lee had thrown him squarely on the defensive; now he was beginning to strike at shadows.

Jackson began his deadly flank march on the morning of August 25, and by evening of that day Pope had been told about it. But he could see only what he wanted to see, and he concluded now that Jackson's men were heading for the Shenandoah Valley once more. It seemed probable, as well, that the rest of Lee's army might follow Jackson, and so Pope notified Washington that he would send a force across the Rappahannock the next day to see about it. If his suspicions were correct he would pitch into the Confederate rear. He was beginning to see that he had problems. Of the three corps which made up his army, he believed that only McDowell's corps really amounted to much. Sigel, who led the men once commanded by Frémont, struck Pope as an incompetent who ought to be replaced, and Banks's corps had been roughly handled at Cedar Mountain, contained no more than 5000 men, and must be kept in the rear until it could be "set up again." Of the Army of the Potomac, Philip Kearny's division from Heintzelman's corps had joined him. It was a good division and Kearny was a first-rate combat soldier who did not share in the feeling that the government was conspiring darkly against McClellan; still, this was only one division, and for his riposte to Lee's feint Pope felt somewhat shorthanded.[7]

Except that it showed a dim awareness of coming trouble, Pope's dispatch gave an imperfect picture. Its appraisal of Sigel and Banks was correct enough: Pope's own army was not yet really an army and it badly needed an overhaul. Still, help was at hand. Heintzelman was coming in with his other division under Joe Hooker, another hard fighter who did not belong to the McClellan clique. Reno was on hand with most of Burnside's force, John F. Reynolds's excellent division from Porter's corps had joined McDowell, and the rest of Porter's corps was drifting about just off the Federal left flank, ready to be used as soon as Porter and Pope learned one another's whereabouts. There were soldiers enough along the Rappahannock but Pope did not seem to know exactly where all of them were, and it was going to be uncommonly hard to mass them for a co-ordinated blow. Finally, and most important of all, Lee's movement was no feint.

This began to dawn on Pope within twenty-four hours. Instead of crossing the river on August 26 to see what Lee was doing, Pope held his position, believing that Halleck wanted him to stand on the defensive until all of McClellan's army arrived; and that evening Stonewall Jackson swept in out of the shadows to strike the Orange & Alexandria Railroad at Bristoe Station, twenty miles behind the Rappahannock, moving on to seize the huge Federal supply base at Manassas Junction.

Jackson had made a prodigious march—more than fifty miles in forty hours—going north from his original position all the way to the town of Salem and then swinging southeast through Thoroughfare Gap to strike Pope's base while Pope still believed that he was moving toward the Shenandoah Valley. With one swift blow he had cut Pope off from his supplies, from his superiors and from his reinforcements, and the first half of Lee's incredible gamble had paid off.

It was only the first half. Jackson was in position to make immense trouble for the Federals, but he was also where he could be in immense trouble himself. He had 24,000 men, Lee and Longstreet with more than 30,000 were far away on the other side of the Bull Run mountains, and John Pope could get between them with 75,000 if he moved promptly. Twenty-five miles northeast of Jackson was the city of Washington, where two corps from the Army of the Potomac were coming ashore prepared to march to Bull Run. Unless he moved fast and befuddled his enemies completely, Jackson and his whole command might well be wiped out.

In the Shenandoah Valley, Jackson had escaped from a similar peril by marching swiftly back out of danger while his enemies were clumsily trying to get at him. But to march away now would be to admit failure. He was not simply making a raid to confuse the enemy, as he had done in the Valley; he was trying to force the unprepared Federals to fight a decisive battle against the united Army of Northern Virginia as far to the north as possible. He could neither wait nor run away; he had to stay, provoke a fight big enough to pin Pope down but not big enough to crush Jackson's own command, and do it all before the gathering Federal hordes came together. The second half of Lee's gamble would not work unless Jackson made no mistakes at all and the Federal generals made several.

That was just what finally happened.

By August 27 Pope realized that the campaign was beginning to turn upside-down. He sent word to Halleck that Lee (who had moved north the day before) had taken position northwest of the Bull Run mountains and had thrust "a strong column" forward to Manassas. Pope accordingly would retire from the Rappahannock and draw up his army on a line going roughly from the hamlet of Gainesville, five miles east of Thoroughfare Gap, to the vicinity of Warrenton Junction; reinforcements coming up from Washington should therefore march toward Gainesville. Lee's own intentions were far from clear, but Pope suspected that the Confederates might try "to keep us in check and throw considerable force across the Potomac in the direction of Leesburg."[8]

As a first step, this was good. The gap between the halves of

Lee's army was well over twenty miles wide, and Pope was going to move into it with all his force. But he would need to call on many separate units to do some rapid marching, and as he learned more about the movements of Jackson and Lee he would undoubtedly have to countermand many orders and issue new ones, and this was just the kind of situation that was apt to lead to large-scale confusion. Furthermore, Pope's dispatches to Washington were not getting through because Jackson had broken the line of communications, and General Halleck had only a dim idea of what was actually happening out beyond Manassas. If Pope himself should misread his enemies' movements; if his orders to corps and division commanders went astray, or were imperfectly understood and obeyed; if delay took the place of rapid movement anywhere between the Rappahannock and Washington—in short if any of the things that were likely to go wrong in a case like this did go wrong—then the mistakes Lee was counting on would occur and Lee's gamble would probably win.

As the only man east of the Bull Run mountains who knew what was going on, Stonewall Jackson was cool and unhurried. He stayed at Manassas all through August 27, to destroy the Federal supplies there and to make certain that Pope understood that it was time to retreat. Since Jackson could carry off only a minute fraction of the tremendous stock of captured Federal goods, the destruction was on a large scale, with huge warehouses and long rows of loaded freight cars set on fire; and after the captured whiskey had been carefully put out of reach Jackson's soldiers were turned loose on the piles of foodstuffs and were told to help themselves. The result was a gigantic picnic whose echoes a century has hardly dimmed. All soldiers are always hungry, and Jackson's were hungrier than most; in the best of times they were usually underfed, and now they had just finished a hard march on exceptionally skimpy rations—and here were all of the edible riches of the earth, from bacon and coffee and hardtack on to sutler's stocks of canned lobster and boned turkey and pie, free to all, without money and without price. For once in their military careers, these soldiers of the Army of Northern Virginia were able to eat beyond their means, and they made the most of it. Fortunately, the overstuffed army was able to march away that evening without leaving behind more than a scattering of moaning stragglers.

When it marched Jackson's force did not go far, but it went around corners in order to confuse the Yankees. Part of the men crossed Bull Run and marched north to Centreville, another part also crossed Bull Run and then sidled upstream, and the rest moved northwest from Manassas, west of Bull Run; and all three parts came together next day, August 28, on a long wooded ridge on the northwestern fringe of the old Bull Run battlefield, a few miles west of the stream itself and a little way north of the turnpike that came down from Washington to Warrenton. It was a good place to defend and also a good place to hide. Jackson got his men in position, pulled them back into the shade out of sight, and awaited developments.

The mistakes Lee had been anticipating were being made.

A man of action rather than of thought, Pope had been responding to all of this with much vigor. Jackson was burning Manassas, so Pope ordered his troops to go there and smash him. But at Manassas the Federals found nothing but a square mile of smoldering debris, a powerful odor of burned provisions, and evidence that Jackson had gone to Centreville. Pope ordered his columns to converge on Centreville, but Jackson was not there, either. He had vanished, going apparently off toward the west, and it seemed to Pope that Jackson was trying to make his getaway, as a sensible man would; and so new orders went out to the weary Federal columns, designed to head him off, to overtake him and to smite him in the flank. In the effort to accomplish this Pope apparently lost sight of the fact that Lee and Longstreet were still west of the Bull Run mountains, and he concentrated on Jackson so zealously that his troops were pulled away from Thoroughfare Gap, leaving that all-important gateway open for Confederate use. And at last, late on the afternoon of August 28, Jackson decided that it was time to make Pope stand and fight.

The sun was just about to set, and one of McDowell's divisions was plodding eastward along the Warrenton Pike within musket shot of the ridge where Jackson's soldiers were hidden. It reached Groveton crossroads, and Jackson himself rode out into the open, all unnoticed, to have a look. There were long intervals between the Federal brigades; he watched one brigade go by and disappear on the way toward Bull Run, and then he suddenly wheeled and spurred his horse back to the ridge at a pounding gallop. His concealed soldiers had been watching and they knew what came next; an officer remembered that as they fell into ranks the woods rang with "a hoarse roar like that from cages of wild beasts at the scent of blood."[9] Confederate artillery trotted out, unlimbered and opened fire. Then brigade after brigade of Jackson's infantry marched from the woods and came down the long slope in parallel columns, battle flags bright in the late afternoon sun; and presently the infantry swung into line of battle beside the guns and began to shoot.

The Federals were surprised but they did not panic. They were westerners led by Brigadier General John Gibbon, and although they had not fought before they had an aptitude for it; they formed their own line of battle without lost motion, Gibbon got some artillery to help and sent off for more infantry. Brigadier General Abner Doubleday's brigade came over to help, and the wild crash of battle echoed across the Manassas plain and a long cloud of dusty smoke drifted down over the Warrenton Pike while Yankees and Rebels fought an engagement that would go into the books as the Battle of Groveton.

It was a strange fight. The opposing battle lines simply stood and fired at each other at close range. Nobody charged and nobody retreated; everyone held his ground and fired as long as he could see anything to fire at, and when full darkness at last made it impossible to fight any longer the battle lines sagged apart by mutual consent, and that night the Federals went sullenly off toward Manassas. Some 2300 young men had been shot—close to one out of every three in action, on the Union side—and nothing whatever had been accomplished; except that in the only way open to him Stonewall Jackson had made certain that there would be a much bigger battle next day.[10]

2: *The Terrible Weariness*

By the time General Pope learned where Jackson had gone into hiding it was too late. He had already lost himself. No matter what sort of battle his enemies might inflict on him Pope would be unable to handle it because he had lost track of what was really happening, and he was moving troops in the light of faulty information. Some first-rate fighting men would do his bidding, but he would send them into action according to a map traced by fantasy; while he contended with shadows they would have to fight real live Confederates, and a great many of them would die of it.

Jackson was in the woods just north of the Warrenton Pike, a short distance west of Bull Run: this was solid fact, unearthed at a price by the fight at Groveton, and after two days in which rumor had been piled on baseless rumor a solid fact was doubtless very welcome. Yet to reason from this fact was difficult, because Pope had already convinced himself that Jackson was running away. Thus it was necessary to bring the Federal Army together with all possible haste, at the price of no matter how much confusion, lost motion, and weariness, because if there was any delay at all Jackson would escape. Pope exulted that if his people moved fast enough "we can bag the whole crowd," and units whose orders had already been changed two or three times in twenty-four hours got additional orders setting new destinations and demanding instant execution. One of Pope's staff officers visited General Porter at dawn with such orders: Porter went to his desk to revise his instructions to his own subordinates, and as he wrote he paused once to ask the staff man how to spell "chaos." The staff man told him, and considered the question most timely.[1]

In one way Pope's instinct was sound. He tried to concentrate his army along the Warrenton Pike, between Gainesville and the Bull Run bridge, in order to overwhelm Jackson, and he had men enough to do the job: between 60,000 and 70,000 within immediate reach.

But because he supposed that his task was to head off, round up, and capture an enemy who was making a desperate retreat he attacked before he was ready. On August 29, the day after the fight at Groveton, Pope got hardly more than half of his troops into action.

Jackson had more than 20,000 men in place, and they held an exceedingly strong position. Along most of Jackson's front, which was about two miles long, there was the line of an unfinished railroad, a long embankment and a series of cuts, with the wooded ridge just behind; an ideal position for a defensive fight, made to order for a tough army whose sole function was to hold on and wait for reinforcements—which, as it happened, were not far away. Lee and Longstreet with 30,000 men marched from Thoroughfare Gap early that morning (the gap being open because Pope was concentrating against Jackson) and around noon the head of this column began to come up just behind Jackson's right flank. By early afternoon the Army of Northern Virginia was solidly united and Lee was preparing for a counterstroke. Believing himself in the act of winning a great victory, Pope was floundering blindly into a shattering defeat.

Coming up from Centreville and establishing headquarters on a hill near the famous Stone House that had been a landmark in the first battle of Bull Run, Pope got his battle started without delay. Most of his divisions were still on the road—these soldiers had done a lot of marching in the last forty-eight hours—but Pope was in a hurry, and he opened the fight with the troops that were at hand, sending Franz Sigel and his 11,000 men in a headlong assault on Jackson's center north of the turnpike. Sigel's men vigorously shelled the woods in front of Jackson's main line, drove out the Rebel skirmishers and then made a slightly incoherent but valiant assault on the railroad embankment. The going was rugged. Jackson once said grimly that although his men sometimes failed to capture a position they never failed to hold one, and today his veterans made his word good. The Federals came up through a killing storm of musketry and artillery fire, some of the brigades drifted apart as they struggled through the woods, and Jackson's men lashed out with sharp counterattacks that threw the assaulting lines into disorder. But a few units pulled themselves together and went on again, reaching the embankment and, for the briefest moment, driving its defenders away.

These men in blue had done better than anyone had a right to expect—after all, they were supposed to be low-morale troops, indifferently led—but they were exhausted and disorganized and when they reached the embankment their attack had spent its force. Jackson's men drove them back, and Sigel asked Pope for permission to withdraw them for a rest and regrouping. Since he had no one to put in their place, Pope refused, and the men hung on in the fringe of the woods, maintained a sporadic fire, and did the best they could.

Then the first team came up—Kearny and Hooker, with 12,000 veterans from the Army of the Potomac, and Reno, with 8000 of Burnside's men, seasoned fighters under first-rate leaders; and Pope ordered a massive assault on Jackson's left, which was posted in a wood over near the Sudley Springs ford. The attack was imperfectly organized; the troops were sent into action piecemeal, and the full weight of a massed blow was lost. Also, Jackson had his own first team in line here, A. P. Hill and his famous "light division," and although the Confederate line was bent backward and in one place was temporarily broken, Jackson's boast was justified once more. Six separate Federal assaults were desperately beaten off, there were flurries of vicious hand-to-hand fighting, Hill's ammunition was almost exhausted and one of his brigades lost all but two of its field officers—officers, that is, of higher rank than captain—but at last, toward dusk, the fighting died down. Hill had just managed to hold his position.

Some of the fighting on this day was as severe as these armies ever had. If Pope had been able to co-ordinate his attacks properly the story might have been different, but co-ordination was lacking; indeed, there were upwards of 30,000 Federal infantrymen who were close enough to the battle all day long to hear it but who never effectively got into it.

Pope had intended to use these men, but this was a day when good intentions did not count. The 30,000 belonged to McDowell and Porter, who that morning were under orders to march to Gainesville and strike Jackson's right flank; and for various reasons, some of them good and some of them bad, this movement was never made. Porter, moving up from Manassas, saw dust clouds ahead and concluded that a large body of Confederates lay in his path. He seems also to have been oppressed by the signs of chaos which he had noted earlier in the day; and in any case he strongly disliked General Pope. So in midmorning he halted his corps behind a little stream and there he took root, two miles from the Federal left, remaining completely inert all day long while the clamor of battle resounded off beyond his right. McDowell did little better, although he at least kept moving. It is hard to feel certain that one knows what any Federal general had in mind on this confused day, but McDowell seems to have felt that he could best support the advance which he supposed Porter was going to make if he backtracked and got north of the turnpike; so he turned his troops around, moved back to the Sudley Springs Road, and then marched north, and by the end of the day only a few of his men had got into any sort of action. In effect, these two corps were wasted. What might have happened if they had actually executed the planned movement is beyond telling; all that is certain is that on this day of battle they were of very little use to John Pope and the Union cause.[2]

Another force which listened to the battle without getting into it was James Longstreet's corps of 30,000 Confederates.

By noon or a little later, Longstreet was getting his troops massed just south of the turnpike, ready for action, and Lee's immediate impulse had been to order an attack. But Longstreet wanted to wait, on the not-illogical theory that the confused Federals would present an even better opening if they were just given more time—and after long discussion and a careful study of the situation Lee let Longstreet have his way. There were times when Lee was strangely reluctant to impose his own will on this stubborn, deeply trusted subordinate, and this may have been one of them; yet it is possible that another consideration was involved. It was clear by now that at least a substantial part of McClellan's army had reached Pope, and the plan to defeat Pope before this happened looked a little different than it had looked a few days earlier. A glimpse at Lee's mind is given in a dispatch he wrote to President Davis after the fighting died down.

So far, Lee said, the campaign had been successful; it had compelled the Federals to leave the Rappahannock and to concentrate between Manassas and Centreville. Meanwhile: "My desire has been to avoid a general engagement, being the weaker force, & by maneuvering to relieve the portion of the country referred to–I think if not overpowered we shall be able to relieve other portions of the country, as it seems to be the purpose of the enemy to collect his strength here."[3] Perhaps, in other words, the moment for a decisive battle had passed; perhaps, after all, this must be a campaign with limited objectives, winning a breathing space rather than trying for a knockout; the general would wait and see how things looked before he made up his mind.

Things looked better before long, largely because certain routine Confederate troop movements brought additional confusion to the mind of General Pope.

Late on the evening of August 29 Longstreet had sent one division down the turnpike on a reconnaissance, and his men skirmished briskly with some of McDowell's troops. After dark these Confederates were withdrawn, and at the same time Hill retired some of his own men who had gone out beyond their own lines after repulsing the attacks Pope had made from his extreme right. These withdrawals were noted in the Federal camp, and to Pope they meant that the Confederates were in retreat. On the morning of August 30 he ordered a vigorous pursuit, detailing part of his army to overrun Jackson's position and forming the rest for an advance straight west along the turnpike. It took time to get everything organized, and the action did not begin until around noon. When it did begin the full truth about the entire battlefield situation was at last made manifest to the Federal commander.[4]

Jackson had not retreated, and the attempt to sweep across his position brought on a tremendous fight. Once again, Federal storming columns charged up to the railroad embankment, hitting so hard that for a short time it looked as if this mishandled battle might turn into a Federal victory. Much against his will, Jackson was obliged to notify Lee that he had to have help if he were to hold his ground. Help was ready. Pope's advance had stripped the Federal left flank nearly naked in front of Longstreet, and when Lee ordered Longstreet to attack that officer obeyed with high enthusiasm and complete competence. With his massed artillery he cut the props out from under the attack on Jackson's line; then he ordered his entire corps to advance and his 30,000 men went rolling eastward on the south side of the turnpike, overwhelming the inadequate Federal force that was posted there and driving on toward the Bull Run bridge. Now Pope was beaten, beyond remedy, and the only question was whether he could save his army . . . that, and the final size of the casualty list.[5]

Longstreet's men never reached the bridge. Now that his illusions were gone Pope handled his army about as well as a man could under the circumstances; at the very least he got everybody into action, and although he could not prevent defeat he was able to avert complete disaster. The battlefront had suddenly doubled in size, and from the Sudley Springs ford all the way down to the hills and fields south of the Warrenton Pike the exultant Confederates were driving forward. In the end, Federal troops were moved over to slow down Longstreet's advance, and toward evening elements from various army corps made a stand around the Henry House hill—the spot where Jackson had made his legendary stand in the first battle of Bull Run, more than a year ago—and there they brought the Southern offensive to a full stop. Slowly, painfully, the battle sputtered out in the twilight. The bridge was safe; Pope could get his men away.

His men were at the point of total exhaustion. They had done much marching and fighting, and in a fortnight's campaigning the army had lost 14,500 men in killed, wounded, and missing. During the night of August 30 they went back to Centreville, numb, dejected, stumbling under the weight of defeat. At Centreville the retreat stopped, and Pope formed a new battle line, rimming the town in a huge semicircle, well entrenched; if Lee proposed to follow up his victory the Federals would make a new fight here. And at Centreville, too, the beaten army saw welcome reinforcements—General William B. Franklin's corps, just up from the peninsula by way of Alexandria, three or four days late but ready for action at last. It was known that General Edwin Sumner's army corps was not far behind.

Pope's men were glad to see these stout fighting men. Now the battle losses at Bull Run would be made good, with strength to spare. Yet there was something deeply disillusioning, almost ominous, about the meeting. Franklin's men had nothing but scorn for the men to whose rescue they had come, and they openly exulted in the fact that these men had been defeated. The spirit that led McClellan to remark that disaster to Pope might mean triumph for himself had seeped down through all ranks, and an officer in one of Pope's brigades remembered that although "our hearts leaped with joy" at the sight of the troops from the peninsula the joy was quickly chilled.

"To them," he wrote, "we were only a part of Pope's beaten army, and as they lined the road they greeted us with mocking laughter, taunts and jeers on the advantages of the new route to Richmond; while many of them in plain English expressed their joy at the downfall of the braggart rival of the great soldier of the peninsula."[6]

Pope's soldiers made no response to the jeers. They wanted nothing except a chance to get a little rest. There was a sullen all-day rain, a good many men had straggled away from their commands, and a Wisconsin soldier spoke for all when he wrote a note to his people to say that he had lived through the battle and added: "I cannot give you particulars or write more now. The terrible weariness of long fight is upon me."[7]

The terrible weariness was also upon the Confederates, for they too had marched and fought to the limit of human endurance, and they had suffered more than 9000 casualties. Lee had no intention of attacking Pope's position at Centreville, but he did think he might flank Pope out of it, and he ordered Jackson to swing out on a wide circling movement to get behind Pope's right. Jackson put his tired men on the road, crossed Bull Run at the Sudley Springs ford, and went north; and although his "foot cavalry" could march so fast, on this day they went at a crawl—the unpaved roads were deep in mud, rations had gone short so that everyone was hungry, the men were all but completely worn out, and not even merciless Jackson could get any speed out of them. They reached the Little River turnpike, which ran eastward toward Alexandria, and turned right to get in Pope's rear, and at last had to camp for the night several miles short of their goal. The next day, September 1, they went on again, and Pope got wind of the move and sent troops out to meet them; and late that day, with a thunderstorm breaking, two Federal divisions attacked Jackson's men on rolling ground near a country estate called Chantilly, a few miles directly north of Pope's camp at Centreville.

It was a racking, bruising fight while it lasted. Brigadier General Isaac Stevens, leading one of Burnside's divisions, picked up a battle flag and rode into action at the head of the column to inspire his men and was shot dead. His battle line wavered to a halt, and the rain began to come down in blinding sheets, and the Federals were not eager to renew the attack. Then Phil Kearny came splashing up through the mud to try to get things in motion once more. The men did not respond, and Kearny cursed them for laggards, and galloped down the line to find more spirited troops. The storm was growing worse, the rain was so heavy that no one could see anything, and Kearny rode into a group of Confederate skirmishers and was killed before he could get away. There was a fire fight after that, with no particular result except that a number of soldiers on each side lost their lives . . . and at last the storm was so bad that even Jackson was willing to call it quits, and the battle came to an inconclusive end. The Federals had lost two of their best generals and about a thousand of other ranks, but they had at least brought the flanking movement to a halt. Pope could stay in Centreville if he wished.

While Jackson was moving off toward Chantilly, Longstreet's corps remained on the Bull Run battlefield to bury their dead, bring in the wounded and pick up small arms and other abandoned Yankee property. The private soldiers, being necessitous, spent as much time as they could looking for food, finding quite a lot of it in the haversacks of dead Federals. One gaunt Virginian, who held that "you cannot hurt the dead by anything of this kind," came upon an apparently lifeless Zouave with a full haversack, and drew his knife to cut the haversack straps and get the rations. The Zouave opened his eyes and begged, "For God's sake don't kill me." Horrified, the Confederate went away, and in a letter to a friend he confessed: "I don't believe I ever felt so bad in my life."[8]

After a day of this, Longstreet's corps followed Jackson, and on

September 2 the whole army rested—which, all things considered, is not hard to understand. Stuart's cavalry probed south and east to examine Yankee intentions, and found that Pope's men seemed to be withdrawing to the fortified lines around Washington; which compelled General Lee to take thought about his next move. The Washington lines were too strong to be attacked, and lack of supplies made it impossible for Lee to remain where he was; as he wrote to President Davis, "we cannot afford to be idle, and though weaker than our opponents in men and military equipments, must endeavor to harass if we cannot destroy them." The surest way to harass the enemy, obviously, was to cross the Potomac and go into Maryland. The army could provision itself there, the people of Maryland were believed to be strongly pro-Confederate and might provide the army with many recruits, and if the army got into Maryland the war would at least be removed for a while from the ravaged state of Virginia. In preparing for this movement Lee had no intention of trying to take and hold a position on northern soil, he was not specifically aiming at the capture of Baltimore or any other city, and he was well aware that his army was not really equipped to invade enemy territory: all of his men were ragged, thousands of them lacked shoes, supplies of food were very low and most of the horses were badly worn down. But the move would harass the foe and relieve Virginia, and there was one additional possibility which Lee never lost sight of. With a Confederate Army in Maryland the Federals would most certainly leave the Washington fortifications and come out looking for a fight. Then the genuinely decisive victory which Lee had been looking for ever since Gaines's Mill might at last be won.[9]

But for the moment the pieces on the chessboard stopped moving. These pieces were living human beings, and the amount of sheer misery some of them endured during the days just after the battle is not pleasant to think about. Many Federal wounded, for instance, were brought back to Fairfax Courthouse, wagon after wagon jolting in along the deeply rutted highways, and at Fairfax there was nothing resembling a hospital; just a huge open field, where people tore apart bales of hay and covered the ground so that the wounded men could lie on something besides bare earth. It was dark and there were no medicines, nothing much in the way of food, and hardly any doctors. There were a few civilian helpers, among them a woman named Clara Barton, and she and a few like her went briskly to work. They found three thousand wounded men lying on the hay in midnight darkness. There was a gusty wind that blew out most of the candles the nurses were carrying, "and the men lay so thick we could not take one step in the dark." The attendants had two water buckets, five dippers and a few boxes of crackers to minister to the wounded men, and as they worked they were haunted by the fear that someone would drop a candle into the hay and burn everyone alive. They managed to get through the night, doing the little they could do to ease suffering; and when morning came the army managed to bring up ambulances and move most of the men back to the capital.[10]

3: *To Risk Everything*

Balance the two campaigns, second Bull Run and the Seven Days. In each case Robert E. Lee first deluded an opponent and then beat him. The retreat from Bull Run was like the retreat from the Chickahominy; the defeated army was led away rather than driven away. The men in the ranks had done their part but the man at the top never quite understood what happened to him. There was a strange similarity in the post-battle protests of the beaten generals. Each man said that he had been foiled by designing men who should have helped him and did not; each asserted that by heroic efforts he had escaped destruction, thereby putting the country in his debt, and each insisted that he would have won if he had been properly reinforced. Even the casualty lists were about the same. In two weeks' campaigning around Manassas the Federals lost almost exactly the number lost in seven days near Richmond. And because these battles had been lost the crisis of the war was at hand at the end of August, and the administration in Washington had to face a baffling problem in leadership.

It was obviously necessary to get rid of General Pope, and that would be attended to promptly. It seemed to many of the administration leaders—among them Secretary of War Stanton—that it was equally necessary to get rid of General McClellan, and it presently developed that this was impossible.

The effort to put McClellan on the shelf had been going on all summer and no one was more aware of it than McClellan himself. He had regarded the elevation of Halleck with suspicion and that of Pope with outright horror, and when he came north from the peninsula he knew very well that his official existence was at stake. The odds seemed to be against him. Most of the cabinet would be glad to see the last of him, and so would the leaders of the Republican majority on Capitol Hill. Mr. Lincoln was aloof; since receiving McClellan's letter of advice at Harrison's Landing he had been withdrawn, and practically all of the general's subsequent communication with the administration had been conducted through General Halleck.

Nevertheless, survival was possible, even probable. If McClellan were removed somebody would have to take his place, and no good candidate was in sight. Pope was out of the question, partly because he was not big enough but also because the Army of the Potomac simply would not have him. Among his many problems, so many of them self-created, Pope also had that one, and it had been a powerful handicap. What had happened to Pope might very well happen to another man. The army's devotion to General McClellan was something the administration could not ignore. It actually seemed possible that at this particular moment no other general could use the Army of the Potomac.[1]

To an extent, the army's devotion for this man had grown up naturally. McClellan had taken thousands of untrained recruits and had made them feel like soldiers. They had been used to confusion and he had given them order and had taught them to be proud of themselves. It could almost be said that he had given ancient traditions to an army that had no past. The long stay in Washington, extended month after month while Congress and the press demanded action, had led the men to feel that this general was on their side, protecting them against the pressure of ignorant politicians. McClellan's personality was magnetic; at the innumerable grand reviews that played so large a part in the first months of the army's life it had been easy to greet him with cheers. This habit of cheering was actively promoted. A Massachusetts officer noted that when the army took to the road McClellan would remain in camp until the entire column had been formed. Then he would ride to the head of the column, preceded by a staff officer who went galloping along the line crying "McClellan's coming, boys! McClellan's coming! Three cheers for McClellan!"[2] The officer who wrote about this considered it "claptrap and humbug," but the men did not; one great reason being that McClellan quite sincerely returned the affection they felt for him. His response to their cheers came from the heart; he identified himself with them just as they identified themselves with him. In their belief that McClellan had their interests at heart and wanted to save and protect them in every possible way the soldiers were entirely correct.

But it went beyond that. Loyalty to McClellan was built up in the army as deliberately as loyalty to a leader is built up in a political organization, and in much the same way. It came down from the top, actively generated by the officers, and one veteran saw the parallel clearly. "His generals," wrote this man, "appointed and promoted through his influence, thoroughly infused a McClellan element into their commands. An army of generals bear very much the same relation to their chief that office holders do to the head of their party. By maintaining him in his position they insure their own, and in promoting his interests they promote themselves." John Pope assured the governor of Illinois that "the praetorian system is as fully developed and in active operation in Washington as it ever was in ancient Rome"; and although Pope's verdict is subject to discount he touched reality in his remark that to encamp a large army around Washington for the better part of a year was to risk corrupting both the army and the government. In its formative period this army had been kept too long too near the capital, and it had been incurably infected with politics. Abner Doubleday believed that Porter was the lieutenant through whom the McClellan influence was most actively promoted, and he wrote bitterly: "The history of everyone who opposed McClellan has been a history of the decline of individual fortunes."[3]

Both by natural predisposition and by good management the army was deeply, passionately attached to its general, and the administration had to take this into account when it planned for the future. McClellan was advised of this while he was on his way up from the peninsula. Allan Pinkerton, who had given him such detailed information about Rebel manpower in front of Richmond, had been in Washington taking soundings, and on August 25 he sent McClellan an appreciation of the political situation. President Lincoln, he said, was already growing disillusioned with Pope—this of course was before the big battle at Bull Run made disillusion complete—and Pinkerton felt that "unless some other military genius appears soon they cannot do otherwise than appoint you to the command though there is no doubt but that this will be very unpalatable and greatly against the wishes of Lincoln, Stanton and Halleck."

Pinkerton went on to underline the moral: "I learn that the rulers more than ever dread doing anything with you since the Army of the Potomac began to arrive at Alexandria. I find that many of the general officers are expressing themselves very strongly in favor of your having moved on Richmond instead of coming here . . . rumors from Alexandria say that the field and regimental officers are very outspoken on this point—all of which tends to increase the fears of Lincoln and his coadjutors, and this is the only point to hope from now."[4]

With this advice in his pocket McClellan opened headquarters in Alexandria on August 27 (the day Jackson destroyed Pope's supplies at Manassas) and wired a report of his arrival to Halleck, who was half a dozen miles away, in Washington; and during the rest of August the general-in-chief and the army commander carried on a long argument, by telegraph, over the matter of reinforcing Pope and making Washington safe. What gave this correspondence a slightly unreal quality was that it nowhere mentioned the one point that neither Halleck nor McClellan ever lost sight of—the question of what McClellan's future status in the army was going to be.

Franklin's army corps was in Alexandria and Sumner's corps would arrive in twenty-four hours, and Halleck greatly wanted them sent on at once to help Pope. A twenty-five-mile march would accomplish this, and McClellan accepted the idea, in principle. Principle, however, was subject to delays. The march was ordered; then the order was countermanded; then it was ordered anew, and delayed again, while McClellan sent to Halleck a record of his doubts. Franklin had no cavalry, his artillery lacked horses; would he be of any use if, thus crippled, he did reach the front? Was Halleck quite sure he wanted him to march? Then McClellan reported that neither army corps was in shape to move and fight, and asked if Sumner should not be retained for the defense of Washington; after which he reported hearing that Lee was in Manassas and that 120,000 Confederates were about to move on Arlington. Again he wanted to know if the advance should be made.

Halleck sent peremptory orders. Franklin began to move, and then halted at Annandale, ten miles out. Halleck angrily told McClellan that "this is all contrary to my orders," and McClellan took offense, icily requesting that he be given very specific instructions about movements henceforth because "it is not agreeable to me to be accused of disregarding orders when I have simply exercised the discretion you committed to me."[5]

In the end, Pope was not reinforced; Franklin and Sumner got out too late to be of any use in battle; and after it was all over President Lincoln told John Hay that it really seemed to him that McClellan wanted Pope to fail. Attorney General Bates wrote to a friend: "The thing I complain of is a criminal tardiness, a fatuous apathy, a captious, bickering rivalry, among our commanders who seem so taken up with their quick made dignity that they overlook the lives of their people and the necessities of their country. They, in grotesque egotism, have so much reputation to take care of that they dare not risk it."[6] But by August 31 the bad news from Bull Run indicated that the moment for a general accounting had at last arrived, and McClellan moved for a showdown, sending this telegram to Halleck: "I am ready to afford you any assistance in my power, but you will readily perceive how difficult an undefined position, such as I now hold, must be. At what hour in the morning can I see you alone, either at your own house or the office?"[7]

McClellan's position was not so much undefined as unstable. He was still commander of the Army of the Potomac, no order relieving him having been issued. By bits and pieces, this army had been sent to, or at least toward, General Pope, and if it was ever brought together again McClellan would presumably remain in charge of it. But a military catastrophe had taken place, and it was clear that somebody was going to be fired . . . and so it was time to touch base with the general-in-chief.

McClellan was not the only one who wanted a showdown. Secretary of War Stanton also wanted one and wanted it intensely. Since Halleck's arrival Stanton had stuck to the administrative routine, but now he got back into action. To Halleck, on August 28, he sent a note asking what orders had been given McClellan regarding the return from Harrison's Landing and the movement of people like Franklin, and requesting the general-in-chief to say whether these orders had been obeyed "as promptly as the national safety required"; after which the Secretary went to call on Secretary Chase to organize the cabinet in favor of putting a new man in charge of the Army of the Potomac. Halleck's reply, which came in on August 30, enclosed copies of his correspondence with McClellan and contained Halleck's official finding that McClellan, all things considered, had not moved as fast as he should have moved.

Stanton and Chase drew up a sort of round robin, which asserted that destruction of the armies, waste of national resources, and the overthrow of the government must inevitably follow McClellan's retention in command. Then they set out to induce the rest of the cabinet to sign it. Attorney General Bates, after getting the document toned down slightly, gave his signature, as did Caleb Smith, Secretary of the Interior. Montgomery Blair was on McClellan's side, Mr. Seward was out of the city (there were those who felt that the Secretary of State had concluded this was a good fight to stay out of) and Secretary Welles said that he was in favor of removing McClellan but would sign no paper putting pressure on the President. Still, a majority did sign; when presented, the paper would serve notice on

Abraham Lincoln that he must either fire a general or lose most of his cabinet.[8]

Now came a contribution from General Pope. From his cheerless camp at Centreville he wrote to Halleck to say that "the unsoldierly and dangerous conduct" of certain Army of the Potomac officers had created an impossible situation. There were brigade and division commanders, he said, who kept saying "that the Army of the Potomac will not fight; that they are demoralized by the withdrawal from the peninsula, etc." Pope correctly believed that this called for action at the top; he told Halleck, "You alone can stop it," and he suggested that Halleck bring all of the troops back to Washington for a general overhaul and reorganization. He warned: "You may avoid great disaster by doing so."[9]

The advice was good but tardy. The great disaster had already occurred. It had been cumulative, five months long, running from the first hesitant pause in front of Yorktown to the last blind battle in the thunderstorm at Chantilly. At the beginning of April it had seemed that the war was all but won; now, at the beginning of September, it began to seem that the war might be all but lost. It would unquestionably be lost unless General Lee, who was about to invade the North, could soon be beaten and driven back. And President Lincoln, whose responsibility it was to say which soldier should be given the task of meeting and defeating Lee, was obliged to recognize a very odd fact.

The most compelling reason for removing General McClellan from command of the Army of the Potomac was precisely the reason that made his removal impossible. The gravest charge against him was at the same time his greatest asset.

It was being charged that McClellan had turned the Army of the Potomac into his own personal instrument. Both his friends and his enemies were saying that the army actually would not fight for anyone else, and this latest dispatch from General Pope could be taken as evidence from a man who had been through the mill. Pope had suggested a remedy, but there was no time to apply it: General Lee was in a hurry, and the Federal Army—not for the last time, either—was going to have to march in step with Lee's drums. If

General McClellan, for whatever reason or combination of reasons, was the only man the army would follow, then he must lead it. If to give him the army was to gamble on an integrity that some men doubted and an aggressiveness that had never yet been in evidence—well, Mr. Lincoln could gamble, just as General Lee could do. There was in fact no other course open.

When McClellan met with Halleck on September 1, President Lincoln was present. He had seen Pope's dispatch, and he brought the matter up—not to administer a rebuke but simply to ask McClellan to use his influence with his friends so that they would loyally serve any superior the government happened to put over them. McClellan gave him what he wanted, and that evening he sent a dispatch to General Porter—as singular a message, from one general to another, as the annals of American wars contain. It went thus:

"I ask of you for my sake, that of the country, and of the old Army of the Potomac, that you and all my friends will lend the fullest and most cordial co-operation to General Pope in all the operations now going on. The destinies of our country, the honor of our arms, are at stake, and all depends now upon the cheerful co-operation of all in the field. This week is the crisis of our fate. Say the same thing to my friends in the Army of the Potomac, and that the last request I have to make of them is that, for their country's sake, they will extend to General Pope the same support they ever have to me.

"I am in charge of the defenses of Washington, and am doing all I can do to render your retreat safe should that become necessary."[10]

The final sentence outweighed all of the verbiage ahead of it. It said that McClellan had won. Putting him in charge of the defenses of Washington, Mr. Lincoln was in effect giving him Pope's army as well as his own. The arrangement was still makeshift, but it would quickly be made formal. On the following day Halleck telegraphed Pope to bring everyone back inside the Washington lines, telling him that McClellan was in charge and that "you will consider any direction as to disposition of the troops as they arrive, given by him, as coming from me."[11]

On September 2 McClellan rode out to take possession of the returning troops and Abraham Lincoln went to a cabinet meeting.

No public announcement of his action in respect to McClellan had been made, and the cabinet ministers knew nothing for certain, although horrid rumors had been circulating. Not until the President himself came into the room and told them what had been done did the men who had prepared that round robin realize that they had been outmaneuvered. Mr. Welles wrote that there was "a more disturbed and desponding feeling" than he had ever seen in a cabinet meeting; Mr. Lincoln was "greatly distressed," but was unyielding. Mr. Chase, who had told Welles that McClellan ought to be shot, warned that what the President was doing was equivalent to making McClellan temporary commander-in-chief, and said that it might be uncommonly hard to get the man out, later on; to all of which the President made the obvious reply—he had to use the Army of the Potomac, and so he had to use McClellan. What he did not say, and never thereafter needed to say, was that army commanders would be named by the President and not by the cabinet. The round robin was not delivered.[12]

McClellan felt that he had done the administration a favor. He told Mrs. McClellan that Halleck had written, "begging me to help him out of his scrape and take command here," and he went on: "Of course I could not refuse, so I came over this morning, mad as a March hare"—what he really meant was that he was angry—"and had a pretty plain talk with him & Abe—a still plainer one this evening. The result is that I have reluctantly consented to take command here & try to save the capital." Secretary Welles was disturbed, a few days later, to note that when a big draft from the Army of the Potomac had to march through Washington it was routed past McClellan's house at 15th and H Streets so that the men could cheer the general, rather than past the White House, where the President would get the cheers. At about the same time Mr. Lincoln told Hay that "McClellan is working like a beaver," and said that "the sort of snubbing he got last week" seemed to have been good for him.[13]

The President did give Halleck a chance to come to his rescue. Late on the evening of September 3 he wrote out and gave to Secretary Stanton, who promptly sent it on to Halleck, a directive instructing Halleck to "proceed with all possible dispatch to organize an army for active operations" against Lee. By its wording, this order was the broadest hint that Halleck himself could take command of field operations if he chose. But Halleck would not do this. He transmitted the order to McClellan, revising it just enough to indicate that the command would be McClellan's; and a few days later, as the reorganization proceeded, Pope's army was formally consolidated into the Army of the Potomac, Pope was relieved and sent out west to Minnesota to fight the Indians, and the rest was definitely up to McClellan.[14]

Pope departed, protesting with extraordinary bitterness and with some logic; unquestionably, the man had been given a hard deal. But nothing could be done about it; the army just was not big enough to contain both Pope and McClellan, it was necessary now to use McClellan, and Pope would have to make the best of it, which he did with very bad grace. He sent long letters to Halleck, denouncing that officer and President Lincoln in unmeasured terms, and Halleck (who was being paid to handle this sort of thing) wrote long, soothing replies in which Pope found little healing. The eastern theater of the war saw John Pope no more.[15]

Meanwhile, President Lincoln was under two great pressures.

In his desk was a paper which undertook to proclaim freedom for Negro slaves—a document which would transform the war and change the future course of American history, if it ever got out, but which would only be a piece of paper unless the Federal Army speedily won a victory; and Lee was north of the Potomac with an army that had never been beaten and was beginning to look unbeatable, moving northwest across Maryland, bent on nothing less than the destruction of the Army of the Potomac.

Lee had raised his sights. He had written to Mr. Davis to say that at the least his move into Maryland would get the war out of Virginia and provide a breathing space, but as he moved he was thinking again in terms of an all-out offensive. (Lee had this hallmark of a great soldier; if he had the slightest warrant for doing so he planned in terms of complete victory.) He had received reinforcements which slightly more than made up for the 9000 men he had lost at Bull Run, and he crossed the Potomac near Leesburg on September 5, moved up to the town of Frederick, Maryland, and planned a new maneuver. Off to his left and rear, posted where it could interrupt his communications with Virginia, was a detachment of 10,000 Federals at Harper's Ferry. Lee proposed to move his army beyond the sheltering screen of South Mountain—that long extension of the Blue Ridge which runs northeast from Harper's Ferry into Pennsylvania—and send Jackson down to capture this annoying outpost. Then he would reassemble his army, seek out McClellan, bring him to battle and defeat him.

Once again he would be taking a long chance. His army was weaker now than at any other time in the war until the final, doomed retreat to Appomattox. It was worn-out, thousands of men had no shoes, other thousands considered that they had enlisted to defend the South and not to invade the North, and Lee had temporarily lost more men by straggling than he had recently lost in battle; all in all, when the time for fighting came he would actually have fewer than 50,000 men of all arms. McClellan, who was slowly moving toward him, might have twice that many, certainly would outnumber him heavily, and the Federals would be much better equipped and supplied. To divide the army in the presence of the enemy was the greatest of risks; it had worked against Pope—would it work against McClellan?

Lee believed that it would. He had supreme confidence in himself and in his soldiers, he knew that McClellan always moved slowly, and he believed that McClellan's army was more or less demoralized. After the war he told a friend that "I intended then to attack McClellan, hoping the best results from the state of my troops and those of the enemy," and another post-war interviewer wrote that Lee said that if he could have kept the Federals in the dark about his own movements for a few days longer "he did not doubt then (nor has he changed his opinion since) that he could have crushed the army of McClellan." Once more, Lee was risking everything in order to win everything.[16]

It might have worked; it is hard to dispute the measured judgment of Robert E. Lee. But no one will ever know about this particular might-have-been; because as the army left Frederick, bound for the sheltering rampart of South Mountain, one of Lee's officers lost the order which set forth all of the movements which Lee's army was going to make, and on the evening of September 13 that order was presented to General McClellan. Now McClellan had the game in his hands.

4: *A Town Called Sharpsburg*

What it came down to was that General Lee had taken forty badly worn infantry brigades north of the Potomac to defeat an army twice as large as his. The odds were forbidding, but they had been carefully calculated. They would swing in Lee's favor if he could get time and space for the maneuvers which would deceive his foes and set them up for the kill. The concealing screen of South Mountain offered an opportunity. West of this long ridge Lee was out of sight, with unlimited room to move and fast-marching men to move in it, and invisibility ought to buy the time he needed. It was true that the Federal infantry could break the screen whenever it really tried–the mountain gaps were held only by Stuart's cavalry, backed by D. H. Hill's infantry–but if past performance meant anything the Army of the Potomac would not move fast against an enemy which it could not even see.

Risky as they seemed, Lee's plans were justified. It was pure freakish chance that tripped him; the fantastic accident which led a nameless Confederate officer to lose a copy of the campaign orders, which led two Federal infantrymen to find that copy, and which placed it shortly thereafter in front of General McClellan. When McClellan read it (to compound the fantasy, he had at his side an officer who recognized the handwriting and so could assure him that the document was genuine) Lee's invisibility ceased to be. Now McClellan knew exactly where Lee was, what he was doing and where he was going to be next.

It seemed to McClellan that Lee had made a great mistake, and in a letter to Mr. Lincoln the Federal commander exulted that Lee "will be severely punished for it." Full of confidence, McClellan explained: "I have all the plans of the Rebels and will catch them in their own trap if my men are equal to the emergency. I now feel that I can count on them as of old."[1]

Before the Federal soldiers could show whether they were equal to the emergency their commanding general would have to do his own part. On the evening of September 13 his opportunity was wide open.

Lee himself was near Hagerstown, Maryland, with Longstreet and nine brigades. Five more brigades, under D. H. Hill, were twelve miles south of Hagerstown, at Boonsboro, a few miles west of Turner's Gap where the National Road crossed South Mountain. All the rest of the army, divided into three separate columns, was off to the south, converging on Harper's Ferry under the direction of Stonewall Jackson, and two of these three columns were south of the Potomac. Lee's army of invasion had split into pieces like an exploding shell, and the Army of the Potomac, massed in and near Frederick, Maryland, was ideally situated to exploit this situation. No Civil War general was ever given so fair a chance to destroy the opposing army one piece at a time.

Not only was the invading army dispersed, it was also in a condition of extreme military destitution. Its soldiers had marched out of their shoes, almost out of their uniforms and far away from their rations—thousands of haversacks contained nothing but green corn and ripe apples gathered from Maryland's fields and orchards—and straggling had been almost ruinous. A New York *Times* correspondent, observing Stonewall Jackson at Harper's Ferry, wrote loftily that this famous general wore a most seedy uniform and had a hat "which any northern beggar would consider an insult to have offered him," and found the men in the ranks much seedier: "Ireland in her worst straits could present no parallel." Long afterward a Confederate veteran wryly confessed that he and his fellows were indeed "a set of ragamuffins," and said that "it seemed as if every cornfield in Maryland had been robbed of its scarecrows." Digging into his memory, the veteran became specific:

"None had any under-clothing. My costume consisted of a ragged pair of trousers, a stained, dirty jacket; an old slouch hat, the brim pinned up with a thorn; a begrimed blanket over my shoulder, a grease-smeared cotton haversack full of apples and corn, a cartridge box full, and a musket. I was barefooted and had a stone bruise on each foot. . . . There was no one there who would not have been 'run in' by the police had he appeared on the streets of any populous city."[2]

So the Army of Northern Virginia was not much to look at; yet it was something special to meet. Lacking all else, it still had those cartridge boxes and muskets, it knew just how to use them, and extreme hardship had swept away everybody except the men who could stand anything. If McClellan meant to round up and destroy these soldiers he would have to work at it.

He tried, and the inspiration born of a look at his opponent's cards lifted him up briefly. He sent his army forward on September 14, and in due time it broke through the South Mountain rampart in two places, at Turner's Gap and at Crampton's Gap six miles to the south, and if he had been just a little more aggressive he would have saved Harper's Ferry, mashed the fragments of Lee's army and won the war before September died. But there were always a few hours to spare. The Federal columns that were to break through the mountain screen were to move tomorrow morning as early as possible—instead of this minute, tonight, before the sun goes down, and if everybody isn't ready march with the ones that are and let the Devil take the hindmost . . . When the Army of the Potomac advanced to seize the South Mountain passes, Lee started to call everything off and get his men back to Virginia while they were still alive; then he found that he would be given half a day or so of grace. On September 15 Jackson captured Harper's Ferry and 11,000 Union prisoners, along with heaped-up supplies, and D. H. Hill's men held Turner's Gap just long enough to make all the difference, and so instead of retreating to Virginia Lee ordered what there was of his army to concentrate at a town called Sharpsburg, down behind the high ground that overlooked Antietam Creek, close to the Potomac, in western Maryland.

Antietam Creek is not much of a stream and Sharpsburg was

not much of a town, and the army that Lee planted behind the creek on September 15 was not just then much of an army; Longstreet and D. H. Hill, mostly, with some guns, perhaps 18,000 men in all, with the rest of the army due to come up after a while from Harper's Ferry; and McClellan got the Army of the Potomac there a few hours later, looked at the guns and the bayonets on the high ground beyond the creek, and concluded that he ought to study the situation. The only way to beat Robert E. Lee was to come and get him, and Lee had his guns ranked on the hills with the leathery, hardcase soldiers in rags lined up with them, and it seemed that this was no time to be hasty. So McClellan's engineers laid out the lines the men were to occupy, and the men filed into them, and the day ended and night came down, and next morning it was September 16, and for a time there was a fog which made it hard to see what the Rebels were up to; and all through September 16 the Army of the Potomac waited, posting artillery on the heights east of the creek, and more and more of Lee's army came up (including Stonewall Jackson in person) and at sundown there was a brief, meaningless clash between McClellan's right wing and Lee's left wing, and the long day in which the Federal Army had a three-to-one advantage in numbers came to an end. There was a drizzling rain that night, and a queer silence lay over the field, and in the morning there would at last be a fight. And still more of Lee's army reached the scene.

For more than a century men have been trying to understand Lee's willingness to stand and fight at Sharpsburg. His army was fearfully overmatched. Even when the last troops came up from Harper's Ferry he would have hardly more than 40,000 men, and McClellan had 87,000 with more coming up.[8] The position overlooking Antietam Creek was strong but it was not invulnerable, and it had one dangerous weakness; fighting there, the Army of Northern Virginia stood with its back to the Potomac and there was only one ford for a crossing. If the Federals ever broke the line and made a really quick Confederate retreat necessary, Lee's army would simply be destroyed. On the face of it there was every reason for a quiet departure without a fight and hardly any reason for remaining and defying the Army of the Potomac to do its worst. And yet . . .

And yet Lee stayed when he did not have to stay and fought when he did not have to fight, and since he was not out of his mind the only conceivable answer is that he believed that he could win.

He had believed this all along. He would not have entered Maryland otherwise; if to fight at Sharpsburg was to risk the loss of his entire army, to go north of the Potomac at all was to take the same risk. Lee wanted an absolute victory, and to get the kind of fight that could bring such a victory he had to run the risk of absolute defeat. To leave Maryland now without putting the matter to the test would be to confess that there could not be the kind of victory that could mean Confederate independence. Perhaps the assignment was just too big. Perhaps the one real chance to sweep the board clean had vanished when McClellan's army got away from the Chickahominy and took refuge in its camp at Harrison's Landing, and perhaps the Confederacy's only course now was to hang on and make the war so expensive that the Yankees would finally get tired of it and quit trying. This might be the case, but Lee would not accept it until he was sure of it. Sharpsburg was where he would find out.

This war saw many terrible battles, and to try to make a ranking of them is just to compare horrors, but it may be that the battle of Antietam was the worst of all. It had, at any rate, the fearful distinction of killing and wounding more Americans in one day than any other fight in the war. If there was any essential difference in the fighting qualities of Northern and Southern soldiers Antietam fails to show it. It was a headlong combat, unrelieved by any tactical brilliance, a slugging match in cornfields and woodlots and on the open slopes of the low hills that came up from the brown creek. Neither commanding general did what he wanted to do; actually, once the fighting got under way neither commander had a great deal to do with it except to stand firm and refuse to call retreat, and in the end it was about as close to a draw as so large a battle could be . . . except that it became the great turning point of the war, meaning more than either general or either army intended, a grim and fateful landmark in American history. American soldiers never fought harder than they did when they fought each other on September 17 on the outskirts of Sharpsburg.

It began in the earliest dawn, with a misty drizzle to obscure the half-light, when Federal skirmishers went prowling southward astride the turnpike that came down to Sharpsburg from Hagerstown. On the left was a big cornfield, with stalks taller than a man's head, and on the right there were open pastures rolling off to hills where Jeb Stuart had planted his horse artillery; and straight ahead, about a mile away, the turnpike went over a bit of rising ground and passed a whitewashed Dunker church, picturesquely framed by an open grove of trees. If the Federals could occupy this ground around the church they would break the left end of Lee's battle line, and McClellan had called for a big attack: one army corps to make the first drive and two more to come in beside and behind to make it a crusher.

The skirmishers were feeling the way for Joe Hooker's corps, on the extreme right of McClellan's line. These troops had been led until recently by McDowell, and in the general reshuffle following Pope's retirement McDowell had been put on the shelf and his command had been given to Hooker, a more dashing general and a far luckier one; florid, handsome, self-centered, coarse of fibre, always ready to fight. Now Hooker had his men moving south toward the Dunker church in a gray rainy daybreak.

Stonewall Jackson was waiting for him, with artillery massed around the Dunker church and solid ranks of infantry in the cornfield and west of the turnpike. The skirmishers probed at the front and found it strong, and the advance drifted to a halt; then Hooker put three dozen fieldpieces in line on a low ridge and had the guns blast the cornfield with a methodical, murderous bombardment that flattened the tasseled corn and the defenders who had been posted in it, and after a while the guns stopped firing and the Federal infantry went forward. It had to fight its way, but the line in the cornfield had been almost blown to bits and the Rebel units to the west were overpowered, and Hooker's corps kept moving; and at last it swept the last of Jackson's infantry out of the way and came up toward the Dunker church.

This was almost it, but not quite. Out of the woods behind the church came a new Confederate battle line—John B. Hood's shock troops, the men angry because they had been sent forward just when they were cooking what would have been their first really good breakfast in a week. (During the night a meat ration had been issued.) This line formed in the clearing and suddenly it was all ablaze with deadly musketry, firing volleys that broke the Federal column apart; then it charged, yelling after the manner of the Rebels, greatly aided by some brigades of D. H. Hill which came in through a fringe of woods and farmlots off to the east. Hooker's men were driven into retreat, some of them going slowly, fighting as they went, others going headlong for any refuge they could find. They went north along the turnpike, whose rail fences were grotesquely festooned with corpses, or back across the cornfield whose torn ground held an unutterable litter of dead and wounded. (Hooker said later that of all the dismal battlefields he ever saw nothing was quite as bad as that wretched cornfield.[4]) At last the Federals got back to their original starting point, Hooker disabled with a bullet in one foot, and the powerful Federal artillery beat the Confederate advance to a halt.

Then McClellan sent in a fresh army corps, the one formerly led by General Banks, commanded now by a white-whiskered old Regular named Joseph Mansfield; and these men drove the Confederates out of the cornfield. Mansfield himself was mortally wounded, but his men kept going, put half of Hood's division out of action, cleared out a plot of woods just east of the cornfield, got one tentacle up to touch the Dunker church—and then came to a sullen halt, bruised and spent and winded.

There was a brief lull, partly because the two corps commanders had become casualties, partly because these two Federal corps had been virtually wrecked. Then a third Federal corps came into action—Army of the Potomac veterans, three big divisions under crusty old Edwin V. Sumner, coming up to break the Rebel line; coming up, by unhappy chance, one division at a time, hitting three moderate blows instead of one crusher . . . and suddenly the pattern for the whole business becomes clear, and the tactical details no longer have much meaning.

The thing really was just about over now, except for the killing, which would go on all day without really changing anything; for the pattern by which the Federals fought on this day made decisive victory impossible.

The Army of the Potomac was fighting the whole battle the way Sumner fought his part of it: that is, it was fighting a series of separate engagements rather than one co-ordinated battle, and so it could never get the proper advantage out of its overwhelming superiority in numbers. Lee's army was never quite stretched past the breaking point.

Thus: Hooker's corps attacked, was used up, and retired. Then came Mansfield's, which did just about the same. Then came Sumner's, one division at a time. The first division, John Sedgwick's, was flanked, routed, and driven from the field (by a Confederate division that had just come up from Harper's Ferry) before the second began to fight. This second division broke its back trying to storm a sunken lane which went zigzag across the Confederate center: a strong position, held by D. H. Hill's people. Then the third division came up, and it flanked and carried this sunken lane and came up against the Confederates' last line of defense—which was so desperately thin by now that Longstreet had his own staff helping to work the guns in a half-wrecked battery, and D. H. Hill had picked up a musket and was trying to rally stragglers. Precisely then and there Lee's army could have been broken.

Sumner's third division was fagged by this time, but it probably would have kept going if its commander, Brigadier General Israel Richardson, had not been mortally wounded. Right behind it, however, there was a fresh army corps, Franklin's, ready to be used; but at this point the Federal high command concluded that its entire right wing was on the verge of disaster and that Lee might at any moment make a big counterattack. Franklin's corps was put on the defensive, and the threadbare Confederate center felt no more pressure. Instead, the Federals attacked on their own extreme left, a mile and a half from the breakthrough point along the sunken road.

This attack was like the others, late and utterly unco-ordinated. It was made by Burnside's corps, which contained four divisions, and these characteristically were sent into action one at a time. This offensive began after all the other offensives had ended, and although it was the weakest of them all it nearly succeeded, and if it had succeeded Lee would have lost his grip on the ford across the Potomac and his army would have been done for. But McClellan was late in ordering the attack, Burnside was slow to execute the order, and coordination was enforced by no one; and finally, well on in the afternoon, A. P. Hill's division came up after a hard seventeen-mile march from Harper's Ferry, and it drove Burnside's advance back almost to Antietam Creek and stabilized the situation. Hill's arrival highlighted one of the strange features of the battle. From the moment the two armies first confronted each other here, Lee had been given forty-eight hours to reassemble his scattered forces, and this last piece slipped into place just when it was most needed.

So the battle ended, at last, and the armies held much the same ground they had held at dawn—except that nearly 23,000 men had become casualties. As always, the night that followed the battle was hideous: from one end of the line to the other the darkness was dreadful with the cries of wounded men who were calling for help. The Federals held the cornfield and the sunken road and the various crossings of the Antietam, and Lee held an unbroken position covering the ford that led back to Virginia; he had lost a fourth of his army but he had not been driven away, and in a narrow tactical sense he had actually had the better of it. Incredibly, he remained in position all of the next day, September 18, and he and Jackson even planned to take the offensive, giving it up at last when a close study of the situation showed that it simply was not possible.[5] McClellan for his part had had all the fighting he wanted. He received 13,000 fresh troops that morning, and he had on the scene two army corps which had hardly been used, but he was willing enough to wait; and that night, while the Army of the Potomac lay in its soiled bivouac, Lee's army rounded up its guns, its stragglers, and as many of its wounded as could be moved and threaded its way back across the Potomac to safety. The Maryland campaign was over.

What it meant could be seen better from a distance than at close range. Whatever might be true of the battle itself, Lee had unquestionably lost the campaign; the attempt to win a decisive victory north of the Potomac had failed. McClellan notified Halleck that

"Maryland is entirely freed from the presence of the enemy, who have been driven across the Potomac," and to Mrs. McClellan on September 18 he sent a thin chirp of pleasure: "The spectacle yesterday was the grandest I could conceive of; nothing could be more sublime. Those in whose judgment I rely tell me that I fought the battle splendidly and that it was a masterpiece of art."[6]

The soldiers themselves knew only that they had been in a terrible fight. The battle had had a strange spectacular quality, because most of it was fought out in the open where everybody could see it, and the veterans remembered what they had seen as well as what they had had to endure. A Northern newspaperman recalled "long dark lines of infantry swaying to and fro, with columns of smoke rising from their muskets, red flashes and white puffs from the batteries—with the sun shining brightly on all this scene of tumult, and beyond it upon the rich dark woods and the clear blue mountains south of the Potomac." A reporter from Charleston told of the immense billows of smoke from the great ranks of Federal cannon (Southern artillerists remembered Sharpsburg forever as "artillery hell") and reflected that the whole of the great Federal Army was in plain sight, assault waves carrying flags up to the Confederate lines, behind them huge columns "so far in the distance that you could recognize them as troops only by the sunlight that gleamed upon their arms." A Wisconsin soldier let it go by calling the whole thing "a great enormous battle—a great tumbling together of all heaven and earth."[7]

They all remembered the terrible guns. One Southerner remarked, with feeling: "Of all mean things the climax is reached when compelled to receive the fury of cannonading with no opportunity to inflict damage," and a Confederate surgeon burst out: "I never was so tired of shelling in my life before. *I hate cannons.*" A Pennsylvanian said the battlefield was "a truly sickening and horrible sight," and added: "No tongue can tell, no mind conceive, no pen portray the horrible sights I witnessed this morning. . . . Of this war I am heartily sick and tired." David H. Strother, the former *Harper's* correspondent who had the odd record of serving first on Pope's staff and then on McClellan's, said that when he crossed the battlefield after the Confederate retreat he found dead bodies hideously swollen and blackened: "Many were so covered with dust, torn, crushed and trampled that they resembled clods of earth and you were obliged to look twice before recognizing them as human beings."[8]

A wounded Mississippian had the last word. After Sumner's men had advanced toward the Dunker church, a Union officer passed over ground covered by Confederate wounded and paused to tell this prostrate Mississippi soldier, "You fought well and stood well." The wounded man looked up at him and said: "Yes, and here we lie."[9]

5: *Taking the Initiative*

General Lee was a hard man to convince. As far as he was concerned the battle had been an incident rather than the end of a campaign. He wanted to resume the offensive just as soon as he could collect his stragglers, and he had a definite plan: recross the Potomac at Williamsport, ten or twelve miles upstream from Sharpsburg, and march northeast to Hagerstown, striking toward Pennsylvania and so compelling McClellan to come up and fight a new battle. Less than three weeks earlier Lee had set out to defeat the Army of the Potomac on Northern soil, and not even the tremendous shock of Antietam had made him abandon this idea. To his uncomplicated but tenacious mind it was the other man's army, not his, that had just brushed the edge of disaster.

When Lee took his army back to Virginia on the night of September 18 the army was extremely weak, but it seemed that it might be possible to strengthen it quickly. Many thousands of men had left the ranks in the last fortnight but they had not gone far and most of them could probably be recalled. On the night of September 17, some five thousand stragglers had been brought back into the ranks, making good half of the loss the battle had caused and enabling Lee to hold his position all of the next day.[1] It was reasonable to suppose that many more would return now that the army was south of the Potomac. As soon as they did the campaign could be resumed.

But it developed that the army had been hurt worse than Lee thought. It was going to take time to recall the missing thousands and bring them back to a fighting pitch. All of the lower Shenandoah Valley was swarming with men who were drifting away toward the South, feigning wounds or sickness, dodging the patrols, compelling Lee at last to admit that "many of them will not stop until they reach their distant homes." An officer stationed at Winchester to halt this exodus reported that it was hopeless to try to do it with less than a full regiment of cavalry, and he predicted that "unless prompt and effective measures are taken thousands will escape up the valley. . . . It is disgusting and heartsickening to witness this army of stragglers." The figures told the story. On September 22 there were hardly more than 36,000 men with the army, not counting the cavalry, and morale was not good. Lee finally had to tell Mr. Davis that although the advance on Hagerstown still looked like the best move, it could not be done: "I would not hesitate to make it even with our diminished numbers, did the army exhibit its former temper and condition; but, as far as I am able to judge, the hazard would be great and a reverse disastrous. I am therefore led to pause."[2]

In plain terms the army had been bled white, and it was not until a week after the battle that Lee realized how serious the situation was. Only then could he accept Antietam as a defeat rather than a check. He had to rebuild his army. The next move would be up to General McClellan if he cared to make one.

Like Lee, McClellan was led to pause. On September 19 he got troops down to the bank of the Potomac, and Fitz John Porter thrust a detachment across the river to see where the Rebels had gone. The next morning this detachment found out that the Rebels had not gone far. A. P. Hill struck it hard, driving it back into Maryland with substantial losses, and thereafter the Army of the Potomac remained in camp and tried to repair battle damages. It had suffered from straggling, too. George Gordon Meade, temporarily commanding Hooker's corps, reported that the corps had fewer than 6000 men present for duty the day after the battle; five days later it numbered more than 14,000. In one division alone, 4000 men returned to the ranks in those five days.[3] Like Lee's army, this army had been hurt.

McClellan had no intention of following up the victory until his army had been fully restored to health; a reasonable idea, in view of his abiding conviction that Lee's army was always larger than his. It did occur to him, however, that he ought to follow up on the political advantages which the victory seemed to offer, and he set out quickly to demand a reorganization of the War Department and a free hand for himself. On September 20, while Lee was trying to find some way to get north of the Potomac and renew the fighting, McClellan wrote to Mrs. McClellan that he had taken his stand: "I have insisted that Stanton shall be removed & that Halleck shall give way to me as Comdr in Chief. I will not serve under him—for he is an incompetent fool—in no way fit for the important place he holds. . . . The only safety for the country & for me is to get rid of lots of them." That evening he sent her another letter along the same line: "I hope that my position will be determined this week. Through certain friends of mine I have taken the stand that Stanton must leave & that Halleck must restore my old place to me. Unless these two conditions are fulfilled I will leave the service. I feel that I have done all that can be asked in twice saving the country. If I continue in its service I have at least the right to demand a guarantee." Meditatively, he went on: "You should see my soldiers *now!* You never saw anything like their enthusiasm. It surpasses anything you ever imagined."[4]

It seemed for a time that some such reorganization would come to pass. The Interior Department clerk and political eavesdropper T. J. Barnett, who had an acute ear for gossip which he was not always able to appraise accurately, wrote to McClellan's friend Barlow on September 19 that things looked bad for the radicals: "McClellan is the acknowledged man. Unless I much mistake me, henceforth he will have a *party* that shall bestride these lilliputians. I think a new and conservative era has commenced; & that the day of little men & demagogues is waning."[5]

To an extent, Barnett was right. One day *was* waning, a long day in the life of the republic, the last of its light going out as the shadows rose out of the valley of Antietam Creek and darkened the heights where men had fought so hard. Morning would bring a new day and not everyone could recognize it immediately. Perhaps the only man who really saw what Antietam meant was Abraham Lincoln, and he could do what neither Lee nor McClellan could do: follow up the opportunity which the battle presented. He had been waiting for a victory, and at last he had one—shaded, incomplete, unexploited, but still a victory. He would give it a meaning which the soldiers could not give it. On September 22 he called his cabinet together to present the final draft of the preliminary Proclamation of Emancipation.

There were no dramatics, because none were needed. Mr. Lincoln even opened the session by reading a chapter from the topical humorist, Artemus Ward, which struck Secretary Stanton as a most unseemly way to behave on so great a day. Then he laid the book aside and took up the proclamation, which he had put into final form the day before, and when he presented it he mused quietly as a man might who, doing a great deed, believed that God's hand had been on his shoulder. As Secretary Welles remembered it, the President said that while he waited for victory over the army of invasion he had made what amounted to a covenant with God: a victory over Lee would mean that God intended the slaves to be free, and the President of the United States would guide himself accordingly. It might seem strange, Mr. Lincoln went on, that he should make such a covenant when his own mind was not really clear about things, but that was how it had been. Now Lee had been beaten, and the meaning was unmistakable: "God had decided this question in favor of the slaves."[6]

As the President spoke, one fear that he had carried ever since Fort Sumter dropped from his shoulders. Montgomery Blair held it up to view for the last time: Would not this action carry the border states over into secession?

Here was the question which always before had brought paralysis. The border states, where slaveowners upheld the Union, had been nursed along with great care. Twice the President had overruled antislavery pronouncements, lest the border be lost because freedom was too great a word; but the border would not listen when he spoke of compensated emancipation, and the hope that a slaveowning society might, under exceptionally favorable conditions, read the signs of the times and adjust itself had finally died. It would never happen, such a society being—because of what it stood upon—too rigid for any adjustment whatever. Answering Mr. Blair, the President simply said that he had thought about the border state problem but that it was too late, and that right now "the difficulty was as great not to act as to act." He had argued with the border state people and it had been in vain, and it seemed to Mr. Lincoln that "slavery had received its death blow from slave-holders—it could not survive the rebellion."[7]

The same thought occurred to Secretary Chase. After the meeting he told John Hay that the behavior of the slave-holders had been "a most wonderful history of the insanity of a class that the world had ever seen." If (Chase went on) the slave states had remained in the Union the peculiar institution might have gone on living for many years; it was protected, and no party, no aroused public feeling in the North, could hope to do much to it. By going to war the slavery people had "madly placed in the very path of destruction" the institution which they insisted must be preserved at any price.[8]

Truly it was too late. Nearly a year earlier the President had told Congress that he hoped to win the war without letting it become "a violent and remorseless revolutionary struggle," but the hope had been vain. Violent enough, in all conscience, the war had been, from Fort Donelson and Shiloh to Gaines's Mill and Antietam, the violence growing greater and deadlier with each battle. As the war grew more violent it grew larger, and as its dimensions were enlarged so also was its meaning; and hereafter it would be revolutionary, waged after the revolutionary manner—without remorse. It was no longer a war to erase a boundary line from a map, but a war fought to erase a word from the books. The Emancipation Proclamation simply ratified a process that had been started long before.

There was a deep continuity at work here. Many years earlier (just about fourscore and seven, as a matter of fact) the people had found it necessary to carry the word "freedom" into a war already begun, and by doing so they had broken an empire and put the world in a ferment. Now they were at it again, and their President was proclaiming freedom "thenceforward and forever" as a rallying cry: and the most vital, disturbing and unforgettable word in the language was being placed at the center of the nation's ideas about the future. Nothing would ever be quite the same after this.

. . . Secretary Seward treated himself to a quiet and mildly rueful chuckle as he reflected on the strange ways of destiny. Years ago he had warned that something like today's business was going to happen because slavery condemned the nation to an irresistible conflict in which a higher law would come into operation, and the words had sounded dangerous and Seward had been denied a presidential nomination as a result. Now he thought about it, and he wrote to his daughter: "Having for twenty years warned the people of the coming of this crisis, and suffered all the punishment they could inflict upon me for my foresight and fidelity, I am not displeased with the position in which I find myself now—of one who has not put forth a violent hand to verify my own predictions." He did hope that the timing of this proclamation was right.[9]

The proclamation was read, commented upon, given a minor correction or so, and at last signed, and on the next day it was made public, to tell all men that the government had changed its policy; and at close range it was hard for many people to see just what had happened and what it meant. David Strother, who called himself a Virginia Yankee and perfectly embodied the border state man who would die for the Union but did not like a fight against slavery, wrote angrily: "The war is going against us heavily. The Revolution is raging at all points while the folly, weakness and criminality of our heads is becoming more decidedly manifest. Abraham Lincoln has neither sense nor principle. . . . The people are strong and willing, but 'there is no king in Israel.' The man of the day has not yet come." In the Army of the Potomac a young Massachusetts officer named Robert Gould Shaw wrote that he could not see what practical good the proclamation could do: "Wherever our army has been there remain no slaves, and the proclamation won't free them where we don't go." One of Barlow's innumerable political tipsters exulted that the proclamation would be "the knell of the Republican party," giving all of the border states to the Confederacy, and Barnett told Barlow that the administration was highly nervous, fearful of what the Army of the Potomac might do, dreading a revolution in the North. The proclamation, he felt, had simply hastened the crisis, and the question now was whether the Democrats would invoke a revolution, striving "to create a chaos in the hope of a more perfect creation."[10]

A great many people worried about what the army might do; and it is worthy of note that in all of the doubt and speculation on this matter "the army" meant, exclusively, the Army of the Potomac. No one ever dreamed or hinted that any other army—Grant's, Buell's, or anybody's—might resist the proclamation, or fall into sulks because of it, or in any other way make it risky for the government to issue and enforce the new pronouncement. It was only this army that raised doubts, and this was in no way accidental; it happened so because only in this army had the high command openly and with passionate devotion aligned itself with the political opposition to the administration.

General Porter, for instance, was writing to Manton Marble of the New York *World* that "the proclamation was resented in the army" and that it had led to expressions of discontent "amounting, I have heard, to insubordination." The men who had to do the fighting, said Porter, "are tired of the war and wish to see it ended honorably by a restoration of the union—not merely a suppression of the rebellion." Such a distinction might be a little too finely drawn for the ordinary soldier to follow, but Porter insisted that the soldier's heroism was offset "by the absurd proclamation of a political coward."[11]

General McClellan was not quite certain what he ought to do; his uncertainty arising primarily from a doubt that this proclamation really applied to him. Three days after the proclamation was published he wrote to his friend, the New York merchant William H. Aspinwall, asking for advice:

"I am very anxious to learn how you and men like you regard the recent proclamation of the Presdt inaugurating servile war, emancipating the slaves & at one stroke of the pen changing our free institutions into a despotism—for such I regard as the natural effect of the last Proclamation suspending the Habeas Corpus throughout the land. I shall probably be in this vicinity for some days, & if you regard the matter as gravely as I do I would be glad to communicate with you." When the two men met the merchant tried to get the general's vision in better focus, and McClellan wrote to Mrs. McClellan that Aspinwall "is decidedly of the opinion that it is my duty to submit to the President's proclamation and quietly continue doing my duty as a soldier." Probably Aspinwall was right, McClellan said; it was at least certain that he was honest in his opinion; and McClellan assured his wife that "I shall surely give his views full consideration."[12]

He would get all the advice he could, first. It was just about now that he invited three generals in for dinner—his old friend Burnside, who had snorted "Treason!" at loose headquarters chatter, one evening by the campfire at Harrison's Landing, and two former Republican politicians, Jacob Cox of Ohio and John Cochrane of New York. As Cox remembered it, McClellan said that he had been urged —by soldiers and politicians of enough stature to give their words weight—to put himself in open opposition to the Emancipation Proclamation. He himself, he said, thought that the war itself would slowly but surely end slavery, but he did not like the abolitionist upsurge behind the proclamation and he considered the document itself premature; also, he had been told that the army was so devoted to him that it would enforce any decision he might make regarding war policy.

Cox and the others quickly told him that people who talked that way to him were his worst enemies, and said that not a corporal's guard would follow him if he actually tried to take the reins into his own hands. McClellan (according to Cox) agreed heartily, and the talk then turned to the question of issuing an order to the Army reminding everybody that their rights as citizens were bound closely to their duties as soldiers. Possibly as a result of this chat, McClellan on October 7 issued General Orders No. 163, drawing attention to the Emancipation Proclamation, remarking that it was the civil authority's responsibility to make policy and the Army's duty to enforce the policy thus made, and suggesting that "the remedy for political errors, if any are committed, is to be found only in the action of the people at the polls." It was altogether a sober, unexceptionable paper, notable only for the fact that it seemed advisable to issue it at all.[13]

Too much loose talk was going around army headquarters, and some of it was heard in the White House. On September 26, Mr. Lincoln sent a stiff note to Major John J. Key, an officer on McClellan's staff, bluntly asking whether Major Key, when a brother officer inquired why Lee's army had not been captured at Sharpsburg, had replied: "That is not the game; the object is that neither army shall get much advantage of the other; that both shall be kept in the field till they are exhausted, when we will make a compromise and save slavery." The President would be happy to have Major Key appear before him at once and demonstrate that he had not used such words.

Major Key came to the White House, along with a Major Levi Turner, to whom the offending words had been spoken. Mr. Lincoln listened to both men, found that Major Key had been correctly quoted, and promptly issued an order dismissing Major Key from the Army; remarking afterward that he did it because "I thought his silly, treasonable expressions were 'staff talk' and I wished to make an example."[14]

The example may have been needed, may not have been needed. Certainly the atmosphere at headquarters had been odd. Too many officers were showing too much contempt for the President and the Secretary of War, and there was altogether too much talk about the need for "a march on Washington." McClellan himself had listened to such talk; he had even suggested such a step, in a letter to his wife, and Major Key had said no more than McClellan had said when he remarked that his defeat in the Seven Days had probably been for the best. There is not much reason to draw a sharp distinction between the attitude of the commanding general and the attitude of his military household. David Strother thought that McClellan had a poor crowd around him. He felt that Fitz John Porter, "with his elegant address and insinuating plausibility . . . and total want of judgment," was the evil genius, and he had bitter words for McClellan's staff: "The people around McClellan . . . were the most ungallant, good-for-nothing set of martinets that I have yet met with. I do not mean that they were inefficient in their special duties, but not a man among them was worth a damn as a military advisor, or had any show of fire or boldness."[15]

The commanding general wanted some resolution of the wearing conflict between desire and duty; wanted, at the least, a clear understanding of what his duty might actually be; and the martinets wanted something which they could not have, so that it was necessary to silence them by cashiering Major Key. And underneath everything, accounting for the loose talk and the desperate groping for advice, was the undeniable fact that a great change had taken place. It was going to be a different sort of war hereafter, and the serviceable Barnett sent Barlow a warning: "Furl your sails." The proclamation, said Barnett, in effect gave the Confederacy one hundred days of grace in which to give up all thought of secession and come back to the Union. Nobody supposed the Confederacy would do anything of the kind, but "from the expiration of the days of grace the character of the war will be changed. It will be one of subjugation determination, if the North can be coerced and coaxed into it. The South is to be destroyed & replaced by new proprietors and ideas." The gist of this, said Barnett, he had from Mr. Lincoln himself.[16]

He may have been tolerably accurate; the qualifying factor being that the President had committed himself to an idea rather than to a specific program. The war would be a revolution from now on, and if revolutionary means were needed to win it they would be used. This, to be sure, had been inherent in the situation from the beginning. The overshadowing fact now was that when he issued his proclamation Mr. Lincoln did in his field exactly what General Lee did in his when he struck the Army of the Potomac at Mechanicsville: he took the initiative, and he would never give it up. All of the Americans who followed this hard road of war would sooner or later have to keep step with him: both those who went with him and those who went against him.

The night after the proclamation was published a crowd came to the White House to serenade the President and to demand a speech.

Never one to say anything of importance on an impromptu basis, Mr. Lincoln did not try to tell them much, and what they heard was no more than a somber warning:

"What I did, I did after a very full deliberation, and under a very heavy and solemn sense of responsibility. I can only trust in God I have made no mistake. I shall make no attempt on this occasion to sustain what I have done or said by any comment. It is now for the country and the world to pass judgment, and, may be, take action upon it."[17]

6: *Nobly Save or Meanly Lose*

Far underneath the war there lay a fear, and the proclamation compelled men to look at it; the fear that the peculiar institution was so dangerous and so unstable that it would explode if it were touched. The declaration that the Federal government would make war to free the slave, and would even turn the freed slave into a soldier to help carry on the fight, seemed to be a threat to take the lid off of the bottomless pit—as if freedom could not be given to millions of bondsmen without bringing terror and the realization of the ultimate peril.

In the days that followed the issuance of the proclamation both houses of the Confederate Congress gave way to bitter oratory as the anger born of this fear found expression. Resolutions to enslave all captured Negro soldiers and to execute their white officers were considered, and discarded. William L. Yancey had urged earlier that Congress resolve that Washington now was making war on the Southern people as well as upon their government, and that individual citizens would thus be justified in shooting Yankee soldiers who tampered with their property. J. B. Jones, the Rebel war clerk who kept such a useful diary, noted at the end of September that "some of the gravest of our Senators favor the raising of the *black flag*, asking and giving no quarter thereafter," and from as sober a soldier as General Beauregard came the same demand.

"Has the bill for execution of abolition prisoners after 1st of January next passed?" he asked, in a letter to Porcher Miles. "Do it, and England will be stirred into action. It is high time to proclaim the black flag for that period. Let the execution be with the garrote."[1]

How England would have responded to a wholesale strangling of prisoners of war was never put to the test. The frothy talk of alarmed super-patriots meant in the end no more than the frothy talk of the martinets at McClellan's headquarters. Yet there were responsible Englishmen who shuddered at the notion that the United States government would fight to end slavery. On October 7 the London *Times* spoke as if the unhappy slave were a subhuman monster who could be liberated only at the price of unspeakable outrages:

"Mr. Lincoln will, on the 1st of next January, do his best to excite a servile war in the states which he cannot occupy with his armies. . . . He will appeal to the black blood of the Africans. He will whisper of the pleasures of spoil and of the gratification of yet fiercer instincts; and when blood begins to flow and when shrieks come piercing through the darkness, Mr. Lincoln will wait amid the rising flames, till all is consummated, and then he will rub his hands and think that revenge is sweet. . . . Sudden and forcible emancipation resulting from the 'efforts the Negroes may make for their actual freedom' can only be effected by massacre and utter destruction."[2]

In 1862 a man did not have to be wholly unhinged to suppose that massacre and utter destruction would accompany emancipation. The most dreadful thing about slavery was the fact that it prepared neither the owners nor the owned for the slightest change in their relationship. It provoked fear on one side, and it was logical to imagine that it provoked desperate hatred on the other; it lived by the invocation of unlimited force, and no one could be blamed for thinking that it would die in the same way. The man who wrote the screed for the London *Times* was doing no more than put quivering, orgiastic prose around a thought that tormented many lesser mortals, in America and in England as well.

Yet the *Times* spoke for nothing but that tortured, dying

thought. The Emancipation Proclamation might flutter the pulses of upper-class Britons who did not in any case expect anything good to come out of America, but once the news of it crossed the Atlantic it began to exert a powerful effect on the attitude of the British government. Mr. Lincoln's opponents found themselves on the defensive: a man who sided with the Confederacy now must at least appear to be siding with slavery. The textile workers of Lancashire who were suffering because the United States fleet kept cotton from the mills would not now demand that their government sweep away that fleet and let the cotton in; the blockade that was ruining the cotton trade was also destroying human servitude, and this meant something even to men thrown on the parish: perhaps *especially* to them. When the war was no more than a bloody struggle between factions there might well be intervention for the sake of the payrolls in the Midlands. Now it was different. If the American Union lived slavery would die, and if it died slavery would live, and although to say this involved a staggering oversimplification the basic issue was clear. Only a ruthless and determined British government could move in now to help the Southern Confederacy.

The British government was neither ruthless nor determined. It was simply old, Prime Minister and Foreign Secretary being both beyond their time. Furthermore—and this was as weighty as the proclamation itself—Lee after all had lost at Antietam, and the South right now did not look like a winner. As Minister Adams had pointed out a year earlier: "Great Britain always looks to her own interest as a paramount law of her action in foreign affairs."[3] It was not in the British interest to bail out a losing cause. When Lee found that he could not go back across the Potomac and force his reluctant antagonist to fight again, the moment for British intervention passed.

There was even more to it than Antietam. The great Confederate counteroffensive had also failed in the west.

When Don Carlos Buell took his army out of central Tennessee and went north toward the Ohio, some sort of opportunity had been briefly offered to Braxton Bragg and Bragg had never quite been able to accept it. His army was just a little too small, Kirby Smith was just a little too far away and too independent, the dire things that would happen if he fought and lost were just a little too easy to see —and, after all, the kind of resolution that drives a man to risk all in order to win all is an uncommon trait; the Confederacy had one army commander who possessed it, and perhaps one was its share. Anyway, the opportunity faded and disappeared. Bragg maneuvered after the time for maneuver had passed. He went to Frankfort and helped to install a true Confederate as governor of Kentucky, and by this time it was too late to win the battle which would have validated the installation. Buell at last was coming to meet him, and on October 8 the two armies collided in a savage, inconclusive engagement near the town of Perryville. More than seven thousand men were casualties, nobody won anything of consequence—so ill-directed was the encounter that the two armies actually fought for hardly more than access to a supply of drinking water, Kentucky's streams being nearly dry at the time—and after it was over Bragg took thought of the length of the odds that were against him. His army had never quite been able to join hands with the army of Kirby Smith, who was also reflecting on the odds; the people of Kentucky had not risen to join him, and the hope that they would do so had been the only thing that really justified the northward march in the first place—and at last Bragg turned about and marched back to Tennessee, Kirby Smith did likewise, and the western invasion came to a dismal end.

Like the eastern invasion, it had ended in a drawn battle which was nevertheless—as a milestone, if as nothing more—profoundly significant. The Southern tide never again rose as high as it was when it touched Antietam and Perryville; and as it ebbed, after those battles, there came a subtle change in Southern hopes. The Confederacy might yet win, by a sudden dazzling stroke, by Northern ineptitude and war-weariness, or simply by dogged refusal to admit defeat, but the old jaunty optimism was gone. President Davis, who was as stout-hearted as any man in the South, reflected the change in a dispatch he sent to Major General T. H. Holmes, who commanded in the trans-Mississippi region:

"The expectation that the Kentuckians would rise en masse with the coming of a force which would enable them to do so, alone justified an advance into that state while the enemy in force remained in Tennessee. That expectation has been sadly disappointed, and the future is to be viewed in the light of our late experiences." This light showed, among other things, that the Confederacy could not reinforce certain vital points which badly needed to be strengthened, and Mr. Davis explained this in a letter to Governor J. G. Shorter of Alabama, who feared that the Federals were menacing Mobile:

"I have felt long and deeply the hazard of its condition and an anxious desire to secure it, but have vainly looked for an adequate force which could be spared from other localities. The enemy greatly outnumber us and have many advantages in moving their forces, so that we must often be compelled to hold positions and fight battles with the chances against us. Our only alternatives are to abandon important points or to use our limited resources as effectively as the circumstances will permit."

At about the same time he notified harassed Governor John Milton of Florida that even though the Yankees seemed likely to overrun that isolated state, "we have no reinforcements that could be spared without injustice to other sections equally important and equally threatened."[4]

Mr. Davis was being forced once more to look at the grim reality which had been so distressingly visible in the spring—the fact that the Confederacy could not resist all of the pressures which the Federal government was able to apply whenever it made unrelenting use of them. This was a reality which Mr. Lincoln had tried in vain to draw to the attention of his generals. Resenting political interference in matters of strategy, they had paid little notice, and as a result Lee and Bragg had carried the war almost to the doorsteps of the North, and Southern prospects had looked much better than they actually were. But now, after two drawn battles and one proclamation, the reality was regaining its visibility. Mr. Davis could see it clearly, and it was time for the Federal generals to see it too.

Among these was General Buell. Far back in January, Mr. Lincoln had written to him, trying earnestly to make the point: ". . . we have the *greater* numbers, and the enemy has the *greater* facility of concentrating forces upon points of collision . . . we must fail unless we can find some way of making *our* advantage an over-match for his . . . by menacing him with superior forces at *different* points at the *same* time."[5] This had done no good. The Federals had had vastly superior forces in Tennessee all spring and summer but they had not menaced anything very much, either singly or in combination, and at last General Bragg with a smaller army had drawn Buell all the way to northern Kentucky, fighting there a battle in which less than half of Buell's army got into action, and marching back to Tennessee afterward with a wagon train full of supplies. Buell made no more than a formal pursuit. He was glad that Bragg was leaving, but he felt that before he could go after him he must rest, reorganize and re-equip his own army, and repeated telegrams from Halleck could not get any speed out of him. One of Buell's soldiers, irritated by the failure to pursue the retreating Confederates, put into words the thought that was unquestionably bothering the President: "The way the hed generals are a doing now I am afraid this war will never end."[6]

Presidential patience ran out at last, and, on October 30, Buell was sent into retirement, command of his Army of the Cumberland going to Major General William S. Rosecrans–red-faced, excitable, "Old Rosey" to his admiring soldiers; an officer who had served with McClellan in western Virginia early in the war and who then and later had shown a considerable talent for two-handed fighting.

As far as Washington could see, Rosecrans had in fact done very well. Commanding troops under Grant in northern Mississippi, he had this fall repulsed General Price in a sharp fight at the town of Iuka, when Price apparently meditated taking his army up to Kentucky to help Bragg. Then Rosecrans had gone to Corinth, that undistinguished railroad junction town which Beauregard had evacuated in Halleck's favor in the spring, and there had fought a tremendous fight against Earl Van Dorn, a battle involving small armies and huge casualty lists; Van Dorn attacked furiously and was driven off in retreat, and what amounted to a third Confederate offensive, to go with those of Lee and Bragg, had failed. If the administration wanted a hard fighter for the Army of the Cumberland it could not help thinking about Rosecrans. His appointment represented something of a rebuff for George Thomas, to whom the command had been offered in September. At the time Thomas had declined the offer, on the ground that a change just then would be fair neither to Buell nor to him, but he had not intended to decline for keeps, and when Rosecrans got the appointment Thomas filed a dignified protest. He withdrew it when Halleck pointed out that Rosecrans ranked him, and if he felt any soreness he kept it to himself, and he gave Rosecrans loyal service as second-in-command; but the fact remained that he had been passed over. Washington seems to have forgotten that he was the one western general who had really wanted to carry out Mr. Lincoln's plan for an invasion of eastern Tennessee. Finding a good fighting man, the government had failed to notice a better one.[7]

The important fact, however, was that the government was replacing a cautious man with an aggressive one. Rosecrans was marching back into Tennessee, and off to the southwest Grant was getting ready to march overland to Vicksburg, and Major General John A. McClernand, the Illinois Democrat, had confidential orders that contemplated the raising of a new army for an amphibious drive down the Mississippi. In the west the Federal power was about to begin tightening the screws once more. If the same thing could be done in the east the Federal pressure might become irresistible.

This led the administration to think anew about General McClellan.

Ten days after Antietam, McClellan told Halleck that his army was not in condition to make a campaign or fight a battle unless Lee made a glaring mistake (which was most unlikely) or "pressing military exigencies render it necessary." It seemed to him that he must reorganize, get much new equipment, watch the Confederates lest they come back north of the Potomac, and get the army into top condition. The fall rains would probably raise the level of the Potomac, making the fords unusable and ending the danger that Lee would make a new invasion. Once that happened, "I propose concentrating the army somewhere near Harpers Ferry and then acting according to circumstances, viz, moving on Winchester, if from the position and attitude of the enemy we are likely to gain a great advantage by doing so, or else devoting a reasonable time to the organization of the army and instruction of the new troops, preparatory to an advance on whatever line may be determined."[8]

This was not good enough. The Confederacy after all was on the defensive again, and the Federals needed men who would take full advantage of that fact; to call for a long refit and to say that the offensive might some day be resumed according to circumstances was to miss the point entirely. The Army of the Potomac had had a rough time, it needed everything from shoes to horses, and new recruits could hardly be fitted overnight into the veteran divisions; but Lee's army was in much worse shape. It was far smaller, its equipment was deplorable, and in relation to its strength it had been much more badly bruised by the recent battle; it needed a breathing spell far more than the Army of the Potomac did, and it stood to gain more by delay. Its stragglers were returning—by October 10 the present-for-duty strength stood at more than 64,000, and others were coming in daily[9]—and it was rapidly getting back into fighting trim. To give this army a month or two for recuperation was dangerous.

About a fortnight after the battle Mr. Lincoln paid McClellan a visit, trying to get the general to see that it was time for action, and the two men seem to have had trouble understanding one another. The general wrote that he urged the President to follow "a conservative course"—which could only mean that he opposed the antislavery war which the President had just announced—and he said that he understood the President to agree with him. He went on confidently: "He told me that he was entirely satisfied with me and with all that I had done; that he would stand by me against all comers; that he wished me to continue my preparations for a new campaign, not to stir an inch until fully ready, and when ready to do what I thought best."

The President remembered it differently. He told John Hay that he "went up to the field to try to get him to move, and came back thinking he would move at once." For confirmation, there is a wire Halleck sent McClellan on October 6: "The President directs that you cross the Potomac and give battle to the enemy or drive him south. Your army must move now while the roads are good." For

Hay, Lincoln summed up what came next: "I peremptorily ordered him to advance. It was nineteen days before he put a man over the river. It was nine days longer before he got his army across, and then he stopped again, playing on little pretexts of wanting this and that. I began to fear he was playing false—that he did not want to hurt the enemy."[10]

Obviously, President Lincoln and General McClellan were not talking the same language. The month of October brought extended bickering between army headquarters and the War Department; McClellan was calling for new equipment and the War Department was calling for action, and neither was satisfied with what was being delivered. On October 9 the Confederate cavalryman Jeb Stuart made this strained relationship worse by setting out on a spectacular raid, in which he got all the way up to Chambersburg, Pennsylvania, destroyed Yankee supply depots and shops, seized a number of good Pennsylvania horses, and got back safely without a man killed and with only a few slightly wounded; once again he had ridden entirely around McClellan's army. It was sheer bad luck that McClellan shortly after this filed a request for more horses, saying that his cavalry mounts were "absolutely broken down from fatigue and want of flesh"; which drew from Mr. Lincoln a dispatch asking, "Will you pardon me for asking what the horses of your army have done since the battle of Antietam that fatigues anything?"[11]

In private, McClellan fumed, and he wrote to Mrs. McClellan: "If you could know the mean character of the despatches I receive you would boil over with anger. When it is possible, misunderstand, and when it is not possible; whenever there is a chance of a wretched innuendo, then it comes. But the good of the country requires me to submit to all this from men whom I know to be greatly my inferior socially, intellectually and morally! There never was a truer epithet applied to a certain individual than that of the 'Gorilla.'"[12]

Halleck was fuming, too. At the end of October he expressed himself in a letter to Governor H. R. Gamble of Missouri: "I am sick, tired and disgusted with the condition of military affairs here in the east and wish myself back in the western army. With all my efforts I can get nothing done. There is an immobility here that exceeds all that any man can conceive of. It requires the lever of Archimedes to move this inert mass. I have tried my best, but without success."[13]

This sort of thing could not go on. No matter where the rights and the wrongs lay, the situation had become impossible; McClellan and the administration could no longer work together, and at last the boom came down. Late in October McClellan began to cross the Potomac, and during the first week of November he marched his army down into Virginia east of the Blue Ridge, heading for a general concentration in the neighborhood of Warrenton. Lee took Longstreet and Longstreet's corps to Culpeper to face him and left Jackson temporarily in the Shenandoah Valley, on the off chance that the old game could be played once more, and, on November 5, Mr. Lincoln concluded that enough was enough. According to one interpretation, he had made up his mind to remove McClellan if the general allowed Lee to get between the Army of the Potomac and Richmond; according to another he had just been waiting for the fall elections to be over; and the point can be argued at anybody's leisure. What is certain is that the War Department, "by direction of the President," issued orders relieving McClellan of his command and turning the army over to Major General Ambrose E. Burnside.

The War Department handled this most carefully, because to remove McClellan was to wrench out of the Army of the Potomac something that went to the very heart, and nobody was sure just what the response was going to be. Secretary Stanton, having heard the loose talk about marching on Washington, suspected that McClellan might not let himself be removed, and he wanted the orders delivered personally by Brigadier General C. P. Buckingham, a staff man assigned to the Secretary's office. He told Buckingham to go to army headquarters at Rectortown, not far from Warrenton, and to see Burnside first. If Burnside flatly refused to take the job Buckingham was to come back to Washington without serving the papers on McClellan; only after Burnside had agreed to serve was McClellan to be notified that he was relieved. The Secretary wanted to have someone legally in command when the removal became effective.

It turned out that Mr. Stanton worried needlessly. General Buckingham had no trouble. He got to headquarters in a snowstorm, late on the night of November 7; Burnside agreed to take the command—reluctantly, for he had a justifiably modest opinion of his own capacity—and McClellan accepted the removal like a good soldier. Stoutly, McClellan wrote to Mrs. McClellan: "As I read the order in the presence of Gen. Buckingham I am sure that not the slightest expression of feeling was visible on my face, which he watched closely. They shall not have that triumph."[14] At Burnside's request, McClellan stayed for a couple of days, to go over headquarters papers with him and explain the plans on which the army had been moving; then he went around the camps to say goodbye to the soldiers.

The soldiers gave him an almost hysterical farewell, cheering themselves hoarse, and doing a power of cursing as well. McClellan said that "many were in favor of my refusing to obey the order and of marching upon Washington to take possession of the government," and European officers who were present muttered that Americans were simply incomprehensible—why did not this devoted army go to the capital and compel the President to reinstate its favorite general? But there never had been much danger that this might really happen, regardless of the loose words that had been uttered; it is extremely hard to imagine McClellan actually leading an armed uprising, even though the idea had haunted him, and it is quite impossible to imagine the Army of the Potomac taking part in one.[15] The goodbyes were finished at last, the echoes of the shouting died away on the wintry plain, and McClellan went off to his home and the army saw him no more. His active part in the war was over.

His departure marked not so much a change in commanders as another change in the war itself. So far the war had been chaotic, formless, a vast tumult which might conceivably be won, lost, or adjusted before it got altogether beyond control. It had been what McClellan always supposed it to be, a limited war for a limited end. Now it was going to be unlimited, and the people who fought it would have to look far into the future for a guiding light because they were bidding goodbye to the past.

It would take a while for them to see this. The fall elections in the North had gone against the administration. The Democrats carried New York, Pennsylvania, Indiana, Ohio, and Illinois—states that had voted Republican in 1860—and although the administration retained its control of both houses of Congress its majorities were sharply reduced. Whether this was the normal off-year reaction against the party in power or the expression of some deep dissatisfaction with the way the war was being fought, it was highly discouraging; it was quite possible to argue that it reflected widespread opposition in the North to the Emancipation Proclamation. Colonel James A. Mulligan, the stout fighter who had unsuccessfully defended the Missouri town of Lexington against Price's army a year earlier, wandered about Washington in a mood of unrelieved dejection.

"This town is filled with littleness," he wrote. "There is not a man in the nation destined to endurance. This great Republic, late the wonder and the envy of the nations, is crumbling into blood-stained fragments because there is no head and hand to guide and light it through the peril. . . . There's no human granite nowadays. It's all clay."[16]

All clay: out of which the spirit might rise, if evoked. The only certainty was that the incalculable was going to happen. To make the slave free was to go on into the unknown; all that could be said was that there was no other place to go. History, as Mr. Lincoln remarked in his message to Congress, was inescapable, and whether they liked it or not people were caught up in something greater than themselves. America was going into the future rather than back into the past, and there was no signpost in anything that had happened earlier. There was nothing but tomorrow to count on; tomorrow, and what people of today really meant.

In his annual message Mr. Lincoln tried to explain it:

"We—even *we here*—hold the power, and bear the responsibility. In *giving* freedom to the *slave*, we *assure* freedom to the *free*—

honorable alike in what we give, and what we preserve. We shall nobly save, or meanly lose, the last best, hope of the earth."[17]

So the armies began to march. In Mississippi, Grant was going south toward Vicksburg, and, at Nashville, Rosecrans would presently set out for an appointment on the banks of Stone's River. And in Virginia, General Burnside was taking the Army of the Potomac down to Fredericksburg.

NOTES

☆ ☆ ☆ ☆ ☆

CHAPTER ONE: *The Leaders and the Led*

1. Tornado Weather

1. *Congressional Globe*, 1st Session, 37th Congress, 1861; 222–23. John J. Crittenden as Senator from Kentucky worked fruitlessly during the first three months of 1861 to bring about a war-averting compromise. His term in the Senate expiring, he immediately won election to the House and sponsored there the resolution which defined Federal war aims.
2. Albert Gallatin Riddle, *Recollections of War Times*, 42.
3. Diary of Charles Francis Adams, quoted in *Charles Francis Adams*, by Charles Francis Adams, Jr., 176, 178. This book, an item in the "American Statesmen" series edited by John T. Morse, Jr., is cited hereafter simply as Adams. See also Henry Adams, *The Education of Henry Adams: an Autobiography*, 104.
4. Letter of Henry Adams in *A Cycle of Adams Letters, 1861–1865*, edited by Worthington Chauncey Ford; Vol. I, 16.
5. For the text of Seward's letters, showing the changes made by President Lincoln, see Roy Basler, *The Collected Works of Abraham Lincoln*, Vol. IV, 376–80. This compilation is cited hereafter as Basler.
6. Adams, 145–46.
7. Ibid., 175, 178, 197–98; *A Cycle of Adams Letters*, Vol. I, 19; John G. Nicolay and John Hay, *Abraham Lincoln: A History*, Vol. IV, 276–77. (Cited hereafter as Nicolay & Hay.)
8. *A Cycle of Adams Letters*, Vol. I, 14, 39.
9. Basler, Vol. IV, 380.
10. Frederick W. Seward, *Seward at Washington*, Vol. II, 575.
11. John B. Gordon, *Reminiscences of the Civil War*, 7–16.
12. Charleston *Mercury*, Aug. 29, 1861; *Official Records of the War of the Rebellion* (cited hereafter as O.R.) Series Four, Vol. I, 505–6; Richmond *Examiner*, Sept. 24, 1861.
13. O.R., Series Three, Vol. I, 167–70.

2. A Mean-Fowt Fight

1. Lyon's activities in the spring and early summer are detailed in *The Coming Fury*, 373–87. For Blair's comments, see the *Report of the Joint Committee on the Conduct of the War, 1863*, Part III, 160–61. (This extensive work is cited hereafter as C.C.W.)
2. Frémont's testimony, C.C.W., 1863, Part III, 33–34. See also his article, *In command in Missouri*, in *Battles and Leaders of the Civil War* (cited hereafter as B. & L.), Vol. I, 279 ff.

3. For Lyon's strength and his appeals for help, see O.R., Vol. III, 394–97. (Series I, unless stated.) There is a good analysis in Wiley Britton, *Civil War on the Border*, Vol. I, 72–73, 75, 77.
4. Frémont to Montgomery Blair, Aug. 9, 1861, in the *Official Records of the Union and Confederate Navies* (cited hereafter as N.O.R.) Vol. XXII, 297. On July 30 Frémont wrote to Lincoln: "I have found this command in disorder, nearly every county in an insurrectionary condition, and the enemy advancing in force by different points of the Southern frontier. . . . I am sorely pressed for want of arms. . . . Our troops have not been paid, and some regiments are in a state of mutiny, and the men whose term of service is expired generally refuse to enlist." (Letter in the Robert Todd Lincoln papers, Library of Congress.)
5. C.C.W., 1863, Part III, 35–36; Frémont Memoirs, 238–39, typescript, by Jessie Benton Frémont, in the John C. Frémont papers, Bancroft Library, University of California. For Confederate strengths and intentions at this time, see the report of Gen. Leonidas Polk to Secretary of War L. P. Walker, O.R., Vol. III, 612–13.
6. Lyon to Frémont, Aug. 9, 1861, O.R., Vol. III, 57.
7. Holcombe and Adams, *An Account of the Battle of Wilson's Creek, or Oak Hills*, 19, 21–22. A description of Lyon's council of war, appraising the difficulties and outlining the arguments that led to the decision to attack, is contained in a report written by Brig. Gen. Thomas W. Sweeney, in the Sweeney Papers at the Huntington Library. See also the report of Maj. Gen. John M. Schofield, O.R., Vol. III, 59. In his book, *Forty-six Years in the Army*, 39, Gen. Schofield wrote that Lyon was greatly depressed by his general situation, by the non-arrival of reinforcements and supplies and by "an evidently strong conviction that these failures were due to a plan to sacrifice him to the ambition of another."
8. E. F. Ware, *The Lyon Campaign in Missouri, Being a History of the First Iowa Infantry*, 339–40, gives an interesting picture of Lyon: "Lyon was a small man, lean, active and sleepless. He was not an old man, although he had wrinkles on the top of his nose. He had a look of incredulity; he did not believe things. . . . I never liked him, nor did any of us as far as I could see, but we did believe that he was a brave and educated officer. He struck us also as a man devoted to duty, who thought duty, dreamed duty and had nothing but duty on his mind."
9. The estimate of numbers is McCulloch's, O.R., Vol. III, 622–23.
10. A most engaging description of Price's army is Thomas L. Snead's *The First Year of the War in Missouri*, B. & L., Vol. I, 269–71. The description of Price is from John Crittenden, *Civil War Letters to His Wife*, Vol. I, 114, in the Eugene C. Barker Texas History Center, University of Texas; original in the possession of Miss Frances Harvey of Arlington, Texas.

11. O.R., Vol. III, 563–64.
12. Thomas L. Snead, *The Fight for Missouri,* 255–57. Snead was present when Price talked to McCulloch, and although his account of the conversation was written after the war, from memory, it probably conveys the substance of what was said.
13. Reminiscences of N. B. Pearce, mss. in the files of the Arkansas History Commission; McCulloch's report, O.R., Vol. III, 104.
14. Ware, *The Lyon Campaign in Missouri,* 310–11; L. E. Meador, pamphlet, *History of the Battle of Wilson Creek;* O.R., Vol. III, 98; Diary of John T. Buegel, 3rd Missouri Volunteers, in the J. N. Heiskell Collection, Little Rock.
15. Sigel's report, O.R., Vol. III, 86–88; Schofield's account of the repulse, 94–95. After the war Sigel wrote that he probably escaped capture on his flight because he wore a blanket over his uniform and had a yellow slouch hat on his head; the Confederates, he believed, mistook him for a Texas Ranger. (Letter of Aug. 10, 1895, to Walter L. Howard, in the Franz Sigel Papers, Western Reserve Historical Society, Cleveland.) In his article *The Flanking Column at Wilson's Creek* (B. & L., Vol. I, 306) Sigel vigorously denied that he became separated from his men after his flanking movement gave way.
16. B. & L., Vol. I, 296, footnote; Snead, *The Fight for Missouri,* 275–76, 285–86; O.R., Vol. III, 57–64; Joseph A. Mudd, "What I Saw at Wilson's Creek," in the *Missouri Historical Review,* January 1913; Ware, op. cit., 323; Schofield, *Forty-six Years in the Army,* 45.
17. Oddly enough, each side claimed that its opponents had been routed. Schofield wrote, "Finally the enemy gave way and fled from the field." Sturgis said that his men held their ground to the last and then "Withdrew at their leisure to return to their provisions and their water." Price asserted that "the enemy retreated in great confusion" and McCulloch said the Federals were last seen, at noon, "fast retreating among the hills in the distance." (O.R., Vol. III, 57–64, 64–71, 98–102, 104–7.) Apparently the battle simply sputtered out, but however it ended it is impossible to interpret it as anything but a Confederate victory.
18. The figures for this battle, as for all others in the Civil War, vary considerably depending on the source used. The writer has followed Snead, *The Fight for Missouri,* 310, 312. Somewhat different totals are in O.R., Vol. III, 72, 101, 106. See also T. L. Livermore, *Numbers and Losses in the Civil War,* 76.
19. William Watson, *Life in the Confederate Army,* 222–23.

3. The Hidden Intentions

1. Letter of Price to Jefferson Davis, Nov. 10, 1861, O.R., Vol. III, 734–36.
2. There are many descriptions of the atmosphere at Frémont's headquarters. See, for instance, Galusha Anderson, *A Border City in the Civil War,* 206–7; John Raymond Howard, *Remembrance of Things Past,* 144; Ida M. Tarbell,

The Life of Abraham Lincoln, Vol. III, 63–64, quoting from accounts by Col. George E. Leighton and General B. G. Farrar; Lieut. Col. Camille Ferri Pisani, *Prince Napoleon in America*, 238–39. (This latter book gives an engrossing picture of Frémont at the height of his power; it is cited hereafter as Ferri Pisani.)

3. Diary of John Hay, quoted in Nicolay & Hay, Vol. IV, 414.
4. Cf. Montgomery Blair's testimony, C.C.W., 1863, Part III, 154–55.
5. William T. Sherman, *Memoirs*, Vol. I, 195–97; testimony of Frank Blair, C.C.W., 1863, Part III, 182–83, naming the men who, in Blair's not unprejudiced opinion, were "in the worst possible repute in California" and denouncing McKinstry as "the worst man that Frémont had about him."
6. Blair was vocal about the contracts. His testimony is in C.C.W., 1863, Part III, 178–80. There is a vast amount of material on procurement practices at St. Louis, indicating pretty clearly the existence of extensive irregularities, in the report of the commission set up by Congress to investigate Frémont's regime. See "War Claims at St. Louis," No. 94 in Executive Documents of the House of Representatives, Second Session, 37th Congress, 1861–62. The commissioners—David Davis, Joseph Holt, and Hugh Campbell—examined 1200 witnesses and concluded that Frémont "virtually ignored the existence of the quartermaster's and the commissary's departments, and of the Ordnance Bureau, and necessarily that of the government at Washington." It added that "the most stupendous contracts, involving an almost unprecedented waste of the public money, were given out by him in person to favorites, over the heads of the competent and honest officers appointed by law." (Op. cit., 34.)
7. Letter of Frank Blair to "Dear Judge," dated Sept. 7, 1861, in the Blair Family Papers, Library of Congress.
8. For a good discussion of the disagreement between Price and McCulloch, and the consequences it entailed, see Snead, *The Fight for Missouri*, 293–97. Snead, who was present as an officer on Price's staff, asserted that the Confederates could easily have captured the Federal army, and estimated that at least 10,000 Missourians could have been armed for Confederate service with the military equipment that could have been taken.
9. Frémont Memoirs, typescript, in the Bancroft Library; Jessie Benton Frémont, *The Story of the Guard*, 84–85.
10. Frémont Memoirs, 240–41. The best account of Grant's trials and lapses in the pre-war years is Lloyd Lewis's in *Captain Sam Grant*.
11. Frémont, *In Command in Missouri*, B. & L., Vol. I, 286.
12. Basler, Vol. IV, 470–71; Comte de Paris, *History of the Civil War in America*, Vol. I, 338; statement of George W. Fishback, managing editor and part owner of the Missouri *Democrat*, in the Ida M. Tarbell Papers, Allegheny College. (From Allan Nevins's notes.)

13. Nicolay & Hay, Vol. IV, 411–12; Diary of Edward Bates, 217; Letter from "S. S." to "Dear Judge," dated Sept. 3, 1861, in the Blair Family Papers, Library of Congress.
14. Ferri Pisani, 238–46.
15. The text of Frémont's proclamation is in O.R., Vol. III, 466–67. The description of his meeting with Mrs. Frémont and Davis is Jessie Frémont's, in a portion of the Frémont Memoirs headed "The First & Second Emancipation Proclamations," in the Bancroft Library.

4. *End of Neutrality*

1. Basler, Vol. IV, 506–7. For the Act of Congress (a copy of which Lincoln thoughtfully enclosed for Frémont's guidance) see the *Congressional Globe*, First Session, 37th Congress, 1861, Appendix, 42.
2. Letter of Frémont to Lincoln dated Sept. 8, 1861, O.R., Vol. III, 477–78.
3. Mss. diary of John Hay, quoted in Nicolay & Hay, Vol. IV, 414. It should be noted that in the Frémont Papers at the Bancroft Library there is a document in Mrs. Frémont's handwriting denying that she ever made any such remark.
4. Jessie Frémont wrote three accounts of her interview. Differing in minor details but making essentially the same statement of material facts, they are with the Frémont Papers in the Bancroft Library. Allan Nevins, in his extremely thorough study, *Frémont, Pathmarker of the West*, (503) holds that "beyond question" Frémont got out his proclamation "simply as a war measure in Missouri, and with little if any thought of its effect outside that state." It takes a brash man to disagree with one of Nevins's considered findings on Frémont, but it is extremely hard to believe that the general did not intend the proclamation to be to at least some extent a political maneuver.
5. Basler, Vol. IV, 531–32.
6. *American Annual Cyclopaedia, 1861*, 396–97.
7. There are interesting references to Buckner in McClellan's *Own Story*, 48–49, and in a dispatch he sent to the War Department from Cincinnati on June 11 (O.R., Vol. II, 674). General Robert Anderson said that Buckner, who had made many "strong attachments" in the officer corps of the pre-war army, did much to win "many young men of the best families and highest influence" in Kentucky to the Confederate cause. (Testimony of Robert Anderson before an army retirement board, in the Papers of the Massachusetts Commandery, Military Order of the Loyal Legion; in the Houghton Library, Harvard University.) For Nelson, see Col. R. M. Kelly, *Holding Kentucky for the Union*, B. & L., Vol. I, 375.
8. Basler, Vol. IV, 497; O.R., Vol. IV, 378, 396–97.
9. O.R., Vol. IV, 179–81. Frémont's orders to Grant, dated Aug. 28, are explicit: "It is intended in connection with all these movements" (i.e., operations in southeastern Missouri) "to occupy Columbus as soon as possible." (O.R., Vol. III, 141–42.) In the

Frémont mss. at the Bancroft Library, Jessie Frémont remarks that by the end of August Frémont felt that it was time either to take Kentucky "or relinquish it into the hands of the rebels," and mentions "the plans with which General Grant had been made acquainted at his interview with General Frémont on the 28th of August." Strangely enough, Grant makes no mention of this in his *Memoirs.*

10. O.R., Vol. IV, 180–81, 189.
11. O.R., Vol. III, 149–50; Vol. IV, 196–97; Grant's *Memoirs*, Vol. I, 264–66.
12. *American Annual Cyclopaedia, 1861*, 399; Moore's *Rebellion Record*, Vol. III, Document No. 45, 129.
13. Nicolay & Hay, Vol. V, 49–50.
14. Basler, Vol. IV, 534, 549; O.R., Series Two, Vol. II, 805–6, 808–9, 812, giving entries from the State Department Record Book, "Arrests for Disloyalty."
15. Buckner to Adjutant General Samuel Cooper, Sept. 13, 1861, O.R., Vol. IV, 189–90.
16. Polk to Davis, Sept. 14, 1861, ibid., 191.
17. William Preston Johnston, *The Life of Albert Sidney Johnston*, 290–91, 306; William M. Polk, *Leonidas Polk, Bishop and General*, Vol. II, 1–3.
18. Johnston to Davis, Sept. 16, 1861, O.R., Vol. IV, 193. As late as mid-November, Johnston's returns show that there were 13,142 present for duty at Columbus and 12,500 at Bowling Green. An earlier return shows 3549 present for duty at Cumberland Gap. On Nov. 10, the Federal returns for the Department of the Cumberland show an "aggregate present and absent" of 49,586, of which more than 23,000 were listed as present for duty. (O.R., Vol. IV, 349, 425, 554, 557.) For details on Johnston's problems and expectations, see William Preston Johnston, op. cit., 316, 333.

5. *Mark of Desolation*

1. The Virginia convention adopted the ordinance of secession on April 17. What is now West Virginia had 46 members in the convention; 9 voted for the ordinance, 7 were absent, one was excused and 29 voted against it. A Unionist meeting at Clarksburg on April 22 summoned a general convention to meet at Wheeling on May 13. This convention was followed by a second, which performed the acts referred to in the text; and by Aug. 20 arrangements were made for a popular vote on the formation of a new state. At a popular election on Oct. 24, the new state was approved, 18,408 to 781. For a résumé of the whole operation, see *West Virginia, a Guide to the Mountain State*, 48–49.
2. Maj. Gen. Jacob Cox, *Reminiscences of the Civil War*, Vol. I, 144–45: "It was easy, sitting at one's office table, to sweep the hand over a few inches of chart, showing next to nothing of the topography, and to say, 'We will march from here to here'; but when the march was undertaken, the natural obstacles began to assert themselves, and one general after another had to find apologies

for failing to accomplish that which ought never to have been undertaken." (This work is cited hereafter as Cox's *Reminiscences.*)

3. Jefferson Davis, *Rise and Fall of the Confederate Government*, Vol. I, 434.
4. Statement by General Rosecrans, C.C.W., 1865, Vol. III, 7–8. The best detailed account of the 1861 western Virginia campaign, that of Douglas Southall Freeman in *R. E. Lee*, Vol. I, 541–604, stresses the great difficulty in getting reliable figures for Confederate strength in this campaign.
5. A. L. Long, *Lee's West Virginia Campaign*, in *The Annals of the War Written by Leading Participants, North and South*, 87–88. The pre-war rank of Loring is set forth in Francis B. Heitman, *Historical Register and Dictionary of the United States Army*, Vol. I, 625, 642. Walter H. Taylor, in *Four Years with General Lee*, 15–16, remarks that Lee did not assume personal command of the army, "although it was understood that Brigadier General Loring was subject to his orders."
6. Long, loc. cit.; Walter Taylor, op. cit., 17; *Cheat Mountain; or, Unwritten Chapter of the Late War*, by a Member of the Bar, Fayetteville, Tenn., 40, 45.
7. Ambrose Bierce, *Ambrose Bierce's Civil War*, 3–7.
8. Jacob Cox, *McClellan in West Virginia*, B. & L., Vol. I, 142–45; Comte de Paris, *History of the Civil War in America*, Vol. I, 376–80. Carnifix is Carnifex on modern maps. Floyd's report (O.R., Vol. V, 146–49) gives a long explanation for his retreat from Carnifix, where, with a force which he puts at 1800 men, his total casualties were 20 men wounded.
9. For a fascinating study of Lee's battle plan and its development the reader is again referred to Freeman. See also Taylor's *Four Years with General Lee*, 20–28. General Reynolds's report is in O.R., Vol. V, 184–86.
10. Taylor, op. cit., 32–33. Anyone who wishes to study the charges and countercharges made by Wise and Floyd (and it is pretty difficult going) will find the dreary record in O.R., Vol. V., 146–49, 149–50, 150–65.
11. E. A. Pollard, *The First Year of the War*, 168. It is interesting to observe that civilian critics, in the North and South alike, grew impatient at any talk of strategy, feeling apparently that all a general needed was a taste for getting close to the enemy and slugging it out. This trait, incidentally, Lee had in full measure, but he had other assets which the civilian critics were slow to recognize.
12. Pollard, op. cit., 168.
13. Robert E. Lee, *Recollections and Letters of General Robert E. Lee*, 51.
14. John S. Wise, *The End of an Era*, 172.
15. Mulligan's account of all of this is in an article, *The Siege of Lexington*, adapted from a lecture he delivered during the war (he was killed in action in 1864) and printed in B. & L., Vol. I, 307–13. Price's report on the campaign is in O.R., Vol. III, 185–88. There is an engaging description of Mulligan and the siege in the

History of Lafayette County, Missouri, by an unidentified author, 337–55. Being scrupulously honest, Price turned the captured money over to the banks from which it had been taken. It seems a pity; his army needed a war chest very badly.

16. Scott to Frémont, O.R., Vol. III, 185. Blair's criticism—voiced some time after the event—can be found in the *Congressional Globe,* 2nd Session, 37th Congress, Part II, 1121–22. A spirited reply to Blair by Schuyler Colfax, asserting that in mid-September Frémont had, in St. Louis, fewer than 8000 men, is in the same section of the *Globe,* 1128–29.
17. McElroy, *The Struggle for Missouri,* 192; John C. Moore, *Missouri,* in Confederate Military History, Vol. IX, 69.
18. New York *Times* for Nov. 4, 1861, printing a dispatch from Warsaw, Mo., dated Oct. 23.
19. O.R., Vol. III, 196, 529–30; *American Annual Cyclopaedia, 1861,* 394; McElroy, op. cit., 187, 232–33, 235–36; Jay Monaghan, *Civil War on the Western Border,* 195–96; *Harper's Weekly,* Nov. 23, 1861, 738.
20. Letters of Mrs. Margaret J. Hays, written from Westport, Mo., in the fall of 1861 and the fall of 1862; in the Civil War Papers of the Missouri Historical Society.

6. The Road to East Tennessee

1. *American Annual Cyclopaedia, 1861,* 682–83.
2. O.R., Vol. IV, 365–67, 369–70; W. G. Brownlow, *Sketches of the Rise, Progress and Decline of Secession,* passim.
3. Ibid., 374, 382; D.A.B., Vol. XX, 659–60; William M. Polk, op. cit., Vol. II, 3–4.
4. Oliver P. Temple, *East Tennessee and the Civil War,* 366–67; Gilbert E. Govan and James W. Livingood, *The Chattanooga Country, 1540–1951, from Tomahawks to TVA,* 170–72. See also E. M. Coulter, *The Confederate States of America, 1861–1865,* 84–85, 96.
5. Richmond *Dispatch* for Nov. 15, 1861.
6. Basler, Vol. IV, 458, 544–45.
7. The narrative here follows the account given by Temple, op. cit., 370–77. In a footnote Temple says he got the details orally from William B. Carter. General McClellan was enthusiastic about the project, writing that Federal occupation of east Tennessee "would soon render the occupation of Richmond and Eastern Virginia impossible to the Secessionists." (McClellan's *Own Story,* 49.)
8. O.R., Vol. IV, 404, 412. In a return dated Sept. 15, Zollicoffer reported 8549 men present for duty. (Ibid., 409.)
9. Notebooks of hearings of Robert Anderson before an Army Retirement Board, in the Papers of the Massachusetts Commandery, the Military Order of the Loyal Legion of the United States, 9–12, in the Houghton Library, Harvard University; General Orders No. 6, Department of the Cumberland, Oct. 8, 1861, O.R., Vol. IV, 296–97.
10. Sherman to Garrett Davis, Oct. 8, 1861, O.R., op. cit., 297.

11. Sherman frankly confessed that at this time "I had no confidence in my ability," admitting that he bluntly told Secretary of War Cameron that "Sidney Johnston was a fool if he did not move from Bowling Green and take Louisville; that our troops could not prevent it." (Inserted comment by Sherman in an extra-illustrated edition of *Sherman and his Campaigns*, by Col. S. R. Bowman and Lt. Col. R. B. Irwin, in the Sherman Collection at the Northwestern University Library.) For an appraisal of Johnston's course, see William Preston Johnston, 362.
12. William Preston Johnston, 362–63; Cleburne to Gen. Hardee, Nov. 13, 1861, O.R., Vol. IV, 545–46.
13. R. M. Kelly, *Holding Kentucky for the Union*, B. & L., Vol. I, 382–83; Temple, op. cit., 377–78, 388; O.R., Vol. IV, 231, 236–37, 294, 335–36, 338–39; Govan and Livingood, *The Chattanooga Country*, 187–88. Thomas proposed the move on Somerset on Nov. 5; he received Sherman's orders to follow a strict defensive policy on Nov. 7; the east Tennessee uprising began on Nov. 9.
14. O.R., Vol. IV, 340–41, 350; A. K. McClure, *Abraham Lincoln and Men of War Times*, 230. Lloyd Lewis, *Sherman, Fighting Prophet*, 195 ff., goes into details about Sherman's nervous instability at this time.
15. For McClellan's vain attempts to get Buell to do something about east Tennessee, see his letters of Nov. 7 and Nov. 25, 1861, and Jan. 6, 1862: O.R., Vol. IV, 342; Vol. VII, 447, 531.
16. O.R., Vol. VII, 701, 760, 764; Series Two, Vol. I, 857–58; Temple, op. cit., 394, 399, 408–11.
17. Sherman's return for Nov. 10 shows an aggregate present and absent in his department of 49,-586. (O.R., Vol. IV, 349.)
18. O.R., Vol. III, 306–10, 327; Grant's *Memoirs*, Vol. I, 269–81; William L. Polk, *General Polk and the Battle of Belmont*, B. & L., Vol. I, 348–55; letter of Charles Johnson to Mrs. Johnson dated Nov. 18, 1861, in the Charles James Johnson Papers, Louisiana State Archives, Baton Rouge; William Preston Johnston, 377. Grant's ideas about the feasibility of using untrained troops were set forth after the war in a speech by John A. Rawlins quoted in this writer's *Grant Moves South*, 72.
19. Isabel Wallace, *The Life and Letters of General W. H. L. Wallace*, 141; O.R., Vol. III, 312.

CHAPTER TWO: *A Vast Future Also*

1. Magazine of Discord

1. Alfred Roman, *The Military Operations of General Beauregard*, Vol. I, 132. This book, which is virtually Beauregard's autobiography, is cited hereafter as Roman.
2. Joseph E. Johnston, *Narrative of Military Operations*, (cited hereafter as Johnston's *Narrative*) 74–76.

3. Mss. account by Gustavus W. Smith, in the Palmer Collection, Western Reserve Historical Society, Cleveland.
4. Jefferson Davis, *Rise and Fall,* Vol. I, 442; editorial in the Richmond *Examiner* for Sept. 27, 1861. Davis's account of the Fairfax Courthouse Conference is in *Rise and Fall,* Vol. I, 499 ff.
5. Letter of Davis to Gov. Letcher dated Sept. 14, 1861, printed in Dunbar Rowland, *Jefferson Davis, Constitutionalist,* Vol. V, 132.
6. Clifford Dowdey, *Experiment in Rebellion,* 99–100. Toombs's brother Gabriel wrote to Vice-President Alexander Stephens urging him to talk Toombs out of the notion of being a soldier: "In this case my brother's zeal blinds his judgment, and is not according to wisdom. He has never been educated in the science of war and has no experience in the business, and besides is physically unfit for camp life." (Annual Report of the American Historical Association, 1913, Vol. II; *The Correspondence of Robert Toombs, Alexander H. Stephens and Howell Cobb,* 573.) For Hunter, see D.A.B., Vol. IV, 403–4, and Dowdey, 100–2.
7. Diary of S. R. Mallory, in the Southern Historical Collection, University of North Carolina, entries for Sept. 4 and Sept. 16; O.R., Series Four, Vol. I, 602, 613.
8. For the vote, see the *American Annual Cyclopaedia, 1861,* 153.
9. Beauregard's report on Bull Run is in O.R., Vol. II, 484–504; Davis's rebuke is in the same volume, 508. The famous letter to the editor of the *Whig* is from the Richmond *Examiner* of Nov. 8, 1861, which reprinted it and denounced it. The whole strange sequence is analyzed by Douglas Southall Freeman, *Lee's Lieutenants,* Vol. I, 99–108.
10. *Journal of the Congress of the Confederate States,* Vol. I, 464. The five commissions were dated thus: Cooper, May 16, 1861; A. S. Johnston, May 30; Lee, June 14; J. E. Johnston, July 4; Beauregard, July 21.
11. O.R., Series Four, Vol. I, 605–8, 611. The case is examined in detail in Gilbert E. Govan and James W. Livingood, *A Different Valor: the Story of General Joseph E. Johnston, C.S.A.,* 66–71.
12. *The Correspondence of Robert Toombs, Alexander H. Stephens and Howell Cobb,* 575–78, 580–81.
13. Mary Chesnut, *A Diary from Dixie,* 108.
14. Diary of S. R. Mallory, entry dated Sept. 4, 1861; Diary of Thomas Bragg, entry for Dec. 6, 1861, in the Southern Historical Collection, University of North Carolina Library.
15. Richmond *Whig,* issue of Nov. 29, 1861; Richmond *Daily Examiner,* issue of Nov. 29.
16. Letter of Jefferson Davis to Gen. G. W. Smith, dated Oct. 24, 1861, in the Jefferson Davis Papers, Duke University Library.

2. *Struggle for Power*

1. In the McClellan Papers at the Library of Congress there is a notebook in McClellan's handwriting, "Extracts from letters written to my wife during the War of the Rebellion." The

letters are not known to exist, and the manuscript represents McClellan's editing of the originals. His autobiography, McClellan's *Own Story*, prints other versions of the letters after still further editing; revealing as the letters in McClellan's *Own Story* frequently are, they are often much less revealing than the document McClellan himself prepared. The manuscript is cited hereafter as McClellan's Letterbook; where the printed volume is referred to it is cited as McClellan's *Own Story*. The quotation in the text is from the Letterbook; the material about Scott is from McClellan's *Own Story*, 66–67.

2. McClellan's Letterbook. A milder version is in McClellan's *Own Story*, 83.
3. Ferri Pisani, 113. The dinner is mentioned in McClellan's *Own Story*, 84. McClellan announced organization of 46 regiments into brigades on Aug. 4; O.R., Vol. LI, Part One, 434–35.
4. George B. McClellan, *Report on the Organization and Campaigns of the Army of the Potomac*, 38–43; giving the text of his Aug. 4 memorandum to the President.
5. Gideon Welles, *Diary*, Vol. I, 242.
6. McClellan's Letterbook, giving his letter of Aug. 8. The ellipsis is McClellan's.
7. McClellan to Scott, Aug. 8, 1861, and Scott to McClellan, Aug. 9, O.R., Vol. XI, Part Three, 3–4.
8. Ibid., 4–6.
9. McClellan's *Own Story*, 85.
10. Ibid., 86–87; McClellan's Letterbook, letter of Aug. 16.
11. McClellan's Letterbook, letter dated Aug. 19.
12. On Aug. 20 McClellan wrote that when he reached Washington the city "could have been taken with the utmost ease" (McClellan's *Own Story*, 88). His work in providing the city with a ring of fortifications was excellent, but the situation at the time of his arrival was not as desperate as he made it appear. The report of Major Henry J. Hunt, chief of artillery, shows that on July 29 the Virginia front was tolerably well protected against any thrust which the Confederates could have made at that time. Fort Corcoran, above Arlington, mounted twelve 8-inch seacoast howitzers, seven 24-pounders, two 12-pounders and two 24-pounder howitzers, and was manned by 200 artillerists and a regiment of infantry. Fort Albany, covering the Fairfax Road, mounted eighteen guns, twelve of which were 24-pounders, and had two companies of artillery and a Massachusetts regiment. Fort Runyon, covering the approach to the Long Bridge, had a 30-pounder Parrott rifle, eight 8-inch seacoast howitzers, ten 32-pounders and four 6-pounder field pieces, and was garrisoned by a New York regiment. Fort Ellsworth, on the edge of Alexandria, mounted two 30-pounders and two 10-pounder Parrotts, with twelve 8-inch howitzers, four 24-pounder siege guns, one 24-pounder field howitzer and three 6-pounder field guns; it contained a company of light artillery and a New York infantry regiment. (O.R., Vol. II, 768–69.)

   Col. Ferri Pisani toured the

defensive positions on the Virginia side on Aug. 4 and wrote that he saw "a series of military works, redoubts, batteries, abatis, carefully constructed and armed with cannons from the Navy dockyard"; he felt that "the whole is well organized and gives the impression of a strong line of resistance." (Ferri Pisani, op. cit., 114–15.) It is of course true that preparations for defense on the Maryland side were much more sketchy, although Map I, Plate VI, in the Atlas Accompanying the Official Records, showing the Washington field works "executed during parts of June and July, 1861," shows some protection on the main roads leading into Washington from Maryland.

13. Letter of Senator Sumner to Gov. John A. Andrew, dated Aug. 11, 1861, marked "private and confidential"; in the John A. Andrew Papers, Massachusetts Historical Society.
14. Letter of Charles Francis Adams to his son, dated Aug. 16; *A Cycle of Adams Letters*, Vol. I, 27–28.
15. John Bigelow, *Retrospections of an Active Life*, Vol. I, 366–67; letter of J. D. Andrus to David Davis, dated Aug. 18, in the David Davis Papers, Illinois State Historical Library, Springfield.
16. McClellan's *Own Story*, 105–7; O.R., Vol. V, 587–89; McClellan to Cameron, Sept. 13, 1861, in the Cameron Papers, Library of Congress.
17. Letter of Winfield Scott to Cameron dated Oct. 4, 1861; letter of Scott dated Oct. 10, quoting orders to McClellan dated Sept. 16 and bearing a notation to Assistant Secretary of War Thomas A. Scott dated Oct. 31 and saying: "I suppose the within is the letter you ask for. A. L."; in the Cameron Papers, Library of Congress. See also O.R., Series Three, Vol. I, 519.
18. Scott's letter of Oct. 10, cited in Footnote 17.
19. William H. Russell, *My Diary North and South*, 205.
20. Jed Hotchkiss, in *Confederate Military History*, Vol. III, *Virginia*, 179–88; O.R., Vol. V, 290; McClellan, *Report on the Organization and Campaigns of the Army of the Potomac*, 77–78.
21. Richard B. Irwin, *Ball's Bluff and the Arrest of General Stone*, in B. & L., Vol. II, 123 ff.; O.R., Vol. V, 308.
22. Nicolay & Hay, Vol. IV, 467–68; McClellan's *Own Story*, 171; Tyler Dennett, ed., *John Hay, Lincoln and the Civil War, in the Diaries and Letters of John Hay*, 31–32.
23. Chandler's letter to Mrs. Chandler, dated Oct. 27, 1861, in the Zachariah Chandler Papers, Library of Congress.
24. There is a moving account of Scott's departure in McClellan's *Own Story*, 173. For the report to the *Tribune's* editors, see letter of Henry Smith to Charles Ray and Joseph Medill, dated Nov. 4, 1861, in the Charles H. Ray Papers, Huntington Library.

3. *The Hammering of the Guns*

1. N.O.R., Vol. XII, 198–201.
2. Rush Hawkins, *Early Coast Operations in North Carolina*, B. &

L., Vol. I, 632–35. Interesting accounts of the bombardment, written by correspondents for the Boston *Journal* and the New York *Herald*, are in Moore's *Rebellion Record*, Vol. III, Documents, 16–26. It is hard to be sure just how many guns the forts contained, the estimates varying all the way from 19 to 35. (B. &. L., Vol. I, 633; C.C.W., 1863, Part III, 282; O.R., Vol. IV, 581–86; D. H. Hill, Jr., *Confederate Military History*, Vol. IV, *North Carolina*, 27.)

3. Butler's testimony of Jan. 16, 1862, in C.C.W., 1863, Part III, 282–83.
4. Butler, *Butler's Book*, 285–88.
5. Dispatch to the Petersburg, Va., *Express* from Raleigh, dated Aug. 30, 1861, in Moore's *Rebellion Record*, Vol. III, Documents, 26.
6. For a summary of the full significance of the action, see J. Thomas Scharf, *History of the Confederate States Navy*, 368–69.
7. Daniel Ammen, *The Atlantic Coast*, 11–13; Nicolay & Hay, Vol. V, 11–14; N.O.R., Vol. XII, 198–201.
8. Welles to Du Pont, Oct. 12, 1861, in N.O.R., Vol. XII, 214–15. The Naval Board had named Port Royal as one of three or four eligible places for occupation, and had quite strongly recommended Fernandina, Florida, as the likeliest spot. After receiving his appointment, Du Pont exercised the discretion which had been given him and chose Port Royal. (Report of Flag Officer Du Pont, Nov. 6, 1861, in N.O.R., Vol. XII, 259–261.
9. James H. Wilson, *Under the Old Flag*, Vol. I, 68–69. It should be noted that Gen. T. W. Sherman was not related to the better-known Gen. William T. Sherman.
10. Nicolay & Hay, Vol. V, 15; Basler, Vol. IV, 527–28.
11. McClellan to Assistant Secretary of War Scott, Oct. 17, 1861, in O.R., Vol. VI, 179. McClellan either withdrew his objection or was overruled; the 79th New York did go south with Sherman.
12. Du Pont's report, N.O.R., Vol. XII, 259–61; Ammen, *The Atlantic Coast*, 13–18; also Ammen's *Du Pont and the Port Royal Expedition* in B. & L., Vol. I, 674.
13. Letter of John Rodgers, in Moore's *Rebellion Record*, Vol. III, Documents, 112; Ammen, *The Atlantic Coast*, 23–24.
14. Reminiscences of Francis T. Chew, in the Southern Historical Collection, University of North Carolina Library.
15. Du Pont, in N.O.R., Vol. XII, 262–65; Moore's *Rebellion Record*, Vol. III, Documents, 304, 318; report of Brig. Gen. Thomas F. Drayton, C.S.A., in O.R., Vol. VI, 8–9; John Call Dalton, *The Battle of Port Royal*, 56.
16. Report of Commander Percival Drayton, U.S.N., (brother of the Confederate general who commanded Fort Walker), in N.O.R., Vol. XII, 272; Ammen, *The Atlantic Coast*, 29–30, 33–35, 40.
17. Sherman's report, O.R., Vol. VI, 3–4; letter of Du Pont to G. D. Morgan, dated Dec. 24, 1861, in the Gustavus V. Fox Correspondence, Box I, 1861, the New York Historical Society; letter of Du Pont to S. H. Shaw of Boston, dated Dec. 30, 1861, in Miscellaneous Papers XXI, Massachusetts Historical Society.

18. O.R., Vol. VI, 4–5.
19. Letter of Mrs. E. C. Anderson, Jr., dated at Savannah, Nov. 9, 1861, in the Wayne-Stites-Anderson Papers, Georgia Historical Society.

4. "*We Are Not Able to Meet It*"

1. Lee's Nov. 9 report, N.O.R., Vol. XII, 299–300; letter of Lee to Governor Pickens, dated Dec. 27, 1861, in the E. M. Law Papers, Southern Historical Collection, University of North Carolina Library; letter of Lee to his daughter Mildred dated Nov. 15, in Robert E. Lee, Jr., *Recollections and Letters of Gen. Robert E. Lee*, 55.
2. For a detailed examination of Lee's problems and conclusions, see Freeman, *Lee*, Vol. I, 609–13.
3. Gen. Sherman's testimony, C.C.W., 1863, Part III, 294.
4. James H. Wilson, *Under the Old Flag*, Vol. I, 71.
5. Lee to Adjutant General Cooper, Jan. 8, 1862, O.R., Vol. VI, 367; Bragg to Jefferson Davis, Oct. 22, 1861, letter in the Palmer Collection, Western Reserve Historical Society, Cleveland.
6. Editorial in the Richmond *Examiner* for Nov. 23, 1861.
7. D.A.B., Vol. XX, 216–17. Gideon Welles wrote that Wilkes was "ambitious, self-conceited and self-willed," and said: "He has abilities but not sound judgment, and is not always subordinate, though he is himself severe and exacting towards his subordinates." (*Diary of Gideon Welles*, Vol. I, 87.)
8. N.O.R., Series Two, Vol. III, 257–64.
9. Ibid., Series One, Vol. I, 148; Thomas L. Harris, *The Trent Affair, Including a Review of English and American Relations at the Beginning of the Civil War*, 19.
10. Mrs. Chesnut's Diary, 160.
11. N.O.R., Vol. I, 154–57, 159; O.R., Series Two, Vol. II, 1107; Theodore Martin, *The Life of His Royal Highness, the Prince Consort*, Vol. V, 347–48; Thornton Kirkland Lothrop, *William Henry Seward*, 323.
12. Charles Francis Adams, Jr., *Charles Francis Adams*, 211–218. For a good account of the receipt of the news at the American Legation see *The Journal of Benjamin Moran*, Vol. II, 913–15.
13. Charles Francis Adams, Jr., op. cit., 231–32; letter of Henry Adams dated Nov. 30, 1861, in *A Cycle of Adams Letters*, Vol. I, 75–76; letter of Charles Francis Adams, dated Dec. 20, 1861, in the same, 88–89.
14. Lothrop, op. cit., 326–28. In McClellan's *Own Story*, 175, McClellan refers to the meeting with Seward thus: "Today is not to be a day of rest for me. This unfortunate affair of Mason and Slidell has come up, and I shall be obliged to devote the day to endeavoring to get our government to take the only prompt and honorable course of avoiding a war with France and England." In a part of this letter omitted from the printed version, McClellan wrote of Seward: "It is a terrible dispensation of Providence that so weak and cowardly a thing as that should now control our foreign

relations–the Presdt is not much better, except that he is honest and means well." (Letter to Mrs. McClellan, dated Nov. 17, 1861, in the McClellan Letterbook, Library of Congress.)

15. Wilkes set forth his argument in a letter to Secretary Welles dated Nov. 16, 1861, in N.O.R., Vol. I, 143–45. See also Adams to Seward dated Nov. 29, 1861, in O.R., Series Two, Vol. II, 1106.
16. Theodore Martin, op. cit., 349–52.
17. Ibid., 350; Spencer Walpole, *The Life of Lord John Russell*, Vol. II, 346–47; W. H. Russell, *My Diary North and South*, 217.
18. John Bigelow, *Retrospections of an Active Life*, Vol. I, 387–90; letter of Scott to Seward dated Dec. 26, 1861, in the William H. Seward collection, Rush Rhees Library, Rochester University.
19. General Horace Porter, *Campaigning with Grant*, 408–9; Benson J. Lossing, *Pictorial History of the Civil War in the United States of America*, Vol. II, 156, citing a conversation Lossing had with Lincoln early in December 1861; *The Diary of Edward Bates*, Vol. I, 177–89, 194–95; *Journal of Benjamin Moran*, Vol. II, 939–40.
20. Letter from Lee to George Washington Custis Lee, dated Dec. 29, 1861, in the R. E. Lee Papers, Manuscript Department, Duke University Library.

5. *Revolutionary Struggle*

1. Varina Howell Davis, *Jefferson Davis*, Vol. I, 165; Richmond *Examiner*, issues of Nov. 29 and Nov. 30, 1861.
2. O.R., Series Three, Vol. I, 775; Series Four, Vol. I, 822; Diary of Thomas Bragg, entry for Dec. 6, 1861, in the Southern Historical Collection, University of North Carolina Library.
3. *Journal of the Congress of the Confederate States*, Vol. I, 467–69, 472.
4. Diary of Thomas Bragg, entries for Nov. 30, Dec. 6, Dec. 7, and Dec. 17, 1861; also O.R., Vol. LIII, 759, 761–63.
5. Charles Francis Adams to his son, letter dated Jan. 10, 1862, in *A Cycle of Adams Letters*, Vol. I, 99.
6. Letter of R. E. Lee to Gov. John Letcher, dated Dec. 26, 1861, in Southern Historical Society Papers, Vol. I, No. 6, 462.
7. Letter to Porcher Miles from Brig. Gen. John S. Preston, written in November or December 1864, in O.R., Series Four, Vol. III, 883.
8. Frémont gave up his command Nov. 2, 1861. For the order relieving him, and Lincoln's general instructions to his successor, see O.R., Vol. III, 553–54. At the time he was relieved, Frémont was in southwestern Missouri groping unsuccessfully toward an encounter with Sterling Price's army, which was not at all where Frémont supposed it to be; the circumstances are set forth in this writer's *This Hallowed Ground*, 65–66. For the original and revised versions of the paragraph in Cameron's report dealing with slaves, see A. K. McClure, *Abraham Lincoln and Men of War Times*, 148–49.

9. The full text of Lincoln's message to Congress is in Basler, Vol. V, 35–53. It is interesting to study Lincoln's earlier exploration of the significance of a free labor system and the relationship between labor and capital in speeches he made at Cincinnati and Milwaukee in the fall of 1859; they are in Basler, Vol. III, 459, 477–78.
10. Diary of Edward Bates, 217; entry for Dec. 31, 1861.
11. David Davis Papers, Illinois State Historical Library, letter of Joseph Casey dated Dec. 11, 1861.

6. *The Want of Success*

1. New York *Tribune* for Dec. 31, 1861.
2. Diary of Fanny Seward, entry for Jan. 1, 1862, in the William H. Seward Collection, Rush Rhees Library, Rochester University; the *Diary of Edward Bates*, 244; Theodore Calvin Pease and James G. Randall, eds., *The Diary of Orville Browning*, Vol. I, 521.
3. Russell, *My Diary North and South*, 205. McClellan's famous snub to Lincoln is detailed in John Hay, *Lincoln and the Civil War, in the Diaries and Letters of John Hay*, 34–35.
4. O.R., Vol. VII, 524, 526.
5. J. W. Schuckers, *The Life and Public Services of Salmon Portland Chase*, 445–46; J. G. Barnard, *The Peninsular Campaign and its Antecedents, as Developed by the Report of Maj. Gen. George B. McClellan and Other Published Documents*, 51–52, 54.
6. *Congressional Globe*, 37th Congress, Second Session, Part One, 194, 200, 206.
7. Ibid., 440–41.
8. Basler, Vol. V, 98–99; O.R., Vol. VII, 533.
9. These odd meetings are described in a memorandum by General McDowell, printed in Henry J. Raymond, *The Life and Public Services of Abraham Lincoln*, 772–77. See also Gen. Meigs, *The Relations of President Lincoln and Secretary Stanton to the Military Commanders in the Civil War*, American Historical Review, Vol. XXVI, No. Two, 292–93; Meigs' Pocket Diaries, Library of Congress; Gen. W. B. Franklin, *The First Great Crime of the War*, Annals of the War, 73–78; McClellan's *Own Story*, 155–58. Lincoln to Halleck and Buell is in Basler, Vol. V, 98–99, as cited in Note 8, above.
10. Diary of Thomas Bragg, entries for Jan. 14, Jan. 17 and Jan. 21, 1862.
11. O.R., Vol. VIII, 508.
12. O.R., Vol. VII, 820; Johnston to Gov. Isham Harris, Dec. 25, 1861, in Southern Historical Society Papers, Vol. IV. No. Four, 185–87.
13. O.R., Series Two, Vol. II, 1169, 1191, 1192.

CHAPTER THREE: *The Military Paradox*

1. Decision in Kentucky

1. Brig. Gen. J. W. Bishop, "The Mill Springs Campaign," in *Glimpses of the Nation's Struggle*, Second Series, 77–78.
2. There is a good account of this battle—Somerset, Beech Grove, Logan's Cross Roads, Mill Springs, or Fishing Creek—in Stanley Horn, *The Army of Tennessee*, 68–70, and in R. M. Kelly, *Holding Kentucky for the Union*, in B. & L., Vol. I, 387–91. In February, Secretary of War Judah Benjamin wrote that "rumors industriously circulated to the prejudice of General Crittenden by the first fugitives from the battlefield are now believed to have been without foundation." (O.R., Series Four, Vol. I, 961.)
3. Landon C. Haynes to Jefferson Davis, Jan. 29, 1862, in O.R., Vol. VII, 849. Crittenden listed his battle casualties at 533 killed, wounded, and missing. (Ibid., 108.)
4. O.R., Vol. VII, 102.
5. *Journal of a Trip to Washington in 1862*, by R. H. Dana, Jr., in the Dana Papers, Massachusetts Historical Society; Albert Gallatin Riddle, *Recollections of War Times*, 179–80.
6. There is an extensive survey of Cameron's regime in A. Howard Meneely, *The War Department, 1861*. See especially 252–79.
7. Diaries of Fanny Seward, Rush Rhees Library, Rochester University; note dictated by Charles A. Dana in the Ida M. Tarbell Papers, Allegheny College.
8. McClellan's *Own Story*, 153; letter of McClellan to Barlow dated Jan. 18, 1862, and letter of Barlow to Stanton dated Jan. 14, both in the Barlow Papers, Huntington Library.
9. McClellan's *Own Story*, 151–52, 176; letter of Barlow to Stanton dated Dec. 11, 1861, in the Barlow Papers; letter of Ward Hill Lamon to Gen. William Orme of Bloomington, Ill., dated Feb. 10, 1862, in the Chicago Historical Society.
10. Donn Piatt, *Memories of the Men Who Saved the Union*, 57–58.
11. War order and supplement are in Basler, Vol. V, 111–12, 115. According to John Hay, Lincoln prepared the order "without consultation." Gideon Welles asserted that such an order had previously been suggested by the Navy Department, while Congressmen Riddle and James G. Blaine credited the idea to Stanton. (Tyler Dennett, ed., *Lincoln and the Civil War in the Diaries and Letters of John Hay*, 36; *Diary of Gideon Welles*, Vol. I, 61; Riddle, op. cit., 181; James G. Blaine, *Twenty Years of Congress*, Vol. I, 355.)
12. Letter of Stanton to the Rev. H. Dyer, dated May 18, 1862, in the Stanton Papers, Library of Congress.
13. Letter of McClellan to Stanton, Jan. 31, 1862, in the Robert Todd

Lincoln Papers, Library of Congress.

14. McClellan to Buell, Jan. 13, 1862, O.R., Vol. VII, 547; Halleck to McClellan, Jan. 20, O.R., Vol. VIII, 508.
15. Letters of Scott to Stanton dated Feb. 1, Feb. 2 and Feb. 6, 1862, in the Stanton Papers, Library of Congress.
16. Letter of Barlow to McClellan, dated Feb. 8, 1862, in the Barlow Papers, Huntington Library; letter of Stanton to Scott, dated Feb. 21, and undated letter of McClellan to Stanton, both in the Stanton Papers. From the context McClellan's letter appears to have been written early in February.

2. *Unconditional Surrender*

1. Letter of Laurent de Give to Blondeel van Cuelebroeck, Belgian Minister, dated Jan. 4, 1862, and forwarded to Lincoln by Seward on Jan. 18; in the Robert Todd Lincoln Papers.
2. William Preston Johnston, *The Life of General Albert Sidney Johnston*, 425–26; Stanley Horn, *The Army of Tennessee*, 78, 80. Buell's Jan. 23 return shows a "total present" force of 72,502, of which he listed 41,563 as infantry present for duty and fit for the field. (O.R., Vol. VII, 563.)
3. Letter of Foote to Gideon Welles dated April 27, 1862, in the Welles Papers, Huntington Library; article in the St. Louis *Democrat*, quoted in Moore's *Rebellion Record*, Vol. IV, Documents, 77; Wilbur G. Crummer, *With Grant at Fort Donelson, Shiloh and Vicksburg*, 21. There is a graphic, detailed narrative of the engagement in Rear Admiral H. Walke, *Naval Scenes and Reminiscences of the Civil War in the United States*, 53–65.
4. Buell's message to Thomas, dated Feb. 2, 1862, O.R., Vol. VII, 580. For his Feb. 1 message to McClellan, telling why it was impossible to go into East Tennessee, see O.R., Vol. XVI, 26. Halleck's anxious dispatches are in Vol. VII, 535, 586–87, 590–91, 593–95.
5. Ibid., 535, 543, 547, 575.
6. James Mason Hoppin, *Life of Andrew Hull Foote, Rear Admiral, United States Navy*, 391 ff.; letter of Foote to Welles, cited in Footnote 3.
7. William Preston Johnston, op. cit., 449; The Missouri *Democrat*, in Moore's *Rebellion Record*, Vol. IV, Documents, 179; Surgeon John H. Brinton in *The Medical and Surgical History of the War of the Rebellion*, Part One, Vol. I, Appendix, 26–28. Brinton wrote that "thousands of the soldiers were broken down" and had to be sent north to hospitals.
8. William Preston Johnston gives a good picture of the odd Floyd-Pillow-Buckner relationship, op. cit., 454–55. See also Buckner's report, O.R., Vol. VII, 330–31, and Arndt M. Stickles, *Simon Bolivar Buckner*, 136–38, 151–56. There is a good description of the fighting in Lew Wallace, *The Capture of Fort Donelson*, in B. & L., Vol. I, 398–428. Johnston's Feb. 15 telegram to Richmond, announcing "Our forces attacked the enemy with energy and won a brilliant victory," is in the Ryder

Collection, Tufts University Library.

9. Adam R. Johnson, *The Partisan Rangers of the Confederate States Army*, 67–68; John Allan Wyeth, *That Devil Forrest*, 40, 50–51.

3. The Disease Which Brought Disaster

1. O.R., Vol. VII, 418; William Preston Johnston, 495.
2. William Preston Johnston, 496–97; dispatch to the Mobile *Tribune*, printed in Moore's *Rebellion Record*, Vol. IV, Documents, 211–12; Adam R. Johnson, *The Partisan Rangers*, 71–72; dispatch from Nashville, apparently written Feb. 23, in the Richmond *Dispatch* for Feb. 27, 1862; O.R., Vol. VII, 427–28.
3. O.R., Vol. VII, 429–31; William Preston Johnston, 496.
4. Letter of Foote to Gideon Welles dated Nov. 13, 1862, summarizing his operations in the campaign, in the Welles Papers, Huntington Library; Hoppin, *Life of Admiral Foote*, 236–38; Halleck to Grant, Feb. 18, and to Stanton, Feb. 21, O.R., Vol. VII, 633, 655; Buell to Halleck, Feb. 21, ibid., 650.
5. Letter of Stanton to the New York *Tribune*, as revised, dated Feb. 19, 1862, in the Stanton Papers, Library of Congress.
6. David Davis, who was investigating army supply and procurement problems, wrote at this time: "Nobody thinks much of Grant. He is in luck, however." (Letter to Leonard Swett dated Feb. 23, 1862, in the David Davis Papers, Illinois State Historical Library.) The sequence in which Halleck tried to put Hitchcock over Grant, and complained about Grant's alleged misconduct, is detailed in this writer's *Grant Moves South*, 193–97.
7. Apparently it is impossible to get a satisfactory figure for the number of prisoners taken at Fort Donelson. Grant strangely enough seems not to have counted them, and estimates range all the way from 8000 to 15,000. John Allan Wyeth made a careful analysis in *That Devil Forrest*, 55. He believed that there were about 15,000 Confederates in Fort Donelson when the battle began, that 400 were killed, 1134 wounded and sent away, and 3000 taken out by Floyd, Pillow, and Forrest. This would make a total of 4534 "not captured" and the number of prisoners would stand at slightly more than 10,000. The Fort Donelson National Military Park pamphlet suggests a figure somewhere between 12,000 and 15,000.
8. Johnston to Davis, March 18, 1862, in O.R., Vol. VII, 260.
9. Ibid., 672, 899–900; letter of Beauregard to Roger Pryor dated at Nashville Feb. 14, in the P. G. T. Beauregard Papers, Duke University Library.
10. Letter of Stanton to Assistant Secretary of War Scott dated Feb. 21, 1862, in the Stanton Papers.
11. John S. Wise, *The End of an Era*, 175–78; O.R., Vol. IX, 111, 114.
12. Burnside's Testimony before the Committee on the Conduct of the War (C.C.W. Report, Part III, 1863; 333–34, 337; McClellan's

Report on the Organization and Campaigns of the Army of the Potomac, 85–86; Comte de Paris, *History of the Civil War in America*, Vol. I, 581–82).

13. Comte de Paris, op. cit., 583–85; D. H. Hill, Jr., in *Confederate Military History*, Vol. IV, *North Carolina*, 34–37; Wise, *The End of an Era*, 179–81; O.R., Vol. IX, 76.
14. O.R., Vol. IX, 112, 121, 190.

4. Time for Compulsion

1. Diary of Thomas Bragg, Southern Historical Collection, University of North Carolina, entry for Feb. 22, 1862; diary of Henry Robinson Berkeley, in the Virginia State Historical Society, entry for the same date.
2. J. William Jones, *Christ in the Camp, or Religion in the Confederate Army*, 148; Varina Davis, *Jefferson Davis, a Memoir*, Vol. II, 180, 182–83.
3. Dunbar Rowland, *Jefferson Davis, Constitutionalist*, Vol. V, 198–202.
4. Diary of Henry Robinson Berkeley, as cited in Footnote 1, above; John B. Jones, *A Rebel War Clerk's Diary*, edited by Earl Schenck Miers, 67–68; Richard Malcolm Johnston and William Hand Browne, *Life of Alexander Stephens*, 413.
5. Diary of Thomas Bragg, entries for Feb. 10, Feb. 19, and Feb. 20, 1862.
6. Dunbar Rowland, Vol. V, 203–5; Robert Garlick Kean, *Inside the Confederate Government*, edited by Edward Younger, 24–26; O.R., Vol. V, 1015, 1086.
7. Joseph E. Johnston, *Narrative of Military Operations*, 89–91; O.R., Vol. V, 1057–58; Freeman, *Lee's Lieutenants*, Vol. I, 122–30.
8. Johnston's meetings with Mr. Davis and the Cabinet are described in Thomas Bragg's Diary, entries for Feb. 19 and Feb. 20.
9. Joseph E. Johnston, op. cit., 96; O.R., Vol. V, 1097, 1083; Davis to James Phelan dated March 1, 1865, in Dunbar Rowland, Vol. VI, 493–94.
10. Johnston's *Narrative*, 97.
11. Editorial from the Washington (Ark.) *Telegraph* for Feb. 26, 1862, in the files of the Arkansas History Commission.
12. Dunbar Rowland, Vol. VI, 216–18.
13. *Journal of the Congress of the Confederate States of America, 1861–1865*, Vol. II, 37, 72–74; H. S. Foote, *The War of the Rebellion*, 356; O.R., Vol. V, 1099; Diary of Thomas Bragg, entry for March 17, 1862; letter of General Lee to Mrs. Lee dated March 14, in the R. E. Lee Papers, Library of Congress; *The Correspondence of Robert Toombs, Alexander Stephens and Howell Cobb*, Annual Report of the American Historical Association for the Year 1911, Vol. II, 590.
14. O.R., Series Four, Vol. I, 986.
15. James D. Richardson, *Messages and Papers of the Confederacy*, Vol. I, 205–6; O.R., Series Four, Vol. I, 1081, 1095–97.
16. O.R., Series Four, Vol. I, 1116–17, 1138; Johnston and Browne, *Life of Alexander H. Stephens*, 414; O.R., Series Four, Vol. II, 43.
17. Dunbar Rowland, Vol. V, 209.

5. *Contending with Shadows*

1. Basler, Vol. V, 144–46.
2. Ibid., 152–53, 160–61.
3. Edward McPherson, *The Political History of the United States of America During the Great Rebellion,* 210–11, quoting from a memorandum written by one of the participants in the conference, J. W. Crisfield of Maryland.
4. *Congressional Globe*, 37th Congress, Second Session, Part II, 1154; Part IV, appendix, 412–13. Shortly after they approved the plan for compensated emancipation, the two Houses of Congress voted to emancipate the slaves in the District of Columbia. Signing the act on April 16, Mr. Lincoln said he was gratified that "the two principles of compensation, and colonization, are both recognized and practically applied" in this act. (Basler, Vol. V, 192.)
5. Letter of McClellan to S. L. M. Barlow dated Nov. 8, 1861, in the Barlow Papers, Huntington Library.
6. Russell, *My Diary North and South,* 210; C.C.W. Reports, 1863, Part I, 129–30.
7. Basler, Vol. V, 88.
8. Russell, *My Diary North and South,* 208; *Harper's Weekly* for Nov. 9, 1861; *Congressional Globe*, 37th Congress, Second Session, Part II, 1662; Richard B. Irwin, *Ball's Bluff and the Arrest of General Stone,* B. & L., Vol. II, 132–33.
9. Testimony given by Stone in February 1863, in C.C.W. Reports, 1863, Part II, 489.
10. James G. Blaine, *Twenty Years of Congress*, Vol. I, 393; Irwin, op. cit., 132; O.R., Vol. LI, Part One, 517.
11. C.C.W. Reports, 1863, Part II, 295 et seq. For a review of the committee's attitude and methods of operation see T. Harry Williams, *Investigation: 1862*, American Heritage, Vol. VI, No. One, 19–20.
12. C.C.W. Reports, 1863, Part II, 427–29.
13. Edward Bates' Diary, 229, entry for Feb. 3, 1862.
14. C.C.W. Reports, 1863, Part II, 510; O.R., Vol. V, 341, 345.
15. C.C.W. Reports, 1863, Part II, 505–9. The messages exchanged by McClellan and Stone on Oct. 21, 1861, the day of the battle, give the story a slightly different cast than the one given in McClellan's testimony before the committee. Informed that Stone's troops had crossed at Ball's Bluff and Edwards Ferry, McClellan wrote: "I congratulate your command"; a little later he asked Stone how big a force would be needed to take Leesburg, adding, "I may require you to take it today" and saying that he could support such a move "on the other side of the river from Darnestown." Later in the day McClellan sent the order, "Take Leesburg," after which he ordered Stone: "Hold your position on the Virginia side of the Potomac at all hazards." (O.R., Vol. LI, Part One, 498–500.)

6. *Forward to Richmond*

1. Diary of Gilbert Thompson, U. S. Engineer Battalion, Army of

the Potomac, entry for Feb. 27, 1862, in the Manuscript Division, Library of Congress.

2. McClellan, *Report on the Organization and Campaigns of the Army of the Potomac*, 113–15; J. W. Shuckers, *The Life and Public Services of Salmon Portland Chase*, 446; O.R., Vol. V, 727–28, 730.
3. Helen Nicolay, *Lincoln's Secretary: a Biography of John G. Nicolay*, 142–43.
4. McClellan wrote to Barlow that the Harper's Ferry move led Johnston to evacuate his Centreville-Manassas line, and felt that history "will, when I am in my grave, record it as the brightest passage of my life that I accomplished so much at so small a cost." (Letter dated March 16, 1862, in the Barlow Papers, Huntington Library.)
5. The cabinet meeting on March 6, at which the use of the new iron-clad was discussed, is from a memorandum by John G. Nicolay in Nicolay & Hay, Vol. V, 221–22. McClellan tells of his interview with Lincoln in his *Own Story*, 195–96.
6. Diaries of Marsena Patrick, Vol. I, entry for March 6, 1862, in the Library of Congress.
7. John Hay, *Lincoln and the Civil War*, 36.
8. Basler, Vol. V, 149–51, for the text of the two war orders. It is significant that none of the new corps commanders was a McClellan man. McDowell had preceded him in command of the Army of the Potomac, and distrusted him; General Marsena Patrick wrote at this time that in a long talk with McDowell he found that McDowell "believes McClellan to be very insincere." (Patrick Diaries, entry for Feb. 28, 1862, Library of Congress.) Heintzelman was a stiff old regular who had fought at Bull Run, and Sumner was even older and stiffer. He had a long service record in the Mexican War and in various frontier posts in the West. Keyes had been Winfield Scott's military secretary, and Wadsworth was a political general in whom McClellan had little confidence. For McClellan's attempts to get Stanton to suspend the order on corps commanders, see O.R., Vol. V, 739, 740–41.
9. Johnston's *Narrative*, 96–97, 101–6; Jubal Early, *Autobiographical Sketch and Narrative of the War between the States*, 53–55; O.R., Vol. V, 1086; Lieut. Col. W. W. Blackford, *War Years with Jeb Stuart*, 59–60; Dunbar Rowland, Vol. VI, 494.
10. Prince de Joinville, *The Army of the Potomac; Its Organization, Its Commander and Its Campaign*, 24.
11. Comte de Paris, *History of the Civil War in America*, Vol. I, 614; Moore's *Rebellion Record*, Vol. IV, Documents, 284–85, quoting a story in the Philadelphia *Inquirer;* notebook containing diary notes and letters of Rufus Dawes, in the Rufus Dawes Papers, courtesy of Rufus D. Beach of Evanston, Ill., and Ralph Newman of Chicago.
12. Basler, Vol. V, 155.
13. Ibid., 157–58.
14. McClellan's *Own Story*, 225. In

his copy of McClellan's book, now in the Oberlin College Library, McClellan's former subordinate in western Virginia, Gen. Jacob Cox, scribbled the marginal comment: "The hollowest of stuff!"

15. Letter of McClellan to Barlow dated at Washington March 16, 1862, in the Barlow Papers, Huntington Library.
16. *Congressional Globe*, 37th Congress, Second Session, Part IV, appendix, 14.
17. Barlow to Stanton, Dec. 11, 1861, in the Barlow Papers, Huntington Library.
18. *Diary of Edward Bates*, 239, 241.

CHAPTER FOUR: *Stride of a Giant*

1. The Ironclads

1. Thomas O. Selfridge, Jr., *Memoirs*, 44–45; H. Ashton Ramsay, *The Monitor and the Merrimac*, 33; Recollections of the sinking of the *Cumberland*, in the Mss. log of Charles William Bishop, Historical Manuscripts Division, Yale University Library; Indianapolis *Sunday Star* for March 20, 1929, printing letter of William Reeder of Company A, 20th Indiana Infantry, describing the sinking of the *Cumberland*.
2. Capt. Catesby ap R. Jones, *Services of the Virginia*, Southern Historical Society Papers, Vol. XI, 65–67; letter of J. L. Porter, constructor, reprinted in the Charleston *Courier* for March 19, 1862, from an earlier issue of the Petersburg *Express;* S. B. Besse, C.S. *Ironclad Virginia, with Data and References for a Scale Model*, 10–13.
3. D.A.B., Vol. III, 206; Charles Lee Lewis, *Admiral Franklin Buchanan*, 184–85; Catesby ap R. Jones, loc. cit.; letter of Buchanan to Mallory dated March 19, 1862, in the Franklin Buchanan Letter Book, Southern Historical Collection, University of North Carolina.
4. Testimony of Gustavus V. Fox in C.C.W. Reports, 1863, Part III, 415; Thomas W. Selfridge, Jr., *The Story of the Cumberland*, Papers of the Military Historical Society of Massachusetts, Vol. XII, 118–20; Mss. log of Charles William Bishop, Yale University Library.
5. Log of Charles William Bishop; Selfridge, op. cit., 123–25; Jones, *Services of the Virginia*, 68–69.
6. H. Ashton Ramsay, op. cit., 34–40; report of Franklin Buchanan, N.O.R., Vol. VII, 41, 44–49; Israel N. Stiles, *The Merrimac and the Monitor*, in *Military Essays and Recollections*, Vol. I, 128.
7. Joseph T. Durkin, *Stephen R. Mallory*, 150; N.O.R., Series Two, Vol. I, 743; John Ericsson, *The Building of the Monitor*, B. & L., Vol. I, 730 ff.; S. B. Besse, U.S. *Ironclad Monitor, with Data and References for a Scale Model*, Mariners' Museum, Newport News, Va.
8. E. B. Potter, *The United States and World Sea Power*, 325–27;

Lieut. S. D. Greene, *In the Monitor Turret*, B. & L., Vol. I. 719 ff.; Ramsay, op. cit., 51–52; N.O.R., Vol. VII, 11, 25; letter of Harry van Brunt, son of Captain Van Brunt, in the Papers of the Massachusetts Commandery, Military Order of the Loyal Legion of the United States, Houghton Library, Harvard.

9. N.O.R., Vol. VII, 27, 78, 100; Frank M. Bennett, *The Steam Navy of the United States*, Vol. I, 307; letter of Lieut. Greene dated March 14, 1862, in the Dana Papers, Massachusetts Historical Society.

2. *The Vulture and the Wolf*

1. Letter of Braxton Bragg to Mrs. Bragg dated March 20, 1862, in the Manuscript Department, Duke University Library. His reference to the evils of universal suffrage is in O.R., Vol. X, Part One, 464.
2. Letter of Mrs. Bragg dated March 12, 1862, in the Eugene C. Barker Texas History Center, University of Texas.
3. O.R., Vol. X, Part One, 463.
4. Walter Lee Brown, "Pea Ridge: Gettysburg of the West," *Arkansas Historical Quarterly*, Vol. XV, No. One, 3–5; William Preston Johnston, 523; O.R., Vol. VIII, 750–52; Gen. D. H. Maury, *Recollections of the Elkhorn Campaign*, Southern Historical Society Papers, Vol. II, No. Four, 180–85; letter of Jefferson Davis to Victor Rose dated Oct. 23, 1883, in the Lawrence Sullivan Ross Letters, the Eugene C. Barker Texas History Center.
5. O.R., Vol. VIII, 755; Wiley Britton, *Union and Confederate Indians in the Civil War*, B. & L., Vol. I, 335–36.
6. Letter of Gen. Curtis to his brother dated Feb. 25, 1862, in the Samuel Ryan Curtis Letters, Huntington Library; O.R., Vol. VIII, 502, 503; D.A.B., Vol. IV, 619–20; Edward A. Blodgett, "The Army of the Southwest and the Battle of Pea Ridge," *Military Essays and Recollections*, Vol. II, 298–99. There is a good account of the army's march by Samuel Prentis Curtis, the general's son and aide, "The Army of the Southwest on the First Campaign in Arkansas," in *The Annals of Iowa*, Vol. IV to Vol. VI.
7. Blodgett, op. cit., 301–9; Gen. Franz Sigel, *The Pea Ridge Campaign*, B. & L., Vol. I, 314–34; John W. Noble, *Battle of Pea Ridge or Elkhorn Tavern*, in War Papers of the Missouri Commandery, Military Order of the Loyal Legion of the United States, Vol. I, 224–42; O.R., Vol. VIII, 206, 285.
8. Letter of Gen. Curtis dated March 13, 1862, in the Samuel Ryan Curtis Papers, Huntington Library.
9. O.R., Vol. X, Part Two, 354, 365, 370–71; William Preston Johnston, 584, 552–53. For an excellent study of Johnston's plans and achievements in the six weeks before Shiloh see Charles P. Roland, *Albert Sidney Johnston and the Shiloh Campaign*, Civil War History, Dec., 1958.
10. William Preston Johnston, 551.

3. *Pittsburg Landing*

1. The circumstances surrounding Beauregard's drafting of the plan of attack are discussed in Roland, op. cit., and in Thomas Jordan, *Recollections of General Beauregard's Service in West Tennessee in the Spring of 1862,* Southern Historical Society Papers, Vol. VIII, August and September, 1880, 404–17. Stanley Horn, *The Army of Tennessee,* 104 ff.; T. Harry Williams, *Beauregard: Napoleon in Gray,* 113 ff.; G. T. Beauregard, *The Campaign of Shiloh,* B. & L., Vol. I, 579–81. A telegram from Johnston to President Davis announcing a corps formation unlike the one actually used is in William Preston Johnston, 554.
2. Jordan, op. cit., 410–11, 414; William Preston Johnston, 561, 568–71; Dunbar Rowland, Vol. V, 227.
3. The attitude is well illustrated by Grant's dispatch to Halleck dated March 21 in O.R., Vol. X, Part Two, 55.
4. Ibid., 93–94; Joseph W. Rich, *The Battle of Shiloh,* 40–41; Ephraim C. Dawes, *The Battle of Shiloh,* Papers of the Military Historical Society of Massachusetts, Vol. VII, 115–16.
5. John G. Biel, ed., *The Battle of Shiloh from the Letters and Diary of Joseph Dimmit Thompson,* Tennessee Historical Quarterly, Vol. XVII, No. Three, 255–56.
6. Beauregard's report on Shiloh, O.R., Vol. X, Part One, 386; Lloyd Lewis, *Sherman, Fighting Prophet,* 232.
7. Diary of A. H. Mecklin, Mississippi Department of Archives and History, Jackson; William Preston Johnston, 569; A. D. Kirwan, ed., *Johnny Green of the Orphan Brigade: the Journal of a Confederate Soldier,* 25.
8. O.R., Vol. X, Part One, 408; letter of Stephen Ellis dated April 11, 1862, in the Department of Archives, Louisiana State University.
9. Letter of Jeff D. Bradford to "My Dear Aunt," dated April 22, 1862, in the Confederate Memorial Literary Society, Richmond.
10. Letter of W. A. Howard, 33rd Tennessee, to Mrs. Howard dated April 11, 1862, in the collection of the Shiloh National Military Park.
11. William Preston Johnston, 613–15.
12. The effect of Johnston's death has been discussed in detail for a century, and the general opinion is that the Confederates would have lost the battle even if he had lived. It may be worth noting that both Polk and Bragg held an opposite view. In his report on Shiloh Polk wrote that when Johnston died "the field was clear; the rest of the forces of the enemy were driven to the river and under its banks. We had one hour or more of daylight still left; were within 150 to 400 yards of the enemy's position, and nothing seemed wanting to complete the most brilliant victory of the war but to press forward and make a vigorous assault on the demoralized remnant of his forces." Bragg's report asserted that "at the moment of this irreparable disaster the plan of battle was being rapidly and successfully executed . . . Great delay oc-

curred after this misfortune, and that delay prevented the consummation of the work so gallantly and successfully begun and carried on until the approach of night induced our new commander to recall the exhausted troops for rest and recuperation." (O.R., Vol. X, Part One, 410, 469–70.)

13. Diary of A. H. Mecklin, cited in Note 7, above.
14. *Johnny Green of the Orphan Brigade*, 28–29; Charles James Johnson Papers, Department of Archives, Louisiana State University; letter of Braxton Bragg, dated April 8, in the Braxton Bragg Papers, Missouri Historical Society.
15. Livermore, *Numbers and Losses in the Civil War*, 79–80, gives fairly accurate figures. He puts Federal casualties at 1754 killed, 8408 wounded, and 2885 missing, for a total of 13,047; Confederate casualties are given as 1723 killed, 8012 wounded, and 959 missing, for a total of 10,694. The armies at Bull Run numbered about 30,000 each, and those at Shiloh were approximately 40,000 each. It should be added, of course, that a much higher percentage of each army was put into action at Shiloh.

4. *Threat to New Orleans*

1. There is a good summary of the operation in John Fiske, *The Mississippi Valley in the Civil War*, 101–7. Pope discussed his campaign against New Madrid in the C.C.W. Supplemental Report, 1866, Part II, 23–24. For Foote's misgivings about Island Number Ten see N.O.R., Vol. XXII, 695–97.
2. There is an engaging account of the creation of this waterway written by Col. J. W. Bissell, *Sawing out the Channel Above Island Number Ten*, in B. & L., Vol. I, 460–62.
3. N.O.R., Vol. XXII, 703.
4. Walke tells about all of this in *The Western Flotilla at Fort Donelson, Island Number Ten, Fort Pillow and Memphis*, in B. & L., Vol. I, 442–45. To "splice the main brace" was of course to give all hands a drink.
5. Letter of Foote to Secretary Welles dated Nov. 13, 1862, in the Gideon Welles Papers, Huntington Library.
6. Alfred Roman, *The Military Operations of General Beauregard*, Vol. I, 358; O.R., Vol. VIII, 809.
7. Ibid., 757, 793.
8. O.R., Vol. VI, 827. Confederate spies were sending such full reports of Federal preparations in St. Louis that the Confederate Navy Department was convinced that the main effort against New Orleans was coming from the north. (Joseph T. Durkin, *Stephen R. Mallory*, 203.)
9. O.R., Vol. VI, 610–11.
10. Construction of the forts is described by Ernest Adam Landry, "*The History of Forts Jackson and St. Philip with Special Emphasis on the Civil War Period*," a thesis written for the History Department of Louisiana State University and made available by the Historian's Office, Adjutant General's Department, Jackson

Barracks, La. For Gen. Mansfield Lovell's comment on the weakness of the guns, see O.R., Vol. VI, 512. Admiral A. T. Mahan draws attention to this point in *Gulf and Inland Waters*, 58–59.

11. Farragut's letter to Secretary Welles dated Dec. 7, 1869, in the Gideon Welles Papers, Huntington Library; Loyall Farragut, *The Life of David Glasgow Farragut*, 219–20.
12. Loyall Farragut, 218.

5. *Fire on the Waters*

1. Lovell's testimony at the Court of Inquiry on the loss of New Orleans, O.R., Vol. VI, 558–59.
2. Ibid., 564; Roman, *Military Operations of Gen. Beauregard*, Vol. I, 153–54.
3. O.R., Vol. VI, 847.
4. Pamphlet, "Correspondence between the War Department and General Lovell relating to the Defenses of New Orleans, submitted in response to a resolution of the House of Representatives passed third February, 1863; and Correspondence between the President, War Department and Gov. T. O. Moore," 105–9; in the Beauregard Papers, Special Collection, Columbia University Library. See also testimony of Nelson Tift, N.O.R., Series Two, Vol. I, 532–38, 546–49.
5. Pamphlet cited in Note 4, above, 114–15; O.R., Vol. VI, 572, 612–13, 811–12.
6. Durkin, *Stephen Mallory*, 206; O.R., Vol. VI, 865, 877.
7. Loyall Farragut, 212; Diary of Oscar Smith, U.S.M.C., in the Manuscript Division, Library of Congress.
8. Welles to Farragut, Jan. 20, 1862, in N.O.R., Vol. XVIII, 7–8.
9. Ibid., 48–49.
10. *Confidential Correspondence of Gustavus V. Fox*, Vol. II, 89–90, 97.
11. See *Butler's Book*, 358; Farragut's report of April 21, in N.O.R., Vol. XVIII, 135; Loyall Farragut, 219. In N.O.R., Vol. XVIII, 372, Porter is credited with firing 7500 shell at Fort Jackson; in *The Opening of the Lower Mississippi*, B. & L., Vol. II, 38, Porter says he fired 16,800.
12. Private diary of Commander Henry Bell in N.O.R., Vol. XVIII, 694–96; George S. Bacon, "*One Night's Work, April 20, 1862*," *Magazine of American History*, March 1886, 305–7; Lewis, *David Glasgow Farragut, Our First Admiral*, 55.
13. *Butler's Book*, 366; letter of Capt. Craven in N.O.R., Vol. XVIII, 198; Farragut's report of April 25, ibid., 154; Diary of Oscar Smith, cited in Note 7, above.
14. N.O.R., op. cit., 152, 177–80. There are a number of graphic accounts of the fighting in B. & L., Vol. II, 22–91. For a general description of the entire campaign, Charles L. Dufour's *The Night the War Was Lost* is warmly recommended.
15. Lovell's testimony at the Court of Inquiry, O.R., Vol. VI, 564.
16. Farragut to Mrs. Farragut, April 25, in the Farragut Papers, David H. Annan Collection.
17. N.O.R., Series Two, Vol. I, 440; O.R., Vol. VI, 608.

6. *Brilliant Victory*

1. *The United Service Magazine*, London, February 1864, cited in J. G. Barnard, *The Peninsular Campaign*, 74–75; Swinton, *Campaigns of the Army of the Potomac*, 99–100; Prince de Joinville, *The Army of the Potomac*, 33–34; O.R., Vol. XI, Part One, 158.
2. Stanton's Act, which certainly must rank as one of the big blunders of the war, was only in part due to overoptimism. He wanted to reorganize the recruiting service–a badly needed reform–and planned to reopen it a bit later. See O.R., Series Three, Vol. II, 2–3, 29; Benjamin P. Thomas and Harold M. Hyman, *Stanton: the Life and Times of Lincoln's Secretary of War*, 201–2.
3. Jacob Cox, *Military Reminiscences of the Civil War*, Vol. I, 265–66; report of Charles S. Tripler, Medical Director, Army of the Potomac, O.R., Vol. XI, Part One, 206–7.
4. D.A.B., Vol. XVII, 106–7; James F. Huntington, *Operations in the Shenandoah Valley*, Papers of the Military Historical Society of Massachusetts, Vol. I, 304; Benjamin P. Thomas, *Abraham Lincoln*, 81–85.
5. Joseph E. Johnston, *Narrative of Military Operations*, 106–7; O.R., Vol. XII, Part Three, 836.
6. O.R., Vol. XII, Part One, 337, 343, 383–84.
7. O.R., Vol. XI, Part Three, 53; Nicolay & Hay, Vol V, 180; Mss. note, Stanton to Lincoln dated March 30, 1862, in the Stanton Papers, Library of Congress.
8. Basler, Vol. V, 184–85; O.R., Vol. XII, Part Three, 16.
9. Basler, Vol. V, 179; O.R., Vol. XI, Part Three, 66.
10. O.R., Vol. XI, Part Three, 76–77; Basler, Vol. V, 182. The interesting part about these messages is that McClellan gave the lower estimate to Wool rather than to Lincoln. If he had been purposely understating his strength in order to get reinforcements, he would of course have given Lincoln the lower figure.
11. Reports and letters of "E. Allen," in the Report and Letter Book of Allan Pinkerton, the Pinkerton Papers, Library of Congress; quoted by permission of Dr. D. F. Boyce, assistant secretary and assistant treasurer, Pinkerton National Detective Agency, 100 Church Street, New York.
12. O.R., Vol. XI, Part One, 268–70.
13. O.R., Vol. V, 57–58.
14. N.O.R., Vol. VII, 99–100; O.R., Vol. XI, Part Three, 63, 67; James Russell Soley, *The Navy in the Peninsular Campaign*, B. & L., Vol. II, 264–66; Alexander S. Webb, *The Peninsula*, 38–41.
15. Aeronautic Report by T. S. C. Lowe, Record Group 94, A. G. O. Checklist entry 126, National Archives.
16. O.R., Vol. XI, Part Three, 68, 71–72; John G. Palfrey, *The Siege of Yorktown*, Papers of the Military Historical Society of Massachusetts, Vol. I, 144–45; Barnard, *The Peninsular Campaign*, 20–22.
17. O.R., Vol. XI, Part One, 272–74, 538–50; George B. McClellan, *Report on the Organization and Campaigns of the Army of the Potomac*, 159, 162–64.

18. McDowell's testimony before the Committee on the Conduct of the War; C.C.W. Reports, 1863, Part I, 260–62.

19. O.R., Vol. XI, Part Three, 71, 74; Webb, op. cit., 60–62; Basler, Vol. V, 226; Prince de Joinville, *The Army of the Potomac*, 47.

CHAPTER FIVE: *Turning Point*

1. The Signs of the Times

1. O.R., Vol. XI, Part Three, 134–35.
2. Livermore, *Numbers and Losses*, 80–81, puts Union casualties at 2239 out of an estimated 40,000 engaged, and says the Confederates had an effective strength of 31,823 and losses of 1703.
3. Letter of Capt. Wilson Barstow to his sister, Mrs. Richard Henry Stoddard, dated May 12, 1862, in the Wilson Barstow Papers, Manuscript Division, Library of Congress; Assistant Secretary of War John Tucker to Secretary Stanton from Fort Monroe, May 13, 1862, Stanton Papers, Library of Congress; O.R., Vol. XI, Part Three, 160, 164.
4. O.R., Vol. XI, Part Three, 145–46, 148–49.
5. Basler, Vol. V, 185.
6. McClellan to Mrs. McClellan dated May 8, 1862, McClellan Letterbook, Library of Congress.
7. Letter of Barlow to McClellan dated April 14, 1862; letter of Samuel Ward to Barlow, marked on verso "Apl/62" but otherwise undated; letter of Barlow to McClellan dated May 10, 1862; all in the Barlow Papers, Huntington Library.
8. Letter of Meagher to Barlow dated April 27, 1862, in the Barlow Papers.
9. Letter of August Belmont to Barlow dated April 27, 1862, in the Barlow Papers; letters of Fitz John Porter to Manton Marble, one written probably in April 1862, the other dated May 21, 1862, in the Manton Marble Papers, Library of Congress; letter of Capt. Wilson Barstow to his sister dated May 20, 1862, in the Barstow Papers, Library of Congress.
10. Letter of Benjamin Stark to Barlow dated April 13, 1862, in the Barlow Papers.
11. Basler, Vol. V, 222–23.
12. McClellan to Mrs. McClellan dated May 23, 1862, in the McClellan Letterbook.
13. O.R., Vol. XI, Part Three, 153–54.
14. William M. Robinson, *Naval Defense of Richmond*, in Civil War History, Vol. VII, No. Two, 167–75; N.O.R., Vol. VII, 356–71.
15. O.R., Vol. XI, Part Three, 150–51; Part One, 26–27.
16. O.R., Vol. XII, Part Three, 66.
17. O.R., Vol. XI, Part One, 27.
18. McClellan to Mrs. McClellan dated May 18, 1862, in the McClellan Letterbook.

2. Do It Quickly

1. For Johnston's proposal regarding an offensive, and Mr. Davis's

response, see O.R., Vol. XI, Part Three, 477, 485.

2. Freeman, *R. E. Lee*, Vol. II, 4–6.
3. Basler, Vol. V, 182; O.R., Vol. XII, Part Three, 865–66, 872; G. F. R. Henderson, *Stonewall Jackson and the American Civil War*, 223.
4. O.R., Vol. XI, Part Three, 477.
5. Toombs to Stephens dated May 17, 1862, in *The Correspondence of Robert Toombs, Alexander Stephens and Howell Cobb*, Annual Report of the American Historical Association for 1911, Vol. II, 594–96.
6. O.R., Vol. XII, Part Three, 142, 149–50, 152.
7. Lee to Jackson, May 6, 1862, in the Headquarters Telegraph Book, Lee Headquarters Papers, Virginia State Historical Society.
8. O.R., Vol. XII, Part One, 462–65, 470, 472–73. According to Gen. Schenck, who says the battle was a delaying action to cover a retreat, the Federal force actually engaged was 2268. Jed Hotchkiss, *Virginia*, in Confederate Military History, Vol. III, 232, says about 4500 Confederates got into action.
9. Edwin E. Marvin, *The Fifth Regiment Connecticut Volunteers*, 97; Milo M. Quaife, ed., *From the Cannon's Mouth: the Civil War Letters of General Alpheus Williams*, 73–74; O.R., Vol. XII, Part Three, 154; Part One, 524–25.
10. Col. John M. Patton, *Reminiscences of Jackson's Infantry*, Southern Historical Society Papers, Vol. VIII, No. Three, 140–41; Jed Hotchkiss, in *Confederate Military History*, Vol. III, 232–40.
11. Mary Anna Jackson, *Life and Letters of General Thomas J. Jackson*, 261–62. General Alpheus Williams (Quaife, op. cit., 78–87) gives a graphic account of the Federal retreat.
12. B. T. Johnson, *Memoirs of the First Maryland Regiment*, 99–100.
13. O.R., Vol. XII, Part Three, 219–21; Basler, Vol. V, 235–36.
14. James F. Huntington, *Operations in the Shenandoah Valley*, 321–22.

3. *The Last Struggle*

1. O.R., Series Three, Vol. II, 44, 70, 109; Thomas and Hyman, *Stanton*, 196. Actually, the War Department telegraphed the Northern governors on May 19, several days before Jackson's spectacular victories in the Front Royal-Winchester area, warning that additional volunteer regiments would be wanted and asking how long it would take the governors to raise and organize them.
2. Jed Hotchkiss in Confederate Military History, Vol. III, 247–52; Huntington, *Operations in the Shenandoah Valley*, 322–26. For Lincoln's orders during this period see Basler, Vol. V, 230–36, 243, 247–51.
3. O.R., Vol. XI, Part One, 32, 33, 35, 37; Fitz John Porter, *Hanover Court House and Gaines's Mill*, B. & L., Vol. II, 319. McClellan's statement of May 25, that his troops north of the Chickahominy were ready to cross as soon as the bridges were completed, disposes of his later argument that he was compelled to hold them there in order to extend a welcome to McDowell.

4. Typescript of letters of C. I. Walker to Miss Ada Oriana Sinclair, dated April 26 and May 10, 1862, in the Eugene C. Barker Texas History Center.
5. Halleck seems to have had reservations about Grant from the beginning, and after Fort Donelson he criticized him so sharply that Grant asked to be relieved of his command; the situation was smoothed out only after Washington intervened in Grant's favor. Details are set forth in this writer's *Grant Moves South*, 186–208.
6. Alfred Roman, *Military Operations of General Beauregard*, Vol. I, 383–90; O.R., Vol. X, Part One, 668–69.
7. After the war Pope tried in vain to get Halleck to set the record straight. His indignant correspondence with Halleck is in O.R., Vol. X, Part Two, 635–36. For his original report, see Part One of that volume, 249.
8. Stanley Horn, *The Army of Tennessee*, 153–54; O.R., Vol. X, Part One, 775–79.
9. Letter of July 12, 1862, signed "G. T. Buenavista," a code name sometimes used by Beauregard in writing to Gen. Jordan; in the Beauregard Papers, Manuscript Department, Duke University Library.
10. Letter of Sumner to R. H. Dana dated May 26, 1862, in the Dana Papers, Massachusetts Historical Society.
11. Correspondence of the Cincinnati *Commercial*, reprinted in Moore's *Rebellion Record*, Vol. V, Documents, 88; Drury L. Armistead, *The Battle in which General Johnston Was Wounded*, Southern Historical Society Papers, Vol. VIII, 186; Francis W. Palfrey, *After the Fall of Yorktown*, Papers of the Military Historical Society of Massachusetts, Vol. I, 176.
12. Davis, *Rise and Fall*, Vol. II, 119–20; Johnston, *Narrative of Military Operations*, 131–32; Steele, *American Campaigns*, Vol. I, 97–98, 104; John B. Gordon, *Reminiscences of the Civil War*, 57; Alexander S. Webb, *The Peninsula*, 97–117; Palfrey, *After the Fall of Yorktown*, 174–205; J. G. Barnard, *The Peninsular Campaign*, 28–29. In *Lee's Lieutenants* (Vol. I, 225–63) Freeman examines the botched Confederate attack in detail and concludes that most of the blame must go to General Longstreet. E. P. Alexander, *Military Memoirs of a Confederate*, 79, 93, remarks that Johnston seemed utterly incapable of handling the army in battle.
13. The figures are from O.R., Vol. XI, Part One, 762, and Livermore, *Numbers and Losses*, 81.

4. *Railroad to the Pamunkey*

1. General Orders No. 13, issued by D. H. Hill on June 26, 1862, original in the Eldredge Collection, Huntington Library; letter of Ed. M. Burrus dated June 14, in the John C. Burrus and Family Papers, George Lester Collection, Department of Archives, Louisiana State University; post-war letter of Longstreet to Jefferson Davis in Dunbar Rowland, Vol. IX, 594–95.

2. Davis to Mrs. Davis, June 11, 1862, in Rowland, Vol. V, 272.
3. Letter of Jackson to Lee from Mount Meridian, June 13, 1862, bearing Lee's note and Davis's endorsement; in the R. E. Lee Papers, Manuscript Department, Duke University Library.
4. An excellent account of Stuart's ride is in H. B. McClellan, *I Rode with Jeb Stuart*, 52 ff. For a good appraisal of what the raid accomplished see John W. Thomason, Jr., *Jeb Stuart*, 153–55.
5. Basler, Vol. V, 276.
6. Rowland, Vol. V, 283–84; O.R., Vol. XI, Part One, 51.
7. Lincoln to Stanton, June 8, 1862, from the Lincoln File, John Hay Library, Brown University; Lincoln to Frémont, June 15, in Basler, Vol. V, 271.
8. There is a tabulation of reinforcements in K. P. Williams, *Lincoln Finds a General*, Vol. I, 216–17.
9. O.R., Vol. XI, Part One, 46–47; J. G. Barnard, *The Peninsular Campaign*, 32–34.
10. McClellan to Lincoln dated June 19, in the Stanton Papers, Library of Congress. As printed in O.R., Vol. XI, Part Three, 233, the letter bears the date of June 18.
11. Francis W. Palfrey, *The Seven Days Battles*, Military Historical Society of Massachusetts, Vol. I, 224–25; Prince de Joinville, *The Army of the Potomac*, 79–82; Diary and Letters of Capt. John Taggart, 9th Pennsylvania Reserve Infantry, Mss. in the Bureau of Research, Publications and Records, Pennsylvania Historical and Museum Commission.
12. O.R., Vol. XI, Part One, 49. This minor engagement is usually counted as the first of the Seven Days Battles.
13. Ibid., 272–74; Part Three, 355. After the campaign ended McClellan protested that he had not, before the Seven Days, been able to base his army on the James because Stanton on May 18 ordered him to prepare to meet McDowell on the Pamunkey. However, he had already established his base at White House when he received that order, and the order in any case became inoperative on May 25, when he was notified that McDowell was marching to the Shenandoah. There was plenty of time to make the change of base if he had wanted to do so.
14. O.R., Vol. XI, Part One, 49; McClellan's Report, 237.
15. O.R., Vol. XI, Part One, 51.
16. O.R., Vol. XI, Part Three, 254.

5. *Seven Days*

1. There are of course many good accounts of the opening of the Seven Days, the best probably being Freeman's, in *R. E. Lee*, Vol. II, 75–121. A good brief summary is in Steele, *American Campaigns*, Vol. I, 99. An oddity about the Seven Days is that they actually were only six—from June 26 to July 1, inclusive. Apparently most people in 1862 began the count with the engagement of June 25, when McClellan's skirmish line made a moderate advance south of the Chickahominy at Oak Grove.
2. O.R., Vol. XI, Part One, 405; Part Three, 455–56.
3. In his memorandum of a post-war conversation with Lee, Col. William Allan of the faculty of

Washington College reports Lee as saying that the attack at Mechanicsville was made "in order to occupy the enemy and prevent any counter movement." In the same way, according to Allan, Lee felt obliged to attack the next day at Gaines's Mill even though Jackson was not ready: "Otherwise, with a large part of his army really farther from Richd. than McClellan was, disaster was to be apprehended." In this account there is no criticism of A. P. Hill for his movements on the afternoon of June 26. The implication, at least, of Allan's version is that the move had Lee's approval. (Memorandum of Conversations of Lee with Col. William Allan: typescript in the Southern Historical Collection, University of North Carolina Library.) Hill's report on Mechanicsville, O.R., Vol. XI, Part Two, 834–36, says flatly: "Three o'clock having arrived, and no intelligence from Jackson . . . I determined to cross at once rather than hazard the failure of the whole plan by longer deferring it."

4. O.R., Vol. XI, Part Three, 257, 259, 260.
5. In McClellan's *Own Story*, 411, McClellan says that he "determined to resist Jackson . . . in the new position near the bridge heads, in order to cover the withdrawal of the trains and heavy guns and to give time for the arrangements to secure the adoption of the James River as our line of supplies in lieu of the Pamunkey." Col. Robert Tyler's account of the moving of the guns is in O.R., Vol. XI, Part One, 272–74. Kellogg's report is in Part Two, 969–72.
6. Letters of James L. Dinwiddie to his wife, dated June 29, 1862, in the Virginia State Library; Reminiscences of Berry G. Benson, 1st South Carolina Volunteers, in the Southern Historical Collection, University of North Carolina Library; diary of J. R. Boulware, 6th South Carolina Volunteers, entries for June 27 and June 28; in the Virginia State Library.
7. Letter of A. A. Humphreys to Mrs. Humphreys dated July 17, 1862, from Vol. 33, the A. A. Humphreys Papers, Historical Society of Pennsylvania. Humphreys wrote: "I was not in the battle on the north side of the Chickahominy nor was Genl. McClellan—we waited for him expecting any moment to mount."
8. Reminiscences of Berry G. Benson, cited in Footnote 6.
9. O.R., Vol. XI, Part Three, 264–66.
10. O.R., Vol. XI, Part One, 60–61; Part Three, 267.
11. O.R., Vol. XI, Part One, 61. It may be as well to remark that McClellan had seen none of the fighting at Gaines's Mill, and that the number of "dead and wounded comrades" he had actually beheld was strictly minimal.
12. McClellan's *Own Story*, 453; David Homer Bates, *Lincoln in the Telegraph Office*, 109–10. Senator Browning noted in mid-July that Lincoln told him he had approved all that Stanton had done in respect to the Army of the Potomac. Browning wrote:

"That immediately after Fitz Jno. Porter's fight McClellan telegraphed to Stanton in very harsh terms, charging him as the author of the disaster—that Stanton came to him with the telegram in his hand and said to him with much feeling 'You know—Mr. President that all I have done was by your authority." (*Diary of Orville Hickman Browning*, Vol. I, 558–59.) This story, of course, fits either the expurgated telegram or the original version.

13. Basler, Vol. V, 289–91; O.R., Vol. XVI, Part Two, 69–70; Vol. XI, Part Three, 270. Dix had been put in command at Fort Monroe early in June, and the former commander, General Wool, had been given Dix's former post at Baltimore.
14. O.R., Vol. XI, Part Three, 274–75, 277; Basler, Vol. V, 293, 295–96. This burst of optimism of course was quite groundless, but it did rest upon a correct appraisal of the possibilities that existed after Porter's corps crossed the Chickahominy. The last word Lincoln and Stanton had from McClellan had said nothing about a retreat; it simply talked of a move "to this side of the Chickahominy."
15. O.R., Vol. XI, Part Three, 280.
16. Alexander S. Webb, *The Peninsula*, 136–37; Prince de Joinville, *The Army of the Potomac*, 91.
17. The failure of Lee's battle plan is examined in detail in Freeman, *R. E. Lee*, Vol. II, 176–99. Jackson's strange failure to measure up to his responsibilities has perplexed all of his biographers, beginning with Col. Henderson; the riddle is most carefully studied in Lenoir Chambers *Stonewall Jackson*, Vol. II, 61–76. No one has ever been able to suggest anything much more definite than that Jackson was physically ailing and at the point of exhaustion—and that like everyone else at the time he was still learning his trade.

6. *Letter from Harrison's Landing*

1. Newspaper account dated July 2, 1862, in a scrapbook of unidentified clippings at the Huntington Library; letter of G. F. Newhall to his father dated July 4, 1862, in the Newhall Letters, Boston Public Library; McClellan's *Own Story*, 442.
2. Lee's report, O.R., Vol. XI, Part Two, 497; letter of Stephen Mallory to Mrs. Mallory, mis-dated May 13, 1862, in the Mallory Papers, Southern Historical Collection, University of North Carolina. Mallory was by no means the only man of that time who used the spelling "McClelland."
3. B. & L., Vol. II, 315, 317.
4. Letter of Beauregard to Thomas Jordan dated July 12, 1862, in the Beauregard Papers, Library of Congress.
5. O.R., Vol. XI, Part Three, 281, 287–88.
6. McClellan's *Own Story*, 483; O.R., Vol. XI, Part Three, 291–92.
7. Basler, Vol. V, 301.
8. O.R., Series Three, Vol. II, 45–46.
9. Basler, Vol. V, 292, 297; Fred Shannon, *Organization and Ad-*

ministration of the Union Army, Vol. I, 269–70.

10. O.R., Vol. XI, Part Three, 294, 298–99; Basler, Vol. V, 305–6.
11. McClellan to Mrs. McClellan, July 6, 1862, in the McClellan Letterbook; Lee to Davis, July 6, O.R., Vol. XI, Part Three, 634–35.
12. Warren W. Hassler, Jr., *General George B. McClellan*, 177–78: McClellan's *Own Story*, 487–89.
13. Two oddly contrasting views of Lincoln's reception by the troops are offered here for whatever they may be worth. A soldier named Felix Brannigan, whose letters are in the Manuscript Division of the Library of Congress, wrote home on July 16 telling about the review and saying: "Talk of McClellan's popularity among the soldiers. It will never measure the 1/100th part of Honest Old Abe's. Such cheers as greeted him never tickled the ears of Napoleon in his palmiest days." On July 17 McClellan, whose Letterbook is also in the Library of Congress, wrote to Mrs. McClellan that "a certain eminent individual is 'an old stick'–of pretty poor timber at that. . . . The army did *not* give him an enthusiastic reception–I had to order the men to cheer."
14. Basler, Vol. V, 309–12, 322. A slightly more detailed discussion of the home-state hospital situation is presented in this writer's *Glory Road*, 126–29.
15. Letter of Warren to his brother, July 20, 1862, in the G. K. Warren Papers, Manuscript and History Section, New York State Library, Albany. Warren's letter calls to mind the bitter outburst of the Abolitionist Congressman Owen Lovejoy, who told the House six months earlier: "We are afraid that we shall hurt somebody if we fight; that we shall get these rebels and traitors so exasperated that they will not return to their loyalty." (*Congressional Globe*, 37th Congress, Second Session, Part One, 194.)
16. McClellan to Mrs. McClellan, July 10, 1862, in the McClellan Letterbook.
17. McClellan to Mrs. McClellan, July 22, in the McClellan Letterbook.
18. Porter to Marble, June 20, in the Manton Marble Papers, Library of Congress; Webb to his father, August 14, in the Alexander Stewart Webb Collection, Historical Manuscript Division, Yale University Library.
19. Letter to Mrs. McClellan dated July 11, and an undated letter to her written late in July or early in August 1862; in the McClellan Letterbook.
20. McClellan to Mrs. McClellan dated July 17, July 18, and July 27, in the McClellan Letterbook. It should be remembered that W. C. Prime, the editor of McClellan's *Own Story*, either omitted or sharply expurgated the most revealing of the letters when he assembled his book.
21. McClellan to Barlow, July 15, in the Barlow Papers, Huntington Library.
22. McClellan to Mrs. McClellan, July 13, in the McClellan Letterbook.

CHAPTER SIX: *Unlimited War*

1. Trade with the Enemy

1. Thomas E. Taylor, *Running the Blockade*, 23, 69; James Morris Morgan, *Recollections of a Rebel Reefer*, 99; J. Wilkinson, *The Narrative of a Blockade Runner*, 123–24; Augustus Charles Hobart-Hampden, *Hobart Pasha: Blockade Running, Slaver-Hunting and War and Sport in Turkey*, 119–23.
2. Taylor, *Running the Blockade*, 11–14; F. B. C. Bradlee, *Blockade Running During the Civil War*, 29–30; Frank Lawrence Owsley, *King Cotton Diplomacy*, 285.
3. Taylor, op. cit., 12; James Sprunt, *Chronicles of the Cape Fear River*, 238–40; Bradlee, op. cit., 118–19.
4. *Diary of Gideon Welles*, Vol. II, 127.
5. Wilkinson, *The Narrative of a Blockade Runner*, 199–202; Sprunt, *Chronicles of the Cape Fear River*, 243–44, 246, 252.
6. C.C.W. Report for 1863, Part III, 611–12.
7. *American Annual Cyclopaedia, 1862*, 765; Joseph H. Parks, "A Confederate Trade Center under Federal Occupation," *Journal of Southern History*, Vol. VII, Number Three, 289–94; O.R., Vol. XVII, Part Two, 123, 140.
8. *Memoirs of William T. Sherman*, Vol. I, 265–68; O.R., Vol. XVII, Part Two, 150; Series Three, Vol. II, 349–50.
9. O.R., Vol. VI, 873–74; Series Four, Vol. II, 151, 173–75.
10. O.R., Vol. XVII, Part Two, 839–40.
11. Ella Lonn, *Salt as a Factor in the Confederacy*, 14–50; Letter of G. S. Denison, Acting Collector and Surveyor for the Port of New Orleans, to Secretary Chase, Nov. 29, 1862, from *Diary and Correspondence of Salmon P. Chase*, Annual Report of the American Historical Association for the Year 1902, Vol. II, 336.
12. O.R., Vol. XVII, Part Two, 179, 186; M. A. DeWolfe Howe, ed., *Home Letters of General Sherman*, 232.
13. Moore's *Rebellion Record*, Vol. VI, Documents, 291–92.
14. *Diary and Correspondence of Salmon P. Chase*, 312–13, 321–24, 346. In his voluminous reports to Secretary Chase, Collector Denison was highly critical of the things that happened in New Orleans but he never quite believed that General Butler was personally dishonest and he greatly respected his administrative ability. He remarked finally that Butler "has great ability, great energy, shrewdness and activity, but he can never acquire a character here for disinterestedness."
15. J. B. Jones, *A Rebel War Clerk's Diary*, ed. by Earl Schenck Miers, 55; O.R., Series Four, Vol. II, 301–2, 334–35.
16. O.R., Series Four, Vol. III, 645–48; "Trade with the Rebellious States," House of Representatives Report No. 24, the Joint Committee on Commerce, 38th Congress, Second Session, 1–3.

2. *The Ultimate Meaning*

1. Letter of John Nicolay to Therena dated July 13, 1862, in the Nicolay Papers, Library of Congress; letter of Attorney General Bates to James B. Eads dated Aug. 2, in the James B. Eads Papers, Missouri Historical Society; letter of Thomas Scott to S. L. M. Barlow dated July 31, in the Barlow Papers.
2. *Congressional Globe*, 37th Congress, Second Session, Appendix, 412–13; Basler, Vol. V, 328–30. For an analysis of the act, see James G. Randall, *Constitutional Problems Under Lincoln*, 358–63. The act was puzzling to army officers. W. T. Sherman was anxious to send fugitive slaves to St. Louis, where the Quartermaster badly needed laborers, and he wrote: "By inviting Negroes to come in, by providing for their families and by providing all with free papers, we could send north any number of slaves, but I would prefer to send none away until after they are declared *free* by a court of competent jurisdiction." (Letter to Capt. Lewis B. Parsons, dated Aug. 30, 1862, in the Parsons Papers, Illinois State Library, Springfield.)
3. Basler, Vol. V, 317–19.
4. Ibid., 342–43, 344–46; F. B. Carpenter, *Six Months in the White House*, 13.
5. Basler, Vol. V, 336–37. An endorsement on the text reads "Emancipation Proclamation as first sketched and shown to the cabinet in July 1862." According to one account, Vice-President Hannibal Hamlin was shown a draft of the proclamation more than a month before the cabinet meeting. Lincoln is said to have invited Hamlin to dinner on the night of June 18, to have read the draft aloud, and to have accepted some of Hamlin's suggestions regarding it. (Charles Eugene Hamlin, *The Life and Times of Hannibal Hamlin*, 428–29.)
6. *Diary of Gideon Welles*, Vol. I, 70–71; Nicolay & Hay, Vol. VI, 125–27; Carpenter, op. cit., 13–15; letter of Secretary Chase to Bishop B. B. Smith of Louisville dated June 24, 1862, in the Salmon P. Chase Papers, New York Public Library; *Diary and Correspondence of Salmon P. Chase*, Annual Report of the American Historical Association for the Year 1902, Vol. II, 48–49. In *The War for the Union*, Vol. II, 165, Allan Nevins shows that Nicolay and Hay overstate the amount of opposition Lincoln met in the cabinet meeting. After the meeting Blair wrote Lincoln that he feared the measure would "depress our financial credit & would add to the enthusiasm of but a small portion of our people & that not the effective portion in war." (Letter of Montgomery Blair dated July 23, in the Blair Family Papers, Library of Congress.) As late as Aug. 10 Lincoln's friend Leonard Swett, who said that the President had talked frankly about his plans, predicted flatly: "He will issue no proclamation emancipating Negroes." (Letter of Swett to Mrs. Swett, in the David Davis Papers, Illinois State Historical Library.)
7. Moore's *Rebellion Record*, Vol. XII, Supplement, 480–83.

8. Basler, Vol. V, 388–89.
9. Ibid., 419–25.
10. Cincinnati *Commercial* for July 11, 1862.
11. New York *Tribune* for Aug. 15, 1862.

3. *A Long and Strong Flood*

1. After his retreat to Tupelo Beauregard wrote that for the immediate future military operations would depend largely on the enemy's movements: "Should he divide his forces, the offensive must be taken as soon as the condition of our troops and our means of transportation will permit." (O.R., Vol. X, Part One, 775.)
2. Basler, Vol. V, 322; O.R., Vol. XVI, Part Two, 143.
3. O.R., Vol. XVI, Part One, 767–70, 792–93, 796–97, 810–11; Stanley Horn, *The Army of Tennessee*, 160–61.
4. One of the oldest Civil War controversies concerns the orders under which Buell moved. Buell argued that Halleck required him to repair and use the Memphis & Charleston line and said that this was chiefly responsible for the delay. In substance, Buell's point was upheld by the Buell Court of Inquiry (whose hearings and findings are recorded in O.R., Vol. XVI, Part One, 6–726); it is set forth in Henry M. Cist, *The Army of the Cumberland*, 40–42. Kenneth P. Williams sharply attacks this thesis (*Lincoln Finds a General*, Vol. IV, 27) and it is even more strongly criticized by George Bruce in *General Buell's Campaign Against Chattanooga*, Papers of the Military Historical Society of Massachusetts, Vol. VIII, 101–22. An interesting account of the march is Capt. Ephraim A. Otis, *Recollections of the Kentucky Campaign of 1862*, also in the Papers of the Military Historical Society of Massachusetts, Vol. VII, 232–36.
5. A. T. Mahan, *The Gulf and Inland Waters*, 90–96; F. V. Greene, *The Mississippi*, 20–23; letter of Welles to Farragut dated May 19, 1862, in the Farragut Papers, David H. Annan Collection.
6. Isaac N. Brown, *The Confederate Gunboat Arkansas*, B. & L., Vol. III, 572–76; C. W. Read, *Reminiscences of the Confederate States Navy*, Southern Historical Society Papers, Vol. I, 349–55; Mahan, op. cit., 98–103.
7. N.O.R., Vol. XIX, 4–5, 19; Charles Lee Lewis, *David Glasgow Farragut, Our First Admiral*, Vol. II, 117–18, 121.
8. Letter of Mrs. Bragg to General Bragg, undated but written in the spring of 1862, in the collection of her letters in the Eugene C. Barker Texas History Center, University of Texas.
9. Letter of C. I. Walker to Miss Ada Oriana Sinclair, dated June 2, 1862, in the C. I. Walker Civil War Letters, typescript in the Eugene C. Barker Texas History Center; Richard Taylor, *Destruction and Reconstruction*, 117; letter of Gen. Bragg to Mrs. Bragg dated July 22, 1862, in the Braxton Bragg Papers, Missouri Historical Society.
10. O.R., Vol. XVI, Part Two, 709–10, 713, 727, 730.

11. There is an excellent study of Bragg's move in Grady McWhiney, *Controversy in Kentucky: Braxton Bragg's Campaign of 1862,* Civil War History, Vol. VI, Number One. See also Robert C. Black, *The Railroads of the Confederacy,* 180–84.

4. *Triumph in Disaster*

1. O.R., Series Four, Vol. II, 34.
2. O.R., Vol. XII, Part Two, 51–52; Part Three, 435, 437, 444, 473–74, 495.
3. Dunbar Rowland, Vol. V, 320–25.
4. Letter of James Gillette, commissary officer in Pope's army, dated July 31, 1862; notes in the possession of Allan Nevins. See also Charles F. Walcott, *History of the 21st Regiment Massachusetts Volunteer Infantry,* 128; Warren H. Cudworth, *History of the 1st Regiment Massachusetts Infantry,* 255; Joseph Keith Newell, *Ours: Annals of the 10th Regiment Massachusetts Volunteers in the Rebellion,* 136; James L. Bowen, *History of the 37th Regiment Massachusetts Volunteers in the Civil War of 1861–1865,* 92–93.
5. Diary of Betty Herndon Maury, entry for May 13, 1862, Manuscript Division, Library of Congress.
6. O.R., Vol. XI, Part Three, 295–96, 306.
7. *Diary and Correspondence of Salmon P. Chase,* Annual Report of the American Historical Association for the Year 1902, Vol. II, 46–47; letters of Fitz John Porter to J. C. G. Kennedy of Washington, dated July 17 and July 29, 1862, in the Fitz John Porter Papers, Massachusetts Historical Society.
8. O.R., Vol. VIII, 508–11.
9. McClellan to Barlow dated "Berkeley, Wednesday 23" (obviously of July 1862) in the Barlow Papers, Huntington Library; O.R., Vol. XI, Part Three, 345.
10. McClellan's *Own Story,* 490–91; O.R., Vol. XI, Part Three, 337–38, 359–60; Vol. XI, Part One, 80–81.
11. Pope's July 31 returns, O.R., Vol. XII, Part Three, 523; Lee's returns for July 20, O.R., Vol. XI, Part Three, 645.
12. *Lee's Dispatches,* 38–40.
13. O.R., Vol. XII, Part Three, 925–26.
14. Freeman, *Lee's Lieutenants,* Vol. II, 1–52; Edward J. Stackpole, *From Cedar Mountain to Antietam,* 55–78. Jackson's report on the battle is in O.R., Vol. XII, Part Two, 180–86; Pope's, 132–36.
15. O.R., Vol. XI, Part Three, 334, 372; Part One, 284.
16. Montgomery Meigs, memorandum on the relations of Lincoln and Stanton, in the Meigs Papers, Library of Congress. (Notes from Allan Nevins.)
17. Letter of Webb to his father dated Aug. 14, 1862, in the Alexander Stewart Webb Collection, Historical Manuscripts Division, Yale University Library.
18. McClellan to Barlow dated July 30, 1862, in the Barlow Papers; McClellan to Mrs. McClellan dated Aug. 21, in the McClellan Letterbook.

5. *The Pressures of War*

1. C. F. Adams, Jr., *Charles Francis Adams*, 240–49.
2. Letter of General Butler to Montgomery Blair dated May 8, 1862, in the Blair Family Papers, Manuscript Division, Library of Congress.
3. *Two Months in the Confederate States, Including a Visit to New Orleans Under the Domination of General Butler*, by an English Merchant, 28–30; Journal of Mrs. Robert Dow Urquhart, entry for May 2, 1862, in the Howard-Tilton Memorial Library Archives, Tulane University; Clara Solomon, *Diary of a New Orleans Girl*, 208, typescript in the Department of Archives, Louisiana State University. The case of the woman who was sent to Ship Island is discussed from Butler's point of view in James Parton, *General Butler in New Orleans*, 438–39; from the prisoner's point of view in Eugenia Phillips, *A Southern Woman's Story of her Imprisonment during the War of 1861–1862*, Manuscript Division, Library of Congress.
4. Butler wrote an interesting defense of his order in a letter to C. C. Garner of New York dated June 10, 1862, asserting: "Since that order, no man or woman has insulted a soldier of mine in New Orleans. And from the *first hour* of our landing, *no woman has complained of the conduct* of my soldiers toward her, nor has there been a single cause of complaint." (Courtesy of Ralph Newman of Chicago.)
5. C. F. Adams, Jr., op. cit., 250–60.
6. Cited in James Ford Rhodes, *History of the United States*, Vol. IV, 84.
7. James A. B. Scherer, *Cotton as a World Power*, 263–64, 267; C. F. Adams, Jr., 268–69.
8. James L. Watkins, *King Cotton: a Historical and Statistical Review, 1790 to 1908*, 19.
9. Dunbar Rowland, Vol. V, 338–39.
10. O.R., Series Four, Vol. I, 1156–69; Rowland, Vol. V, 292–93.
11. O.R., Series Four, Vol. I, 1127; N.O.R., Series Two, Vol. II, 243–44, 535.
12. O.R., Series Four, Vol. II, 881–83; Series Three, Vol. V, 1003; Charles W. Ramsdell, *Behind the Lines in the Southern Confederacy*, 94–98; Robert C. Black, *Railroads of the Confederacy*, 294–95.
13. Rowland, Vol. VIII, 42–43; *American Annual Cyclopaedia for 1863*, 205.
14. There is an excellent discussion of the Confederacy's financial problems in Ramsdell, op. cit., 7–14, 115–16. See also Emory Hawk, *Economic History of the South*, 400–5, 409–10.
15. Rowland, Vol. V, 209, 301–3, 342–43.
16. *DeBow's Review*, May–August, 1862, 77; Victor S. Clark, *History of Manufactures in the United States*, Vol. II, 52.

6. *Scabbard Thrown Away*

1. London *Times* for Aug. 5, 1862, bearing a story from New York dated July 22.
2. Fred A. Shannon, *The Organization and Administration of the Union Army, 1861–1865*, Vol. I, 275–77; O.R., Series Three, Vol.

V, 609; William B. Hesseltine, *Lincoln and the War Governors,* 201–2; Report of Secretary Stanton, *Congressional Globe,* 37th Congress, Third Session, Part Two, 28.
3. William E. Dodd, *Jefferson Davis,* 283; Rowland, Vol. V, 313; letter of W. T. Sherman to T. Ewing from Chewalla, Tenn., in the Ewing Family Papers, Library of Congress.
4. Chicago *Morning Post* for July 1, 1862, bearing a Memphis dispatch dated June 26; letter of E. L. Acee to Governor Pettus dated July 29, in the John J. Pettus Papers, Mississippi State Archives, Jackson, Miss.
5. Letter to August Belmont from a Dr. Mercer of New Orleans dated Aug. 22, 1862, copy in the Barlow Papers, autograph collection, Huntington Library.
6. Davis's ideas about the western campaign are presented in fair detail in a July 28 letter to Kirby Smith (Kirby Smith Papers, Southern Historical Collection, University of North Carolina) and an Aug. 5 dispatch to Bragg (Rowland, Vol. V, 313). The President believed that success against Buell would mean the recall of Grant's army.
7. O.R., Vol. XVI, Part One, 471. Perhaps the best succinct analysis of Bragg's campaign is Grady McWhiney, *Controversy in Kentucky,* Civil War History, Vol. VI, Number One, 11 ff.
8. W. L. Gammage, *The Camp, the Bivouac and the Battlefield; being a History of the Fourth Arkansas Regiment,* 38, 45–47; letter of Smith to Bragg from Lexington dated Sept. 3, 1862, in the Palmer Collection, Western Reserve Historical Society, Cleveland.
9. Robert S. Harper, *Ohio Handbook of the Civil War,* 25; "The Siege of Cincinnati," in the *Atlantic Monthly* for February 1863; O.R., Vol. XVI, Part Two, 524.
10. Arndt Stickles, *Simon Bolivar Buckner,* 201–3; O.R., Vol. XVI, Part One, 209–10, 967, 982.
11. Letter of Bragg to Mrs. Bragg from Munfordville dated Sept. 18, in the Braxton Bragg Papers, Missouri Historical Society; Journal of Captain W. L. Trask, in the possession of Mr. and Mrs. Gordon W. Trask of Oak Park, Ill.; O.R., Vol. XVI, Part One, 208, 961.
12. O.R., Vol. XVII, Part Two, 628, 667–68.
13. Letter of Smith to Bragg dated Sept. 23, in the Palmer Collection, Western Reserve Historical Society.
14. Journal of Capt. W. L. Trask, cited in Footnote 11: O.R., Vol. XVI, Part Two, 876.

CHAPTER SEVEN: *Thenceforward and Forever*

1. Recipe for Confusion

1. For a detailed study of Lee's moves between his departure from the peninsula and Pope's retirement behind the Rappahannock, the reader is referred to Freeman,

R. E. Lee, Vol. II, 259–90: also E. P. Alexander, *Military Memoirs of a Confederate*, 186–90.

2. There is a good time-table of the Army of the Potomac arrivals in Peter S. Michie, *General McClellan*, 383. See also O.R., Vol. XII, Part Two, 412; Part Three, 613–14, 617, 620.
3. Letter of Lee to Mrs. Lee dated Aug. 25, 1862, in the R. E. Lee Papers, Library of Congress.
4. Letter of Mallory to Mrs. Mallory dated Aug. 31, in the Stephen R. Mallory Papers, Southern Historical Collection, University of North Carolina.
5. O.R., Vol. XI, Part Three, 345–46, 359–60.
6. Ibid., 378–80.
7. O.R., Vol. XII, Part Three, 653.
8. Ibid., 684.
9. W. W. Blackford, *War Years with Jeb Stuart*, 121.
10. There is a good sketch of the Groveton fight in Edward J. Stackpole, *From Cedar Mountain to Antietam*, 158–63.

2. The Terrible Weariness

1. O.R., Vol. XII, Part Three, 704; Cecil D. Eby, Jr., ed., *A Virginia Yankee in the Civil War: the Diaries of David Hunter Strother*, 91–92.
2. The argument over Porter's inaction continues to this day. The dust cloud which caused him to halt was raised by Stuart's troopers, who worked hard to make Porter think exactly what he did think. Longstreet got his corps into position by noon or a little later, and when Pope at 4:30 P.M. peremptorily ordered Porter to attack Jackson's right flank such a move was wholly impossible. Porter was cashiered for his failure to obey this order; long after the war a Court of Inquiry reconsidered the case and exonerated him, and his commission as an army officer was returned to him. Pope unquestionably based his plan of battle on a misunderstanding of the real situation.

   At the same time it is hard to acquit Porter of having been an extremely reluctant dragon. General Lee noted the presence of Porter's corps some time before Longstreet's corps came up and directed Stuart to make a demonstration in order to prevent an attack—a fairly clear indication that energetic action by Porter in the middle of the morning would have harmed the Confederates. After the war, Lee remembered that Porter's troops were "peaceable looking" and said that he did not think them disposed to attack. (Memorandum by Col. William Allan of a conversation with General Lee on Feb. 18, 1870, in the Southern Historical Collection, University of North Carolina.) The case for Porter is energetically and exhaustively argued in Otto Eisenschiml's *The Celebrated Case of Fitz John Porter*. For an opposing viewpoint see K. P. Williams, *Lincoln Finds a General*, Vol. I, 324–30.

   There are interesting sidelights on the case in the John A. Logan Memorial Collection, Illinois State Historical Library, Springfield. In 1880, as a member of Congress, Logan made a speech opposing the attempt to exonerate General

Porter, and this collection contains six volumes of letters from former soldiers commending his speech. Written long after the event, when the case had become a hot political issue, the letters have only sketchy value as evidence, and yet their weight is rather impressive. They at least show that many hundreds of the men who fought at Bull Run felt in 1880 that Porter had willfully refused to join in the fight at a time when his help was greatly needed, and they deserve a critical examination.

3. Lee to Davis, Aug. 30, 1862, in *Lee's Dispatches*, 56–59.
4. Pope's aide, David H. Strother, wrote in his diary that on the night of August 29 "Pope was firmly of the opinion that Jackson was beaten and would get off during the night." It is interesting to note that Pope apparently realized that Longstreet's corps had arrived; on the morning of Aug. 30 he wrote Halleck that he had fought the previous day against "the combined forces of the enemy." He added: "The news just reaches me from the front that the enemy is retreating toward the mountains. I go forward at once to see." (*A Virginia Yankee in the Civil War*, 94; O.R., Vol. XII, Part Three, 741.)
5. Actually, the Army of Northern Virginia had not yet formally adopted the corps formation, and technically Longstreet commanded one wing of the army. To all intents and purposes, however, this was an army corps and it is so referred to in the text.
6. Brig. Gen. Charles F. Walcott, *The Battle of Chantilly: the Virginia Campaign of 1862 under Gen. Pope*, Papers of the Military Historical Society of Massachusetts, Vol. II, 143.
7. Letter from Frank Haskell to his brother dated Aug. 31, 1862, in the Haskell Papers, State Historical Society of Wisconsin, Madison.
8. Letter of John F. Sale, 12th Virginia Infantry, dated Jan. 31, 1863, in the Archives Division of the Virginia State Library, Richmond.
9. O.R., Vol. XIX, Part Two, 590; memorandum by Col. William Allan of a conversation with Gen. Lee on Feb. 15, 1868, in the Southern Historical Collection.
10. Letter from Clara Barton to "Mr. Shaver" of Washington, dated Sept. 4, 1862, B. & L., extra-illustrated edition, Vol. VII, in the Huntington Library.

3. To Risk Everything

1. The comment of Jacob Cox is worth recalling: "Pope's introduction to the eastern army was an unfortunate one; but neither he nor anyone else could have imagined the heat of partisan spirit or the lengths it would run. . . . There was abundant proof that the wounded *amour propre* of the officers and men of the Army of the Potomac made them practically a unit in intense dislike and distrust of him. It may be that this condition of things destroyed his possibility of usefulness in the east." (*Military Reminiscences of the Civil War*, Vol. I, 248.)

2. Charles E. Davis, Jr., *Three Years in the Army: the Story of the 13th Massachusetts Volunteers from July 16, 1861, to Aug. 1, 1864*, 156–57.
3. David W. Judd, *The Story of the 33rd New York Volunteers*, 217; letter of Gen. Pope to Gov. Yates of Illinois dated Sept. 21, 1862, in the John Pope Papers, Chicago Historical Society; sketch of the life of Gen. Doubleday, written by his wife and with notes by the general, sent by him to Frank I. Bramhall of New York on Dec. 18, 1864; now in B. & L., extra-illustrated, Vol. X, Huntington Library.
4. Pinkerton to McClellan dated Aug. 25, 1862, from the Allan Pinkerton Papers, notes by Allan Nevins, courtesy of Howard Swiggett.
5. O.R., Vol. XII, Part Three, 688–89, 691, 709–10, 722–23.
6. Tyler Dennett, ed., *Lincoln and the Civil War in the Diaries and Letters of John Hay*, 45; letter of Attorney General Bates to Francis Leiber dated Sept. 2, 1862, in the Francis Leiber Collection, Huntington Library.
7. O.R., Vol. XII, Part Three, 773.
8. Ibid., 706, 740; Nicolay & Hay, Vol. VI, 21–22; *Diary of Salmon P. Chase*, 62–63; Benjamin P. Thomas and Harold Hyman, *Stanton*, 219–20.
9. O.R., Vol. XII, Part Two, 83.
10. O.R., Vol. XII, Part Three, 787–88. An account of Lincoln's state of mind at this meeting is in Nicolay & Hay, Vol. VI, 21.
11. O.R., Vol. XII, Part Three, 797.
12. *Diary of Gideon Welles*, Vol. I, 105; *Diary of Salmon P. Chase*, 63–65.
13. Letter of McClellan to Mrs. McClellan dated Sept. 2, 1862, in the McClellan Letterbook; *Diary of Gideon Welles*, Vol. I, 111; *Lincoln and the Civil War in the Diaries and Letters of John Hay*, 47.
14. The Lincoln-Stanton order to Halleck, and Halleck's order to McClellan, are in O.R., Vol. XIX, Part Two, 169. For the relief of Pope and the consolidation of the armies see the same volume, 183, 188.
15. For Pope's furious correspondence with Halleck see his letters to Halleck dated Sept. 30 and Oct. 20, 1862, in the John Pope Papers, Chicago Historical Society. An angry letter to V. B. Horton, the general's father-in-law, dated March 9, 1863, containing bitter denunciation of Lincoln, is in the Pope Papers, New York Historical Society. A long letter from Halleck to Pope dated Oct. 10, 1862, is in the Halleck Papers, Chicago Historical Society.
16. Memorandum of Col. William Allan, reciting a conversation with Gen. Lee on Feb. 15, 1868, and giving also a memorandum by the Rev. Mr. E. C. Gordon describing a conversation with Lee on the same date; in the Southern Historical Collection. Lee's letter to Mr. Davis is in O.R., Vol. XIX, Part Two, 590–91.

4. *A Town Called Sharpsburg*

1. O.R., Vol. XIX, Part Two, 281. The literature on the lost order is extensive. There is a good treat-

ment of the case in Hal Bridges, *Lee's Maverick General: Daniel Harvey Hill*, 96–99.

2. Diary of J. R. Boulware, assistant surgeon, 6th South Carolina, in the Virginia State Library, Richmond; Moore's *Rebellion Record*, Vol. V, Documents, 444; Alexander Hunter in Southern Historical Society Papers, Vol. XXXI, 40.
3. In his report (O.R., Vol. XIX, Part One, 151) Lee says that he had 40,000 men in the battle. Livermore (*Numbers and Losses*, 92) thinks the figure too low, arguing that to accept it is to admit that Lee's army had had fantastic temporary losses from straggling during the fortnight before the battle. The fact is, however, that straggling had been fantastic, and the careful study in Freeman *R. E. Lee*, Vol. II, 402, indicates that Lee's total is approximately correct. McClellan gives his own strength as 87,000 (O.R., Vol. XIX, Part One, 67). John C. Ropes, *The Story of the Civil War*, Part Two, 376, points out that only about 46,000 of McClellan's men were seriously engaged.
4. "Every stalk of corn in the northern and greater part of the field was cut as closely as could have been done with a knife, and the slain lay in rows precisely as they had stood in their ranks a few moments before"—Hooker's report, O.R., Vol. XIX, Part One, 218.
5. Cf. Jed Hotchkiss, *Confederate Military History*, *Virginia*, Vol. III, 357: "Lee was not only willing but eager to renew the battle, in which he was earnestly seconded by Jackson." The best appraisal of casualties indicates that the Federals lost upwards of 13,000 men on September 17 and the Confederates rather more than 10,000.
6. O.R., Vol. XIX, Part One, 68; McClellan's *Own Story*, 613.
7. Albert D. Richardson, *The Secret Service, the Field, the Dungeon and the Escape*, 284; dispatch in the Charleston *Courier* dated Sept. 17, cited in Moore's *Rebellion Record*, Vol. V, Documents, 472–75; letter of Frank Haskell dated Sept. 19, in the Haskell Papers, State Historical Society of Wisconsin. It might be noted that the rain which began the day soon ended, and there was clear sunlight throughout most of the battle.
8. Bell Wiley, ed., *Reminiscences of Big I*," by Lieutenant William N. Wood; diary of J. R. Boulware, cited in Footnote 2; diary and letters of Capt. John Taggart, 9th Pennsylvania Reserves, in the Pennsylvania Historical and Museum Commission, Bureau of Research, Publications and Records; David H. Strother, "Personal Recollections of the War, by a Virginian," in *Harper's Magazine*, Vol. XXXVI, February 1868, 282.
9. Strother, *A Virginia Yankee in the Civil War*, 124.

5. *Taking the Initiative*

1. Jed Hotchkiss, Confederate Military History, *Virginia*, Vol. III, 357; O.R., Vol. XIX, Part Two, 626–27.

2. Lee to Davis dated Sept. 25, in O.R., Vol. XIX, Part Two, 626–27; letter of Brig. Gen. John R. Jones dated Sept. 20, in B. & L., extra-illustrated, Vol. VIII, Huntington Library; Allan, *The Army of Northern Virginia in 1862*, 451. A Sept. 22 return on the army's strength in infantry and cavalry is in O.R., Vol. XIX, Part Two, 621.
3. O.R., Vol. XIX, Part Two, 348.
4. Letters to Mrs. McClellan, both dated Sept. 20, one marked "9 p.m.," in the McClellan Letterbook.
5. Barnett to S. L. M. Barlow dated Sept. 19, in the Barlow Papers, Huntington Library. Barnett needs a little study. A friend of Caleb Smith, he held a job of some sort in the Interior Department and served also as a newspaper correspondent and as a lobbyist, devoting much of his time to writing gossipy letters to Barlow on political developments. He apparently knew Lincoln personally, and some of his letters to Barlow reflect his conversations with the President.
6. *Diary of Gideon Welles*, Vol. I, 143.
7. Nicolay & Hay, Vol. VI, 162–63, quoting Welles in *The Galaxy* for December 1872, 846–47.
8. *Lincoln and the Civil War in the Diaries and Letters of John Hay*, 50.
9. Frederick Seward, *Seward at Washington*, Vol. III, 135–36.
10. Strother, *A Virginia Yankee in the Civil War*, 116–17; letter of Robert Gould Shaw to his mother dated Sept. 25, from the Robert Gould Shaw letters, privately held, transcribed by Allan Nevins; Samuel Butterworth to Barlow, Sept. 23, and Barnett to Barlow, Sept. 25, in the Barlow Papers.
11. Letter dated Sept. 30, in the Manton Marble Papers, Library of Congress.
12. McClellan to William H. Aspinwall dated Sept. 26, in B. & L., extra-illustrated, Vol. VIII, Huntington Library; McClellan's *Own Story*, 655.
13. Jacob Cox, *Military Reminiscences of the Civil War*, Vol. I, 359–61; O.R., Vol. XIX, Part Two, 395–96.
14. The correspondence on the case of Major Key is in Basler, Vol. V, 442–43, 508–9; Nicolay & Hay, Vol. VI, 186–88. Major Key's brother, Col. Thomas Key, Democratic leader in the Ohio Senate at the outbreak of the war, was appointed to McClellan's staff in August 1861, and was in no way involved in Major Key's difficulties.
15. Strother, *A Virginia Yankee in the Civil War*, 129. In the John Hay Papers, Illinois State Historical Library, are two newspaper clippings—one from the New York *Tribune*, undated, and one from the Washington *Capital* for March 21, 1880, reprinting the *Tribune* article. This is an interview with Nathaniel Paige, then a Washington lawyer but at the time of Antietam a *Tribune* correspondent. Paige asserts that Thomas Key, at the time of the battle, told him that members of McClellan's staff had been talking about "a plan to counter-march to Washington and intimidate the President." According to Paige, McClellan knew nothing about

this, and the harebrained scheme (if it did exist) was dropped because of Key's opposition.

16. Undated letter to Barlow, apparently written early in the fall of 1862, in the Barlow Papers.
17. Nicolay & Hay, Vol. VI, 164; Basler, Vol. V, 438–39.

6. *Nobly Save or Meanly Lose*

1. *Journal of the Congress of the Confederate States of America*, Vol. II, First Congress, Second Session, 231, 469. Jones, *Rebel War Clerk's Diary*, 101; O.R., Series Two, Vol. IV, 916. In the end Congress adopted a comparatively mild resolution asserting that Mr. Lincoln wanted to stir up a slave revolt and promising to sustain Mr. Davis in any retaliatory measures he considered necessary.
2. London *Times* for Oct. 7, cited in Rhodes, Vol. IV, 343, n.
3. *A Cycle of Adams Letters*, Vol. I, 39.
4. Rowland, Vol. V, 356–7, 361, 366.
5. Basler, Vol. V, 98–99.
6. Letter of John E. Haley to John Martin dated Oct. 19, in the Civil War Papers at the Missouri Historical Society.
7. O.R., Vol. XVI, Part One, 657, 663.
8. O.R., Vol. XIX, Part One, 70.
9. O.R., Vol. XIX, Part Two, 660.
10. McClellan's *Own Story*, 627; *Lincoln and the Civil War in the Diaries and Letters of John Hay*, 218; O.R., Vol. XIX, Part One, 72.
11. O.R., Vol. XIX, Part Two, 52–54, 484–85; Basler, Vol. V, 474.
12. Undated letter written sometime in October, in the McClellan Letterbook.
13. O.R., Series Three, Vol. II, 703–4.
14. Buckingham's account of this is in the Comte de Paris, *History of the Civil War in America*, Vol. II, 555–56. McClellan's letter, dated Nov. 7, is in the McClellan Letterbook.
15. McClellan's *Own Story*, 652; Allan Nevins, ed., *A Diary of Battle: the Personal Journals of Col. Charles S. Wainwright*, 125.
16. Journal of Col. Mulligan, entry for Oct. 31, Chicago Historical Society.
17. Basler, Vol. V, 537.

BIBLIOGRAPHY

☆ ☆ ☆ ☆ ☆

The following bibliography for *Terrible Swift Sword*, Volume II, The Centennial History of the Civil War, has been condensed from the list of research materials used in writing this volume. Only entries *not* in the bibliography of *The Coming Fury*, Volume I, The Centennial History of the Civil War, have been included. The bibliography consists of four parts: I. Resources. II. Primary manuscript collections consulted. III. Principal newspapers. IV. Books, pamphlets, and periodicals of which substantial material has been extracted or used as reference. Space has permitted the recording of only the major sources used. Many hundreds of additional manuscripts, newspapers, books, and articles contributed to the research notes for the Centennial History.

SECTION I: *Resources*

In addition to the institutions listed in *The Coming Fury*, the following were consulted for *Terrible Swift Sword*. All the major battlefields and many of the secondary ones pertaining to this volume were visited. Appreciation is extended to all those in the libraries and on the battlefields who so generously aided the research.

Beach, Rufus D., Evanston, Ill., private collection.
Civil War Commissions. The United States Civil War Centennial Commission, Allan Nevins, James I. Robertson, and others, along with many of the state and local Centennial Commissions.
Civil War Institute, Gettysburg College, Gettysburg, Pa., John Howard Knickerbocker.
Colorado Historical Society, Denver.
Columbia University Library, New York.
Fitting, Mrs. Robert D., Midland, Texas, private collection.
Hoffman, Mal, Park Forest, Ill., private collection.
Louisiana Historical Association, Confederate Memorial Hall, New Orleans.
New York, Museum of the City of, Philip Rees.
New York State Library, Manuscript and History Section, Albany, Charles F. Gosnell, Donald C. Anthony, Stephen A. Powell.

Otis, Mrs. J. D., Oak Park, Ill., private collection.

Shiloh National Military Park, Pittsburg Landing, Tenn., manuscript collection.

Trask, Mr. and Mrs. Gordon W., Oak Park, Ill., private collection.

U. S. Army, Corps of Engineers, Vicksburg, Miss.

Vicksburg National Military Park, manuscript and map collection, Edwin C. Bearss.

Wilgus, Walter, Arlington, Va., private collection.

SECTION II: *Manuscript Collections*

This lists only a portion of the major manuscript collections consulted:

Allan, William, Conversations with Lee, William Allan Collection, Southern Historical Collection, University of North Carolina.

Ammen, Jacob, Diary, Illinois State Historical Library.

Bailey, J. B., The Story of a Confederate Soldier, 1861–1865, Texas State Archives.

Barlow, S. L. M., Autograph Collection, Huntington Library.

Barstow, Wilson, Papers, Library of Congress.

Barton, Clara, Letter, Battles and Leaders of the Civil War, extra illustrated, Huntington Library.

Beauregard, P. G. T., Papers, Columbia University Library, New York.

Berkeley, Henry Robinson, Diary, Virginia State Historical Library.

Bishop, Charles William, Log of a Cruise in the Gunboat Port Royal in 1862, Yale University Library.

Blair Papers, Library of Congress.

Boulware, J. R., Diary, Virginia State Library.

Bourlier, Emile, Letters, Western Reserve Historical Society.

Bradford, Jeff D., Letter, Confederate Memorial Literary Society.

Bragg, Braxton, Papers, Western Reserve Historical Society.

Bragg, Braxton, Papers, Duke University Library.

Bragg, Braxton, Papers, Huntington Library.

Bragg, Edward S., Papers, The State Historical Society of Wisconsin.

Braxton, Fannie Page (Hume), Diary, Virginia State Historical Society.

Brock Collection, Huntington Library.

Buchanan, Franklin, Letterbook, Southern Historical Collection, University of North Carolina.

Burrus, John C., and Family, Papers, George Lester Collection, University of North Carolina.

Butler, Benjamin F., Eldridge Collection, Huntington Library.

Butler, Benjamin F., Letter, Ralph G. Newman Collection.

Cameron, Simon, Papers, Pennsylvania Historical and Museum Commission, microfilm from Historical Society of Dauphin County, Harrisburg, Pa.

Chamberlain, Joshua L., Papers, Library of Congress.

Chandler, Zachariah, Papers, Library of Congress, Nevins' Notes.

Chase, Salmon P., Miscellaneous File, Huntington Library.
Chase, Salmon P., Papers, Chicago Historical Society.
Chase, Salmon P., Papers, Historical Society of Pennsylvania.
Chew, Francis T., Reminiscences, Southern Historical Collection, University of North Carolina.
Civil War Papers, Missouri Historical Society.
Cox, Jacob D., Letter, Battles and Leaders of the Civil War, extra illustrated, Huntington Library.
Cram, George F., Letters, Loring Armstrong Collection.
Curtis, Samuel Ryan, Papers, Huntington Library.
Dana, Charles A., Papers, Library of Congress.
Dana Papers, Massachusetts Historical Society.
Davis, Jefferson, Letters to Marcus Wright, Palmer Collection, Western Reserve Historical Society.
Davis, Jefferson, Letters to Varina H. Davis, Confederate Memorial Literary Society.
Davis, Lawson L., Account of Mumford Flag Incident, Louisiana Historical Association.
Dawes, Rufus, Papers, Courtesy Rufus D. Beach, Evanston, Ill., and Ralph G. Newman.
de Coppet, Andre, Collection, Princeton University Library.
Dinwiddie, James L., Letters to his Wife, 1862, Virginia State Library.
Doolittle, James R., Papers, State Historical Society of Wisconsin, Nevins' Notes.
Doubleday, Abner, and Mrs. Doubleday, Sketch of his life, Battles and Leaders of the Civil War, extra illustrated, Huntington Library.
Douglas, Henry Kyd, Papers, Manuscript Department, Duke University Library.
DuPont, S. F., Miscellaneous Papers, Massachusetts Historical Society.
Ellis, E. J., and Family, Papers, Louisiana State Department of Archives, Louisiana State University.
English, Edmund, Papers, Huntington Library.
Farragut, David Glasgow, Letter, Battles and Leaders of the Civil War, extra illustrated, Huntington Library.
Farragut, David Glasgow, Papers, David H. Annan Collection.
Fessenden, Samuel, Miscellaneous Papers, Huntington Library.
Floyd, John B., Papers, Duke University Library.
Fox, G. V., Correspondence and Papers, New York Historical Society.
Frémont, Jesse Benton, Papers, Chicago Historical Society.
Frémont, John Charles, Papers, Bancroft Library, University of California.
Gamble Papers, Missouri Historical Society.
Goldsborough, Louis M., Papers, Duke University Library.
Grant, Ulysses S., Papers, Chicago Historical Society.
Grant, Ulysses S., Papers, Illinois State Historical Library.
Grant, Ulysses S., Letter, Sang Collection.
Greeley, Horace, Papers, Chicago Historical Society.

Greeley, Horace, Papers, Library of Congress.
Halleck, H. W., Papers, Chicago Historical Society.
Halleck, H. W., Papers, Huntington Library.
Harrison, Burton, Papers, Library of Congress.
Hay, John, Papers, Illinois State Historical Library.
Hill, D. H., Papers, Virginia State Library.
Hitchcock, E. A., Papers, Missouri Historical Society.
Hotchkiss, Jed, Papers, Alderman Library, University of Virginia.
Howard, W. A., Letter, Shiloh National Military Park Collection.
Humphreys, A. A., Collection, The Historical Society of Pennsylvania.
Jackson, T. J., Letter, Simon Gratz Autograph Collection, The Historical Society of Pennsylvania.
Jackson, T. J., Papers, Southern Historical Collection, University of North Carolina.
Johnson, Charles James, Papers, Louisiana State Dept. of Archives, Louisiana State University.
Johnston, Albert Sidney, Papers, Chicago Historical Society.
Johnston, Albert Sidney, Scrapbook, Barker Texas History Center, University of Texas.
Jones, John R., Letter, Battles and Leaders of the Civil War, extra illustrated, Huntington Library.
Lamon, Ward Hill, Letters, Chicago Historical Society.
Law, E. M., Papers, Southern Historical Collection, University of North Carolina.
Lee, Robert E., Letter, Battles and Leaders of the Civil War, extra illustrated, Huntington Library.
Lee, Robert E., Letters, André de Coppet Collection, Princeton University Library.
Lincoln, Abraham, Unpublished Lincoln File, Lincoln Collection, John Hay Library, Brown University.
Lincoln, Abraham, Papers, New York Historical Society.
Longstreet, James, Letters, Battles and Leaders of the Civil War, extra illustrated, Huntington Library.
Longstreet, James, Papers, Duke University Library.
McClellan, George B., Letters, Huntington Library.
McClellan, George B., Sang Collection.
Marble, Manton, Papers, Library of Congress, Nevins' Notes.
Meade, George G., Papers, The Historical Society of Pennsylvania.
Mecklin, A. H., Diary, Mississippi Department of Archives and History.
Meigs, Montgomery C., Papers and Diaries, Library of Congress.
Mulligan, Col. James A., Diary and Journal, Chicago Historical Society.
Nicolay-Hay Papers, Illinois State Historical Library.
Parsons, Lewis B., Papers, Illinois State Historical Library.
Patrick, Marsena, Diaries, Library of Congress.
Pearce, Gen. N. B., Reminiscences of, Arkansas History Commission.

Pettus, John J., Correspondence, Mississippi Department of Archives and History.
Phillips, Eugenia, A Southern Woman's Story of Her Imprisonment During the War of 1861–1862, Library of Congress.
Pinkerton, Allan, Papers, Library of Congress.
Pope, John, Papers, Chicago Historical Society.
Pope, John, Letters, Huntington Library.
Pope, John, Papers, New York Historical Society.
Porter, Fitz John, Letter, Western Reserve Historical Society.
Porter, Fitz John, Papers, Massachusetts Historical Society.
Ray, Charles H., Letters, Huntington Library.
Ross, Lawrence Sullivan, Letters, Barker Texas History Center, University of Texas.
Ryder Collection, Tufts University Library.
Sherman, William Tecumseh, Papers, Huntington Library.
Sigel, Franz, Letters, Huntington Library.
Sigel, Franz, Papers, Western Reserve Historical Society.
Smith, E. Kirby, Letter, Western Reserve Historical Society.
Smith, G. W., Papers, Duke University Library.
Smith, G. W., Papers, Western Reserve Historical Society.
Smith, Oscar, Papers, Library of Congress.
Smith, W. F., Papers, Walter Wilgus Collection.
Solomon, Clara E., Diary of a New Orleans Girl, 1861–1862, Louisiana State Department of Archives, Louisiana State University.
Stuart, James Ewell Brown, Papers, Duke University Library.
Stuart, James Ewell Brown, Memoranda, Ryder Collection, Tufts University.
Taggart, John, Diary and Letters, Pennsylvania Historical and Museum Commission.
Tarbell, Ida M., Papers, Allegheny College, Nevins' Notes.
Thompson, M. Jeff, Letter, Battles and Leaders of the Civil War, extra illustrated, Huntington Library.
Thompson, M. Jeff, Reminiscences, Southern Historical Collection, University of North Carolina Library.
Trask, W. L., Wartime Journal, Mr. and Mrs. Gordon W. Trask Collection.
Urquhart, Mrs. Robert Dow, Journal, Tulane University Library.
Van Brunt, Harry, Letters, Massachusetts Commandery, Military Order of the Loyal Legion Papers, Houghton Library, Harvard University.
Warren, G. K., Papers, New York State Library.
Wayne-Stites-Anderson Papers, Georgia Historical Society.
Webb, Alexander Stewart, Collection, Yale University Library.

SECTION III: *Newspapers*

Extensive use has been made of newspapers covering the period treated in this volume. In some cases, quotations have been taken from newspapers, articles or editorials reprinted in such volumes as Moore's *Rebellion Record.*

BIBLIOGRAPHY

All prominent papers of Charleston, S.C., Chicago, Cincinnati, New York, and Richmond, Va., have been directly consulted. In addition, other papers such as *Harper's Weekly*, London *Times*, and Washington (Ark.) *Telegraph* for the war years have been used, as have articles in postwar papers up to the present time.

SECTION IV: *Books, Pamphlets, and Periodicals*

Adams, Charles Francis, The Trent Affair, 1861–1862, Massachusetts Historical Society Proceedings, Vol. XLV, Oct. 1911–June 1912.

Adams, Ephraim Douglass, Great Britain and the American Civil War, two vols., Gloucester, Mass., 1957.

Allan, William, The Army of Northern Virginia in 1862, Boston, 1862.

Allan, William, First Maryland Campaign, Southern Historical Society Papers, Vol. XIV, Jan.–Dec. 1866.

Allan, William, History of the Campaigns of T. J. (Stonewall) Jackson in the Shenandoah Valley of Virginia, Philadelphia, 1890, 1912.

Allan, William, Strategy of the Campaign of Sharpsburg or Antietam, Vol. III, Military Historical Society of Massachusetts, Boston, 1895.

Ambrose, Stephen E., Halleck: Lincoln's Chief of Staff, Baton Rouge, 1962.

Ammen, Daniel, The Atlantic Coast, New York, 1883–85.

Andreas, Alfred T., The "Ifs and Buts" of Shiloh, Military Essays and Recollections, Vol. I, Chicago, 1891.

Annals of the War Written by Leading Participants North and South, Philadelphia, 1879.

Armistead, Drury L., The Battle in Which General Johnston was Wounded, Southern Historical Society Papers, Vol. XVIII, 1890.

Bacon, George S., One Night's Work, April 20, 1862, Magazine of American History, March 1886.

Badeau, Adam, Military History of Ulysses S. Grant, three vols., New York, 1868.

Barnard, J. G., The Peninsular Campaign and Its Antecedents, New York, 1864.

Bearss, Edwin C., The First Day at Pea Ridge, March 7, 1862, Arkansas Historical Quarterly. Vol. XVII, No. 2, Summer, 1958.

Bearss, Edwin C., Maps of Pea Ridge.

Bearss, Edwin C., Unconditional Surrender, The Fall of Fort Donelson, Tennessee Historical Quarterly, March & June 1862.

Bedford, M. L., Fight Between the Batteries and Gunboats at Fort Donelson, Southern Historical Society Papers, Vol. XIII, Jan.–Dec. 1885.

Bennett, Frank M., The Steam Navy of the United States, two vols., Pittsburgh, 1897.

Bennett, L. G. and Haigh, Wm. M., History of the Thirty-sixth Regiment Illinois Volunteers, Aurora, Ill., 1876.

Bernard, George S., War Talks of Confederate Veterans, Petersburg, Va., 1892.

Bernard, Montague, A Historical Account of the Neutrality of Great Britain During the American Civil War, London, 1870.

Besse, S. B., U.S. Ironclad Monitor, Newport News, Va., 1936.

Besse, S. B., C.S. Ironclad Virginia, Newport News, Va., 1937.

Bierce, Ambrose, Ambrose Bierce's Civil War, Chicago, 1956.

Bill, Alfred Hoyt, The Beleaguered City, New York, 1946.

Bishop, J. W., The Mill Springs Campaign, Glimpses of the Nation's Struggle.

Black, Robert C., The Railroads of the Confederacy, Chapel Hill, 1952.

Blackford, W. W., War Years with Jeb Stuart, New York, 1945.

Blair, Montgomery, Opening the Mississippi, The United Service, Jan. 1881.

Blake, Henry N., Three Years in the Army of the Potomac, Boston, 1865.

Blodgett, Edward A., The Army of the Southwest and the Battle of Pea Ridge, Military Essays and Recollections, Vol. II, Chicago, 1894.

Bloss, John M., Antietam and the Lost Dispatch, Talks in Kansas, Vol. I, Kansas City, 1906.

Bowman, S. M., and Irwin, R. B., Sherman and His Campaigns, New York, 1865.

Boynton, H. V., Sherman's Historical Raid, The Memoirs in the Light of the Record, Cincinnati, 1875.

Bradlee, Francis B. C., Blockade Running During the Civil War and the Effect of Land and Water Transportation on the Confederacy, Salem, Mass., 1925.

Bridges, Hal, Lee's Maverick General: Daniel Harvey Hill, New York, 1961.

British and Foreign State Papers, 1860–1861, also 1861–1862, Compiled by the Librarian and Keeper of the Papers, Foreign Office, London, 1868.

Britton, Wiley, Civil War on the Border, two vols., New York, 1890.

Brotherhead, W., General Frémont, and the Injustice Done Him by Politicians and Envious Military Men, Philadelphia, 1862.

Brown, Junius H., Four Years in Secessia, Hartford, 1865.

Brown, Walter Lee, Pea Ridge: Gettysburg of the West, The Arkansas Historical Quarterly, Vol. XV, No. 1, Spring, 1956.

Brownlow, W. G., Sketches of the Rise, Progress and Decline of Secession, Philadelphia, 1862.

Bruce, George A., The Donelson Campaign, Military Historical Society of Massachusetts, Vol. VII, Boston, 1908.

Bruce, George A., General Buell's Campaign Against Chattanooga, Military Historical Society of Massachusetts, Vol. VIII, Boston, 1910.

Bruce, George A., The Twentieth Regiment of Massachusetts Volunteer Infantry, 1861–1865, Boston, 1906.

Bushnell, Rev. Samuel, The Story of the Monitor and the Merrimac, no date.

Butler, Benjamin F., Private and Official Correspondence of Gen. Benjamin F. Butler During the Period of the Civil War, five vols., Norwood, Mass., 1917.

Callahan, James Morton, The Diplomatic History of the Southern Confederacy, Springfield, Mass., 1957.

Callender, Eliot, What a Boy Saw on the Mississippi, Military Essays and Recollections, Vol. I, Chicago, 1891.

Carpenter, F. B., Six Months in the White House, Watkins Glen, N.Y., 1961.

Carse, Robert, Department of the South, Hilton Head Island in the Civil War, Columbia, S.C., 1961.

Catton, Bruce, Grant Moves South, Boston, 1960, and other works as cited.

Chalmers, James R., Forrest and His Campaigns, Southern Historical Society Papers, Vol. VII, No. 9, Sept. 1879.

Chambers, Lenoir, Stonewall Jackson, two vols., New York, 1959.

Cheat Mountain: or, Unwritten Chapter of the Late War, By a Member of the Bar, Fayetteville, Tenn., Nashville, 1885.

Church, William Conant, The Life of John Ericsson, two vols., London, 1890.

Cist, Henry M., The Army of the Cumberland, New York, 1890.

Civil War History and Civil War Times Illustrated, various issues.

Clark, Charles, The Trent and San Jacinto, London, 1862.

Clark, Victor S., History of Manufactures in the United States, two vols., New York, 1929.

Coffin, Charles Carleton, My Days and Nights on the Battlefield, Boston, 1887.

Confederate Military History, twelve vols., Atlanta, Georgia, 1899.

Confederate Veteran, various issues.

Conger, A. L., The Rise of U. S. Grant, New York, 1931.

Connolly, James A., Three Years in the Army of the Cumberland, The Letters and Diary of Major James A. Connolly, edited by Paul M. Angle, Bloomington, 1959.

Costi, Michele, Memoir of the Trent Affair, London, 1865.

Coulter, E. Merton, The Civil War and Readjustment in Kentucky, Chapel Hill, N.C., 1926.

Cox, Jacob Dolson, Military Reminiscences of the Civil War, two vols., New York, 1900.

Crummer, Wilbur C., With Grant at Fort Donelson, Shiloh and Vicksburg, Oak Park, Ill., 1915.

Cudworth, Warren H., History of the First Regiment Massachusetts Infantry, Boston, 1866.

Curtis, Samuel Prentis, The Army of the South-West, and the First Campaign in Arkansas, The Annals of Iowa, Vol. IV–VI.

Dabney, R. L., Life and Campaigns of Lieut.-Gen. Thomas J. Jackson, New York, 1866.

Dalton, John Call, John Call Dalton, M.D., U.S.V., Cambridge, Mass., 1892.

Davis, Charles E., Three Years in the Army, The Story of the Thirteenth Massachusetts Volunteers from July 16, 1861 to August 1, 1864, Boston, 1894.

Davis, Charles W., New Madrid and Island No. 10, Military Essays and Recollections, Vol. I, Chicago, 1891.

Davis, George B., The Antietam Campaign, Vol. III, Military Historical Society of Massachusetts, Boston, 1895.

Dawes, Ephraim C., The Battle of Shiloh, Vol. VII, Military Historical Society of Massachusetts, Boston, 1908.

De Trobriand, Regis, Four Years with the Army of the Potomac, Boston, 1889.

Dewey, George, Autobiography, New York, 1913.

Dowdey, Clifford, Experiment in Rebellion, Garden City, N.Y., 1946.

Dufour, Charles L., The Night the War Was Lost, Garden City, N.Y., 1960.

Edmands, Thomas F., Operations in North Carolina, 1861–1862, Vol. IX, Military Historical Society of Massachusetts, Boston, 1912.

Eisenschiml, Otto, The Celebrated Case of Fitz John Porter, Indianapolis, 1950.

Eisenschiml, Otto, The Story of Shiloh, Chicago, 1946.

An English Merchant, Two Months in the Confederate States, including a Visit to New Orleans Under the Domination of General Butler, London, 1863.

Farragut, Loyall, The Life of David Glasgow Farragut, First Admiral of the United States Navy, Embodying His Journal and Letters, New York, 1879.

Foote, H. S., War of the Rebellion, New York, 1866.

Force, M. F., From Fort Henry to Corinth, New York, 1908.

Ford, Harvey S., Van Dorn and the Pea Ridge Campaign, Journal of the American Military Institute, Vol. III, No. 4, Winter, 1939.

Frémont, Jessie Benton, The Story of the Guard: A Chronicle of the War, Boston, 1863.

Fry, James B., Military Miscellanies, New York, 1889.

Fry, James B., Operations of the Army Under Buell from June 10th to October 30, 1862 and the "Buell Commission," New York, 1884.

Gift, George W., The Story of the Arkansas, Southern Historical Society Papers, Vol. XII, Nos. 1–5, Jan.–May 1884.

Gordon, A. C., Hard Times in the Confederacy, Century Magazine, Vol. XXXVI, No. 5, Sept. 1888.

Gordon, George H., History of the Campaign of the Army of Virginia, Boston, 1889.

Govan, Gilbert E., and Livingood, James W., The Chattanooga Country 1540–1951, New York, 1952.

Govan, Gilbert E., and Livingood, James W., A Different Valor, The Story of General Joseph E. Johnston, C.S.A., Indianapolis, 1956.

Government Contracts, House Report No. 2, two vols., 37th Congress, 2d Session, Washington, 1862.

Green, John William, Johnny Green of the Orphan Brigade: The Journal of a Confederate Soldier, A. D. Kirwin editor, Lexington, 1956.

Greene, Francis Vinton, The Mississippi, New York, 1882.

Hamlin, Charles Eugene, The Life and Times of Hannibal Hamlin, Cambridge, 1899.

Harper, Robert S., Ohio Handbook of the Civil War, Ohio Historical Society, Columbus, 1961.

Harper's Monthly, various issues.

Harrington, Fred Harvey, Fighting Politician: Major General N. P. Banks, Philadelphia, 1948.

Harris, Thomas L., The Trent Affair, Indianapolis, 1896.

Hartje, Robert G., A Confederate Dilemma Across the Mississippi, The Arkansas Historical Quarterly, Vol. XVII, No. 2, Summer, 1958.

Hassler, Warren W., Jr., General George B. McClellan: Shield of the Union, Baton Rouge, 1957.

Haven, Franklin, Jr., The Conduct of General McClellan At Alexandria in August, 1862, Vol. II, Military Historical Society of Massachusetts, Boston, 1895.

Hawk, Emory Q., Economic History of the South, New York, 1934.

Hay, John, Letters of John Hay and Extracts from Diary, Washington, 1908, printed but not published.

Heysinger, Isaac W., Antietam and the Maryland and Virginia Campaigns of 1862, New York, 1912.

Hill, D. H., The Lost Dispatch, The Land We Love, Vol. IV, Feb. 1868.

Hinman, Wilbur F., The Story of the Sherman Brigade, no place, 1897.

History of Lafayette County, Mo., no author, Missouri Historical Society, 1881.

Hitchcock, Ethan Allen, Fifty Years in Camp and Field, New York, 1909.

Hobart-Hampden, Augustus Charles, Hobart Pasha, Blockade-Running, Slaver-Hunting, and War and Sport in Turkey, edited by Horace Kephart, New York, 1915.

Holcombe and Adams, An Account of the Battle of Wilson's Creek or Oak Hills, Springfield, Mo., 1883.

Horn, Stanley, The Army of Tennessee, Indianapolis, 1941.

Howard, John Raymond, Remembrance of Things Past: A Familiar Chronicle of Kinsfolk and Friends Worth While, New York, 1925.

Huntington, James F., Operations in the Shenandoah Valley from Winchester to Port Republic, March 1–June 9, 1862, Vol. I, Military Historical Society of Massachusetts, New York, 1895.

Johnson, Adam R., The Partisan Rangers of the Confederate States Army, edited by William J. Davis, Louisville, Ky., 1904.

Johnston, A. S., Correspondence between General A. S. Johnston and Governor Isham G. Harris, Southern Historical Society Papers, Vol. IV, No. 4, Oct. 1877.

Johnston, William Preston, The Life of General Albert Sidney Johnston, New York, 1878.

Jones, Catesby ap R., Services of the "Virginia" (Merrimac), Southern Historical Society Papers, Vol. XI, No. 2–3, Feb. and March 1883.

Jones, J. William, Christ in the Camp, Atlanta, Ga., 1904.

Jones, J. William, Reminiscences of the Army of Northern Virginia, Southern Historical Society Papers, Vol. IX, Nos. 7–8, July and Aug. 1881.

Jones, J. William, Reminiscences of the Army of Northern Virginia, How Frémont and Shields "Caught" Stonewall Jackson, Southern Historical Society Papers, Vol. IX, No. 6, June 1881.

Jones, Virgil Carrington, The Civil War at Sea, three vols., New York, 1960, 1961, 1962.

Jordan, Donaldson, and Pratt, Edwin J., Europe and the American Civil War, Boston, 1931.

Jordan, Thomas, Recollections of General Beauregard's Service in West Tennessee in the Spring of 1862, Southern Historical Society Papers, Vol. VIII, Nos. 8 and 9, Aug. and Sept. 1880.

Judd, David W., The Story of the Thirty-third N.Y.S. Vols., Rochester, N.Y., 1864.

Kelley, Wm. D., Lincoln and Stanton, New York, 1885.

Kellogg, Sanford C., The Shenandoah Valley and Virginia, 1861 to 1865, A War Study, Washington, 1903.

King, Horatio, The Trent Affair, Magazine of American History, March 1886.

Kreidberg, Marvin A., and Henry, Merton G., History of Military Mobilization in the United States Army, 1775–1945, Washington, 1955.

Landry, Ernest Adam, The History of Forts Jackson and St. Philip, thesis, Louisiana State University, Baton Rouge, La., 1938.

Leake, Joseph B., Campaign of the Army of the Frontier, Military Essays and Recollections, Vol. II, Chicago, 1894.

Lee, Robert E., Lee's Dispatches to Jefferson Davis, edited by Douglas Southall Freeman and Grady McWhiney, New York, 1957.

Leland, Edwin Albert, Organization and Administration of the Louisiana Army During the Civil War, thesis, Tulane University, 1938.

Lewis, Charles Lee, Admiral Franklin Buchanan, Baltimore, 1929.

Lewis, Charles Lee, David Glasgow Farragut, two vols., Annapolis, 1943.

Lewis, Lloyd, Captain Sam Grant, Boston, 1950.

Lewis, Lloyd, Sherman Fighting Prophet, New York, 1932.

Livermore, Thomas L., The Conduct of Generals McClellan and Halleck in August, 1862, and the Case of Fitz-John Porter, Vol. II, Military Historical Society of Massachusetts, Boston, 1895.

Long, A. L., Lee's West Virginia Campaign, The Annals of the War Written by Leading Participants North and South, Philadelphia, 1879.

Lonn, Ella, Salt as a Factor in the Confederacy, New York, 1933.

Lothrop, T. K., William Henry Seward, Boston, 1896.

McClellan, H. B., I Rode with Jeb Stuart, edited by Burke Davis, Bloomington, Ind., 1958.

McCordock, Robert Stanley, The Yankee Cheese Box, Philadelphia, 1938.

McDonald, Mrs. Cornelia (Peake), A Diary with Reminiscences of the War and Refugee Life in the Shenandoah Valley, 1860–1865, Nashville, 1936.

McWhiney, Grady, Braxton Bragg at Shiloh, Tennessee Historical Quarterly, March 1962.

McWhiney, Grady, Controversy in Kentucky; Braxton Bragg's Campaign of 1862, Civil War History, Vol. VI, No. 1, March 1960.

Mahan, A. T., Admiral Farragut, New York, 1916.

Mahan, A. T., The Gulf and Inland Waters, New York, 1883, 1885.

Martin, Theodore, The Life of His Royal Highness the Prince Consort, five vols., New York, 1880.

Marvin, Edwin E., Fifth Regiment Connecticut Volunteers, Hartford, Conn., 1889.

Marshall, Albert O., Army Life: From a Soldier's Journal, Joliet, Ill., 1883.

Maury, D. H., Recollections of the Elkhorn Campaign, Southern Historical Society Papers, Vol. II, No. 4, Oct. 1876.

Maury, Dabney H., Recollections of Campaign Against Grant in North Mississippi in 1862–63, Southern Historical Society Papers, Vol. XIII, Jan.–Dec. 1885.

Meador, L. E., History of the Battle of Wilson Creek, Springfield, Mo., 1938.

Michie, Peter S., General McClellan, New York, 1901.

Military Historical Society of Massachusetts Papers, fourteen vols., Boston, various dates, many important articles used.

Mindil, George W., The Battle of Fair Oaks, A Reply to General Joseph E. Johnston, Philadelphia, 1874.

Monaghan, Jay, Diplomat in Carpet Slippers, Indianapolis, 1945.

Moore, Albert Burton, Conscription and Conflict in the Confederacy, New York, 1924.

Moran, Benjamin, The Journal of Benjamin Moran, 1857–1865, edited by Sarah Agnes Wallace and Frances E. Gillespie, Chicago, 1948.

Morgan, James Morris, Recollections of a Rebel Reefer, London, 1918.

Mudd, Joseph A., What I Saw At Wilson's Creek, Missouri Historical Review, Vol. VII, Jan. 1913.

Munford, T. T., Reminiscences of Jackson's Valley Campaign, Southern Historical Society Papers, Vol. VII, Jan. to Dec. 1879.

Myers, William Starr, General George Brinton McClellan, New York, 1934.

Nevins, Allan, Frémont; Pathmarker of the West, New York, 1955.

Nevins, Allan, The War for the Union, two vols., 1959, 1960.

Newell, J. K., Ours, Annals of the 10th Regiment Massachusetts Volunteers, Boston, 1875.

Newton, Lord, Lord Lyons, A Record of British Diplomacy, two vols., London, 1913.

Newton, Virginius, The Confederate States Ram Merrimac or Virginia, Richmond, 1949.

Nicolay, Helen, Lincoln's Secretary, A Biography of John G. Nicolay, New York, 1949.

Noble, John W., Battle of Pea Ridge or Elkhorn Tavern, War Papers of the Missouri Commandery, Vol. I, 1892.

Noel, Theophilus, Autobiography and Reminiscences of, Chicago, 1904.

O'Connor, Thomas H., Lincoln and the Cotton Trade, Civil War History, Vol. VII, No. 1, March 1961.

Otis, Ephraim A., Recollections of the Kentucky Campaign of 1862, Vol. VII, Military Historical Society of Massachusetts, Boston, 1908.

Palfrey, F. W., The Antietam and Fredericksburg, New York, 1882.

Palfrey, F. W., The Siege of Yorktown; After the Fall of Yorktown; The

Seven Days' Battles to Malvern Hill; The Battle of Malvern Hill; The Battle of Antietam, Vols. I and III, Military Historical Society of Massachusetts, 1895.

Parker, William Harwar, Recollections of a Naval Officer 1861–1865, New York, 1883.

Parks, Joseph H., A Confederate Trade Center Under Federal Occupation; Memphis, 1862 to 1865, Journal of Southern History, Vol. VII, No. 3, Aug. 1941.

Parks, Joseph Howard, General Edmund Kirby Smith, C.S.A., Baton Rouge, 1954.

Parton, James, General Butler in New Orleans, New York, 1864.

Patton, John M., Reminiscences of Jackson's Infantry ("Foot Cavalry"), Southern Historical Society Papers, Vol. VIII, No. 3, March 1880.

Piatt, Donn, Memories of the Men Who Saved the Union, New York, 1887.

Pierson, Charles Lawrence, Ball's Bluff: An Episode and Its Consequences to Some of Us, Salem, Mass., 1913.

Pirtle, John B., Defence of Vicksburg in 1862–The Battle of Baton Rouge, Southern Historical Society Papers, Vol. VIII, June and July 1880.

Pisani, Camille Ferri, Prince Napoleon in America, Bloomington, Ind., 1959.

Provost Marshal General Report, Washington, 1866.

Poague, William Thomas, Gunner with Stonewall; Reminiscences of William Thomas Poague, edited by Monroe F. Cockrell, Jackson, Tenn., 1957.

Polk, William M., Leonidas Polk, Bishop and General, two vols., New York, 1915.

Pollard, Edward A., The Lost Cause, New York, 1867.

Pollard, Edward A., The Second Year of the War, New York, 1864.

Porter, David Dixon, Incidents and Anecdotes of the Civil War, New York, 1886.

Potter, E. B., editor, The United States and World Sea Power, Englewood Cliffs, 1955.

Putnam, Mrs. Sallie A., Richmond During the War, New York, 1867.

Quint, Alonzo H., The Potomac and the Rapidan, Boston, 1864.

Quint, Alonzo H., The Record of the Second Massachusetts Infantry, 1861–65, Boston, 1867.

Ramsey, H. Ashton, The Monitor and the Merrimac, Confederate Veteran, July 1907.

Raymond, Henry J., The Life and Public Services of Abraham Lincoln, New York, 1865.

Read, C. W., Reminiscences of the Confederate States Navy, Southern Historical Society Papers, Vol. I, No. 5, May 1876.

Reminiscences of the Women of Missouri During the Sixties, Gathered, Compiled and Published by Missouri Division, United Daughters of the Confederacy, Jefferson City, Mo., no date.

Report of the Commissioner of Agriculture, 1862 through 1866, Washington, various dates.

BIBLIOGRAPHY

Report of Committee on Ordnance and Ordnance Stores, Senate Executive Document 72, 37th Congress, 2d Session.

Report of the Special Committee on the Recent Military Disasters at Forts Henry and Donelson and the Evacuation of Nashville, Richmond, 1862.

Rice, Allen Thorndike, Reminiscences of Abraham Lincoln by Distinguished Men of His Time, New York, 1888.

Rich, Joseph W., The Battle of Shiloh, Iowa City, Iowa, 1911.

Richardson, Albert D., The Secret Service, The Field, The Dungeon, and The Escape, Hartford, Conn., 1865.

Roberts, A. S., The Federal Government and Confederate Cotton, American Historical Review, Vol. XXXII, No. 2, Jan. 1927.

Robinson, William M., Jr., Drewry's Bluff, Naval Defense of Richmond, 1862, Civil War History, Vol. VII, No. 2, June 1961.

Roland, Charles P., Albert Sidney Johnston and the Loss of Forts Henry and Donelson, Journal of Southern History, February 1957.

Roland, Charles P., Albert Sidney Johnston and the Shiloh Campaign, Civil War History, Dec. 1958.

Ropes, John Codman, The Army Under Pope, New York, 1881.

Rosin, Wilbert Henry, Hamilton Rowan Gamble, Missouri's Civil War Governor, Dissertation, University of Missouri, Columbia, 1960.

Saltonstall, William G., Personal Reminiscences of the War, 1861–1865, Vol. XII, Military Historical Society of Massachusetts.

Sands, Francis P. B., A Volunteer's Reminiscences of Life in the North Atlantic Blockading Squadron, 1862–1865, War Paper 20, Commandery of the District of Columbia, 1894.

Schenck, Martin, Up Came Hill, The Story of the Light Division and Its Leader, Harrisburg, Pa., 1958.

Scherer, James A. B., Cotton As a World Power, New York, 1916.

Schofield, John M., Forty-six Years in the Army, New York, 1897.

Seitz, Don C., Braxton Bragg: General of the Confederacy, Columbia, S.C., 1924.

Selfridge, Thomas O., Jr., Memoirs of, New York, 1924.

Selfridge, Thomas O., Jr., The Story of the Cumberland, Vol. XII, Military Historical Society of Massachusetts, Boston, 1902.

Semmes, Raphael, Memoirs of Service Afloat, Baltimore, 1869.

Shaler, Nathaniel S., The Kentucky Campaign of 1862, Vol. VII, Military Historical Society of Massachusetts, Boston, 1908.

Sheridan, P. H., Personal Memoirs of, two vols., New York, 1888.

The Siege of Cincinnati, Atlantic Monthly, Feb. 1863.

Smith, Ernest Ashton, The History of the Confederate Treasury, Southern History Association, Harrisburg, Pa., 1901.

Smith, G. W., Confederate War Papers, New York, 1884.

Smith, J. L., Philadelphia's Corn Exchange Regiment, History of the 118th Pennsylvania Regiment Volunteers–from Antietam to Appomattox, Philadelphia, 1888.

Smith, William Farrar, Shiloh, Magazine of American History, April 1886.

Sorrel, G. Moxley, Recollections of a Confederate Staff Officer, edited by Bell I. Wiley, Jackson, Tenn., 1958.

Southern Historical Society Papers, Richmond, Va., various issues and dates.

Speed, Thomas, The Union Cause in Kentucky, 1860–1865, New York, 1907.

Sprunt, James, Chronicles of the Cape Fear River, Raleigh, 1914.

Stackpole, Edward J., From Cedar Mountain to Antietam, Harrisburg, Pa., 1959.

Stanley, D. S., The Battle of Corinth, Personal Recollections of the War of the Rebellion, Second Series, Vol. II, New York, 1897.

Stevens, Hazard, Military Operations in South Carolina in 1862, Against Charleston, Port Royal Ferry, James Island and Secessionville, Vol. IX, Military Historical Society of Massachusetts, Boston, 1912.

Stickles, Arndt, Simon Bolivar Buckner, Borderland Knight, Chapel Hill, N.C., 1940.

Stiles, Israel N., The Merrimac and the Monitor, Military Essays and Recollections, Vol. I, Chicago, 1891.

Stone, Henry, The Battle of Shiloh, Vol. VII, Military Historical Society of Massachusetts, Boston, 1908.

Stone, Henry, The Operations of General Buell in Kentucky and Tennessee in 1862, Vol. VII, Military Historical Society of Massachusetts, Boston, 1908.

Strother, D. H., Personal Recollections of the War, Harper's, Vol. XXXVI, Feb. 1868.

Strother, David Hunter, A Virginia Yankee in the Civil War, The Diaries of David Hunter Strother, edited and with an introduction by Cecil E. Eby, Jr., Chapel Hill, N.C., 1961.

Tarbell, Ida M., The Life of Abraham Lincoln, four vols., New York, 1909.

Taylor, Thomas E., Running the Blockade; A Personal Narrative of Adventures, Risks and Escapes During the American Civil War, London, 1896.

Taylor, Walter H., Four Years with General Lee, New York, 1878.

Thomas, Benjamin P., and Hyman, Harold M., Stanton, The Life and Times of Lincoln's Secretary of War, New York, 1962.

Thomason, John W., Jr., Jeb Stuart, New York, 1948.

Thompson, Joseph Dimmit, The Battle of Shiloh, Tennessee Historical Quarterly, Vol. XVII, No. 3, Sept., 1958.

Trade with Rebellious States, Report No. 24, House of Representatives, 38th Congress, 2d Session, Washington, 1864–65.

Vandiver, Frank E., Confederate Blockade Running Through Bermuda 1861–1865, Austin, Texas, 1947.

Van Horne, Thomas B., The Life of Major-General George H. Thomas, New York, 1882.

Wainwright, Charles S., A Diary of Battle, edited by Allan Nevins, New York, 1962.

Walcott, Charles F., The Battle of Chantilly, Vol. II, Military Historical Society of Massachusetts, Boston, 1895.

Walcott, Charles F., History of the Twenty-first Regiment Massachusetts

Volunteers in the War for the Restoration of the Union, 1861–1865, Boston, 1882.
Walke, H., Naval Scenes and Reminiscences, New York, 1877.
Walker, Peter Franklin, Command Failure; The Fall of Forts Henry and Donelson, Tennessee Historical Quarterly, Vol. XVI, No. 4, Dec. 1957.
Wallace, Lew, An Autobiography, two vols., New York, 1906.
Walpole, Spencer, The Life of Lord John Russell, two vols., London, 1889.
War Claims at St. Louis, Executive Documents of the House of Representatives, 37th Congress, 2d Session, 1861–1862, Vol. VII, Washington, 1862.
Watkins, James L., King Cotton, A Historical and Statistical Review 1790 to 1908, New York, 1908.
Watson, William, Life in the Confederate Army, London, 1887.
Webb, Alexander S., The Peninsula, McClellan's Campaign of 1862, New York, 1881.
Weber, Thomas, The Northern Railroads in the Civil War 1861–1865, New York, 1952.
Weld, Stephen M., The Conduct of General McClellan At Alexandria in August, 1862, Vol. II, Military Historical Society of Massachusetts, Boston, 1895.
Welles, Gideon, Admiral Farragut and New Orleans, Galaxy, Nov. 1871.
Welles, Gideon, The Capture and Release of Mason and Slidell, Galaxy, May 1873.
West, Richard S., Jr., The Second Admiral; A Life of David Dixon Porter, 1813–1891, New York, 1937.
West Virginia, A Guide to the Mountain State, New York, 1941.
Wherry, William N., The Campaign in Missouri and the Battle of Wilson's Creek, 1861, Publications Missouri Historical Society, St. Louis, 1880.
White, E. V., The First Iron-Clad Naval Engagement in the World, Portsmouth, Va., 1906.
Wilkinson, J., The Narrative of a Blockade Runner, New York, 1887.
Williams, Alpheus S., From the Cannon's Mouth; The Civil War Letters of General Alpheus S. Williams, edited by Milo M. Quaife, Detroit, Mich., 1959.
Williams, T. Harry, Investigation: 1862, American Heritage, Vol. VI, No. One.
Wise, John S., The End of an Era, Boston, 1901.
Wood, William Nathaniel, Reminiscences of Big I, edited by Bell I. Wiley, Jackson, Tenn., 1956.
Worden, J. L., Samuel Greene, and H. Ashton Ramsay, The Monitor and the Merrimac, New York, 1912.
Wyeth, John Allan, That Devil Forrest, New York, 1959.
Yearns, Wilfred Buck, The Confederate Congress, Athens, Ga., 1960.

★ ★ ★ ★ ★

ACKNOWLEDGMENTS

☆ ☆ ☆ ☆ ☆

Several hundreds of persons and institutions have contributed in scores of ways to the research for The Centennial History of the Civil War. It is impossible to list or record all their names, but it is the wish of the author and the research director personally to express their gratitude.

Many of those who unstintingly gave of their knowledge and aid were mentioned in *The Coming Fury*, Volume I, of the Centennial History. Others are presented in the lists of resources found in the bibliography of each volume.

Collectors, librarians, historians, and others all over the nation gave freely of their time and allowed use of their valuable documents. Among those deserving special mention is Allan Nevins of Huntington Library, San Marino, Calif., who allowed us full access to his own voluminous research notes. In addition, he read the manuscript and made many valuable suggestions. Others who read the manuscript in preparation were Edwin C. Bearss, Carl Haverlin, Ralph G. Newman, T. Harry Williams, Bell I. Wiley, and Frank Vandiver. Mr. Newman also made available his collection of manuscripts and books, among countless other services. Stanley Horn read the work in galley proofs.

The following are among those whose names should be added to the roll call of helpers:

Henry B. Bass, Enid, Okla.; James L. Borroum, Corinth, Miss.; B. F. Boyce, New York, for permission to use certain papers of Allan Pinkerton; Chester D. Bradley, Fort Monroe, Va.; Thomas D. Clark, Lexington, Ky.; Monroe F. Cockrell, Evanston, Ill.; Mrs. William Hunter de Butts, Upperville, Va., for permission to use certain papers of R. E. Lee; Mrs. Henry Clinton de Rahm, Garrison-on-Hudson, N.Y., for permission to use various manuscripts; Allen M. Ergood, Silver Spring, Md., for permission to use the Diary of John Price Kepner; Gilbert Govan, Chattanooga, Tenn.; Donald Hamill, North Olmsted, Ohio; Henry B. Hunt, Jr., Baltimore, Md., for permission to use certain papers; T. S. Kennedy, Pensacola, Fla., for use of the S. R. Mallory Papers; Donald W. Krummel, Newberry Library, Chicago; L. E. Meador, Springfield, Mo.; Thomas E. Mulligan, Jr., Albany, N.Y.; Ray D. Smith, Chicago, for making available his extensive index to the *Confederate Veteran;* Enoch Squires, Albany, N.Y.; Frederick Tilberg, Gettysburg, Pa.; Lawrence W. Towner, Newberry Library, Chicago; Justin Turner, Los Angeles, Calif.; John Vela, Triumph, La.; Ray Williams, Cleveland, Ohio; Robert Waitt, Richmond, Va.; Miss Emily Warren, Newport, R.I.

★ ★ ★ ★ ★

INDEX

☆ ☆ ☆ ☆ ☆

INDEX

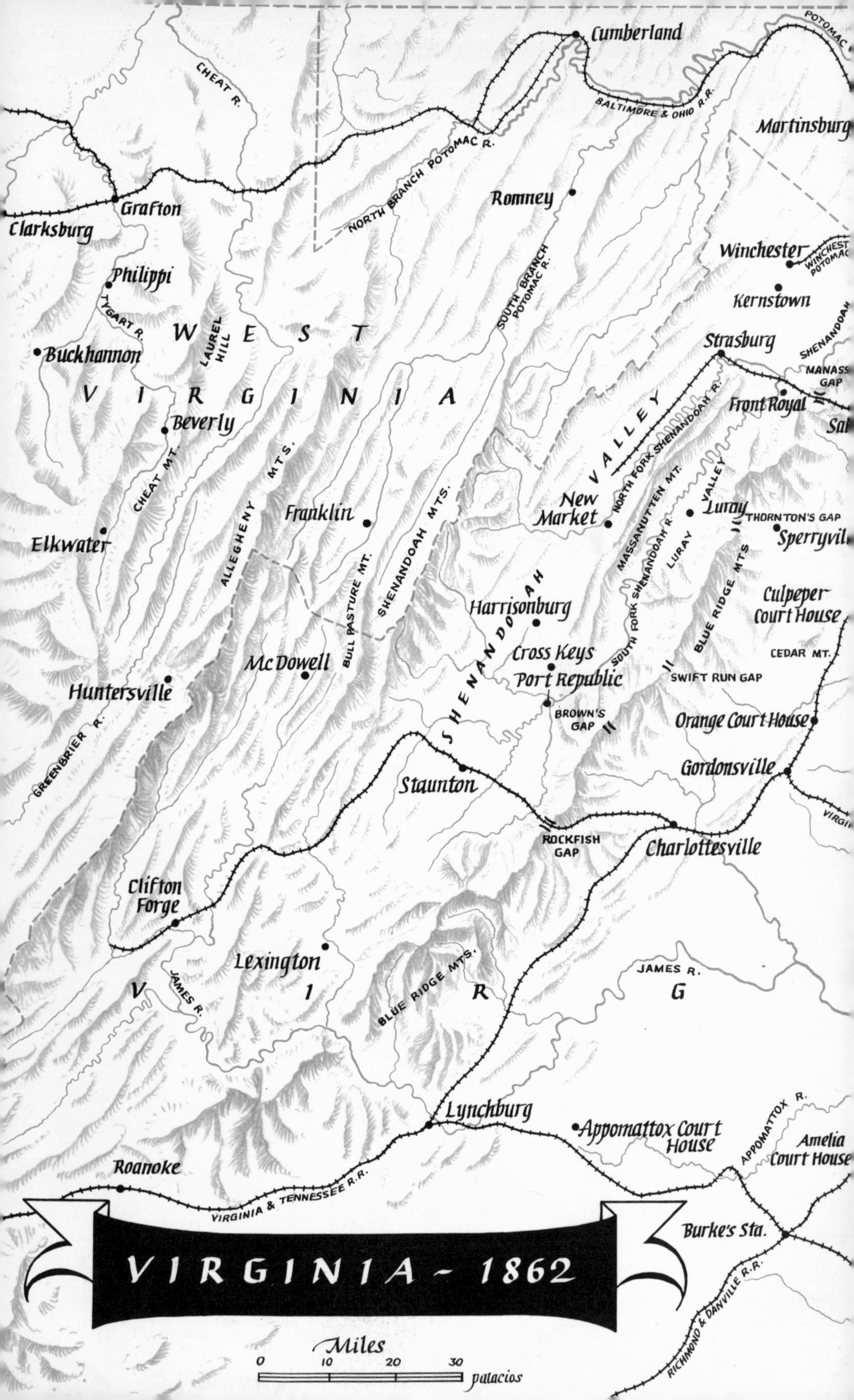

VIRGINIA - 1862
Cumberland
POTOMAC R.
CHEAT R.
BALTIMORE & OHIO R.R.
Martinsburg
NORTH BRANCH POTOMAC R.
Romney
Grafton
Clarksburg
Winchester
Philippi
SOUTH BRANCH POTOMAC R.
Kernstown
TYGART R.
LAUREL HILL
W E S T
V I R G I N I A
Buckhannon
Strasburg
SHENANDOAH
MANASSAS GAP
Front Royal
Beverly
VALLEY
NORTH FORK SHENANDOAH R.
CHEAT MT.
ALLEGHENY MTS.
SHENANDOAH MTS.
New Market
MASSANUTTEN MT.
VALLEY
Luray
THORNTON'S GAP
Franklin
Elkwater
LURAY
SOUTH FORK SHENANDOAH R.
BLUE RIDGE MTS.
BULL PASTURE MT.
SHENANDOAH
Harrisonburg
Culpeper Court House
CEDAR MT.
Cross Keys
Port Republic
McDowell
SWIFT RUN GAP
Huntersville
BROWN'S GAP
Orange Court House
GREENBRIER R.
Staunton
Gordonsville
ROCKFISH GAP
Charlottesville
Clifton Forge
Lexington
JAMES R.
V I R G
BLUE RIDGE MTS.
JAMES R.
Lynchburg
Appomattox Court House
APPOMATTOX R.
Amelia Court House
Roanoke
VIRGINIA & TENNESSEE R.R.
Burke's Sta.
RICHMOND & DANVILLE R.R.
Miles
0 10 20 30
palacios